THE DIARY OF
SIR EDWARD WALTER HAMILTON
1880–1885

THE DIARY OF
SIR EDWARD
WALTER
HAMILTON
1880–1885

EDITED BY

DUDLEY W. R. BAHLMAN

VOLUME I

1880–1882

OXFORD
AT THE CLARENDON PRESS
1972

Oxford University Press, Ely House, London W. 1

GLASGOW NEW YORK TORONTO MELBOURNE WELLINGTON
CAPE TOWN IBADAN NAIROBI DAR ES SALAAM LUSAKA ADDIS ABABA
DELHI BOMBAY CALCUTTA MADRAS KARACHI LAHORE DACCA
KUALA LUMPUR SINGAPORE HONG KONG TOKYO

PRINTED IN GREAT BRITAIN
AT THE UNIVERSITY PRESS, OXFORD
BY VIVIAN RIDLER
PRINTER TO THE UNIVERSITY

CONTENTS

PLATES

PREFATORY NOTE

WHAT appears here is the text of Sir Edward Hamilton's diary from its beginning in 1880 until the fall of Mr. Gladstone's second ministry and Hamilton's departure from Downing Street in the summer of 1885. I have not excised any part of the text within those limits except where Hamilton himself has crossed out passages because they were repetitious. (Some other passages that are crossed out in the manuscript I have restored, either in the text itself or in a footnote, when the passage seemed to have any interest.) I have printed the text in this degree of completeness not because every part of the diary is of obviously enduring interest but because I wished to avoid at all costs having to write those chilling words: 'I have omitted passages that could be of little or no interest to anyone.' Therefore, this is not 'selections' from Hamilton's diary but the full text, the valuable and the trivial alike.

After 8 May 1883, the date on which Hamilton started to write on only one side of the page, thereby leaving a page available for him to write additions to his entries, I have indicated such additions by enclosing the words written on the verso in brackets of this type < >.

With many entries for 1883 and 1884 there are marginal comments written in by Hamilton's fellow secretary, Horace Seymour. I have printed these—even when they have been crossed out—in the footnotes in so far as they are legible.

I have normalized the dates at the beginning of each entry. Hamilton, as a rule, wrote down the day of the week, month, and date, putting the year at the top of the page. In some entries he has written a day of the week and a date which do not agree. Usually (but as the entry for 24 April 1883 shows not always) he has the day right and the date wrong. Where internal evidence offers no certain guide I have assumed that it is the date that should be altered. In each case the change is noted in a footnote.

I have followed Hamilton's spelling exactly in most cases. What may appear to be American spellings of such words as 'favor' and 'honor' are Hamilton's when they appear. (See the first paragraph of 28 July 1880, and the entry for 23 June 1880 where both 'favor' and 'favour' are written.) Hamilton had a tendency to write 'that' for 'than' and vice versa; I have silently corrected all such obvious slips of the pen. His manner of writing 'these' and 'those' tends to make the two words indistinguishable. In each case I have made what seems to me the most likely choice between them. I have tried to regularize his spelling of proper names—especially foreign names—using the spelling ordinarily that he himself finally settled upon. For example, he could not make up his mind how to spell Kandahar or Kabul, but he ended by using the 'K' rather than the 'C' as the initial letter. In the

entry for 28 July 1880 he wrote, in the second paragraph, 'Candahar' and
five lines later 'Kandahar'; in order to avoid confusion and to simplify the
index I have used Kandahar throughout. I have handled other such incon-
sistencies in the spelling of proper names in the same way. Hamilton's use of
capital letters was erratic; it is often difficult to tell whether he has capitalized
a letter or not; I have therefore been guided by what seemed to me the most
desirable usage in this matter. I have retained one of Hamilton's irregular
practices in the cases of his references to the Queen where, especially in the
entries after 1880, he tends to capitalize personal pronouns referring to her.
The difference of emphasis and intonation imparted to the text of the diary
by this practice is of some importance in reading it. Hamilton's punctuation
is often erratic, even by nineteenth-century standards; I have been guided
by his practice but I have not hesitated to alter his punctuation in the interests
of clarity.

For a diarist Hamilton used remarkably few abbreviations. Any reader of
the diary in its manuscript form would be struck by the care with which it is
written and the painstaking way in which Hamilton has tried to make himself
clear and the diary a handsome and orderly thing. On the relatively informal
handwritten pages such abbreviations as Hamilton uses do nothing to impair
the clarity or appearance of the text; to attempt to reproduce those abbreviations in type would tend to give the text a cluttered and slapdash look.
Therefore I have expanded most of Hamilton's abbreviations without comment and without dotting the pages with brackets. But the reader should
remember that as often as not Hamilton wrote out 'House of Commons',
'Lord', and other such words and titles.

Because of its extraordinary fullness and clarity the diary requires relatively little annotation of an explanatory kind; because of its close relationship to the letters and papers passing through 10 Downing Street it invites
extensive references to manuscripts in the Gladstone papers and other similar
collections. Since the relationship between passages in the diary and readily
identifiable letters is so explicit and since the Gladstone papers are so well
arranged and indexed that finding almost all of the documents Hamilton
refers to would present no difficulty to someone with access to the Manuscripts Room of the British Museum—who, then, could also read the diary
in its original form—I have not made footnote references to the manuscripts.
Instead, assuming that this printed text will be of most use to readers who
do not have ready access to the Museum, I have tried to refer the reader to
a printed version of the documents Hamilton made use of. But readers
should be warned of two obvious hazards: one is that I have certainly not
found and have not attempted to find *all* the printed versions that are available
—especially of documents printed in Parliamentary Papers—and the second
is that no one should assume that the printed version to which I direct the
reader is either accurate or complete. I must assume that most readers will

dip into the diary and not read it through; therefore, perhaps to the annoyance of more knowledgeable or more extensive readers, I have repeated
identifications of the persons who are mentioned in the text by title—e.g.
Archbishop of Canterbury—rather than by name. I have tried to strike the
difficult middle ground between being helpful in these matters without being
insulting; in general in text and notes I have tried to be clear and accurate
first, regarding consistency as of secondary importance.

It was when I was in England in 1957–8, with the help of a Morse Fellowship granted by Yale University, that I first saw the diary and, finding it
extremely useful and interesting, thought of preparing part of it for publication. Generous grants and a sabbatical leave from Williams College
enabled me to acquire the diary on microfilm and then with the support of
a fellowship from the John Simon Guggenheim Memorial Foundation, to
return to England to do further work for the introduction and notes. I am
most grateful to these institutions and the Foundation for their support.

Many individuals have been of assistance to me. I am especially grateful
to Sir Walter Moberly, Sir Edward Hamilton's nephew, for at the outset
gaining for me the permission of Sir Edward's heirs to publish the diary;
but beyond that in numerous letters and in two conversations he has provided me with invaluable information and advice. The staff at the Manuscripts Room at the British Museum, Miss Jane Langton and her colleagues
in the Round Tower at Windsor, and Miss Juanita Terry and others of the
staff of the Williams College Library have all given me important assistance
with unfailing courtesy and admirable skill. Both editor and readers can be
grateful for Miss Delight Ansley's heroic work on the Index.

The following have in various ways been generous with their time and
helpful with their expert advice: Lady Bland, Hamilton's niece; Dr. James
Bull; Dr. Edwin Clarke; Dr. Macdonald Critchley; Dr. Robert K. Davis;
W. J. Derbyshire of the Treasury; M. R. D. Foot; Charles Fuqua; Gordon
S. Haight; Henry Hamilton of Aberdeen; George McLean Harper, Jr.;
Walter E. Houghton; Drs. Richard Hunter and Ida Macalpine; J. F. A.
Mason, Librarian of Christ Church; Sir Otto Niemeyer; Henry Roseveare;
and Miles Shepherd, Borough Librarian of Middlesbrough.

My wife has helped most patiently with the work of proof-reading. She
discovered—as other readers will—what Eddy Hamilton himself discovered,
somewhat to his surprise, when he looked back through the diary in 1885:
'I have', he wrote, '. . . been reading over (almost for the first time) a part of
this Journal, and I confess it is interesting and reads better than I ever
expected.'[1]

Williamstown, Massachusetts
January 1969

[1] Diary, 29 Dec. 1885, Add. MS. 48642, f. 64.

LIST OF ABBREVIATIONS

DNB	*Dictionary of National Biography*
Childers	Spencer Childers, *The Life and Correspondence of the Right Hon. Hugh C. E. Childers 1827–1896*. 2 vols. London, 1901.
Fitzmaurice	Lord Edmond Fitzmaurice, *The Life of Granville George Leveson Gower, Second Earl Granville K.G. 1815–1891*. 2 vols. London, 1905.
G. E. C.	Vicary Gibbs, ed., *The Complete Peerage of England, Scotland, Ireland, Great Britain and the United Kingdom by G. E. C.* 12 vols. London, 1910–59.
Gardiner	A. G. Gardiner, *The Life of Sir William Harcourt*. 2 vols. London, 1923.
Garvin	J. L. Garvin, *The Life of Joseph Chamberlain*. 3 vols. London, 1932–4.
Guedalla	Philip Guedalla, *The Queen and Mr. Gladstone*. 2 vols. London, 1933.
Gwynn and Tuckwell	Stephen Gwynn and Gertrude M. Tuckwell, *The Life of the Rt. Hon. Sir Charles W. Dilke Bart., M.P.* 2 vols. London, 1917.
Hammond	J. L. Hammond, *Gladstone and the Irish Nation*. London, 1938.
Knaplund	Paul Knaplund, ed., 'Letters from the Berlin Embassy. Selections from the Private Correspondence of British Representatives at Berlin and Foreign Secretary Lord Granville, 1871–1874, 1880–1885', *Annual Report of the American Historical Association for the Year 1942, Vol. II*. Washington, 1944.
Letters	George Earle Buckle, ed., *The Letters of Queen Victoria. Second Series, 1862–1885*. 3 vols. London, 1926–8. *The Letters of Queen Victoria. Third Series, 1886–1901*. 3 vols. London, 1930–2.
Medlicott	W. N. Medlicott, *Bismarck, Gladstone, and the Concert of Europe*. London, 1956.
Morley	John Morley, *The Life of William Ewart Gladstone*. 3 vols. London, 1903.
Parl. Deb.	*Hansard's Parliamentary Debates, Third Series*.
Ramm	Agatha Ramm, ed., *The Political Correspondence of Mr. Gladstone and Lord Granville 1876–1886*. 2 vols. Oxford, 1962.
Temperley and Penson	Harold Temperley and Lillian M. Penson, *Foundations of British Foreign Policy from Pitt (1792) to Salisbury (1902)*. Cambridge, 1938.
Wemyss Reid	T. Wemyss Reid, *Life of the Right Honourable William Edward Forster*. 3rd edition. 2 vols. London, 1888.

INTRODUCTION

ON 24 April 1880 Edward Hamilton began to keep a journal. For eight shillings and sixpence he had purchased a handsome black morocco-bound notebook with a metal lock containing 135 leaves of lined paper and measuring 9 inches by 7 inches. When, owing to his rapidly failing health, he had to give up his journal in May 1906, it consisted of 54 volumes, all, with two exceptions, of the same kind. The fifth volume is maroon instead of black; the twenty-seventh volume has 170 leaves instead of the usual 135 and lacks the number 36 stamped in the leather at the base of the spine, which all the other volumes have. Every volume has a lock.

In spite of the locks, the diary is not of a highly personal or private nature. Hamilton intended it to be 'a journal of events', one that avoided gossip or scandal, which he thought of as generally inaccurate or exaggerated; he hoped to create 'a trustworthy record' and 'a contribution to history'.[1] This diary is of the kind one would allow friends to read, as indeed Hamilton did. Horace Seymour, one of Hamilton's fellow private secretaries during Mr. Gladstone's second ministry, not only read the diary but, while reading entries for 1883 and 1884, wrote in comments of his own.[2] In 1888 Hamilton made extensive extracts from the diary for the period March to May 1882 for Mr. Gladstone to read;[3] twice, once in 1889 and again in 1893, he let Rosebery borrow a volume[4] but on another occasion copied out a long extract for Rosebery's use.[5] When in 1897 John Morley was writing up an account of the Home Rule question and again in 1902 and 1903 when Morley was at work on his biography of Mr. Gladstone, Hamilton let him browse through the diary and borrow what seemed to him important volumes.[6] His readers then were unanimous in their praise of the diary's accuracy and interest, Morley declaring himself '*entranced*' by the three volumes he borrowed in 1897.[7]

Entrancing sometimes, useful always, the journal has proved of great value

---

[1] Diary, 27 Jan. 1891, Add. MS. 48655, f. 8. When referring to a part of the diary here published I refer simply to the date of the entry; when, as here, I refer to an unpublished part of the diary, I add to the date of the entry a citation of the MS. in the British Museum.

[2] See, for example, Diary, 20 and 23 Nov. 1883 and 16, 28, and 30 Apr. 1884.

[3] EWH to G., 31 July 1888, Add. MS. 44191, f. 132 and the extracts, ff. 133–49. G. to EWH, 8 Aug. 1888, Add. MS. 48608. When I read the correspondence in the Hamilton MSS. it was in bundles and the folios were not numbered; therefore reference to that correspondence will take the form followed above in the letter of 8 Aug. 1888.

[4] Diary, 16 June 1889, Add. MS. 48651, f. 16 and 6 Feb. 1893, Add. MS. 48659, f. 108.

[5] Rosebery to EWH, 22 Mar. 1895, Add. MS. 48611.

[6] Morley to EWH, 20 Oct. 1897, 28 July 1902, 15 Feb., 8 Nov., and 31 Dec. 1903, Add. MS. 48619. Diary, 19 Oct. 1897, Add. MS. 48672, f. 24 and 12 Aug. 1903, Add. MS. 48681, f. 37.

[7] Morley to EWH, 20 Oct. 1897, Add. MS. 48619.

not only to those few who saw it during Hamilton's lifetime, but to the scholars who have used it since it became available for study at the British Museum in the mid 1950s. Even at its dullest, when Hamilton lists dinner guests or records minor appointments, the diary has its uses; the appointments, for example, serve to remind the historian of the extent to which a Prime Minister and his staff have to concern themselves with sometimes petty and often troublesome, time-consuming matters of patronage, at the expense of far more important matters of state. With a Prime Minister who, like Mr. Gladstone, took questions involving *persons* so much to heart[1] and the duty of advising the Crown on appointments—especially ecclesiastical appointments[2]—so very seriously, the diary's occasional resemblance to the *Gazette* is not all to the bad. During the years he was in Downing Street, Hamilton often made his entries a résumé of the contents of letters that Mr. Gladstone had written or received. With the presence of the incoming letters themselves and copies of the outgoing letters (often in Hamilton's hand) available in the British Museum, these parts of the journal diminish in importance. The scholar will wish to get beyond Hamilton's account to the letters themselves; but he will find Hamilton's journal an excellent guide to the Gladstone manuscripts and a valuable reminder of the concurrence of events. When, in addition to describing the contents of letters, Hamilton records what Mr. Gladstone said or in what mood he read or wrote his correspondence, the journal acquires a unique value. Now in this published version of the diary during the years with Mr. Gladstone, these descriptions of letters will serve the reader who cannot be in the Manuscripts Room of the British Museum. Hamilton was a first-class private secretary, excellent at singling out the important points made in letters and reports; though not infallible, his summaries are extraordinarily accurate and just, as a reader can discover by turning to published versions of some of the documents Hamilton describes. His summaries are an excellent second-best source of information.

But fortunately together with the listing of names and beyond the description of documents and speeches, there are throughout the journal—but increasingly so with the passage of time and the development of Hamilton as a civil servant and as a diarist—the astute observations of one in a remarkable position to know men and events, with wonderfully balanced powers of judgement, and possessed of the uncommon perseverance needed to keep a journal alive. He did not have the literary skill of some of the greatest diarists. His journal lacks the verve or the tension of Charles Greville's; Hamilton was too happy in his position and too charitable toward those around him to etch his portraits with acid. But Hamilton had the combination of skill and industry that enabled him to create a great diary—one that is not simply useful to historians specializing in the period but one

[1] See Diary, 1 Feb. 1883 and 21 Apr. 1885.
[2] See, for example, Diary, 4 Jan. 1884.

that can attract any reader with an interest in English politics and society in the late nineteenth century. In the part of the diary published here, Hamilton has recorded a fascinating account of the melancholy history of Mr. Gladstone's second administration. Along with the day-to-day narrative of events Hamilton sketches skilful portraits of some of the principal figures in that history. Some, like Hartington, are seen at a distance, mainly through their letters. The Queen, though rarely sketched from life, emerges with clarity, and Hamilton's commentary provides an admirable accompaniment to the already published correspondence of the Queen and her Prime Minister. Hamilton's dislike of Forster and his distrust of Chamberlain sharpen the lines of his pictures of them. Rosebery was one of Hamilton's closest friends and Hamilton's intimate knowledge of him makes his diary a document of prime importance for understanding that brilliant and complex man; his affection for Rosebery did not induce Hamilton to avoid sketching the darker aspects of his character.

But all other persons take a subordinate place in the journal to Mr. Gladstone himself. Inevitably in this section dealing with the years when Hamilton was in close daily contact with 'the Great Man', he appears in almost every entry. Through these pages we get to know him well—and that was what Hamilton obviously intended. What Hamilton did not so obviously intend was to present himself so prominently. But try as he might to conceal himself behind the word 'one' in an effort to avoid the use of 'I', Hamilton created a self-portrait along with his massive portrait of 'Mr. G.'. The conscientious reader will get to know Hamilton well and will understand why Eddy Hamilton came to have so large a number of devoted friends.

Edward Walter Hamilton was born on 7 July 1847, the second child but first son of Walter Kerr Hamilton.[1] At the time of his birth his father was a canon of Salisbury Cathedral. His mother had been Isabel Lear, whose father had been archdeacon and then dean of Salisbury and whose elder brother, Francis, was to become an archdeacon of that diocese. Walter Kerr Hamilton was made bishop of Salisbury in 1854 on the nomination of Lord Aberdeen.

W. K. Hamilton and W. E. Gladstone had been close friends since their days together at Eton. When the vacancy at Salisbury occurred on the death of Edward Denison, Aberdeen had first recommended Professor Blunt, the Lady Margaret Professor of Divinity at Cambridge, who refused the offer on the grounds that he was at 57 too old to take on a bishopric. Then Aberdeen recommended Canon Hamilton, knowing that Hamilton had been the stated choice of Bishop Denison on his deathbed.[2] The Queen approved but much to her distress started 'to *hear* from *all sides* that he [Hamilton] is considered extremely High Church in his views'.[3] It was too

[1] See Appendix II.
[2] Aberdeen to the Queen, 16 Mar. 1854, Royal Archives, Windsor, A 23/79 and 22 Mar. 1854, A 23/81.
[3] The Queen to Aberdeen, 21 Mar. 1854, Add. MS. 43048, f. 313.

late to stop the appointment; from this time forward the Queen was to be more cautious in accepting the recommendations for ecclesiastical appointments even of trusted Prime Ministers like Lord Aberdeen. She probably suspected that Hamilton's friend, Gladstone, a leading member of Aberdeen's government, had had a hand in the appointment. The appointment of Bishop Hamilton, which Mr. Gladstone jocularly called 'the sin of Sarum',[1] was an important part of the background of the conflict over church appointments during the ministry which the bishop's son describes in such interesting detail in his diary.[2]

The ties with Salisbury were strong; the city was always 'home' to Eddy Hamilton. After his father's death his mother (until her death in 1886) and unmarried sisters lived there and one of his sisters, Alice, married R. C. Moberly, who was the son of W. K. Hamilton's successor as bishop, strengthening the link not only with the city but with the cathedral. At Salisbury the Hamilton's ten children were born; of these ten, eight grew to be adults. After his sister Mary's death in 1859 Eddy was the oldest, and with his father's death in 1869 he became at 22 the head of the family. His mother was left with an income of £800 a year; but there were debts and eight children (the youngest of whom, Sidney, was four) to provide for.[3] The five daughters, it is clear, were all a source of pride and strength to Eddy and his mother. Ethelinda, the oldest, was 20 when her father died; she never married, and became as her brother wrote, 'a sort of rock on which all the sisters and brothers have leaned'.[4] The other sisters, Alice, Eleanor, Maud, and Constance, were married between 1880 and 1890, three of them to clergymen. Of the three sons only Eddy played a role in holding the family together. Clement, who was 15 when his father died, became a source of anxiety to the Hamiltons; when he was 21, he went off to Australia, but from time to time—once in 1888 and again in 1897—he returned to England, much to the distress of some who regarded him as a problem—'lack of backbone' was the phrase used by members of the family.[5] When Sidney, the youngest, grew to manhood he took none of the burden from his brother; he was something of an invalid and never had a permanent occupation.[6] In 1883, Hamilton counted among his blessings 'a divine (in every sense of the

[1] Paul Knaplund, ed., 'Gladstone–Gordon Correspondence, 1851–1896', *Transactions of the American Philosophical Society*, New Series, li (1961), p. 14.

[2] See D. W. R. Bahlman, 'The Queen, Mr. Gladstone, and Church Patronage', *Victorian Studies*, iii (1960), 349–80.

[3] Lady Herbert to G., 31 Aug. 1869, Add. MS. 44212, ff. 162–3. In this letter she told G. of plans to raise money for Mrs. Hamilton.

[4] Diary, 10 Dec. 1895, Add. MS. 48668, f. 40.

[5] EWH to G., 30 Dec. 1875, Add. MS. 44189, f. 15; Diary, 30 Mar. 1888, Add. MS. 48648, f. 66; Rosebery to EWH, 9 Apr. 1888 and 16 Feb. 1889, Add. MS. 48610; E. W. T. Hamilton to EWH, 19 Dec. 1890 and 13 Jan. 1896, Add. MS. 48620; Kingscote to EWH, 27 Dec. 1889, Add. MS. 48625.

[6] Diary, 28 Sept. 1886, Add. MS. 48644, f. 131.

word) mother, together with most loveable and attractive sisters'; his brothers are conspicuously absent.[1]

In September 1860 Eddy went off to Eton and in January 1866 he matriculated at Oxford. Like his father and his father's friend, Mr. Gladstone, he went to Christ Church and was reported by Lady Herbert a year later as 'doing admirably there'.[2] But Eddy Hamilton was not to shine in traditional academic pursuits. Music was his passion. Latin, Greek, English literature interested him little. He took a B.Mus. degree in 1867 and in 1868 was seeking an appointment as a civil servant. On 8 April 1868 Bishop Samuel Wilberforce wrote Disraeli, then the Prime Minister: 'Will you let me ask the favour of your directing the name of Edward Hamilton of Ch Ch Oxford, and eldest son of the Bishop of Salisbury, to be put down as candidate for a clerkship in the Treasury. He is a remarkably pleasing young fellow.'[3] Although Disraeli was apparently 'disposed to look favourably upon the Bishop's application', it came to nothing.[4] It was not until after his father's death in August 1869, that Hamilton in January 1870 finally received from Mr. Gladstone a nomination to a post at the Treasury.[5]

But then in December 1870 another tempting offer came to him. On the, advice of Dean Liddell of Christ Church, the head of Hamilton's old college, the Prince of Wales sounded out the possibility of Hamilton becoming the tutor of his oldest son, Prince Albert Victor, who was then 6. To a young man in a junior position at the Treasury and with heavy responsibilities toward his family, the offer was attractive. When he sought his mother's advice she recognized its value and was pleased (and knew that her husband would have been pleased) that Dean Liddell should have shown his confidence in Hamilton in this way. As she said, 'in a worldly point of view one is inclined to accept the offer'. But then she expressed some fears. 'This is of course strictly between ourselves but from time to time I have heard things said about the Prince of Wales that make me afraid that he himself and those about him are not what they ought to be, and it is a very grave question whether it is right to place oneself in an atmosphere of evil for any consideration on the other side.' She advised her son, therefore, to stall for time and to seek the opinion of Bishop Hamilton's examining chaplain and devoted admirer, the new canon of St. Paul's, Henry Parry Liddon.[6] Liddon wrote that 'decidedly you *should* accept the post'. At the Treasury, he said, the prospects of advancement were uncertain, but the Prince of Wales would 'take care to provide for you handsomely when you have done your work with his boy'.[7]

[1] Diary, 12 Dec. 1883.
[2] Lady Herbert to G., 22 Dec. 1866, Add. MS. 44212, f. 138.
[3] Disraeli Papers, Hughenden, B/XXI/W/371.   [4] Diary, 27 Dec. 1882.
[5] Gurdon to G., 4 Jan. 1870, Add. MS. 44182, f. 22.
[6] Mrs. Hamilton to EWH, 13 Dec. [1870], Add. MS. 48622.
[7] H. P. Liddon to EWH, 16 Dec. 1870, Add. MS. 48622.

As always careful and methodical, in a highly characteristic fashion Hamilon wrote down the grounds on which 'one's' decision should be made.

Pro—supposing salary to be good

(1) Immediate advantage.
(2) Position for oneself and to aid others.
(3) Whether, circumstanced as one is, one ought not to allow present advantage to outweigh consideration of future, so as to enable one to assist family, trusting to Providence for the future.
(4) Mr. Liddon's urging one to accept the post, partly on account of his thinking it would have been my dear father's wish.
(5) Throwing one into best of society.
(6) Somewhat gloomy prospects of future in Treasury.
(7) Making a bold stroke—'Nothing venture nothing have.'

Con

(1) Uncertainty of future and giving up profession.
(2) Sacrifice to a certain extent of independence, and making one dependent on one individual who in his present position is unable to do much for those in his service.
(3) Discouragement of Herbert Fisher; and no direct encouragement from my mother, Uncle Edward &c.
(4) Entire inexperience of teaching.
(5) Great responsibility; and incompetence of oneself to discharge duties accordingly.[1]

Before Hamilton had to make his decision, the Prince of Wales, to Dean Liddell's annoyance, decided that it was 'as yet premature to engage the services of a tutor of high grade'.[2] But since the Prince of Wales had been most favourably impressed by the reports he had had of Hamilton, the subject was not closed. The offer was renewed in July 1871 and this time, mainly on the advice of his Uncle Edward and Mr. Gladstone, Hamilton refused.[3]

But in the end he was to play a formal role in the education of the Prince of Wales's heir. In 1894 the Duke of York, who was now, owing to the death of his older brother, the Prince of Wales's oldest son, told Lord Rosebery that he wanted some instruction in English Constitutional history; Rosebery replied that what was important was to learn about the machinery of government and suggested Hamilton as a well-qualified instructor. Hamilton's entry in his diary for 14 March 1894 tells of his first encounter with the future George V:[4]

I received a summons to go to York House this morning; and I obeyed it. The Duke of York said he was anxious to act on Rosebery's suggestion and have some talks with me about government machinery. He was reading Bagehot's book on the

[1] Undated note by EWH, Add. MS. 48622.
[2] Liddell to EWH, 29 Dec. 1870, Add. MS. 48622.
[3] H. P. Liddon to EWH, 11 July 1871, Add. MS. 48622.
[4] Add. MS. 48663, f. 35.

Constitution with a professor; but he found it difficult to follow and hardly gave him the information he wanted. I found him very easy to talk to, because he asked so many questions; and the easiest way of imparting knowledge is by answering questions. He confessed that he had read very little and knew very little. He could not remember what he read and he had no power of assisting his memory with notes. Our talk this morning mainly related to the powers of the Sovereign, the constitutional checks upon those powers which were now mainly nominal, the popularity of the monarchy, the influence which may and the influence which may not be exercised by the Crown. He also discussed the relative advantages of a King and a Queen and referred very sensibly to the difficulties which might have arisen had the life of the Prince Consort been prolonged.

Again in March and three times in April Hamilton visited his student and took him on tours of the Bank of England and the Mint. He found him 'quick and intelligent'.[1]

But to return to his early career; Hamilton was soon rewarded for his decision to stay at the Treasury. Robert Lowe, Mr. Gladstone's brilliant and difficult Chancellor of the Exchequer from 1868 to 1873, chose Hamilton to serve him as a second private secretary in February 1872. He remained with Lowe until unfortunate circumstances forced Lowe from office in August 1873. Brief though the experience was, Hamilton found it most pleasing and rewarding.[2] In this short time he and others saw how excellently qualified he was to be a private secretary. Lowe rated his qualifications as 'very high'. Hamilton had been put to the test at the end of May 1873 when Horace Seymour met with an accident that prevented his continuing in Lowe's service. Lowe wrote that during June and July, 'these two most trying months in the year, Mr. H. did the work of 2 secretaries with great ability, perfect accuracy, and great despatch. I am satisfied that in him the Treasury has a most valuable and useful officer'.[3]

With this endorsement Hamilton became a member of Mr. Gladstone's secretarial staff; his handwriting appears for the first time on the docket of a memorandum of July 1873 concerning Cabinet changes.[4] Copies of the Prime Minister's letters to the Queen start to appear in Hamilton's hand in October.[5] But then from November 1873 until January 1874 he went off to Ireland to serve as secretary to the Irish Civil Service Committee,[6] and upon his return the death of Mr. Gladstone's first government was at hand.

His journey to Ireland coincided with what was probably his first—

[1] Diary, 17 Mar., 17, 19, and 25 Apr. 1894, Add. MS. 48663, ff. 38, 75–6, 78, 83. Though Hamilton found the Duke 'charming' at this time, it is clear that he was aware of some limitations. He saw him at close range again in 1902 and found him 'much improved. He has lost that silly laugh and has broadened out enormously'. Diary, 7 Nov. 1902, Add. MS. 48680, f. 47.

[2] Diary, 29 July 1892, Add. MS. 48658, f. 75.

[3] Lowe's memorandum copied in EWH's hand, 11 Aug. 1873, Add. MS. 48622.

[4] Add. MS. 44761, f. 157.

[5] G. to the Queen, copy, 4 Oct. 1873, B.M., Res. MS. 25/15.

[6] Memorandum, 1 Dec. 1874, Add. MS. 48622.

but, as we shall see, not his last—disappointment in love. He had become attached to the older daughter of Dean Liddell—Lorina, known as Ina, for whose sister Alice *Alice in Wonderland* had been written. He had probably seen something of her while he was at Christ Church; they had written one another in a formal way—she always addressing him as 'Dear Mr. Hamilton'. It was thus that she addressed him in her letter of New Year's Eve 1873 informing him of her engagement to Willie Skene, a fellow of All Souls.[1] His closest friends knew to what extent his hopes had been dashed. Lord Pembroke and his sister, Maude Parry, wrote Hamilton consoling letters, she being glad that Hamilton was off to Dublin. 'You will bear it better there away from your friends.'[2]

With the fall of the government in 1874 Hamilton went back to his clerk-ship at the Treasury.[3] Occasionally, as in December 1875, he would perform informal secretarial tasks for Mr. Gladstone.[4] But for the most part his life seems to have been one of routine work. His excellent qualities as a civil servant gained the recognition of the permanent secretary of the Treasury, R. R. W. Lingen, and of the parliamentary secretary, Sir Henry Selwin-Ibbetson; he gained special commendation for his work on a report for the Board of Works for Ireland in 1878.[5]

The formation of Mr. Gladstone's second ministry in the spring of 1880 marks the beginning not only of Hamilton's diary but of the happiest years of his life. Some of the men who had served Mr. Gladstone as private secretaries in the past—Algernon West, W. B. Gurdon, and Lord Frederick Cavendish—now held other posts; Mr. Gladstone turned to those who had held junior posts in his earlier secretariat. As his principal private secretary in 1880 he chose Arthur Godley, who had joined Mr. Gladstone's staff upon West's departure in 1872 as third private secretary.[6] Godley was a natural choice. He was the Prime Minister's equal or even perhaps superior as a classicist and had qualities that marked him at Balliol and after as one who would have a distinguished career in the civil service. Years later Asquith was to describe him as 'a highly cultivated man with a vast knowledge of literature, but with all the characteristic limitations of the Civil Servant type, amongst which is excessive caution and non-commital-ness'.[7] When Godley left the secretarial staff in 1882, he went first to the Inland Revenue Board and then in 1883 he became the Permanent Under-Secretary at the India Office, where he was, according to Asquith, 'the real Governor of India under

[1] Lorina Liddell to EWH, 31 Dec. 1873, Add. MS. 48622.

[2] Pembroke to EWH, 15 Jan. 1874 and Maude Herbert Parry to EWH, Add. MS. 48621.

[3] See G.'s letter commending the service of his secretaries, 28 Feb. 1874, Add. MS. 48607.

[4] EWH to G., 30 Dec. 1875, Add. MS. 44189, ff. 14–15.

[5] Testimonials of Lingen in 1876, Selwin-Ibbetson and Mitchell Henry, 1878, and the letter from Lingen to EWH, 5 Apr. 1880, Add. MS. 48622.

[6] W. C. James to G., 12 July 1872 and G. to James, 10 Aug. 1872, copy, Add. MS. 44265, ff. 121–3; Godley to G., 10 Aug. [1872], Add. MS. 44222, ff. 1–2.

[7] H. H. Asquith, *Memories and Reflections 1852–1927* (Boston, 1928), ii. 241–2.

a succession of viceroys and secretaries for the best part of thirty years'.[1] Mr. Gladstone had the greatest respect for Godley's talents; he even thought of making him viceroy of India in 1893.[2] After Mr. Gladstone's death Godley was the first choice of the Gladstone family to be the official biographer.[3] In 1909 Godley was elevated to the peerage as Lord Kilbracken.

Next to Godley in the secretariat in 1880 came Hamilton himself; therefore when Godley moved on in the summer of 1882 Hamilton became the principal private secretary. Between Hamilton and Godley there existed strong ties of friendship and mutual respect. As Godley's departure from Downing Street became imminent Hamilton wrote: 'It is impossible to over-rate his charm as a colleague; always ready, never put out, never excited; while his modesty, simplicity, genuineness, unselfishness, and brilliancy are irresistably attractive'.[4] And Godley thought of Hamilton as 'the best of all possible colleagues'.[5] Later on Godley described Hamilton as 'not in the first class for intellectual gifts, but he was very industrious, painstaking, accurate, and obliging, and in every way pleasant to work with'.[6] To Godley, Hamilton left in his will all his papers, including his diary, asking him to advise his trustees concerning possible publication of the diary and select and present to the British Museum those papers which in Godley's judgement had historical value.[7]

Next to Hamilton in the Downing Street hierarchy was Horace Seymour, who was four years older and who had been at the Treasury four years longer than Hamilton. That he was passed over and outpaced by Hamilton wounded Seymour. When Godley left Downing Street and Hamilton took the first place on the staff in August 1882, Seymour wrote to him: 'It is 9 1/2 years ago since you and I first started as colleagues together. The end of that time finds us in reversed positions. I suppose a case without any precedent. I have gone down, and you are come up over me.'[8] In spite of the bitterness he felt he assured Hamilton that he could work as his subordinate loyally and harmoniously. And so he did until he left the staff to become a Commissioner of Customs in December 1884.[9] That this harmony could exist is the most telling evidence of Hamilton's tact and of the respect which his personal and professional qualities inspired in those near him, for Seymour was a bitter, disappointed man who grumbled openly about all of his fellow workers except Hamilton.[10] Of Godley he wrote that 'we all know that he

---

[1] Ibid. ii. 241.   [2] Diary, 3 Aug. 1893, Add. MS. 48661, ff. 19–20.
[3] Lord Kilbracken, *Reminiscences* . . . (London, 1931), pp. 224–8.
[4] Diary, 17 July 1882.
[5] Godley to EWH, 18 July 1882, Add. MS. 48616.
[6] Lord Kilbracken, *Reminiscences* . . . (London, 1931), p. 121.
[7] Extract from EWH's will, Add. MS. 48628 and EWH to Godley, 21 Mar. 1887, Add. MS. 48616.
[8] H. Seymour to EWH, 13 Aug. 1882, Add. MS. 48615.
[9] Diary, 7 Nov. and 24 Dec. 1884.
[10] Seymour to EWH, 27 Aug. 1883 and 8 Sept. 1884, Add. MS. 48615.

does not allow his official work to hinder him from taking his leisure'.[1] Seymour especially disliked Spencer Lyttelton, Mrs. Gladstone's nephew, who joined the staff upon Godley's departure.[2] Seymour found him 'a sadly selfish idle dog',[3] and Lyttelton, in turn, found Seymour 'not particularly congenial'.[4] Irritable, lacking confidence in himself, nursing wounds real and imaginary, Horace Seymour was the one member of the secretariat who found little joy in working for Mr. Gladstone.[5]

In 1880, in addition to Godley, Hamilton, and Seymour, there were on Mr. Gladstone's staff as assistant private secretaries his son, Herbert, and Lord Granville's nephew, George Leveson Gower. Herbert Gladstone worked only sporadically at Downing Street; his duties as an M.P. and after 1881 his appointment as a Lord of the Treasury occupied most of his time.[6] George Leveson Gower remained as a junior member of the staff throughout the ministry; Hamilton found him 'an excellent fellow and a good workman'.[7] Near the end, in order to replace Horace Seymour, Henry Primrose, Rosebery's cousin and one of Hamilton's close friends, joined the staff.[8] In addition to these formally appointed secretaries Mary Gladstone played a role especially in the difficult area of minor church patronage.[9]

The work of the private secretaries was, according to George Leveson Gower, 'like Sam Weller's knowledge of London, . . . "extensive and peculiar"'.[10] The first private secretary—what Godley had been and Hamilton was after 1882—had an especially important role. He stood in a position of extraordinary closeness to the Prime Minister and to those with whom the Prime Minister most often worked. Through him the Queen, the Queen's private secretary, the members of the Cabinet, and others in both public and private life could find a uniquely valuable channel to the Prime Minister. In the opinion of Reginald Welby, who through long experience as a civil servant was qualified to judge, the first private secretary's position transcended the essentially private and personal character that marked the other secretaries. 'I have seen enough of [his] duties to convince me that they are higher and more delicate, and further more of a public character than the

---

[1] Seymour to EWH, 11 Jan. 1883, Add. MS. 48615.

[2] Diary, 6 Aug. 1882.

[3] Seymour to EWH, 9 Sept. 1884, Add. MS. 48615.

[4] S. Lyttelton to Mary G., 4 Sept. 1884, Add. MS. 46232, f. 102.

[5] Seymour to EWH, 12 Aug. 1883 and 3 Sept. 1884, Add. MS. 48615. See also Diary, 25 June 1902, Add. MS. 48679, f. 113, for EWH's remarks on the occasion of Seymour's death.

[6] G. to Lord Houghton, 19 Aug. 1881, Add. MS. 44901, f. 145.

[7] Diary, 16 Sept. 1880.

[8] Diary, 5 Dec. 1884; EWH to G., 9 Dec. 1884, Add. MS. 44190, f. 125. Actually Primrose had been one of the original members of the staff in 1880 but very soon went off to India to serve as Lord Ripon's private secretary. It was with his departure that Horace Seymour came to Downing Street. See 27 June 1880.

[9] See the correspondence of Spencer Lyttelton to Mary G., Add. MS. 46232.

[10] George Leveson Gower, Years of Content, 1858–1886 (London, 1940), p. 154.

Mr. Gladstone and his secretaries *circa* 1883
(Standing left to right: Horace Seymour, Spencer Lyttelton, George Leveson Gower, and EWH)

duties of his colleagues. . . .'[1] Of the extraordinary range and importance of
the first secretary's duties Hamilton's diary after 1882 gives the best evidence.[2] In addition to a capacity for hard work, the position required those
qualities of tact and discretion which Hamilton possessed to a high degree.
Indeed, Hamilton came to be known as *the* private secretary, the man in
England most completely possessing the peculiar qualifications necessary for
the post. In 1891 the Liverpool *Daily Post* stated that 'an ideal private secretary . . . has been defined as Mr. Gladstone's Mr. Hamilton, plus the power
of writing shorthand'.[3]

In addition to the special personal responsibilities of the principal private
secretary he shared with the others the daily routine of work—and a very
heavy amount of work it was. The secretaries opened the incoming letters,
although whether they opened *all* of the incoming letters was a question on
which Godley and Hamilton disagreed in later years. In his little monograph
on Mr. Gladstone, written in 1898 just after the Prime Minister's death,
Hamilton emphasized that there were no secrets between Mr. G. and his
private secretaries. They saw everything, he said.[4] But when Godley saw the
draft of Hamilton's essay he urged Hamilton to qualify his statements. 'In
my time we did not open letters from Cabinet Ministers, nor from a few
other privileged persons whose handwritings were well-known to us. Perhaps this was afterwards changed.'[5] In the same letter Godley noted that
Hamilton was wrong to imply that all the private secretaries were equally in
Mr. Gladstone's confidence. 'Of course this was very far from being the case.'
On this last point Godley was certainly correct. He and Hamilton had enjoyed
the confidence of Mr. Gladstone in a way that Horace Seymour could not.
But on the matter of all papers passing through the hands of the secretaries
Hamilton let his statement stand because in fact the secretaries, as the diary
makes clear, saw most of the correspondence of the ministers (and the Prime
Minister's replies) just as they saw the correspondence of lesser persons.
From the evidence of the diary it seems that the only exception was in the

---

[1] Welby to EWH, 11 June 1885, Add. MS. 44338, f. 287.

[2] For Mr. Gladstone's opinion on this, see Diary, 28 July 1883.

[3] From a clipping enclosed in a letter from W. Wilton Phipps to EWH, 3 Mar. 1891,
Add. MS. 48619. See also Randolph Churchill's reference to him in the House of Commons
on 4 Aug. 1884, *Parl. Deb.*, 3rd ser., vol. 291, pp. 1596–7. And the essay on Hamilton written in 1890 by George W. Smalley in his *London Letters and Some Others* (London, 1890),
ii. 489–94. What the remuneration of the private secretaries was the Hamilton MSS. do
not reveal. In 1874 Mr. Gladstone paid Gurdon, his principal private secretary, £400, but
he had another £430 in salary as Clerk in the Treasury. The second private secretary then
got £200. When Disraeli came into office in that year, Northcote, his Chancellor of the
Exchequer, advised him that he could give his first secretary, Montagu Corry, a salary of
£500 since Corry held no other post, and that he could give his second secretary £300.
Northcote to Disraeli, 27 Feb. [1874], Add. MS. 50016, ff. 161–2. The Gladstonian scale in
1880 was probably along these lines.

[4] Edward W. Hamilton, *Mr. Gladstone. A Monograph* (London, 1898), p. 79.

[5] Godley to EWH, 28 Sept. 1898, Add. MS. 48616.

case of those who were invited to write Mr. Gladstone by means of the 'double-envelope system'. In these cases only the outer envelope would be opened by the secretary and the inner passed on unopened. It would seem that this system was used mainly by those concerned with Mr. Gladstone's 'rescue work'; in the diary the practice appears in connection with Mrs. Langtry.[1]

In his monograph on Mr. Gladstone Hamilton described the way in which correspondence outside the double-envelope system was handled. His account explains the folds and marks that one finds in the Gladstone Papers in the British Museum. Incoming letters had to be folded in a certain way so as to make them as much as possible of uniform size, that is 'the size given by note-paper which, when both sides of it are laid out, folds into three—a size to which the folding of larger paper conveniently adapts itself'.[2] Once folded the letters had to be docketed. If the secretary judged that Mr. Gladstone should read the letter in full, he would put a + in the upper left-hand corner. Otherwise the secretary would make a brief note of the contents of the letter on the outer fold. For all correspondence of importance Mr. Gladstone would write the reply in full and the secretaries would write a copy of the reply either into a letterbook or on a separate sheet of paper depending on whether Mr. Glad-stone had put ✓ on the incoming letter (indicating a letterbook copy) or ✓✓ (for copying on a separate sheet). In replying to letters of minor importance Mr. Gladstone would use what his secretaries called a 'head and tail letter'. Mr. Gladstone would jot on the docket of the incoming letter a very brief note indicating what the nature of the reply should be; then on a blank piece of Downing Street stationery he would write 'My dear Sir' or 'My dear Bright' and about half way down the reverse side of the sheet he would write 'Faith-fully yours W. E. Gladstone' and then write the name of the recipient. The secretaries were to compose a reply that would fill up the space in between.[3]

The number of letters passing through the secretaries' hands could be very large. During one week in May 1882, after the assassination of Lord Frederick Cavendish, the letters came in on the average of 200 a day.[4] But in more ordinary times Hamilton regarded 70 a day as a heavy load.[5] The unfortunate events of 1884 increased the tempo; in March Hamilton calcu-lated that 500 letters were arriving each week and in December he estimated the year's receipts at 20,000.[6] When the pressure of work was extremely

[1] See Diary, 20 Apr. 1882.

[2] Edward W. Hamilton, *Mr. Gladstone. A Monograph* (London, 1898), p. 80.

[3] See Godley's example of a 'head and tail' letter, G. to H. H. Fowler, 24 Apr. 1882, Add. MS. 44902, f. 152; and one in which Hamilton wrote the body of the letter, G. to Bright, 21 Nov. 1884, Add. MS. 43385, f. 332.

[4] Diary, 17 May 1882.   [5] Diary, 25 Mar. 1883.

[6] Diary, 3 Mar. and 6 Dec. 1884. EWH to G., 15 Dec. 1884, Add. MS. 44190, f. 127. EWH wrote down the numbers of incoming letters during certain periods in 1882, 1883, 1884, and 1885 at the end of the 'secretarial book of knowledge' (see below) which is now in the possession of his nephew, Sir Walter Moberly.

heavy, as it was in 1885, Hamilton would have to work for 11 hours a day.[1]

To aid the secretarial staff in handling routine matters such as using the proper wording for announcing appointments, for responding to requests from clergymen for preferment, for 'declining Presidency of Clubs', or for making the necessary arrangements for a railway trip to or from Hawarden, there was compiled a volume known as the 'Book of Knowledge'. During Mr. Gladstone's first ministry W. B. Gurdon, recognizing that for the Prime Minister and his staff there was 'no department to fall back upon for information, as in the case of other Cabinet minister's', worked at compiling information 'for the guidance of the freshmen'.[2] Hamilton and his colleagues found the book of great value and with characteristic industry Hamilton, with some help from Seymour, produced a tidy revised version.[3]

In view of the amount of secretarial work and Hamilton's heavy duties in coping with it, the additional task of keeping up a diary, especially one so carefully and fully written, was very burdensome. To have spent a long day summarizing incoming letters and copying outgoing letters and then to end by writing out the sort of detailed résumé that Hamilton's diary is, would weigh on most men beyond endurance. But as a diarist and as a secretary Hamilton displayed extraordinary persistence. At first he thought that his self-imposed chore of journalizing might be impossible.[4] He hated to have breaks in it; a gap of a week or more in the diary was in his view 'a horrible hiatus'.[5] By 1884 he found 'the difficulty of writing up my diary becomes greater and greater. It is a very heavy tax on my spare minutes, which are few. But I may be repaid by it someday; so I struggle on determinedly'.[6] But in spite of the heavy official work of that year and what was by then a remarkably active social life, Hamilton not only struggled on but made his diary fuller than it had been in the past.

His ordinary method of keeping his journal, it appears, was to write directly into the bound volume on the day in which the entry was dated. The frequent alterations, deletions, and corrections in the diary are evidence that the entries are first drafts and were not copied in from another draft. It is also clear that in writing the entry for one day he usually had no idea what might happen the next; the entries for 5 May and 8 May 1882 concerning Lord Frederick Cavendish are the most dramatic examples of this. But then during the busy days of 1884 he found it difficult to keep up and he referred

[1] Diary, 10 Feb. 1885.
[2] Gurdon to G., 15 Aug. 1872, Add. MS. 44182, ff. 49–50.
[3] Hamilton's version is a small notebook of less than 100 pages containing forms of letters written out mainly in his hand. It is in the possession of his nephew, Sir Walter Moberly, in Oxford. See also EWH to Ponsonby, 11 Nov. 1881, Add. MS. 45725, ff. 23–4 and Seymour to EWH, 22 Aug. 1882, Add. MS. 48615.
[4] See, for example, Diary, 16 June and 10 July 1880.
[5] Diary, 22 Nov. 1881. See also Diary, 6 Jan., 22 May, 17 June 1881 and 20 June 1882.
[6] Diary, 18 May 1884. See also 31 Oct. 1884.

often to 'writing up' his journal as if in a quiet moment—usually Sunday—he would go back and, probably out of his recollection but perhaps from notes, reconstruct the entries for past days.[1] Only in one instance is there a section of the diary surviving on separate sheets of paper; the entry for 13 May 1884 is written on four pages of paper inserted in the volume with only the last paragraph written into the bound volume. Hamilton had left two sheets of the volume blank prior to the last paragraph but he had never copied in the entry.[2] If it were his usual practice to write entries on separate sheets and then copy them, these sheets and this gap would probably not exist; it is because it was not his usual practice that he left inadequate space for this entry by writing in the sections around it.

The diary had begun with the formation of Mr. Gladstone's ministry and with the fall of that ministry Hamilton thought of giving it up. On 30 June 1885 he wrote:

I am beginning to doubt whether it is any longer worth my while to keep up my diary. So long as one was behind scenes, I felt it a duty, and a very irksome duty it has been at times. But now I shall have little to relate but what is common to everybody else. I shall probably, for a while at any rate, endeavour to jot down a few things and see whether 'the game is worth the candle'.[3]

He soon discovered that his life as a civil servant at the Treasury, though lacking some of the drama of his work at Downing Street, was full of activity worth recording. His continuing relationships with the Gladstone family, with Rosebery, and now with major figures in the Conservative party, kept him close to the world of great events. But he also discovered that 'journalizing had become a part of one's ordinary life', a habit which he could not readily give up.[4] Even when ill health had made it almost impossible for him to write legibly, he went on with the diary because 'his fingers itched' to be at their old work.[5] But for him the great years of the diary—and of his life—were the years with Mr. Gladstone, the years from 1880 to 1885. Doing work he loved for 'the kindest, the most thoughtful'[6] of masters, Hamilton was brought into a world where he could be 'a somebody',[7] where he could be close to politics—a field in which he did not wish to act but which he took delight in observing. In his article on 'The Private Secretary', published in 1891, Hamilton wrote:

It is said that there are only two happy days in the term of Ministerial office—the day on which the Minister accepts office and the day on which he lays it down. With the private secretary it is otherwise. It is probable that to him the day on

[1] See Diary, 9 Mar., 27 July, and 7 Dec. 1884 and 31 May 1885.
[2] Add. MS. 48636, ff. 76–81.   [3] Diary, 30 June 1885.
[4] Diary, 23 Aug. and 28 Sept. 1886, Add. MS. 48644, ff. 98, 130.
[5] Diary, 1 Sept. 1905, Add. MS. 48683, f. 64. See also Appendix I.
[6] Diary, 26 Dec. 1881. See also Diary, 17 and 29 Dec. 1882 and, above all, for a tribute to Mr. Gladstone, see 23 June 1885.   [7] Diary, 23 June 1885.

which he is apprised of his confidential appointment will be the day of his life on which he will look back with the greatest pride and that the day on which he has to give up that appointment will be the day which will be tinged with most regret.[1]

Along with his delight in his work Hamilton found special pleasure in the company of his friends, old ones from Salisbury, or Eton and Christ Church like Lord Pembroke, William Wilton Phipps, or Lord Rosebery, and new ones like their wives and all sorts of people in the political and diplomatic world with whom his position now brought him into touch. The diary includes striking evidence of the steady enlargement, outward and upward, of Hamilton's sphere of friendships. His remarkable talents as a private secretary were matched by an extraordinary capacity to attract and hold the respect and affection of both men and women. Described by T. H. S. Escott as the 'most musical, most cheery, most *répandu* of men',[2] Hamilton came to be increasingly in demand at dinners, dances, and week-end house parties. In July 1883 he discovered that he had dined out 39 out of the last 42 nights; in July 1884 he 'found that out of 56 nights I had only dined at my own expense alone once'.[3] The pace could be exhausting but he loved it; never did it break the regularity or efficiency of his work at Downing Street and only rarely did it prevent him from keeping up his diary, although it is usually the pressure of his social rather than his official life which made for gaps.[4]

At the centre of his social life was the group of friends for whom Wilton House was the focus. Bishop Hamilton and his family naturally visited there often with Sidney Herbert's widow, and Edward Hamilton became a close friend of George Herbert, who had been Lord Pembroke since he was twelve.[5] After Pembroke's marriage in 1874 Hamilton was a devoted friend of both husband and wife and of Pembroke's brother Sidney Herbert and his wife; he was a frequent guest at Wilton and at Lady Herbert's house in London. The Herbert family, Hamilton, and other friends regularly had a dinner at the time of the Eton–Harrow cricket match, a cricket week at Wilton, and an annual row on the Thames; they called themselves the Bilton Waggers, a Spoonerized version of Wilton Baggers, and jocular references to the Waggers appear occasionally in the diary and frequently in the correspondence between Hamilton and Pembroke.[6] To Pembroke, Hamilton was in 1870 'Ted' or 'Ned'; to others in early years he was 'Hab'; to some, so George Leveson Gower wrote, he was 'The Cob, partly on account of his strong, compact little figure, and partly on account of his cheeriness and great

---

[1] [Edward W. Hamilton], 'The Private Secretary: His Life and Duties', *The New Review*, v (July–Dec. 1891), p. 453.

[2] T. H. S. Escott, *Society in the Country House* (London, 1907), p. 472.

[3] Diary, 4 July 1883 and 25 July 1884.

[4] See, for example, Diary, 14 Oct. 1882, 15 and 31 July 1883.

[5] Lady Herbert to G., 21 Aug. 1867, Add. MS. 44212, f. 141.

[6] Add. MS. 48621. See also George Leveson Gower, *Years of Content, 1858–1886* (London, 1940), p. 155, and Diary, 15 Aug. 1880, 15 and 28 Aug. 1881, 15 July 1883.

capacity for work'.[1] To all eventually he became 'Eddy'; even Mr. Gladstone as early as 1882 gave up 'My dear Hamilton' for 'My dear Eddy'.[2]

In 1883 when Hamilton was visiting Panshanger the guests were amused not only by the 'lawn tennis and bowls' that Hamilton mentioned in his diary[3] but by a phrenologist whose reading of Hamilton's head might encourage one to believe that there was more to the art than we in later times have been willing to accept. In listing the various qualities, the phrenologist gave a '7 large' to Hamilton in music, perceptive faculties, and 'ideality'; for 'amativeness' there was written 'so-so' but it was crossed out and the quality assigned the number '6'. Then there was the evaluation:

This is what I should describe as a strongly marked head, especially in respect of the natural (or as they are termed animal developments). Yet it is a full head mentally—the perceptive organs are stronger than the brain organs, and I should judge that though a clever head, *certainly*, most of the knowledge it contains has been gained through experience and observation rather than deep study—the character *must be* a fine one and the brain quick. I should judge that *great tact* and a sensitive refined nature with good strong judgment and ability, and with much kindliness of disposition form the chief characteristics—and that he would be a true firm friend—Ideality and music are strongly marked.[4]

Whether through his head or through his host, Lord Cowper, some of Hamilton's leading traits had become clear to the phrenologist.

'*Great tact*' was indeed one of Hamilton's gifts. In his relations with his fellows on the secretarial staff, with ministers, and with Mr. Gladstone himself, it was his tact, his sensitivity to the feelings of others, that made him the perfect private secretary. It is in his friendship for Lord Rosebery that Hamilton's talents in dealing with difficult personal situations become most clear, and that he shows himself to be 'a true firm friend'. Throughout the period of this ministry and beyond, Hamilton acted the part of emissary and buffer between Rosebery and Mr. Gladstone. Hamilton and the Prime Minister both found Rosebery attractive but mysterious; Mr. Gladstone saw his intellectual brilliance and political capacity, tried to play the role of a political patron, but discovered that Rosebery did not respond in a comprehensible way. Hamilton, so the diary shows, was the man who most effectively played the role of interpreter between the two—and yet, close as he was to Rosebery, he too found the man beyond his grasp. In 1883 Hamilton wrote of Rosebery to Ponsonby:

I have known him intimately for 23 years—we were next each other at Eton for about 5 years and a half and afterwards at Christ Church together;—and yet I have never really understood him. He is an extraordinary mixture. He has brilliant

---

[1] Add. MS. 48621 and George Leveson Gower, *Years of Content, 1858–1886* (London, 1940), p. 154.   [2] G. to EWH, 11 May 1882, Add. MS. 48607.
[3] Diary, 15 May 1883.
[4] Written on Panshanger stationery, dated 15 May 1883, Add. MS. 48623.

abilities and in many ways special aptitude for political life; but I fear his over-sensitive, thin-skinned nature will sadly stand in the way of a really successful political future.[1]

Along with his tact went an unusual degree of patience.[2] Horace Seymour's whining, Rosebery's instability, Harcourt's boorishness, Mr. Gladstone's inconsiderateness were all fully observed and understood; and to all these different and often sharply differing men Hamilton remained loyal, a devoted friend, whose friendship for one did not involve the betrayal of another.

As the phrenologist detected, it was these human qualities of the heart rather than those of the mind that set Hamilton apart. But he was aware of possessing certain mental abilities that made him unusually adept at tasks especially appropriate to the private secretary and civil servant. His powers of summing-up were remarkable, as the diary illustrates again and again and as his memoranda show. In September 1885 Mary Gladstone, in begging Hamilton to come and visit, recognized that there was 'nobody exactly who can gather together all the leading points of importance and interest' in recent events as he could.[3] Hamilton knew that he had a valuable talent for clear, written—not oral—exposition;[4] with characteristic modesty he ascribed this talent to his possession of moderate rather than superior intellectual powers. In 1891 the Chancellor of the Exchequer, Goschen, felt his budget statement had been a failure in part because Hamilton's health had prevented him from assisting in its preparation. Stephen Spring-Rice, who had distinguished himself in the classical tripos at Cambridge, and was principal clerk in the Treasury, played the leading role in advising the Chancellor. Hamilton found it 'quite comforting to feel that moderate abilities without any pretence to cleverness can stand up against such remarkable talents as Spring-Rice possesses. What I do pride myself upon is being clear in exposition; and the reason why I am clear is that I must explain things clearly in order to make them intelligible to myself'.[5]

More and more often as the years go on the diary offers numerous examples of Hamilton's wise and balanced judgements of men and events based on experience and intuition rather than on unusual powers of analysis. Ireland, and particularly the Home Rule question, were issues on which Englishmen felt strongly and on which devoted Gladstonians especially had difficulty in

[1] EWH to Ponsonby, 5 June 1883, Add. MS. 45725, f. 67. For Hamilton's role as buffer and interpreter, see his note of 7 Mar. 1883, Add. MS. 44189, f. 201 and his notes to G. of 6 Apr. and 14 Aug. 1883, Add. MS. 48607.

[2] This quality was one that Mrs. Gladstone took special note of. See, for example, her letter to EWH, 1 Oct. [1898], Add. MS. 48609.

[3] Mary G. to EWH, 4 Sept. 1885, Add. MS. 48609.

[4] Later, when as a Treasury official he had to appear to testify before the Public Accounts Committee, he became 'conscious of having far less power to explain with my tongue than my pen, which is far the readier of those two instruments'. Diary, 19 Mar. 1886, Add. MS. 48643, f. 45. See also Diary, 25 Apr. 1888, Add. MS. 48648, f. 83.

[5] Diary, 28 Apr. 1891, Add. MS. 48655.

holding moderate opinions. But read what Hamilton wrote in his diary in February 1888 after two Gladstonian liberals had been returned to the House of Commons in by-elections in West Southwark and West Edinburgh:

Nothing daunted with the result of the recent elections, the *Times* actually says: 'We are convinced that the policy which Mr. Balfour is carrying on in Ireland will be completely successful.' This is a bold conviction. It means neither more nor less than the complete re-establishment of law and order in Ireland and the entire disappearance of the Home Rule cry. It is difficult to say which of the two doctrines it is most foolish to propound—that Home Rule is dead or that there will be a Home Rule government in office within a few months' time, as many people elated by Southwark and West Edinburgh declare. Lady Aberdeen for instance whom I saw yesterday was quite annoyed at my venturing to say that the present government would probably last another three years. Home Rule will, in some form or other, of course be tried; but not for a little while; and moreover I am not one of those who believe that when the trial takes place it will mean a millenium for Ireland. The fact is, most remedial measures fall short of the expectations of the promoters and authors of them. This is not so much to be wondered at; for such measures conduce generally more to remove the *sense* of a grievance than a grievance itself, and to produce a *sense* of amelioration more than to produce an actual state of things for the better.[1]

The willingness to view so cooly an issue so hot explains in itself why Hamilton, though always fascinated by politics, had no wish to participate actively in political life. Indeed, he was of the opinion that civil servants like himself should not vote, should even be denied the franchise by law.[2] But as he said: 'One cannot of course help having one's own opinions; but that is [a] quite different thing to giving practical expression to them.'[3] Hamilton's own opinions were very much those of a loyal Gladstonian, but he was not an enthusiastic advocate of every Gladstonian policy. Not only was he luke-warm on Home Rule but even a major piece of legislation like the Irish Land Bill of 1881 he regarded as 'a disagreeable necessity'.[4] On finance, however, and on Free Trade he was strong in the faith, regarding tendencies away from Liberal policies with horror. As the London society in which he took such delight became more and more virulently opposed to Mr. Gladstone, Hamilton had to sit through some uncomfortable dinners, welcoming those, like that given by the Dowager Duchess of Montrose in February 1885, where 'politics [was] excluded out of consideration for me'.[5] Wedded to the idea of the neutrality of the civil servant and in his own view 'a poor partisan', Hamilton was nevertheless strongly attached to certain political causes and,

[1] Diary, 21 Feb. 1888, Add. MS. 48648, ff. 25–6. Even in the fever heat of 1886 Hamilton could write: 'I have never been carried away with the idea of Home Rule . . .', Diary, 12 July 1886, Add. MS. 48644, ff. 61–2.
[2] Diary, 7 Apr. 1883; 14 Sept. 1886, Add. MS. 48644, f. 122; and 11 July 1888, Add. MS. 48649, f. 12.
[3] Diary, 11 July 1888, Add. MS. 48649, f. 12.
[4] Diary, 9 June 1881. For Home Rule see Diary, 26 Mar. 1886, Add. MS. 48643, ff. 55–6.
[5] Diary, 8 Feb. 1885.

above all, to Mr. Gladstone.[1] When Hamilton had returned to the sanctuary of the Treasury in 1886 he found that with the formation of Mr. Gladstone's third government, he could not keep his 'fingers out of the political pie altogether, and so have been giving a helping hand on the sly in starting; but must now stand aside'.[2]

Hamilton's moderation, balance, and growing knowledge of the political world made him wonderfully effective as a buffer between Mr. Gladstone and others—a salutary restraining force. Even as early as September 1880 Hamilton took the liberty of calling to Lord Granville's attention the use of an inflammatory adjective—'short-sighted'—in Mr. Gladstone's description of the action of the House of Lords on the Compensation for Disturbance Bill.[3] And throughout the part of the diary published here, Hamilton's role as a go-between and peace-maker becomes clear, especially in the Prime Minister's dealings with Hamilton's friend, Rosebery.[4] According to Ponsonby, the Queen felt Hamilton's absence at Downing Street upon Mr. Gladstone's return to power in 1886; 'she declares that now that I [Hamilton] am no longer at Mr. G.'s elbow there is not a soul left to keep him in check'.[5]

As he himself had sensed, it was his lack of brilliance, the absence in himself of the kind of temperament that made and marred Rosebery's career, that qualified Hamilton to play so effectively the part he did. A modern reader of his diary will probably be amused by some of the examples of his provincialism, but the reader should remember that Hamilton's attitudes, while not perhaps those that a more sensitively introspective man might have, were appropriate to a clubbable Englishman of his time. Take, for example, his remark of November 1880 relating to the problem of settling the territorial changes agreed to at Berlin: 'Dulcigno matters continue *in statu quo*. If the Sultan has the smallest spark of good feeling left in him, he ought to see to the transfer being completed by Lord Mayor's Day. The Government on that occasion certainly ought to be able to point to its policy abroad having actually borne fruit.'[6] What Hamilton regarded as humour was usually less than witty and usually had a punning element. Two examples will serve.

[1] See especially his eloquent defence of the Liberal Government, Diary, 11 Jan. 1885.

[2] EWH to Ponsonby, 2 Feb. 1886, Add. MS. 45725, f. 148, and Diary, 14 Sept. 1886, Add. MS. 48644, f. 122. See also Hamilton's declaration that even if Treasury officials should have to administer a policy of protection, they 'would work, heart and soul', to solve the problems surrounding what was to most of them an abhorrent departure from free trade principles. Diary, 30 June 1903, Add. MS. 48681, ff. 17–18.

[3] Ramm, i. 179–80. 'Please do not blow up Hamilton for the indiscretion of his suggestion', wrote Lord Granville, and G. replied that he would 'willingly give up short sighted'.

[4] And see also EWH's letter to Dilke, 21 Apr. 1885, Add. MS. 43913, ff. 128–30, urging Dilke not to resign and thus upset G.

[5] Diary, 4 Mar. 1886, Add. MS. 48643, f. 34.

[6] Diary, 4 Nov. 1880. Another example of the same sort of straight-faced obtuseness can be found in the entry for 5 Apr. 1882: 'Another terrible murder in Ireland this week;—this time a woman of the Upper Class is the victim, which makes the deed the more atrocious.'

He recorded the termination of Gladys Lonsdale's engagement to Luke White by saying: 'Experience of it converted her attraction for Luke White into *Luke* warmness.'[1] In 1888 he went to visit the Cowpers at Wrest Park in Bedfordshire and wrote in his diary: 'After the season there could be no more appropriate place to come than (W)*rest* in Bed(s).'[2] In this respect Hamilton's humour was quite in tune with Mr. Gladstone's, which was also based on puns, though with a characteristic classical turn, as in the case of Lady Florence Dixie's improbable tale of being attacked by knife-wielding Irishmen, which Mr. G. called 'an Ipsa *dixit*'.[3] Like Mr. Gladstone, Hamilton also enjoyed discussions of the use and misuse of words.[4] The favourite object of Hamilton's pedantic concern in this field had to do with the use of the word birthday. In 1890 he wrote: 'Mr. G. celebrated the 81st anniversary of his birth yesterday. (People will always talk of his 81st birthday; it really is his 82nd birthday, and the 81st anniversary of it.)'[5]

Another one of Hamilton's interests that made him a welcome member of the world of London society, and also a major element in contributing to his own enjoyment of life, was his love of music and his talent as a performer and composer. The degree he had received at Oxford was a degree in music, and during the seventies Hamilton sought opportunities to further his musical education. In 1876 he had asked Arthur Sullivan to be his musical mentor but Sullivan had declined;[6] Stainer was the man under whom Hamilton formally studied and it was from Stainer that Hamilton thought he had learned what little he knew.[7] During the seventies Hamilton had some of his compositions published; there were some songs—'By the River Side. A Ballad' and 'A Set of Singing Quadrilles'. Even as early as 1868 he had published 'a sacred cantata', *Praise the Lord O My Soul* and in 1870 he had set a poem by his friend Lord Pembroke to music.[8] *Six Sketches for the Pianoforte* of 1878 show a strong influence of Schumann. The piano was his instrument; his sisters Constance, who played the cello, and Maud, a violinist, comprised with him an excellent trio.[9] Throughout his busy years with Mr. Gladstone he could find time for 'a little outburst of music'.[10] Listening to music was a part of many of the evening parties he attended; occasionally he and a singer—Lady

---

[1] Diary, 7 Oct. 1883.

[2] Diary, 31 July 1888, Add. MS. 48649, ff. 32–3.

[3] Diary, 31 Mar. 1883. Hamilton rarely made use of Latin phrases or classical allusions. His favourite and, it seems, sole specific allusion to a classical work is to the line in Horace's *Ars Poetica* concerning the mountain and the mouse. He uses it three times in the diary—7 Nov. 1880, 31 Dec. 1893, and 11 Feb. 1894 (Add. MS. 48662. ff. 34, 104).

[4] See, for example, Diary, 22 Nov. 1883.

[5] Diary, 30 Dec. 1890, Add. MS. 48654, f. 111.

[6] A. Sullivan to EWH, 8 Oct. 1876, Add. MS. 48622.

[7] Diary, 1 Apr. 1901, Add. MS. 48678, ff. 24–5.

[8] *The Hollow Elm Tree*, beginning, 'Once when my heart was riven.' For this and other references to his published music see the Music Catalogue at the British Museum.

[9] In addition to numerous references in the diary, see Mary Gladstone's diary, 17 Nov. 1880, Add. MS. 46259, f. 79.   [10] Diary, 6 Jan. 1881.

Breadalbane or Miss Santley—or he and his sisters would provide part of the musical entertainment. In the section of the diary now published he describes writing for Miss Santley a setting of Thomas Moore's 'When through Life Unblest We Rove';[1] in his setting he matches the sentimentality of the verses. Later, in 1892, when Hamilton was dining with John Morley, for whom music was also a special delight, Hamilton played some of his recently published *Sketches in Music* and moved Morley to say that 'he would give up all politics tomorrow if he could play decently well on the piano'.[2]

As his frequent comments on music in the diary show, he took great interest in the development of English music, and he played an important role in the founding and support of the Royal College of Music. Aside from his admiration for the work of Stainer and Sullivan, he had the highest regard for the work of his close friend and contemporary, Hubert Parry, whose father had married as his second wife Hamilton's aunt. In 1881 he went to Cambridge to hear a performance of Parry's *Prometheus*:

It was a grand performance, of which the work itself was nobly worthy. No music ever stirred me so much. I felt quite overcome at the end. Making a liberal allowance for the natural excitement of hearing so advanced a work so admirably performed of one of one's oldest and dearest friends, I cannot but attribute the main part of my emotion to the intrinsic merit of the work. Certainly it could not have been produced by any other English living composer; and I doubt if it does not rank almost first of English works in its high standard, its breadth, sublimity and pathos, its mastery over the orchestra and other high qualities combined.[3]

Later on when Elgar began to dominate the English musical scene, Hamilton, who had heard *The Apostles* but had found it unrewarding, expressed his wish to organize a festival for Parry 'on the lines of the one organised last year in honour of Elgar, whose talents don't approach those of H.P.'.[4]

By 1904 he had brought himself to engage in the 'horrible extravagance' of a box at Covent Garden; by then operas were his chief musical interest. His 'omnibus box' in that year cost him £72 and he calculated that, as he had gone about 40 times during the year, each night had cost him almost £2. Melba and Caruso in *La Bohème*, for him the best of Italian operas, had attracted him most often. But his real liking was for German opera, and especially for Wagner.[5] In his enthusiasm after a performance of *Götterdämmerung* in 1903 he wrote: 'I remember once seeing Wagner. He is the greatest man on whom I ever set eyes.'[6] A surprising assertion from Mr. Gladstone's private secretary.

Music, friends, Downing Street work—these were the principal ingredients

[1] See Diary, 20 Aug., 29 Sept., and 20 Nov. 1883.
[2] Diary, 29 Jan. 1892, Add. MS. 48657, f. 48.
[3] Diary, 28 May 1881.
[4] Diary, 26 June 1904, Add. MS. 48682, f. 57.
[5] Diary, 26 July and 2 Aug. 1904, Add. MS. 48682, ff. 72, 74.
[6] Diary, 16 May 1903, Add. MS. 48680, f. 132.

of the joyous years Hamilton recorded in the opening volumes of his diary. Living and working in 11 Downing Street, winning more and more friends through his position and engaging qualities, coming ever closer to his beloved chief, Mr. Gladstone, Hamilton fully recorded in his diary the events—mainly public—that engaged his attention during the years of Mr. Gladstone's second ministry. The private or personal landmarks of these years were the enlargement of his circle of friends, his entry into the clubs that were the foundation of his social life—Brooks's to which he was elected in 1881 and the Cosmopolitan which he entered in 1883[1]—but most dramatically his attachment to Venetia Cavendish-Bentinck.

A daughter of George Cavendish-Bentinck, who had been the parliamentary secretary of the Board of Trade and Judge Advocate-General during Disraeli's ministry, a great-granddaughter of the 3rd Duke of Portland, Venetia seems to have become acquainted with Hamilton in the summer of 1882 when he recorded that 'Miss Venetia is an excellent girl'.[2] Thereafter the mention of meetings with Mrs. Cavendish-Bentinck and her daughter increase in frequency. Their house in Grafton Street was one of his favourite resorts. Mrs. Cavendish-Bentinck was an active and ambitious hostess;[3] her husband, in addition to being, in Hamilton's view, 'a typical high Tory', was an enthusiastic collector who filled the house with fine French, Italian, and English paintings and other objects of art.[4] Hamilton found their daughter Venetia fascinating. His friends could see that his hopes for matrimony, while high, were to be dashed. In November 1883 Spencer Lyttelton wrote Mary Gladstone: 'I hear Venetia Bentinck has not much money so that it is probable she will not be allowed by Penelope [her mother] to marry Eddy.'[5] And the diary for 1884 and 1885 tells the unhappy story bearing out Lyttelton's prediction. Through the first half of 1884 the tempo of Hamilton's references to Venetia accelerates, culminating in the entries for 1 and 2 July where he records his 'hideous resolve' which is, apparently, to give up seeing her until she should give him an answer to his proposal of marriage. But after this sudden crescendo there is the resigned resumption on 9 July 1884 of their old friendly terms and then the gradual waning of hope. By December 1884 Hamilton was properly alerted to the danger of a rival; it was Arthur James, who could offer Venetia a house in Warwickshire and an income that Hamilton could never dream of matching. Hamilton's chief confidante in this matter, Mrs. Stanley Clarke, warned him of the danger

---

[1] *Memorials of Brooks's* . . . (London, 1907), p. 220; Diary, 6 Apr. and 4 July 1883.
[2] Diary, 26 Aug. 1882.
[3] See, for example, Henry Drummond Wolff, *Rambling Recollections* (London, 1908), ii. 122.
[4] Diary, 9 Nov. 1886, Add. MS. 48645, f. 29 and 11 Apr. 1891, Add. MS. 48655, ff. 67–8. Upon Venetia's death in 1948 the National Gallery and the Victoria and Albert Museum fell heir to the paintings and furniture. See *The Times*, 30 June 1948, p. 6a.
[5] Spencer Lyttelton to Mary G., 12 Nov. 1883, Add. MS. 46232, f. 90.

and the pressure on Venetia 'to make some confidential promise'.[1] But in spite of his continued attention and the support of Mrs. Clarke, Venetia was lost to him. On 2 October he 'received a "death warrant" in the kindest possible terms' and three days later he 'had a touching interview . . . in Grafton Street'.[2] In December Venetia married Arthur James and became the mistress of Coton House, Rugby, in Warwickshire; indeed she and her husband took on the Grafton Street house after her father's death in 1891, altering and renovating it, and putting in, to Hamilton's distress, 'a *red marble staircase*'.[3] Hamilton remained on friendly terms with the Jameses; they entertained him and she called on him while he was convalescing in Brighton in 1891.[4] As Mrs. Arthur James, Venetia came to be known as one of the most brilliant, though eccentric, hostesses of her time. Generous, witty, domineering, kindly though outwardly hard, notoriously devoted to small economies, especially of fuel, Venetia has left her mark in the memoirs of her contemporaries. She was, like Hamilton, interested in music, and in her later life 'played the organ and gave the congregation a deafening lead in the hymns'.[5] She died in 1948 at the age of 86, having then been a widow for 30 years.

But the dashing of his hopes of marriage with Venetia were the only serious blot on these years of Mr. Gladstone's second ministry. The only other disappointment he faced was his failure to be appointed to the Secretaryship of the Admiralty—'one of the few places I should really like'. But in 1884 he learned that it was 'out of the range of practical arrangements, and it is probably best and as it should be'.[6]

Other possibilities offered themselves while he was in Mr. Gladstone's service. In the autumn of 1884 his superiors at the Treasury dangled a promotion in front of him if he would return.[7] In early 1885 the Commissionership of Woods was vacant and Lord Richard Grosvenor, the Chief Whip, suggested Hamilton for the post; but Hamilton wrote Mr. Gladstone that 'it would take more than one Commissionership to induce me to leave your privileged service, so long as I can be of any use. This has been an old resolve of mine; and one which could not easily be shaken'. In reply Mr. Gladstone wrote: 'I am a vanishing quantity and you should not be governed in considering your own future by any regard to it.'[8] But, aside from his loyalty to the Prime Minister, he admitted that the Commissionership had 'no very special attractions' for him.[9]

[1] Mrs. Stanley Clarke to EWH, 26 Dec. 1884, Add. MS. 48624.
[2] Diary, 2 and 5 Oct. 1885, Add. MS. 48641, ff. 92, 94.
[3] Diary, 14 July 1893, Add. MS. 48660, f. 129.
[4] Diary, 26 Apr. 1891, Add. MS. 48655, f. 77.
[5] Sonia Keppel, *Edwardian Daughter* (London, 1958), pp. 187–8; Edward Cadogan, *Before the Deluge* . . . (London, 1961), pp. 167–9.
[6] Diary, 25 July 1883 and 22 Mar. 1884.
[7] R. R. W. Lingen to EWH, 9 Oct. 1884, Add. MS. 48624 and Diary, 18 Oct. 1884.
[8] EWH to G., 13 Jan. 1885 and G. to EWH, 14 Jan. 1885, Add. MS. 48608.
[9] Diary, 15 Jan. 1885.

He stayed with Mr. Gladstone to the end of the ministry, when he had to face the effects for himself of the Government's resignation: 'I lose the most interesting, responsible, and important place I can ever hold. I am turned out of house and home as well as office.'[1] His friend Rosebery felt what a blow it was to Hamilton and offered the best cushion he could—an invitation to stay with the Roseberys at Lansdowne House 'for the present' and a characteristically extravagant reminder of the bond that existed between them since their schooldays at Eton: 'Do you know that next September we shall have been friends for a quarter of a century? It will then be twenty-five years since we trembled together in the upper school yard and were united in affection by the bonds of terror and awe. A quarter of a century! it took only that for Pitt to be begotten and receive the seals of Prime Minister, and there are only seventy-five of them since the birth of Christ.'[2] Hamilton gratefully accepted the Roseberys' invitation to take up residence with them, but felt deeply the 'kick downstairs' that made him a 'nobody' after being a 'somebody'.[3]

On Mr. Gladstone's recommendation, the Queen made him a Companion of the Order of the Bath. 'I am so glad', Pembroke wrote, 'you are going to tub with the Queen.'[4] But more than this honour, it was Mr. Gladstone's letter of thanks that served as a reward for his service. Hamilton had written Mr. G. on 29 June 1885 to say that the new Tory Government had made him the Principal Clerk of the Finance Division of the Treasury—'their first job' as he had written in the diary.[5]

'I feel', he continued in his letter to Mr. Gladstone:

that I owe my advancement in a great measure to yourself and to the experience I have derived from my service under you. One of the many great advantages of that service has been to make me proof against fear of responsibility and excess of work; . . .

The only drawback to my accepting the post is that it places me, I fear, in a position which will disqualify me from any further personal service to yourself.

During these last few trying days, I have felt quite unable to give expression to you of my feelings. As they have been under little control, I have not dared to do so. It has been a dreadful blow to me, I confess, to have had to terminate my highly privileged service in Downing Street. But I am very sensible of the good fortune I have had in being allowed to work for you as long a time as five years; and your kindness, in addition to the kind things done and the kind words said by others, has helped to break my fall.

[1] Diary, 9 June 1885.

[2] Rosebery to EWH, 11 June 1885, Add. MS. 48610.

[3] Diary, 23 June 1885. In the entries for 25 and 26 June 1885 he repeated (but then crossed out) the 'somebody' and 'nobody' theme.

[4] Pembroke to EWH, 25 June 1885, Add. MS. 48621.

[5] Diary, 29 June 1885—although in his letter to Mr. G. he wrote that since it was an appointment 'from the other side' it could not 'be set down as a job either by the Department or by people outside'. EWH to G., 29 June 1885, Add. MS. 44191, ff. 21-2.

This period of five years will always be looked upon by me as the most privileged time of my life; and, though I have been fully alive to the great honour I have been deriving all this while, I shall never be thankful enough, or at any rate shall never be able to show adequately my sense of thankfulness for all I owe to you.

There never could be such a master to serve: never an unkind word, never the smallest loss of temper, and constant remarks of approbation. I am afraid I have taken a very large share of the 'plums' of the service just terminated; but I never could have done even as well as I have done—and I am conscious of plenty of shortcomings—if it had not been for the very valuable assistance and ready co-operation always afforded to me by my colleagues who have been most considerate and forbearing to me, one and all.[1]

To this Mr. Gladstone replied in a letter which Morley quoted extensively.

Since you have in substance received the appointment, I am unmuzzled, and may now express the unbounded pleasure which it gives me, together with my strong sense (not disparaging anyone else) of your desert. The modesty of your letter is as remarkable as its other qualities, and does you the highest honour.

I can accept no tribute from you, or from anyone, with regard to the office of Private Secretary under me except this, that it has always been made by me a strict and severe office, and that this is really the only favour I have ever done you or any of your colleagues, to whom in their several places and measures I am similarly obliged.

As to your services to me, they have been simply indescribable.

No one I think could dream, until by experience he knew, to what an extent in these close personal relations devolution can be carried, and how it strengthens the feeble knees and thus also sustains the fainting heart.

I am afraid that all is over and that I am now no longer on addresses the familiar name which for nearly sixty years has been dear to me.[2]

God bless you.

As Hamilton wrote in his diary: 'It makes the colour come to one's cheeks. It is a real heir-loom.'[3]

From Sir Henry Ponsonby, the Queen's private secretary, Hamilton received a tribute all the more telling for its spontaneous informality. 'If I had my way', Ponsonby wrote, 'I would give you the G.C.B., for you deserve much more than a C.B. and I am indeed really and truly sorry to lose—for a time only I trust—my correspondence with you, for you have helped me greatly in all the difficult and troublesome questions that have arisen between us—and which thanks to your good management have almost always been satisfactorily settled. I didn't mean to say all this when I began my letter—but it came out as I really felt it.'[4]

On 'Black Friday'—26 June 1885—Hamilton moved out of his Downing Street rooms and took up residence with the Roseberys at Lansdowne House. During the few days when his future at the Treasury was uncertain

---

[1] EWH to G., 29 June 1885, Add. MS. 44191, ff. 21-4.

[2] By which he meant presumably 'W. E. Gladstone, M.P.'.

[3] G. to EWH, 30 June 1885, Add. MS. 48608. See also Morley, iii. 210-11. Diary 1 July 1885.

[4] Ponsonby to EWH, 23 June 1 85, Add. MS. 48603.

he had looked into the possibility of a career in private business, but by the time he had moved he knew that there was a fair chance of his succeeding to Reginald Welby's place at the Treasury and three days later he learned that he had been promoted over some other first-class clerks to the post of Principal Clerk of the Finance Division.[1] The prospect of working under men different from Mr. Gladstone in both stature and politics made Hamilton uneasy, but, as he wrote in his diary, 'Loyalty toward one's political masters should be the first object of a public servant', and therefore he assured himself that even if Lord Randolph Churchill should, as rumour had it he might, become the Chancellor of the Exchequer in 1886, 'one would be able to get on with him'.[2] And when Churchill in fact did become the Chancellor Hamilton found him, to his surprise, an admirable chief; Hamilton was sorry when Churchill's sudden departure from office severed their official connection, and even though he recognized that Goschen, Churchill's successor, was a man 'from whom one would be able to learn', Goschen's orthodoxy and the 'humdrum budget' it would produce was not, in Hamilton's view, a favourable exchange.[3] But then he discovered that Goschen too was a bold and artful Chancellor. Goschen's conversion of the 3 per cent consols in 1888–9 was a masterpiece of financial management and was for Hamilton 'the biggest and most interesting job in which one will ever be concerned'.[4] So interesting did Hamilton find this episode that he published in 1890 a history of it—*Conversion and Redemption*, 'the title of which', he noted, 'is exciting the curiosity of the evangelical world'.[5]

In each Chancellor in turn he found something to admire. Harcourt, in spite of his '*tantrums*' and 'ungentlemanlike' behaviour toward Rosebery, was a Chancellor he would miss when the change in government came in 1895.[6] Since Hicks-Beach was 'a gentleman, a very straight man', without '*fads* or heterodox notions' Hamilton was sure he could get on with him—and he did. Indeed he thought that 'his measures and the way he expounded and conducted them will secure him a place not far off such men as Pitt, Peel, and Mr. G.'.[7] But then with C. T. Ritchie in 1902 a new sort of man started to preside at the Treasury. Hamilton had always thought that being a gentleman and being also of independent means were of the greatest importance for a politician.[8] 'The first qualification required', he wrote of the

---

[1] Fife to EWH, 25 June 1885, Add. MS. 48624 and Diary, 26 and 29 June 1885.
[2] Diary, 27 July 1886, Add. MS. 48644, f. 85. The reader will have noticed that Hamilton was in the habit of referring to himself as 'one' and often carried this seeming effacement of self in his diary to ludicrous extremes. See, for example, the first paragraph of 24 Sept. 1884.
[3] Diary, 9 Jan. 1887, Add. MS. 48645, f. 78.
[4] Diary, 7 July 1889, Add. MS. 48651, f. 37.
[5] Diary, 8 Mar. 1890, Add. MS. 48652, f. 80.
[6] Diary, 26 June 1895, Add. MS. 48667, f. 45.
[7] Diary, 28 June 1895, Add. MS. 48667, f. 49 and 14 July 1902, Add. MS. 48679, f. 129.
[8] See, for example, Diary, 5 June 1881 and 17 Mar., 9 and 23 May 1882.

office of Chancellor of the Exchequer, 'is to be a gentleman.' He had, therefore, lodged a protest in advance against the appointment of Ritchie, whose
'blood is not of the bluest'.[1] Likewise Austen Chamberlain proved to be
a disappointment. 'I have served many Chancellors', wrote Hamilton in
1904, 'but by none have I been so little taken into confidence as by the
present. This is probably owing in great measure to his bourgeois bringing
up at Birmingham.'[2]

During these years of service in the Treasury Hamilton lived first with the
Roseberys at Lansdowne House but then moved to a flat in Park Lane. In
1891, however, he had left his flat and for some months had been at Brighton
recuperating from pneumonia; when he returned to London, W. H. Smith,
the First Lord of the Treasury, allowed him to lodge in 10 Downing Street
itself. Lord Salisbury, the Prime Minister, used the Foreign Office as the
centre of his government, and Hamilton found himself using the Cabinet
Room at No. 10 as his sitting-room and the adjoining room, 'which used to
be the Gladstone's dining room', as his bedroom.[3] Rosebery, when he heard
of Hamilton's new living arrangements, wrote: 'If you really sleep in the old
Cabinet Room, your powers of somnolence must be much greater than mine
. . . I think you will see visions of one of my portliest colleagues [Harcourt]
objecting, objecting, objecting, in the stillest watches of the night.'[4] In August
1892 the formation of Mr. Gladstone's fourth ministry forced Hamilton to
move out of Downing Street. He took a flat in Half Moon Street until the
new flats in Whitehall Court were ready.[5] Finally, in November 1892 he
moved into some rooms in the new building, Whitehall Court, where he
hoped eventually to get a flat overlooking the river. For a year, at a rent
of £260, he had '3 fair sized rooms looking toward the Horse Guards' while
the flats toward the river were being completed;[6] then in February 1894 he
moved into the rooms on the fifth floor of No. 4 Whitehall Court where,
although he had to pay £300 a year, he felt himself settled for life—as he was
—and where he had the 'most beautiful view in London'.[7]

His return to the Treasury in 1885 ended his official connection with
active political life, but the strong personal ties that had developed with the
Gladstones and with other political figures continued and the pace of his

[1] Diary, 14 July 1902, Add. MS. 48679, f. 128 and 25 Aug. 1902, Add. MS. 48680, f. 12.
[2] Diary, 8 Nov. 1904, Add. MS. 48682, f. 106.
[3] Diary, 24 June 1891, Add. MS. 48656, f. 7.
[4] Rosebery to EWH, 25 June 1891, Add. MS. 48610.
[5] Diary, 15 Aug. 1892, Add. MS. 48658, ff. 101–2. Hamilton was mildly put out to discover that Mr. Gladstone, who liked 'to concentrate his thoughts and directions on one
individual', 'was already engaged with Algy West who will evidently monopolise him'
when Hamilton went to offer his aid during the period preceding the formation of the
Government. Diary, 29 July 1892, Add. MS. 48658, f. 71.
[6] Diary, 26 Nov. and 15 Dec. 1892, Add. MS. 48659, ff. 41, 54.
[7] Diary, 7 and 12 Feb. 1894, Add. MS. 48662, ff. 97, 107–8. In 1902 Mr. Gladstone's
son, Henry, also lived at No. 4 while in No. 3 lived Lord Herschell, Haldane, and Gerald
Balfour.

social life accelerated. In addition to Wilton, Herbert House, Mentmore, and the Durdans—houses of friends from his youth—he came to be a regular visitor at Chatsworth and eventually Sandringham. Through the Roseberys he became a close friend of Ferdinand and other Rothschilds; his special liking for Americans—and especially for American women—brought him into another sort of moneyed circle. In August 1901 he sailed as a guest of the Anthony Drexels on their yacht *Margarita* from Cowes to Philadelphia and then visited Washington, Niagara Falls, Atlantic City, and Newport. After a visit to New York he sailed back to Liverpool on the *Umbria*, a regular steamship.[1]

At the Treasury he rose from post to post in a way that at first he found most satisfying. He was gratified and surprised when, in 1892, in the last days of the Conservative Government's life, Goschen revived for Hamilton's benefit the post of Assistant Financial Secretary to the Treasury, which carried a salary of £1,500.[2]

Two months after Rosebery had succeeded Mr. Gladstone as Prime Minister in 1894, Rosebery wrote a letter which gave Hamilton intense pleasure. Rosebery was, as Hamilton wrote, 'a master in writing nice letters'.[3]

My dear E.

I have many burdens and few compensations in this office, but you can give me one pleasure in connection with it.

Almost my first thought when I assumed my present post was to offer you the K.C.B. But I doubted on account of my affection for you, and I feared that I might be charged with favouritism. But these scruples have gradually melted away and I don't see why you should suffer because of my attachment and lose the due of your public services. Give me then this rare happiness. I have known you long enough to be sure that I can make no worthier appointment. It is near 34 years ago since we first stood together, pale and awed, in the Schoolyard at Eton. Since then in joy and sorrow, in good report and evil report, you have been the truest of friends to me and mine, so I hope that you will not hesitate or deny this great kindness to

Your affectionate old friend
R[4]

Hamilton felt the same scruples in accepting that Rosebery had felt in offering the honour; he wished to make sure that the award had the concurrence of Harcourt, his immediate chief. But of course he was delighted. 'What attracts me most about the proposal', he wrote in his diary, 'is that I should have the offer made to me after barely 24 years' service and before I have completed my 47th year. I think there will be only one younger K.C.B. in the

[1] Diary, 8 Aug. to 22 Sept. 1901, Add. MS. 48678, ff. 89–100.
[2] Diary, 12 Aug. 1892, Add. MS. 48658, f. 99.
[3] Diary, 15 May 1894, Add. MS. 48663, f. 112.
[4] Rosebery to EWH, 14 May 1894, Add. MS. 48610. Hamilton recorded the letter in his diary.

civil service, and that is Arthur Godley, after whom I can well afford to come'.[1] He accepted and became Sir Edward.

A few months later he was not disappointed when he failed to succeed Welby as Secretary to the Treasury. He told Harcourt that 'it would be monstrous if [Sir Francis] Mowatt were not put in Welby's place: he has strong prior claims both as regards age and service; he is much better fitted for the work; and I prefer infinitely my present post'. He did, however, wish to have it made clear that he was second to Mowatt.[2]

In October 1894 Harcourt offered Hamilton the post of Comptroller-General of the National Debt Office, but Hamilton 'told him that I infinitely preferred staying where I was: I held the most interesting post in the Civil Service; the National Debt Office would be very dull and I should feel that I was shelved'.[3] Similarly he refused the Clerkship of the Council when it was offered him in 1898.[4]

From 1896 onward Hamilton was in demand to serve on commissions and committees dealing with technical financial questions; thus he served on the Local Taxation Commission of 1896; in 1899 Henry Chaplin, the President of the Local Government Board, made him the chairman of the departmental committee to examine the proposals of the Commons' Committee on the Aged Deserving Poor; and he was a member of the Royal Commission on Indian Expenditure, formed in 1896 and reporting in 1900.[5]

Beyond these appointments and promotions of an official sort Hamilton was also a man to whom people in high places turned for informal and unofficial advice and aid. In the summer of 1892 when Mr. Gladstone's last ministry was in the making, the Prince of Wales suggested to the Queen that Hamilton was the man to whom she should turn for aid in dealing with both Mr. Gladstone and Rosebery. Therefore the Queen's secretary, Ponsonby, was in close touch with Hamilton throughout the tense days of July during which the government was formed with Mr. Gladstone at its head and Rosebery at the Foreign Office.[6] Again, at the time of the succession of Edward VII, Hamilton was the man who, through being both a friend of the King and a Treasury official, could best carry out the negotiations over the Civil List, which was not an easy job with a monarch of Edward's extravagant taste.[7]

But Hamilton's career at the Treasury, his enjoyment of society—and his ability to keep a diary—began to be affected seriously by the onset in 1889 of

[1] Diary, 15 May 1894, Add. MS. 48663, f. 113.
[2] Diary, 6 Mar. 1894, Add. MS. 48663, f. 18.
[3] Diary, 31 Oct. 1894, Add. MS. 48665, f. 31.
[4] Diary, 29 June 1898, Add. MS. 48673, f. 68 and Sir Almeric Fitzroy, *Memoirs* (N.Y., 1925), I. x.
[5] See *Parl. Papers*, 1899, xxxv. 733–832; 1900, x. 1–148 and also xxix; 1902, xxxix. 9–37.
[6] Diary, 17, 19, 23, 26, 29 July, 4 and 15 Aug. 1892, Add. MS. 48658, ff. 52–104. See the interesting account of these days, largely based on Hamilton's diary, in Robert Rhodes James, *Rosebery* . . . (N.Y., 1963), pp. 247–51.
[7] Diary, 20 Feb. 1901, Add. MS. 48677, ff. 123–5.

a number of symptoms of vascular disease which were at first uncomfortable and inconvenient, then from time to time disabling, and finally completely crippling. Throughout most of his younger years he had been robust, rightly regarding good health as one of the principal ingredients of happiness.[1] Quite suddenly, however, while enjoying his customary holiday in Scotland and the shooting that was a part of it, his right foot became numb and cold and his use of the leg was restricted. He cut his holiday short, but his leg got no better.[2] He sought medical advice and received a variety of explanations of the condition but no relief. In April 1890 he resolved on his doctor's advice to 'imprison' himself for three weeks and give his leg a complete rest, but that radical curtailment of activity did no good.[3] In the summer of 1890 with '43 years completed' his spirits were low; he visited friends but found that the part he could play in a beloved sport like lawn tennis was seriously curtailed.[4] Then almost exactly a year after his right leg had been affected his left was similarly attacked and again he had to cut his holiday in Scotland short.[5]

He started a series of visits to specialists—Barlow, Gowers, Lister—and then with the financial aid of Rosebery, Hamilton, accompanied by his regular physician, Manley Sims, went to see Charcot in Paris.[6] Charcot, diagnosing the case as one of clodification of the arteries of the legs, gave Hamilton some hope for eventual improvement and prescribed a prolonged period during which he was not to use his legs at all.[7] On 10 December 1890 upon his return from Paris he began his 'imprisonment', which was marked by the appearance of further complications, first phlebitis in his left leg in January and pneumonia in February. The latter condition brought about a long gap in the diary from 12 February to 15 March 1891. He was cared for during this time by his sister, Maud, his servant, Springett, and a nurse, provided—as were other conveniences—by Rosebery, in as unobtrusive a way as possible.[8] Aside from Rosebery's aid, Hamilton's illness provided the occasion for a remarkable outpouring of concern on the part of his friends. In a small *Letts's Diary* Hamilton kept a list of those who had called during his lying-up; long and distinguished, it is a remarkable testimony to the devotion of his friends.[9]

---

[1] Diary, 12 Dec. 1883. In 1875 he had experienced some lameness in the knee, ascribed by his friend, Wilton Phipps, to 'devotion to football at Eton' but no mention of that condition appears in the diary.

[2] Diary, 12 and 18 Sept. 1889, Add. MS. 48651, ff. 91–3, 96; 22 Dec. 1889 and 6 Apr. 1890, Add. MS. 48652, ff. 15, 106.

[3] Diary, 23 Apr. 1890, Add. MS. 48652, ff. 125–6; 7 and 11 May 1890, Add. MS. 48653, ff. 6–7.

[4] Diary, 8, 20 July and 11 Aug. 1890, Add. MS. 48653, ff. 63, 83, and 102.

[5] Diary, 7 and 21 Sept. 1890, Add. MS. 48653, ff. 115, 126–7.

[6] Diary, 24 Oct., 9 and 30 Nov., 7 Dec. 1890, Add. MS. 48654, ff. 20, 32, 68, 75–6.

[7] Diary, 7 Dec. 1890, Add. MS. 48654, ff. 75–6.

[8] Diary, 15 Mar. 1891, Add. MS. 48655, ff. 30–1 and Rosebery to G., 16 Apr. 1891 Add. MS. 44289, f. 139.

[9] Add. MS. 48684 and also Diary, 24 June 1891, Add. MS. 48656, ff. 8–10.

Fortunately the long period of rest, prescribed by Charcot and enforced by acute illness and convalescence, brought some improvement; almost four months in Brighton for recuperation completed his time of absolute rest which had lasted from December 1890 to June 1891. In late June he returned to London; in early July he 'donned a white tie . . . for the first time in seven months and went to dinner' at the Rothschilds.[1] In August Rosebery wrote Mr. Gladstone: 'Eddy Hamilton walked cheerfully into my room and dined with me. . . . I cannot tell you what a joy this is to me, and I know to you'.[2]

Improved though he was, he still could not take part in the sports he loved, although he could visit the houses where lawn tennis was played and where he could shoot—but only by riding from box to box on a pony.[3]

But then in September 1894—and again in Scotland—his left leg was attacked and he had to take to his bed; it was not until December that he could return to his duties.[4] There was improvement so that in October 1895 he could shoot pheasants at Tring—his first shots in two years—but always the threat of relapse.[5] Riding was his exercise and his principal means of locomotion; in order to avoid riding around on the pavement from White-hall Court to the Treasury, he liked to ride through the Horse Guards, and, as he wrote in his diary, 'though I am seldom challenged, and when I give my name I am allowed to pass through, I hate usurping a right. So I determined to ask Bigge [the Queen's secretary] if he could secure permission for me from the Queen to ride through the guarded archway, having first ascertained from Francis Knollys [the Prince's secretary] that the Prince of Wales thought I might . . . reasonably prefer the request on the ground of my living so close to the Horse Guards and of my official position. Bigge has written to me to say that, though the privilege is still jealously guarded, the Queen consents, . . . So my scruples now of a morning will be removed'.[6]

Dramatic episodes of his disease became rarer after 1894 but he was increasingly aware of a general physical deterioration. When he completed his 55th year in 1902 he wrote: 'I often think I am going down hill rather fast—that I am prematurely old, as I undoubtedly am.'[7] Just after Christmas 1902 he began another period of complete rest. While he was at Chatsworth for Christmas he had written: 'My nervous system has broken down; there is what they call a want of "co-ordination". This may easily be seen in my hand-writing. It is not a want of power, but a want of being able to properly control

---

[1] Diary, 24 June and 3 July 1891, Add. MS. 48656, ff. 7, 17.

[2] Rosebery to G., 7 Aug. 1891, Add. MS. 44289, f. 145.

[3] Diary, 31 Jan. 1892, Add. MS. 48657, f. 50 and 24 Sept. 1892, Add. MS. 48658, f. 133.

[4] Diary, 1, 3 Sept., 21 and 29 Nov. 1894, Add. MS. 48664, ff. 99–100, 107; Add. MS. 48665, ff. 60, 71, 80.

[5] Diary, 17 Oct. 1895, Add. MS. 48667, ff. 133–4; 10 and 13 May 1896, Add. MS. 48669, ff. 43, 46.

[6] Diary, 10 Mar. 1896, Add. MS. 48668, ff. 134–5.

[7] Diary, 8 July 1902, Add. MS. 48679, f. 122.

one's writing power. The same with my walking and talking, which partakes of that of a drunken man.'[1] Indeed his handwriting had been deteriorating; there are sections of the diary after 1900 where it is very irregular followed usually by some improvement but never a return to the firm legible hand of the eighties. His two-month rest cure proved of little effect, but in February 1903 he returned to work and, in spite of his continuing symptoms, he felt he could do his work effectively. 'So long as I can keep my work and my friends', he wrote in 1903, 'life will be perfectly tolerable.'[2] But as his condition grew worse, it became increasingly difficult to stay at his work, maintain any kind of social life, and keep up his spirits. In July 1904 he wrote: 'In two years' time I shall be in my sixtieth year. But a man is as old as he feels, and I feel much more like 75 than 57, though one ought to be very thankful (and I am) that I only suffer discomfort and no pain.'[3] He continued his search both in England and on the Continent for a doctor who could effect a change but nothing helped.[4] While his intimate friends remained kind and helpful, he found that 'physical decadence' involved 'social decadence'. 'Out of sight is out of mind in the social world. I used to be a good deal in request. Now I am at a discount.'[5] For the first time in 23 years he didn't go to the Devonshire House party after the Derby in 1905 because he was not invited, and in June of that year he decided that 'social gatherings are not for me any longer' and that 'Londonderry House shall be my last party'.[6] But he still attended week-end parties and in September 1905 visited Balmoral.

His physical condition—as might be expected—adversely affected his career at the Treasury. In 1902 Sir Francis Mowatt, the Permanent Secretary of the Treasury, was due to retire, and Hamilton assumed that he would be asked to succeed him. But he received what he called 'a knock-down blow'; Mowatt was asked by Balfour and Beach to stay on beyond retirement age. 'I have no right of complaint', he wrote,

for I have no right of succession. But I confess I am greatly disappointed. I have held my present post for 16 1/2 years; nearly 8 years ago Sir W. Harcourt practically apologised then to me for not putting me in Welby's place; Mowatt when appointed declared he should only remain on a short time (5 years at the outside) and now he is to stay indefinitely. My promotion now, if it comes at all, will come too late. But what I dislike most is that the continuance of Mowatt as Permanent

[1] Diary, 25 Dec. 1902, Add. MS. 48680, ff. 70–1.

[2] Diary, 18 Aug. 1903, Add. MS. 48681, f. 41.

[3] Diary, 7 July 1904, Add. MS. 48682, f. 62.

[4] In Sept. 1904, for example, he went to see the famous Dr. Frenkel at Heiden in Switzerland where he was assured that his condition was not 'locomotor ataxia' but received little else of benefit. Diary, 11 Sept. 1904, Add. MS. 48682, f. 81 and see also Rosebery to EWH, 26 Apr. 1904, Add. MS. 48611.

[5] Diary, 18 Nov. 1904, Add. MS. 48682, f. 113. Hamilton felt that even Rosebery was drawing away from him—but confessed that it might be his imagination. Diary, 1 Mar. 1904, Add. MS. 48681, f. 135 and 20 Mar. 1904, Add. MS. 48682, f. 9.

[6] Diary, 31 May and 9 June 1905, Add. MS. 48683, ff. 56, 59.

Secretary beyond the prescribed age can only be open to one construction—that there is no one competent to succeed him. I don't believe either A. Balfour or Beach intend it to be a reflection on one's competency, but I don't see how it can be held to be otherwise.[1]

By August 1902 Hamilton had been invited to entertain the novel arrangement of being one of two secretaries of the Treasury. Beach, who was about to retire from the post of Chancellor of the Exchequer, told Hamilton that he felt that he 'was not strong enough to take Mowatt's place and at the same time keep an eye on finance'. But Beach recognized Hamilton's right to succeed Mowatt, if he could do it 'without killing' himself. Beach had decided that there should be two secretaries—'one doing the expenditure or administrative side of the work, the other doing the revenue or financial side of it'.[2] And that was the arrangement that was made; Hamilton became the Financial Secretary of the Treasury and Sir George Murray the Administrative Secretary. It was not the position of unquestioned primacy in the Civil Service for which he had hoped but he could take comfort in Godley's opinion that most men in his physical condition, lacking his pluck, would have thrown in the sponge and that his was 'the higher of the two thrones'.[3] The state of his health made it difficult for him to perform even half of the work of the Permanent Secretary but he persevered. His ability to walk around and to write deteriorated but his mind was clear. His long experience in government service and his qualities of mind continued to command respect. When Sir Henry Campbell-Bannerman became Prime Minister in 1905 Hamilton served quite naturally as a kind of king-maker in the realm of private secretaries; Henry Higgs, who became C.-B.'s private secretary, had had his name put forward by Hamilton.[4] Respected and loved though he was, his usefulness and effectiveness diminished. By 1906 his handwriting had become so bad that his diary became illegible even to himself and his letters from the Treasury had to be written out by someone else.[5] A man who began his career in the Treasury in 1906 recalls that 'his handwriting had all the appearance of being written with a crossed nib, almost illegible like that of most of his contemporaries in the Treasury'.[6] Finally, on 13 May 1906 he wrote what was to be the penultimate entry in his diary: 'Very low. What I feel most I think is that I have come to the end of my career. I can't get higher; but I may easily go lower.'[7]

And the rest of his story is indeed a sad one. Reluctantly at last in October 1907 he retired from his post at the Treasury. When he heard of his intention

---

[1] Diary, 14 and 19 Dec. 1901, Add. MS. 48679, ff. 6, 8.
[2] Diary, 5 Aug. 1902, Add. MS. 48680, f. 2.
[3] Godley to EWH, 9 Aug. 1902, Add. MS. 48616.
[4] Memorandum by Henry Higgs, Dec. 1919, Add. MS. 41252, f. 146.
[5] See, for example, his letters to Dilke, 4 and 9 May 1906, Add. MS. 43919, ff. 61–3, 66.
[6] Sir Otto Niemeyer to D. W. R. Bahlman, 13 Jan. 1966.
[7] Diary, 13 May 1906, Add. MS. 48683, ff. 117–18.

to retire Balfour wrote him that he would 'have the comfort of knowing that you carry with you not merely the high esteem but the warm affection of everyone with whom you have served, and that you have added lustre to the greatest Department of the Greatest Civil Service in the World'.[1] But Hamilton found little to comfort him on his retirement; indeed he felt that along with the pain of departure from a post he loved he was made to feel that his services had not fully been appreciated. 'We must draw an honorific Treasury minute on his retirement', wrote Asquith to the Prime Minister; and Hamilton had sensed the hollowness of the remarks praising his 22 years of service at the head of the financial side of the Treasury, 'a longer term', so the Minute said, 'than has fallen to any of his predecessors'.[2] He felt a special blow in having to give up along with his post at the Treasury the Auditorship of the Civil List, a position that gave him a formal and cherished connection with the King. The poignancy of his retirement—and the attitude of his friends towards it—is best conveyed in a letter that Sir George Murray, who was now to become Permanent Secretary, wrote to Knollys, the King's private secretary:

Eddie's last day here is Saturday; and I am dreading it more than anything I have been through in my life. His present idea is not to leave London; so that on Monday morning he will be wondering why he is not coming across here as usual. I think it would be an immense thing if somebody could be got to invite him for the week-end and a few days after, so as to make the break less obvious.

I suppose you won't be at Windsor then? Perhaps Mrs. Leo [Rothschild] would get him down to Ascott, but I do not know what her movements are. Any place within reach of his motor would do quite well.

Can you think of anything that would help? I am going to Wynyard this afternoon, but shall be back on Friday. I am almost glad to be away for these last few days of his official life.

He is giving sittings for a portrait we are having done for him; and he would have to suspend these for a few days if he went away; but I don't think that would matter. The portrait was his own idea. I should myself have chosen something else; but he is quite delighted with it.[3]

The portrait was, as Murray suggested, an unfortunate request. The painter could only succeed by producing an image of a prematurely senile, partially paralysed, and unwillingly pitiful man.[4] Early in 1908 the portrait was finished, and, much to the distress of Murray and others at the Treasury, it was Hamilton's wish that he be carried over to the Treasury for a formal 'presentation' and 'reply' from him.[5]

[1] A. J. Balfour to EWH, 11 Sept. 1907, Add. MS. 48628.
[2] Asquith to Campbell-Bannerman, 7 Oct. 1907, Add. MS. 52519 and Minute of 26 Oct. 1907, Add. MS. 48628.
[3] Murray to Knollys, 21 Oct. 1907, Windsor, RA W. 65/110.
[4] A photograph of da Costa's portrait is in the files of the National Portrait Gallery.
[5] Lord Esher to Knollys, 17 Jan. 1908, Windsor, RA W. 41/20.

Another event of the final months of his illness brought out what the diary hints at by its silence: that Hamilton had for a long time ceased to share with his father and with Mr. Gladstone a feeling of devotion for the Church of England and a belief in orthodox Christianity. His friend, Edward Stuart Talbot, then Bishop of Southwark, came to his flat hoping to offer him in his extremity the comforts of the Church. 'In a frank and simple way' Hamilton had refused his ministrations, not wishing, as Talbot put it, to turn 'in the time of weakness to what in your strength you did not accept'. Hamilton told Talbot that 'after mature consideration and a good deal of reading' he had become what he called a devout sceptic.[1]

On 7 June 1908 Asquith wrote Hamilton to offer him a privy councillorship on the occasion of the King's birthday.[2] But Hamilton was in no condition to rejoice in this honour. On 2 September 1908 Edward Hamilton died at the Hotel Metropole in Brighton, where he had spent many months in past years resting and convalescing. His sister, Maud Ottley, was with him at the time of his death.[3] Two months earlier he had passed, as he would have put it, the sixty-first anniversary of his birth. At the funeral, which took place at St. Martin's Church in Brighton, Sidney Greville represented the King, Sir Arthur Bigge the Prince of Wales. Lord Rosebery and his sons, Wilton Phipps, and Lord Herbert, the son of his old friend Sidney Herbert, attended the service which his brother-in-law, Canon Ottley, conducted. 'Poor Eddy', wrote Lord Rosebery, 'one could only rejoice at his release for which he so longed.'[4]

To record the story of his own life and to sketch a self-portrait was not Hamilton's chief purpose when he began his diary in 1880. During the years 1880–5 the diary was to be—and is—a detailed report of what went on at Downing Street and, above all, an account of what 'Mr. G.' did, said, and wrote.

Seen close up, Mr. Gladstone, though always to Hamilton 'the Great Man' and an object of worship, becomes a man of extraordinary but still mortal proportions. His talents were manifold and for Hamilton the object of wonder, but what gives the diary's portrait of 'the Great Man' its peculiar value is that the diarist described both consciously and unconsciously the flaws that make the titan lifesize and the hero human. The qualities of greatness and the moments of glory Hamilton records, for example, in connection with 'the mastery of detail . . ., the tact, judgment, and good temper . . ., the outbursts of eloquence . . ., and last (and not least) the extraordinary physical power he has exhibited' in conducting the Irish Land Bill of 1881 through committee or with Mr. G.'s great speech in favour of the Affirmation Bill in 1883. 'No statesman ever made a finer defence of civil rights. No Archbishop

[1] Talbot to EWH, 17 Apr. and EWH to Talbot (typewritten copy), 18 Apr. 1908, Add. MS. 48628. [2] Asquith to EWH, 7 June 1908, Add. MS. 48612.
[3] EWH's Death Certificate, General Register Office, Somerset House.
[4] Rosebery to Mary Gladstone Drew, 11 Sept. 1908, Add. MS. 46237, f. 177.

ever put forward a more powerful plea on behalf of religion. . . . It was indeed a privilege to have heard it.'[1] But then Hamilton took note of the moments of exhaustion when the heroic endurance gave way. During the New Year holiday of 1883 when Hamilton was visiting at Longleat Mrs. Gladstone followed a telegram with a characteristically rambling letter urging him to come to Hawarden. She had not told her husband that she had asked Hamilton. Mr. G., she wrote, 'has been unusually worried take *Rosebery* worst of all then *Archbishops* appointment with management of H.M. then Dilke, and now Bishop's appointment and he has in consequence had no Holyday in fact I never remember such a time as calling itself Holyday. The strain has shewn itself for several nights in more or less *want of sleep*. A new sign'. She asked Hamilton to come as if for purely social reasons. 'He thinks you are coming here as more of a *Holyday* or he would not consent.'[2] No one knew better than Hamilton that Mr. G.'s 'grandness', his breadth of view, his seeming detachment from petty things, left him, in fact, highly vulnerable to a '*personal* question'; for as Hamilton discovered Mr. G. was 'always far more bothered over personal matters like appointments than over any amount of national crises'.[3] His greatness lay, for Hamilton, not only in his skill in the Commons, his command of measures and men, but in the resilience which could bring him from exhaustion, induced sometimes by overwork or sometimes by involvement in a personal question, to the buoyant and confident mastery of affairs that marked his political life even into what would be for anyone else old age.[4] Above all what Hamilton found in Mr. Gladstone was the capacity to be what Mr. G. called a 'ferocious master' but at the same time, from Hamilton's point of view, 'the kindest, the most thoughtful, and the most ready to give credit when credit is due'.[5]

Hamilton does not dwell on the heroic aspects of Mr. G.; no day-by-day account could. What gives Hamilton's diary in this period a unique value is his demonstration of Mr. G.'s 'greatness' through its description of his daily accomplishments. Take, for example, Hamilton's account of the Gladstonian routine while at Hawarden, away from the immediate demands of Downing Street:

His life is very regular. He rises a little before 8 o'clock and walks off to service

---

[1] Diary, 24 July 1881 and 26 Apr. 1883. In connection with the speech on the Affirmation Bill Hamilton wrote in 1893 that 'Asquith and I both agreed that the greatest speech made in modern times—say in the latter half of this century—was Mr. G.'s speech on introducing the Affirmation Bill in 1883'. Diary, 8 Mar. 1893, Add. MS. 48660, ff. 3-4.

[2] Mrs. G. to EWH, 2 Jan. [1883], Add. MS. 48609 and Diary, 8 Jan. 1883.

[3] Diary, 1 Dec. 1883 and 21 Apr. 1885.

[4] A passage from the diary in 1887 illustrates the point: 'I notice one respect in which I think he has changed within the last year. He is no longer the "old man *in a hurry*." He recognises time as the essential element of a settlement [of the Irish issue]. He is full of confidence in the strength of his cause and in its eventual consummation; but he will be content to have initiated it.' Diary, 20 Mar. 1887, Add. MS. 48645, f. 135.

[5] Diary, 26 Dec. 1881.

at the parish church. On his return he opens his letter-bag and after giving it a glance reads the *Pall Mall Gazette*, the only paper he can be got now to look at. He then comes in to breakfast, at which he is always specially agreeable, and which he does not hurry over. After breakfast he returns to his own room—'the temple of Peace' as it is called—and gets to work. His letters with occasional dives into books occupy him till luncheon, when he again gives one the benefit of his conversation. He returns to his letters and books till about 3:30, when he goes out either for a walk or for a 'chop' in the woods, returning in time for 5 o'clock tea, which is a special fondness of his. Having devoted about half an hour in the drawing room to a cup of tea and a little chat, he once more goes back and alternates reading with his letters up till dressing time (which he makes a marvelously short business of). At dinner, though in a general way he perhaps hardly lays himself out so much for conversation as at breakfast, he is never silent and is always bright. The power of throwing off all his work and anxieties is among his chief wonders. If one fails to take into sufficient account this power, one might be tempted to think that the cares of government and responsibilities of office sit too light upon him, in almost an unbecoming manner. After dinner he soon resumes his book again, which will occupy him till bedtime (11:30). I doubt if any public man ever read one tenth part of the amount he does. It is simply marvelous the masses of books which he gets through, especially considering that he is not a rapid reader; on the contrary he reads everything, no matter what, with the greatest deliberation, as the pencil marks in the margin show; it is the amount of time he daily, hourly, and minutely devotes to books of every kind, from the 'tuppeny' tract to the stiff theological work, that enables him to get through the amount he does.[1]

Such orderly habits of life are not unexpected; but what is surprising is to learn that when Mr. G. left for Hawarden in September 1882 'he was quite disappointed at leaving before the guns in honour of the Egyptian victories had been fired, which was his own suggestion, and about which he was quite childishly keen'.[2] Was the G.O.M. a Jingo?

Of course not. But he was a man of a passionate temperament, enthusiastic, sensitive, possessed of strong feelings. Especially on religious and ecclesiastical subjects, Mr. Gladstone felt deeply. The Public Worship Regulation Act of 1874, a statute for which Archbishop Tait, Disraeli, and the Queen were responsible in varying degrees, was an '"iniquitous" act' which demonstrated that the Archbishop, while 'a great Christian and . . . an excellent speaker . . . was no real statesman and . . . had been a man greatly overrated'.[3] Once at Hawarden when Lord Ripon, a convert to Roman Catholicism, and John Morley, an agnostic, were visiting their chief 'they were both unceremoniously thrust out of the room in which they were sitting by Mr. G. himself who planted them in another room with a solitary candle. They could not understand Mr. G.'s strategic movement. The explanation was that it was the hour

---

[1] Diary, 25 Nov. 1881. See also 15 Jan. 1883.
[2] Diary, 16 Sept. 1882. See also the comment on the pride he took in remembering in 1890 the naval demonstration against Turkey ten years earlier. Diary, 17 June 1890, Add. MS. 48653, ff. 43-4.
[3] Diary, 23 Nov. 1881 and 28 Mar. 1895, Add. MS. 48666, f. 75.

of family prayers; and the banishment of both men—one because he believed too much and the other because he believed too little—was indispensable in in Mr. G.'s eyes'.[1]

A similar abhorrence of religious error coloured Mr. Gladstone's relations with the Queen. On this subject the diary is most informative; it reveals how much, for example, the problem of church patronage contributed to the bad feeling that arose between them.[2] She distrusted his high-church tendencies; he feared that in her desire to assure 'safe' appointments she was willing to upset what he regarded as the proper and necessary relationship between Sovereign and Minister. It was Mr. Gladstone's impression in retrospect that the turning-point in his relations with the Queen had occurred in 1873 over the issue of creating a royal residence for the Prince of Wales in Ireland—an issue which had actually come to the fore in 1872.[3] By the time of the formation of the second ministry in 1880 the Queen's hostility had matured in proportion to her increasing devotion to Lord Beaconsfield. As the diary shows there were a host of questions that provided occasions for unpleasantness between Mr. Gladstone and herself: appointments and promotions of 'republicans' like Dilke, 'renegades' like Lord Derby in addition to all the 'extreme' Churchmen for whom, in the Queen's eyes, Mr. Gladstone had such a regrettable liking; 'errors' in colonial and foreign policy beginning with the recall of Frere and culminating in the disaster in the Sudan and the death of Gordon; then there was Mr. G.'s refusal to share with the Queen full accounts of the proceedings of the Cabinet; his unwillingness, as she thought, to put proper curbs on unruly Cabinet members like Chamberlain; and his lack of courtesy toward her in, for example, sailing off to meet foreign rulers in Copenhagen in the summer of 1883 without asking her permission in advance. All of these disagreements upset Mr. Gladstone profoundly—more, in Hamilton's view, than they should have because he thought that Mr. G. 'imagines the relations more strained and the estrangement greater than is really the case'.[4] But Mr. Gladstone thought that the Queen would never be happy until she had hounded him out of office.[5] Admiring the institution of the monarchy as he did, revering—or wishing to revere—the Sovereign, Mr. Gladstone found distressing the Queen's pettiness, her 'warped' judgement, and her overt Toryism.[6]

In seeking the foundations of the Queen's feelings, Mr. Gladstone and Hamilton came to the conclusion that it was 'jealousy pure and simple. She takes offence', wrote Hamilton to his chief, 'at the big type in which the

---

[1] The story is one that Rosebery told EWH. Diary, 18 Oct. 1887, Add. MS. 48647, f. 34.
[2] For this subject see D. W. R. Bahlman, 'The Queen, Mr. Gladstone, and Church Patronage', *Victorian Studies*, iii (1959–60), 349–80.
[3] Diary, 30 Apr. 1880 and 10 Nov. 1893, Add. MS. 48661, ff. 119–21; Guedalla, i. 359–67.
[4] Diary, 8 Jan. 1883.
[5] Diary, 9 May 1882.
[6] Diary, 11 Mar., 23 May, and 25 Aug. 1883 and 27 Apr. 1885.

newspapers head "Mr. Gladstone's Movements" and the small type *below* of the Court Circular. These are not unnatural feelings, especially when the monarch is a woman'.[1]

Had Mr. Gladstone been what the Queen and many of his enemies thought him, a politician indifferent to traditional values and willing to pursue any course, however radical, that would perpetuate his own power, he would not have been so concerned about Victoria's feelings. But, as Hamilton points out repeatedly, Mr. Gladstone was always a conservative, though not since 1839 or perhaps 1841 a Tory; Peel was 'anything but a Tory' and therefore Mr. G.'s adherence to Peel and the Peelites marked his loyalty to progressive conservatism which the Conservatives had rejected.[2] The Queen had once, so they thought, understood the distinction between conservatism and Toryism but Disraeli had made her—and many like her—forget it. Thus Mr. Gladstone found himself in 1886 saying: "'I am . . . an absolute worshipper of the hereditary principle—hereditary titles and possessions; but would that it were not so often abused as it is in certain hands!'"[3]

Mr. Gladstone felt very deeply—as Hamilton did also—that the Queen and others who enjoyed hereditary positions of power and influence were debasing the tone of political life in a dangerous fashion. Both men commented frequently on the bad manners, vulgarity, and obstructiveness that marked the actions of men in politics who, because of their birth, should have behaved quite differently.[4] Mr. Gladstone late one evening in 1887 turned to Hamilton and said 'very solemnly and in a low voice' that if he 'were in a dying condition' he would have one great apprehension in his mind; it would not be Ireland—'that difficulty will be solved'; nor would it be 'the character of the measures of the future: the good sense of the people will take care of them. It is the men of the future, personalities of the stamp of Randolph Churchill and Chamberlain who have no principles'.[5]

Nothing demonstrated to Mr. Gladstone the absence of principle in the new breed of politicians so much as the indiscretion of some of his Cabinet in dealing with newspapers. 'Leakages' were one of the many unpleasant and unhappy characteristics of the history of his second ministry. Forster, Chamberlain, and Dilke were the men—the new men—who were suspected of being indiscreet, partly through ignorance but also through calculated indiscretion. In the autumn of 1881 the *Standard* reported that it had 'good grounds' for predicting that in the next session of Parliament a measure of county government involving County Boards would be a chief measure. Mr. Gladstone circulated the paragraph to members of his Cabinet asking if any

---

[1] EWH to G., 27 Sept. 1883, Add. MS. 44189, f. 249 and Diary, 27 Sept. 1883. See also the comment on the burden of royal correspondence, Diary, 9 May 1885.
[2] Diary, 5 May 1888, Add. MS. 48648, ff. 89–90.
[3] Diary, 22 July 1886, Add. MS. 48644, f. 80.
[4] See, for example, Diary, 9 Feb., 17 Mar., and 23 May 1882 and 26 Jan. 1884.
[5] Diary, 6 Nov. 1887, Add. MS. 48647, ff. 60–1.

of them could explain its appearance, which they said they could not. Hamilton, however, thought that the leak came from his least favourite minister, Forster, and probably through his adopted son and private secretary, H. O. Arnold-Forster.[1] Again in the spring of 1882 a leakage occurred for which Arnold-Forster was suspected; 'I think you will have observed', wrote Mr. G. to W. E. Forster, the Chief Secretary for Ireland, 'that this leakage happens specially in Irish matters?'[2] Later the news of A. W. Peel's appointment as Speaker and of Rosebery's admission to the Cabinet leaked out to the press, upsetting Mr. Gladstone but distressing Hamilton in particular because the leakages could reflect on him.[3] In the end it was Chamberlain and Dilke who, in Mr. Gladstone's view, 'were the only two men to whom he could impute the betrayal of Cabinet secrets . . .'.[4] These men lacked 'principles'.

And 'principles' were what Mr. Gladstone always claimed to hold most dear; publicly he would often parade a loyalty to principles designed to set off what he regarded in his opponents as cynicism and baseness. In the diary Hamilton subscribes, as often as not, to Mr. Gladstone's own appraisal of himself and of his opponents. But he also makes vivid how, behind the genuine concern for great principles and exalted causes, there lay sometimes an incongruous preoccupation with petty things; but also, more importantly, in Hamilton's portrait of his chief, real weaknesses and faults receive their due.

We learn from the diary, for example, that Mr. Gladstone prided himself on having invented a symbol 'm̅ . . . to represent millions'.[5] And we also learn that he had an almost childish concern with the length of time he had held office by comparison with others—but especially by comparison with Lord Beaconsfield. Arthur Godley, knowing his former chief to the core, hit the proper note on this subject in the midst of the third ministry: 'Pelham', he wrote, 'was Prime Minister for 10 years and 7 months (less one day). You have today been Prime Minister for 10 years, 6 months and 20 days. If therefore you can keep your grasp of power until the end of the [Easter] recess, you will have beaten him and will have started in pursuit of Lord North (12 years and 2 months)'.[6]

Beyond his comments on Mr. Gladstone's concern with small things, which

---

[1] *Standard*, 14 Nov. 1881; Add. MS. 44765, ff. 139–42, 163–4; and Diary, 23 Nov. 1881.
[2] Diary, 24 Apr. 1882 and G. to Forster, 24 Apr. 1882, letterbook copy, Add. MS. 44545, f. 127.
[3] *Daily News*, 10 Dec. 1883, pp. 4–5; Diary, 11 and 14 Dec. 1883; H. Seymour to EWH, 18 Dec. 1883, Add. MS. 48615. *Standard*, 17 Nov. 1884, p. 5 and *Pall Mall Gazette*, 15 Nov. 1884, p. 3; EWH to G., 17 Nov. 1884, Add. MS. 48608. Diary, 20 Nov. 1884.
[4] Diary, 10 Dec. 1891, Add. MS. 48656, f. 166.
[5] Diary, 18 June 1881; and E. W. Hamilton, *Mr. Gladstone* (London, 1898), pp. 105–6.
[6] Godley to G., 19 Apr. 1886, Add. MS. 44223, f. 80; and see Diary, 14 Feb. 1882, 14 Feb. and 11 June 1885; Seymour's memorandum, Add. MS. 44775, f. 255; Godley's notes and G. to Godley, 1 Jan. 1883, Add. MS. 44900, ff. 25–8; Godley to G., 14 Feb. and 5 June 1885, and 25 Nov. 1893, Add. MSS. 44223, ff. 52–5, 59–60; 44775, ff. 249–50, 255.

served to make the Great Man human in his proportions, Hamilton noted much in his diary that was critical of Mr. G.; Hamilton, though a worshipper, was not blind to Mr. Gladstone's faults. In spite of his admiration for the Prime Minister as an employer, Hamilton, in discussing the unfortunate timing of Mr. Gladstone's retirement in 1894, stated it to be a 'fact that he [Gladstone] is not a considerate man. Consideration for the convenience of others has never been numbered amongst his best qualities'.[1] In addition, Mr. Gladstone was too often blind to things that were clear to everyone around him—blind to things that a great minister should not have ignored. The advancement of Herbert Gladstone, for example, was something that the world, but not Mr. G., would regard as nepotism; in a matter like this Mr. G. could combine *naïveté* with what amounted to a shocking degree of insensitivity. If he wished to attend a séance, he should have been prepared for the adverse comment on his doing so just as he should have understood how the world would view his 'rescue work' or his friendship with Mrs. Langtry.[2] In his dealings with Parnell through Mrs. O'Shea, Mr. Gladstone, as Hamilton saw, demonstrated an unworldliness that approached stupidity.[3] Similarly Mr. Gladstone was much too willing to accept favours from people whom he refused to regard as self-seeking; 'he never can see', wrote Hamilton, 'that he ought to pick and choose among those from whom he receives favours'.[4]

Hamilton also saw a flaw of character in Mr. Gladstone's extraordinarily changeable attitudes toward holding office. During 1881 Mr. Gladstone spoke constantly of his imminent departure from office; he called himself a 'bird of passage' and harped 'too much' on his retirement.[5] Pressure from his family, from Granville and Hartington, the course of events, and his own changing attitude toward himself and his powers kept Mr. Gladstone in office and by July 1883 Hamilton saw that he had 'abandoned the idea of immediate retirement',[6] but he still accepted a bet, which he lost, that the letterbook begun by the secretaries in November 1883 would be adequate for recording the remainder of Mr. G.'s letters as Prime Minister in that government. In April 1885, when yet another letterbook had to be opened, Hamilton paid George Leveson Gower half a crown.[7] In 1887 Hamilton recalled these vagaries in a conversation with Sir Henry James. 'Would Mr. G. ever resume office?

[1] Diary, 13 Jan. 1894, Add. MS. 48662, f. 60.
[2] Diary, 1 Apr. 1882; 7 Nov. 1884, and 9 and 10 Feb. 1882, and 30 June 1884.
[3] Diary, 20 June 1882 and 3 Feb. 1891, Add. MS. 48655, ff. 21–2; but notice the irony of singling out O'Shea himself as one Irishman who 'does seem like a gentleman'. Diary, 9 May 1882.
[4] Diary, 4 Jan. 1888, Add. MS. 48647, f. 114.
[5] Diary, 17 June and 25 Nov. 1881. In 1901 Morley told EWH that he thought that Mr. G. should have retired in 1881, that he had confessed in 1883 that, while speaking was no effort to him, 'the construction of measures' was now beyond him. Diary, 4 May 1901, Add. MS. 48678, ff. 40–1.
[6] Diary, 29 July 1883.   [7] Add. MS. 44547, flyleaf.

I hoped not; but I told him that of all the things that puzzled me about Mr. G. nothing ever puzzled me more than Mr. G.'s constant change of mind in this respect.'[1] Even then, as Mr. G. approached his eightieth year, he had surprises 'in this respect' for his friends and the others.

These are a few of the aspects of the remarkable portrait of Mr. Gladstone that Edward Hamilton left for posterity.[2] It is one of the many valuable elements of his greatest legacy, the diary itself.

[1] Diary, 21 Dec. 1887, Add. MS. 48647, f. 95.

[2] It should be noted here that Hamilton also took pride in leaving a collection of like-nesses of all the First Lords from Walpole onwards, which he had been at great pains to gather, to No. 10 Downing Street, where, I am told, they still hang. Diary, 16 Mar. 1893, Add. MS. 48660, f. 14; 22 July 1894, Add. MS. 48664, f. 57; and 26 Nov. 1894, Add. MS. 48665, ff. 65–6.

1880

Saturday, 24 April. According to general expectation, Lord Beaconsfield tendered his resignation to the Queen on Wednesday afternoon last. The following day Lord Hartington received a summons to attend at Windsor. The reasons which induced Her Majesty to send for him will probably never be known. It may have been at the instigation of Lord B[eaconsfield], in the hope that it was more likely Lord Hartington would consent to form an administration irrespectively of Mr. Gladstone than Lord Granville.[1] But whatever the true explanation may be, the act was an undoubted slight to Lord Granville who, being the recognised leader of the party, was the natural person to be sent for. On returning from Windsor, Lord Hartington had interviews with Lord Granville and Mr. Gladstone, and the supposition was that he had asked leave of H.M. to be relieved of the responsibility of forming a Government.[2] The surmise proved correct. Lord Hartington and Lord Granville the following day (Friday) proceeded together to Windsor in the morning and on their return repaired at once to Mr. Gladstone in Harley St.[3] Within an hour Mr. Gladstone had started himself for Windsor and during his interview kissed hands on assuming *de facto et de jure* the First Lordship of the Treasury combining with it the seals of the office of Chancellor of the Exchequer.[4]

This morning, therefore, the country was definitely apprised that Mr. Gladstone, for whose services the country had so distinctly called, had been entrusted with the formation of an administration. It must have been a bitter pill for the Queen to swallow. It has been made no secret that of recent years she has entertained a strong personal dislike for him, and great credit must be given to H.M. for preferring public interests to private prejudices.

The assumption by Mr. Gladstone of the additional office of Chancellor of the Exchequer is an indication that finance is to be given a foremost place

[1] Beaconsfield thought that the elections had given the Whigs and moderate Liberals enough seats to make a Hartington administration possible. Therefore he advised the Queen to call Hartington. See W. F. Monypenny and George E. Buckle, *The Life of . . . Disraeli* (N.Y., 1911–20), vi. 536.

[2] 'and to consult the two' is crossed out.

[3] The Gladstones were living at 73 Harley Street.

[4] See G.'s description of the interview, Morley, ii. 626–8; and the Queen's, *Letters*, 2nd ser. iii. 84–5. G. held the two offices until Dec. 1882 when Childers became Chancellor of the Exchequer. See 4 Dec. 1882.

in the programme of the new ministry. It is only to be hoped that the two offices will not be too much for him.

Godley came down early to the Treasury and informed me that Mr. G. had intimated his intention to take me as his Private Secretary. I can honestly say that if I had been given the choice of every civil employment in the service this is the one I should have singled out for myself. It has therefore been a notable day in my life.

I went up to Harley St. in the middle of the day with a Cabinet key and some boxes, but did not see Mr. G. himself.

Cabinet-making has been going on all day. Lord Granville is to go to the Foreign Office; Childers to the War Office; Lord Northbrook to the Admiralty; Lord Hartington to the India Office; Sir W. Harcourt to the Home Office; Lord Selborne becomes Lord Chancellor; Forster goes to Ireland as Chief Secretary. Mr. Bright is to have a seat; and the Duke of Argyll, Lord Ripon, Dodson, and Stansfeld are, I believe, to have places.[1]

I am not by any means satisfied with the allotment of places. Childers will not be welcomed by the Duke of Cambridge in Pall Mall[2] and will not command the confidence of the Army. Harcourt will be unpopular at the Home Office. I should have passed over Stansfeld's claims and not admitted Dodson's. I hope the Queen will not accept Childers for the War Office.[3]

Dined with the Algy Wests. I omitted to note that Mr. Lowe is to be offered a peerage without office. I am afraid his nerve is failing him, but there are no signs of his mental powers being impaired. He is not an ambitious man and therefore will probably be content, but Mrs. Lowe told me the other night they had no wish to be relegated to the Upper House. He was much concerned at the commencement of the crisis for fear that Mr. Gladstone was not to be summoned. He characteristically described the prospects of the party, under such belief, in the phrase—'We shall be rotten before we are ripe'.[4]

---

[1] Bright became Chancellor of the Duchy of Lancaster, Argyll Lord Privy Seal, Ripon Governor-General of India. Dodson became President of the Local Government Board with a seat in the Cabinet. Stansfeld had been the President of the Local Government Board 1871-4 and held the post again in G.'s 3rd ministry after Chamberlain's resignation. He refused the offers of lesser posts that were made to him in the course of this ministry.
[2] i.e. at the War Office.
[3] Her reluctance to do so was clear to G. at his first interview but she did accept him. Childers wanted to be Chancellor of the Exchequer; the War Office, according to his wife, 'was *the* one of all the great offices he did not wish to have'. Childers, i. 268-9. Harcourt similarly was disappointed with the offer of the Home Office. Gardiner, i. 362-3.
[4] G. wanted Lowe to be made a viscount at this time. The Queen thought 'more than a baron would be objectionable'. Guedalla, ii. 91. This seemingly petty disagreement disturbed G.'s sleep and at 7 a.m. on 30 Apr. he dashed off a letter arguing for Lowe's viscountcy; in reply the Queen rather ungraciously agreed to it. Guedalla, ii. 91-3. See 25 and 30 Apr. 1880. Lowe became Viscount Sherbrooke.

Sunday, 25 April. Went up to Harley St. in the afternoon. Found Mrs. Gladstone, Mary, and Harry,[1] with whom I had some talk. Picked up but little additional news. Goschen has been offered the Governor-Generalship [of India] as advocated by the *Economist* but has refused.[2] Layard has telegraphed from Constantinople that the Turk is becoming really alive to the necessity of 'putting his house in order'—(if that broken-down establishment will admit of repair). No further information respecting the manufacture of that delicate piece of political furniture, the Cabinet. Horace Seymour and Henry Primrose are the two between whom the other private secretaryship lies.[3] Both are excellently well fitted for the post, but I am inclined to regard Primrose favourite, as the award of the place to him would be a graceful compliment to Rosebery, who, to his honour, has (I believe) declined any appointment in the administration. Mr. Lowe has accepted the peerage gratefully.

The great man is, I fancy, prepared to launch out at once into financial reforms. I only hope it will not be with too great a rush. He is keen about the Malt tax about which he has so often chaffed the other side as giving themselves out to be the 'farmer's friend'.[4]

People very kind about congratulations.

Thursday, 29 April. Not had a moment since last Sunday for jotting anything down. Dined with the Gladstones on Monday. It was a financial dinner— Lord F. Cavendish, West, Welby, and Gurdon—to discuss the question of Malt duty v. Beer duties.[5] Finance seems quite a recreation to Mr. G.

The Cabinet is complete—14 in all.

First Lord and Chancellor of Exchequer	Mr. Gladstone
Lord Chancellor	Lord Selborne
Lord President of the Council	Lord Spencer
Lord Privy Seal	Duke of Argyll
Home Secretary	Sir W. Harcourt
Foreign Secretary	Lord Granville
Indian Secretary	Lord Hartington
War Secretary	Mr. Childers
Colonial Secretary	Lord Kimberley

[1] i.e. G.'s children Mary, later (1886) Mrs. Drew, and Henry Neville, later (1932) Baron Gladstone of Hawarden.

[2] See 'The Need for a Financial Viceroy in India', *The Economist*, 24 Apr. 1880, pp. 462–3.

[3] Primrose, who was Rosebery's cousin, became one of G.'s private secretaries but then consented to go to India as secretary to Lord Ripon. See 29 Apr. and 9 June 1880. Horace Seymour took his place on G.'s secretarial staff. See 27 June 1880.

[4] The repeal of the Malt tax would remove a burden from the already distressed agricultural community and would embarrass the Tories, who had wished to repeal it but had not found the means of doing so. In his Budget of June 1880 G. replaced the tax with a duty on beer and a 1*d.* increase on the income-tax. See 9 and 10 June 1880.

[5] 'financial' because Cavendish, Welby, and Gurdon were experienced Treasury officials and West was at the Board of Inland Revenue.

First Lord of the Admiralty	Lord Northbrook
Chancellor of the Duchy of Lancaster	Mr. Bright
Chief Secretary for Ireland	Mr. Forster
President of the Local Government Board	Mr. Dodson
President of the Board of Trade	Mr. Chamberlain

A strong and representative Cabinet, but like every other Cabinet open to criticism. Mr. Childers is a very 'round' man for the 'square' place at the War Office. The Queen takes considerable exception to this appointment. He has, however, secured Neville Lyttelton for his Private Secretary, and he could not get a better man—popular in the Army and free from all taint of Jingoism. Mr. Whitbread would have been far more popular at the Local Government Board than Dodson, but he declined; he is apparently nervous about his health. I have not yet definitely found out why Chamberlain has been preferred to Dilke; apparently it was at the latter's request. No doubt it was absolutely necessary to have in the Cabinet a representative of the Extreme Left, but Chamberlain has neither from his parliamentary experience nor from his party conduct deserved such a lift.[1] Fawcett's physical infirmities[2] seemed to have placed him 'out of court' for the Cabinet, but he has been secured for high office—the Post Office—and I am very glad of it. I was afraid at one time he might have been left out. Mr. G. has never forgiven him for his conduct in 1873 in connection with the Irish Ed[ucation] Bill.[3]

Primrose comes to Downing St., which completes the recognised staff of Private Secretaries. Herbert G. will work with us later on.

Today's Press has been generally favourable about the construction of the administration. Most of the minor appointments have been made; and they are, I think, satisfactory. Lord Cowper has been offered Ireland—a first-rate move—and a great improvement on the original proposal of sending Lord Carlingford there.

It is wonderful the power that Mr. G. has of writing 'letters of offers'. He must have written nearly 50 of such during the last few days and every one is expressed happily and differently—not only in different terms, but each is built on wholly different lines.

Shoals of congratulations to Mr. G. from every part of the country and every quarter of the globe arrive hourly.

Parliament met at two o'clock, and the House of Commons proceeded to the election of a Speaker. The choice could have fallen on no one but Mr. Brand,

---

[1] The complicated negotiations that led to Chamberlain's admission to the Cabinet and Dilke's acceptance of subordinate office are described in Gwynn and Tuckwell, i. 303–10 and Garvin, i. 293–303.

[2] i.e. his blindness.

[3] Fawcett had been a sharp critic of G.'s Irish University Bill in 1873; his attacks on the bill were among the chief causes of its defeat, which fatally weakened G.'s ministry. See Morley, ii. 434-45 and Leslie Stephen, *Life of Henry Fawcett* (London, 1885), pp. 277-85.

and on the motion of Sir T. Acland and Sir P. Egerton he was duly elected without opposition.

Friday, 30 April. Almost all the minor posts are now filled up. Lord Cowper goes to Ireland, which ought to be an excellent appointment. The question of substituting for the present viceroyal [*sic*] a Prince of the Royal Blood has not apparently been revived by Mr. G. When he ventilated the question with H.M. in 1873 the proposal did not meet with Her Royal favour.[1] She is too jealous of the Royal prerogative. Lord Kenmare (an R.C.) becomes Lord Chamberlain; Lord Richard Grosvenor, Whip; and the other appointments do not call for remark. There must, I fear, be many a disappointed candidate for office.

The Queen thinks a Barony '*ample*' for Mr. Lowe. Mr. G., however, has argued for a Viscountcy.[2]

Mr. G. came down to Downing St. this afternoon for the first time and went over the two official houses. No. 11 is, I think, settled to be his residence; and No. 10 will be appropriated to the Secretariat.[3]

A curious revelation—Lord Robert Montagu has thrown himself on the mercy of Mr. G. He says that in 1872–3 Dizzie made overtures to him and promised him the post of Comptroller and Auditor General if he went in for Home Rule with a view to forming a Conservative Catholic Irish party. He did so—poor deluded creature—and, when 1874 came, he was thrown over. He has now the want of 'gumption' to crave the favour of the appointment from Mr. G.[4]

The *Pall Mall Gazette*, which has taken so strong and decided an anti-Gladstonian line for so many years is to change hands and become a Liberal paper. Greenwood, the editor, who for the first time in his life was introduced to Mr. G. the other night, has written to announce the event. The change is a sign of the times, as is also the change in the tone towards Mr. G. and his followers of almost all the London papers.

Saturday, 1 May. Minor appointments in the Household have been proceeding today. They are always difficult to fill up in order to combine efficiency

---

[1] On 25 June 1871 G. spoke to the Queen concerning a Royal Prince becoming Lord-Lieutenant of Ireland. At that time the Queen, though wishing to think over the question, was not entirely opposed. *Letters*, 2nd ser. ii. 137–8. But the matter was dropped as was the related question of establishing a royal residence in Ireland. See Guedalla, ii. 284–97, 387–8, and Add. MS. 44760, ff. 40–5, 67, 74–5. When Lord Spencer thought of retiring as Viceroy in Aug. 1873, G. might have thought of broaching the subject once more, but there is no evidence in his letters to the Queen or to Lord Granville that he then raised the question. [2] See 24 Apr. 1880.

[3] In the event the reverse of this arrangement was made. See 4 May 1880.

[4] In his letter to G. of 28 Apr. 1880 Lord Robert stated that Disraeli had promised that 'he would, as soon as he should come into power, either give me Cabinet office or else increase the Audit Office to £3000 a year with an ex officio seat in the House'. Add. MS. 44463, ff. 234–5.

in the administration with the wishes and likes of the Queen. Lord Charles
Bruce much pleased with the Vice-Chamberlainship.

Mr. Osborne Morgan is to be Judge Advocate General, and Lord Wolverton
is to be given the Paymaster-Generalship in order that he may be formally
associated with the Government. His loyalty to Mr. G. certainly deserves
recognition, but a less judicious adviser it is impossible to conceive.

There is a remarkable article in the *Fortnightly* on the 'Conservative Collapse', in the shape of a letter from a Liberal to an old Conservative signed
'Index'. It is, I think, unmistakeably the product of the pen of Mr. G. himself.
He has not admitted the authorship of it directly, but he sent copies yesterday
to Lady Lothian and Lord Bath, which I consider to be pretty conclusive
evidence of whence the article owes its origin.[1]

The work in Downing St. is almost appalling.

The Russian Ambassador[2] called on Mr. G. this afternoon. This reminds
me he had a letter the other day from 'O.K.'—Madame Novikoff, who was
termed the Russian spy. He does not seem to appreciate her over-much as
a correspondent. Her letter, however, seemed frank and straightforward,
rejoicing at the change of Government, but not asking on behalf of Russia
any indulgence. She only claims to be treated without suspicion and hopes
that a spirit of 'co-operation' between the two countries will be established
in lieu of the recent regime of suspicion and estrangement.

Sunday, 2 May. A very bustling day. Went down to Downing St. in the morning; up to Harley St. for luncheon. Herbert G. returned from Leeds after
a magnificent and probably unprecedented reception.[3] Over 25,000 people
present—great enthusiasm and extraordinary unanimity. He certainly promises to make his public mark in the world, but however great may be his
promises, I am glad it has been decided not to give him a 'billet' in the
Government. It would not have done with his father Premier. If he waits
a short time so as to win his spurs inside the walls of Parliament, he will then
merit a place. Certainly no young fellow of his age ever had a finer start, and
I don't think he will abuse it. His father is evidently very much pleased and
touched, and no wonder. The other sons have not proved themselves up to
the mark of such a father. Mrs. Brand told me today that, in writing to the
Speaker during the election time, Mr. G. said, apropos of the only opportunity he had had of hearing Herbert speak, (which was when he (Herbert)
was received at Hawarden), that 'his son in speaking appeared to have none

---

[1] 'The Conservative Collapse Considered in a Letter from a Liberal to an Old Conservative', signed Index, and dated 17 Apr. 1880, *Fortnightly Review*, xxvii (New Series),
1 May 1880, pp. 607–24. G. was the author; see 2 May 1880 and Morley, ii. 345 n.

[2] Prince Lobanov-Rostovsky.

[3] G. was elected at the top of the poll in both Leeds and Midlothian. When he opted
to sit for Midlothian, his son Herbert, who had been defeated in Middlesex, was returned
for the vacant seat at Leeds without opposition. Morley, ii. 611–12, 617.

of the faults of his father'. All over Gladstone, and his modesty about himself.

The Prince of Wales, who always does the right thing, has asked Mr. and Mrs. G. to dine on Wednesday next, which I think has much pleased them. It is always to be remembered to the credit of H.R.H. that, in connexion with that overt slight of the Queen in not bidding Mr. G. to the Duke of Connaught's wedding two years ago, the Prince did his utmost to get Mr. G. included in the list of Royal Guests.

The Austrian Ambassador—Count Karolyi—has written to demand, in effect, an apology from Mr. G. for his untoward remarks in Midlothian about the Emperor of Austria and the conduct of Austria as a nation. Mr. G. has submitted his draft reply to Lord Granville, in which he tenders most frankly his regret for having used the words he did in the heat of the moment and owing to misinformation. The matter will doubtless be smoothed over, but the statement was very devoid of tact, and the accusation apparently groundless.[1]

Mr. Gladstone was evidently the author of the article on the 'Conservative Collapse' in the *Fortnightly Review*. He wrote it in answer to a letter from Lord Bath apropos of the situation.[2]

Monday, 3 May. Evelyn Ashley has been offered and has accepted the Secretaryship to the Board of Trade. I gathered from him that he apprehended no difficulty about getting on under Chamberlain. With the exception of the offers of Lordships-in-waiting to the Peers whom Her Majesty has selected from a list submitted by Mr. G., the work of forming the administration is over.

There was a Council at Windsor this morning at which the new members of the Household took over their 'whips, staffs, sticks, &c' of office.

The first Cabinet was held this afternoon. Mr. G., in writing to the Queen afterwards, gave an outline of the business discussed. The question of whether, owing to Lord Lytton wishing to delay his departure from India, Lord Ripon should start at once was talked over and it was decided that it would be best that Lord Ripon should go out immediately.

Indian finance seems to have formed the other principal topic. Mr. G. said that the finances were in a serious, if not alarming state. Exact information is apparently not forthcoming as yet, but, owing to some misstatement of the accounts, he seems to apprehend a deficit of 'several millions'. There is no imputation that the misstatement has been intentional.

---

[1] In his speeches in March and Apr. 1880—and especially in the Edinburgh speech of 17 Mar.—G. spoke harshly of Austria as an enemy of freedom and accused the Emperor of Austria of openly seeking the victory of Lord Beaconsfield in the election. See *Annual Register*, 1880, p. 47; Fitzmaurice, ii. 200–7. See also 15 and 18 May 1880, and 17 Nov. 1884. [2] See 1 May 1880.

It is evidently Indian affairs which present the greatest difficulties immediately. As regards Europe the policy of the present Government will, no doubt, be on the lines of the Berlin Treaty and differ from that of the late Government in one respect only—namely, that the provisions of that Treaty shall be carried out more rigorously.

In reading over the draft despatches to our representatives abroad, I noticed that a remarkable statement is credited to the Turkish Ambassador over here. In his conversation with Lord Granville Musurus seems to have implied that, in his opinion, had the Liberals been in power when the Eastern difficulties first arose, the Turks would have escaped the disastrous war.

Who is to go to Constantinople is occupying Mr. G.'s thoughts. He is not in favor of pressing Lord Carlingford. Mr. Goschen is the man who commends himself to Mr. G.'s judgment. Mr. G. has also in his mind's eye Lord Monck.

According to the *Daily News* the rejoicing in the Ottoman Empire is not confined to the Christian races. It extends even to the Turkish populations.[1]

Rosebery has declined all office. With the very prominent part he has taken about Mr. Gladstone and Midlothian it is probably most wise that he should clear himself in the eyes of the world from the charge of ambition and self-interestedness. At the same time it is a pity that, in his over-scrupulousness, the Liberal administration should be deprived wholly of his services, which, in the natural course of events, would have been certainly secured in some capacity or other by Lord Granville or Lord Hartington.

Tuesday, 4 May. I omitted yesterday to note that the Cabinet decided against the recall of Sir B. Frere in South Africa.

Went up early to Harley St. and transacted work with Mr. G. While at breakfast he told me two incidents relating to my father.[2] Sir F. Doyle, in speaking of my father years ago, said, '"Bashel" Hamilton is not the milk of kindness, but the *butter* of kindness'. As true as it is witty. Mr. G. said that my father was the first of his friends who advocated disestablishment of the Church.[3] When walking with Mr. G. in Pall Mall some 30 or 40 years ago, my father (according to Mr. G.) said, 'It would be far better for us were you to make us unfettered and untrammelled by Establishment'.

There has been a change in the Downing St. programme. The Gladstones are to live in No. 10, and we are to be relegated to No. 11,—on the whole a good move for both Prime Minister and the Secretariat.[4]

[1] There is a long article to this effect in the *Daily News* of the next day, 4 May 1880, p. 6.
[2] Walter Kerr Hamilton, after 1854 Bishop of Salisbury, a contemporary of G. at Eton and Christ Church, Oxford, and one of his dearest friends.
[3] EWH emended this sentence imperfectly. It actually reads: 'Mr. G. said it that my father was. . . .' He originally had written: 'Mr. G. said it was my father who . . .' but he altered the 'was' and the 'who' without removing the 'it'.
[4] See 30 Apr. 1880.

Mr. G. has written to the Austrian Ambassador an ample apology which I hope will square matters.[1]

This afternoon Mr. G. held a conclave on the question of Beer duties v. Malt tax. He is evidently very keen about the proposal. It would no doubt be hailed as a great boon by the farmers; but will the change really be as beneficial as supposed? It would of course cut the ground from beneath the feet of the Tories; but is it wise to plunge into financial readjustments so immediately? I doubt it.

Saturday, 8 May. I have not had a moment these last few days to jot down a line. The work is tremendous.

There was another Cabinet on Wednesday, and the measures on which it may be expedient to legislate this session were considered. These were (1) a Burials Bill, on which the Lord Chancellor is to communicate with the Archbishop.[2] It will probably be a moderate measure, on the lines of Osborne Morgan's Burials Bill.[3] (2) A Game Laws Bill, with special reference to Scotland.[4] (3) A measure for strengthening the purchase clauses of the Irish Land Act, so as to encourage more largely a peasant proprietary.[5] (4) A possible Bill to provide for the appointment of a Royal Commission for ascertaining the property of the City Companies.[6]

Lord Derby, it appears, was asked to join the Government, but he declined. He expressed himself most willing to give a loyal and cordial support to the Government, but thought (and very properly so) that the acceptance of office so immediately after his conversion would be too glaringly open to the charge that his change of policy had selfish and personal motives.

Mr. Gladstone's own account of his interview with the Queen, on being summoned, is intensely interesting. She seems to have received him well and kindly, to have told him flatly he must take the consequences of his hard words in opposition. 'She was', as he put it, 'if I may say so, natural but under reserve'.

[1] See 2 May 1880. The apology was printed on 10 May. See 15 and 18 May 1880.

[2] i.e. Lord Selborne is to communicate with Archbishop Tait of Canterbury. For Selborne's letter and some ensuing correspondence between the two see Randall T. Davidson and William Benham, *Life of . . . Tait* (London, 1891), ii. 391–3.

[3] The matter of the law governing burials had been the subject of prolonged and heated controversy. The best brief account of the subject is in Francis Warre Cornish, *The English Church in the 19th Century* (London, 1910), ii. 334–6. See 29 May 1880.

[4] This emerged as the Hares and Rabbits Bill or, as it eventually was called, the Ground Game Bill which received the Royal Assent 7 Sept. 1880. See 29 May 1880.

[5] This question was not taken up in earnest in the 1880 session, which, as far as Irish matters were concerned, was devoted largely to the unsuccessful Compensation for Disturbance (Ireland) Bill. It was the Irish Land Bill of 1881 that attempted a large alteration of the Land Act of 1870 mentioned here. See 16 June 1880.

[6] No bill was necessary since no extraordinary powers were sought. See *Parl. Deb.*, 7 June 1880, cclii. 339–40. A Royal Commission was appointed in the usual way. It reported in 5 volumes in 1884 ('Report of Royal Commission on the Livery Companies of the City of London', *Parl. Papers*, 1884, xxxix. parts I–V). See also 14 July 1880.

The disclosures about Indian finance have a very ugly appearance. We have yet to learn the explanations of the late Government on the subject, but it is impossible to relieve them of the responsibility of the errors of their subordinate officials and difficult to acquit them of a failure to disclose the real facts at the time of the election.

The only minister opposed on re-election has been Harcourt, and he has been beaten today at Oxford by a majority of 54. The imprudently boastful language he has used all along has probably contributed to his defeat, which was not unexpected. It is presumed a seat will be found for him.[1]

Goschen is to go out to Constantinople as Ambassador Extraordinary,—Sir H. Layard being relieved temporarily. He [i.e. Goschen] ought undoubtedly to have gone to India as was originally proposed to him. It is there where we may expect greatest troubles. If, owing to the deficiency, we are bound to take on our own shoulders part of the war expenses, this will inevitably lead to an increase of taxation. Mr. G. takes a gloomy view of revenue prospects and doubts if Sir S. Northcote's figures will be realised.

Mr. G. gone to Mentmore for Sunday.

It seems settled that I am to live in No. 11.

Sunday, 9 May. At work almost all day. Went to luncheon with the Knatchbull-Hugessens. He is certainly the most delightfully conceited self-assured man living. He evidently does not wholly relish being polished off by a peerage. He expected at least a seat in the Cabinet and the Home Secretary-ship. On this expectation he purchased a house in Queen Anne's Gate in order to be handy to his office and the House of Commons. Moreover, according to him, now that he can no longer take an active part in politics, Kent, or rather his part of Kent, will be lost to the party—his influence and popularity have been so great.[2]

I have been offered and have undertaken the post of Chief Wine Butler to Mr. G., which I hope will secure something rather less nasty in his cellars.

Tuesday, 11 May. Read yesterday two interesting despatches (or rather private letters to Lord Granville) from our Ambassadors at Berlin and St. Petersburg.

According to Lord O. Russell, Bismarck has always been favourable to any settlement of the Eastern question to which the agreement of the European powers could be secured. Joint action is in fact what he has always aimed at. Since the Treaty of Berlin was passed, he has been and is determined

---

[1] Samuel Plimsoll, M.P. for Derby, resigned his seat as soon as he heard of Harcourt's setback at Oxford, and Harcourt was elected in his place. Gardiner, i. 364–5.

[2] Edward Knatchbull-Hugessen, who later in May was created Baron Brabourne, owned, in 1883, 4,173 acres in Kent in the area between Ashford and Folkestone. He lived at 3 Queen Anne's Gate.

to defend it, and it has been with a view to resist any encroachments against that Treaty by Russia that he has formed an Austro-German alliance. Personally he wishes for a predominance of Austrian influence in the Balkan peninsula. He considers that Turkey has been given a sufficient breathing time to warrant a presumption that the outstanding questions connected with the Eastern question may be peaceably settled. He—I mean Bismarck all through—evidently inclines towards Austria. He regards Goschen's mission to Constantinople as most important.[1]

According to Lord Dufferin, the Emperor of Russia is weak and the administration incompetent, thoroughly second-class. Now that Gortchakoff is on the shelf Mr. Giers is the man who superintends everything. General Milutine and Louis Melikoff are the two most important personages on the political scene. The Cesarevitch has displayed recently great rudeness towards the Germans in St. Petersburg. Schouvaloff seems entirely shelved. The alarm at Nihilism may act as a preventive against troubles abroad, but there need not be apprehended a revolution at the back of it. There is no inclination on the part of Russia to disturb the Treaty of Berlin; she is only anxious that outstanding questions in the East should be wound up. The inability of Turkey to occupy the Balkans has been chiefly instrumental in removing the sting of mortification felt at the Berlin Treaty having superseded the San Stephano Treaty. As regards Central Asia, the desire of the Russians is to avenge their own defeat by the Turkomans. They are anxious to come to an understanding with us on the Central Asiatic business. Their chief cause for anxiety consists in the line taken by the Chinese. At the same time, an agreement on our part with Russia ought only to be taken as collateral security:— the Executive in St. Petersburg is so slack and powerless that there is no saying what her agents may do. There is no fear of an actual invasion of India by Russia; the outside that can happen is the establishment of an Asiatic base, whence in case of hostilities between the two countries she might annoy us. The return of a Liberal Government in this country is (as is only natural) hailed by Russia with much delight.

Layard at Constantinople seems to be making up to the present Government. It is presumed he does not like the idea of temporary supersession by Goschen. He (Layard) maintains that the days of Turkish rule in Europe are numbered, and that his contention has always been that the Christian races should have been allowed to work out their destiny for themselves in conjunction with the Mussulmen. The question now is, how far to avoid a sudden collapse of the Porte, so that some little time may be gained in order to prepare for the change which sooner or later is inevitable. He denies ever having led the Turk to believe that help would be forthcoming from England. The Sultan[2] appears to be an able, subtle man; at times not in his right mind, being crazy by his dread of harm to himself.

[1] Knaplund, pp. 140–2.   [2] Abdul Hamid II.

Mr. G. still at Mentmore, ruminating over the Malt tax. He has written an interesting letter to his old friend Sir F. Doyle, reviewing his own political life. He maintains that it has been experience which has changed his politics, but that he is not open to the charge of inconsistency as much as is supposed; in his original Tory days his sympathies were really on the side of Liberalism. As regards the recent electoral struggle, so far as the main issue has been concerned, the Liberals fought the fight against ideas and practices neither Liberal nor Conservative, and (I would add) not English.[1]

Wednesday, 12 May. The Gladstones took up their abode in No. 10 Downing St. today for the first time. There was a Cabinet in the afternoon. The topics discussed (and which apparently are most likely to figure in the programme of this session) were the Burial Laws, the Game Laws, and the Employers' Liability. Instructions have been sent out to Sir B. Frere to the effect that the Transvaal will be maintained, but that on no pretext is any further annexation in that part of the world to be projected.

The Malt tax still occupies the 'Great Man's' mind.

Thursday, 13 May. The Bradlaugh committee met yesterday to consider whether Bradlaugh might 'affirm' in lieu of taking the usual oath. The committee were evenly divided, owing to Hopwood having gone against the line taken by the Government, and the chairman[2] gave his casting vote against admitting Bradlaugh on affirmation. Consequently, either Bradlaugh must swallow the oath, or a special Act with special provisions to meet the case must be passed.

Had a talk with Forster this evening at the Algy Wests on Irish affairs. The distress, though partially very extreme, has been much exaggerated.

Lord Ripon has started for India. His appointment has evidently given great offence among the Dissenting orders.[3] Those orders are certainly the most uncharitable of people.

Saturday, 15 May. Another Cabinet yesterday. The Peace Preservation Act or Coercion Act (as it is more commonly called) is not to be renewed. The fact is it expires next month, so the Government had not much choice in the matter. But it is certainly desirable, if possible, to make a commencement towards placing Ireland on a footing similar to Great Britain. It is presumable that the late Government contemplated 'dropping' the Act; otherwise, they must have left this important matter out of consideration when they determined on the dissolution of Parliament, for they could not have expected to secure the renewal of the Act within such a limited time with

---

[1] A small part of the letter is quoted in Morley, ii. 631.   [2] Spencer Walpole.
[3] Lord Ripon became a convert to Roman Catholicism in 1874. For a discussion of the criticisms of the appointment see Lucien Wolf, *Life of . . . Ripon* (London, 1921), i. 318–19.

a powerful array of Irishmen against them. Flogging in the Army is to be abolished; the rules and regulations of the service are to 'accord with those in foreign countries'. (I was not aware that there was no flogging abroad.)

Bradlaugh is to take the oath, reserving to himself the right to bring the question before the House.

The Karolyi correspondence has given rise to much discussion. The apology, according to the Opposition Press, is a humiliation. According to the other side, it is merely a frank confession that, on the assurance that Austria had no intention of interfering with the development of the Eastern Provinces, Mr. G. is willing to accept her statement.[1]

Tuesday, 18 May. According to Layard, Musurus over here is not to be trusted. Goschen's special mission to Constantinople has frightened the Sultan and his ministers out of their wits. They regard it as a first step towards placing Turkey under foreign tutelage. Layard, however, says that Goschen must be on friendly terms with the Sultan. It is his only chance of doing anything with the 'sick man'. There is a hope that a better set of ministers may be the outcome, but in any case Goschen will find a most unpleasant state of things confronting him—penury, distress, utter confusion, and anarchy.

The Emperor of Austria is not only extremely gratified but greatly struck by the way in which Mr. G. has removed whatever unpleasant impression his words in Midlothian may have created. H.M. [i.e. Francis Joseph], in short, thinks Mr. G. has behaved 'like an English gentleman', and that in Austro-Hungary no trace of sore will be found to exist.[2]

It will not be known to the world at large, but I believe myself that Mr. G.'s words about Austria were carefully weighed; that they were meant as a rejoinder to Lord Salisbury's famous allusion in the autumn to the 'glad tidings of great joy' consequent on the supposed alliance between Germany and Austria, which implied that it was Austria, instead of Russia, who was to divide the spoils, and that it was only on the assurance (which Mr. G. wished to evoke) that Austria had no motives of aggrandisement in the Balkan Peninsula, that he consented to withdraw his words and to write what is termed 'an apology'.[3]

The Queen's Speech 'goes in' for the execution of the Berlin Treaty, for endeavouring to place Afghanistan on friendly terms, for a reform of the

---

[1] See 2 and 4 May 1880.

[2] See 2, 4, and 15 May 1880.

[3] In mid Oct. 1879 Lord Salisbury travelled to Manchester where he addressed a large gathering at the Pomona Gardens. He defended the Government's foreign policy against the charges that were then issuing from G. in Midlothian, and he referred to the rumours of an Austro-German alliance as 'glad tidings of great joy'; the phrase became widely known and Lord Salisbury was criticized for his irreverence. Lady Gwendolen Cecil, *Life of Salisbury* (London, 1921–32), ii. 369–70.

Game Laws, for a Burials Bill, for the extension of the suffrage to Ireland, for a continuance in a reformed manner of the Ballot Act. The Queen does not like the idea of a non-renewal of the Coercion Acts, and has impressed on Mr. G. the necessity for not trusting to the Emperor of Russia.[1]

Sunday, 23 May. The Parliamentary dinner on Wednesday evening went off very well, I think, on the whole. It pleased the guests and pleased Mr. G. with one exception, viz., the absence of the sauterne. He is extraordinarily conservative on small points like that of wine and does not readily fall in with the current of modern fashion. I sat between Lyon Playfair and O. Morgan, and near Fawcett and Dilke. The latter greatly 'took' me—good-looking, charming-mannered, quick &c.

Parliament opened on the Thursday (20th). Albert Grey and the seconder— Hugh Mason—both acquitted themselves well. There was good humour on the side of the Opposition. Mr. G.'s speech was moderate, straightforward, and effective; and, though the Irishmen, or rather the Irish Extremist party, moved an amendment regretting the absence in the speech of any mention of the land question in Ireland, there was no bitterness or obstruction shewn.

Friday—the 21st—was mostly devoted to the Bradlaugh case which is a delicate and difficult question. The original Committee having reported against his substituting an affirmation for an oath, he presented himself at the table in the usual way. Thereupon Sir H. Wolff,[2] who seems bent on making himself notorious and disagreeable, protested against Bradlaugh, who had given out that he merely regarded the oath of allegiance as an empty form, taking his seat. This led to a lengthened discussion which promised to travel over a wide range—political as well as legal, which was the point at issue—and Mr. G. suggested a further reference to a committee. We have not heard the end of it, as the debate was adjourned.

The other most important point discussed was the retention of Sir B. Frere at the Cape. Courtney violently attacked the Government for (apparently) so flagrant an act of inconsistency. It was, however, decided in the Cabinet yesterday not to recall him, but I expect his retention will be for a limited time only. The defence of the Government is that Sir Bartle cannot by any possible means land us into further difficulties like the Zulu War, and that as he is more conversant than any '*remplaçant*' could be with the important question of confederation, he had better be left to carry that through. It is not a wholly satisfactory state of things.[3]

The Gladstones seem to have been favourably [impressed] with their visit to Windsor last Sunday. Mrs. G. said the Queen was very cordial. There is no doubt, however, that Lord Beaconsfield was very genial to the Queen. The

---

[1] Guedalla, ii. 95.   [2] EWH has written 'Woolf'.
[3] And it became increasingly less satisfactory. Late in July 1880 the Cabinet decided to recall Frere. See Guedalla, ii. 107–9; and see 27, 30 July, 3 Aug., and 10 Sept. 1880.

Dean of Windsor told my uncle that Lord B[eaconsfield] had ingratiated himself more in Royal favour than probably any other Prime Minister of her reign.

A secret despatch from Saxony makes out that the Liberal victory has caused considerable disappointment, amounting almost to dismay, in Germany. This seems due to a fear that the Berlin settlement will be undone, and that, by a tolerance of Slav propaganda in the Balkan peninsula, fresh outbreaks may be excited and Russia encouraged to make further attempts on the Bosphorus. This fear is intensified by an apprehension lest we may be jealous of Austria. Germany is said to be anti-Russian to a man. Dizzie exercised a sort of fascination over the German mind.

Saturday, 29 May.[1] It is very difficult to find time to jot down anything. Nearly a week elapsed since my last entry. Meanwhile I have taken up my abode in Downing St., and I find it most pleasant, far pleasanter than I expected. I feel the benefit of more room and fresher air.

Bradlaugh and Frere have been the main centres of interest during the last week.

Mr. G. took the opportunity at the beginning of the week of making a statement about South African affairs which has to some extent diminished the outcry against the non-recall of Frere.[2] The Queen has expressed a strong desire that the Government will be firm about him. The Government will be so, unless the feeling in favour of recalling him becomes intensified enough to paralyse his influence in South Africa. H.M. evidently has a strong impression that Sir G. Wolseley has not played his part out there so as to ensure confidence in him.

The Bradlaugh business has so far advanced that the Committee of Inquiry has been agreed to; but last night Sir S. Northcote played a 'fast and loose part.' It was arranged that the Whips should nominate the members who were to serve on the Committee. This was done, but in spite of this arrangement he never gave the smallest assistance to the Government but walked out of the House.

Goschen has arrived in Constantinople. En route he had an interesting interview with the Emperor of Austria who expressed much gratification at the act of the new English Government. He spoke warmly on behalf of Greece, but deprecated any material intervention for ensuring a settlement of the frontier question. H.M. seems to look forward to the Albanians quieting down in the Montenegro business. As to Turkey, the Emperor agreed that her end must come unless reforms be introduced. Great care, however, must be taken to prevent the Porte from being driven into the arms of Russia. Austria seems well disposed towards France and Italy and would continue to support Germany, but not in a dangerous sense. The Emperor is not easy

---

[1] EWH wrote '*Saturday May 31st*'.   [2] *Parl. Deb.*, 25 May 1880, cclii. 455-64.

about Russia and assured Goschen that Austria had no selfish objects in view herself.

Baron Haymerle spoke in a similar strain.

Two measures promised in the Queen's Speech have been introduced during the week: the Burials Bill in the House of Lords, the Ground Game Bill in the House of Commons. The Burials Bill is not framed on extreme lines, but on the lines of Osborne Morgan's annual bill and of the amendment proposed two years ago in the House of Lords by Lord Harrowby. Every churchyard and cemetery is to be open to everyone, and the alternatives for those who are not content with the Church of England Burial service will be no service, or a service of a 'Christian and orderly character'. The Bill ought to secure a settlement of this long-outstanding, vexed question.

The Ground Game Bill provides that the occupier of the soil shall have an inalienable right, concurrent with that of the landlord, to kill hares and rabbits himself or by some duly appointed person or persons. It is probable that in the House of Commons the Bill or at any rate the principle of the Bill will be accepted; but it remains to be seen what will be done with it in the higher assembly of landlords.[1]

Monday, 31 May. Sir H. Elliot reports that Goschen has left excellent impressions behind him at Vienna. Haymerle is strongly in favor of 'decentralisation' for the Balkan provinces and of freeing them from Palace control, but great care must be taken that the majorities do not tyrannise over the minorities.

An interesting despatch from Lord Odo Russell came under my notice this afternoon. The gist of it was this—Bismarck has for long been desirous for an alliance with England, but his offers of co-operation were never met cordially by the Conservative Government. His last offer was made when we were under Russian difficulties (or supposed Russian difficulties) in our Northwest frontier of India. While rejoicing at the offer, we declined it. Thereupon Bismarck in despair turned to France, seemingly with a view to secure the alliance of this country indirectly. France appears to have readily accepted the German overtures. Russia has felt the blow keenly. Since the change of Governments in England, he has become more cordial towards Russia and may possibly endeavour to revive the Triple Alliance. Bismarck's preference for England is founded on a conviction that, by her great moral influence, she is best fitted to keep the peace of Europe, so necessary to consolidate the German Empire and keep the general peace.[2]

Tuesday, 1 June. Apropos of H.M. apprehensions lest the policy of the present

---

[1] The Lords passed the bill, having successfully limited the number of those who might shoot for the occupier. See *Parl. Deb.*, 3 Sept. 1880, cclvi. 1192–9. Their attempt to provide for a close season was unsuccessful. Ibid., pp. 1199–1207. See 1 Sept. 1880.

[2] The letter of 29 May 1880 is printed in full in Knaplund, pp. 144–5.

Government should lead to a threatening of force against Turkey without acting on it, the Queen expressed herself in quite unmeasured terms against Lord Derby. She seems to regard him as the most unsatisfactory minister she ever had about her. Today is the anniversary of Prince Imperial's death. The Queen evidently looks back on the event with inexpressible horror, both on account of the disgrace that attached to the British name by reason of his having been deserted by an Englishman, and on account of the end which his death put to the only man who might have re-established monarchy in France.[1]

Saturday, 5 June. (Salisbury) Goschen has now been some days in Constantinople. The Sultan seems to be playing his old game, and I fear English difficulties will be great about bringing the Porte to account. Musurus[2] is out there, having before his departure been posted up with the views of Mr. Gladstone. Previous to his starting he had an interview with Mr. G., the result of which seems to have been this: —Musurus pitched very high the practical progress of Turkey since '39. He said autonomies meant anatomies for the Turkish Empire—in other words 'vivisection'. He thought the Governors of the various provinces might be appointed for 5 years; he seems to fear the influence of Russia and still more the plans of Austria. Mr. Gladstone laid stress on the fact that maintenance of the Turkish Empire, however much it might be desired, was not a 'sine qua non' to English interests and regretted that Turkey had relied on British support in the last resort.[3] Musurus admitted that Lord Beaconsfield's Government had encouraged the idea and had in reality done nothing. What the English Government desire is that the supremacy of the Sultan shall be maintained, but conditionally upon effective reforms being carried out by means of 'administrative, not political autonomy'. The tie, in short, between the Porte and the Provinces should be light. Musurus seems to have been satisfied with the policy thus foreshadowed. It remains to be seen whether he will be able to induce the Sultan to realise his position, or whether we shall get the stereotyped form of answer from the Porte—'*non possumus*'.

Parliament has been getting to work. The Burials Bill has been read a second time in the House of Lords, and the Employers' Liability Bill has reached a similar stage in the House of Commons. The latter Bill will no doubt undergo considerable modifications. This Employers' Liability question is a most difficult one. On the one hand, the employers are greatly

---

[1] The Prince Imperial, the only son of Napoleon III, went off to the Zulu War against the wishes of Beaconsfield and the Cabinet but with the Queen's encouragement. He was killed in a small skirmish.

[2] The Turkish Ambassador to England.

[3] The memorandum of 'proposed language of Mr. Gladstone to Musurus Pasha' is printed in Temperley and Penson, p. 398, although the date ascribed to it there is incorrect; see Ramm, i. 127 n. 4.

alarmed at the prospect of being held liable for accident caused not only by their own negligence, but by the negligence of their foremen and all who are in any way placed in authority. On the other hand, the workmen will be satisfied with nothing short of complete liability.

Sunday, 6 June.[1] (Salisbury) Down here for Sunday, mainly to talk over arrangements about Alice's wedding.[2] I wish the day were over, as I dread it for her, Mother, and the other sisters. Had a talk with the Bishop[3] on the Burials Bill. He shewed no signs of hostility towards the measure in its present form. The question of exempting Cathedral Cloisters which has been raised might, he thinks, be best met by closing them. If, according to the Bill (as I understand it), the Unitarian (say) will render himself liable to a misdemeanour by casting obloquy by any inscription of a gravestone against the Trinitarian, will the Trinitarian render himself equally liable to the committal of a misdemeanour if he casts obloquy on the Unitarian?

Monday, 7 June.[4] An important despatch is going out to Goschen.[5] It is to put him in possession of the views of the Government on the subject of the Anglo-Turkish Convention, which was broached some little back by Musurus Pasha. It seems that the Turkish Government would be glad to cancel it. They don't object to the part relating to our tenure of Cyprus; indeed, they would be glad to commute the revenue and get rid of the fee simple of the island. What they do resent is the right of local interference with the internal administration of the Asiatic dominions of the Porte, which is claimed by the consular authorities in virtue of H.M. engagement to introduce reforms. Accordingly, they would like to release England from her engagements in Asia Minor.

It is an established fact that the acquisition of Cyprus has been no single advantage to us either from a political or military point of view, while the transaction had an evident appearance of its origin arising from motives not wholly disinterested.

To restore Cyprus to Turkey would be disliked by the inhabitants; they have probably had a sufficient taste of Turkish rule, and it seems probable that the Porte would be glad to arrange the entire transfer of the island to Turkey [*sic*] on the tribute being commuted for so many years' franchise.

[1] EWH wrote '*Sunday, June 5*'.

[2] EWH's sister Alice (1851–1939) married the Revd. R. C. Moberly, vicar of Great Budworth, Cheshire, on 29 June 1880. See 10 July and 4 Nov. 1880.

[3] i.e. Bishop Moberly of Salisbury, successor of EWH's father in that position, and the father of Alice Hamilton's fiancé.

[4] EWH wrote '*Monday, June the 6th*'.

[5] The dispatch, of which the following entry is a paraphrase, is printed in Temperley and Penson, pp. 400–5. It was sent to Goschen on 10 June. While the Queen gave formal approval to the document, she disagreed with its contents. *Letters*, 2nd ser. iii. 111–13. See also Ramm, i. 129–34.

As regards Asia Minor, no practical reforms have been introduced, and in the absence of all money there is little hope that much, if anything, will be done in this direction. This being the case, the majority of the Cabinet are evidently and strongly in favor of our terminating the agreement so far as we have any concern with Asia Minor. We are not less desirous of seeing an amelioration of the Turkish subjects attained, but considering how little is likely to come out of our separate engagements in Asia Minor by reason of the Anglo-Turkish Convention, we may as well fall back on the general article in the Berlin Treaty affecting our interests in it, retaining of course complete liberty of action in certain eventualities.

Wednesday, 9 June. Mr. G. has finally made up his mind to make his financial proposals tomorrow. A Beer tax is to take the place of malt. This will involve a loss of something like $1\frac{1}{2}$ million the first year, and to make this good as well as to secure a margin, 2^d is to go on to the Income Tax for the last half year, equivalent, of course, to an additional 1^d practically. With a margin, he intends readjusting the scale of wine duties in order to induce the French to give us better terms in the new commercial treaty, and what remains will go to meet contingencies. I am very sorry he does not seize this opportunity of giving some substantial assistance to India. It must come in the long run, and now is the right moment to do it, when people are all hot about the Indian financial troubles. He thinks, however, it is premature, because we do not know sufficiently how the land of Indian finance lies, thus sacrificing expediency to what he calls right. I am rather afraid that exception will moreover be taken to the fact of his giving a pull to the indirect taxpayer at the entire expense of the direct (income) taxpayer.

The Queen has taken alarm at the growing tendency of the House of Commons to meddle too much with the Executive, and to arrogate its rights. Mr. G. admits the tendency, and that it has increased greatly during the last half century, but doubts whether this particular Parliament or late Parliaments have made any very great advances more distinctly in this direction. The most important and alarming phase of this tendency has, he thinks, reference to public charges, with which the Executive constitutionally without doubt takes the initiative. A very large portion of the increased expenditure during the last 25 years is due to the repeated demands made by classes, more especially the landed interest and soldiers, who force the Government of the day into relieving their particular burdens or improving their individual positions at the expense of the community.[1]

Henry Primrose is to go out to India as private Secretary to Lord Ripon. A better choice could not have been made, but he will be a great loss to us in Downing St. We shall lose a charming colleague.

---

[1] The letters of the Queen and G. on this subject are printed in Guedalla, ii. 100–2.

Thursday, 10 June. **Mr.** Gladstone propounded his great Budget this afternoon. It was a truly magnificent and masterly exposition. The proposals appeared to be met with great favour in the House—perhaps too favourably for eventual adoption. Roughly speaking, they amount to this, financially:

Dr.		Cr.	
Supplemental Estimates	200,000	Present Estimated Surplus	180,000
Drawback on Malt	1,100,000	Increased License charges	310,000
Expenses	40,000	1^d Income Tax	1,450,000
Allowance for Wine Duties	300,000		
Surplus	300,000		
	1,940,000		1,940,000

The Malt duty, of course, gives way to the Beer duty, which, though there is for this year a loss of £1,100,000 on account of drawback, is estimated to yield next year about £350,000 more than the present Malt tax.

Wednesday, 16 June. It is almost useless to attempt a diary of events. I never get a moment to jot anything down.

We had an unpleasant fright after last Saturday's Cabinet. The proposals made in connection with the grant of compensation for ejectment of the Irish tenant for non-payment of rent could not be swallowed by the Duke of Argyll; and I feared we were to have a crisis. He actually placed his resignation in Mr. Gladstone's hands, but has been since prevailed upon to think better of his impulsive step, after being partly met—that is, any extensive amendment of the Land Act is to be postponed till a small Commission has reported on its operation, while a clause will be inserted in the Irish Relief Bill empowering the judge, in a somewhat modified form, to award compensation for eviction if the non-payment of rent is clearly the result of the distress in Ireland.[1]

On Monday there was a great rumpus in the House. O'Donnell attributed all kinds of foul deeds to the new French Ambassador-designate. Mr. Gladstone 'took the bull by the horns' and moved that O'D be not heard. This created great excitement, resulted in an angry discussion the whole of the sitting, and caused a horrible waste of time.[2]

---

[1] Argyll's letter of resignation as Lord Privy Seal and the responses to it of G. and Granville are printed in Argyll's *Autobiography and Memoirs* (London, 1906), ii. 349–54. He withdrew his resignation, but his objections to the Irish Land Bill of 1881 forced him finally to resign. See 6 Apr. 1881.

[2] On 14 June in the House of Commons O'Donnell formally asked Sir Charles Dilke, Under-Secretary for Foreign Affairs, if the future French Ambassador, M. Challemel Lacour, was the Prefect of the Provisional Government of 4 Sept. 1870 who 'ordered the massacre of Colonel Carayon Latour's battalion in the telegram "Fusillez-moi ces gens-là"'. *Parl. Deb.* cclii. 1904.

Wednesday, 23 June. Another week and not a line written! The Berlin Conference for settling the Greek frontier appears to have made satisfactory progress.[1] All the Western powers, viz. France, Italy, Austria, and Germany seem agreed as to the line which the new boundary is to take. Russia's policy has been kept dark, but it appears that her game is to go in for Greece—become the champion of the Hellenes. In short she supports the frontier which the Greeks have sketched out for themselves, so as to 'take the wind out of the sails' of France, England, Italy, and Austria. The majority of the powers, however, will largely outvote Russia in favour of the line advocated by France, and Russia will then claim to have 'broken a lance' in favor of Greece and go in for establishing a protectorate over Greeks, as well as over the Slavs in Turkey. (This sort of behaviour is not best calculated to remove that distrust of her which this country has so long entertained; and at a time too when we are willing to be on frank and friendly terms with her!) Lord Odo Russell, one of, if not *the*, best of our Ambassadors abroad, evidently thinks that this Government is on the right track by aiming at an 'European Concert' in spite of such a concert being so sneered at by Lord Salisbury. (I notice in the last volume of the life of 'Prince Consort' that he alludes to the 'Concert' being the only possible and safe programme for ensuring to Europe peace.)[2] As regards the resort to material force in the event of the Sultan not accepting the fiat of the Powers, it seems that Bismarck, though unwilling to 'sacrifice a single Pomeranian soldier' in the cause of Greece, will give Germany's moral support, at any rate, to a demonstration. In what that demonstration is to consist with any real effect and without leading to bloodshed seems to be a debateable point and is, I fear, a big 'rock ahead'. The Emperor of Germany appears to favour the Powers acting in concert.[3]

Saturday, 26 June. The great excitement of the week has been that wretched Bradlaugh business. Instead of treating the matter as purely one of law, the majority of the House have made it the occasion of parading their religious fanaticism and of embarrassing the Government. What are the facts? The first Committee by a majority of one decided against Mr. Bradlaugh being allowed to make an affirmation. The second Committee had a majority in favour of permitting him to make the affirmation and then testing the legality of his affirmation by the High Court of Justice. The House by carrying Sir

[1] This conference of the great powers met first on 16 June 1880, and its decisions were embodied in collective notes to Greece and Turkey, 15 July 1880. For an account of the conference see Medlicott, pp. 83–4, 97–112.

[2] The 'he' refers presumably to Prince Albert, not to Lord Salisbury who is mentioned in the biography (v. 289) but only in passing. EWH may have in mind the passage from Prince Albert's letter to the King of Prussia in which he talks of the safeguards of Europe's peace, but the passage cannot be considered an endorsement of the 'Concert'. Theodore Martin, *The Life of . . . the Prince Consort* (N.Y., 1875–80), v. 260.

[3] Throughout this entry EWH has drawn on Russell's letter to Granville, 19 June 1880, printed in Knaplund, pp. 148–9.

H. Giffard's resolution have refused to allow him either to take the oath or to make an affirmation.[1] Therefore the House have assumed the authority to settle the legal question and have succeeded in settling nothing. The reason why Mr. Gladstone and the Government generally declined to accept this resolution was that they feared that the House would be entangled in difficulties of a serious character by assuming a jurisdiction in a case of this kind where they had no jurisdiction; and their apprehensions have been fully realised. In one way, no doubt, the majority have triumphed, inasmuch as they have forced the hands of the Government by necessitating their doing something to disentangle the House out of the difficulties which it has got itself into. The decision of the Cabinet was to be arrived at this afternoon; and what appears most probable that they will do is to move a Resolution which will enable a member to affirm if he scruples to take the oath. It has been a wretched business. It has led to the Government's policy being entirely misrepresented, and it has done no credit to the Opposition. It has certainly been an unfortunate occurrence for the Government.

What with this and other occurrences the Government start has not been a very successful one. What I am most apprehensive about and am concerned at is Forster's Irish Bill empowering the award of compensation to tenants ejected for non-payment of rent. It may not be a revolutionary one, more especially as its object is limited and intended merely to tide over a year of special difficulty resulting from the recent Irish distress. But the principle is one which not unreasonably excites territorial fears, and the measure is calculated to be regarded by the land agitators as an instalment for 'better things to come'.

Sunday, 27 June. Henry Primrose started off for India on Friday, which has involved the loss of a great friend and a charming colleague. However, I feel sure he is the right man in his new appointment of Private Secretary to Lord Ripon; and we have obtained a very nice substitute for him in the shape of Horace Seymour.

The Berlin Congress seems to have prospered, at any rate so far, and to the extent of establishing an agreement among the powers in the matter of the Greek frontier. It remains to be seen whether their proposal will be accepted by the Porte; and if not, what means and measure of force are to

---

[1] On 21 June 1880 Labouchere moved that Bradlaugh be allowed to make an affirmation instead of taking the oath. Sir Hardinge Giffard then moved an amendment stating that Bradlaugh should not be allowed to affirm or swear. *Parl. Deb.* ccliii. 443–55. After a long debate the House, on 22 June, defeated Labouchere's motion 275 to 230 and accepted Giffard's resolution. Ibid., pp. 624–8. G., however, did not let the matter drop. On 1 July 1880 he introduced on behalf of the Government a resolution which would permit any duly elected person to make an affirmation instead of taking the oath. The House passed the motion 303 to 249, and on 2 July Bradlaugh took his seat. *Parl. Deb.* ccliii. 1267–1347. This action by no means ended the Bradlaugh case; for an account of which see Walter L. Arnstein, *The Bradlaugh Case* (Oxford, 1965).

be applied. Moreover, there is the great danger about the Albanians rising. In fact, the Eastern corner of Europe is in a most uncomfortable state. Wilfrid Blunt, who is really quite an authority on the Eastern question, at any rate as far as the Asiatic Provinces of the Empire are concerned, maintains that no solution of the difficulties is possible [but] one, and that *one* is the deposition of the Sultan, and the substitution of a less powerful, less clever, and less deceitful man—a nonentity in fact, after the fashion of what has been done in Egypt.

Saturday, 10 July. It is certainly hopeless endeavouring to keep up a diary; nearly a fortnight's blank.

Dear Allie's marriage was a great success.[1] Everything went off to perfection from the weather downwards, and everybody behaved most bravely. I believe I was one of the most 'quaky', for which I felt quite ashamed.

We have been living in troublous times. That wretched bill of Forster's[2] has done incalculable harm to the party. It has frightened the landlords; brought discredit on the Government, and satisfied no one. The proposed new *explanatory* clause of the Irish Attorney General,[3] which purports to make it clear that the tenant who has been given the option of selling his good will is excluded from compensation, has opened the eyes of the Irishmen to the really limited scope of the bill, and while it has excited their hostility to the bill, it has done little to calm the apprehensions of the alarmists. Lansdowne has resigned.[4] He would not be contented with anything short of the withdrawal of the bill. I am not sure that the withdrawal of the bill might not, from a party point of view, be the lesser of two evils; but it is doubtful whether that or the throwing out of the bill might not do more harm in Ireland by creating a peg whereon to hang renewed anti-rent agitation. Altogether it has been and is a wretched business, miserably mismanaged. It is true the Irish Government—Burke—said that they would not be responsible for the peaceable government of the country without some such measure; and it was on that advice that Forster apparently acted. But it was, I believe, bad advice, and Forster ought to have seen through it. Things in general and this bill specially haunt me like a nightmare and entirely take away from the pleasure of one's Downing St. work. Oh! for being landed safely into a prorogation of Parliament.

Mr. G. has offered Lansdowne's place—the Under-Secretaryship at India Office—to Rosebery who is abroad for his health; but I doubt his accepting the offer in spite of the 'reek' of the election (as Mr. G. put it to him) being over.[5] Probably Camperdown, in the event of Rosebery refusing, has best

---

[1] See 6 June 1880.

[2] The Compensation for Disturbance (Ireland) Bill, which came before the House of Commons for the first time on 18 June 1880.

[3] Hugh Law.   [4] Lord Lansdowne was Under-Secretary for India.

[5] Rosebery refused the offer. See 21 July and 25 Aug. 1880. Lord Enfield accepted the position. See 25 July and 25 Aug. 1880.

claims; but I am not sure, considering his position and his ability, Fife would not be the best man. The Conservatives are greatly on the crow.

Tuesday, 13 July. Matters are going better, at any rate abroad, for the Government. The Concert of Europe has been maintained, and all the Powers seem determined that their decision shall be carried out by the Porte as regards the Greek frontier. Goschen seems to be doing excellent work at Constantinople. His views of the situation now are something as follows: He thinks the Porte will not accept the proposed frontier if the verdict of the Powers is merely presented in the form of mediation. He is doubtful whether even Europe's *will* will be executed peacefully; a mere *wish* would certainly be set aside. The Turks feel the award to be unjust, and they may think that they could never justify themselves in the eyes of the Turkish population except by some exhibition of force. To allow the decision of the Berlin Conference to remain a 'dead letter' would be a death-blow to European influence. It has been represented to the Porte, more especially by the French Ambassador at Constantinople,[1] that dismemberment of the Empire would be the certain result of resistance by the Turks, as well as the union of Eastern Roumelia with Bulgaria. The probability seems to be that, under all the circumstances, the Porte will content itself with encouraging the Albanians to resist the occupation of the new frontier by the Greeks; in which case it is fair to assume that Greece would be able to hold her own provided that the command of the sea is secured to her by the other Powers. All the Powers seem willing to join in a naval demonstration, but they won't commit themselves to *landing* forces.

The Irish Bill[2] makes no progress, and the further amendments proposed by the Government, if they are calculated to calm the apprehensions of the moderate Whigs, are tantamount to an admission that the Government does not properly know the meaning of its own bill.

Wednesday, 14 July. Government having 'bagged' Wednesdays and Tuesdays for their own business, they went to work again at that wretched Irish bill.[3] They made no progress. They partly accepted an amendment of the front Opposition Bench which will limit the operation of the bill to holdings under £20, but the more they vary the original provisions of the bill the more they tend to fall between two stools. They don't satisfy those of their own party who are discontented or frightened, and they alienate the Irish party or the

---

[1] C. J. Tissot.

[2] i.e. the Compensation for Disturbance Bill.

[3] On 12 July G. moved that 'for the remainder of the Session Government Orders have priority on Wednesday and that on Tuesday the 20th July and every succeeding Tuesday, Orders of the Day have precedence of Notices of Motions, Government Orders having priority'. The House agreed to the motion. *Parl. Deb.* ccliv. 180–93. The Irish Bill referred to is again the Compensation for Disturbance Bill.

bulk of it. They seem, however, determined to fight it out. I am not at all sure myself whether the lesser of the two evils would not be to drop it now, despite all the waste of time it has caused. Anyhow what is the good of going on with a measure which is certain to be rejected by the Lords?

Dined at the Goldsmiths—the trial of the Pyx.[1] Went down to City with Mr. G. Sir W. Harcourt made a very clever, telling speech, and all the old wardens and members of City Companies came away, I believe, more than happy about the inquisition which it is proposed to hold into their affairs.[2] He said in effect, why should there not be 'tit for tat'? The Goldsmiths Co. have been inquiring into the wares of the Chancellor of the Exchequer—Master of the Mint—his coins; why should he not inquire into their wares—their property and their administration of it?

By the bye, the Queen seems to have been much pleased with Chamberlain, who dined at Windsor the other night.

Friday, 16 July. The Irish Disturbance Bill—(I am almost inclined to apply to it the description given to the 'Burials Bill' by that old bigot—Dean Burgon—'that cursed Bill')—dragged his weary course through the whole of last night's sitting and this morning's sitting. A little progress, but very gradual, a great deal of obstruction and very bitter. Mr. G. made a brilliant speech last night, which had a sensible effect on the House (I am told), in reply to Gibson, the late Attorney General for Ireland, who is a rare fighter and appears to be the backbone of the front Opposition Bench. The amendment which was the principal battlefield last night was the question of the limitation of the provisions of the bill to holdings under a certain amount. £15 was proposed and negatived. £30 was what the Government adopted but subsequently determined to reconsider, on a £50 limit being pressed on them. Granted that the bill is right in principle, what can be the good of forcing down people's throats a measure which is liked cordially by no one, which is opposed tooth and nail by the Opposition, which frightens the moderate section of the party, and which is 'next door to certain' to being thrown out in the House of Lords?[3] The only defence is that the consequences of not going on with the bill may be worse than anything that can result from its passing; and so the last state of the measure may be worse than the first.

Lord Fitzwilliam has made one more final appeal to Mr. G. about proceeding with the bill. He holds strongly that the bill will be destructive of

---

[1] This traditional testing of the quality of the coins issuing from the Mint was at this time held under the provisions of the Coinage Act of 1870 (33 & 34 Vict. c. x) which stated that 'a trial of the pyx shall be held at least once in every year in which coins have been issued from the Mint' and that there be 'a jury of not less than six out of competent freemen of the mystery of goldsmiths of the city of London or other competent persons'. The trial had been for many years the occasion of a banquet at Goldsmiths' Hall.

[2] See 8 May 1880.

[3] As it was on 3 Aug. 1880. See 4 Aug. 1880.

the moral and social welfare of Ireland; that it is the cunning and want of self-reliance of the Irishman which is the country's besetting sin; that the bill will place a premium on idleness and poverty, whether real or assumed; that it is impossible to ascertain men's real circumstances; that the bill will retain in the country those who ought to be shipped off to America; that many of the landlords literally have not the money to pay the compensation, if cast in damages; and that it will be impossible to get Paddy to resume the habit of paying rent at the end of the time.

The people who are, I believe, most responsible for this bill must be Bright and Forster. Forster may be an able and an honest man, but my faith (never very great) in him has been severely shaken when he absolutely proposed 'en grand serieux' that the damages of the ejectment should be charged to the Consolidated Fund!

The Queen has been asked to send an autograph line to the Sultan to impress upon him the risk he will run if he fails to abide by the decision of the Berlin Congress.[1]

Wednesday, 21 July. Rosebery has declined the offer of Lansdowne's place. His doctors say he must have further rest and not, for the present, take to an official life. But for this he evidently would now be pleased to take office.[2]

There have been further resignations—Listowel and Zetland.[3] What with these withdrawals and many others who will vote against the Government, which in any case is in a minority in the Upper House, the prospects of the Irish bill are absolutely *nil*, and I see no other possibility than its being rejected by an overwhelming majority. The responsibility will then, I presume be thrown on the House of Lords, which will in any case be unfortunate. I think, were I in the House, the line I should take would be this—that while disapproving the measure in principle, I should support the Government in taking extraordinary steps to meet extraordinary circumstances on the ground that they were better able to judge of the necessity of such steps, and in the belief that they would not take them were it not for the necessity.

The Queen has been rendered very frantic about Briggs' motion being carried the other night against the proposal to erect a monument to the Prince Imperial in Westminster Abbey.[4] The Government dealt with the

[1] The Queen was reluctant to communicate with Abdul Hamid, the Sultan, but she finally agreed to send a telegram; *Letters*, 2nd ser. iii. 120. For letters concerning this communication see Ramm, i. 145–7; *Letters*, 2nd ser. iii. 118–20. See 30 July 1880.

[2] See 10 July, 25 Apr., and 3 May 1880. See also Rosebery's letter to G. of 14 July 1880, Lord Crewe, *Lord Rosebery* (N.Y., 1931), pp. 109–10.

[3] The final resignations of these two Lords-in-waiting were put off until August. They were ultimately replaced by Lords Dalhousie and Sandhurst. See Ramm, i. 149–51, 156. See 25 July, 23, 29, and 31 Aug. 1880.

[4] See the Queen's letters on the subject. Guedalla, ii. 105–7. W. E. Briggs, M.P. for Blackburn, brought forward his motion against erecting the memorial to Prince Louis Napoleon on 16 July 1880. It was carried 162 to 147, G. and the other ministers having

matter as 'tenderly' as possible, voting first for going into supply and then, when the amendment became a substantive motion, abstaining from voting.

Good progress has been made with the Budget Bill, but the brewers are frantic.[1]

Matters are going fairly well abroad, but the French seem to be 'hanging fire' rather. It will be too bad if, when the European powers are 'discoursing' so excellently well in time together at the European Concert, France of all nations should disturb the harmony.

Sunday, 25 July. The Budget Bill has 'run the gauntlet' of Committee this week with success, handled of course by its author in the most masterly of manners. The only serious opposition it encountered was from the brewers. They take exception to it chiefly on two grounds: (1) They maintain that the specific gravity of beer is taken too low; (2) They assert that they were led by Mr. G. to suppose that the equivalent, and the equivalent only, of the Malt, duty would be imposed, whereas some £7 or £800,000 more than the equivalent, as they say, will be the result of the proposed tax on beer. The financial arrangements at any rate have been *one* redeeming feature of the session and will redound to the honour of the great financier.

There was an interesting discussion on Friday about Armenia, raised by Bryce.[2] The Government seem quite prepared to take the question up and force some real reforms on the Porte. Some little time, however, must be given for the collection of facts, as it must be according to the result of the census of the Province that any new organisation is framed. In fact, the question at issue is are the Armenians—the Christians—or the Mahometans in a majority in the Province? Wilfrid Blunt goes in 'hot and strong' for making the Province a sort of independence, that is, for giving it an independent government, so as to act as a sort of buffer between Russia and the Asiatic provinces of the Porte, and so as to take away from Russia excuse for advancing southwards in Asia, which so long as the present system of mis-government prevails she has good reason for doing.

The resignation of the Lords-in-waiting seems to be suspended.[3] The Queen is anxious to retain them, and if the bill is to meet with no support practically from the House of Lords, they may just as well remain on and be excused voting. The Under-Secretaryship at the India Office has not been filled, but Enfield seems first favourite.[4]

withdrawn to a room behind the Chair just before the Division—an act which caused Sir Henry Drummond Wolff and Lord Randolph Churchill to question the conduct of the ministers. *Parl. Deb.* ccliv. 698–735.

[1] See 25 July 1880.

[2] See *Parl. Deb.*, 23 July 1880, ccliv. 1260–1301.

[3] i.e. Lords Listowel and Zetland, who were opposed to the Compensation for Disturbance (Ireland) Bill. See 21 July 1880.

[4] The office was vacant through Lord Lansdowne's resignation and Lord Enfield succeeded to the office. See 25 Aug. 1880.

Wilfrid Blunt (whom I look upon as a considerable authority on Asiatic matters) goes in for our indirectly encouraging the establishment of a new Caliphate, that is, for separating the spiritual from the temporal power of the Sultan. His idea is that it is the fact of the Sultan's being Caliph which really attaches importance to him so far as our interests are concerned, and that if some Arabian were to displace him in the Caliphate we might turn our eyes from the northeastern corner of the Mediterranean with perfect composure.[1]

News from India seems satisfactory. Abdur-Rahman has been recognised Amir at Kabul.

Tuesday, 27 July. On last night the Irish Disturbance Bill was read a third time by a majority of 67,—a falling off from the 2nd Reading, chiefly due to a larger number of Tories coming up to the scratch. Sixteen Liberals—'eldest sons' almost entirely—voted against the bill, and there must have been some 60 or 70 abstentions. Went down and heard the end of the debate. Clarke (whose election for Southwark just before the general election created such dismay and exultation respectively in the Liberal and Conservative camps, and who during his short innings made a considerable sensation with his maiden speech on the Licensing Laws) was the first man I heard. I was disappointed at his effort. There was great fluency no doubt, but a want of animation and force, and though he put some of his points well, most of them were *rechauffées* of the arguments in the London papers during the last week or two. Hicks Beach spoke tamely and lamely and was listened to with evident and almost indecent impatience. The Great Man then got up. He was grandly forcible, most temperate, and well received. I doubt if he has ever made a greater succession of fine speeches in any session previously; and certainly his oratorical powers are very far from waning with his increasing years. Every time one hears him the more marvellous does he seem. Thus ended, thank goodness, the stormy career of this wretched little bill. I feel inclined to wish that its sins may be visited on its 'For(s)ter mother's' head. However necessary it may have been considered for the peaceable government of Ireland, it is impossible to conceive that some other means less calculated to excite apprehensions and create universal dislike could not have been devised. Its fate in the House of Lords must be assured.

I see Layard is averse to Armenian autonomy. He holds that the Armenians when compared with Mussulmen are in a minority, however exaggerated that minority may be by the Porte; and that Armenia would never submit to a purely Christian government. Armenia he looks upon as but a geographical expression, the Armenians being widely scattered and therefore there being extreme difficulty in forming a province composed of Armenians.

Goschen has telegraphed that he thinks the Powers should be prepared to

[1] Ramm, i. 154 n. 7.

land troops in Montenegro, not to act on the offensive but merely to defend the Montenegrin frontier against attack, so as to free the whole Montenegrin force for operations necessary to carry out the Dulcigno plan. He also thinks that the best way of averting bloodshed over the Greek question will be to consent to the exchange of Janina for other territory; the Porte's honor would then be saved on the most vital point, and the Greeks at the same time would get a substantial set-off. The Porte seems to be floundering and would gladly catch at this straw. But will the other Powers assent to any departure from the Berlin award? And as regards the Montenegrin business, France certainly, and Austria probably, will never agree to the disembarkation of troops. We may, then, have very critical times in prospect.

There at last seems to be a good prospect of the recall of Sir B. Frere.

Wednesday, 28 July. The Queen is doubtful whether the Lord Lieutenancy of Aberdeenshire should be conferred on Huntly. He has got into such frightful pecuniary scrapes; would not Aberdeen be a more respectable recipient of the honor? No doubt; but he has not near such claims on the party or such position in the county or Scotland as Huntly has; and if we can make out that he is turning over a new leaf, I daresay we shall get H.M. to consent.[1]

Horrible intelligence has reached us from India. The annihilation of an entire brigade in the direction of Kandahar.[2] No particulars known, but seemingly Ayub Khan, who has been stealing down from Herat southwards, surprised our forces; and it is supposed that our losses are something between 2000 and 3000 men, with Kandahar probably in danger. It is just like the foolhardiness of the British, not keeping a sufficiently good look out, which must have been the immediate cause of the disaster; for how, with ordinary watchfulness, can 12,000 men sweep down without warning? The 'original sin' however must lie with the authors and initiators of the Afghan War.[3] It makes one's blood boil to think of the iniquity of that undertaking. And all this has come just when at last something like an end to the wretched business seemed at hand.

This afternoon the report of the Budget Bill was taken, and a parting shot was fired at it by George Hamilton who moved the omission of the income tax clause. He was supported by Northcote! who had taken no exception to the popular part of the financial scheme—the repeal of the Malt tax—and

---

[1] Ultimately, though G. had decided to recommend Huntly (ibid., pp. 148–9), his name was not submitted and Lord Aberdeen was appointed instead. In Jan. 1881 Huntly was appointed to the captaincy of the corps of Gentlemen-at-arms, but he had to resign that post in June 1881 in order to live abroad, his financial position making residence in England impossible. Ibid., pp. 229, 239, 280. See 10 Jan. and 17 June 1881.

[2] This was the battle of Maiwand, 27 July 1880, where a brigade of 2,500, including one British infantry regiment, under the command of General Burrows was set upon and badly defeated by an Afghan force numbering 15 or 16,000. For an account of the events leading up to the engagement, see Lucien Wolf, *Life of . . . Ripon* (London, 1921), ii. 25–32.

[3] i.e. especially with Lords Beaconsfield and Lytton.

then goes and votes against the unpopular part without which the whole scheme must have fallen to the ground. If the Government have not made a particularly successful start, there is one satisfactory set-off against this, namely the hopeless '*conduct*' of the Opposition.

In a letter from Goschen sent over from Foreign Office today he evidently thinks the Turks will *not* yield and therefore that there is great risk in exacting a literal fulfilment of the Berlin decision. Is then Janina (say) worth a general conflagration in the Eastern peninsula?—a tremendous crisis which is quite on the 'cards'. On the one hand it would seem best to accept from the Porte an equivalent of territory for Greece elsewhere; but on the other hand any departure from the terms of the Berlin award would be stultifying the united mandate of Europe.

It appears from the latest telegrams that the Porte's reply has been sent in and that she has declined to accept the award as it stands. Goschen's apprehensions, therefore, have been fulfilled, and we shall have to face an armed resistance or agree to a compromise.[1] I should prefer the latter alternative to a horrible kick-up which is probably a certainty.

Friday, 30 July. Last night's sitting was occupied entirely with the adjourned debate on the 2nd Reading of the Hares and Rabbits Bill. I confess the principle of the bill was never quite to my liking. Apart from its interfering with the freedom of contract—though it is not so sacred and inviolate as it is alleged to be by many—I am apprehensive of its effects; it may create a bad feeling between landlord and tenant; it may depreciate and in some cases destroy the value of a certain property (the letting value of shooting); it may tend to discourage leases. However it is a difficult question, no doubt. The common sense remedy would probably be to provide that those who indulge in the luxury of keeping up a head of ground game must pay for it, but then it is most difficult to assess damages and award compensation. On the whole the principle of the Bill has been generally admitted in the House, and the opposition to it is more latent than avowed. The fact is few like it, but still fewer dare to oppose it. It ended this afternoon in the 2nd Reading of the Bill without a division; Harry Brand's resolution in favor of substituting the omission from the Game Laws of Hares and Rabbits being withdrawn.[2] Harcourt appears to have wound up with a more conciliatory speech than usual and amused the House generally.

---

[1] See Medlicott, pp. 104–5.

[2] Brand's amendment, introduced on 29 July 1880, gave support 'to the principal recommendations of the Select Committee on the Game Laws, 1872–3' but declared 'that it is not expedient to restrict or interfere with the freedom of contract' in the way that the Government's Bill would do. In his speech he stated his intention, if the Bill got into Committee, 'to move an amendment declaring that hares and rabbits should not be deemed game within the meaning of the Game Laws'. He withdrew his amendment on 30 July 1880. *Parl. Deb.* ccliv. 1681–2, 1836.

Not much further intelligence received from Afghanistan, but latest accounts shew that 'annihilation' was a considerable exaggeration. It was a defeat and a serious defeat, but no more.[1] Reinforcements are to go out at once.

The Queen strongly deprecates the recall of Sir B. Frere on the ground that Colonial Governors ought not to have confidence withdrawn from them because of a change of their political allies at home. H.M. will, however, have to give way to the strong feeling there is about the matter. In fact it was partly owing to the well-known wishes of the Sovereign that the Cabinet have shewn such long-suffering.[2]

The Sultan has replied to H.M. telegraphic message. After expressions of cordiality he intimates that he will do his best to comply with the provisions of the Berlin Treaty.[3]

Tuesday, 3 August. On Friday night Mr. G. complained of feeling very seedy; he was dining at Lord F. Cavendish's. Fortunately a 'count-out' enabled him to go to bed.[4] He slept well and got up Saturday morning rather late, transacted some business, but looked wretchedly ill. He complained of feeling very shivery. Dr. A. Clark was sent for and on coming ordered Mr. G. straight to bed just at the time fixed for the Cabinet. Clark seemed anxious. He told me it was 'serious',—the temperature being 103; but did not like to commit himself. I went out of Town—to Charters[5]—in the afternoon, as arranged, but very reluctantly. In the train on Monday morning the accounts in the paper—'Serious illness of Mr. G.'—alarmed me much. It appeared that he was suffering from a certain amount of congestion of the lung and fever consequent thereupon. Temperature continued very high, and though there were no alarming symptoms, yet his state gave good cause for anxiety. I went in to see him for a minute or two in the morning. He was very calm and quite himself. I got him to let me take a message from him to Lord Hartington to ask that Lord H. would act as temporary Leader in his (Mr. G.'s) place. Anxious inquirers flocked to the door all day, and telegrams streamed in from all parts of the country. Intensely nice feeling was shewn from the Queen downwards, including political opponents of all shades. He passed a tolerably good night, and this morning disburdened his mind of a letter (by dictation) to Lord G[ranville] anent the rejection of the Disturbance Bill in the House of Lords.[6]

---

[1] See 28 July 1880.   [2] Guedalla, ii. 108–9   [3] See 16 July 1880.

[4] On 30 July 1880 when the House of Commons resumed its sitting at 9 p.m. formal notice was taken that a quorum did not exist; the House was counted and, there being fewer than the necessary 40 members, the House adjourned at 9.05 p.m. *Parl. Deb.* ccliv. 1836–7.

[5] Charters, Sunningdale, Berkshire, was the house of EWH's uncle, Edward W. T. Hamilton.

[6] See Ramm, i. 155. The Lords debated the Compensation for Disturbance (Ireland) Bill at length on 2 and 3 Aug. 1880 and rejected it 282 to 51. *Parl. Deb.* cclv. 110–13. See 4 Aug. 1880.

It seemed to relieve his mind. The substance of it was that he viewed naturally with regret the use which the Lords had (or rather were sure to have) made of their undoubted power to reject the Bill. He went on to say, however, that the question would not be finally disposed of; much of course would depend on the harvest; the course of law must be firmly upheld; and should the exercise of proprietary rights in Ireland become dangerous and strengthen the hands of the agitators, resort would have to be had to the re-assembling of Parliament in the autumn. Meanwhile he invoked the aid of all 'good citizens' and would encourage the people of Ireland to rely on the wisdom of Parliament.

Mr. G. has passed a good day; the temperature is lower and the general symptoms continue favourably. Clark told me he hoped that the beginning of the end had come. The universal feeling of sympathy is not abated, and general expression has been given to it. Mr. G. told me tonight he felt much touched.

As to political matters—Frere has been recalled and I think rightly. Sir H. Robinson is his successor designate. The Queen is in favour of leaving Janina to the Porte because proposal adopted by Berlin Conference would be hard on the Porte, and because it may lead to compulsion of unwilling population.[1] The Cabinet seemed to think, when the question was debated, that, after the part taken by H.M. Government at Berlin, we could not take the initiative of departing from the terms of the new proposals made at Berlin. Another question seems to have been discussed as to whether a union of Kabul and Kandahar was not desirable.

Latest news from Afghanistan somewhat disquieting I fear.

Wednesday, 4 August. Mr. G. progressing most favourably. Congestion disappeared and fever subsided. Of course he is left weak, but this is only natural. It is hardly likely, however well he goes on, that he will be able to resume his place in the House this session; so they will have to get on as best they can without him. They have been making tolerable progress with the Employers Liability Bill, and it appears that at the Cabinet today it was determined to proceed with Hares and Rabbits and also Burials Bill.

The Lords last night threw out the Irish Disturbance Bill with even a larger majority than was expected—231! An appalling majority. Fifty-one only voting for it, which is less by 2 than the number of Liberals or ordinary supporters of Lord Granville who voted against the bill! This unfortunate bill therefore met with a crushing end. Lansdowne seems to have spoken very well; Lord Cairns also very powerfully, lengthily and argumentatively, against the bill; but Lord Beaconsfield somewhat tamely and hesitatingly. Lord Granville seems to have defended the measure with his accustomed moderation, good tact, and ability, and the Duke of Argyll to have made a slashing oration. The other most noteworthy speech apparently was that of Lord

[1] See Ramm, i. 154 n. 4.

Derby who, while disapproving the principle of the bill, preferred its passing in an amended form to its total rejection by the Upper House.[1]

So much exaggeration has been spent on the aim, scope, and effect of the bill that it is worthwhile jotting down what it really and honestly was intended to provide for, and provide for only.

The Land Act of 1870 recognised a certain ownership or co-partnership of the tenant in his holding, i.e. recognised the fact that the labour of his hands must go to give the land some of its value. The 'Ulster tenant right' had already recognised the tenant's right to compensation for improvements and to the sale of his good will or ownership in the event of his leaving or being ejected from his holding, and this tenant right was legalised by the Land Act of '70. When such tenant right did not exist, the Act recognised the right of a tenant to compensation for improvements, and also his right to claim compensation for the loss of his holding in cases of capricious, unjust, or unreasonable eviction, excepting only the case of non-payment for rent. The Bill of this session sought (so to speak) to except under the exceptional circumstances this exception; that is, if a man owing to the failure of his crop was unable to pay his rent, under the exceptional circumstances of famine time, he should not forfeit his claim to compensation, to which he would have been entitled but for the 'act of God'. The bill was thus intended merely as a measure of relief of distress, to apply only in the specially distressed districts and to apply only for a limited time. And the exceptional claim, too, which the tenant was to have was not to be absolute but merely one which could be raised before a County Court Judge. This is the substance of the measure which has raised such a storm in a 'teacup', and it seems to me that, if the case had been clearly made out that ejections for non-payment of rent during these famine times had assumed a formidable proportion, then the bill was perfectly defensible. My only doubt is whether this case really was made out beyond all question.

Tuesday, 10 August. (Windsor) The Great Man has progressed fast and steadily. He came down to Windsor yesterday—the Deanery—whither I have followed him today.[2] Clark came down by same train, and as Mr. G. had imprudently gone to church this afternoon as well as come down to luncheon and driven, Clark found him rather disappointingly weak. Had a charming walk with the Dean[3] in the private grounds of the Castle this afternoon. He received me most cordially—he had a great reverential affection for my father—and was charmingly agreeable in conversation and delightfully attentive in

[1] Granville expected only about 50 Liberal peers to support the Bill, but he did not expect so many Liberal peers to vote against it. See his letter to the Queen, 27 July 1880, *Letters*, 2nd ser. iii. 122–3. See also the Queen's and Beaconsfield's appraisal of the defeat, ibid., pp. 127–30.

[2] The Queen was in residence at Osborne at this time.

[3] Gerald Wellesley, Dean of Windsor from 1854 until his death in 1882.

shewing me all the charms of the Castle grounds, which I had not partaken in since Eton days when I used to be taken about by cousin Caroline Grey.[1] Mr. G. appeared in the drawing room after dinner, and for an hour and a half 'discoursed' in his usual charming and interesting manner. I wish I had been able to take down his talk by shorthand. He travelled over every conceivable subject, historical and political. The four English sovereigns, and the only four, he holds in contempt are Richard III, Henry VIII, Charles II, and George IV. He believes the strength and vitality of the monarchy is solely dependent on the individual on whom the crown rests. He sees no signs of its hold in this country being materially weakened. Certain it is that it gathered great strength during the first part of the Queen's reign. It may, however, have been somewhat affected by the establishment of republicanism in France. The statesmen who in modern times are usually accredited with the greatest political courage are probably Palmerston and the late Lord Derby. Mr. G. for his part would place first and foremost Peel, Russell, and Dizzie. He questioned the Dean as to the probable successor of Lord Beaconsfield in the leadership of the Conservative party. The Dean seems to think that Lord Salisbury is 'Hobson's choice'. Mr. G. thinks the Opposition would fare better in Cross's hands than in Sir S. Northcote's. Though Northcote is far the ablest of the two, he is much less straightforward, less courageous, and less strong. Mr. G. does not anticipate that the disestablishment question in England will ripen for many years to come. If it did come to the front in his time, which is extremely unlikely, he should make a strong fight for retaining in the present hands the edifices. The question is not even ripe in Scotland; but if it were so, one remarkable result would probably be that disestablishment would lead to the reunion of 6/7ths of the Presbyterian sects. Mr. G., though admitting that there are very numerous reforms which the good of this country demands, does not think that the coming political generation will have any such interesting subjects and such important subjects to deal with as have fallen to the lot of those who have taken a leading part in politics during the last 40 years. The two leading and cleverest men on the opposition side he regards to be George Hamilton and E. Stanhope. These are a few of the many subjects which the Great Man touched upon. The Dean in conversation this afternoon referred to Mr. G.'s accepting the two offices of First Lord and Chancellor of the Exchequer; he (the Dean) appears to have remonstrated with his friend at the time for taking upon himself such overwhelming duties; Mr. G. told him that he felt it was incumbent upon him to undertake the double duties; he had not sufficient confidence in the financial judgment of his colleagues; he might have acted otherwise had he had a man like

---

[1] Caroline Eliza, woman of the Bedchamber to Queen Victoria, wife of General Charles Grey (1804–70), private secretary to Prince Albert 1849–61 and to the Queen 1861–70. Caroline Grey was the daughter of Sir Thomas Farquhar, 2nd baronet; EWH's paternal grandmother was Charity Graeme, daughter of Sir Walter Farquhar, 1st baronet and father of Sir Thomas.

Northcote to whom to delegate the duties of finance.[1] It is probable that he considered Northcote to be possessed of great financial qualifications and to be more free from crotchets than men like Childers and Goschen (who was temporarily out of the running).[2]

Thursday, 12 August. Transacted a considerable amount of business with Mr. G. yesterday morning. Among other things he delivered himself at some length in the shape of a memorandum which I took down by dictation on the introduction into the Burials Bill of a reference to Convocation, his argument being that there are many precedents for Parliament delegating to such bodies as Convocations and Commissions the consideration of extraneous or special subjects, and to its adopting by name their recommendations.[3]

Returned to Town in the afternoon by Mr. G.'s desire.

Obstruction in the House, chiefly emanating from what is termed the 'Fourth party' (composed of Randolph Churchill, Elcho, Chaplin),[4] has been the order of the last few days.

Sunday, 15 August. (Wilton) Came down to Wilton yesterday afternoon to take part in the annual cricket week, always about the most enjoyable week in the year.

The Great Man came up from Windsor yesterday morning. He has made considerable progress and is regaining strength as evidenced by his handwriting being much as usual again. He did not attend the Cabinet, but saw Lord Granville, Childers, and Hartington. He wrote a letter to the Queen expressing his appreciation of the kind interest Her Majesty had evinced throughout his illness.[5] I am afraid, however, it would take a good many of such letters to establish him really in royal favor. Her Majesty never has been suited by him and never will be. He was 'forced upon her' (to use the Dean of Windsor's phrase) by Lord Granville and Lord Hartington, and being a good constitutional Queen she accepted him.

An excellent despatch has been written by Lord G[ranville] to Goschen. The gist of it was this: the Porte is deluding itself about the European Powers not being in earnest in enforcing their demands as to Montenegro and Greece, and more especially as to the latter. How can the Porte expect to appeal with

---

[1] Northcote had had Gladstonian training, having been G.'s private secretary 1842–6. G. admired Northcote's book *Twenty Years of Financial Policy* (1862). Morley, i. 516–18; iii. 356, 465–6.

[2] Goschen's opposition to the extension of the county franchise, which was part of the Liberal programme in 1880, made a Cabinet position for him impossible. Arthur D. Elliot, *The Life of . . . Goschen* (London, 1911), i. 196.

[3] Ramm, i. 158.

[4] This is an erroneous listing of the members of the 'Fourth Party'. It actually consisted of Lord Randolph Churchill, J. E. Gorst, Sir Henry Drummond Wolff, and Arthur Balfour. See Harold E. Gorst, *The Fourth Party* (London, 1906).

[5] Guedalla, ii. 109–10.

any success or forcible argument against the award at Berlin? The Porte's argument is that the Greek question was left open in the Berlin Treaty, but this was only so long as Greece and Turkey could not agree to a frontier among themselves; and as such agreement has not been brought about, the argument falls to the ground. It is the old story of procrastination. The Porte relies on the breaking up of the European concert; it overlooks the probability in the event of the existing state of affairs continuing, of an outbreak in the misgoverned provinces. Another point on which the Porte relies is the difficulty about finding (as she thinks) a successor to the Sultan, but she had better not flatter herself this is an insuperable difficulty. H.M. Government would be very glad to see the Sultan attain a better hold over his empire, but this feeling has its limits. The Porte would do well to bear in mind that resistance on her part to the Berlin award may very likely encourage the tendency of Bulgaria and Eastern Roumelia to unite. On the other hand, a compliance with it will enable the Porte to consolidate reforms and will ensure the Powers resisting the demands made upon her by smaller states.

The question has been raised and discussed in the Cabinet as to whether in consequence of the unusual drain upon the Imperial forces caused by the demands of India, it may not be necessary, as a temporary expedient, to call out some portion of the reserves or embody some portion of the militia.

Monday, 23 August. A whole week's idleness away from Downing St. at Wilton. During this time some fair progress has been made with public business. The Employers' Liability has been read a 3rd time and sent up to the Lords. The Ground Game Bill has been got through committee, and Lord Hartington has made, and seemingly made very well, his Indian Budget.

The Queen has selected out of four names submitted to her C. Lyttelton and Dalhousie to succeed Listowel and Zetland as Lords-in-waiting resigned.[1] The former declines.

At the Cabinet on Saturday, which Mr. G. came up from Holmbury to attend, [it was] determined to persevere with the important measures now before Parliament. There was an idea started of adjourning to November, but it has been dropped, and wisely I think.

The Cabinet approved the language of Lord Granville's telegrams for the purpose of putting forward the concert of the Powers on the subject of the Montenegrin frontier in regard to which the recent proposal of the Porte seems to throw a disagreeable light both on the methods and on the intentions of the Turkish Government.[2]

It was also agreed that Lord G[ranville] should hold a conversation with the Russian Ambassador[3] and point out to him that information had reached H.M. Government of the presence with Ayub Khan of officers who had been trained in the Russian army and should also notice the unfriendly spirit which

---

[1] See 21 and 25 July 1880.   [2] Medlicott, p. 146.   [3] Lobanov.

is to be traced in the correspondence of General Kauffmann; expressing at the same time confidence that the two Governments are agreed in believing that the choice of wise and temperate agents on both sides is of great importance with a view to a good understanding in Central Asia.[1]

Mr. G., according to present arrangements, is to go for a sea trip on one of Donald Currie's ships on Thursday. The 'Enchantress'—admiralty yacht—has been given up, and I think wisely. Ill-natured people would have been sure to say unkind things about his taking a trip at the public expense. I should have preferred his accepting Brassey's offer of the 'Sunbeam'; (it is paying too great a compliment to Donald Currie, who is a fawning and troublesome man, that Mr. G. should place himself under such an obligation; but the size of the ship in comparison with a yacht seems to weigh with Mr. G.).

A Garter is vacant by death of Lord Stratford de Redcliffe, and it would be a timely and well-deserved honour to bestow it on Lord Hartington.[2] Lord Palmerston is a precedent for a commoner receiving a KG.

The Gladstones are in trouble about the dangerous illness of their niece Mrs. Hardy.[3]

Apropos of the Greek frontier question, it appears from a recent despatch of E. Fitzmaurice that according to the trustworthy authority of an intelligent Albanian, Upper Albania consists for the most part of Roman Catholics, Middle Albania of Mahometans entirely, and Lower Albania of half Greeks and half Mahometans. According to the same authority, Janina is *not* Albanian really as is alleged by the Porte; and it appears that what the Albanian movement aims at is at leaving the Sultan merely suzerain and promoting a large Albania with an independent Prince brought in from the 'outside world.'

Wednesday, 25 August. The Queen fears that nothing satisfactory will be elicited from the Russian Ambassador[4] about the employment of officers trained in the Russian Army. It is extraordinary what amount of Russophobism pervades the royal mind. I am convinced that we shall do no good if we show signs of distrust towards Russia. After the way she has been treated the last few years, our only chance of securing her good behaviour and real friendship is to be open with her and not to impute to her all kinds of sinister motives. If, after being so dealt with, she plays us false, then by all means let us show her the cold shoulder.

Mr. Gladstone has submitted Lord Derby's name for the Garter vacant by the death of Lord Stratford de Redcliffe. The Queen will not at all like the

---

[1] Ramm, i. 163–4.

[2] See 25, 29 Aug. and 7 Sept. 1880.

[3] Lucy Marion, daughter of G.'s brother John, married Reginald Hardy (after 1888 Sir Reginald) in 1876. She died in 1921.

[4] Lobanov.

idea, and I hope myself he will have the same good taste to refuse it as he had to refuse office. I regret the offer being made.[1]

Rosebery having finally made up his mind that he is unable to take the Under-Secretaryship at the India Office, Lord Enfield has been chosen for the post—a somewhat mild and commonplace appointment.[2] Lord Hartington would have been glad to take Courtney with a view of securing his services in the Government. Lord H. seems to attach great value to the man—clever, no doubt, but tiresome and bad-mannered, and he had the offer of office when the Government was being formed.[3]

Adam is to succeed Duke of Buckingham as Governor of Madras Presidency which becomes vacant in the autumn. Who is to succeed Adam as First Commissioner of Works? F. Cavendish? He could be ill spared from the Treasury.[4]

Russia declares that, though regretting the policy which resulted in separation of Bulgaria from Eastern Roumelia, she will do nothing to upset the arrangements arrived at in Berlin 2 years ago.

Nubar Pasha thinks that the Turks will settle the Montenegrin business and then procrastinate about Greece. Meanwhile the union of Bulgaria and Eastern Roumelia would take place. He regards the Russian empire as too straggling and disorganised to prevent such organisation.

Palermo is suggested as the rendezvous for the joint fleets. The Austrian and other Governments would delegate the Commandership-in-Chief to the English admiral.[5]

I don't like the tone of Goschen's private letter, received a day or two ago, to Lord Granville. He seems to think he has not been very fairly treated and has not been consulted sufficiently. He evidently is far less sanguine about the Concert of Europe and Turkey's giving way on merely a naval demonstration. Mr. Goschen would almost like to be replaced at Constantinople.

Thursday, 26 August. The Great Man has gone off with Donald Currie on board one of his big steamships, 'Grantully Castle.' He is accompanied by Mrs. G., Helen, and three sons, one of the Ladies Campbell, Walter James, Sir James Lacaita, the Arthur Godleys, &c. They went off at two o'clock from Charing Cross, whither I accompanied them, to Gravesend where they embark. I wish I had been of the party. However, having been away last week, I felt bound to waive my claim in favour of Godley and Seymour. The first

---

[1] See 23, 29 Aug., and 7 Sept. 1880.

[2] See 10 and 21 July 1880.

[3] See 23 May and 28, 29, 30, 31 Dec. 1880.

[4] See 22 Sept., and 12, 26, 28, 30 Nov. 1880. G. J. Shaw Lefevre got the post.

[5] EWH refers here to the plans for a naval demonstration on the part of the Concert of Europe designed to coerce the Sultan into surrendering Dulcigno to Montenegro. Sir Beauchamp Seymour was the English admiral commanding the Mediterranean fleet. Ragusa was eventually decided upon as the rendezvous. See 28, 29 Aug., 11 Sept. 1880; and Medlicott, pp. 149–55.

point at which they are to touch is Dartmouth. Mr. G. is getting wonderfully well, and a week's sea air ought to put on the final polish to complete convalescence. I presume Donald Currie aspires at least to a baronetcy.[1]

Saturday, 28 August. The cruising party reached Dartmouth yesterday in the middle of the day. With the exception of being for a short while befogged and subjected to the annoyance of the fog horn, they seem to have had a most prosperous voyage thus far. They went on last night to Plymouth; this morning to Falmouth; and proceed thence to Kingstown, after which they will go to the west coast of Scotland.

Henry Primrose inclosed yesterday a memorandum from Lord Ripon, written to defend himself against charges of insufficient wariness about Ayub Khan and of false moves on Ayub's approach. Constant rumours had reached the Indian Government that Ayub was going to sally forth out of Herat, but they always came to nothing. It was on the 22nd July that authentic news of Ayub's forward movements was received, confirmed this time by our Minister at Teheran.[2] Thereupon Lord Ripon immediately consulted the military authorities. All recommended the despatch of troops from Kandahar to the Helmund to meet Ayub. Reinforcements were at once ordered up to Kandahar, more than Primrose (the soldier) in command of the Kandahar garrison asked for, and more than the Commander-in-Chief[3] thought necessary. On the Wali[4] (of Kandahar) regular infantry turning out untrustworthy, when they reached the Helmund, and Ayub was drawing near, General Burrows, who was in command of the advancing force, was told to act on his own judgment as to disarming them and as to making any change in his tactics. Lord Ripon, therefore, seems to have acted cautiously and in time, and to have acted on the best military advice he could get, and to have allowed no political reasons to interfere with military necessities. The situation in Afghanistan at the present moment is much as follows: Stewart is retiring from Kabul towards the frontier; Roberts is marching rapidly southwards to Kandahar and should be within sight of the city in a day or two; Primrose is invested at Kandahar, having made one rather expensive sortie; reinforcements are moving up from the Southeast; Ayub seems to be moving away from Kandahar, perhaps fearing to risk a battle against the combined forces and thinking that his retreating will give us more trouble, which it will do, than were he to remain and take his beating outside the city walls.

To turn to Europe, matters are not altogether very satisfactory. France is still chary and fearful of joining the demonstration off the Montenegrin coast, though they *will* join it if the Porte shews bad faith and refuses to deliver over Dulcigno. The French profess to be anxious to work in concert with our

---

[1] Currie was knighted in 1881, but he never received a baronetcy or peerage.
[2] Ronald F. Thomson.   [3] Sir Frederick Haines.
[4] Sher Ali Khan.

Government, but they are sadly afraid that England will go farther than they will under present circumstances venture to follow her. France seems to regard her position at home as peculiar, and therefore to be apprehensive of running counter to popular opinion. All the other powers are unanimous and will consent to be under command of the English senior officer (who is Seymour). France's temerity is certainly awkward. The only thing to do is to try and conceal as far as possible her divergent views.

There was a Cabinet today. Lord Beaconsfield appears to have made a communication with Lord Granville with a view of ascertaining how far the Opposition in the Upper House might amend the Ground Game Bill on condition they assented to the 2nd Reading. The amendments they want are (1) to limit the number of people whom the occupier may appoint to kill for him, and (2) to obtain a close season. The Cabinet decided that a close season was out of the question, considering how and by whom the idea in the House of Commons had been rejected;[1] but that the bill would not be sacrificed were some gun amendment only introduced. The Government will be unable to accept the Lords' amendments to the Employers' Liability Bill, and no wonder, as they have the effect of disembowelling the bill.

Sunday, 29 August. The Queen won't hear of the Garter being given to Lord Derby. I knew she wouldn't; and I am sorry his name was ever submitted. His connection with the Liberal party is too short. Mr. G. has withdrawn the proposition in deference to H.M. wishes and has made the offer of the Blue Ribbon to the Duke of Bedford. I doubt his accepting it as he refused it before when offered to him by Mr. G. before 1874.[2] Mr. G. has justified his original proposal (with a view to paving the way for submitting Lord Derby's name on a future occasion) on the ground that from the point of view taken by the Government Lord Derby's vote and speech on the Irish Disturbance Bill was not only an act of courage and decision on his part but also a considerable service to the public in connection with the anxious duty of administering the law and maintaining the peace.[3]

Loch, the Governor of the Isle of Man, is to be a KCB, and if it were not for the fact of his having asked for the favour himself through Sir W. Harcourt, it would not be a bad honour bestowed. There ought to be a rule that no one should ever be submitted for any honour or place which he

---

[1] On 19 Aug. 1880 in the House of Commons Mr. Sclater-Booth proposed a close season amendment but it was soundly defeated 148 to 58, a number of Conservatives voting with the Government against it, a point emphasized by Harcourt when the Lords' amendment for a close season came before the Commons. *Parl. Deb.* cclv. 1659–81, cclvi. 1199–1200. See 29 May 1880.

[2] Bedford accepted. See 7 Sept. 1880. See also 1 June, 25 Aug., 1 Sept., and 4 Nov. 1880.

[3] See Guedalla, ii. 111–12; and 4 Aug. 1880. The opinion of Derby's speech held by Beaconsfield, and passed on by him to the Queen, was quite different. *Letters*, 2nd ser. iii. 129.

himself has asked for. It would be astonishing what a decrease of honours this rule would ensure.

Charles Lyttelton has definitely declined to be a Lord-in-waiting. He declines on some private and I believe sufficient grounds.

Sandhurst I am glad to say is to get a Lordship. Considering his surroundings, his political virtue merits reward.[1]

The Burials Bill was got through Committee yesterday at the Saturday sitting. Harcourt seems to have put his foot into it. He got up on the spur of the moment and unknowingly opposed an amendment which O. Morgan on behalf of the Government had intimated his intention to accept.[2]

The programme for the naval demonstration in connection with Montenegro, to which all the powers with the exception of France have agreed, seems to be this: the rendezvous to be Ragusa; the English senior officer[3] to be Commander-in-Chief, who is to summon the Governor of Scutari[4] and the local authorities of Dulcigno to deliver up Dulcigno to Montenegro; if the agents of the Porte give their consent to this, the Prince of Montenegro[5] is to be told to take possession of the place; should the Turkish authorities decline to give it up and declare they have no instructions, or should they profess to agree in the transfer in principle but declare it to be unpractical in consequence of the opposition of the Albanians, then, after a respite of 3 days to be granted to Turkish authorities to obtain instructions from the Porte, the Prince of Montenegro is still to be informed that he is to take possession with an assurance of support from the joint fleet. In this case the Commander-in-Chief is to be authorised to order, on his own responsibility, such military measures to be taken by all or part of the fleet as may appear conducive to supporting the Prince from the side of the sea.

Colonel Wilson who is reporting on the state of the Bulgarian and Eastern Roumelian provinces finds in such districts as he has visited a better state of affairs than he expected. He says the population moves about freely, and the women even are to be found working alone. There *are* evils but both Moslem and Christians have their share. The Moslem has to supply recruits for the army; the Christian cannot get his evidence regarded in the law courts. The Christians no doubt have suffered much from the brutal manner in which the search for arms has been conducted.[6]

Reviewing generally the Balkan peninsula, one may say that Servia seems to

---

[1] See 21, 25 July, 23 and 31 Aug. 1880. Sandhurst, like Lyttelton, was one of the fifty-one peers who voted in the minority for the Compensation for Disturbance (Ireland) Bill.

[2] On 28 Aug. 1880 Mr. H. H. Fowler offered an amendment to the Burials Bill which Mr. Osborne Morgan, the Judge Advocate-General, who was shepherding the bill through Committee, did not oppose. Harcourt spoke against it and had to be reminded by Osborne Morgan of the Government's policy. Harcourt then withdrew his objections. *Parl. Deb.* cclvi. 576–89.

[3] Sir Beauchamp Seymour.   [4] Riza Pasha.   [5] Nicholas I.

[6] See *Parl. Papers*, 1880, lxxxii. 49–212.

have every intention of remaining quiet; and Russia is determined *at present* not to encourage the union of Bulgaria and Eastern Roumelia.

Continued good news of the cruising party. They were at Kingstown today and were to proceed thence this afternoon to Oban.

I omitted to note the extraordinary long sitting of the House over the Irish Constabulary vote on Thursday which lasted from 4 on Thursday till nearly one o'clock the next day. In spite of the malicious obstruction of the Irish quorum, the discussion seems to have been conducted in an orderly and good-humoured fashion.

I hear from all sides universal praise bestowed on Lord Hartington's leading powers; everyone admires his sound judgment, his good sense, his sterling ability and unruffled temper.[1]

Monday, 30 August. Lord Dufferin is convinced that Russia wants to keep things quiet in the Balkans for the present, but, though he appears to believe in her sincerity so far as the immediate future is concerned, he nevertheless thinks that she will never cease to prepare for the *ultimate* establishment of Bulgarian ascendancy in all provinces surrounding Constantinople. My own belief is that the way to treat Russia is to treat her firmly but *openly*; and then if she plays one false in the long run, England will not be able to reproach herself with a corresponding insincerity, but will have at her command not only material but likewise moral force.

Adams from Paris confirms again the apprehensions of France of being forced into something more than what she considers prudence dictates in her present position. He hears that the Porte is becoming convinced that the Ambassadors are relaxing their efforts and that the Concert of the Powers will be defeated. He admits, however, that the naval demonstration is the best move that can be made, and only wishes it were to be held at the Golden Horn so as to frighten the Sultan.

Read today some interesting Indian despatches proving clearly that the withdrawal from Kabul never was made dependent on our establishing a friendly Amir, or on the adjustment of friendly relations, however desirable, with the rulers of Kabul. The early and prompt retirement of our forces has been held to be the main object of all political and military measures. There was never to be a bargain struck or even discussed with Abdur Rahman and the Indian Government. All the undertaking we have ever given or even intended to give was that, assuming his dealings towards us to be in good faith and in a friendly spirit, we would, on his being recognised Amir, give him our countenance and political support but no cooperation by British troops; that we would meet his *immediate* wants with artillery and money; that with certain points (notably Kandahar) held in reserve, he should have the same

[1] Lord Hartington acted as Leader of the House of Commons during G.'s illness.

authority as his predecessors; and that we would not force upon him an European resident.

Tuesday, 31 August. Sir John Adye, the Surveyor General of Ordnance, is regarded, I believe, as a tip-top soldier. His opinion therefore on Afghan policy should carry great weight. He evidently thinks the whole 'forward' policy inaugurated by Lord Lytton, commencing with the occupation of Quetta in 1876 and ending in our getting as far as Kandahar in 1878, a great mistake. From beginning to end it has involved our advancing 400 miles, which means our having to keep up that lengthened line of communication through defiles and across deserts, without supplies and with a population not to be relied on. Kandahar no doubt is itself an important position both commercially and strategically, but it involves our retaining there a force of 5000 troops and a probable (because practically unavoidable) extension of our influence and proportionately of our responsibilities. Its retention too is fatal to our establishing a strong, friendly, united, and independent Afghanistan, which is one of our avowed objects. Further, the retention of the place which is on the main road to Herat tends to isolate the latter place and to leave it open to anarchy. The three proverbial courses open to us in our present position are (1) to hand Kandahar over to the ruler of Kabul; (2) to maintain a native ruler at Kandahar independent of Kabul; and (3) to establish ourselves at Kandahar permanently.

All things considered, Sir J. Adye regards the first alternative as the only feasible one in the interests of peace.[1] He is also strongly in favor of our wholly abandoning the so-called 'scientific frontier' in the Northwest in all events.

Cardwell declines taking the vacant GCB. He seems to be rather less sore than he was and professes to be gratified at the offer made to him. He believes himself to be getting strong and well again, and therefore his recovery may bring with it a return of soreness at having been left out.

Dalhousie (Ramsay) will, if wanted, accept a Lordship-in-waiting, but he is not much bitten with the idea.[2]

Lord Granville has 'rated' the Russian Ambassador[3] about there being in Ayub's army officers trained in the Russian army and has commented on the Kaufmann correspondence found at Kabul. He [the Russian Ambassador] has assured Lord G[ranville] that his Government desires to cultivate the most friendly relations with us in Central Asia, and in proof of this has instanced the refusal of Russia (contrary to precedent) to allow an embassy of congratulation being sent to Abdur Rahman. Lord G[ranville] formulated

---

[1] This was the alternative adopted by the Government. See 6 Jan. 1881.

[2] See 21, 25 July, and 23 Aug. 1880. The Earl of Dalhousie sat in the House of Lords as Baron Ramsay, Dalhousie being a Scottish title.

[3] Lobanov.

no demand on the Russian Ambassador, but Prince Lobanoff has evidently taken a hint that it is Kaufmann whom we should like to see recalled, and he will do what he can to further this object.

Wednesday, 1 September. Her Majesty has recurred to the subject of Lord Derby and the Garter. She maintains that the Garter is the highest of all the European Orders, and as such should not be looked upon as a mere political reward at the disposal of the Prime Minister of the day, but should only be bestowed on account of general 'patriotic conduct', coupled or not (as the case may be) with high rank and character. She looks upon Lord Derby's conduct in office as being very far from what could be approved by 'any Government'. She refers to his betrayal of secrets to his wife who repeated them to the Russian Ambassador, and his making public in the House of Lords despatches of the most confidential character without the permission of his Sovereign. She hopes therefore it will be some time before Lord Derby's name is again submitted for such an honour.[1] This little outburst on behalf of the Queen against a man of Lord Derby's ability, sound sense, and high position betokens much. It shews how thoroughly she has become imbued by the jimcrack imperialist idea and how thoroughly hoodwinked she has been by Dizzie. Her prejudices evidently owe their origin to Lord D[erby]'s having parted company with the late Government in 1878. I am beginning to think one misses the sound judgment and calm impartiality which one used to regard as characteristic of her letters.

The House of Lords have passed the Ground Game Bill, but not without some material amendments. I regard with no little apprehension a possible conflict between the two Houses and a consequent outcry in the country against the Peers as a legislative body if they continue to place themselves as rejectors and mutilators of the Commons' bills. They would do well to remember that they are representative of only one class, whereas the other House represents all classes; and will do wisely to put themselves more in harmony with the expressed wishes and wants of the nation.

Sunday, 5 September. France continues to 'hang fire'. The French Foreign Minister[2] told Adams at Paris the other day that he was afraid France would be frightfully abused when it was known that even her ships had proceeded to take part in the demonstration *for Montenegro*. It was therefore impossible she should go the whole length which the other Powers were prepared to do, and he expressed himself as 'chagrined' at the terms of disappointment of which Lord G[ranville] made use. France seems to leave out of consideration the effect which any departure from the Concert of Europe on the part of France, occupying as she does now again a foremost position, may have on the French mind.

[1] Guedalla, ii. 112.   [2] Charles de Freycinet, Premier and Foreign Minister.

Gambetta seems to have made an injudicious speech the other day—some reference to Alsace and Lorraine. It was probably a slip of the tongue after dinner, but it has created apprehension at Berlin, and the Emperor of Germany seems disquieted and to attach some significance to it more especially as it occurred simultaneously with the change come over France about Eastern affairs.[1] The Emperor distrusts Gambetta.

There is a scheme, which appears to be seriously projected by certain Greek merchants, to hand over to the Porte an indemnity of £2,000,000 in compensation for loss of territory and by way of conducing to a peaceful settlement of the Greek frontier question. The project is regarded as a matter of £ s d; that is, a sum down would be a better bargain for Greece than the expense of a standing army for an indefinite time and a possible war with Turkey. The money would only be handed over to the Porte on proper guarantees being received of its beneficial application. Lord Granville does not look unfavourably on the idea.[2] As a matter of mutual accommodation it seems a good one.

Good news from Afghanistan; Roberts' march from Kabul to Kandahar completed without a mishap, and on his arrival an attack was made on Ayub which appears to have ended in the complete rout of his army. This ought to terminate our troubles in Afghanistan, if only the Government has courage enough to retire in due course wholly out of the country including Kandahar. There will, I foresee, be considerable difficulty in total withdrawal from the 'forward' policy, but in the long run I am convinced it is the wise one. Colonel East, believed to be a great authority on this question, counsels it strongly. He takes his stand on the collapse of the native armies which the Afghan campaign has produced and on the breakdown of the transport. On the other hand, I see the Duke of Cambridge is not at all convinced as to the adviseability of giving up Kandahar. He maintains that on its retention depends not only our general position and influence in the East, more particularly in Central Asia, but even our hold on India. The place, he thinks, might be made a real emporium of trade, and he attaches great importance to it as a military position. Retain Kandahar and we might then look on the occupation of Merv, on which the Russians are bent, with equanimity.

Mr. G. returned yesterday. I though he looked somewhat pale, but he regards himself as completely recovered. He attended the Cabinet and afterwards the House (for the first time); he even spoke.

---

[1] On 9 Aug. 1880 Gambetta, who, together with President Grévy and other officials, was at Cherbourg for a naval review, spoke extemporaneously to a group of commercial travellers who had invited him to a 'Punch' and referred to France's supposed worship of her army. That worship, he said, arose not from a warlike spirit but from necessity, and in veiled terms he indicated that France may hope to see her just place in the world restored. This brief and rather harmless speech was taken up by the German press, especially by the *Norddeutsche Allgemeine Zeitung*, and caused some furore in Germany.

[2] Ramm, i. 167.

Forster put his foot into it terribly on Friday night by speaking in the most injudicious tone against the House of Lords.[1] I hope, and I have every reason to believe, that he was thoroughly well hauled over the coals by Lord G[ranville] and Mr. G. He is the man who will upset the coach sooner or later, depend upon it. He is vanity itself; honest no doubt and exceedingly able, but without a particle of tact or taste; a very 'bear' in manners and a 'bull' in measures. I sometimes wish we were rid of him; and this is the man who 6 years ago was pitted against Hartington for the leadership!

The Queen's Speech was agreed upon finally yesterday. It is rather duller than usual.

Tuesday, 7 September. The Duke of Bedford has accepted gratefully the Garter, in spite of his having declined it on a former occasion.[2] He is willing to assist his brother, Lord Odo Russell, on his (the brother's) being given the peerage which Mr. G. is willing to recommend him for as soon as the Greek matter is settled.[3]

There was a farewell Cabinet yesterday. The ministers seem to have been chiefly occupied with the situation in the East and in India. Lord Hartington was to submit a telegram to the Queen about our future Afghan policy which I hope and believe includes the approximate, if not the immediate, evacuation of Kandahar.[4] The weight of military opinion is against its permanent retention, and now that Ayub has been so completely smashed up, there is a golden opportunity not only for our retiring without loss of prestige but also for our setting up Abdur Rahman as ruler over an united Afghanistan.

Lady Burdett-Coutts is really going to marry that fellow Ashmead-Bartlett. I call it a 'disgusting' proceeding on her part, and Mr. Gladstone told me yesterday he entirely agreed; he would only add another epithet to the step she is taking, which is loathsome. He was much exercised in his mind at getting a letter from her yesterday asking for an interview, evidently with a view to 'explain'. Mr. G. has fought shy of seeing her and has told her so, whereupon she says she will be satisfied if she sees Mrs. G., which she is to do.[5]

---

[1] *Parl. Deb.* cclvi. 1210–14. [2] See 29 Aug. 1880.
[3] i.e. Bedford was willing to settle a sum of money on Lord Odo. See 25 Sept. 1880. Lord Odo was created Baron Ampthill in Mar. 1881. See 24, 26, and 29 Nov. 1880. Lord Odo had been offered a peerage in 1878 by Beaconsfield. At first he accepted, but his brother, the Duke of Bedford, thought it improper to accept such an honour from a Conservative Prime Minister, and refused to endow Lord Odo, who consequently refused the peerage. W. F. Monypenny and George E. Buckle, *The Life of . . . Disraeli . . .* (N.Y., 1911–20), vi. 346, 385.
[4] *Letters,* 2nd ser. iii. 137.
[5] Baroness Burdett-Coutts was an enormously wealthy woman active in philanthropic causes; she had been raised to the peerage in her own right in 1871. She now made known her intention to marry William Lehman Ashmead-Bartlett who was almost 40 years her junior. They were married 12 Feb. 1881 and he assumed the name Burdett-Coutts. See 10 Sept. 1880.

Breakfasted this morning with Mr. G. in company with Algy West, who wanted to see which way the financial wind was blowing so as to be prepared for next year's budget campaign. Mr. G. talked much of the Succession and Probate duties, but nothing definite was elicited from him. He evidently thinks those duties are mixed up so with land reform and land burdens generally that one subject cannot be touched without the other; so whether he deals with these duties will depend much on next year's programme. Apropos of Mr. Lowe's attempt to deal with the subject some 8 years ago, Mr. G. remarked how curious it was that a man of such gifted talents and prodigious power of assault should be so destitute of means of defence when attacked himself as Mr. Lowe (or rather Lord Sherbrooke) is, which is quite true.

Thank goodness, the session is at an end, and if it had not been for that unfortunate Irish Disturbance Bill, I think we should have done well. Almost every measure mentioned in the Queen's Speech and more besides have been carried.

Mr. G. is pretty well his old self again, and I have all my work cut out for me.

Wednesday, 8 September. Mr. G. today wrote a friendly letter to Sir A. Gordon, recently appointed Governor of New Zealand, of whom the Great Man has a very high opinion, hardly justified, I think, by ordinary contact with him or by general hearsay. It was a very interesting letter as in it he expressed himself freely on the topics of the day. Reviewing the course of the Government since their accession to power, he said he considered the results of the Parliamentary session 'as they have been hardly earned, so have they been wonderfully satisfactory'. He referred to our activity in the East, and to the Turk being found to be worse than ever, especially the Turk as embodied in the Sultan, who (to use Mr. G.'s own words) 'is perhaps the greatest and certainly the most indefatigable liar upon earth'. He looked hopefully to a settlement of the Montenegrin business, after which we shall have to go forward with the Greek frontier and the reforms which, as he fears, are hopeless. He went on to say that 'one thing we can and will do, that is to put an end to imposture in our dealings with Turkey and to let the facts stand out in the light of day'. He told Sir Arthur that he regarded the progress we had made in Afghanistan as satisfactory, and that he hoped for further and greater progress to come. He evidently thinks Lord Ripon is doing extremely well.[1]

The Government seem firm about Kandahar, but the Queen is very loathe to consent to its abandonment.[2]

[1] A small part of the letter is printed in Paul Knaplund, ed., 'Gladstone–Gordon Correspondence, . . .', *Transactions of the American Philosophical Society*, New Series, li (1961), pp. 82–3.
[2] See the telegram of the Queen to Hartington, 7 Sept. 1880 and Ponsonby's letter to Hartington, 8 Sept. 1880, *Letters*, 2nd ser. iii. 137–9.

Friday, 10 September. Mr. G. dined on Wednesday night at the Russian Ambassador's (Lobanoff) to meet the Grand Duke Constantine who appears to have been most agreeable and to [have] expressed a strong desire for friendly and frank relations with England.

Lady B. Coutts has never turned up yet, in spite of Mrs. G. giving her an appointment. There still seems some chance of her extricating herself from the meshes of Ashmead Bartlett; though if [it] is to be done I presume it can only be done for some enormous pecuniary consideration. It is stated on good authority that the man made up to and proposed to a young lady who was a sort of ward of Lady B[urdett] C[outts] and that he suddenly broke the engagement off in order to catch the larger and more elderly 'gold and silver fish'.[1]

Lord Wolverton was talking over the session yesterday with Mr. G. He referred to the amount of caste which Forster has lost (and certainly lost) since the commencement of affairs. Mr. G. was willing to admit that F[orster] had made great mistakes, but he thought immense allowance ought to be made for the very difficult circumstances in which he has been placed; and one gathered from what Mr. G. said that he attaches great value to F. mainly on the ground that F. combines great manliness with a childlike simplicity. My own belief is that F.'s besetting sin is vanity, and accordingly in order to attempt to gratify it, he tries to please everybody all round, and instead of pleasing them succeeds not only in not pleasing them but in rubbing them up the wrong way.

Sir B. Frere's despatch on his recall has been received. He pleads that he was not aware of any divergence (such as is attributed to him) in principle between his views and those of the present Government. He still believes that the view he has taken of affairs in South Africa has already been proved to be the correct one. According to him, his ministers did what they could to secure the South African union, and they are persevering in an attempt which they could hardly have made had they known that they would have had the authority of Home Quarters against them. He maintains that the assurance (which they had) that they did not command the confidence of the Home Government materially influenced the Colonial Parliament in considering the Union question. He nevertheless seems confident that there is, under fair conditions, a possibility still of the Union being brought about. He only hopes his recall will not affect the maintenance of peace in Basutoland. He evidently thinks himself indispensable to the welfare of South Africa.

Saturday, 11 September. Mr. G. left town yesterday for Hawarden, calling on his way at Mentmore. Before he left he indited a letter to Lord Ripon to express not only his own entire satisfaction but also the entire satisfaction of the Cabinet at large at the manner in which he considered the Viceroy had borne himself since his arrival in India amidst the extraordinary difficulties of his

---

[1] See 7 Sept. 1880.

position. As to Kandahar, he told Lord Ripon that the Cabinet cordially assented to his evident wish for its evacuation; that they wanted to convey by telegram at once their agreement with his opinion; but that a reference to Her Majesty seemed necessary, the result of which had been the offer of resistance under the name of a request for information and delay. Mr. G. agreed that this was not the first case of obstruction from that quarter, nor did he regard it as likely to be the last. Since his last Government he observed a serious and unhappy change; nor could he fail to conjecture to whose influence such change was due. What specially struck Mr. G. was the decline of practical understanding with which the change was attended. The high mind and love of truth, however, he felt sure remain unimpaired; and it was these on which the present ministry must rely. The change to which Mr. G. referred is to my mind most evident. I remember, in reading over H.M. letters written in 1868–74, being so much impressed with the sound judgment, the impartial tone, and the practical suggestions which pervaded the writing. Now it is all grumbling and finding fault; and even approval is forced. I greatly deplore the change, mostly for the sake of the monarchy and next for the sake of the gracious lady herself. Time and usage may bring her more in harmony with the present Ministry; but if it does not, and consequences of a serious nature result therefrom, there is one man[1] to whose door will rightly be laid the charge among other things of having been the first to cause a blow to be struck at the monarchy.

Consent to Lord Ripon's ideas has been now fortunately wrung out of H.M.

It was proposed the other day, on the recommendation of the Commander-in-Chief,[2] that a new division of the Order of the Bath should be created for the Volunteers, but the Queen doubts the expediency of the proposal. She is sure such a division in the Order would be considered an inferior class, and moreover it would be bestowed, or rather might be bestowed, on officers, formerly regulars, who from never having seen active service would not under present arrangements be entitled to receive Military Orders. In lieu of this proposal H.M. suggests the addition to her aides-de-camp of 4 Volunteers.

Lord Thurlow (of whom I know nothing) has been offered and has accepted the remaining Lordship-in-waiting.[3]

The ships of all the Powers have arrived off Ragusa to 'demonstrate'.

I have, I think, never noted the appointment of Adam to the Governorship of Madras.[4] His place will have to be filled up at the Office of Works. I should like to see Arthur Peel placed there. Baxter has crossed Mr. G.'s mind for the

---

[1] i.e. Lord Beaconsfield.
[2] George, Duke of Cambridge, who was Grand Master of the Order of the Bath.
[3] Created by Enfield's appointment as Under-Secretary for India. See 25 Aug. 1880.
[4] EWH had mentioned it; see 25 Aug. 1880.

post, but I trust the idea will not seriously be entertained. I reminded Mr. G. of the villainously bad impression Baxter left behind him at the Treasury before.[1]

Monday, 13 September. It seems that the French Minister for Foreign Affairs[2] is anxious as to the present state of Europe. He *professes to be* more than ever in favour of the maintenance of cordial relations between France and this country. He thinks that Mr. G., in the speech he made the other day about foreign affairs, takes too optimistic a view of the situation and is too enthusiastic about Montenegro.[3] He appears to be apprehensive of Bismarck's taking up too prominent an Oriental position. He sees traces of it in Germany's allowing her officers to take employment in the Turkish service. He maintains that Russia always had, and has, an *arrière pensée*. I don't believe in Russia's openly doing anything to upset the Berlin Treaty arrangements; but that the real danger is, apart from Russia, that, if the Greek question is opened and leads to giving Greece a sensible lift in the world, then the Slavs will be making some sort of countre-movement as a set-off against their rivals for Constantinople—the Greeks.

The Kandahar question is the most important one just now. Even the *Times*, I am glad to say, goes in for an evacuation of the town.

Tuesday, 14 September. There are fresh ministerial changes at Constantinople. Cadri and Abedine have been dismissed.[4] Goschen's version of the crisis (which is probably the correct one) is that Musurus had drawn up a violent protest to the Powers against the naval demonstration, which they fought hard against and attempted to tone down, but in vain. Consequently the Sultan's particular protege—Said—returns to power, which Goschen regards as a strong slap in the face against England. There is this consolation, however, he says, which is that we shall now know that we are dealing with the ruling Sultanic (one might as well say Satanic) spirit; for it appears that Said is the man who has all along been pulling the Palace strings and been overruling the decision of the ministers. Goschen says we must now take a very decided line.

The Archbishop of Canterbury[5] has written to Mr. G. to disburden his mind on a subject which he says has occupied it much of late. It is the increasing tendency there is of the distinction between the upper and lower classes

---

[1] William Edward Baxter was joint secretary to the Treasury 1871–3. G., over Lord Wolverton's objections, wished to offer him the Post Office in Oct. 1873.

[2] Charles de Freycinet.

[3] i.e. G.'s spur-of-the-moment speech in the House of Commons on 4 Sept. 1880 defending Montenegro and the Government's actions in enforcing the Berlin settlement in favour of Montenegro against the criticisms of Joseph Cowen, M.P. for Newcastle-on-Tyne. *Parl. Deb.* cclvi. 1318–27.

[4] The change of ministry occurred on 12 Sept. 1880. See Medlicott, p. 151, for an explanation of its causes.   [5] A. C. Tait.

becoming more and more marked. He observes the tendency specially in the two Presses—the one for the rich, the other for the poor; and rightly perceives that with this divergent expression of opinions there can be no congruity in the views of the various classes. Can no remedy be found by raising the standard of the Press which reaches the lower classes and bringing it more into harmony with that which affects the upper classes?

Our Minister at Copenhagen[1] has had an interview with the King of Greece.[2] The King appears to be very grateful towards England and is evidently very keen that the Berlin decision should be carried out in its entirety. He professes to be unable to give way about Janina, which he declares is as much Greek as Athens is, and he anticipates that, unless the question can be finally settled, war is certain to break out by next spring. It is curious that there should be so many conflicting opinions as to the real component parts of the territory which according to the Berlin decision is to be ceded to Greece. It was only today I was reading a long interesting letter of Sir George Bowen, Governor of Mauritius, who from his antecedents seems to be a considerable authority about that part of the world (I mean the Balkan peninsula), and he goes in strongly for extending the frontier of Greece by handing over to her Crete and other Aegean islands in decided preference to any part of Thessaly and Epirus, which he maintains is not really Greek—exactly therefore the reverse of the opinion of the King of Greece and others.

The Duke of Cambridge's presence at the German manoeuvres seems to have afforded great satisfaction at Berlin.

According to Lord Odo Russell, Russia is bent on regaining the good will of Germany, and so we need not anticipate surprises from that quarter.[3]

Bismarck is supposed to maintain that if Austria had, from the beginning of the Eastern complications, favoured the Bulgarian movement instead of opposing it, the Bulgarians would be much less Russian than they now are. He wishes Austria and Russia to be well occupied in Turkey but not to fight.

Lord Dufferin reports favourably of the situation of affairs in Russia.

The opinions as regards Kandahar of Generals Stewart and Roberts have been taken.[4] As might be imagined, neither of them favour its evacuation. Stewart is at any rate against any undue haste being displayed in the matter of the evacuation; and Roberts lays great stress on the strategical importance of Kandahar. It will require great strength and firmness on the part of the Government to give effect to what they really believe is on balance the best for the public good of India—namely our leaving Kandahar.

---

[1] Sir Charles Lennox Wyke, minister in Copenhagen 1867–81.   [2] George I.

[3] For Russell's letter of 11 Sept. 1880 see Knaplund, pp. 157–8. EWH draws on it for his remarks about the Duke of Cambridge's visit, the relations of Russia and Germany, and for Bismarck's views concerning Austria, Bulgaria, and Russia.

[4] In Ponsonby's letter to Hartington, 8 Sept. 1880, written on behalf of the Queen, the opinions of Napier, Stewart, and Roberts are specifically requested. *Letters*, 2nd ser. iii. 138–9.

Thursday, 16 September. That infernal old liar—the Sultan—tells Goschen that he has dismissed his ministers[1] because they were 'incapable' of bringing about a satisfactory solution of the Montenegrin question, and he has the impudence to say that he is *anxious* to find a means of peaceably surrendering Dulcigno, which he asserts can only be done on the Powers promising that the Porte should not be asked to make further concessions to Montenegro. Of course, it may seem to be hard to bring compulsion on the Porte to surrender portions of dominion—*nolens volens*—to Montenegro and Greece, but the real point to bear in mind is this: that, when *in extremis* and at the absolute mercy of Russia, the Porte consented to have terms made by the Great Powers assembled at Berlin two years ago; that under those terms much was saved to the Porte which would have been taken from it under the Treaty of San Stephano; that, in return for this, the Porte by accepting the Berlin decision distinctly stipulated that there should be extensions of territory made to Montenegro and Greece; and that now the Porte refuses to carry into effect so much of the Berlin decision which is naturally distasteful to her.

I yesterday read a letter from an Indian officer who has been engaged in the front. He is strongly against the retention of Kandahar. He says it can't be occupied without 10,000 additional men to our European army and as many additional natives. He regards the native army [as] in a deplorable condition which is a very serious affair.

I find that working this place with only one assistant—George Gower, an excellent fellow and a good workman—is as much as I can manage.

Friday, 17 September. As to the ministerial changes at Constantinople, Mr. G. only regards them as one in a long series of blinds and frauds used with ingenious variation of form by the Sultan to evade the fulfilment of his engagements. In short, Mr. G. thinks that too much importance must not be attached to these changes. He has urged on Lord Granville the necessity for prompt action in view of the advancing season, which will not admit of ironclads lying off the coast in the Adriatic much longer. It won't surprise him if it is necessary to employ the ship force on shore. Such a step would probably not command unanimous assent, but he does not suppose Lord G[ranville] will shrink from it.[2]

Mr. G. in a letter to Lord Reay this morning lays down the ideas of the Government on the present situation in the East. 'We are,' he says, 'for the Concert of Europe; we hope it will continue; we think it *will* prevail, for surely Europe will not run away from the Turk with its tail between its legs? It would be bold, however, to say the union will be maintained. It was in 1853 and 1854 but not in 1855. Should it be broken up now,' he adds, 'two duties

[1] See 14 Sept. 1880.
[2] See G.'s letter to Granville, 16 Sept. 1880, Ramm, i. 173.

will remain—one, to let it be known who has broken it; the other, to see whether enough remains to be sufficient for our aim in view.'[1]

In referring to Stewart's and Roberts' opinions on the Kandahar question, Mr. G. remarked today to Lord Hartington that sometimes a military opinion is (a very bad) political one 'with a military garnish'. In a case of this kind much must depend on the general basis of policy to be assumed, which is *not* a military question.[2]

Sunday, 19 September. The Sultan declares that he changed his ministers because he wanted the pending question about Montenegro to be promptly carried out. This is probably an audacious lie or blind.

I see that Austria (and I don't wonder at it) contrasts the course followed by the Powers towards Turkey and towards Bulgaria. In the one case, extreme steps, she maintains, are being taken to enforce the provisions of the Treaty of Berlin in its entirety; in the other, no protest has been lodged against the open disregard of it. Bulgaria has hardly performed one of its obligations; there is the tribute to pay, the share of Turkish debt and railway engagements to assume, the neutrality of the Danube to observe, the fortresses to demolish. All these have been disregarded; and when Bulgaria can find the means of preparing an army, it is idle to excuse her on the ground of her pauper state. Too much impartiality cannot, I feel sure, be shewn; and I am glad to see that Mr. G. has suggested that a remonstrance should be lodged at Sophia and Phillipopolis, accompanied by a suggestion to the Porte that this state of things may be due to her own delays and evasions.[3]

The Queen is evidently much annoyed with our anti-Turkish activity in the East. She is convinced that public opinion will not stand undue pressure being put upon the Porte, and that among the European Powers Russia alone is desirous of pushing matters to extremities. She contemplates the probability of the combined fleets retiring in the event of the Porte refusing to listen to their united voice, and to Russia proceeding to war alone. She regards the state of affairs as unsatisfactory in the highest degree and regrets we should have placed ourselves in such a position.[4]

Lord G[ranville], instead of 'riding the high horse' in return (which he was evidently inclined to do), has replied to H.M. calmly and argumentatively. He maintains that nothing has been done which is inconsistent with what She herself and the Cabinet have sanctioned; that there would be great indignation if the Government were, by weakness and vacillation, to retire from the policy of carrying out the conditions of the Treaty of Berlin; and that, though our endeavours may fail, the failure must not be attributed to this country.[5]

---

[1] See the letter, described as of 16 Sept. 1880, as printed in Temperley and Penson, pp. 407–8.   [2] See 14 Sept. 1880.   [3] Ramm, i. 177.
[4] Guedalla, ii. 113.   [5] Ramm, i. 175.

One can't help sympathising more or less with the position of H.M. Here are two distinct, and most important, almost entire reversals of the policy of the late Government—(1) anti-Turkish in Europe, (2) anti-'forward' in India. The result is H.M. finds herself in this position: either She must disagree with the lines taken by the present Government, which in Her position as a constitutional Sovereign it is difficult for her to do; *or* she must admit that, in having given her assent (which must be applied) to the opposite policy which under the late régime was pursued, She committed an error of judgment.

As regards our present line of action in the East, of course all those of the Russophobist turn of mind are inclined to charge the Government with playing indirectly into Russia's hands. They forget that the more the growth and building up of the fabrics of the Principalities in the Balkan peninsula is encouraged, the better and surer means of really resisting her encroachments southwards is being brought about.

The question of the Prince of Wales and his income out of the Duchy of Cornwall estates is coming to the front again. Some means will have to be found for placing him in better funds. The drains on his purse are no doubt materially enhanced by the additional expenses to which he is put consequent on the 'retirement' of the Queen. This additional drain is estimated at £10,000 per annum. Mr. G. seems to think it might be possible to attain the end by the Government taking over the estates like the Crown Estates, by so effecting an economy in their management, and thereby being able to afford to give him an annuity which would exceed the present income he derives directly from the estates.

Tuesday, 21 September. H.M. was not quieted by Lord G[ranville]'s excellent letter, but on Sunday reverted to her fears that we were pushing matters to hostilities at Constantinople. She declares she will not consent to any steps which will lead to war with England's old ally, Turkey; she *will not* sanction a reversal of the policy of the last few years, to which she had willingly assented in the belief that it was the policy best calculated to serve the interests of this country. She maintains we are playing into the hands of Russia. She refers to the fact that Lord Granville assured Prince Leopold on the accession to power of the new ministry that H.M. need be under no apprehension as to foreign affairs. She says she feels aggrieved and will 'never consent' to what will tend to a rupture with the Porte.[1]

Lord Granville has again replied calmly and admirably. The gist of his argument is this: on the formation of the Government, contrary to general expectation perhaps, he had certainly assured H.M. and Prince Leopold that they need be under no misapprehension; and they (the Government) have been true to their word—instead of destroying the Treaty of Berlin they determined, and have been endeavouring, to carry out its provisions. To attain this

[1] *Letters,* 2nd ser. iii. 141.

end they considered it could best be done, and could only be done, by the Concert of Europe; and on this policy of the Concert of Europe they have faithfully acted. Whether it succeeds or not, a great deal depends on the amount of firmness shewn. Turkey is not likely to declare war against *Europe*! and considerable pressure, even of a material nature, may be exercised by Europe without going to war. There is no intention of doing anything singly; and as to H.M. Government being accused of being in alliance with Russia, such an alliance is absolutely untrue. The Cabinet decline to act alone in a matter which concerns all Europe. It would, however, be inconsistent with their duty as responsible ministers of the Crown to advise that under all contingencies this country should not join the other Powers in putting some compulsion on the Porte to settle the questions which are left open and which really endanger the existence of the Porte.[1]

Mr. G. is greatly pleased with Lord G[ranville]'s letter. In expressing his approval he referred to words he made use of at the last Cabinet to the effect that in their discussions the Cabinet should not wholly exclude from view the possibility of H.M. turning upon them and declaring she had no further use for their services—a most serious affair no doubt, but one to be considered. Mr. G. says the present case carries him back to George III's time and to the pledge he exacted from the Whigs that they would not stir the Roman Catholic question.[2]

An impetuous and injudicious step now taken by H.M. might in short endanger the monarchy. This is what we have come to, then, after 6 years of imperialist doctrine instilled into the Sovereign's ears, though there are rumours that Lord B[eaconsfield] even had difficulty in restraining H.M.

The Lord Chief Baron—old Kelly—is dead.

I heard last night a good thing attributed to the late Lord Derby. He was asked the answer to the riddle—no new one—about the similarity between a bald head and heaven, to which the orthodox reply is to the effect that a bald head is a holy shining place where there are no partings. Lord Derby paraphrased this by giving as the answer that the reason why a bald head resembled heaven was because it was a place without '*Whigs*'!

A remarkable statement, by the by, was made the other day by Artim Effendi, the Turk, to our Consul, St. John. He said: 'There are only two ways of dealing with us Turks, gold or firmness. Your principles will not allow you to make use of the first alternative; therefore, you must resort to the second. The Palace party is now persuaded that England is Turkey's greatest enemy. I do not believe it. On the contrary, I believe England to be Turkey's best friend, because she is more disinterested than any other Power; the salvation of the Turkish empire depends on firmness being maintained against her.'

Wednesday, 22 September. Affairs are most critical at Constantinople.

[1] Ibid., pp. 141-2.   [2] Ramm, i. 179-80.

Goschen has impressed on the Turkish Prime Minister that concessions alone can save the existence of Turkey; and I believe the ministers if left alone *would* concede, at any rate if they had some kind of assurance that concession meant the abandonment of the naval demonstration. But the Sultan won't listen to reason; he is as stubborn as he is deceitful and persists in making the most preposterous conditions. I can't help suspecting that the French Ambassador at Constantinople[1] is playing the other Powers false. The Sultan seems to be getting at him. Goschen evidently fancies His Imperial Majesty is touched in the head.

Lord Granville is in favor of making Dilke First Commissioner of Works in the place of Adam when he leaves England, and of giving Dilke therewith a seat in the Cabinet.[2] No man certainly has so good a title for promotion. It seems absurd that he should be outside the Cabinet and Chamberlain inside it. One of the objections to this proposal would be the enlargement of the Cabinet which is already if anything too big.

Lord Coleridge is in favor of rearranging the Supreme Court of Judicature and having only one head, the Lord Chief Justice, dispensing with the Lord Chief Barony (vacated by old Kelly) and the Lord Chief Justiceship of Common Pleas as soon as Lord Coleridge retires himself.[3]

Thursday, 23 September. The crisis has come at last at Constantinople. The Sultan declares he cannot surrender Dulcigno except on certain specified conditions. One is that the naval demonstration should be abandoned, not only for Montenegro but for Greece; the second is that the *status quo* be maintained everywhere; the third is that the property of Mussulmen should be respected.

Friday, 24 September. The situation in the East is, of course, exceedingly awkward, and it looks as if the united voice[4] of Europe is likely to have been raised in vain. The stubbornness and wild infatuation of that old Sultan is extraordinary but perhaps not surprising. He may fairly think that he has nothing to lose in his European Empire and everything (or a good deal) to gain in the estimation of his Mussulmen subjects.

The Concert of Europe, however, is still maintained. Austria, for instance, is even warming up apparently; therefore, as things now stand, the next stage in the proceedings will be the real commencement of the naval demonstration off Dulcigno; and if the presence of the fleet is not of itself sufficient

---

[1] C. J. Tissot.   [2] See 29 Apr., 25 Aug., and 11 Sept. 1880.

[3] The reform was accomplished when the Lord Chief Justice of the Queen's Bench, Cockburn, died on 20 Nov. 1880 and Coleridge was promoted from Chief Justice of Common Pleas to the position now formally entitled Lord Chief Justice of England. See 23 Nov. 1880, and Ernest Hartley Coleridge, *Life . . . of John Duke Lord Coleridge* (N.Y., 1904), ii. 283–4.

[4] EWH originally wrote 'united force' but altered the letters.

to overawe the Porte, there will be material force applied, I presume, to the extent of a gunshot or two fired. H.M. has, I understand, yielded so far as to consent to a show of material force to this limited extent. If that does not succeed, the Powers will probably have to retire, and our fleet have to turn tail with the others. It will be an ignominious result, no doubt; but it must be remembered that it will be *Europe*, not England, befooled by the Porte. We can't then be laughed at; for if all Europe are in the same boat there will be no one to laugh at us but the Turks themselves, and this limited amount of derision we ought to be able to stand, shared as it will be by the other Powers.

Musurus seems to have been in the first rank of obstructives, which is not a little surprising considering his long acquaintance with Western ideas and the feeling more especially of England.

I confess myself I wish the Government had contented themselves with saying, when they came into power, they would, of course, accept the Treaty of Berlin settlement, but would hold their hands and wait and see what turned up, instead of plunging *in medias res* and playing so prominent a part in advocating the claims of Montenegro and Greece.

George Lefevre has applied for a Privy Councillorship which ought to put his claims 'out of court' for a while. He has a good case, and therefore ought to have been[1] all the more scrupulous about urging it himself.

Saturday, 25 September. Lord O. Russell is to have his peerage whenever he and his brother, the Duke, like. The Duke has settled or rather will settle £100,000 upon him.[2]

But little news from the East. The fleets are to proceed to Dulcigno early next week. Sir B. Seymour, who is recognised as Commander-in-Chief, is to have full discretion. He is to manoeuvre as much as possible without having recourse to military measures except on absolute necessity. Whatever may be said against the foreign policy of the present Government, they can't be charged with a want of activity abroad. The Sultan's appeal, which he has made to the German Emperor, has been of no avail. The Emperor has courteously told him he cannot now do anything which will entail the withdrawal of Germany from the united action of the Powers.[3] This is satisfactory. At present, therefore, the Powers still hang together, and to have kept them in unity even thus far reflects great credit on Lord Granville.

Lord Ripon held his council in India yesterday. He found so powerful a majority against him on the question of withdrawing from Kandahar that he postponed, and wisely I think, coming to a direct issue on the main question. It would be awkward for him to overrule his council. Accordingly he has adjourned the discussion and will have the political state of affairs at

---

[1] EWH has written 'ought not have been'.
[2] See 7 Sept., 24, 26, and 29 Nov. 1880. [3] See Medlicott, p. 152.

K[andahar] investigated. He thinks that after such an investigation he may possibly find more to agree with him. The ardour of the military element on the council will perhaps by that time have abated.

Sunday, 26 September. The Sultan seems hard pressed. He has now tried on an appeal to Russia and has merely got a reply that the naval demonstration could not be abandoned unless the demands of the Powers were fully complied with. The argument of Russia is as forcible as it is ingenious: 'If', she says to the Porte, 'you wish to give up Dulcigno but have not the power to force the Albanians, then you ought to be grateful for the assistance we Powers give you. If you have the power but not the will, you would then do well to take the hint that the wisest thing to do will be to obey the dictates of Europe. If you have neither the power nor the will, then you can't be surprised at Europe carrying out her decision for herself in lieu of leaving it to you to do'.

I fear it is possible we may have troubles in store for us with the Basutos and possibly a repetition of a Zulu War. The enforcement of the disarmament act seems a monstrous act of injustice and is mainly attributable to the handiwork of that 'fire-eating' Sir B. Frere. Here are a fine native race who have always lived on peaceable terms with our colonists and are suddenly told that they must lay down their arms, because if they have no intention of fighting they can't possibly want them. Why, it would be difficult to conceive a proceeding more calculated to wound the pride of a high spirited race.[1] Moreover, instead of handing over, or rather back, to them the strip of land occupied by Moirosi, one of their own minor chiefs, after he had been 'brought to book' for securing the escape of his son (I think) who had been convicted of some offence, we go and put the land up to auction for small settlements. These two circumstances are sufficient to stir up the Basutos, and if thoroughly stirred up, numbering as they do (I believe) some 30,000 men, we shall have a tough job, as tough as, if not tougher than, the Zulu business. We tell, of course, the colonists they must look after themselves, but it will inevitably end in our having to give them a helping hand.

Ireland seems quieting down. Childers writes cheerfully of the country and says the good harvest has worked wonders. As regards the harvest, we have no cause of complaint about it in this country, which ought to give a lift both to the revenue and to the landlords.[2]

---

[1] By an act of the Cape Parliament in 1878 the Government was given the power to disarm native tribes when necessary. The Government, interpreting the act broadly, announced in 1879 that it would apply the act to the Basutos and formally proclaimed the disarmament on 8 Apr. 1880. The attempt to enforce the disarmament led in September to armed conflict between the Cape Government and the Basutos—a conflict that dragged on until Apr. 1881. See *Annual Register*, 1880, pp. 334–42; 1881, pp. 387–8.

[2] For three weeks in Sept. 1880 Childers left his duties in the War Office and toured the distressed districts of Ireland collecting information on the land question in Ireland. Childers, i. 277–9.

Tuesday, 28 September. It could only have been a few hours before I wrote the words above as to 'Ireland quieting down' when the unfortunate murder of Lord Mountmorres took place.[1] It seems to have [been] a purely agrarian outrage of a most dastardly kind. The old story: a harsh landlord, who had evicted and likewise refused to give an abatement of rent, waylaid by masked assassins, riddled with shot, and the murderers clean gone.

Matters in the East yesterday assumed a most serious aspect. We received intelligence to the effect that the Montenegrins had been told by the Turkish commander[2] that the advance of their troops would be considered by the Porte a *casus belli*, and further that the Prince of M[ontenegro] declined to incur the risk of war before knowing what amount of material support he would obtain from the Powers beyond the mere presence of the fleets. I wired down to Hawarden the gist of the telegram. Mr. G. communicated with Lord Granville at Balmoral and in pursuance of their directions I issued an order for a Cabinet Council at 12 o'clock on Thursday. Considering the gravity of the question I think it was only right that the ministers should be summoned. On the one hand, of course, a sudden meeting of the Cabinet always gives rise to alarm. On the other hand, the absence of responsible ministers from headquarters naturally causes an impression abroad in the diplomatic world that after all we (England) 'don't so much care' about the issue of events in the East.

Wednesday, 29 September. There is a slight turn of the tide today. The Porte seems alarmed at the sternness of the Powers as evinced by their last collective note. The Sultan's ministers never dared, it appears, to shew the exact terms of it to the Sultan, but he has become rather more amenable. He promises to settle definitely the question connected with the Treaty of Berlin by next Sunday and hopes that it is a settlement that will satisfy the Powers. In return he trusts the naval demonstration will be then given up.

Italy now seems to be hanging fire somewhat, and Austria is most anxious not to take any step which is likely to lead to active hostilities.

However, the European Concert is still maintained, and so long as that is the case the Government can 'do no wrong'.

Thursday, 30 September. No material change in the situation. There was a report this morning that Dulcigno had been burnt; this has subsequently been contradicted. Goschen is in favour of strong measures, and even goes so far as to hint the advisability of sending the joint fleets through the Dardanelles.

[1] Lord Mountmorres was murdered on 25 Sept. 1880 while returning to his house, Ebor Hall, from a meeting of magistrates at Clonbur, co. Galway. Vicary Gibbs writes: 'He appears to have been neither cruel nor unjust, but merely a man of business who expected his tenants to keep their engagements or go. His assassination was probably part of a deliberate attempt to secure better terms for the tenantry by intimidation.' *G.E.C.* ix. 357.

[2] Riza Pasha. See Medlicott, p. 154.

The Cabinet sat today from 12 to 4 o'clock. Nothing very definite appears to have been decided beyond that a telegram should be despatched to Goschen to the effect that the delay till next Sunday for which the Sultan has asked may be granted, but that if that delay does not suffice to procure an 'advantageous arrangement', the matter will not stop there. What ulterior measures could or would be taken must be entirely dependent on the mood of the other Powers. If backed by the others, we should probably be prepared, if not for the despatch of the fleet within sight of the Sultan, at any rate for the seizure by sea of certain places by way of material guarantees. But all hinges on what the Powers will together agree to. I am glad to say the Cabinet strongly deprecate solitary action, or action with any individual Power. It is the maintenance of the European Concert which is the primary object of the Government.[1]

Forster brought the question of Ireland before the Cabinet. He seems to report a highly unsatisfactory state of affairs in certain parts of the country, and it has been suggested that, if the Law Officers find the Land League to be illegal, Parnell will be arrested and tried.

No further Cabinet seems likely to be held for several days.

Lord Northbrook is strongly opposed to the retention even of Pishin. He attaches no great weight as to the time of withdrawal from Kandahar. He feels sure this is an occasion when it is the proper function of the Home Government to check the impulse of public opinion in India.

Friday, 1 October. The order of the day is still 'marking time' with these two exceptions: (1) France seems to be taking a little heart and asserts that the rumours respecting her withdrawal from the union of the Powers are absolutely false; (2) Austria seems to be hanging back, to be in favor of milder measures or a compromise, the danger of which is that, if her advice is not followed, she will find an excuse for retiring; and if she takes the lead, Europe will not succeed in carrying into effect its [*sic*]

Saturday, 2 October. Mr. G. went down to Holmbury with Lord Granville and Lord Northbrook. He had previously put on paper his ideas of the line which should be taken with Austria:—in the event of some new illusory proposals or shifts on the part of the Porte, some action must be taken; but H.M. Government are anxious to do nothing which will re-open generally the Eastern question; and therefore by way of avoiding the infliction of a general shock to the Porte, action should be local, that is, confined to certain points or places agreed upon. This might advantageously be gained by taking certain material measures in connection with Dulcigno. Would the Austrian Government push forward a force for the temporary purpose of securing the Montenegrin frontier against invasion, while the army of Montenegro was

---

[1] See Memorandum by G. for the Cabinet, 30 Sept. 1880, Ramm, i. 190–1.

engaged in giving effect to the decision of the Powers laid down in the Treaty of Berlin? By this means probably Dulcigno might be occupied by the Montenegrins. Without, however, the concurrence of Austria, there could be no satisfactory method of taking local action on the Albanian coast.[1]

Meanwhile we are waiting for the further reply of the Porte.

Monday, 4 October. Up till late this afternoon nothing transpired from Constantinople. There was an informal meeting of a quorum of ministers at 3:30. No news from the Porte could hardly be interpreted to mean good news, and facts have now proved that this assertion is not always to be relied on. About 6:30 news did come, and it was as about as unsatisfactory as it well could be. The reply of the Porte amounts to little more than a reiteration of their former professions and conditions; in short, they refuse to do anything unless the naval demonstration is absolutely given up; and if that is done, Dulcigno, it is true, will be transferred, but the other questions—Greek and Armenian—are to be indefinitely shelved. The proposal which Lord G[ranville] has now made to the other Powers is that we shall send the united fleets to Smyrna, hold the place and impound the revenues. I doubt much if the other Powers will agree; but either some strong measure of this kind must be taken, or else the Powers must acquiesce in being befooled by the Porte. The former alternative is one which in my opinion will constitute the climax of the Concert of the Powers; the latter alternative is somewhat humiliating. Mr. G. is very stern, and on my saying that I questioned the support of the country to any strong line, he merely said he would gladly throw the whole thing up.

Mr. G. wrote Goschen today a charming letter of encouragement which doubtless will, in the trying circumstances, be very acceptable.[2]

Herries is to have a KCB, and West a CB ostensibly on the ground of the Board of Inland Revenue having, successfully as we hope, converted the Malt duty into a Beer tax. Mr. G. accompanied the offer with notes such as he only can write.

The Lord Chancellor[3] in this country has given his opinion about the Land League in Ireland, and he considers proceedings can and should be taken.

Tuesday, 5 October. I was not quite easy about Mr. G. yesterday. He was evidently not himself, apparently having caught a chill. I got him to put off dining with Count Münster, and today, though he seemed better, I induced him to see Dr. Clark who thinks it is merely a stomach derangement, and with a little care no troubles need be apprehended.

[1] This undated memorandum is printed in Ramm, i. 189–90 as a memorandum for the Cabinet, 30 Sept. 1880. EWH's manner of referring to it is evidence for assigning the memorandum to some time after the Cabinet meeting on 30 Sept. and before G.'s departure for Holmbury on 2 Oct. 1880.

[2] Arthur D. Elliott, *The Life of . . . Goschen* (London, 1911), i. 201–2.

[3] Lord Selborne.

Italy thoroughly approves the Smyrna proposal, and, considering the action of the Porte an insult to Europe, will cooperate with us in any energetic measures through thick and thin. France has been sounded, and though she has not replied formally yet, the new Foreign Minister[1] did not seem averse to the proposition. Bismarck will apparently do nothing but give his moral support to the Concert of Europe.

Mr. G. is evidently willing to go to Smyrna if only he can get two others to follow our lead. There would probably be Italy and Russia; and that would never do in this country.

The Porte's answer now that it has been received more *in extenso* is in effect this:—'Give up,' says the Sultan, '*all* demonstrations, and in return I will do my best to hand over Dulcigno; I have sketched out a very nice little frontier for Greece,' (apparently a small triangular slice of land without a scrap of additional seaboard), 'which I will in due time take care is carried out; I shall be very glad to see my creditors in Constantinople, and I will have a look round in Armenia.'

Hengelmüller, the Austrian Chargé d'Affaires, told me tonight he was immensely impressed with his interview yesterday with Mr. Gladstone.[2] He had been brought in contact with Bismarck and the other big men in Europe, but no one had so impressed him with his charm of manner, frankness, and greatness as Mr. G.

Wednesday, 6 October. The answers of the Powers have not yet been received except that of Italy yesterday and Russia today, the two Powers most likely to be willing to follow our lead, but with whom it will *not* do to act alone,[3] even if the other Powers give their tacit assent to the action.

Quite recently the following views on the situation of European affairs were attributed to Prince Bismarck:[4] So long as the Concert of Europe is maintained there need be no apprehension of war. The duration and influence of that Concert depends on the initiative being taken by England. With regard to the other Powers, England can reckon on the support absolutely of Russia and Italy (as proved by both these Powers being the first to acquiesce in the proposal of the Cabinet). From Austria, England can only expect reluctant support—she has so many political dangers at home to encounter. France's attitude will depend in greatest measure on the minister for the time being. The chief obstacle to the future leadership of the Concert of Europe is the

---

[1] On 19 Sept. 1880 the Freycinet Government resigned and on 23 Sept. Jules Ferry formed a new Government in which Jules Barthélemy St. Hilaire was the Foreign Minister.

[2] G. found Hengelmüller 'pleasant and frank'. See G.'s letter to Granville, 4 Oct. 1880, Ramm, i. 192.

[3] EWH has written 'whom he will *not* do to act alone'.

[4] By Lord Odo Russell who had 'been privately informed on reliable authority that in his last report to the Emperor on foreign affairs' Bismarck had submitted the views which EWH outlines. See Russell's letter to Granville, 2 Oct. 1880, in Knaplund, pp. 159-60.

rapid change of public opinion to which the country is subject (too true). If England is not allowed to go as far as armed interference with Turkey, Russia may be tempted to interfere by herself on behalf of the Christian subjects of the Porte. Germany would then do what she could to harmonise the interests of Austria and Russia. Negotiations with Russia would be easier during the life of the Czar. Bismarck would insist, if Russia went to war again with Turkey, on her conveying her troops by sea only. This he thinks would tend to localise any such war.

This is a high compliment paid to the policy of European concert, a policy which the Opposition are endeavouring to turn into ridicule and are daily praying may fail in order to strike a blow at the ministerial programme!

Thursday, 7 October. Mr. G. has kept his bed today, but Clark thinks he will be all right again immediately.

No further replies received from the Powers beyond that Germany says her line of action is entirely dependent on that of Austria, and according to private intelligence from the Austrian Chargé d'Affaires, Austria will probably respond favourably to England's proposition.[1] This looks hopeful.

I received a very gloomy account today of the state of Ireland from Willie Compton, Lord Cowper's Private Secretary. He goes in for the strongest of measures—the suspension of the Habeas Corpus. Forster, he says, is gradually becoming looked upon as a failure and is producing a bad impression by the gross ignorance he displays of Irish affairs.

Friday, 8 October. The much looked-for reply from Austria has at last arrived late this evening. While approving of the proposal to proceed to Smyrna and lay hold of the revenues of the Porte and suggesting that a portion of such revenues should be handed over to the Prince of Montenegro to recoup him partially for the expenses he has been put to, Austria declares her inability to send her own ships there. She cannot take any step which may eventually result in war with Turkey. This, of course, means that neither will Germany send her ship to Smyrna. Accordingly we shall have either to drop the Smyrna proposal, or to proceed there alone with Russia and Italy, which would certainly wear the appearance of the break-up of the Concert of Europe, and likewise leave us nearly single-handed with Russia—for I take it to be nearly certain France won't go further than Germany and Austria. I have no doubt Mr. G. will wish to go forward all the same, but I am convinced it will be a step which will not be approved by this country. Therefore, I earnestly trust some other proposal will be devised, or else that we shall leave the old Turk to rot to pieces of his own accord. The Smyrna proposal, too, having leaked out,[2] it will be difficult to have recourse to any other alternative without a

[1] Ramm, i. 194.
[2] The *Pall Mall Gazette* published an account of a proposal to seize ports on the Turkish mainland on 8 Oct. 1880, p. 7. See Medlicott, pp. 162–3 and Ramm, i. 194.

confession of failure. Altogether it is a bad business, and I wish I could see a good way out of it. Mr. G. won't give up the Smyrna plan readily. He is very keen about it. He likened it this morning to castor oil from which he said he had derived so much good as a 'mild but efficient prescription'.

Fife has resigned his Captaincy of the Gentlemen-at-Arms not on political but on private grounds. Lord G[ranville] thought the resignation should be accepted with regret, and accordingly Mr. G. has accepted it. But I am very sorry. His leaving the ranks of the Government will do harm. I am strongly in favor of his being asked to retain his post till after Adam goes to India, and I should then put A. Peel at the Works and Fife at the Home Office as Under-Secretary.[1]

I had a talk tonight with Lord Vernon on Ireland, who has lately been there on the business of the Agriculture Commission[2] and had accordingly heard much evidence bearing on the state of the country. Ready as he is, and right as he feels it, that some remedial measures should be taken, he is convinced that such measures must be prefaced by a very strong administration of the law, ordinary if not extraordinary. What with Ireland and Turkey, these are very anxious times, and I don't at all like the outlook.

Monday, 11 October. (Mayen) I am writing from Mayen whither I came yesterday.

In consequence of the Austrian reply, which Mr. G. termed 'shabby', and the awkward predicament which the refusal of Germany as well as of Austria to take an *active* part in the Smyrna proposal, a Cabinet was summoned on Saturday for today. The question for the Cabinet to decide was whether under the circumstances England should in conjunction with Italy and Russia act as mandatories of Europe, or whether all action should be dropped. There seems still a faint hope whether the Turk will not now cave in; he is reported to have expressed his willingness to cede Dulcigno at once adding a hope that the demonstration will therefore be given up—these are very different terms to those which[3] the *last* note of the Porte contained. If this should fortunately come about, the disagreeable alternatives before the Cabinet will today not necessarily have come to the front. If they were the only courses open to us, we should certainly be in a disagreeable fix. To give up all action would be a great failure, and a stultification of Europe, tantamount to implying that Europe could not lift up her voice with Turkey and get a hearing. To proceed with Italy and Russia would be regarded as our walking arm in arm with Russia (which is still regarded with such suspicion in this country) with Italy merely thrown in as a 'chaperon'.

---

[1] See 17 and 28 Dec. 1880. Lord Huntly finally received Fife's post. See 28 July, 30 Dec. 1880, and 10 Jan. 1881.

[2] i.e. the Richmond Commission, 1879–81, of which Vernon was a member.

[3] EWH has written 'to those while the *last* note'.

Wednesday, 13 October. (Mayen) The hope of the Turk caving in has been realised; and today's newspapers announce the willingness of the Sultan to cede Dulcigno at once, practically without conditions, though he expresses a hope that the naval demonstration and other coercive measures will be given up.

I hear daily from Godley. It appears that until noon yesterday no official announcement had arrived from the Porte about Dulcigno, though rumours were afloat. Mr. G. and Lord G[ranville] were very low in their mind. At 12 o'clock Lord G[ranville] came across to announce the good news himself to Mr. G. Lord G[ranville] stole into the room unobserved and proceeded to make known the intelligence by dancing about Mr. G.'s room in a wild state of delight. Mr. G. said, 'God Almighty be praised; I shall go to Hawarden by the 2:45 train.' All's well that ends well, but I am afraid the time and mode of surrender by the Porte can hardly be regarded a very triumphant climax to the European Concert. Thank goodness the immediate anxiety on the latest phase of the European [Eastern?] question is over. The Sultan has afforded the Government a not discreditable means of escape, and I should be glad, were it possible, that we should now take up a more neutral non-intervening position. We have got quite enough to do at home, notably as to Ireland.

Forster the other day put the *pros* and *cons* together about taking legal proceedings against those wretched Land Leaguers.[1]

(1). *Pros.* (1) A prosecution is the only thing to be done without fresh legislation.

(2) It will be a means of punishing great criminals.

(3) It will shew up the absurdity which some people have got hold of that the Government are either afraid of the agitators or are in league with them.

(4) It will assert *the* law in place of Parnell's law.

(2). *Cons.* (1) A prosecution will produce great enthusiasm for Parnell, subscriptions &c, &c.

(2) The Land Leaguers and nationalists would shake hands.

(3) The moderate Home Rulers might be induced to join Parnell.

(4) There is the probability of an acquittal.

(5) There is no likelihood of securing an immediate trial.

All the Law Officers have now delivered their opinions; and as the majority are favourable to a prosecution, a prosecution will commence. I fear, however, the advisability of it is doubtful. A state trial of that kind leads to a disagreeable dilemma. If it succeeds, those prosecuted become martyrs. If it fails they become heroes. However, the taking of legal proceedings will at any rate disabuse the mind of some Irish landlords, who believe that the Government

---

[1] See Forster's letter to G., 8 Oct. 1880, Wemyss Reid, ii. 255-8.

are more or less countenancing the agitation of the League in order to strengthen their hands against the inevitable Irish Land Bill next session.

If the prosecution does not (and it may not) check outrages, the only alternative will be to summon Parliament and ask for some special powers. What those special powers should be it is difficult to say, and the Government are not helped out of their difficulties by any suggestions in the shape of prescriptions for Irish ills from the landlords themselves.

Sunday, 17 October. (Mayen) Matters seem quiet in Downing St., and the Government to be satisfied with the course of events. The Opposition, of course, regard the result of the very tardy yielding of the Sultan, at a time when it appeared too that his obstinacy had got the Powers into difficulties, as a very insignificant result of the naval demonstration, enough only 'to swear by' as Sir S. Northcote put it the other day. At the same time it is an incontestable fact that the Sultan has distinctly given out that he surrenders in the hope of avoiding such a demonstration, and therefore it is surely not unfair to regard the coercive policy so far as it had proceeded, accompanied with rumoured intentions of more active measures, to have succeeded in its object.

Thursday, 21 October. (Mayen) It is difficult to find time to jot anything down up here and to find anything at this distance from Headquarters worth jotting down.

There are, I fear, doubts, suspicions, and delays about the final surrender of Dulcigno; but perhaps not more, or rather I hope not more, than might be expected from that shifty, crafty fellow, the Sultan.

I hear the drawback on malt turns out to amount to £300,000 more than the estimate—or £1,250,000 instead of £950,000—which will rather upset Mr. G.'s calculations and has falsified the sanguine expectations of the Inland Revenue people.[1] But their revenue promises well, and Mr. G. appears not to be at all depressed by the excess, for which he was not unprepared, knowing by experience that such estimates as drawbacks on stocks in hand must necessarily be made very much in the dark. Moreover the estimate was reduced £200,000 on the special representations of the principal brewers; and so we shall have a good score off them if they open their mouths next session.

Dilke, who has been over in Paris and who is, I hope, pretty well recovered, seems to have sent over an interesting account of his conversations with Gambetta in Paris. Gambetta appears to be pro-English and anti-Turkish.

We are having regular winter weather up here, quite deep snow and sharp frost.[2]

[1] See 10 June 1880.   [2] Mayen House is in Banffshire, near Rothiemay.

Received today a letter from Henry Primrose. He has sent me Primrose's (no relation) and Burrows' despatches (but which have not reached me yet) from which he says it is shewn that the advance to the Helmund which led to the terrible disaster with Ayub Khan[1] was recommended by General Primrose before he received any orders about it from the Indian Government, and that neither he nor General Burrows showed any sign of fearing that the Brigade would be overmatched. So that the Indian Government are to be acquitted of blame in this respect. H. W. P[rimrose] says that the confidential accounts of the battle and retreat are more pitiful reading than even the official ones, and that the officers do not come out of the unfortunate business at all well. The troops, it seems, were so utterly demoralised that they huddled together like sheep, and the Ghazis took them by the turbans and sliced off their heads without any resistance being offered. The only wonder is that any got away.

H. W. P[rimrose] likes Lord Ripon immensely and thinks very highly of his abilities. He says he is immensely popular out in India.

Sunday, 24 October. (Mayen) Dulcigno has not yet been finally delivered over. There are still shifts and quibbles, but there does not seem to be any apprehension in Downing St. as to the result.

The Greek question must now necessarily come to the front. The King of Greece has returned to Athens, and the speech from the throne bears a very decided warlike tone. There are now over 40,000 men under arms, and these are supposed to be capable of being increased to 70,000. Whatever, however, may be the numbers which Greece may be able to put into the field, it is hardly possible she can single-handed achieve the end she has in view with Turkey. The Powers, therefore, must either stand by, and after more or less inciting her to fight, or after admitting the justice of what she will be fighting for—the new frontier—be content to witness her defeat; or they will have to interfere. But who is to interfere? Who is to take the initiative? It ought to be France after the leading part she has taken in the Greek business, and after the marked manner in which she has played the part of God-mother to Greece. But France hangs back. Austria, who according to her Crown Prince[2] does not wholly exclude from view the possibility of eventually going herself to Salonica, is not likely to be very anxious to take any active steps which will increase the power of a possible rival for that place some day. Germany has never shewn any very pro-Hellenic tendencies, and Russia is naturally without doubt anti-Hellenic—that is, she is jealous of any Power which is likely to interfere with, or become a rival of her special protegés, the Slavs. So it is improbable she will intervene very actively on Greece's behalf; and it is remarkable that Baron Jomini told our Chargé d'Affaires[3] the other day at St. Petersburg that, though she would go anywhere with England so long

---

[1] i.e. the battle of Maiwand. See 28 July 1880.   [2] Archduke Rudolph.
[3] Probably Francis Richard Plunkett, secretary of the embassy at St. Petersburg, 1877–81.

as there are three Powers taking active measures, she would with a less number hold back and join the other Powers in constituting Great Britain their mandatory. (This probably has special reference to Greece.) As no great dependence can be placed on Italy, it seems that what we come to is that England is the only Power on which Greece can the least rely, or rather can the least look to for material support. I trust, however, the Government will not for one moment entertain the idea of acting in Greece as the mandatory of Europe, no matter how strongly the other Powers request her to 'do their dirty work for them,' which it would amount to. Maintain the Concert of Europe by all means and require the execution of the Treaty, but don't plunge this country into war.

Thursday, 28 October. (Mayen) The Attorney-General[1] has refused the Lord Justiceship vacant by the death (sadly premature) of Thesiger; and it has now been offered to Lush.[2]

Mr. G. has drawn up a very important memorandum about his plan for relieving the work of the House of Commons by means of Grand Committees, which would be appointed for the various parts of the U.K., and to which would be delegated portions of the present Parliamentary work. It is, I believe, grounded on a suggestion of Sir T. E. May.[3]

Forster has drawn up a memorandum anent the intended prosecutions of the Land Leaguers. The gist of it is this: the Government are not actuated by any attempt to interfere with the liberty of speech at public meetings, because the speakers demand legislative changes. If the Land Leaguers were merely trying to obtain support to a Land Bill, they would be let alone. But the leaders of the agitation avow their object to be to abolish landlordism. By declaring what the tenant should pay by way of rent and by threatening landlords if they exercise their legal rights, they aim at bringing the landlord on his knees, and by deteriorating the value of his property, at making it easy to buy him out of his property compulsorily. Further, the Land Leaguers aim at replacing the law by what Parnell calls their 'unwritten law', i.e. they determine how much of a legal debt shall be paid. This action is held to be illegal, and in the face of this how could the Government do otherwise than prosecute? Moreover, violent physical outrages follow the Land League meetings, and with the application of such means to attain their end, we have a 'reign of terror'. Many demand the suspension of the 'Habeas Corpus' or

---

[1] Sir Henry James.
[2] Sir Robert Lush (1807–81) accepted the offer.
[3] This memorandum, dated 23 Oct. 1880, is printed in Hammond, pp. 198–204. G.'s scheme of Grand Committees as propounded at this time was a step in the direction of devolution and Home Rule, and was different from the Grand Committees on Trade and Law that were introduced to expedite parliamentary business in 1883. G.'s proposal was supported in the Cabinet on 15 Nov. 1880 by Bright and Chamberlain but was rejected by G.'s other colleagues. Joseph Chamberlain, *A Political Memoir 1880–92* (London, 1953), p. 9.

some such strong measure, but if this were substituted for the prosecutions, what would Parliament say to taking away from the Irish tenant the greatest safeguard which law now gives him of his personal liberty and to allowing the leading men of influence to defy and break the law with impunity?

Whatever, however, may be said against strong measures, I believe they will have to be taken sooner or later (and better sooner than later) in addition to the chief agitators being prosecuted.

Thursday, 4 November. (Great Budworth) Left Mayen on Sunday after a very pleasant 3 weeks. It is like a small miniature Wilton; that is to say, a small liberty hall and an absolutely unselfish host. Slept at Carlisle on Sunday, and on Monday proceeded to Hawarden. I had a most agreeable little stay there. Mr. G. was in the greatest force, and I never remember to have seen him more vigorous or more pleasant. The party consisted of Lord and Lady Bath, Lord and Lady Odo Russell, Lord Dufferin, Mr. Leveson Gower and George Leveson G[ower], and Mr. MacColl. One ought to have been shorthand writing all day and all night, so much worth was most of what one heard said and discussed. I am afraid I shall be able to retail but little of it. Lord Odo R[ussell] is certainly an extremely agreeable man, so well-informed and able to bring out his information in so pleasant and interesting a manner. Lord Bath was likewise in a specially agreeable humour. It is a thousand pities that a man of his abilities, position, and information should be so isolated in politics. On ordinary topics one would imagine him to be a strong Liberal, but he will not avow himself to be so-minded. He still talks of 'you' not 'us' about Government policy. I should like to see him turned to account as a diplomat. If it were not that he has committed himself so strongly on Eastern affairs and is therefore a little too much of a party man in this respect, I can conceive no man better fitted for a high diplomatic post—say Constantinople in succession to Mr. Goschen. His charming wife too doubly befits him for such a post.

Conversations naturally turned specially on foreign politics. Lord O. Russell regards the present situation as one of the most interesting and eventful of foreign crises. He as well as Lord Bath and, I think, Lord Dufferin seem to think that nothing will be wrung out of the Turks except by coercion. Coercion, however, is not likely to be accepted by all the Powers, though all the Powers would probably acquiesce in seeing England and one or two only of the others acting as mandatories of Europe.

I asked Lord O. Russell how he accounted for an apparent change of front in Bismarck. A few months ago Bismarck (I reminded him) had strongly advocated the European Concert led by England; and now he (Bismarck) appeared to sneer at the Concert and to hang back. Lord O. Russell attributed this change of front to Bismarck's jealousy of Mr. Gladstone's European influence, which struck me as being a remarkable admission. It is curious to think of Gladstone, the non-interventionist who has always been so ridiculed on the continent, acquiring an influence of which even Bismarck himself is afraid.

Lord Bath told me after prolonged conversations with the Ambassadors—Lord O. R[ussell] and Lord Dufferin—that he thought he had now obtained a mastery of the European situation. The conclusion to which he had come was that what Bismarck's real game now was to force on Austria in the south-east of Europe; and on my replying if that was his game he was playing the game apparently of aggrandising Austria, Lord Bath, while admitting the force of this, thought the aggrandisement of Austria in the direction of Slav territories was the very thing which Bismarck was secretly fostering in order to convert Austria mainly into a great Slav power and thereby to abstract from Austria her German-speaking provinces for the German Empire.

Many interesting incidents of the Constantinople Conference and the Berlin Congress transpired,[1] which I only imperfectly remember. Lord O. Russell said that the impression which Lord Beaconsfield made at Berlin was extraordinarily great, and that it was impossible to overrate the extreme ability with which he conducted much of the Congress business. The other representatives were evidently afraid of him, and of all the marked men assembled there, no one was regarded with so much curiosity or treated with so much deference.

Lord Bath (I think it was he) said he believed that had Lord Salisbury had his own way at Constantinople the Conference would have succeeded, and that its failure was due to his being overruled at home by Dizzie and other and higher authorities.

Lord Bath regarded the orders about the moving up of the fleet and the summoning of Indian troops[2] in a great measure directed as means of getting rid of Lord Derby at the dictation of supreme authority. I can well believe this.

Lord Dufferin seems to be entirely in favour of our withdrawing from the advanced frontier in Northwest India. He seems to entertain no distrust of Russia, and he ought to be a good judge.

I had a long talk with him on Ireland, and his authority on Irish matters is very high. He has much studied the question and is a disinterested landlord, for he got rid of almost the whole of his Irish property some years ago. I am afraid he does not see his way to any materially beneficial changes in the Land Laws. He was a supporter of the Land Act of 1870 and thinks that in many ways it has worked beneficially. But he could not advocate—he would

---

[1] i.e. the Constantinople Conference of Dec. 1876–Jan. 1877 and the Berlin Congress of 1878.

[2] EWH refers to the decision of Beaconsfield's Cabinet, 27 Mar. 1878, 'to send an expedition from India to occupy Cyprus and Scanderoon'. The decision was the occasion of Lord Derby's resignation from the Cabinet. W. F. Monypenny and George E. Buckle, *The Life of . . . Disraeli . . .* (N.Y., 1911–20), vi. 264–8.

strongly oppose—an extension of the Ulster tenant right throughout Ireland. He gave me several instances of the very unjust way in which the Ulster custom works. I think he would be for some coercive measures, but at the present moment he thought much good might be done by a firm word or two next Tuesday (Lord Mayor's dinner) from Mr. Gladstone, so that those who are being misled by the Land Leaguers may be shewn that they are really running their heads against brick walls, and likewise that the proprietary class may be convinced that the Government is not, as they (he believes) to a great measure seriously and honestly believe, countenancing this agitation.

Mr. G. seemed to be annoyed with the remarks which Chamberlain made the other day about the Irish Land Laws and required amendments.[1]

One evening Mr. G. was lamenting the change of feeling as regards economy which had crept over the country since the Crimean War. Before that time there was a genuine earnestness that economy should be exercised in the administration of this country. Of all men whom Mr. G. would like to see back in their place in the House of Commons, Joseph Hume is the man whom Mr. G. regards as the politician who did in a modest way more good to the cause of economy and the general interest of the public than anyone during the last century. He gave me a curious instance of the difficulty of getting ministers to assent to a reduction of their estimates. In 1861 (I think) Sir G. Cornewall Lewis, then Secretary for War, resisted strongly the pressure Mr. G. put upon him for some reduction in the Army Estimates. Sir G. C. [Lewis] was supported in the Cabinet, and Mr. G. had to accept the Estimates as they stood. A few weeks later notice of a motion was given against the excessive expenditure of the Government, and what happened? £2,000,000 was at one fell swoop knocked off the Army Estimates.[2]

Lord O. Russell furnished one morning some interesting facts regarding the state of religion in Germany. There is practically no such thing as church-going there, and there is a general falling off of all ecclesiasticism. The Germans are inclined to sneer at this country for all its church tendencies. Germany seems to be a remarkable instance of morality flourishing without religion.

I went over from Hawarden to see Eaton.[3] It is a huge pile; it is like a small town, and the principle on which it has been rebuilt and enlarged is curious—there is the big house for entertaining purposes, and then tacked onto it and semi-detached are one or two buildings which are complete small houses in

[1] Chamberlain spoke on Irish policy at the opening of the Birmingham Liberal Club on 30 Oct. 1880.

[2] G. was probably referring to 1862 when Stansfeld put forward a motion urging the reduction of public expenditure, especially for military and naval purposes. In that year, however, Sir G. C. Lewis's Estimates passed, in spite of G.'s misgivings. Morley, ii. 50–1; *Annual Register*, 1862, pp. 88–96; and Philip Guedalla, *Gladstone and Palmerston . . .* (N.Y., 1928), pp. 217–28. EWH refers to this subject again on 25 Feb. 1886, Add. MS. 48643, ff. 26–7, giving the date as 1862.

[3] The property of the Duke of Westminster.

which the Duke and Duchess, the Grosvenors, and others would live separately, so that the big house would never be used except for guests. I rather agree with Lord Bath when he says he does not see the use of having a large house unless you have the benefit of it and enjoy its capaciousness.

I find everything very nice here in Alice's new home—an ugly house, but comfortable and cosy inside. She looks very happy and seems very well.[1]

Princess Beatrice is supposed to have said in reference to Her Majesty losing Lord Beaconsfield's services: 'Yes, we shall miss him much; he was so kind to Mama.'

Dulcigno matters continue *in statu quo*. If the Sultan has the smallest spark of good feeling left in him, he ought to see to the transfer being completed by Lord Mayor's Day.[2] The Government on that occasion certainly ought to be able to point to its policy abroad having actually borne fruit.

Sunday, 7 November.[3] Returned to Town yesterday. One of the first things that has met my eye is a fresh outburst of Jingoism from Balmoral over a draft despatch to Sir H. Elliot in which Lord G[ranville] sounds Austria as to what should be the next step in the East and expresses a hope that the Concert of Europe may be maintained in regard to the other Turkish questions. H.M. reiterates her inability to approve any policy towards the Porte which is un-settling a question that had, according to her, been laid to sleep for a time. She can only warn and deprecate, but will go as far as declining to give her assent to any active coercion which might lead to war at a time when, what with Ireland and the Cape difficulties, it would be madness for us to land this country into a state of warfare. H.M. again harks upon her *bête noir* Russia, who she considers is playing a double game and into whose hands she main-tains we are playing. This royal effusion is to Lord Granville. Had Mr. G. to answer it, he would say that it would be inconsistent with their duties as Ministers of the Crown were the Cabinet not to 'advise' according to the principles of policy they have all along advocated in and out of office. He would add a hope that such principles may be applied so as to maintain peace, but that no other principles (he is convinced) could maintain it or save the Ottoman Empire, which the Sultan is daily and surely destroying.[4]

Goschen is evidently very anxious to return home. He says he notices a decided change of tone in the attitude of Lord G[ranville], and if there is to be no further application of material pressure on the Porte, which is the only means of making the smallest impression on the Sultan, the game is up, the object for which he was sent out is at an end, and he may therefore just as well come back. Now that we have gone as far as we have—in short, blown hot—it will look very foolish now to blow cold and retire

---

[1] See 6 June and 10 July 1880. [2] 9 Nov.
[3] EWH wrote '*Sunday. 6: Nov:*'.
[4] EWH here paraphrased G.'s letter to Granville, 6 Nov. 1880, in which G. tells Gran-ville how he would have replied to such a letter. Ramm, i. 216–17.

before the triumphant Turk. In short, all that we have got out of the mountainous parturition is the 'ridiculus mus'—Dulcigno—and that only at present in embryo![1]

Monday, 8 November. Mr. G. arrived in Town this afternoon to be ready for the Lord Mayor's dinner tomorrow night. I hear that there never was a greater rush for invitations than on the present occasion, and I feel quite nervous as to what the Great Man may and may not say. The subject on which most interest will naturally be centered is Ireland. Forster's latest reports are certainly bad; last month seems to have been one of the worst months, statistically as regards agrarian crime, since the great famine times. Though diminishing in atrocity, the outrages are gathering strength numerically. Forster is himself still against the suspension of the Habeas Corpus. It would, he maintains, weaken the law of the land, be a bad precedent, and a temptation to rely on despotic power rather than on law. He does not, however, deny that such a step would be effectual. Lords Emly and Monck, also Lord Cowper and Burke, are in favor of resorting to it at once, and Forster himself seems to think that a measure, which will empower the arrest of suspected people, necessary to tide over the winter months, which the Irish Government dread so much. We therefore seem to be 'within a measurable distance' of a summoning of Parliament. Forster thinks good would result were a threat held out that no Land Bill will be forthcoming unless the country is quiet, and this is the line which I want Mr. G. to take up tomorrow night, though I fear he will not, on the ground that the violence of the few must not be allowed to sacrifice the interests of the many.

As regards such a measure—I mean a Land Bill—no shape can be given to it till the Land Commission[2] has reported, but at present Forster goes in for the 3 F's, viz. *f*ree land, *f*air rents, and *f*ixity of tenure. E. O'Brien, son of Smith O'Brien, says there *must* be a strong land measure. He, like Forster, believes that good would result were any remedial measure made conditional on the re-establishment of peace and order. He regards the Land League in the light of wind-bag which when once pricked would disappear. On the whole he approves the prosecutions. Never had a Government a more difficult problem to solve than that of Ireland at the present moment. I am glad I am not responsible for finding a solution. Ireland no doubt is the rock ahead for the Government.

A report has reached Lord Odo Russell that Turkey is seriously thinking of taking steps to secure the services of German officers against another war with Russia. The Porte seems to have more dependence on Germany than on any other Power.[3]

[1] 'parturient montes, nascetur ridiculus mus', Horace, *Ars Poetica*, line 139.
[2] i.e. the Bessborough Commission.
[3] Knaplund, p. 169.

Wednesday, 10 November. There seems to be Turkish intriguing going on in Arabia. Goschen does not attach much importance to it, but there appears to be some unity and continuity of policy in the intrigues. A certain outlaw of India is said to be at the bottom of it—Said Fazl Pasha—on whom the Porte has recently bestowed honours. Goschen has given a hint that two can play the game of currying favor with the Arabs. The Arabian question should no doubt be left in view, as is maintained by Wilfrid Blunt, and all Turkish pretensions to extend Turkish influence in Southern Arabia should be resisted. The Sultan is of course intending to work mischief in India via the Arabs; he is frightened at the possibility of losing the Khalifate.

The Russian military influence in Bulgaria is undoubtedly strong; there are over 700 Russian commissioned and non-commissioned officers in the country. The Bulgarian Prime Minister[1] evidently contemplates union with Eastern Roumelia on the first favourable opportunity, such as war with Greece would offer, and with the union a part of Macedonia would be incorporated. In short the Bulgarians aim at the position assigned to them by the Treaty of San Stephano. Vincent, who reports this, says no fear need be entertained of Russia ever taking Bulgaria. The Bulgarians seem to hate Austria.

It is reported from St. Petersburg that Haymerle's speeches have produced a bad effect in Russia, and the feeling in Russia has suddenly become much changed—more warlike. Jomini now advocates a Russo-English alliance, which is remarkable after the recent statement that Russia could go nowhere alone with England for fear of offending her 'big neighbours'.

The Lord Mayor's dinner last night was a great success so far as Mr. G.'s reception and the speeches generally are concerned. There seems to be a general consensus of opinion that Mr. G. spoke in a statesmanlike way. The banquet no doubt is a fine sight and the occasion most interesting, but it would be difficult to overestimate the badness and paucity of food and the general discomfort entailed by overcrowding. Lord Hartington also spoke well.

There was a Cabinet today. The principal matter discussed was naturally Ireland. No decision was actually come to as regards the necessity for summoning Parliament, but I fear it will have to end in the Government asking Parliament this autumn for some extraordinary powers. The latest reports are bad. In October alone there were 266 outrages—more than the aggregate in the 6 years before 1878—and 80 men are under personal protection.[2] Much as Lord Cowper and Forster dislike the idea of coercion, they are both in favor of the suspension of the Habeas Corpus or some Peace Preservation Act. They prefer the former, which gives power to arrest more summarily. The question will have to be decided this week, as the Council for further proroguing Parliament has to be held on Tuesday next.

---

[1] Dragan Zankoff (or Tsankov).
[2] Wemyss Reid, ii. 263–6.

Friday, 12 November. The question of who is to be Adam's successor at the Office of Works has come to the front again. There is to be consultation about it next week. Trevelyan has written to Lord Hartington urging his claims for office, which are undoubtedly strong; but after having broken company with the last Liberal Government and declining Mr. G.'s offer last April of the Secretaryship at Board of Trade, he has no right to show himself aggrieved. He would do well, I think, at the Works, but there are many alternatives open to the Government. Shaw Lefevre might be put there;[1] F. Cavendish might be moved there (I don't think he would consent to leave the Treasury, so long at any rate as Mr. G. retains Chancellorship of Exchequer); Arthur Peel would not be [an] unsuitable man for the post. Another idea which has been broached is to transfer Enfield from the India Office and put Courtney in Enfield's place; but it would never do to have a peer—the principal *raison d'être* of a First Commissioner is to defend the Works Estimates in House of Commons.

An excellent despatch has been drafted to Governor-General of India[2] on the Kandahar question, the gist of which is this: The Government state their strong objections to the permanent occupation of the place. The primary reason for its retention is not that our relations with the neighbouring tribes make it necessary now, any more than formerly, for us to have a military protectorate over K[andahar], but that it is required as a measure of defence against Russia. The Government, however, has no apprehensions of foreign invasion as would warrant the heavy additional military expenditure, strain the native army, and lead to future complications. As to the advance of Russia in Central Asia, it was foreseen in the days of the 'old frontier' policy and has secured her no additional strength. The difficulties of occupying Afghanistan have been too fully exemplified. The occupation of Kandahar would not only mean the occupation of the place itself but of the surrounding provinces, which would mean 20,000 men probably. Moreover, after expressly stating that the object of the expedition was to punish an act of the Amir and not of the Afghan people, nothing but the strongest necessity for self-preservation could justify the annexation of the people against their will. A scrupulous adherence to declarations will be sure to impress our native allies and remove apprehensions as to the Government being weak. The real thing to do is to restore Kandahar to the Amir and take no account of the Wali. Again, what guarantee have we that we should be able to stop at Kandahar were it acquired? There would rise up fear against *its* security, and then we should have to push on somewhere else. The only reason why the Afghans have preferred, and are likely to prefer, Russia and Persia has been and would be the fear of loss of freedom, which our recent policy has inspired, which if removed

---

[1] Ultimately he was. See 26 and 28 Nov. 1880.
[2] Lord Ripon.

may convert the Afghans into useful allies. Withdrawal then from Kandahar is to be made on the earliest suitable occasion.[1]

It is a great comfort to have such sensible words outspoken. Bitter as may be the pill to swallow for those who have advocated the forward policy, and mortifying as it may be to think that all this blood and money has been expended without tangible results, I am convinced Lord Hartington is right.

The one thing to 'draw' Russia is an allusion to the occupation of the Balkans by the Porte; and it is difficult to avoid it in advocating a strict fulfilment of the provisions of the Treaty of Berlin. The Russians cannot bear being taunted about the matter, and though it is essential that the enforcement of the Treaty should not be one-sided, the Russians no doubt have plausible excuses. They maintain (and there is no reason to doubt their word in this instance) that what they want above all things to do is to avoid a premature explosion in Bulgaria, which according to them would be certain to result from the occupation of the Balkans.

The union with Eastern Roumelia is no doubt what would be popular in Bulgaria. At the same time the Bulgarians seem to be sensible enough of not resorting to any steps which would lead to bloodshed. The Union question seems to depend almost entirely on whether the Porte gets involved in war, say with Greece. Whenever the Union is taken in hand, it is bound to include a great part of Macedonia.

Sunday, 14 November. More agrarian murders, and Lord Cowper has written again very strongly in favor of coercive measures. He seems very apprehensive. He even goes so far as to contemplate the possibility of a general massacre of landlords and agents. Great allowance must of course be made for alarmist notions on the spot, but I don't see how the Government can now avoid having recourse to some such step as the suspension of the Habeas Corpus, or if not how Lord Cowper can avoid resigning. The inclination of the Cabinet last Friday was evidently against the immediate summoning of Parliament. This was the gist of an article in the *Standard* yesterday (which by the way is gradually becoming more friendly towards the Government every day). Mr. G. was much astonished at the article as it expressed so accurately the deliberations of the Cabinet; and who could have prompted it in this way still remains a mystery.[2] It pointed to a sort of compromise; namely, the meeting of Parliament in January.

Thursday, 18 November. Here we are in the midst of a ministerial crisis; early

[1] See the description of and quotations from this dispatch from Hartington to Ripon, 11 Nov. 1880, in Bernard Holland, *The Life of . . . Devonshire* (London, 1911), i. 306–9.
[2] *Standard*, 13 Nov. 1880, p. 4. See 19 Dec. 1880. According to Chamberlain, both he and Forster had intimate connections with the *Standard*, Forster through Mudford, the editor, and Chamberlain through Escott, then a writer for the paper. Joseph Chamberlain, *A Political Memoir 1880–92* (London, 1953) p. 9. See 6 and 10 Apr. 1881.

days for this certainly. It surely never was the fate of a ministry before to be troubled so much in their early career;—first Ireland (last session), then the Montenegrin business, and now Ireland again. The rumours which have been so curiously and mysteriously rife the last few days as to dissensions in the Cabinet are unfortunately too well founded. The question is—Shall there be coercion or not? Forster backed by the Lord Lieutenant declares he cannot be responsible for the government of Ireland without some extraordinary powers. Chamberlain, on the other hand, says that resort to such powers *pur et simple* must entail his resignation, reluctant as he would be to part company with his great Leader. He contends that the proposal to suspend the Habeas Corpus is so wrong in principle and bad in policy, according to his ideas, that he could not even give it silent support; that redress of acknowledged grievances should precede or at any rate accompany the suspension of the safeguards of liberty; that the Irish disaffection proceeds from causes of just complaint and that it is empirical to try and crush it out without first inquiring into and dealing with the causes. He cannot admit that the necessity for destroying the constitution is proved by facts. The actual number of serious outrages due to agrarian discontent is not numerically great. He believes that a definite statement of the intentions of the Government would stay the disaffection and that a suspension of the H[abeas] C[orpus] would not be really effectual. His objections would be modified were it possible to accompany coercive measures with a strong bill; but then comes the difficulty of introducing a measure which must necessarily be at present crude and framed irrespectively of the recommendations of the Land Commission.[1] He suggests that if a coercive measure be absolutely necessary, it might at any rate be possible to insert a clause in it suspending evictions for (say) 3 months.[2]

The question which must be decided tomorrow is certainly a most difficult one. In the interests of the Government it would probably be better that Mr. G. (provided he were supported by Lord Granville and Lord Hartington and the majority of the Cabinet) should split with the head than with the tail, that is, rather with Forster than with Chamberlain, which would include Dilke. On the other hand, it is difficult to set aside the deliberate opinion of those who are directly responsible for the administration of Irish affairs.

Supposing, however, some such compromise were agreed to as a coercive measure accompanied by a remedial measure or a distinct promise of it, there would still be great difficulties in connection with such a course. Apart from the formidable opposition and stubborn obstruction with which the Government would be met by the whole of the Irish party, it would be hardly possible to introduce a coercive bill without referring it to a Select Committee, according to usual precedent. That means a very appreciable addition to delay.

[1] i.e. the Bessborough Commission.
[2] This description of Chamberlain's views EWH drew, often verbatim, from Chamberlain's letter to G., 16 Nov. 1880, quoted in Garvin, i. 328-9.

Moreover, the Introduction of such a measure must be supported by arguments, and how could those arguments not contain pointed references to the action of the Land Leaguers who are on their trial, whose case is *sub judice*, and whose action consequently should not be prejudged?

It would indeed be lamentable if a split cannot be avoided. A few hours will, however, put us out of our suspense.

Friday, 19 November. The crisis is, I fear, hardly over. A *modus vivendi* has, it is true, been provided for the moment, for the simple reason that matters remain much *in statu quo*, no definite decision having been arrived at, and (in order to meet the immediate necessity) Parliament having been prorogued till Thursday the 2nd December in the ordinary way, that is, without reference to 'despatch of business'.

A memorandum which Mr. G. circulated yesterday about referring any coercive bill to a Select Committee came back this morning, and, as it drew out the views of most of the Cabinet, one is enabled to see better how the ministerial land lies.

Lord Granville and Lord Hartington would evidently like to dispense with resort to coercion but feel the difficulty of doing so in view of the assertion of the Irish Government that they cannot without some special powers undertake to maintain peace and order.[1]

Sir W. Harcourt thinks coercion would be fatal to the Government and the party, and hopes in the interests of the Government and party Forster will see his way to do without it. He doubts whether a sufficient case has been made out for having recourse to such strong measures as a suspension of the Habeas Corpus Act. He would, however, bow to the decision of the majority of his colleagues. What is politic, and not what is really right, is evidently uppermost in his mind.

Lord Spencer thinks that what is required is that a case should be made out for general coercive steps. He is, however, against attaching too much weight to outside opinion; and, on the face of it, some parts of Ireland, according to his views, clearly point to the necessity of coercive measures.

Childers is in favour of the Habeas Corpus being suspended as soon as a Land Bill can be introduced—say early in January, or if that is not possible he thinks that any coercive measure should be accompanied by resolutions pledging the Government to a large remedial measure.

Duke of Argyll desires to support the Irish Government, but considers that every possible concession should be made all round to prevent disagreement, as he regards it as little short of being 'shameful' that there should be a split in these early days of the Administration.

---

[1] Hartington wrote G. on 19 Nov. 1880 that he would have to resign if the Government did not give Forster the extra powers he thought necessary. Bernard Holland, *The Life of . . . Devonshire* (London, 1911), i. 330.

Chamberlain cannot believe that the suspension of the Habeas Corpus would be efficacious.

The Cabinet did not sit for long this afternoon, and separated as above stated without coming to any definite decision beyond proroguing Parliament for a week, and thus giving time for further reflection. This will at any rate make it clear to the outside world that unremitting attention is being given by the Government to the state of Ireland and act as a warning to the Irish folk that unless they behave some ulterior measures will be forthcoming.

In his letter to the Queen[1] Mr. Gladstone remarked that the Irish matter was one of greater complexity and difficulty than ever he remembered throughout his experience as a Cabinet Minister since 1843. He wrote at greater length than usual, which was partly to make up for what H.M. considered very meagre news in his account of the last Cabinet.[2] He referred to the advantage which would attach to the Government being able to proceed simultaneously with land reforms in Ireland, which were probably necessary, and any measure for maintaining order such as might become indispensable. As to the prosecutions, if they failed, they would strengthen the hands of the Government in proposing coercion; if they succeeded, the state of affairs could not fail to be improved thereby. Mr. Gladstone drew attention to the fact that the agrarian offences against property had increased, yet those endangering life so far from increasing had on the contrary somewhat diminished, and consequently it would be difficult at present to show that anything had happened to justify the supersession of the determination of the Government since the Guildhall speech.[3] Whatever differences of opinion there may be in the Cabinet are apparently solely due to the doubt as to the efficaciousness of the suspension of the H[abeas] C[orpus]. It is assumed that Parnell & Co. could not be arrested while their case is still *sub judice*. It might take some of the small 'tools' out of the country, and by their removal civilised rights, now paralysed, might be revived. On the other hand, the conspiracy against property is too widely spread to be repressed by the very limited way in which arbitrary imprisonment could be put in force by the suspension of the Habeas Corpus.

Tuesday, 23 November. The chief event within the last few days has been the death of Lord Chief Justice Cockburn. His end was very sudden, and so he was probably spared the mortifying thought that he would have to surrender his high office to Mr. Gladstone, of whom he for long seems to have entertained so deadly an aversion. I believe the aversion owed its origin to his not being made Lord Chancellor by Mr. G. in 1868. His moral life was supposed at the time to put him out of court for holding the Great Seals. An attempt was made at the time, as I have always understood, to gild this pill for him

---

[1] Guedalla, ii. 122–4.   [2] Ibid., p. 121.
[3] i.e. G.'s speech at the Lord Mayor's banquet, 9 Nov. 1880.

by the offer of a peerage; but that he declined it on the ground that if he was not good enough to be made Lord Chancellor, he was not good enough to be made a peer.[1]

The Attorney General[2] has waived whatever right he may possess to the reversion of the Lord Chief Justiceship so as to enable an important reform to be carried out, namely to have one Lord Chief Justice only in the person of Lord Coleridge transferred from the Common Pleas and to have all the other judges Puisne judges.[3]

The all important question about Ireland stands over for Thursday, when the Cabinet will really have to make up their minds. Forster has gone over to Dublin again, and I shall be surprised if he comes back less keen for coercive measures, to which the Queen thinks it high time to have resort.[4] Lord Spencer, who is a calm sensible-minded man and whose opinion on Ireland is from his lengthened experience at the Viceregal Lodge entitled to considerable weight, wrote yesterday and expressed himself very strongly in favor of coercion. All things considered, I have come to the reluctant conclusion that the Government ought to try the effect of suspending the Habeas Corpus, and on the introduction of such a measure move certain resolutions pledging the Government on general terms to a Land measure, of which all men from Conservative landlords downwards seem to admit the necessity. Such a course ought to get over the scruples of Chamberlain and Bright about coercion. If I had, however, to prophecy, I should say the Cabinet will decide to postpone the summoning of Parliament and the taking of action till January. This would probably involve losing Forster.

Wednesday, 24 November. Lord Cowper has written again. It appears that he and Forster feel so strongly in favor of trying the effect of suspending the Habeas Corpus that unless some coercive measures are taken they will have to resign. They will, however, postpone doing so till January, by which time at any rate it is probable that something will have to be done in that line. So by this means we shall probably avoid losing them, which would be very awkward.

Several appointments have been submitted to Her Majesty today,—Lord Odo Russell for his peerage, Lord Herries for the Lord Lieutenancy of East Riding of Yorkshire in the room of the late Lord Wenlock, and Lord Coleridge for Lord Chief Justiceship.

Heard from Henry Primrose today. He says it enrages him to think how the folly of Lytton & Co. could have gratuitously involved us in all this trouble and expense in Afghanistan, and that what surprises him most is to find how few people now have a word to say for the 'scientific frontier'. He had always supposed that the Anglo-Indian was a worse Jingo than his

[1] Ramm, *Gladstone–Granville Correspondence, 1868–76*, i. 1–2.   [2] Sir Henry James.
[3] See 22 Sept. 1880.   [4] Guedalla, ii. 124–5.

brother of the English public service, but that one does not often meet anyone in India who thinks the Lyttonian policy was right.

Friday, 26 November. The final die on the immediate Irish question was cast
yesterday by the Cabinet. Parliament is not to be summoned till the 1st week
in January. This will enable the Government to approach the question as
a whole. By that time they will have been able to shape to some extent their
Land Bill; and accordingly will be able to proceed, if necessary, *pari passu*
with remedial and repressive measures. The ministerial crisis for the moment
is accordingly over, and the Cabinet ministers are again a happy family.
They don't meet again before the 15th of next month.

Mr. G. expressed his view on the situation in a letter to the Speaker yesterday. This was the gist of it:—the Irish question is supposed by some to be
simple and would be solved by clapping 2 or 3 scores into prison without the
necessity for bringing them to trial. This is not his opinion. The immediate
duty of the Government is most difficult; there are so many circumstances to
be taken into consideration. There is the novelty of suspending the Habeas
Corpus for agrarian crime stimulated by a *public* society; and the rather
serious difficulty of obtaining Parliamentary sanction to such a course; and
still more there is the grave doubt whether it would reach the great characteristic of the state of affairs, namely, the paralysis of the most important civil
and proprietary rights, and whether the immediate proposal of a remedy,
probably ineffective and even in a coercive sense partial, would not seriously
damage the prospects of that arduous and comprehensive task which without
doubt Parliament will have to undertake.[1]

The postponement of any active measures to reduce the chaotic condition of
affairs to order imposes a horrible responsibility on the Government in the event
of matters getting worse, of which the most sensible and moderate-minded
men are apprehensive; for even did such measures as suspending the Habeas
Corpus prove ineffective, at any rate the Government would then have a
clear conscience of having done the utmost within the power of the Executive.

There is of course the hope that the Land Leagues will, so far as outrages
are concerned, do their best to prevent their band from resorting to violence
when they see that actual aggression for the moment is not aimed at them;
and moreover there is not the risk of retaliatory measures, which might ensue
from immediate coercion.

Shaw Lefevre is to be offered the First Commissionership of Works.[2] He
has earned his promotion; and George Trevelyan is to succeed him at the
Admiralty. No exception, I think, can be taken to these appointments, and
one disappointed man[3] will be provided for, which is something.

[1] This letter to Mr. Speaker Brand, 25 Nov. 1880, is printed in part in Morley, iii. 51.
[2] See 25 Aug., 11, 22 Sept., 8 Oct., 12 and 28 Nov. 1880.
[3] i.e. Trevelyan. See 12 Nov. 1880.

Lord Odo Russell's name has been submitted for his peerage; and the Queen has approved, but she evidently is rather annoyed to think that Lord Odo should accept what he refused to receive at the hands of the late Government.[1]

Dulcigno is practically surrendered at last. Whatever may be sent [*sic*] to the contrary, the cession is an undoubted triumph for the policy of an united coercion, even if only threatened.

Goschen is to come home for a fortnight, but is prepared to go out again for a month or two. A talk over matters will come opportunely.

Sunday, 28 November. Mr. G. left Town yesterday. He proceeded first to Windsor for the Council and an audience; and then went on to Hawarden.

George Lefevre has accepted the First Commissionership of Works, though he seems rather jumpy about the probability of having a contest at Reading.

Dulcigno has been actually surrendered, and yesterday afternoon there arrived a telegram from the Prince of Montenegro to Mr. G. thanking him for having taken the initiative in settling this vexed question. The cession came in opportunely for Lord Granville who had to speak yesterday down in the Pottery country.

There are rumours that Lord Salisbury intends joining the 'Fourth Party' and throwing over Lord Beaconsfield. I can believe anything of that man.

Monday, 29 November. Mr. G. is beginning to ruminate over his Budget for next year. He wants to go in for a fling at the Death Duties—probate and legacy. He said the other day he should like to tackle them by way of making a *final* financial stroke. That means that as at present minded he only intends retaining the Chancellorship of the Exchequer over one more Budget.

Lord Odo Russell is back at Berlin. He says that Bismarck virtually directs the foreign policy of France and Austria, and that he is becoming more all-powerful than ever in Germany, the old Emperor having lost the power even of passive resistance. His main object seems to be to obtain the leadership of the European concert;—(his jealousy of Mr. G. is peeping out again) —so that he may be playing first fiddle in the event of a collapse at Constantinople.[2]

Tuesday, 30 November. It seems that Her Majesty was very 'kindly and agreeable' at the audience she gave Mr. G. last Saturday, and that as to Ireland she was quite fair and willing to listen to reason. She appears to have rather shied at Trevelyan's appointment at the Admiralty. H.M. and Mr. G. both forgot to mention the Odo Russell peerage case.[3]

---

[1] The Queen wrote Beaconsfield, 1 Dec. 1880: 'I was much surprised, and I *may* say, annoyed when Mr. Gladstone proposed a peerage for Lord Odo Russell *just* as if it had *never* been *mentioned* before, . . .', *Letters*, 2nd ser. iii. 160–1. See 7 Sept. 1880.

[2] Knaplund, pp. 170–1.

[3] See 7 Sept. and 26 Nov. 1880. The audience took place on 27 Nov. See also Ramm, i. 222–3.

The Irish land question evidently weighs heavily on Mr. G. The failure of the Act of 1870 seems to be a grievous disappointment. He had hoped that he had touched the question once and for all. He thinks it is going to be a great crux for the Government, which certainly it will be. He is afraid of Forster 'getting a twist'. Forster is evidently in favor of very strong measures. Mr. G., on the other hand, would like to proceed temperately on the lines and basis of the old act. What he would prefer would be practical security for the tenant rather than theoretical fixity. His mind is turning on free sale by tenant of interest in his occupation. He favours Judge Longfield's scheme, which was detailed in the *Fortnightly Review* of August or September last, whereby the Irish occupier would be given increased security of tenure, and yet the mischief of recurrent state interference for determining rents would be avoided.[1] He dreads a seriously divided report of the Land Commission.

I am afraid from what I hear that Adam left the country for India rather hurt. He seems to have considered that his 'whipping work' was insufficiently appreciated and requited. He wanted a peerage.

There have of late curiously been some leakages.[2] My own belief is that men like Chamberlain and Forster (specially) are most unguarded in their language outside. I heard tonight for instance that in applying for more troops for Ireland he[3] remarked to Sir Charles Ellis that the sooner civil war came the better!

Lord Beaconsfield's *Endymion* has, of course, excited immense curiosity, but it does not seem to be at all up to the mark of *Coningsby* or even *Lothair*.

Thursday, 2 December. Mr. G. is hard at work devolving something in the shape of a Land Bill. He says fixity of tenure does not improve on nearer acquaintance.

I had an interview this afternoon with Mr. Errington M.P.—a moderate Home Ruler. He takes a gloomy view of affairs in Ireland. I was surprised to learn that he was so in favor of coercive measures. He expressed his belief that the suspension of the Habeas Corpus a month or two ago would have arrested the evil, and as things now are the only course to take is to 'run' two measures side by side the moment Parliament meets—one [a] coercive measure on the principle of the Westmeath Act;[4] the other a remedial measure, a strong Land Bill based on the '3 F.'s'. I feel convinced it will have to come to

[1] M. Longfield, 'Land Tenure in Ireland', *Fortnightly Review*, 1 Aug. 1880, xxviii (New Series), pp. 137–46. Longfield proposed in opposition to Ulster tenant right a scheme that he called 'parliamentary tenant right', which would provide by statute for ten years' tenure at a freely determined rent and a payment of 7 years' purchase for the tenant right by the landlord on the termination of occupancy.

[2] For example, see 14 Nov. 1880.

[3] i.e. Forster.

[4] This act of 1871 (34 & 35 Vict., c. 25) gave the Viceroy and Chief Secretary the power to commit without trial anyone suspected of being a member of the Ribbon Society in the county of Westmeath and a few adjacent areas.

this, and I am not at all sure now that it won't go hard with the Government for not already taking such steps. Mr. Errington fully anticipates that the Lords will throw out any strong land measure, and that we shall have to appeal to the country in the autumn next year. He said Sir Charles Dilke shares his opinion.

The Carnarvonshire election was very satisfactory.[1]

Goschen has written at length his views on the Greek situation. He hopes the Government will not dissuade the Greeks from going to war; for what reward will she get in return for moderation? She must make an effort and run a risk as Italy did. He has a scheme which is that we should promote negotiations between Greeks and Albanians. He believes that the accession of a large part of Albania by a dynastic tie would be of infinitely greater importance to Greece than the disputed possession of Epirus. Albania would be of great use to Greece; and yet Greece would with her superior intelligence be able to hold her own and would be the governing power. He thinks that the union of Greece and Albania would, from an European point of view, be of great advantage as a counterbalancing force to the Slavs. Albania, as it is, is quite out of the Porte's hands. Mr. G. does not 'mislike' (as he terms it) this idea.[2]

Saturday, 4 December. There are few subjects, out of the many which the Great Man studies and is conversant with, which interest him so much as theology, or of which he knows more. You have only to send him a tract or book on some disputed point of theology, and you are sure to draw him for an answer. He won't, however, admit that he is fond of polemics and refers to 'Vatican Decrees'[3] as his solitary performance in this respect. He believes more harm than good is done by proselytism. He regards Christianity as on its trial.[4]

Willie Compton continues to write despondingly of the state of things subsisting in Ireland; and outrages, according to the latest made up account, have undoubtedly increased, but fortunately almost entirely in respect of *property* and not life, which marks the leading feature of the present agitation.

To turn to foreign affairs. A lengthy and well drawn up despatch is just going out to Vienna reviewing the situation and the relations between this country and Austria. It appears that Austria still declares that she sees no reason why her policy should separate her from the English Government, and

---

[1] Charles James Watkin Williams, M.P. for Carnarvonshire, vacated his seat as a result of being appointed to the Bench. William Rathbone, a Liberal, beat his Conservative opponent 3,180 to 2,151 in the by-election on 29 Nov. 1880.

[2] Ramm, i. 226.

[3] i.e. G.'s pamphlet *The Vatican Decrees in their Bearing on Civil Allegiance. A Political Expostulation*, which was published in Nov. 1874.

[4] EWH here echoes what G. wrote in a letter to Margaret deLisle on 30 Nov. 1880, copy, Add. MS. 44544, f. 102, in reply to her letter of 27 Nov. 1880 accompanying a copy of Abbé Martin's book on *Anglican Ritualism*, Add. MS. 44467, ff. 62–3.

that she does not abandon the cause of Greece. She thinks, however, that the Concert of Europe which she still favours should be of a purely diplomatic character. Her primary consideration is peace, and she still believes in the efficacy of steady moral pressure on the Porte. She doubts if the Greeks have the power to fight the Turks, or that any other Power would single-handed undertake an expedition in aid of Greece. Lord Granville thinks that the Concert should be one in which each Power should place in due subordination its smaller direct interests and concentrate its efforts on general points of great magnitude. He disabuses Austria of the idea she seems to entertain that, while she is all for peace, this country is burning for war. He reminds her that the extension of the naval demonstration for the Greek question was agreed to by all the Powers. He is prepared to recommend prudence and moderation to Greece, but the question is, does Europe abandon or maintain the Berlin decisions, and on this depends whether encouragement can in good faith be offered to Greece if she keeps quiet.

For any real progress in the Greek question, Mr. G. considers that there are but two contingencies to look to. One, a change in the line of the French Government; the other, the pressure which Greece may bring to bear on Europe by going to war.[1]

Sunday, 5 December. There is a further despatch going out to India. Hope is expressed that it may be found unnecessary to prolong the occupation of Kandahar beyond the winter, and the Home Government consider that the arguments against the retention of Kandahar apply equally to Pishin. So we shall be retiring from that place as well before long probably, and thus after spending some £17,000,000 of public money in marauding expeditions, get home again. As Lord Hartington forcibly points out, the true defence of India consists not in the acquisition of strategic positions at a distance from our frontier, nor in competition for influence in Central Asia with any other Power, but in the good government of India itself, the development of her resources, and the perfecting of her military organisation.

Tuesday, 7 December. The Irish 'soup' (as Mr. Gladstone terms it) is 'thickening' and becoming what the brewers would call 'Treble X'.

In writing to Mr. Bright, Mr. G. says the question as regards the Irish land problem is whether to act on the principles of the Land Act of 1870 and limit the exercise of proprietary rights for the safety of the country, or whether to set out on a new principle and convert the landlord virtually into a rent-charger or incumbrancer and give over in the main to the occupiers a proprietary character.

Mr. G. is evidently alarmed at the outcome of the inquiry of the Land

[1] Ramm, i, 226–7.

Commissioners.[1] They are divided in opinion, and accordingly, instead of being assisted in solving the Irish problem, the Government may be only embarrassed by them.

Dowse seems to be in favour of the '3 F.'s'—fixity of tenure on a rent determined periodically by a Land Court.

On the other [hand], the O'Conor Don[2] regards a compulsory measure of that kind to be sure to work injustice to the landlords and to fail to give satisfaction. He is convinced that what is wanted is extended ownership rights, of which owing to their being possessed by so few are very imperfectly understood. The '3 F.'s', according to him, would, as undoubtedly it must, convert the landlords into rent-chargers, which would be tantamount to making them mere tax receivers. Moreover, fixity of tenure and fair rents are next to an impossibility because of the dissimilarity of rents and the necessity of raising some. He thinks it would be much better to buy out the landlords (not compulsorily) by the intervention of the State and to sell back to the occupiers at low rents. He is convinced that no smaller measure will be of any real avail.

Mr. G. regards such a plan as wild and cannot think that either the Cabinet or Parliament would agree to confiscate or charge the English Exchequer with a huge liability as the price of a Land Act.

Wednesday, 8 December. Lord O. Russell appears to be delighted with the Hanley speech of Lord Granville. A compliment seems to have a magic effect on the most conceited man of the most conceited nation. Lord O. R[ussell] believes that Bismarck will now wish to be on intimate terms with the English Government, so as to share the laurels with them in carrying out the Berlin award.[3]

Thursday, 9 December. Forster's ideas for a remedial measure proceed on the basis that we must admit the contest between law and equity in the ownership of land in Ireland. That is, the law makes the landlord sole owner; equity makes the tenant part-owner, because he has given to land much of present value. But if for Ireland, why not for England? Provided the tenant in Ireland be given substantial credit for all improvements, the only argument for drawing a distinction between England and Ireland presumably consists in the fact that in the latter country the proprietor of the soil holds to a very large extent the monopoly of means of 'liveable' employment; that is, that while in England agricultural employment is only one of many employments, in

---

[1] i.e. the members of the Bessborough Commission.

[2] Dowse, a judge of the Irish High Court, and the O'Conor Don (Charles Owen O'Conor) were members of the Bessborough Commission.

[3] See Russell's letter to Granville, 4 Dec. 1880, Knaplund, pp. 171–2. Granville spoke at Hanley on 27 Nov. 1880 and praised Germany for her restraint in relation to the Eastern question and her loyalty to the Concert of Europe and the decisions of the Berlin Conferences.

Ireland it is almost the sole employment, and the State has a right to inter-fere and practically take away a part of the proprietary rights of a landlord, quâ holding a monopoly.

Forster has no hope of being able to dispense with a Coercion Bill. He says the Land League rules and rules by fear of outrages, as the law when upheld rules by fear of punishment. The organisation of the League is so complete that it will not avail merely to put down meetings and prevent speeches. His programme is to mention coercion and land reform in the Queen's speech, give immediate notice of a Coercion Bill and also resolutions pledging the Government to amend the land laws, proceed with the former, and on its passing introduce the remedial measure.

Mr. G. practically accepts Forster's programme.

Bright thinks it is clear that Parnell & Co. want to provoke revolt, and that their purpose is more revolution than mere reform of the land system. If this is so, he might consistently be a little less sentimental about suspending constitutional rights.

Friday, 10 December. The latest letter which came to hand here of Forster's was calculated to make one feel most uneasy. The outrages in Ireland are, he says, greatly on the increase, and he maintains that his warning against allow-ing the Executive to be defied has already been more than justified. He thinks it has become a question of whether Parliament ought not be summoned at once without waiting for the 6th prox°. Every week makes the restoration to order more difficult. This is what I have always felt, and that in this consisted the enormous responsibility undertaken by the Government of postponing taking action. In commenting upon the deplorable state of the community, Mr. G. asks whether there is no hope of the community itself doing something against the League, of some strong countre-association? The landlords only howl and whine.

Since the morning it appears that Forster has pressed for an early Cabinet, and I received a telegram to summon one for Monday. If it comes really to a question of immediately calling together Parliament, what will be said, and rightly said, of the vacillating course of the Government?

As an instance of the extraordinary versatility of the Great Man, it is worth noting down that while he is 'up to the eyes' in this Irish business, while he is ruminating over Death Duties, and has to get through all his ordinary work and correspondence, he finds time to go through the Memoirs of Mr. Herries, once Chancellor of the Exchequer, father of Sir C. Harries, and has written to Sir C. H[erries] 3 letters criticising historical points, evidently having com-pletely mastered the 2 volumes.[1]

[1] Edward Herries, *Memoir of the Public Life of the Right Hon. J. C. Herries . . . with an Introduction by Sir C. Herries,* 2 vols., London, 1880. In fact G. wrote four letters to Herries about the *Memoir* between 3 and 9 Dec. 1880. See copies, Add. MS. 44544, ff. 105, 106, 108.

Sunday, 12 December. Lord Dufferin yesterday sent a valuable and interesting contribution to the Irish land question in the shape of an exhaustive memorandum. He maintains that if the landlords are converted into rent-chargers, which would be the effect by the adoption of the '3 F.'s', the change will quickly be followed by a strike against all rent on the first available plea of a bad harvest or American competition. The '3 F.'s' mean nothing short of turning the Irish tenantry into copyholders and the complete severance of owners from the control of their property. Landlords would, in short, be worse off than the mortgagee. They would get lower interest and be subject to the operation of bad seasons, and at the same time to the disagreeableness of ejectment as the final 'amenity'. Again, supposing the landlord has bought up the tenant right, is it to be returned to the tenant? Moreover, the present occupiers would pocket large sums to which they are not properly entitled. The '3 F.'s' would, too, hit the peasant proprietor. The Land Act, of course, might be amended in certain respects, as for example, by regarding a rise of rent as a disturbance and enlarging the provisions of the equity clause by setting up a travelling court to superintend the operation of the Act. The real thing to aim at is to extend ownership. Let the rent represent the interest of the capital employed by the State for this purpose, and let it be converted into a fixed charge or land rate colligible by local authorities, more or less on the Russian system.

Wednesday, 15 December.[1] I have not had a moment to jot down any of the events of this interesting week.

The Cabinet met on Monday. They listened to Forster's tale, and a sorry tale it must have been. They were all united as to the necessity of resorting to coercion; but what with the Land League trials and the Christmas holidays, it was not deemed advisable to accelerate the meeting of Parliament before the 6th prox°. The Government will then introduce at once a measure to suspend the Habeas Corpus or to give the Executive other and more efficacious special powers, accompanying such a measure with the promise of a Land Bill. The Government will not, I think, go in for the '3 F.'s', except in some modified form on the lines of the Act of '70, with special provision to create a more extensive system of peasant proprietorship. I should be afraid the measure may be one that will please nobody and displease everybody. I wish the Government could see its way to going in for some more drastic plan, more on the principle of O'Conor Don's and Lord Dufferin's views, which would give landlords a chance, if they pleased, of getting out of their property on fair and reasonable terms. But Mr. G. seems to think such a scheme too wild. He admits that Lord D[ufferin]'s suggestions command his sympathy, but he is against expropriation of landlords covert or open. He thinks tenant right should consist of the right to transfer by assignment, two things,—one,

---

[1] EWH wrote '*Wednesday. Dec: 16:*'.

his (the tenant's) improvements; the other, his interest in his occupation as a means of livelihood. The question of what constitutes property in hand must not be begged. He seems to be inclined to define it thus: that a proprietor is the person who either occupies or has the choice of occupying; and that, once part with that choice, and the occupier ceases to be proprietor. Hence, he thinks, has probably been the origin of long leases. He gave an instance the other day of a miracle in the way of leases. He said Lord Meath is his own sub-tenant under 4000 years' lease![1]

One of the most extraordinary parts of the present state of Ireland is the utter helplessness of the right-minded part of the community. Why cannot they make some countre-combination against the League. All the government on earth cannot do for a community certain things that it ought to do for itself.

Friday, 17 December. Ministers have dispersed again after yesterday's Council, at which they seem to have discussed the provision for a new Ballot Bill specially intended to check corrupt practices and lessen election expenses, and also Childers' army reform proposals, which have for their main object the lengthening of service with the Colours, the establishment of what Mr. G. calls 'double battalioned territorial regiments,' the abolition of honorary colonelcies, and the improvement of the status of non-commissioned officers. The Cabinet also, of course, talked much of Ireland and considered the best means whereby to extend the system of a peasant proprietary. I believe Bright's and Chamberlain's schemes are very wild. They would buy up properties wholesale at an expenditure of some £5,000,000 a year, out of which to carve small holdings or rather properties. Such schemes, of course, cannot be entertained. The British tax-payer must be taken into consideration as well as the Irish peasant.

I heard on excellent authority yesterday that the figure lately cut by Forster at the Athenaeum has been painful in the extreme. He seems to have been conducting himself more like an inebriated or demented man than one merely who has lost his nerves, and to have talked wildly and confusedly before men like Morley and Chenery, as if he had not been conscious of their presence. No wonder such extraordinary rumours get abroad, and such stories leak out.

Lord Cowper seems to be losing the confidence of the Government as Lord Lieutenant and to be wholly unequal to present emergencies. One may well ask, how will he be equal to manage affairs when Forster and the Law Officers have to be over here in attendance on Parliament? Forster is supposed to have made it a condition of his accepting the Chief Secretaryship that he should have a cypher as Viceroy. His condition seems to be in course of strict fulfil-ment. Childers has hinted strongly at the desirability of removing Lord C[owper].

[1] Ramm, i. 229.

The Irish Executive from the Lord Lieutenant down to the lowest constable seems to be completely paralysed. What answer will there be to the attack, if made, on the helplessness of the Irish Government to make any material use of the extraordinary powers they already possess? The constabulary seem to be entirely cowed. This was fully confirmed by Lord Kenmare's agent, whom I saw the other day, and more than borne out by facts, when with all the outrages committed, the threatening letters received, and the terrorism exercised, not a single arrest is made! Mr. Hussey, the agent, like Lord Kenmare, is a refugee in this country. He takes the most despondent of views of the situation. He looks upon the Land Act of '70 as a dead failure and scouts the idea of any extension of tenant right. He thinks the threat of the suspension of the Habeas Corpus may lead to retaliatory measures. The only remedy he has the least faith in is peasant proprietorship.

I saw Boycott by the by last week, whose name has now become a household word and has been foisted into the dictionary. He came to present a letter appealing for Government aid, not, however, with much expectation of getting it. He looked a surly little beggar, calculated to incur any amount of odium of his fellow creatures.

It came round to my eyes yesterday that Lord G[ranville] said that no other human being could have kept the Cabinet together over the Irish business save Mr. G. himself, whose tact and influence with others is something certainly extraordinary.

Mr. and Mrs. G. seem to have been pleased with their visit to Windsor, and said Her Majesty was very gracious and kind.

Camperdown is to be offered Fife's place. I doubt Camperdown accepting. I think he is too aggrieved.[1] Fife, though he does not swerve from his allegiance to the party, was evidently a little mortified at Enfield's being preferred to him for the India Office. This is probably the true explanation of his throwing up his Household appointment.[2]

Sunday, 19 December. (Wilton) There have been some very disagreeable leakages lately, and I believe they must be in the main traceable to Chamberlain and Forster. The articles in the *Standard* have over and over again been under evident inspiration, and I understand Chamberlain has an intimate liaison with the Editor.[3] In evidence of Chamberlain's indiscreetness, Pembroke casually told me last night that while he was staying at Lady Lothian's 3 weeks or so ago, during the time of the penultimate sittings of the Cabinet, [John] Morley, who was of the party, made no secret of having received from Chamberlain the following telegram—'Situation unchanged; no coercion.'

---

[1] See 10 July and 30 Dec. 1880.   [2] See 8 Oct. and 28 Dec. 1880.
[3] W. H. Mudford. The *Standard* printed what purported to be the text of the Land Bill agreed upon by the Cabinet. See Joseph Chamberlain, *A Political Memoir 1880–92* (London, 1953), pp. 9–10, for Chamberlain's exoneration of himself and Forster.

If Chamberlain can be guilty of such indiscretions and Forster can blurt out his anxieties so openly,[1] no wonder we have revelations of Cabinet secrets.

Mr. G. can't get over Bright's and Chamberlain's wild land schemes. He said in writing to the Duke of Argyll yesterday that their scheme was certainly the most naif (he reserved all more pungent epithets) that he ever heard promulgated, nay the most naif by far.

Apropos of rumours that by way of solving the Greek question a countre-proposal has been or is being put forward that Crete should be handed over to Greece in lieu of Thessaly and Epirus, Mr. G. evidently thinks that after all that has been said and done it should be impossible to have those provinces as they now are under direct government of the Porte; that they ought at least to have a tributary autonomy. The idea has crossed his mind whether we might not hand over Cyprus to Greece.[2]

Wednesday, 22 December. (Wilton) All the delights of this place with its hunting and shooting cannot drive that wretched Ireland out of my head; and I am not made more comfortable today by hearing from Downing St. that Lord Hartington has written pressing *strongly* the necessity of immediate and very effective repressive measures in Ireland when Parliament meets. Indeed, without these he could no longer remain in the Government as he has not approved one single step (except the institution of legal proceedings) which has been so far taken, or not taken.[3] I am not surprised. I only wonder that he has not spoken out his mind sooner, and I think it is much to be regretted that he has not done so. No single member of the Cabinet, bar its head, is entitled to speak with as much weight as he is. I am willing to admit that taking everything into consideration there was much to be said against the Government plunging hurriedly into coercion. They were bound to give a fair trial to a policy of not resorting to unconstitutional means. They were even bound, I think, to take into account the serious consequences of a split in the Cabinet, followed as it might have been by a downfall of the Government at a time when of all others it was impossible to appeal to the constituencies, and followed as it must have been by a greatly weakened Government at a time when of all others a strong Government is required. But a fortnight ago, when Forster unfolded his latest tale and renewed his appeal for extraordinary measures, I think it would have been far wiser at all risk and inconvenience to summon Parliament at once. (It might have been then sitting today). It would have shewn the country that the Government was really impressed with the gravity of the situation and were determined not to let Ireland get completely out of hand, which seems to be the risk now that the Government is running. I don't believe that the party will withdraw

---

[1] See 17 Dec. 1880.   [2] Ramm, i. 230.
[3] Hartington's letter of 19 Dec. 1880 is printed in Bernard Holland, *The Life of* . . . *Devonshire* (London, 1911), i. 334–6.

its support from the Government, because a change of Government would be fatal to mending the present state of affairs and would be playing directly into the hands of the Land League. But I am very apprehensive—and this I feel very keenly—that the Cabinet and more especially the Great Man himself cannot possibly emerge with credit out of the crisis.

We are threatened with troubles in the Transvaal. The Boers have set up a republic.[1] This means either fighting or surrendering—not pleasant alternatives.

Monday, 27 December. Back again in the Metropolis. Transvaal matters promise to give trouble. We have had another Isandhlwana[2] on a smaller scale, and a regiment surprised and cut to pieces.[3] We shall be driven to send out reinforcements. I only hope that when we have retrieved the disaster we shall be able to surrender what we had no business ever to have taken. All our troubles in South Africa I believe arise from a total neglect of affairs in that part of the world by the Home Government while their time was wholly monopolised by their Imperial policy in Eastern Europe and India.

Courtney has been offered the Under-Secretaryship at the Home Office in place of A. Peel, resigned on account of health. I am rather sorry the offer has been made, for desirable though it is to secure his services, it looks rather like an attempt to buy up his opposition by office.[4]

Irish affairs remain *in statu quo.* The Queen has again expressed herself strongly against the announcement of any details whatever regarding a remedial measure till a Coercion Bill has been passed and the supremacy of the law been reasserted. She finds much fault, though it is rather late in the day, with Bright and Chamberlain for their recent speeches.[5] It is probable that her mind has been turned to this by Lord Carnarvon's public letter to Bright the other day, which seemed wholly uncalled for and written in bad taste.[6]

Mr. G. is evidently somewhat low in his mind about Ireland and the situation of the Government. It will evidently require all his and Lord G[ranville]'s tact to keep up a spirit of entire concord in the Cabinet. Any withdrawal, however, now from resort to coercive measures would entail the resignation of the whole of the Whig element of the Cabinet.

Bright has answered Lord Carnarvon today very characteristically.

---

[1] The proclamation of the Republic was the result of a great gathering of the Boers at Paardekraal, 13–15 Dec. 1880. The Transvaal had been annexed on 12 Apr. 1877.

[2] The battle of Isandhlawana, 22 Jan. 1879, was, for the British, the most disastrous engagement of the Zulu War.

[3] On 20 Dec. 1880 250 men of the 94th Regiment were surprised and over 100 of them killed by the Boers between Middelburg and Pretoria. *Annual Register,* 1880, pp. 332–3.

[4] See 23 May, 25 Aug., and 28, 29, 30, 31 Dec. 1880.　　[5] Guedalla, ii. 127–8.

[6] In a long letter dated 8 Dec. and published in *The Times* on 24 Dec. 1880, p. 6, Carnarvon criticized Bright's speech on Ireland delivered before the Birmingham Liberal Club on 16 Nov. 1880. Bright replied in a letter to *The Times,* 28 Dec. 1880, p. 7.

Tuesday, 28 December. Courtney has accepted the Under-Secretaryship at Home Office in spite of the exceptions he has taken to part of the policy of the Government. He has made a reservation as regards the Transvaal—that is, that he must abstain from supporting the Government on that question—which Mr. G. has accepted. Courtney will add strength to the Government, no doubt; but it savours of a purchase of valuable support by a bribe. Moreover, it puts Fife's chances out of court, and I should have been glad to see his political services rewarded, though Harcourt was evidently averse to the proposal. He was huffed at Fife not notifying to him his resignation, and maintains that Fife manifested no interest in his office work and would never come near the place.

Stuart Rendel has been offered and has accepted the duties of moving the Address. Armitstead has been asked to second it, but has not sufficient confidence in himself to undertake the task.

A despatch from St. Petersburg represents on good authority that war between Germany and Russia is inevitable on death of Czar, if not sooner.

Forster says he must in his coercive bill provide for the suspension of the Habeas Corpus, because the failure of evidence is the chief cause of the failure to protect.[1] He must also have an enactment about arms. He seems very grateful to Mr. G. for his help during these very anxious times.

Mr. G. has been sounding Shaw Lefevre on the Irish land question, on which Lefevre is one of the best authorities. He maintains that no scheme will be of use, unless it is approved by the Ulstermen. There must, he says, be some legal restrictions on rent; otherwise, the interest of the tenant is whittled away. In fact, he would go in for a general extension of the Ulster custom as defined the other day by Castlereagh. The absence of an interest in the holdings in other parts of Ireland is traceable in rent; for in Ulster where such interest exists the rent is higher than elsewhere, and this therefore would be the defence for extending or rather creating a tenant right after the fashion of the Ulster custom. Lefevre's recommendations then are these:

(1) He would appoint a Land Commission with power to buy up properties and to resell them to tenants advancing 4/5 or 3/4 of purchase money.

(2) He would extend the Ulster tenant right unless refused by the Commission.

(3) He would let the Commission decide the rent on application of the landlord or the tenant.

(4) He would empower the Commission to buy out those landlords who object to new terms of tenure.

Mr. G. cannot be brought to stomach the '3 F.'s', the adoption of which would, he maintains, be an admission that the Act of '70 had totally failed. This is no doubt a disagreeable admission, but if the '3 F.'s' are advocated by the Ulster men, Conservative as well as Liberal, and by many

[1] Wemyss Reid, ii. 284–5.

landlords in other parts of Ireland as well as by all Radicals, my belief is any milder measure will fail. If by force of events, the '3 F.'s' gain still more popularity, we shall be giving the Conservatives perhaps another opportunity of 'dishing the Whigs,' which I suppose they would not be loath to avail themselves of.

Wednesday, 29 December. The Great Man's birthday. He has completed his 71st year. Godley and I presented him with a 'Gladstone Bag' with which he seemed to be much pleased. He arrived in Town this afternoon, physically very well, but in his gravest 'official' demeanour as Mrs. G. calls it; and no wonder. He holds a position of the greatest responsibility. He has the whole weight of Ireland on his shoulders, and in the Cabinet he stands between the two fires of the right and the left wing. In writing to Lord G[ranville] yesterday, he said he fulfilled the Christian dictate of turning the left cheek when he was smitten on the right. He is smitten today to the right on coercion; tomorrow to the left on land. He appears to contemplate the possibility of any land plan, built as he would like on the lines of the Bill of 1870, falling to the ground 'between the Grey[1] (Whig) stool and that of the "3 F.'s"'.

There was in the same letter a sort of tendency displayed towards Home Rule; for he said he was not sure whether it would not be the smaller evil to let Irishmen knock their heads against one another on questionable theories, either in Grand Committees or some other way, rather than introduce them into Imperial Legislation.[2]

Forster goes in for the '3 F.'s' hot and strong; so there is likely to be very brisk discussion in the Cabinets this next week. It is curious that the landlords should arrive by totally different reasonings at the same conclusion as Bright and Co.—namely the buying out of landlords.

The Queen strongly objects to Courtney for the Home Office on the ground of his being an advanced radical.[3] She considers that Mr. G. has recruited lately quite enough from the radical ground, the last selection being G. Trevelyan. Her refusal to accept Courtney is a somewhat delicate matter, for it has leaked out indirectly that he has been offered the appointment.

Sir H. Ponsonby has been written to in reference to the exception recently taken by H.M. regarding the utterances of Bright and Chamberlain at Birmingham. Mr. G. presumes H.M. refers to the terms in which Bright made allusions to the House of Lords. 'It certainly,' Mr. G. said, 'is not the business of a Minister to raise or suggest questions respecting the root of a body, which, while opposed to every Liberal Administration, (excepting Lord Aberdeen's, under which it showed great wisdom), yet is undoubtedly

---

[1] i.e. the great Whig leader Lord Grey and his following, especially Albert Grey, in the House of Commons.

[2] Ramm, i. 238.

[3] See Ponsonby's letter to G., 29 Dec. 1880, Guedalla, ii. 130. See 28, 30, and 31 Dec. 1880.

a coordinate historic portion of the legislature. On the other hand Mr. **Bright** is an exceptional man, without any official traditions.'[1]

Thursday, 30 December. Mr. G. had symptoms of a lumbago attack this morning, but by keeping his bed in the forenoon he got the better of it. He was bright and cheerful when I went in to see him, and, after recurring to the presentation bag,[2] asked after my sister Ethie.[3] He never forgets anybody, and his attentions in small ways are not the least remarkable and endearing part of him. I remember 2 years ago when he was in the midst of waging war against the late Government and she was lying ill in London, he found time to come and see her.

He seemed satisfied with the Cabinet today. Coercion was agreed upon under the strong belief of the necessity of it in order to re-establish order and a peaceable exercise of civil rights in Ireland. The Habeas Corpus Act is to be suspended, as the principle repressive measure. Lord Spencer said the Cabinet were almost too strong for coercion, even for him. I hope they won't overdo it. Her Majesty ought to be pleased.

Mr. G. wrote to Sir H. Ponsonby today combating with great dexterity on the question of Courtney. The fact is, his political principles would be rather hard to define, and, being a man of great self-assertion, he will undoubtedly be less formidable on the Government benches, muzzled as he will be in a subordinate office, than at large below the Gangway.[4]

Camperdown has declined the Captaincy of the Gentlemen at Arms. I expected he would, but he declined in a becoming manner, without signs of mortification.[5] I understand Duke of St. Albans regrets having refused the offer of a Household appointment, so his claim will be considered. Lord G[ranville] regards Huntly and Carrington as the two peers with the next claims.[6]

Slagg, M.P. for Manchester, has been booked to second the address.[7]

Carrington and Yarborough are to do the moving and seconding of it in the House of Lords.

The Duke of Westminster has, in consequence of the Duchess's death, offered to relinquish the duties of the Mastership of the Horse. The Queen's pleasure is being taken on the matter. If his resignation is accepted, I presume Lord Cork would be first favourite for the post, and then Wolverton might have the Buck Hounds, or perhaps, better still, Carrington.[8]

[1] With a few minor variations and omissions this is a quotation from G.'s letter to Ponsonby, 28 Dec. 1880, Guedalla, ii. 129.

[2] See 29 Dec. 1880 and 10 Jan. 1881.

[3] Ethelinda Hamilton (1849–95) was the oldest surviving daughter of Bishop Hamilton.

[4] Guedalla, ii. 130.

[5] See 17 Dec. 1880.

[6] Huntly was offered the post and accepted. See 28 July 1880 and 17 June 1881.

[7] In place of Armitstead. See 28 Dec. 1880.

[8] The Duke was persuaded not to resign.

Friday, 31 December. Another satisfactory Cabinet. Mr. G. seemed in good spirits after it. They determined as regards a remedial measure for Ireland to proceed on the basis of the Land Act of 1870, by an attempt to supply the defects of it and strengthen it where it is weak. While endeavouring to provide against the abuse of power, their intention is to avoid tampering with the basis of property in land and attempting to reconstruct society by ambitious plans. My fear is that such a measure will, while alienating the landlord interest by taking a further slice out of their property, give insufficient satisfaction to the majority of the party and will be treated with absolute contempt by the Irish folk.

Mr. G. in writing to the Queen admitted that the remedial and coercive measures determined on were two most grave decisions—graver than any two ever taken by a Government in his recollection. The measure of coercion will undoubtedly be opposed by an overwhelming majority of Irish members; but besides the amount of virulent obstruction such a measure will give rise to, there is this further consideration, which evidently Mr. G. much apprehends, namely, that it will be the first time on which such measures will be carried by English and Scotch members in defiance of the Irish vote, and this may lead to a severe straining of the relations of Ireland with Great Britain.

The Cabinet also decided to introduce a measure for promoting local self-government.

What with this, coercion, and land reform, the session promises to be wholly Irish.

The Queen has given way about Courtney. She could not in fact do otherwise.[1]

Mr. G. is about to surrender the Newcastle Trust with which he has so long been connected, and about which he has worked so hard.[2]

The year 1880 is just closing. It will indeed be a noted year in my history. How little did I think a year ago that in the next 12 months I should be installed in Downing St. and again the servant of the Great Man.

[1] See 28, 29, and 30 Dec. 1880.

[2] G. was a trustee of the estate of his great friend and Cabinet colleague the 5th Duke of Newcastle (1811–64). See Morley, ii. 151; see also 7 Jan. 1881.

1881

Thursday, 6 January. The New Year has begun badly with me as regards my diary. Nearly a week elapsed in silence, partly owing to exceptional press of work and partly to my few spare minutes having been devoted to a little outburst of music, which does not often now assert itself.

Here we are with Parliament actually met again. We had a tremendous tussle with Her Majesty over the Queen's speech yesterday, or rather over one paragraph of it, relating to the withdrawal from Kandahar. The draft speech was sent down on Tuesday night, and yesterday morning the Queen telegraphed to say she could not assent to the announcement of any definitive intention to retire from that post. Mr. G., after consulting with Lord Granville and Lord Hartington, replied by referring to former letters on the subject and pointing out that She had already assented to the policy by allowing the despatches to the Viceroy to go forward.[1] Meanwhile Lord Spencer and Harcourt, who went down to attend the Council, could not get the speech approved. H.M. declared that She could only assent on receiving an assurance from them that the Cabinet would retain Kandahar if subsequent events made its retention appear desirable; and in spite of their pointing out the impossibility of pledging their colleagues and themselves in the future, H.M. stood out till 4 o'clock. She had not seen them, but had made Ponsonby the means of communicating her wishes to them. Mr. G.'s telegram apparently had its effect, and She at last sent a message to Lord Spencer and Harcourt to say that, though highly displeased with them at their not complying with her desire to have the speech altered or that they should give some kind of undertaking, she would hold a Council. Her assent to the speech was accordingly wrung out of Her. She was evidently immensely put out, mostly it seems at not having been apprised beforehand that the question of Kandahar would be mentioned. I believe She declared She had never been so treated by Ministers since She came to the throne. Poor woman! as Mr. G. said. It was certainly rather hard that She should be made to express satisfaction at the withdrawal from a place to which only a few months ago she had by Her late Ministers been made to attach so much importance.

The Parliamentary dinner went off fairly well. Mr. G. read out in his best voice the speech. He admitted that it was the most difficult thing to compose

[1] For the exchange of telegrams see Guedalla, ii. 133. See also Gardiner, i. 597–600.

he had ever had to do. I thought considering those difficulties it was exceedingly good. What with the worry of the Osborne tussle and the strain of work, Mr. G. was terribly fagged, but he got through the evening all right.

Friday, 7 January. Mr. G. seems to have been satisfied on the whole with the first night on the Address. Both the attack and the defence seem to have been forcible and good. There was, as might have been expected, some disappointment as regards the Land Bill, so far as it was foreshadowed, among the radicals and the more moderate Home Rulers. My fear is that the Bill, though it is so entirely in embryo at present, will be too mild. It will please no one and displease many. There is every prospect of the fight, which will be shewn by the Irish members, being most formidable. The Coercion Bill or Bills will, of course, bring together the moderate Irishmen and the ultra Land Leaguers; and without the '3 F.'s' there is no chance of disarming the moderate Irishmen on the Land question.

The Queen sent up Sir H. Ponsonby yesterday with a letter expressing her strong disapproval at the Kandahar paragraph in the Queen's speech, and saying She had assented to the speech on the condition that an assurance would be given that, should circumstances hereafter prove the necessity for the retention of Kandahar, it will be retained. Mr. G. has on the part of the Cabinet given her today such an assurance, and tried to make his peace by expressing his regret that H.M. should have been taken by surprise about the intended announcement respecting Kandahar.[1]

Mr. G. has the last few days been greatly anxious to secure out of the Newcastle Estates some increased allowance to the wife of his old friend the Duke of Newcastle, who went wrong, married a foreigner, and is now Lady Susan Opdebeck.[2] Mr. G.'s intercession seems to have been successful, which has pleased him greatly.

Monday, 10 January. On Friday night the Parnell party played their first game of obstruction by moving the adjournment of the House on a question relating to a Land League meeting. It was a little forecast of what we may expect. Parnell resumed the debate on the Address, after this little episode, in a speech of what Mr. G. termed 'much candour and much ability'. The two important points he made were: one, that the object of the Land League was to punish those who offended against the 'unwritten law'; the other, that the Disturbance Bill, inadequate as he regarded it, would, had it passed, have crushed or at any rate greatly reduced the agitation. Forster spoke ably and

---

[1] See Guedalla, ii. 133–4.

[2] Lady Susan was the Duke of Hamilton's daughter and had been until 1850 the wife of G.'s close friend, Lord Lincoln, who became 5th Duke of Newcastle. It was in search of her that G. in 1849 made his extraordinary journey to the Continent. See Philip Magnus, *Gladstone* . . . (London, 1954), pp. 92–4. In 1860 she married M. Opdebeck of Brussels and died in 1889.

vigorously in defending himself against the double fire of the Coercionists and the anti-Coercionists. Gibson followed with a very forcible speech describing and denouncing the Land League.

On Saturday Mr. G. worked hard at the Land Bill. He is throwing himself into it *con amore*. There is a manifest feeling gaining ground daily that to be of any use the Bill must be 'double X'. Any bill of a mild description will receive but a very half-hearted support from the moderate Irish party, the Radicals, and many Liberals; and as any measure must be distasteful to the Lords, a mild one sent up luke-warm will be as liable to be roughly handled by them as a strong bill enthusiastically supported in the Lower House.

I have hopes that there are signs of Mr. G. being willing to make further concessions in the direction of the '3 F.'s', but a radical departure from the Land Act of '70 will go much against the grain with him, as he holds very un-radical views on anything touching landed property.

Mr. G. has made his peace with the Queen over the Kandahar contretemps in connection with the Queen's speech.

Huntley has been offered and has accepted Fife's Captaincy of Gentlemen at Arms. Camperdown has been given the refusal of the First Civil Service Commissionership, which is still held by Enfield.[1]

Monday, 17 January. All my spare time—and that is little enough—has been taken up in drawing up a memorandum about Scotch banks.

The debate on the Address is still proceeding. The end of the first stage was concluded on Friday. Mr. G. was prevented, owing to a cold, from going down to the House and winding up the debate. The division was considered satisfactory—only 8 English members voting with the Irishmen. Justin McCarthy's amendment is the next stage. The patience of all right-minded men is becoming rapidly exhausted, but it is, of course, eminently desirable that there should not be taken too hasty steps. The Cabinet are evidently quite prepared to strike hard, when the right moment comes, with very strong measures aimed at obstruction.

The Land Bill is only slowly hatching. A measure which falls much short of the '3 F.'s' will disappoint greatly. I expect, however, it will be of a more drastic nature than is generally anticipated.

The latest forlorn hope of the Tories is said to be the breakdown of Mr. G.; that Hartington succeeding him will dispense with the services of Bright and Chamberlain; and that will ensure the downfall and split up of the party.

Lord Hartington's speech, by the way, last week was considered by everyone quite first rate, the best he ever made.

Thursday, 20 January. Mr. Gladstone got down to the House on Monday, his cold being better, and made a slashing speech on McCarthy's 'truly

[1] See 30 Dec. 1880 and 17 June 1881.

extraordinary' amendment as he called it. He nettled the Parnell party greatly and proportionately delighted the right-minded people. McCarthy's amendment amounted to a prayer to H.M. that She would withhold the aid of all military and civil forces from the enforcement of rent in Ireland until a new Land Bill became law, which Mr. G. told H.M. was tantamount to asking her to become the chief lawbreaker of the country; it was a motion wholly without precedent, not to say an insult to the throne. Mr. G. seemed pleased at the energetic support tendered very briefly by Lord J. Manners.

Meanwhile, the debate founded on the various amendments to the Address is still dragging its weary way, and the House is slowly but surely moving towards the point at which some stringent measures for dealing with obstruction will be necessary.

The Speaker[1] has been called into counsel, and Sir S. Northcote has been sounded. There are many proposals on the tapis, but the one which seems to be favoured most is a simple resolution empowering the Speaker to move at his discretion that the debate on hand be closed, whereupon if 40 members are clearly agreed on this point the question under debate will be put without further discussion.

The news this week from India tends to show that the announcement of the early evacuation of Kandahar is causing some uneasiness on the spot. Her Majesty is greatly exercised on this point, and presumably rejoicing inwardly that her fears, as she supposes, have been realised, owing to her warnings being unheeded. I am sorry She should have this temporary crow, but it is probable that the report emanates solely from Jingo quarters, and that effect has been greatly exaggerated.

We have been having the most extraordinary severe weather, almost unprecedented severity of frost and almost unprecedented heavy falls of snow.

The Land Bill is making progress, but is being only slowly developed. The Agricultural Commission have reported seperately on Ireland. There is a majority report of Duke of Richmond's, somewhat halting and feeble, but which goes the lengths, much to Mr. G.'s surprise, of recognising the necessity of the interposition of some kind of tribunal between the landlord and tenant for the purpose of fixing rent. There is, likewise, a minority report of Lord Carlingford, which goes in hot and strong for the '3 F.'s'.[2]

Friday, 21 January. The debate on the Address and the several amendments was brought to a close last night. The Report on the Address was under the circumstances, though contrary to precedent, proceeded with at once. Parnell caved in. It looks as if he had got wind that strong measures were in contem-

---

[1] H. B. Brand.

[2] Carlingford and five other members of the Commission signed the minority report advocating free sale, fair rent fixed by a land court, and fixity of tenure. Thirteen commissioners signed the majority report. *Parl. Papers*, 1881, xv. 9, 20–4.

plation, and as if he wished to put himself and his followers a little less in the wrong than they have hitherto been.

While almost the whole of one's attention is naturally centered on Ireland and the obstructive Irish, foreign affairs are anything but pleasant. The fresh negotiations instituted by France for a peaceful settlement of the Greek question have broken down. Greece is assuming a bellicose position and gives out that nothing but the award of Berlin in its entirety will satisfy her. Lord Granville has now as a sort of last hope suggested to Bismarck in flattering terms that he should assume the initiative and use his influence towards securing some basis or other for further negotiations. If nothing comes of that, war will probably be Hobson's choice. Kirby Green[1] does not at all look upon it as a certainty that the Greeks will be thrashed by the Turks, what with the independent line the Albanians are sure to take up, and what with the probable troubles in Bulgarian regions which an outbreak of war will probably bring about.

Saturday, 22 January. Last night was taken up with a discussion on the Transvaal affair. Mr. G. spoke, and his speech seems to have been well received. The bent of it was, that though he had disapproved of the original annexation he was bound to accept the situation and to reassert the authority of the Crown.

At today's Cabinet nothing of any great interest transpired. They seem to have agreed to apply some form of the cloture, if obstruction shewed itself next week at all virulently.

They agreed to support the Archbishop[2] in his intended prayer to the Crown for the appointment of a Royal Commission to inquire into the constitution and working of the Ecclesiastical Courts, in consequence of the unsatisfactory operation of the Public Worship Regulation Act of 1874.

Mr. G. has been in great force and was unusually charming at dinner, at which my mother and sisters were present, and after which we made some music with which he seemed specially delighted.

Tuesday, 25 January. Frost still continues without any perceptible break.

Mr. G. proposed to H.M. that the Duke of Cambridge should be offered the Constableship of the Tower, which Sir W. Codrington had declined; but the Queen did not like the idea, and rightly I think. It would have been an appointment attributed to royal nepotism; would have given no satisfaction to anyone and given offence to a great many.

Last night Mr. Forster introduced his first coercive measure, providing for suspension of the Habeas Corpus in Ireland in such districts as may be

[1] William Kirby Mackenzie Green was the consul-general for Montenegro from 1879 to 1886.
[2] i.e. Tait of Canterbury.

proclaimed by the Lord Lieutenant. Mr. G. thought the debate was as satisfactory as could be expected. He thought Mr. Forster's speech an admirable
exposition of the case, and it was considered by all to be very effective. He
seemed to produce a beneficial effect upon the House at large and even to
carry some dismay into the ranks of Mr. Parnell's friends. However, the
Government are prepared against a renewal of obstruction, and arming
themselves with a resolution in the sense of a modified cloture, which they
will keep ready to bring out on the expected emergency arising, provided the
Conservative leaders will promise it their support.

Lord Granville is trying his diplomatic hand with Bismarck to see if by
flattery he can get the conceited man to make a move on the Grecian
board. The result of Lord Odo's negotiations with Bismarck seems to come
to this—Bismarck has little faith in the settlement of the Greek question by
negotiation; he thinks war inevitable and perhaps even not undesirable in the
interests of the King of Greece; he has agreed with Austria and Russia to
step in, after war has made Greece amenable to reason, with a proposal that
will retain Janina and Metzovo for the Porte, and substitute Crete for what
Greece fails to get on the mainland.

Wednesday, 26 January. Mr. G., in a very moderate, closely argued, and
pointed short speech, yesterday brought forward his resolution to give precedence to Forster's coercive measures so as to enable them to be got through
de die in diem. At the commencement of the sitting things promised to go
fairly smoothly, but after dinner Biggar ran riot, and after being called to
order repeatedly by the Speaker was finally named and suspended from
the sitting. This nettled the Parnellites, and they intimated they would fight
to the death. The Government, on the other hand, expressed themselves
determined to sit on until they got a division on Mr. G.'s resolution. On they
sat throughout the night and up till two o'clock today, by which time the
Irishmen caved in. Thereupon the sitting was suspended. The Parnellites have
now piled up the agony, and the Government ought to carry all right-thinking
men of every shade of opinion with them in applying their cloture scheme,
which I trust they will do. The waste of parliamentary time has reached such
a pitch that Parliamentary machinery has become completely out of gear and
we are becoming the laughing stock of the world.

The trials[1] terminated yesterday in Dublin as was to be expected, and perhaps even better than could be expected, namely, the jury could not agree.
They characteristically maintained that they were unanimous as to their
inability to agree.

Jos. Cowen made a bitter speech, by the way, against the Government. He
has thrown his lot in now entirely with Parnell & Co., which is rather amusing

[1] Of Parnell and other leaders of the Land League. See 13 and 28 Oct. 1880.

considering that he was the man whom the Tories just before the General Election tried to play off as their trump card on their foreign policy.

Sunday, 30 January. Communications with the Conservative Opposition in regard to the means of encountering obstruction have made no advance in the last few days. Northcote won't even now promise his own individual support to any form of the clôture however modified, nor has he any alternative to suggest. So much for the patriotic opposition. This change of front on the part of Sir Stafford—(for at first he was quite inclined to view the Government proposals with favour)—is characteristic of the timidity and shabbiness of the man. His conduct in this instance corresponds with the epithets Mr. G. once applied to him—'flabby and shabby'. Who has he to fear? Certainly not his own immediate colleagues. Cross told the Lord Chancellor he would support the Government proposal, which he had been communicated to him by the Speaker. Mr. W. H. Smith, moreover, the night before last gave me to understand from the strong language he applied to Parnell & Co. that he was prepared to accept strong measures. Northcote, therefore, is presumably frightened at the Fourth Party. Her Majesty is much concerned at the deadlock to which the machinery of Parliament has been brought, and is willing herself to act as a sort of negotiator between the Government and the Opposition. If negotiations fall wholly to the ground, the Government can only resort to patience or else act independently of the Opposition, and let Northcote and his followers, if they like, accompany Parnell and his friends into the same lobby.

On Thursday night, when the debate was resumed on Forster's resolution for leave to bring in his Protection Bill, Bright spoke with great vigour and vindicated his conduct in becoming responsible for the Bill mainly on the ground that the Land League were by their proceeding completely demoralising Ireland.

On Friday Mr. G. spoke, and spoke magnificently. The speech produced a profound impression in the House. I don't remember ever hearing a finer effort from him. What with his powerful reasoning, his perfect temper, his high-bred bearing towards those miscreants, he quite carried one off one's legs. In spite, however, of his powerful appeal, the debate was further adjourned. When is it ever to end? Sir W. Harcourt told me yesterday he did not entertain any very serious apprehensions as to the upshot of this obstruction, but I fear he is too sanguine. What he did fear was that the Land Bill would not be 'screwed up high enough'. I am afraid his fears in this respect may be realised, for the Cabinet yesterday decided to give directions for a bill framed on Mr. G.'s own lines, which I am sure will not satisfy. It is too permissive in its character.

To turn to foreign affairs. The European concert seems to be well maintained, but most of the Powers are only half-hearted about Greece. The pourparlers which are in contemplation among the RR.[1] of the Powers at Constantinople will probably come to nothing and will merely give the Porte a further pretext for delay.

On the general Eastern question there seems to be no doubt that Bismarck's oriental policy is based on a desire to favour the extension of Austria towards the South, and in so doing to preserve and protect her against any complications with Russia. He has privately admitted that he hopes some day to see the Austrian Empire extend to the Aegean. Though he seems to wish to prolong the existence of the Turkish Empire, yet, if the collapse can no longer be postponed, his favourite solution to the Oriental problem is the peaceful division of influence in the Balkan peninsula between Austria and Russia.

It appears that when the present Government assumed office, Bismarck apprehended 3 things:

1. A special understanding between England and Russia.

2. The consequent damage to Austrian interests.

3. The diminution of his personal influence in Europe by reason of the European concert.

His fears, however, especially as regards Nos. 1 and 2 were groundless.

As regards Central Asian affairs, the Russian Ambassador says that all the correspondence between Kaufman and Shere Ali, of which so much was said and made, had been ordered home by the Emperor. A perusal of it, he maintains, shewed that it was simply of a complimentary character until 1878, when war with this country was considered imminent. Anything of a disagreeable nature written subsequently to the Treaty of Berlin has been written before the news had reached General Kaufman. A complete denial is given to Russian assistance to Ayub Khan, and the Russian Government strenuously asserts that they are anxious to put an end to all antagonism between the two countries founded on mutual prejudice. The fact is, their interests in Central Asia are identical. As regards the Russian expedition against the Turcomans, it has been pressed on under absolute necessity.

Wednesday, 2 February. Today will always be a noted day in the annals of Parliament. The House had been occupied up till nine o'clock this morning ever since Monday by a continuous sitting on the debate for leave to introduce the Protection Bill. At 9 o'clock this morning the Speaker[2] resumed the chair and, according to arrangement, interfered by taking upon himself to put the question. The secret had been admirably kept, and a rare mine was sprung on the Irish miscreants. Mr. G. was ecstatic over the way in which the Speaker acquitted himself in the climax of the difficulties, so much so that he wanted to shower on the Speaker's head a G.C.B. However, I don't think it will do

---

[1] i.e. presumably Representatives.
[2] H. B. Brand.

for one moment to entertain the idea. It would bear marks of decided partisanship. After the Speaker's interference, Mr. G. gave notice of his intention to move a resolution which embodies the cloture system in a modified form by empowering the Speaker to declare that public business is urgent and by throwing open thereupon the regulation of the debate. The Opposition are not properly supporting the Government in their endeavours to prevent the occurrence of these sad and monstrous proceedings. They even tried to force the authority of the Chair last night, though conscious of what the Government intended doing.

Friday, 4 February. Yesterday I witnessed the proceedings of one of the most extraordinary nights ever known in the annals of Parliament.

Mr. G. was to move his resolution aimed against obstruction, which provides that, in the event of urgency being voted under certain conditions, the Speaker shall have absolute power to regulate the proceedings of the House.

Before he rose, it had been announced by Harcourt in answer to Parnell that Davitt, the chief organiser of the Land League, had been arrested, the condition of his ticket of leave having been deemed by the Law Officers to be broken. This announcement was, perhaps unhappily, greeted with a tempest of cheering which exasperated past all bearing some of the Parnellites.

Accordingly Dillon, supposed to be one of the most sincere but also of the most violent and excitable, rose in the midst of Mr. G.'s first sentence and remained obstinately standing up without attempting to speak 'to order', and in despite of the Speaker who required him to sit down. For this conduct he was named by the Speaker under the order of February, '78.[1] Mr. G. moved that he should be suspended from the House for the rest of the sitting. A division took place and authority having thus been obtained Mr. Dillon was required to withdraw, and on his refusal to do so, was removed with a show of force by the Serjeant-at-Arms—Old Gossett, who shook all over in discharging his duty.

Mr. G. then resumed his broken sentence, but had hardly finished it when Mr. Parnell rose and moved that he be no longer heard. 'The extreme brutishness', as Mr. G. called it, of such a proceeding when taken without any kind of Parliamentary reason, enabled the Speaker to treat it as an offence of 'wilful and persistent obstruction' outright, and the same process as had taken place in the case of Dillon was repeated first with Parnell and then with Finigan.

Had the same course been pursued by Parnell's chosen few one after another separately, numbering as they did some 35 or 36, it would have taken the best part of 18 hours to dispose of the lot individually. But fortunately the

---

[1] EWH should have written 'February, '80'. The rule concerning the suspension of a member after being named by the Speaker became a Standing Order on 28 Feb. 1880. *Parl. Deb.* ccl. 1706–8.

tactics of the party were so suicidal as to relieve the House from this embarrassment. From the second division onwards, some 26 or 27 of these men determined that in sheer contumacy they would neither vote in the lobbies nor quit the House, which on every occasion of a division the Speaker orders that all members shall do.

On the first time of their acting thus, the Speaker reported it to the House. But there was no list of the offenders, and at first there was doubt as to the manner of treating them. However, Mr. G. had given a general notice that such conduct could not be borne, and a method was soon suggested. On the next occasion the Speaker addressed them and required them to leave their places, which they refused to do. Upon this the whole batch of them were named, probably to their great surprise. Mr. G. made one motion, dispensing them all from the service of the House for the evening. Their case was thus fortunately able to be disposed of by a single division, and all were removed by the Speaker. They all 'declined respectfully' to withdraw except by the aid of superior force. On the Serjeant, however, touching them they walked out. It was a truly melodramatic scene, and their proceedings were as comic in effect as they were serious in deed.

A few more cases having been individually disposed of, the total of suspended members removed from the House amounted to 35. The back of obstruction then became fairly broken.

Mr. G. then proceeded to propose his resolutions, and the debate was conducted in the ordinary decorous fashion.

In order to secure 'moral unanimity' the Government at once accepted and incorporated some of Sir S. Northcote's modifications, emasculating even as they did the measure. Ultimately late in the sitting, the resolutions were carried without division and amidst the liveliest expressions of general satisfaction.

Throughout the great difficulties which he had to encounter, the Speaker acquitted himself in a masterly way. Mr. G. said it was impossible to overrate the Speaker's 'firmness in mind, his suavity in manner, his unwearied patience, and his incomparable temper under a thousand provocations'.

Mr. G.'s own speech in moving his resolutions produced a profound impression in the House, and the peroration with which he wound up moved many an eye to tears.

Sunday, 6 February. Mr. G. has not suffered, I hope, from the great fatigue and excitement of the last week.

The Tories are a little sore in two ways about the proceedings of the week. They thought that considering the support they had given to the Government they were entitled—at any rate the front Opposition bench—to be apprised of the step the Speaker intended taking on Wednesday morning. Barring Sir S. Northcote, who was under a pledge of secrecy, not a soul on the other side had been given a hint, but no more had any of the followers of the Government been told anything, so great was the importance of keeping matters dark. The Tories also feel a little aggrieved at the assistance which the Speaker has given to the Government, and comment on the difference in the measure of support *they* obtained from him when they were confronted by obstruction; but the real fact is they were never serious about putting down obstruction; they merely played with it.

We are—bad luck to it—threatened with further troubles. There seems to be every probability of hostilities breaking out again in the Gold Coast.

Russia emphatically repudiates the idea of any advance upon Merv.

Monday, 7 February. Outrages in Ireland are greatly on the decline. The introduction of the Coercion Bill has told wonderfully already. The 2nd Reading of the Bill is proceeding quietly and decorously.

Goschen's call at Berlin on his way back to Constantinople seems to have been a success and productive of good. He has got Bismarck to assent to take the initiative and make a proposal, which the representatives of the Joint Powers at the Porte are to press on the Sultan. The proposal will be in effect to accept the massacre of the Berlin award (which is termed in diplomatic phraseology 'La St. Barthelemy de St. Hilaire'),[1] and to suggest a new line with equivalents by way of compensation to Greece in the shape (say) of Crete; and if Greece assents to promise her jointly moral support, approximating perhaps to indirect material assistance, such as conveyance of her troops by sea to the points at which she requires to concentrate her forces.

Wednesday, 9 February. The debate on the 2nd Reading of the Protection Bill dragged on till today, when it was read a second time by a good and satisfactory majority. The last 3 sittings have been conducted in an ordinary and quiet manner. Nothing could have been more satisfactory than the working of the new power in the Speaker's hands. The Parnellites have been reduced to their proper place and liberty of speech has been restored to the rest of the House. The speeches have been dull and noteworthy [*sic*], if we except Cowen's speech which contained a violent attack on the Government for arresting Davitt and on Mr. Bright specially for supporting the Bill. Mr. G. seems in better spirits as to the outlook. He thinks the general feeling and the aspect of affairs in the House is thoroughly good.

His mind is now specially turned on the Land Bill which is in course of being drafted. Thring—no mean judge—considers the scheme too complicated. I fear it will be too mild. The gist of it seems to be that there will be two courses open to the Irish landlords: (1) either to work on in much the same way as is provided for by the Land Act of 1870, only with heavier

---

[1] The name of the French foreign minister, Jules Barthélemy St. Hilaire, provided the occasion for this pun.

penalties against rent-raising; or (2) to adopt one of three alternatives: (a) to grant 31 years' leases, (b) to go in under the Court for rent purposes, (c) with consent of himself and his tenant, to give the '3 F.'s'.

Monday, 14 February. Since Wednesday the Protection Bill has been going through or rather creeping through Committee. Progress has been very slow. What with a question of privilege, as to Land League members being charged with being in receipt of pay, raised by the Parnellites, and Fowler's motion against the abolition of the Chief Barony and the Chief Justiceship of Common Pleas, little time on Thursday was left for the Committee on the Bill. On Friday the amendments as to the retrospective action of the Bill and bringing within its scope treasonable practices took up the whole evening. The largest minority did not much exceed 60. In short, the countenance given to the opposing minority by English and Scotch members has been very limited. This remark applies equally to the 2nd Reading when the number of the minority was composed almost wholly of Irish members, and was less than that which opposed the Coercion Bill of Lord Grey's ministry in 1833. Moreover, the Irish minority is not *quite* a majority of Irishmen, which is a more favourable result than had been anticipated before the introduction of the Bill. In short, by the patience and good judgment displayed by the Government, the distasteful Coercion Bill has gone down in the country well. Judging from the innumerable resolutions of confidence we have received from every quarter of Great Britain, the country has intimated its willingness most distinctly, though regretfully, to entrust the present Executive Government with the extraordinary powers it has demanded, which is more than the country would have done had these powers emanated from a Conservative Government.

Parnell has disappeared, and his movements are not known. His disappearance has naturally excited much comment and given rise to many stories. Some attribute it to a fear (an ungrounded one) of being arrested; others to something in connection with a misappropriation of the Land League funds; others to the charms of women to which he is supposed to be much addicted; and another story is that he has gone out of his mind and has been quietly detained somewhere by his friends.

Her Majesty generally approves the draft Land Bill, the spirit and intention of which Mr. G. himself says are 'to meet existing needs within the bounds of reason and justice; to avoid any shock to the social system with its relation of class; to afford scope and encouragement to intelligence and conscientiousness among landlords as well as tenants; to confine within the narrowest bounds the operation of exceptional expedients called for by the peculiar state of Ireland; and to eschew the establishment of precedents which might hereafter be susceptible of a dangerous application outside that particular sphere'.

Monday, 21 February.[1] The whole of the last week's Parliament was consumed by the Protection Bill discussion in Committee which consisted for the main part in what Mr. G. called 'veiled obstruction'. On Friday, or rather Thursday, in view of this persistent obstruction, the Speaker laid on the table some more stringent rules aimed at terminating this interminable discussion. In deference to legitimate criticism on the part of the Opposition, these rules underwent certain amendment, and today a motion was passed providing for the termination of the debate at 12 o'clock, after which such of the amendments as have not been reached are to be taken without discussion and settled simply by dividing on them.

At the Cabinet on Saturday it was decided not to proceed with the Arms Bill in immediate succession to the Protection Bill. This step will, of course, be looked upon by many as something akin to shilly-shallying, but in view of the very marked change in things in Ireland brought about by the coercive measure, and the lengthened delay which has already taken place in proceeding with other business, the change in front may probably be politic and unattended with risk.

This ought to secure the introduction next week of the Land Bill, if it can be got ready. In its present shape I fear it will fall short of expectations and reasonable expectations. However, there is a hope of its being 'screwed up'.

It has been the fashion with some reason to criticise the conduct of Playfair in the Chair in Committee. But he has had most difficult times to contend with, and Mr. G. thinks he has improved lately. Mr. G. has gone as far as to say that Playfair is shewing himself equal to coping with the numerous and trying questions with which he is overwhelmed.

The vacant canonry at Westminster has been offered to Dr. Barry, who holds a stall at Worcester; and if he accepts, the canonry he will vacate will be offered to Dr. Bradley, Head of University College.

Mr. G. has been down to Brighton for the Sunday and was much amused at being brought up today by an engine christened 'Beaconsfield'.

The outlook in the East is brightening. It was an evidently happy idea of Lord Granville's to flatter the vanity of Bismarck and to induce him to take the lead in the Greek question. His ideas are: (1) to be ready with compensation for what Greece does not get on the mainland by the cession to her of Crete, (2) to obtain the assent of Greece to this first, and (3) to have resort to defensive measures if necessary.

Austria is evidently much indisposed to acquiesce in Bismarck's views, but she will be bound to follow his lead.

Bismarck, according to Goschen, thinks a good deal of the Albanians and of the possible account to which they may be turned on the break-up of the Ottoman Empire. He disbelieves in any serious Bulgarian movement, more especially as it is not Russia's interest to do any more crusading work at

[1] EWH wrote 'March' instead of February.

present; what she wants is peace whereby she may recover the effects of the war. Bismarck spoke strongly to Goschen on the Transvaal question in the sense that anything—even loss of military prestige—is better than fighting the 'white man'. He appears to be quite envious of the parliamentary excitement in this country and would evidently quite like the chance of taking part in such frays. He characteristically observed that in the English Parliament a man could call his enemies by strong names, whereas in diplomacy it was all soft words.

Tuesday, 22 February. The Committee on the Protection Bill was definitely closed last night in consequence of the new rule, the operation of which was supported by an enormous majority, only some 10 Conservatives and some half-dozen radicals voting in the minority. The Parnellites had their final fling of obstruction over that stage of the Bill by persisting in taking one or two absolutely superfluous divisions.

Canon Barry has accepted gratefully the Westminster stall.

Fife is most properly to have the Order of the Thistle vacant by the death of Lord Seafield, and will accordingly receive the 'emblems' which his father wore.

There was an informal Cabinet today to consider the draft Land Bill. Little or no progress was made. Each minister aired his own ideas again, and Mr. G. was quite low-spirited. One thing must in any case be done, and that is the simplification of its provisions. At present the complications are much too great.

Friday, 25 February. The night before last on his return from Marlborough House[1] Mr. G. slipped in the melted snow on the paved footpath from the Park entrance and fell on the back of his head. He cut his head severely and bled profusely, but never lost consciousness for a moment. The wound was deep, but fortunately no serious consequences need be apprehended. He is making most favourable progress. Sir J. Paget said to me this morning that it was marvellous how well Mr. G. was going on, that his physical powers were, in short, proportionate to his intellectual powers. Intense interest has been evinced, and marked sympathy evoked from all sides. Telegrams of inquiry and congratulations have been coming in from various parts of Europe, notably Italy and the 'oppressed nationalities'. It is marvellous the position that man occupies in Europe and the World. I doubt if ever—or certainly since the days of Pitt—a man held so commanding a position in this country. Meanwhile, of course, the Land Bill is hung up.

This evening the last stage of the interminable Protection Bill was closed, and the Bill has been read a third time.

Whether the Arms Bill is to be proceeded with has again become an open

[1] The residence of the Prince of Wales.

question. The Government stands between two fires—or on the horns of a dilemma—what with the opposition with which it is confronted from the Conservatives if the Bill is abandoned or withdrawn, and from the Parnellites and some few radicals if it is pushed forward.

Accounts from Constantinople continue fairly good. Greece appears to be amenable, and Turkey not so absolutely obstinate as might have been expected, or according to her wont.

Sunday, 27 February. Nothing could be more satisfactory than Mr. Gladstone's progress. He got up for the first time today and moved into his sitting room where I went and had a little talk with him. Except that his head was all bandaged up, he looked much himself and declared he felt little the worse for the shake and the cut in the head. He was much pleased at the result of the Cumberland election yesterday for three reasons—the proverbial 'three'. (1) The gain of a seat, (2) the exclusion of a man like Jim Lowther, for whom he can have no possible respect, to say the least of it, (3) the admission of a good Liberal like G. Howard. The actual figures giving a majority of only 30 were not much to boast of, but the constituency has always been evenly balanced, and the Tories could not have run a stronger man politically and locally. Mr. G. was touched at hearing of the arrival of the telegrams from the various Hellenic communities, and apropos of the cause of Greece being taken up by Bismarck he remarked of the great German that, glad as he was he should be taking up the line he now is, he believed Bismarck would sell anybody or anything for a sixpence.

The Cabinet met yesterday, notwithstanding Mr. G.'s absence. They decided—I am inclined to think unwisely on the whole—to proceed with the Arms Bill after all. Lord Granville said Chamberlain was 'very angry' at the decision, and though Bright was less so, he (Bright) had commented severely to Lord G[ranville] after the Cabinet at the departure from the former decision in the absence of Mr. Gladstone, who, however, had placed himself on this question unreservedly in the hands of his colleagues.

I called this afternoon on Lady Cork among other people. She is certainly a most agreeable woman, full of political gossip. She referred to the very marked way in which, as she felt assured (to my surprise), Lord Granville had forfeited the confidence of the Royal family. It must probably be due to the line he took in 1875 on the Royal Titles Bill.[1] She and Lord Cork appear to think Lord Spencer a very bad man to advise on Ireland—a sentiment in which I wholly disagree. She told me Lord Beaconsfield is supposed to have expressed his great surprise that a man like Lord Spencer should have been preferred to Lansdowne for the Cabinet. Lord Beaconsfield's strong point is certainly

---

[1] In Feb. and Mar. 1876 Lord Granville, as the leading spokesman of the Liberal Party owing to G.'s retirement, voiced in his letters to the Queen the objections that most Liberals had to the title of Empress. See Fitzmaurice, ii. 159–63.

judgment of character, but as things have turned out, Lansdowne's presence in the Cabinet must have been very brief, considering his views on Ireland.

Monday, 28 February. Bad luck certainly dogs the steps of the present Government. I was woke up this morning with a stream of telegrams announcing a horrible disaster to the British troops in Transvaal, comprising the almost complete annihilation of some 600 men taken up by Colley to a height commanding the position of the Boers at Laingsnek, and the killing of the poor General himself. His expedition appears to have been within an ace of a great coup, and terminated only in destruction for the want of ammunition. We must await further details before judging his proceedings, though at first sight it seems to have been a foolhardy undertaking, resulting in murderous bloodshed the consequences of which may be fearful. One would imagine his tactics must have been actuated from a feeling (perhaps unconscious) of doing something off his own bat to re-establish his prestige as a general.

The news was broken this morning to Mr. G. who is going on wonderfully well, the wound being well nigh healed.

Thursday, 3 March. The Arms Bill has made somewhat better progress than might have been expected. Very few English members voted even against the application of 'urgency' to it, and none to its introduction. It was read a first time the first night (Tuesday).

Mr. G. has practically recovered. He recommenced work yesterday, and in the afternoon had a long conversation with the Inland Revenue authorities on the Death Duties, with which he was satisfied, but I am afraid it did not lead to any very practical conclusions. I don't believe it will do to tinker them up. Either he must go in for one uniform duty a la Dodds,[1] or else leave them alone. Mr. G. was 'pleased', as he said, with his head, which stood him in its usual marvellous stead throughout the discussion.

Sir G. Wolseley has been submitted to Her Majesty for a peerage, mainly on the ground that his services on Army matters are greatly wanted in the House of Lords. I don't expect the Queen will accede with much willingness. The proposal will be, in Mr. Gladstone's words, 'a nasty pill for Her'. If Her assent *is* obtained, the honour will certainly not be popular.

Mr. G. reappeared in the House this afternoon, and his reappearance was warmly greeted.

Saturday, 5 March. As I expected, Her Majesty has refused point blank to entertain the idea of a peerage for Wolseley.[2] She maintains he has already

---

[1] i.e. J. Dodds, M.P. for Stockton, who argued for the Death Duty being treated as a charge on the capital of the testator at a uniform rate rather than a charge to be paid by the legatees at differing rates. See *Parl. Deb.* cclx. 604–6.

[2] For the exchange of letters between G. and the Queen on this subject between 2 and 5 Mar. 1881, see Guedalla, ii. 141–5.

been amply rewarded for his military services and will not admit the necessity of his presence in the Upper Chamber to assist the Government in their Army measures; but more than this, H.M. accuses him of direct insubordinate conduct towards the Commander-in-Chief,[1] and she holds to this in spite of Mr. G. expressing his disbelief in its existence. It comes to this, then—putting aside the question of the peerage—that either Wolseley, if he is guilty of insubordination, must go, or, if not, that the Duke, 'the great boulder of obstruction', as I believe Wolseley calls him, must apologise or himself resign. Mr. G. agreed with me when I said [this] this morning and was evidently greatly annoyed at the whole business. He has put it to the Queen that the circumstances demand immediate investigation. I think it is a pity to make too much of it. It is probably more a woman's whim than anything else.

Childers' statement on Thursday night as to what he intended doing in the shape of army reform was received with a chorus of approval. The main features of his scheme are: (1) while retaining the short service system, to extend somewhat the duration of the service, (2) to introduce double battalions, (3) to increase the pay of non-commissioned officers, (4) to raise the minimum age for enlistment, (5) to abolish paid colonelcies of regiments.

I was present at the Kandahar debate in the House of Lords last night. The speeches that impressed me most were those of Lord Cranbrook and Lord Granville. I never heard Lord Cranbrook so good. Lord Beaconsfield was as usual laboured. Lord Lytton's motion was, of course, carried by a large majority, but I cannot but regard the tactics of the Conservatives [as] unfortunate and injudicious. It seems to be, on the part of the Lords, courting voluntarily their own effeteness. The result can only weaken their position in the country.

Tuesday, 8 March. The principal news of the last day or two has been the armistice with the Boers, which E. Wood, following out the instructions given to his poor predecessor, Colley, has secured. They do not seem disinclined to stop further bloodshed, but it will be difficult to find terms which they will accept and to which we can honourably accede.

The Wolseley business is not yet settled. The 'witness for the Crown' who charged Wolseley with general disloyalty (not amounting to insubordination) declines to come forward, and the Duke of Cambridge has, I believe, waived his objections to the peerage provided Wolseley be made to vacate his office,[2] so that it may not be converted into a political one. But the Queen stands out and asks that the question may at any rate stand over for the present. The *Morning Post* yesterday had a short article on the grant of the honor.[3] How in the world it leaked out Heaven only knows.

---

[1] i.e. the Duke of Cambridge. [2] He was Quarter-Master General.
[3] *Morning Post*, 7 Mar. 1881, p. 4, col. 6.

The Land Bill is making some little progress, and in the right direction I trust.

Sunday, 13 March. One cannot help being haunted by the terrible tragedy that befell poor Rob. Meade a week ago—to lose two wives within a year of his marriage in each case and to lose them from the same cause is too cruelly sad.[1]

The Arms Bill was read a 3rd time on Friday night after an unwise speech from Randolph Churchill denouncing the Bill 'which as Sir W. Harcourt shewed in a caustic reply he had long and hotly invited', as Mr. G. put it. Thus the coercion debates have at last reached their close, and the outwearied assembly has bidden farewell, for some little time to come it is hoped, to that disagreeable discussion.

That horrid Transvaal business is now uppermost in political thoughts. It has been most unfortunate for the Government. They are reaping the fruits of the initial mistake they made, which was not to have faced the difficulties when they first came into office by sending Commissioners out to inquire into the real feeling of the Boers regarding their annexation to this country. The Colonial Office have been misled from the first. For this they have to thank partly Sir B. Frere, and partly the military administrator of the Colony. Had, however, the Government had the full courage of their own convictions on this subject, they never could have induced Her Majesty either to assent to the immediate recall of Frere or to the taking of any step which might have involved the reversal of the policy of their predecessors. Hence the present mess. The actual conduct too of the war has been more than unlucky, —first that our troops should have suffered three reverses, and 2ndly, that negotiations should have been *opened* by the Boers just at the moment *after* the disaster at Majuba Hill.[2] We have consequently just had enough fighting to wound all the susceptibilities of the Peace Party; and just stopped short, momentarily, to kindle up all the Jingo feelings afresh. We have in short fallen between two stools; and to this circumstance coupled with the Irish difficulties is probably attributable the loss of the seat at Coventry.

A curious letter came the other day from Duleep Singh expressing admiration of Mr. Gladstone's magnanimous conduct towards the Boers. Mr. G. first thought the letter a hoax; but it proved on investigation to be clearly genuine. He was pleased and interested by it. His reply was in effect as follows, which shews his own views on the situation: The Government will be careful of the true honor of the Crown and will sedulously avoid whatever might in their judgment tend to impart a new shock to the social and political system in South Africa. But subject to these obligations, they will continue to study

[1] Both of Meade's wives died after childbirth.
[2] The two italicized words are underlined in pencil and in a manner different from that usually practiced by EWH. After the word 'opened' there is also a pencilled question mark.

the interests of peace, humanity, and freedom, and will not allow themselves to be drawn aside from the pursuit of these aims either by material or personal vain glory, or other considerations unworthy of the Christian name or regard of any manly or right-minded person of whatever race or creed.

The wretched Bradlaugh business has come to the front again. The judge[1] has decided that the right to affirm instead of taking the oath has not been established. Consequently Bradlaugh has incurred the penalties and has no *locus standi* in the House. Gorst intends moving for the issue of a new writ tomorrow; but it is probable that until the appeal has taken place the discussion of the seat cannot be resumed. At the same time, sooner or later the matter will cause trouble to the Government and they will probably be forced to take some step regarding it. There is simply no end to their persistent bad luck.

Tomorrow will have to be decided the question as to whether urgency shall be voted for supply. The Government have only two disagreeable alternatives —one, to have recourse to the exceedingly objectionable method of obtaining votes under the urgency rules—the other, to allow the financial machinery of the country to be thrown completely out of gear. It is doubtful whether the Opposition will support the Government, but to vote urgency is probably the lesser danger of the two, and I expect the required majority will be obtained somehow or other.

The Wolseley peerage business promises, I fear, no end of troubles. H.M. thinks Mr. G. is forcing it upon Her without listening to or caring for her objections. I trust wiser counsels will prevail and the matter dropped for the moment. But he and Childers are very hot about it. I expect her real objections arise from the fact of Wolseley having written an anti-Kandahar memorandum.

The other peerage (of Prince Leopold) which Mr. G. sounded Ponsonby about must, according to H.M., emanate from Herself, and She does not intend to suggest it yet.

I had a long interesting talk with Lord Bath on Friday. He is much exercised in his mind as to the Greek question sending to the wall the interests of Servia. He maintains that Austria is daily acquiring more absolute influence and control over the little principality, and that the reason why we dare not interfere is that we are so desirous of maintaining the concert of the Powers intact in order to settle the Greek question, and that the price we have to pay for that is that we cannot preach 'Hands off' to Austria.

Monday, 14 March. I came up from Harry Brand's this morning; and on reaching the station was startled by the horrible news in the paper of the assassination of the Emperor of Russia.[2] Apart from the horrors of the deed,

---

[1] Mr. Justice Mathew.   [2] Alexander II.

his death may have a most important effect on general European politics. His successor, Alexander III, is known to be anti-German and pro-Slav.

Another piece of news which took one by surprise was Sir S. Northcote's manifesto deprecating resort to the urgency rules of which Mr. Gladstone had given notice for supply this evening. There was considerable force in his arguments, but he overstated and misstated his case. In consequence of these tactics on the part of the Tories, the Government of course failed this afternoon to get the necessary majority to vote urgency. The division, however, was not unsatisfactory. It was on strictly party lines, which in itself was a gain; and a majority of 84 on such lines for the Government was not bad. I am afraid the Government has committed a mistake. They would probably have done better to commence supply under the ordinary rules of the House, and on getting into difficulties to have asked the House to give precedence to supply over all orders of the day and every day. If that step failed, then recourse might have been had to urgency. I can't believe Northcote would have taken the step he did had the Irish party not been more or less squared. As things turned out, the Government got at once into Committee of Supply and have made excellent progress with the Civil Service Supplementaries during the evening. This may, however, be due to the air being cleared by the division; and it is premature to count on the collapse of obstruction, especially at a moment when there never was a better opportunity of bringing the Government into difficulties by obstructing.

Saturday, 19 March. Nothing could have been better than the conduct and whole tone of the House during the week; and nothing could have been more satisfactory than the progress made with supply. The House has resumed its old appearance, and obstruction has become a thing of the past,—which one can look back upon as a 'hideous dream' (so were Mr. G.'s words). What does this mean? Time alone can show. The minority of course may have merely sought to show that 'urgency' as proposed by the Government last Monday was needless; and no one can say how long this remarkable forbearance will be prolonged. There is no doubt, however, that in their way the Opposition gained a victory, and it is probable that the vote of Monday produced a considerable moral effect. Anyhow the Government have gained their point which was to get money voted for the service of the country in time to prevent the financial machinery being thrown out of gear, and they have gained it without resort to extraordinary means.

On Tuesday Mr. Gladstone moved votes of condolence to the Queen and the Duchess of Edinburgh on the occasion of the tragic end which befell the Czar last Sunday. Nothing could have exceeded the good taste and the impressive eloquence with which Mr. Gladstone prefaced his motion, and he said he never saw more marked signs of deepened unanimous feeling in the House.

The Wolseley peerage has come again to the front disagreeably. The Queen holds out, and rightly I think, though her last words do not forbid the peerage provided Sir Garnet relinquishes his office of Quartermaster General.[1] I think this offers a fair compromise, but Mr. G. is very firm and I doubt his yielding an inch. If the Sovereign is ever to have her say, this seems to be a legitimate opportunity for her so doing, as the matter affects the two subjects in which she has special concern, namely, the army and the peerage.

The Cabinet have decided today to bring on both the Land Bill and the Budget before Easter, that is, before the 8th when they propose to adjourn the House till the 25th. The Government could hardly fail to introduce the land measure before the holidays, considering the temper of the House, the anxiety with which the Bill is regarded, and the pledges they have given that their remedial measures should follow as closely as possible upon their coercive measures. The Easter recess will afford about the legitimate interval required between the 1st and 2nd readings of the Bill. There will, however, be this great danger, that the Irish members will be free during that time to stump the country and possibly to expose the inadequacy of the provisions of the Bill. The Bill I think is gaining strength and simplicity, but the fear will be that it will be too strong for the Tories and Whigs to swallow and not strong enough to secure the enthusiastic support of the Radicals and Irish; and accordingly it will run the risk of falling between two stools.

The Budget has made a little move this week. Mr. G. can't be got to adopt the reform of the Probate and Legacy Duties which we have so pressed upon him, viz., the substitution of one uniform Probate Duty of 4% in lieu of the present complicated system of Probate *and* Legacy Duties. He attaches immense importance to, and lays great stress on, the 'natural expectation' which a son has to succeed to his father in comparison with all other legatees. What he is prepared to do is to reduce the Legacy Duty scale by 1% all round, and to add 1% to the Probate Duty. This will be an important administrative reform, doing away as it will with all the reversions arising from sons taking after the widows (for widows will be subject to a tax like sons) and of these there are many. We shall also get an additional revenue in 1881–2 by this means.

Monday, 21 March. The Great Man is in tremendous force, and he requires to be so with the prospect a fortnight hence of expounding his Budget and introducing his Land Bill during the same week. He enjoyed his quiet Sunday at the Durdans with the Roseberys plus MacColl, who is always congenial to him. (That is a remarkable little man.) This evening I dined quietly with the Gladstones. Mr. G. was anxious to hear all about Friday's proceedings at Salisbury in connection with the uncovering (as it were) of the memorial tomb of my father. The proceedings were quiet and gratifying. Lord Nelson, on the part of the subscribers, (who has been the prime and entire mover in the

[1] See Ponsonby's letter to G., 19 Mar. 1881, Guedalla, ii. 149–50.

business), and the new dean,[1] on the part of the Cathedral body, did their respective parts in exceedingly good taste. I was very glad to have been present. At dinner this evening Mr. G. was in good spirits at the news from the Transvaal promising a peaceful issue. If that wretched war can be terminated without further fighting, it will redound greatly to the credit of the Government and certainly not to the dishonour of this country. The Radical party have certainly behaved extremely well under the trying circumstances. Their conduct is really no doubt due to the extraordinary confidence they have in the Government, more especially its Head. Apropos of their behaviour, Mr. G. remarked tonight that he never remembered the Liberal party— certainly for the last 30 years—as a whole in a more satisfactory state.

Mr. G. is to be subpoenaed in the Lawson–Labouchere case. He does not seem bored with the prospect. Labouchere evidently much impressed him this evening when he was apologising for giving him this trouble, by saying that he had proved that Lawson, or rather the *Daily Telegraph*, had made £30,000 out of the insertion of obscene advertisements! The particular point on which Mr. G. is to be examined concerns the Negropontine correspondence during the time of the Eastern question. In connection with this Mr. G. observed how remarkable was the manner in which men after renouncing the tenets of a political creed continued to cling to all the prejudices and antipathies belonging to their late creed. To this fact he attributed the line of policy adopted by Lord Beaconsfield and endorsed by the *Daily Telegraph* on the Eastern question, both being actuated by a feeling of anti-Judaism, though they[2] had long since renounced the tenets of the Jewish religion.

Mr. G. was much pleased today by a little present he received from the Princess of Wales in the shape of a pencil case designed like an axe, and by the pretty words with which She accompanied the gift.[3] She said she presented this pencil case to the 'great people's William' because of the many trees he had axed in his lifetime, and of the many questions he had been 'axed', and in the hope that he would not 'cut down' the Greek frontier by another yard.

I fear the Greek question does not prosper. Bismarck seems to be playing the truant and to be falling very far short of the programme to which he committed himself when interviewed by Goschen. A small slice of Thessaly with the addition of Crete seems to be the miserable pittance which the RR[4] of the Powers have wrung out of the Porte, and which most of them seem to be willing to accept—shame to them. It is hardly possible to conceive that Greece can submit to so paltry an award, after all she has been led to expect. So the

[1] G. D. Boyle, who had become dean in May 1880.
[2] i.e. Lord Beaconsfield and Edward Levy-Lawson, the editor of the *Daily Telegraph* which had transferred its support from G. to Lord Beaconsfield in 1879. Lawson had brought a suit for libel against Labouchere for statements that had appeared about Lawson in *Truth* of which Labouchere was the editor. On 28 Mar. the case came to an end with the jury unable to agree.   [3] See also 27 Mar. 1881.   [4] See 30 Jan. 1881.

consequence may, and probably will be, war after all, when peace might be secured, were the Powers to do what they are in duty bound to do and to show a little firmness.

I had an interesting talk the other day with Sir T. Tancred, the son of the old friend[1] of Mr. G. and my father, who has been tendering for the Servian Railway contract. Having raised the money, he seems to have a fair chance of getting his tender accepted, and of thus 'bowling out' the Austrians. Servia is already immensely overshadowed by Austrian influence; and were the Austrians to get the contract that influence would become paramount. The importance of the proposed line is enormous, connecting as it will the Hungarian capital with Belgrade, and then establishing communication through the heart of Servia southwards, thus opening up all the resources of the Principality, until it has formed the connecting line with the Turkish lines leading (a) to Constantinople and (b) to Salonica. It is probable that when this line has been made, Salonica may take the place of Brindisi for mail purposes eastward, shortening as it will the time of communication between this country and Egypt by some 20 hours or more.

Saturday, 26 March. On Tuesday last the news arrived that Sir E. Wood had concluded terms of peace with the Boers, thus bringing a most unsatisfactory business to a somewhat unsatisfactory close. The terms provide for the dispersal to their homes of the Boers, the recognition of the suzerainty of the Queen, the retention of a British resident at the capital of the Transvaal, the control of foreign affairs by the British Government and the appointment of a commission to arrange for the complete self-government of the Boers. Anything is better than the continuance of the wretched war; but its termination under the circumstances grates somewhat on the feeling of John Bull and has strongly aroused the sentiments of the Jingos. Had it been possible to insist on a military march to Pretoria, it would have been far better; and it is difficult to give any plausible answer to the very natural question why, if the Government concede now that for which the Boers rose in rebellion, we did not at the outset grant their demands and thus avoid all bloodshed. The best construction to place upon the policy which has been pursued is to assume that the Boers would not have submitted until they had become fully alive to the undoubted superiority of our arms by the presence of a really appreciable force. Of course, the real mistake committed was not to have given the Boers self-government or independence many months ago before they had resort to an appeal to arms. But the difficulties were immense; and, as it was the Queen who resisted most strongly any step which would practically have rescinded the annexation, these difficulties were such as could not be made known to the public. Accordingly, public opinion must somewhat unfairly judge the Government. Nothing, however, will ever justify the annexation

[1] Sir Thomas Tancred (1808–80), 7th bart.

and the grossly bad way in which the colonial authorities allowed themselves to be misinformed as to the real feeling of the Boers. The Queen much resented the acceptance of the terms of peace; but she could not refuse. Among the Radicals and with a very large section of the multitude, the termination of the war has been most popular, as is only natural; and there is for all the redeeming point that the Government has had the courage to show that in a bad cause it is not afraid of being thought afraid—the worst of all fears.

All supply was got through within the proper time, and there has been no return of the obstruction disease. Tuesday was taken up with Chaplin's motion in favor of making the provisions regarding the prevention of the landing of animals from countries 'reasonably suspected' of harbouring foot and mouth disease more stringent; but the Government resisted the motion on the ground that the restrictions were already burdensome enough, that they gave already practical security, and that any change in the direction of the resolution would too seriously interfere with the supply of food to this country.

Thursday and Friday were devoted to the Afghan debate raised by E. Stanhope's motion censuring the Government for withdrawing now from Kandahar. Mr. G. thought Stanhope displayed judgment and talent in attacking; and he considered the speech of Dilke who was put up to reply one of 'singular ability'. Herbert G[ladstone] made his debut as a parliamentary speaker on the first night—Thursday—and acquitted himself very well. He was very nervous as was only to be expected; but he made some good points. He was exceedingly well received and was deservedly complimented by Gibson who succeeded him and by Sir S. Northcote later on in the debate. I think he is certain to make his mark in the House. He has remarkable power of putting his thoughts together clearly and ably, has an excellent delivery, and inherits much of his father's charm of voice. Baring also the same evening made a successful maiden speech. George Hamilton led off on Friday, and Mr. G. considered that he fully sustained his reputation as a 'ready, able, and effective speaker'. Fawcett followed and spoke powerfully. Lord Hartington wound up for the defence in a speech with what Mr. G. termed 'really masterly and crushing force, his speech being little less than a textbook of the whole argument'. Sir S. Northcote, who had the last word, was somewhat tame, and more than usually unpleasant in his voice and delivery, without making any attempt to reply to Lord Hartington's arguments. The Government got a rattling majority of 120, thus exceeding the most sanguine expectation formed of the result of the division. I met Mr. G. in Downing St. on returning from the House, and on my remarking to him about the magnificent majority, he said, 'Yes, but not so magnificent as Hartington's speech'. Mr. G. was evidently very anxious that Lord Hartington should have the full credit for the affair, and was greatly gratified at the very masterly way in which Lord H. had played the leading part. He thought that there was a great display of ability on both sides throughout the debate, but it struck him that there was something 'unreal' in it to Liberals, considering that the resolution or rather vote of censure 'simply took exception to the moment of quitting Kandahar, with the appearance of utter uncertainty as to the principle on which, or as to the time for which, the evacuation should be delayed'.

From a party point of view the tactics of the Tories on this question have been singularly beneficial to the Government and the Liberal party generally, and proportionately damaging to the Opposition, the result of these tactics being to have voluntarily placed the House of Lords in direct antagonism with the Lower House and to have united the Liberal party almost to a man. There were only some half dozen defaulters.

Sunday, 27 March. At the Cabinet yesterday they made considerable progress with the Land Bill. They also agreed to institute legal proceedings against the Socialist organ called the *Freiheit* on the 'wicked and shameful character' of which Mr. G. expatiated to the Queen. It contained a most outrageous article of exultation on the assassination of the Czar, and its sale in this country is a reflection on England.

As regards the Greek frontier, the Cabinet evidently attach greater weight to keeping the Concert of Europe intact than to risk it by attempting to extort better terms for Greece. What the Powers have agreed to is to the award to Greece of nearly the whole of Thessaly and to the razing of the fortifications of Prevesa. Greece by this arrangement would get some 8000 additional square miles and the free navigation of the Gulf of Arta, which amounts to about 2/3 of the Berlin award. It is presumable that Turkey will accede to this, but it remains to be seen whether Greece will accept the terms. The odds are, I think, that she will.

The Wolseley peerage business still hangs fire. Her Majesty has, however, given way to the extent of expressing her willingness to creat Sir G[arnet] a peer provided he resigns his office of Quartermaster General. This seems to me a fair and reasonable compromise; but Childers won't have it. He considers himself pledged and his honor staked to the recommendation in its entirety. It is an unfortunate, disagreeable, and unsatisfactory business.

Mr. G. has written to the Princess of Wales to thank for her present of the pencil case.[1] He said his tree-felling days were all but over, but that her remembrance of his propensity would 'gild their decline'. Apropos of the play on the word 'axes' of which H.R.H. made use in her letter to Mrs. G., Mr. G. inclosed the following lines which were an impromptu of the famous Theodore Hook:

> There sits Mr. Winter,
> Collector of Taxes;
> I advise you to pay him
> Whatever he '*axes*'.

[1] See 21 Mar. 1881.

For he is a gentleman
As won't stand no flummery,
And though his name's Winter,
His proceedings are '*summery*'.

As an instance of his never losing an opportunity of expressing his
sympathy with those in trouble, Mr. G. made time yesterday in the midst of
his Budget work, Land Bill, and Cabinet proceedings to write a charming
letter to Mr. Reed on the occasion of the death of his father Sir Charles
Reed, M.P.

Wednesday, 30 March. The Cabinet met on Monday and again on today to
consider the Land Bill. They have made satisfactory progress and 'prosecuted
with great diligence the revision' of the measure, as Mr. G. told the Queen.
He is evidently in good heart about it. The Duke of Argyll is 'stumbling' over
Free Sale, and it is still uncertain whether he will swallow the pill.[1] The Lord
Chancellor,[2] in spite of the line he took in 1870, has bolted it with avidity.
I feel in good heart about the Bill. Certainly on no measure were greater pains
ever bestowed. The draft itself, irrespective of the notes or heads for the Bill,
has undergone nearly 20 revisions.

I don't feel at all happy, on the other hand, about the Budget, though it
seems absurd and presumptuous not to have implicit faith in any financial
proposals emanating from the Great Man. But I am very uncomfortable
about the changes he intends making with regard to the Probate and Legacy
Duties. If the expenditure for the new year is taken with the income on its
present basis, there will be some £1,300,000 to spare. This is about the sum
which 1^d taken off the income tax—the 1^d imposed solely to enable the malt
duty to [be] repealed last year—will absorb; and in order to enable him to
have a good working balance, he proposes to put on 1% to Probate and take
off 1% for Legacy duties, thereby doing away with a certain number of the
reversions arising from lineals taking after the widow, and thus accelerating
the revenue together with taxing widows to the extent of some £600,000. He
will also allow debts to be deducted and make the Probate Duty an uniform
percentage. This plan will be exceedingly complicated; the idea of taxing the
widow will be very unpopular, and Mr. G. will, after his speeches last year in
Midlothian inveighing against Sir S. Northcote's proposals,[3] lay himself open
greatly to retort.

[1] He didn't. See 6 Apr. 1881.
[2] Lord Selborne, who, as Sir Roundell Palmer, had been an opponent of many aspects
of the Land Act of 1870, acquiescing in it only reluctantly. See his *Memorials Part II
Personal and Political 1865–1895* (London, 1898), ii. 25–7.
[3] Just before the dissolution of Parliament in 1880 Sir Stafford Northcote, as Chancellor
of the Exchequer, had introduced as part of his budget proposals a Probate Duty Bill,
which G. had then attacked in his Midlothian campaign prior to the General Election.

Mr. G. has offered Welby what he calls the 'blue ribbon' of the Treasury—the Auditorship of the Civil List,[1] vice Law—as a deserved mark of honour.

Thursday, 31 March. This morning Mr. G. had a long interview with the Inland Revenue people, and most interesting indeed was the conversation. He will on Monday be able to give a most satisfactory review of the beer duty. There never was seemingly a greater financial feat and success. It is extraordinary how he bowls over all the difficulties connected with financial proposals, and on the whole I was made happier as to the prospects of the Budget. He will anyhow have a somewhat larger margin to work on than we originally anticipated, and this evening the idea has crossed his mind of reducing the income tax by $1\frac{1}{2}$d to $4\frac{1}{2}$d. He is evidently on his metal [*sic*] about his financial statement, and we shall at any rate be assured of a magnificent exposition.

The Duke of Argyll says he must go.[2] He can't swallow Free Sale. There is still some hope that, by a little judicious talk over with the Lord Chancellor, who is somewhat of his mind, he may be prevented from taking the plunge of resignation. Mr. G. has begged that in any case he will say nothing about it till after the introduction of the Bill. His resignation would not of itself be a great blow to the Government, but the effect his leaving them might have on the Lords would very likely jeopardise the Bill in the Upper House. If he does go, I suppose we shall have Lord Derby to succeed him. That might create difficulties with the Queen.

Lord Beaconsfield has been and is seriously ill. His illness has stirred up a universal feeling of sympathy in much the same manner and degree as did Mr. G.'s illness last year. Mr. G. has been most attentive in calling. He has been twice to the house himself and has sent up every morning.

Lord Lytton made a curious admission to Harry Brand the other day. Harry Brand remarked that the terms of Stanhope's motion the other day about Kandahar practically constituted a throwing up of the sponge. In this Lord Lytton entirely agreed. If we are to leave Kandahar, he admits that the sooner we get out of the place the better. What he goes in for is permanent occupation, not postponement of the step.

Friday, 1 April. There is evidently no hope of saving the Duke of Argyll. His resignation is very serious. Not only will it embolden the Lords to oppose the Land Bill, but it is a sign of the times in regard to the action of the Whigs. He is a thoroughly representative Whig; and the party whom he represents, whether in the Upper or Lower House, will or probably will follow suit. In short, I foresee great trouble ahead regarding the Bill. It appears that it is not only Free Sale over which the Duke is stumbling, but likewise the interference

---

[1] A post that EWH was to hold in the last years of his career at the Treasury.
[2] See his *Autobiography and Memoirs* (London, 1906), ii. 370–1.

of the Court,[1] a principle which even the Tory Commission of the Duke of Richmond admitted. This *may* be a possibly hopeful symptom. It is certainly a matter greatly to be deprecated—the possible, if not probable, conflict between the two chambers, and if the Opposition are to lose the counsel of Lord Beaconsfield, they may run wholly riot in the Upper House. Though better, Lord B. is still in an anxious state, and there is little chance of his coming to the front again for a long time. Therefore it is quite possible the question of the Leadership of the Conservative Party may crop up immediately. I think the 'first favourite' for this, on the whole, is Lord Cairns, but he is a man of whom not 1 out of 1000 electors have ever heard. If he does succeed to Dizzie, it will certainly be curious that the aristocratic party should be again led by what is practically an upstart, who has without antecedents made his own way.

Sunday, 3 April. At the Cabinet yesterday, surprising though it may seem, Mr. G.'s financial proposals were not accepted, i.e. they took exception to the way he proposed to deal with the Death Duties, to the suggestion [of] $\frac{1}{2}$d off the income tax in addition to the 1d, and to the idea of taxing settled personalty more heavily. It was rather 'cheek' perhaps their taking this line, but I think they were right, and the proposals now are far more satisfactory to my mind, though I don't know to whom they are attributable. The Probate Duty is to be raised $\frac{1}{2}$% all round, and the 1% (lineals) in the Legacy Duty scale is to be abolished; accordingly lineals will all benefit to the extent of $\frac{1}{2}$%, and all others, widows and widowers included, will pay $\frac{1}{2}$% more all round. One penny is to come off the income tax.

The Land Bill underwent its final revision at the Cabinet.

Matters at Athens are critical. All the Powers are agreed to the line they have extorted from the Porte, viz. practically the whole of Thessaly, a small slice of Epirus, and the demolition of the fortifications of Prevesa at the mouth of the Gulf of Arta, so as to secure the free navigation of the Gulf. Greece kicks, as she is probably bound to do, and it is natural that she should do; but one hopes that she will, on being pressed, accept the verdict of Europe. It is not a satisfactory settlement in itself, but anything is better than an outbreak of war and the break-up of the Concert of Europe.

The Queen still holds out about Sir G. Wolseley. She declines to make him a peer if he retains his Quartermaster Generalship. If the Government must have military assistance in the House of Lords, She suggests a man like Sir N. Chamberlain.

Monday, 4 April. Budget day. Great bustle all the morning. Sir C. Herries 'turned' in his Probate Lesson early. What with his deafness and the state of

---

[1] i.e. the Land Court provided for by the Bill.

his health, he is getting passed his work, at any rate when Mr. G. is Chancellor of the Exchequer. Poor Algy West in a terrible state of mind, and no wonder; for he is in an awkward position. He knows what the Great Man's ways and requirements are, and yet it is difficult for him to take the lead out of his Chairman's hands.[1]

After the usual hustle and bustle on a Budget day, went down to the House. Mr. G. was in his happiest financial vein, for he interested and almost entranced his audience for $2\frac{1}{4}$ hours, while he had but poorish materials with which to deal. If his budget this year will not rank among his great financial feats, at any rate it will not show any falling off in his extraordinary powers of exposition. The construction alone of his speech was ingenuity personified. It is premature to say how his proposals will be received, but there seems every reason to suppose that they will be accepted without much criticism. The Opposition are probably disappointed at his being enabled to take off the 1[d] income tax he put on last year for the purpose of converting the malt duty into a beer tax.

Wednesday, 6 April. The Duke of Argyll has taken the final plunge and today Mr. G. has submitted his resignation to the Queen. It is a blow to Mr. G. parting with the Duke, but no great surprise. Mr. G. says he expected it from the commencement. He loses a great personal friend, and the minister of whom he is probably most fond. The Duke is the only man in the Cabinet to whom Mr. G. subscribes himself as 'affect[ly]'. Mr. G. has proposed to H.M. that Lord Carlingford should take the office of Privy Seal, and probably this is the wisest appointment he can make. Lord C. will be of immense use on the Irish Land Bill.

We were all startled this morning by the appearance in the first leading article of the *Standard* of an accurate resumé of the Land Bill.[2] The writer evidently had the latest revise of the Bill, or of the analysis, which did not contain the 'occupying ownership' clauses and the provisions relating to reclamation and emigration. Suspicion at once points her finger to Chamberlain through whom undoubtedly extraordinary revelations have appeared now and again in the *Standard*.[3] This suspicion is confirmed by what F. Lawley told Lord Northbrook, viz. that Chamberlain had intimated his intention to communicate a copy of the Bill to that paper. It is a bit of downright treachery, and I hope it will be brought home to him. A Cabinet is to hold an inquiry into the matter on Friday, and if it were not for the disastrous

---

[1] Herries was the Chairman of the Board of Inland Revenue of which West was one of the commissioners. West was to succeed Herries as Chairman later in the year. See 9 and 11 Nov. 1881.

[2] *Standard*, 6 Apr. 1881, p. 4, cols. 6–8.

[3] Chamberlain thought that Forster, who had close contact with Mudford of the *Standard*, had been responsible. See Joseph Chamberlain, *A Political Memoir 1880–92* (London, 1953), pp. 9–10. But see 10 Apr. and 3 Dec. 1881.

effects of losing another member of the Cabinet, Chamberlain according to his deserts ought to be required to go. Mr. G., though much annoyed, has taken it calmly, but considering that the announcement, which was put in so authoritatively as to make every one believe in its authenticity, has taken the greater part of the wind out of Mr. G.'s sails tomorrow, he might well resent it still more. It is vexatious and degrading to say the least of it to think that any member of the Cabinet should commit such a breach of confidence.

Certainly it is extraordinary the continued series of excitements one witnesses here. It must be remembered, however, that nothing is as yet proved.

A good deal of disappointment has been expressed as to the unheroic character of the Budget, but it has on the whole given great satisfaction.

Thursday, 7 April. The much looked for Land Bill has at last been introduced. The exposition of it by Mr. G. was masterly and clearness itself. He wound himself up magnificently at the end. It seemed to be well received, but it is useless to speculate at present as to how it will be received. It is so complicated that everybody must necessarily reserve judgment about it. Moreover, 'first thoughts' as to measures are by no means a good criterion of ultimate thoughts.

At question time, the Attorney General[1] slated and crumpled up Randolph Churchill in a truly delightful manner over a charge he brought against Dilke and T. Brassey as to their subscribing to the nihilist paper, the *Freiheit*. The charge of course was wholly without foundation.

Lord Beaconsfield was worse today. I should doubt now his getting over it. It is whispered that he is really suffering from a far more serious disorder than appears on the face of the bulletins, i.e. 'Bright's disease'.

Sunday, 10 April. Lord Beaconsfield still struggles on. He has made one or two rallies, but his strength seems to be gradually failing.

Comments on the Land Bill in the press are very favourable. No marked hostility has been displayed against it by the Tories, and the Irish party seem not disinclined to accept it. What I fear is that, though the purport of the Bill may be liked, it will break down through its complexity and cumbersomeness when it comes to be analysed and put to a working test. The principle criticism seems to be that too much responsibility and discretion is placed in the Court and the Land Commission, and more especially that exception will be taken to the local courts proceeding from distrust in their being unbiassed. On the one hand, there seems to be a disposition on the part of landlords to take advantage of the selling powers offered in the Bill; yet on the other hand, the more security you afford to the tenants, the less will they be disposed

---

[1] Sir Henry James.

to resort to buying, when you practically give them what they want without their saddling themselves with the burden of purchase money. Lord Cork, with whom I was talking this afternoon, held much the same view.

As far as the evidence regarding the leak in the *Standard* the other day is capable of being sifted, ministers seem to be acquitted, which will absolve Chamberlain. A careful comparison of the article with the various drafts of the Bill seeems to prove that the writer must have had draft No. 16, which was *not* circulated. At the same time, even if ministers are cleared as regards the *Standard*, they have to account for the fact that Hayward had a copy of the Bill which he shewed in the Athenaeum on Thursday, and Hutton (*Spectator*) had another copy in his hands admittedly 'given him by a Cabinet minister'. For this Sir H. Thring can vouch.[1]

The Queen has made known her wishes that She intends conferring a peerage upon Prince Leopold under the title of the 'Duke of Albany'.

Mr. G. went down to Hawarden yesterday in great spirits. He is none the worse for his great week, which comprised the Budget as well as the Land Bill.

Lord Carlingford has accepted the Privy Seal vice the Duke of Argyll.

Monday, 11 April. Mitchell Henry writes to me today in raptures over the Land Bill. 'It is the greatest work of all the great works of Mr. Gladstone'. This looks as if the Bill will at any rate be cordially supported by the Irish Liberal party, as distinguished from the Parnellites.

The Duke of Argyll's resignation has not produced any sensible impression. The Tories have not crowed over it, and the Liberals have not lamented over it, while the Radicals silently regard it as a good omen of the efficacy of the Bill. Apropos of his resignation, Lord Hartington said the other day he sympathised with him (the Duke), as he (Lord H.) had found the Bill a difficult morsel to swallow. However, he seems quite safe, and though he asks not to be put to the front in the discussion over it more than can be helped, he is willing to support it and defend himself.

The Prince of Wales has written to Mr. G. an account of his experiences in Russia during his visit there.[2] Mr. G. was greatly interested by it, and in writing to H.R.H. he said 'the way to put down nihilism is without doubt to enlist the community on the side of the supreme power and of the person bearing it'. He (Mr. G.) has evidently confidence in the new Czar and his good intentions. Lord Dufferin, on the other hand, says the Czar is not a man of any ability, that he is obstinate, rough and shy, and is without any experience of men and affairs owing to his recluse habits.[3]

[1] See 6 Apr. and 3 Dec. 1881. The memorandum of 8 Apr. 1881 describing the process by which EWH and Thring deduced that the source of the article was Draft No. 16 is in Add. MS. 44189, ff. 63–5. The Cabinet ministers' letters of denial of having handed drafts to Hayward or Hutton follow on ff. 73–83.

[2] The Prince had represented his mother at Alexander II's funeral.

[3] See Sir Sidney Lee, *King Edward VII. A Biography* (London, 1925), i. 507 n.

The Prince of Wales has recommended for baronetcies 4 men, of whom Freake is the only one known to ordinary fame. It is perhaps hardly fair to say so, but these recommendations have rather an ugly look about them. A respectable clergyman wrote not long since to say that he was in possession of information, to which he could swear, that there were certain persons who were scheming for hereditary honours in consideration of bribes, and bribes to people in very high life.[1]

Sunday, 17 April. Had a very busy week of it. The fact is, that when Mr. G. is away, which almost always means one or two of the secretaries being away, work is at higher pressure than when he is here and we are all in full swing. If it were not that there were less interruptions in his absence, it would be impossible to carry on the business. As it is, Seymour and myself have hardly managed to keep our heads above water, in other words, to escape from getting into terrible arrears.

In one way, in Mr. G.'s absence, the work is almost more interesting. Separation from his colleagues means more letters, and from letters one gets perhaps the best insight into his mind.

While at Hawarden, he has been much taken up with literature, more especially theological works. People pour in books upon him. He finds time to thank some with his own pen, and to peruse, if not read, mostly all.

His avidity for books, expecially theological, is simply extraordinary. By this I mean his greediness to acquire books. He goes carefully through catalogues of sales of old books, marks lots, and buys. Nine out of ten of these are theological. His library must have assumed enormous proportions.

During the last week we have had a renewal of correspondence with the Duke of Argyll.[2] Mr. G. was touched greatly by the Duke's parting words and reference to himself in the House of Lords when he made his short explanatory statement regarding his resignation.[3] In writing to express his feelings on

[1] The Revd. H. W. Bellairs, vicar of Nuneaton, wrote G. on 21 Feb. 1881 to warn him of some information that had come to him from a gentleman who had been offered a baronetcy both by the Carlton Club in return for a payment to its election fund and by 'an emissary of the Prince of Wales . . . on condition that he would pay the sum of £30,000 to the Prince's agent on receiving the title'. Add. MS. 44468, ff. 149–51. In the Prince's letter to G. of 9 Apr. 1881 he asks G. to consider 'the names of the four gentlemen who I spoke to you about in February last' for baronetcies. In this letter he mentions no names but in reply to a letter from G. questioning the claims and political loyalties of the candidates the Prince mentioned Mr. Antony Gibbs as 'a strong Liberal' and Mr. Freake as having no 'special politics'. See letters of 9, 10, and 12 Apr. 1881 in B.M. Res. MS. 25/28. In Mar. 1882 the Prince brought up the case of Freake again calling attention to Freake's generosity in relation to the new Royal College of Music, and in April G. included Freake in a list of men to be made baronets. See letters of 8 Mar., 15 and 16 Apr. 1882, B.M. Res. MS. 25/28. Antony Gibbs (1842–1907), a member of the Junior Carlton, became Sheriff of Somerset in 1888 but never received a title. See also 8 and 20 Apr. 1882.

[2] See some extracts in the Duke's *Autobiography and Memoirs* (London, 1906), ii. 371–2.

[3] *Parl. Deb.*, 8 Apr. 1881, cclx. 993–4.

this incident, Mr. G. let fall that he was anxiously looking 'for the first door open to him by which he may escape from office and bid it a final farewell'. He considers that his occupation, more than any other, 'demands a space between the arena and the grave'. He told the Duke that 'every remnant of his energy' should be addressed to the prompt settlement of the question of land legislation for Ireland. The Duke said he regarded it as most unfortunate that Mr. G. has had, or should at least now intend, to throw all his personality into the Irish land question. It was, the Duke maintains, no part of of Mr. G.'s programme, (nor more it was); it has been mismanaged, and Mr. G.'s energies will be spent in what the Duke believes will be no settlement, but an unsettlement. The Duke, however, admits that Mr. G. has been more conservative on this question than many others. Mr. G. argues that there is no doubt that his personality *is* pledged over head and ears to the Irish Land Bill and to pass it this session, but that he himself did not so pledge it —it pledged itself. He says that with a country under coercion and only just escaped from anarchy, after such an antecedent history with men like the Land Leaguers, and an institution like the Land League to confront and overcome, he holds that it is a question of the peace of Ireland and perhaps of the union of the three kingdoms, and that were he the greatest 'poltroon' on the face of the earth, he should necessarily be 'driven forward' by forces. Moreover, Mr. G. reminded the Duke that, besides themselves, 6 ministers wished to go *further*—(probably meaning Forster, Harcourt, Bright, Chamberlain, and query the other two), and that the one who in all the later stages had most sympathised with the Duke had at the earlier stages proposed a plan far more radical than the Bill—evidently referring to Lord Hartington.

Mr. G. is evidently afraid—and no wonder—that the Duke will prove very formidable in the House of Lords when the Bills get up there. The Duke ought, out of regard for his late colleagues, [to] hold his tongue; it is one thing to have to support a measure and another thing to take no part or responsibility on it.

At present, however, the Duke's resignation has produced little or no adverse effect on the Government or the Bill. The fact is, he has been rather a thorn in the side of the Cabinet and has worried Mr. G. out of his life by his reiterated scruples in perpetual letters. So his departure will not be an unmixed evil. Mr. G. said to Lord Spencer the other day that the Duke had 'learnt less' since he had become a minister than any more inferior to him would have done; he had, in short, never thoroughly given himself to politics.

The Land Bill still continues to be favourably received by all parties, and Mr. G. is pleased beyond expectation thus far; but thus far, as he said himself the other day, does not mean everything.

During the last few days Lord Beaconsfield has made a wonderful rally and seems on a fair way to convalescence; he has certainly made a wonderful fight of it. Mr. G. is, I believe, conscientiously pleased.

Mr. G. has been much exercised in his mind at Hawarden at the fact that he observes snowdrops on the ground together with daisies, buttercups, and primroses. If this is an extraordinary phenomenon, I presume it is due to the lengthened spell of extraordinarily dry weather and the consequent backwardness of the country.

Tuesday, 19 April. I was woke up this morning by the news of Lord Beaconsfield's death. Until yesterday he seemed in a fair way to recovery, but late in the afternoon weakness increased and spasms returned, resulting in a collapse terminated early this morning. Thus ends one of the most remarkable and eventful careers in English history. One cannot help feeling that by his death a prodigious blank is made in politics. They will be now denuded of half their brilliancy, interest, and excitement. One of 'the two great gladiators' in the 19th century is gone, and the remaining one will, I know, greatly feel the disappearance of the other. Most conspicuous of all the qualities of Lord Beaconsfield comes his courage,—his courage in long adversity, his courage against his foes, and his courage against his political friends, many of whom up till within the last few years of his life longed to be rid of him. Next to his courage would probably come his extraordinary dexterity and ingenuity, and after that his sagacity and knowledge of character.

I have noted nothing during the last week about the Greek question. The latest and dwindled award of the Powers sitting in conclave at Constantinople has been accepted by Greece, but under great reserve. There seems a fair hope of their acquiescing in the decision and taking the award as an instalment, and at any rate of peace [*sic*]. Mr. G. is afraid that Bismarck will hold everything subordinate to his favourite purpose of troubling the East and of setting the Powers at loggerhead. He (Mr. G.) thinks that Turkey under the circumstances should be urged in her own interests to give the Epirotes some measure of self-government, such as Crete enjoys.

There has been, and still is, a disagreeable Tunis affair. France is in process of exacting by force of arms reparation for some raid by the Tunisians in Algeria, not being satisfied with the assurance given by the Bey of Tunis that he can and will punish the marauders. France desires an excuse, and she thinks she has now got it, of asserting herself in North Africa. The consequence is Italy, jealous of any extended influence of another power in the Mediterranean, professes to be hurt and alarmed; and she sees, or imagines she sees, an evident desire on the part of France to annex Tunis. She is confirmed in this idea by something which apparently fell from Lord Salisbury's lips at Berlin at the time of the Congress. It has transpired that, when the question of our acquiring Cyprus was first mooted, he hinted to France that if she wanted an equivalent acquisition in the Mediterranean she had better lay hold of Tunis, to which we should not object. There has been no categorical denial to this, and so reckless and dangerous an encouragement to 'bag' does not reflect much to the credit of Lord Salisbury. In connection with this affair, Mr. G. the other day referred to the marked manner in which his (Lord S.) character has suffered of late—the character of a man whose 'good fame used to be regarded as part of the national estate'.

In view of the *West Cheshire* election, Mr. G. congratulated Tomkinson, the Liberal candidate, the other day in taking the bull by the horns on the Transvaal matter in his address, and said that he himself should adopt no apologetic tone when he comes to discuss it in Parliament and defend the action of the Government. It was a question, he maintains, of 'saving the country from sheer blood-guiltiness'. True; but, if so, why was there any blood shed at all? One knows the difficulties surrounding this disagreeable question, but I fear there are many weak points in the defence.

Mr. G. reverted the other day to the question of giving the Speaker the GCB. Lord Granville agreed. Knowing, however, that the Speaker's conduct had, though most undeservedly, been regarded in Tory circles as rather biassed, and believing that an honour conferred now would tend to confirm the opinion that he had shewn more willingness to assist his own friends, the Liberals, in their difficulties than the late Government, when they were similarly confronted by obstruction, I took upon myself to suggest the advisability of at any rate postponing this step till the end of the session, a suggestion which I am glad to say has been acted on.

Friday, 22 April. Came down yesterday to Longleat. Nobody here but Wetherall (Lord G[ranville]'s former Private Secretary), Mr. Jackson (a clergyman), and Mr. Chany, a sort of old dilettante. It is certainly a magnificent place, and it is very pleasant getting a few days breathing in the country, but that horrid East wind continues. Lord Bath very agreeable and pleasant. Lady Bath as charming and beautiful as ever.

The question of a public funeral for Lord Beaconsfield has been finally given up. I am very glad the offer was made; and I am also glad it has been refused, though there would certainly be something peculiarly appropriate to the termination of such an extraordinary career in a grand funeral ceremony in Westminster Abbey. I had a talk with Sir P. Rose on the subject on Wednesday, and I think it is clear that the executors could have come to no other conclusion than they did. They were evidently much gratified at Mr. Gladstone's writing to make the offer; but, besides the wording of the will which was explicit, and directed that Lord Beaconsfield should be buried quietly at Hughenden, there was a letter of Lady Beaconsfield, which influenced them much, which she had left to Lord B. with her will, and on which he had set great store.[1] That letter—Sir P. Rose shewed me a copy of it—implored 'her Dizzie' in most touching terms to be laid beside her, no

---

[1] Sir Philip Rose was one of the executors of Beaconsfield's will. See also George E. Buckle, *The Life of . . . Disraeli . . .* (N.Y., 1920), v. 232 and vi. 619.

matter where he might die. The country will no doubt be disappointed. Sir P. Rose told me that Lord Beaconsfield had never himself had the least hope of recovery from the very first day of his illness. He appears to have shewn great courage and patience throughout it, and to have displayed immense consideration for all those around him. Assured of such immortality, he could afford to die bravely.

The funeral is to take place on Tuesday at Hughenden. Mr. G. is, I believe, to be asked to adjourn the House from Monday after the necessary 'funeral orations' till Wednesday. I doubt if there are precedents for this. Mr. G. is evidently anxious as to what he shall say on Monday. It certainly will be a most difficult and delicate task, but yet there is no one who can perform a task of difficulty and delicacy in such good taste and with such dexterity. His letter to the Queen yesterday probably foreshadows the line of thought he will take.[1] He said that such an occasion of deep and national interest was entirely beyond the reach of controversy which belong to differences of political parties; and, though he could not dissemble the amount or character of the separation between Lord B. and himself, yet it did not at all blind him to the extraordinary powers of the deceased statesman, and to 'many remarkable qualities, in regard to which he was well aware of his own marked inferiority, and the example of which he could only desire to profit by'.

Sir Dudley Marjoribanks has returned to his application for a peerage. There is something singularly indecent and vulgar in these personal requests for honours. What are honours, unless gratuitously conferred? And what are the particular claims of Marjoribanks, except money and a certain amount of loyalty to his party? I wish it were a rule, and a known rule, that anybody who applied personally on such matters should *ipso facto* go down to the 'bottom of the list'.

Mr. G. is pleased with the 2nd volume of Bishop Wilberforce's life done by R. Wilberforce. He thinks it successful and satisfactory. I am rather surprised, as, though I have not yet read the book, I have glanced at it sufficiently to show that there are some grave indiscretions more especially affecting Mr. G. himself.

It appears that Rosebery positively was mortified at the idea of not having been consulted about the succession to the Privy Seal.[2] Really to set up such a claim is preposterous. I am very sorry for it, for I believed better things of him. Mr. G. is extremely concerned. What Rosebery evidently wants is to be lifted straight into the Cabinet without subordinate office; and, if that is not feasible, to be taken into consultation regarding the constitution of the Cabinet!—on which Cabinet ministers themselves are not consulted except such men as Lord G[ranville] and Lord Hartington.

[1] Guedalla, ii. 153.
[2] The office resigned by Argyll to which Lord Carlingford was appointed. See Lord Crewe, *Lord Rosebery* (London, 1931), p. 112.

By the way Queensberry wrote the other day to beg to be made an English peer now that his pronounced extreme religious opinions have ousted him from the select circle of representative peers in Scotland.[1] It is needless to say Mr. G. declined. It is bad enough to have a Bradlaugh case in the House of Commons not of your own creation, but to go and place of your own free will a man of similar opinions in the Upper House would be to invite a rare outburst of religious squalling.

Sunday, 24 April. (Longleat) Had much talk with Lord Bath especially about Land Bill. He does not like it, as might be expected; but he regards it as a political necessity and the inevitable sequel to the Act of 1870. He takes the line, which most of the landlords seem to be taking up, that if the condition of land tenure is to be so revolutionised they ought to be given the option of getting out of their properties, or else to be entitled to compensation; and still more that at any rate they shall be secured in future against a recurrence of the agitation and the cessation of rent payments. But whatever is done, or is not done, what Lord Bath insists most upon is the inadvisability of the Lords throwing out or mutilating the Bill.

Monday, 25 April. Returned to Town after much enjoying my little outing at Longleat, the principal feature of which was the agreeable conversation. It is a pity Lord Bath has been and is thrown away for public life. He is a man undoubtedly of great ability, well read, and keenly interested in politics. He is a keen Liberal partisan as regards men, and at heart a real Conservative as regards measures.

The funeral orations on Lord B[eaconsfield] have been put off until the resolution which Mr. G. intends moving a fortnight hence in favor of a monument in Westminster Abbey. Lord B. has, I understand, left everything to his nephew, a young son of his brother Ralph.

We shall now have nothing but the Land Bill, and I confess I feel anxious about its fate. If any amendments are accepted in the interests of the landlords, it will divorce the Irish party; and if any amendments are accepted in the line which the Irish party will advocate, we shall meet with difficulties from the Whigs and the Conservatives. It seems therefore that it must be the Bill, the whole Bill (practically as it stands), and nothing but the Bill.

Wednesday, 27 April. The debate on the 2nd Reading of the Bill was not very satisfactory. Gibson led off and assailed the Bill as a measure of confiscation, but did not say he would vote against it. As it was thought that those who had amendments on the paper would lead off, it was not expected that anyone would have to speak on the Government side early in the evening, and what

[1] Queensberry was a secularist with opinions similar to Bradlaugh's. See *G.E.C.,* x. 706, note d.

with this and the absence of Mr. G. at the commencement of the sitting, the debate nearly collapsed about dinner time, and the collapse was only staved off by a motion for adjournment. Forster replied after dinner to Gibson 'with great temper and ability' (as Mr. G. thought), having been preceded by an able speech—'admirable' according to Mr. G.—from Lymington.

Last night was again sensational. Bradlaugh came forward to take the oath and was objected to by Sir S. Northcote. The Conservatives had sent out a very strong whip. The Government declined to make it a party question, and argued strictly on the line that the taking of the oath by Mr. Bradlaugh was legal, however bad taste on his part it might be, which it was not for the Government to question. The Tories maintained that after what happened last year, it was derogatory to the dignity of the House and making the oath a farce in letting the man do what he declined to do last year on the ground that the oath had no meaning in it to him. The House was in an excited, heated state. Bright and Mr. G. pleaded the case with great good temper and moderation as well as with arguments which apart from the question of conscience appeared to me to admit of no flaw. Besides the strictly legal view of the case, which was supported by the highest authorities including the Speaker and Sir E. May, there was the unanswerable plea that if the right to question a man's judgment in such a matter and to take exception to a man's belief or disbelief were once admitted, there was no saying where it might end. But the Tories saw they had the chance of playing effectively the part of defenders of the faith and of putting the Government in a disagreeable hole, and accordingly they had made up their minds to follow blindly the injudicious lead of Northcote and chance the consequences. Northcote's conduct in the matter just at this time savoured strongly of a bid for the leadership of his party. The outward conduct of the Opposition throughout the evening, commencing with the most ill-mannerly interruptions while Davey who followed Northcote moved his amendment, and continued by violence and general discourtesy as well as accompanied by all kinds of base imputations, made my blood boil. The result was a triumph to the Tories, Northcote carrying his motion by a majority of 33. It can't be called a defeat to the Government, as they declined to make it a party question though they acted in concert with one another, but in the country they will be discredited by a supposed alliance and sympathy with Bradlaugh. Mr. G. was greatly worried and distressed in the matter.

Thursday, 28 April. Yesterday the House cooled down a bit over the Bradlaugh business. There was less virulence and bumptiousness on the Tory side, and a greater disposition on the part of the Government to come to the help of the Tories in the mess to which they had brought the whole House. The Government are prepared to lend a helping hand to a Bill to remove the anomaly about the oath and to enable anyone to affirm in lieu of taking the oath; and as Northcote admitted that he had no objection to the presence of Bradlaugh in the House, if the difficulty about the oath can be removed, he can hardly do otherwise than support such a Bill.

The *Morning Post* today gave an authoritative credence to the rumour that Northcote is to be leader of the party.[1] Mr. G. said to me this morning he should much regret that, if it is to be. He holds it to be most material to the welfare of both parties that neither should have a weak leader, which he considers Northcote would be. I doubt, however, if anyone will be proclaimed recognised leader of the party. It is more likely that they will go on with Northcote as leader in the Commons, elect a leader of the Lords, most probably the Duke of Richmond, and leave the leadership of the party to the chance of events.

Walter Northcote has been sounding Mr. G. through Algy West as to securing for Sir Stafford the political pension vacated by Lord Beaconsfield. Walter Northcote says his father can't maintain his position as Leader of the Opposition without living on his capital which is but very limited. Mr. G. sees difficulties in the way. He believes it is without precedent to confer a political pension on a member of the Opposition and thinks he should lay himself open to the charge of bribing his opponent. He has consulted Lord Granville, as he always does on everything.[2]

The Queen has been exercised in her mind as to Mr. G. not being present last Monday himself to give notice of the resolution about the memorial to Lord Beaconsfield, and as to nothing having been said in the House in the nature of a lamentation over the decease of her great statesman. The proceedings were, however, strictly in accordance with the precedent of Lord Palmerston and had the concurrence of Sir S. Northcote.

There is a row in the diplomatic world. Goschen's almost immediate return creates a vacancy at Constantinople, which is to be filled by Lord Dufferin. Dufferin's place at St. Petersburg was offered to Sir A. Paget, but he declines to quit Rome. He pleads a lame excuse on the ground of health, and Lord G[ranville] has evidently got his back up and is determined to be very firm and give Paget the choice of the British Embassy at St. Petersburg or nothing.[3] Paget is terribly aggrieved, but I expect will be beaten and have to quit the calling of an ambassador. I fear Lord G[ranville] has Rome in his mind for Layard in order to get over the difficulty about Layard's pension, but his re-appointment to an Embassy will raise a great outcry among Liberals. It would be looked upon as a reward, or at any rate as a condonation, for Jingoism.

A small instance of Mr. G.'s consideration came under one's notice yesterday. He offered a living in Cornwall to Mr. Knox Little, a High Church

[1] *Morning Post*, 28 Apr. 1881, p. 5, col. 1.   [2] Ramm, i. 267.
[3] Sir Augustus Paget remained as ambassador in Rome until 1883 after which he went to Vienna.

clergyman of some notoriety in Manchester, of limited means. Mr. Little did not find himself able to accept the offer, but having to go down and inspect the living incurred necessarily some expense. Mr. G. yesterday sent a cheque to the Dean of St. Paul's,[1] who knows Mr. Little well, with a request that the Dean will slip the cheque into Mr. Little's pocket as coming from an unknown friend, by way of reimbursing him in his expenses.

Lord Dufferin, who always writes well, described in a letter which came under one's notice today his interview with Bismarck on his way home from St. Petersburg. Bismarck appears to like much the idea, which I believe emanated from himself, that this country should act as a broker between Turkey and Greece, and receive the ceded country from the Porte to hand over to Greece. Bismarck rejoices in the Tunisian business. He is glad that France should be occupied with undertakings in the Mediterranean which will withdraw her attention from Germany. As to Italy, he likens her to a jackal inciting his neighbours to quarrel in the hope of picking up something herself.

I am glad to see St. Vallier[2] strongly condemns the proposal of Russia about a Nihilistic conference, because *cui bono*? We therefore shall not stand out alone in our refusal.

Friday, 29 April. The Tories have at last shewn their hands a little about the Land Bill. Lord J. Manners gave notice of an amendment last night on the 2nd Reading. It is singularly vague and judging from this morning's press has given satisfaction to none of the Tory party. It is very far from being a direct negative; it expresses a willingness to recognise existing tenant-right and to amend the shortcomings of the Act of 1870, and then proceeds to assert that the condition of Ireland is more likely to be ameliorated by developing the resources and industries of the country than by any fundamental changes in the land laws. From a party point of view, I think it is just as well that the question should be brought to a more or less direct issue. But for the country, I doubt if it is wise to do anything which will imperil a measure intended to be an efficient settlement. Failing that, there is no saying to what, short perhaps of revolution, the present grave state of affairs may lead.

The debate on the 2nd Reading of the Land Bill was continued last night. Lord Elcho led off. He stated the extreme landlord's point of view and stated it, as Mr. G. thought, in great good humour. C. Russell followed him and very ably supported the general outline of the Bill.

Wednesday, 4 May. Pursuant to decision of Cabinet last Friday, Dillon has been arrested. On the whole the arrest has been well received. But we are sure to have a row with the Parnellites and they may revenge themselves by not supporting the 2nd Reading of the Land Bill.

[1] R. W. Church.   [2] The French ambassador at Berlin.

Had a long talk last night with Lord Dufferin. He can't swallow the Bill. He admits that there are many good points in it, but he took forcible exception to the general character of the measure and assailed bitterly the indiscriminate Free Sale provisions. I am bound to admit that from a purely argumentative point of view those who assail the Bill stand on the firmest ground, but the real point is that something must be done, and is there any real alternative that would have the smallest beneficial effect?

The Society papers and Society at large are abusing Mr. G. and imputing to him the most mean and unworthy motives regarding his conduct and action in connection with Lord Beaconsfield's death. If he *had* gone to the funeral, of course they would have accused him of being a humbug.

Sunday, 8 May. Society is still rampant about the Beaconsfield incident. What is the truth of the whole story?

The very day on which Lord B. died, Mr. G. wrote and offered a public funeral. This was for very good reasons declined. Thereupon Mr. G. determined to follow the precedent of Lord Palmerston and move a resolution in the House in favor of erecting a monument in Westminster Abbey. On Monday the 25th, notice of this resolution had to be given, and following closely on the Palmerston precedent, it was determined that all speechifying on the resolution should be postponed till the day arrived on which it was to be moved. In this course Sir S. Northcote concurred. Meanwhile the executors of Lord Beaconsfield invited, admittedly *pro formâ*, Mr. G. to the funeral at Hughenden. Mr. G. wrote back and said he was afraid his engagements would not admit of his attending. Considering that the funeral was of a private character, it would have been going out of his way for Mr. G. to have gone down; and had it been desirable for him to have been present, there were urgent considerations against it, namely, the pressure of his work and his health. Had it been a public funeral, I feel sure Mr. G. would have gone *ex officio*; and this would have been in excess of what was done by the leaders of the Tories in the case of Lord Palmerston, none of whom, I believe, attended the ceremony. I admit that I think it would have been better had Mr. G. been present in the House to give notice of the monument resolution (he deputed Lord R. Grosvenor to do the formal act) and had he accompanied the notice with a single sentence expressive of the blank which Lord B.'s death had caused in the political world. But with this exception, no reasonable fault can be found with the course he has pursued. He has, on the contrary, done and offered to do more in honor of the late Prime Minister than the majority of precedents would have warranted. The outcry has been truly monstrous. It well demonstrates the intensely bitter feeling which the Tories entertain against the Great Man.

Mr. G. took immense pains with the wording of the resolution about the monument. He was anxious not 'to sail too near the wind' as he put it. 'Rare and splendid gifts and devoted labours in Parliament and in great offices of State' were truthful and ingenious words.

And so Lord Salisbury is to be leader after all—ostensibly leader of the House of Lords, but practically this will mean leader of the party, for he must absorb Northcote. I believe the choice is wise. There is no greater misfortune to either party and to the country than that one of the two parties should be led by a weak man, which certainly would have been the case had the Duke of Richmond led the Peers and Northcote the Commons on the Conservative side; for this would have meant *two weak* leaders. With Lord Salisbury, whatever objections there may be to him, there will be *one strong* man.

I was much surprised yesterday by an application arriving from Sir R. Cross for the political pension. I always imagined him to be a rich banker. It is curious that there should be such impecuniosity among the aristocratic leaders. We have now Lord J. Manners in receipt of a pension, and Northcote and Cross in want of another one.[1]

Mr. G. has been seedy the last few days. He has had one of his old diarrhoea attacks, brought on I fully believe by excessive mental worry, of which he has plenty.

Monday, 9 May. Mr. G. returned this morning from The Durdans quite set up again. Went down in the afternoon to hear him move his resolution in favor of a public monument to the memory of Lord Beaconsfield. He discharged his difficult task with most consummate skill. His speech was in perfection of taste, very forcible, and grandly impressive. He defended his proposals by reference to precedents, carefully avoided all contentious matter, pointed out the traits in Lord Beaconsfield's character which even his enemies must admire and would do well to imitate, and wound up by a touching conviction that the deceased statesman, however much he might have opposed him (Mr. G.), bore no personal antipathy to himself. Northcote seconded the resolution rather tamely. Labouchere followed by moving the previous question in a lengthy speech most impatiently listened to. The only other speaker was A. O'Connor.

Wednesday, 11 May. There has been one general chorus of approval of Mr. G.'s speech on the Beaconsfield monument from the Queen downwards. She wrote quite gushingly in expressing her pleasure at what Mr. G. said about her 'departed friend' and 'great statesman', and maintained that the speech will redound greatly to his honor.[2] The division was better than was expected. If ever a speech does influence votes, I believe it did in this instance to the extent of diminishing the minority considerably.

Lord Granville did his part in his different way as well as Mr. G. did. It was the essence of good taste. Lord Salisbury was somewhat heavy and

---

[1] See 28 Apr. and 4 Sept. 1881.   [2] Guedalla, ii. 155-6.

laboured, but complimentary speaking is not his *forte*; he ought to have had to criticise Lord Beaconsfield's character.

The Bradlaugh business is shelved momentarily. On his presenting himself again at the table to take the oath yesterday, Sir S. Northcote moved that Bradlaugh be not admitted within the precincts of the House until he gave an undertaking that he would not interrupt its proceedings by asserting his right to swear. Mr. G. accepted the situation and bowed to the will of the majority; whereupon the motion was agreed to without a division and Bradlaugh withdrew under protest. He has appealed to the country and to the Speaker. The Lord Chancellor was 'drawn' on the subject the other day and has written an excellent letter which has sent him up 50% in my estimation.[1]

Sunday, 22 May. Nearly 10 days have elapsed and nothing has been noted. This time of year what with going out in society and going down to the House one's evenings get terribly demoralised.

The principal item of news in the week has been the conclusion of the debate on the 2nd Reading of the Land Bill. Mr. Gladstone spoke on Monday night very forcibly and endeavoured to clear up some of the moot points in the measure. I missed his speech owing to his getting up being delayed by the usual adjournment of the House at question time. According to some, it was one of his finest efforts. He 'riled' the Opposition a good deal by lecturing them on the position they were taking up which he contrasted very unfavorably with Dizzie's line of conduct in 1870. On the last night (Thursday) Chaplin made a very telling speech and one of 'considerable ability and eloquence' as Mr. G. admitted. He represents the current feeling of the ordinary Tory landlord and of the ordinary London Society, which is to denounce the Bill in unmeasured terms as one of confiscation and robbery. They forget that by far the greatest innovation and the most radical provision in the whole Bill, namely, the regulation of rents by public authority, was distinctly countenanced by the Duke of Richmond and his colleagues on the Agricultural Commission, and on them must rest some of the responsibility of this recommendation, however much they may repudiate it.[2] I know this was the point on which Mr. G. himself had the greatest scruples, which the report of those landlords contributed not a little to surmount. On the same evening Parnell spoke—very tamely, I thought, and certainly not immoderately, very differently to the way in which he speaks on the Land League platform. The burden of his song was that the Bill was entirely unsatisfactory as a restitution to Ireland, and to mark his sense of its inadequacy he

---

[1] For an expression of Lord Selborne's opinion on this matter at this time, see his *Memorials Part II. Personal and Political 1865–1895* (London, 1898), i. 491–3.

[2] In the 'Preliminary Report from H.M. Commissioners on Agriculture' dated 14 Jan. 1881 the commissioners, with only one exception, stated that 'legislative interference to protect him [the tenant] from arbitrary increase of rent does not seem unnatural'. *Parl. Papers*, 1881, xv. 8.

declined to support the 2nd Reading. The only remedy for Ireland is to turn out of the country bag and baggage all Dublin Castle officials, the constabulary and the executive generally. Such was the way in which he wound up. Northcote followed. He was on the whole moderate and attempted to explain the action of his party. He failed, however, to give sufficient reason for voting against the Bill. Now and then he made use of a strong expression, but in a general way his speech was delivered tamely and received tamely. Hartington followed, and had no difficulty in forcibly exposing the hollowness, inconsistency, and impolicy of the tactics of the Tories. The division soon followed, and the result wholly eclipsed the most sanguine forecasts— a majority of 176! Quite overpowering. The debate throughout was tame and listless, no doubt partly to be accounted for by the evident foregone conclusion which was to be the issue. Its length, however, extending over 9 nights as did the debate, demonstrates forcibly how the parliamentary machinery is breaking down. What took 4 nights (I think) in 1870, when the Bill then was almost as great a new departure comparatively as the present Bill, now takes more than double that time. The prospects of Committee, where the real fight will begin, are simply appalling.

Almost nightly now the House is adjourned at question time by the Irish in order to have a Forster-bait in which men like Randolph Churchill join. The only object in view which these persons who take part in such proceedings have is to inflict discredit and dishonour on Parliament, to damage the Government, and to intercept the application of remedies to the condition of Ireland.

The outlook is certainly most grave outside as well as inside Parliament. Matters get worse in Ireland instead of better. Forster in short has been a lamentable failure. One can't help feeling the greatest pity for the man, as he is bent on doing good to the country, but he is the wrong man in the wrong place. Instead of striking quickly and indiscriminately under the Protection Act, he has struck too late and too fitfully. His arrests have lost none of their irritating effect and all their deterrent effect. Some strength must be given to the Irish executive. Forster hinted the other day at the desirability of getting Lord Spencer to take the Viceroyalty, but my belief is that, instead of a new Lord Lieutenant, what is wanted is a new Chief Secretary. Sir R. Blennerhassett, with whom I had a long talk this evening, would like to see Forster replaced by a man like Dilke or Courtney.

Pembroke sent me a Memorandum a day or two ago summarising the position of the Tory peers in the House of Lords, a Memorandum which Mr. G. said did 'great honor to his acumen and his prudence'. He wants—and I believe he speaks the feeling of many others—to see the House of Commons amend the Bill in the interests of the landlords, so that the Peers may be able to accept the measure *en bloc*.

The Queen has made an extraordinary proposal which is that a baronetage shall be conferred on Lord Beaconsfield's brother, Mr. Ralph Disraeli, father of Coningsby, the heir.[1] There is no precedent for conferring an honour on the collateral relatives of a deceased notability, and the brother was purposely and markedly passed by altogether in the will. Mr. G. said he could not oppose H.M. wishes, but expressed doubts as to the expediency of the proposal. The Queen seems to have got Beaconsfield on the brain, which reached its culminating point in the arrival of the peacocks at Windsor from Hughenden.

The Tunis question has occupied a good deal of attention. It is most extraordinary conduct on the part of France. It is a distinct revival of Imperialistic days, and is really playing Bismarck's game. The one thing of all others to please him is that France should be occupied in the Mediterranean instead of the Eastern frontier. The Tories would like to make a vigorous attack on the Government, but they dare not, owing to the correspondence in Lord Salisbury's reign which has now appeared.[2] In that correspondence there is a distinct though informal undertaking given that this country would not mind much if France not only exercised a protectorate over but even occupied Tunis.

Thursday, 26 May. That unfortunate Wolseley business has been stirred up again. H.M. maintains, and I think with some reason, that to create the Quartermaster General a peer is to make a military office a political one, and to give a political colour to the Army.[3] Of course it is awkward for Childers and even Mr. G. to recede. Retraction would mean humiliation to Childers and a distinct reflection upon him, and likewise make his position towards Wolseley very awkward. At the same time, the proposal was a mistake, and it is worth considering whether the admission of a mistake would not be better than pursuing a matter which the Sovereign strongly disapproves, which the Army would resent, and which the House of Lords would not welcome. Mr. G., while holding his ground, says he will defer to H.M. wishes to the extent of postponing the further consideration of the matter until business is more advanced. What I should like to see now would be that Wolseley should intimate that under all the circumstances he would refuse the offer if made to him.

Saturday, 28 May. Queen's birthday with its usual demoralising effect, what with parade in the morning and the visitors it brings, the stunning guns, and the bustle and fuss of 2 big dinners in the evening.

Never noted my visit last week to Cambridge to hear Hubert Parry's

---

[1] See her letter of 18 May 1881, Guedalla, ii. 157.
[2] Correspondence of July 1878 concerning Lord Salisbury's encouragement of France in Tunis was published in *Parl. Papers*, 1881, xcix. 501–6.
[3] See her letter of 23 May 1881, Guedalla, ii. 158–9.

Prometheus. It was a grand performance, of which the work itself was nobly worthy. No music ever stirred me so much. I felt quite overcome at the end. Making a liberal allowance for the natural excitement of hearing so advanced a work so admirably performed of one of one's oldest and dearest friends, I cannot but attribute the main part of my emotion to the intrinsic merit of the work. Certainly it could not have been produced by any other English living composer, and I doubt if it does not rank almost first of English works in its high standard, its breadth, sublimity and pathos, its mastery over the orchestra and other high qualities combined.

The Land Bill has got into Committee, though it has not yet made any progress in that stage. The number of amendments of which notice has been already given almost surpasses calculation, and the Tories mean fighting to the death. Their main points of attack will be (1) definition of Fair Rent, which the Cabinet think it will be best to eschew, (2) provision for the landlord to apply to the Court of his own accord, (3) compensation to landlords *or* the option of selling their estates, and (4) possibly, further restrictions on Free Sale.

Forster's account today was not hopeless, though far from reassuring.[1]

Monday, 30 May. The 'Birthday dinners' on Saturday were a success. The Prince of Wales was very gracious and, according to Rosebery who sat next him, was greatly delighted by Mr. G. The arrangement of the guests was very successful. We placed the Duke of Argyll next to Lord Ailesbury as a penance for leaving the Government, a little joke which Mr. G. 'spotted' and entered into thoroughly.

Another long letter this morning from Forster.[2] He is thoroughly alive to strengthening the Irish executive. He has 3 alternatives—(1) to get Lord Spencer to replace Lord Cowper as Viceroy, who is I fear lamentably weak and a mere cypher, (2) to remain himself over in Ireland altogether outside Parliament as it were—impracticable, (3) to remove that broken reed, Lord O'Hagan, from the Lord Chancellorship and substitute Sullivan, the Master of the Rolls. The latter alternative, though certainly desirable, would probably be insufficient of itself; and I am afraid difficult as it would be, and moreover painful, the removal of Lord Cowper is the right course. Possibly, too, a fourth alternative should be considered—the replacement of Forster himself by a stronger man.

Ponsonby wrote to me again this morning. He says the postponement of the Wolseley business is all very well as far as it goes, but the Queen is determined not to give her assent to making Wolseley a peer so long as he retains the Quartermaster Generalship, no matter how long the question is postponed. So we shall have further trouble over this a little time hence.

There seems to be a good prospect of a further break up among the Land

---

[1] See Wemyss Reid, ii. 320–1.   [2] See ibid., pp., ii. 321–2.

Leaguers. When O'Connor Power takes to calling Egan, the Secretary of the League, a swindler and a coward, there must be something hideously wicked in the constitution of the most advanced Land Leaguers.

Thursday, 31 May. The Queen has written a frantic letter to Lord G[ranville]. She says she is greatly annoyed and displeased about the decision of the Transvaal boundary, which the Cabinet adopted the other day in deference to the majority of the Transvaal Commission. Her Majesty then launches out generally against the Government. She maintains that the policy of the Cabinet is nothing but surrender after surrender, and all to satisfy the Radicals (!); that the promise given by Mr. Gladstone when he acceded to office about recognising accomplished facts has been broken and cast to the winds; and what with India, South Africa, and Ireland, she contends that the Government have been at any rate 'eminently unsuccessful'. She takes credit to herself in discharging her duty about giving warning which, however, has all been in vain! And this from a constitutional monarch! If Dizzie did no other harm, he certainly did the greatest possible harm to his Sovereign and the Crown generally of this country.

There was an informal meeting of ministers today about the Irish executive. They were all of opinion that Lord O'Hagan ought to be removed from the Chancellorship, but doubted whether this move would be adequate. Mr. G. is to call on Lord Cowper for an explanation of his views on the condition of Ireland, and on the nature of that explanation will probably hang his fate.

Wednesday, 1 June. Mr. G. sent for his letters before the usual time, and, as it was Derby Day, it looked quite suspicious. However, though he did disappear all mid-day, he did not get as far as Epsom.

The House still sticks to marking the Blue Riband day of the Turf, and insisted upon adjourning after 2 smart speeches, one from each side of the House—Power and Lawson. When every day is precious and when private members are screaming out about the curtailment of their rights and privileges, it really is too silly to cut off 6 hours work for a set purpose, of which probably not one member out of thirty takes advantage.

Lord Lyons writes anxiously about France.[1] He regards the recent action of France in Tunis of singularly bad omen. The military preparations were not considered very creditable. It has been a high-handed bullying policy, and yet hailed by the French with delight. They are evidently very sensible of having gained the approval of the German Government. Gambetta's autumn speech at Cherbourg was the first glass of wine administered to a convalescent patient.[2] The Tunis business is the second and stronger glass. What will the third be? Lord Lyons hints at the probability of France resorting to other

[1] This refers to Lyons's letter to Granville of 13 May 1881, Lord Newton, *Lord Lyons* ... (London, 1913), ii. 243–4.   [2] See 5 Sept. 1880.

annexations which will wound English feeling indirectly. It behooves us, he says, to be specially watchful about Egypt.

Nothing settled yet about the Governorship of Madras, vacant by the death of poor Adam. Among those of whom Lord Hartington has thought are Lefevre, Grant Duff, Trevelyan, Morley, and Enfield.

Sunday, 5 June. The House adjourned on Friday. Mr. G. went down the same evening to The Durdans. Rosebery was anxious he should come in for the tail-end of his Derby party in order to show the Great Man to them. I will undertake to say that those who conversed with him for the first time left The Durdans with a very different impression of him to that which they probably held before.

Sir R. Cross has written again *in formâ pauperis* about obtaining the vacant political pension.[1] I presume he little knows that Northcote is a candidate. It is certainly a great misfortune that the three foremost men on the front Opposition bench should be dependent on State aid—Lord J. Manners already in receipt of a pension, Northcote and Cross candidates for other pensions. (It seems rather strange that Cross should not have consulted his own leader before applying.) Politicians ought to be independent in means in order to be thoroughly independent in politics.

Lord Cowper wrote yesterday, but confined himself chiefly to remarking how much worse matters would have been without a Coercion Act. Mr. G. in replying has taken the opportunity of asking Lord C[owper] to expound in detail his views on the grave situation. I wish it were possible to turn Goschen's services to account in the Irish executive. He would be a first class man for the post. Mr. G., I am glad to say, consented to write one of his nice notes to Goschen congratulating him on his return to this country after so successful a mission in the East. Few know the difficulties with which that man has had to contend, and few give him sufficient credit for his work at Constantinople. He certainly has shewn throughout his time there consummate ability, great firmness, excellent tact, and great good judgment.

Monday, 6 June. Accounts from Ireland no better. It is a sad condition of affairs. Poor Forster is working away over in Dublin. Considering how vain a man he is, his tenure of office must be a woeful disappointment to him. If it were not for the grave objections of 'swapping horses &c', I wish he could be moved for his own sake, for the sake of the Government, and for the sake of the country.

In spite of all the amendments of which notice has been given and the little progress yet made, Mr. G. has pluck enough to be hopeful about the Bill. He is greatly pleased with the general disposition and behaviour of the Party under the trying circumstances.

[1] See 8 May 1881.

Thursday, 9 June. Mr. G. came up from The Durdans today, flourishing and refreshed by his blow at Epsom. The place just suits him. They leave him alone and yet look well after him. He delights in Rosebery, and Rosebery delights in him and has the art of 'drawing' him.

Political speeches have been the order of the day during the short Whitsun recess, mostly from the Opposition. Lord Carnarvon bitter and intemperate; Cross prolix and rather washy, dwelling at length on the supposed disunion of the Government of which there is not a word of truth; Stanhope 'cheeky' and inaccurate, not to say mendacious; Hicks Beach Boer-wild. On the other hand, Chamberlain broke out on Tuesday with a very slashing speech, bold, incisive, powerful, and exhaustive. He clearly shewed himself to be a man of great parts, gave evident indication of statesmanship. He took all the fences in slashing style and altogether much impressed me.

Accounts don't improve from Ireland. It is clear that the crisis is very severe. If only landlords would forego their right to evict pending the fate of the Land Bill, we should have comparative quiet, and I fully believe the landlords themselves would benefit. They would allay the bitter class feeling, and would lose nothing, for by evictions they can only assert the law without getting any corresponding benefit, that is, when they have turned out the defaulting tenant, they can get no one to take the farm from which they have evicted.

The general feeling towards the Land Bill is curious. The majority of people don't believe in its real efficacy; and yet there are few Tories of Tories who avow themselves in favour of rejecting the measure. The long and short of it is this—that the Bill is a disagreeable necessity.

Another judge dead. Lord Justice James. The mortality among judges of late has been extraordinary. Mr. G. as usual has not neglected to let the family of the deceased judge know that they have his sincere sympathy.

Forster is not to return till Monday. The question then of strengthening the Irish executive must seriously come to the front. I still hanker after Goschen.

Friday, 17 June. Another vacuum in the Diary, what with dissipating at Ascot and other things. Had a very pleasant 4 days racing;—good company and capital weather.

The House of Commons has been since Whitsuntide hard at the Irish Land Bill at morning and evening sittings, and though the progress made has not been rapid, it has been appreciable. The greatly disputed Free Sale clause (No. 1) has been got through, and with the exception of one amendment (Heneage's) which sought to exempt from the Bill 'English-managed estates', the majorities have been good. The Committee at any rate seem to have settled down to work. Hope is entertained of the Bill being sent to the House of Lords about the third week in July.

Goschen was offered the GCB on his return, but has declined. He would not like to become Sir George and considers the plain 'Right Hon.' is the most honourable title he can hold. How unlike the late administration who all jumped at being 'ribanded' and 'Sirred'!

Huntly has had to resign his Household appointment.[1] He appears to have got into a very shady financial scrape by having given as security 'mortgaged property'. He had only partially white-washed himself by taking office, and now he goes and makes a bigger fool of himself then ever!

I note the ever-recurring wish expressed by Mr. G. in letters to his private friends that he may escape soon from office. When he consented to form an administration I remember his saying that he considered himself merely a 'bird of passage' in Downing St., and I am afraid the extraordinary cares and anxieties of office this time have not made him the keener to remain in harness.

Old 'Mother Hubbard' (Mr. J. G. Hubbard) sent Mr. G. the other day a speech of his with reference to the Bradlaugh case in which Mr. H[ubbard] contends that atheism and conscience are incompatible terms. Mr. G. answered Mr. H. by admitting that Bradlaugh had committed a gross error, but so also did Lady B. Coutts in marrying;[2] and how could Mr. G. interfere on that account? (It is rather amusing that Bradlaugh and Burdett Coutts should be classified together.) He could not query her legal right to do a moral wrong; nor could he similarly query Bradlaugh's right. Mr. G. holds that the House of Commons has acted illegally. Bradlaugh fulfilled the law or he [did] not fulfil the law. If he had fulfilled the law, he should take his seat; if he has not, the Law Courts should correct him. Mr. G. went on to challenge Hubbard's contention that atheists have no conscience. How could it be so with such brilliant examples of men who have preached the highest morality and yet been unable to believe in a God in the ordinary acceptance of the term and the ordinary conception of the being? Reverting to the Bradlaugh case, Mr. G. maintained that the only thing now to be done is to recognise frankly that religious differences to not entail civil disabilities.

Saturday, 18 June. The Duckworth case has come to the front again. Just before the late Government went out, Canon Duckworth formally resigned his living of St. Mark's; and Lord Beaconsfield proceeded to fill the vacancy by appointing Dr. Flood of Leeds who resigned his living accordingly. Just before the legal formalities were completed, Canon Duckworth withdrew his resignation on account (it appeared) of some disagreeable rumours affecting his personal character to which he thought his resignation would give credence. Meanwhile, Dr. Flood's successor had been appointed, and Dr. Flood was left high and dry without preferment owing to an undoubted breach of

[1] He was the Captain of the Gentlemen at Arms. See 10 Jan. 1881.
[2] See 7 and 10 Sept. 1880.

faith on the part of Duckworth. Dr. Flood has now renewed his appeal *ad misericordiam* to Mr. G. as dispenser of Crown patronage. Mr. G. has called on Duckworth for an explanation, which is eminently unsatisfactory, and Mr. G. is greatly annoyed with such conduct.

Lord Hartington thinks of offering the Governorship of Madras to Grant Duff. It is to be hoped he will accept. He is no great strength to the Government except that he is one of the few Scotch members who hold office. He is too dictatorial and priggish in the House, and is perpetually rubbing people up the wrong way. The two men to my mind who on their merits, abilities, and standing in the House have best claims to office are E. Fitzmaurice and Harry Brand. The objections to them would be that they are not very sound on the Irish question and neither of them are Scotch. As regards, however, the first objection, want of loyalty to the Government is often considered by no means as a disqualification for office.

The idea of making changes in the Irish executive seems for the moment to be in abeyance. Mr. G. was not dissatisfied with Lord Cowper's exposition of the present situation, though it did not contain any practical recommendation.

O'Shea made an extraordinary proposal the other day.[1] As a strong Home Ruler, without being a Land Leaguer, he offered to effect a compromise between the Government and the Parnellites. The terms were to be these: the Government to permit Irish rents to be reduced to the Poor Law Valuation, which O'Shea maintains will alone allay dissatisfaction, but which he admits would reduce rents throughout Ireland by one third from 15m̂* to 10m̂*, and which would therefore entail compensation out of public funds to the landlords; the Parnellites to accord a hearty support to the Government in and out of Parliament, and to stay outrages. It is needless to say that the Government will not 'look at' such a proposal. How could they demean themselves to bargain with such a fellow as Parnell, were the terms even feasible and fair?

A sensible letter was sent here for inspection the other day from Alan Gardner who was out in the Zulu War, is now out in the Transvaal, and accordingly had considerable experience of South African affairs. He takes a much more hopeful view of the outlook in that part of the world than do most people. His idea is that there is a much better chance of an improved feeling between the white races now that one of them—the Boers—have shewn that they are not the despicable people which their rivals have held them to be. This change of feeling was not possible so long as one race dominated over the other, any more than was it possible for the English and

---

* This m̂ was invented by Mr. G. to represent millions—an invention on which he much prides himself. [EWH]

[1] See Hammond, pp. 221–3.

Scotch to live and lie down together, while the latter were tyrannised over by the former; but now there is a good chance of a change for the better.

Saturday, 25 June. A despatch received the other day from St. Petersburg says that the programme of the new Czar[1] is to be at peace with all his neighbours, to direct attention to the internal condition of his country, and to introduce economy everywhere more especially in army expenditure, though this last reform may create much discontent in military circles.

Foreign affairs are tolerably quiet. The feeling, however, towards France for the part she has played in Tunis is not over agreeable. Nothing but the fact that the mouths of the Opposition are closed on account of the *carte blanche* which Lord Salisbury gave France when he was in Berlin prevents an angry outburst against her behaviour in Africa.

The Prince of Bulgaria[2] has been playing the fool, overriding his constitution, and staking his retention of the throne on his having his own way. The fact is, he is bored by having to rule a semi-barbarous small state, and would gladly find himself back again in Germany resuming military life.

Had a talk the other day with Gould,[3] who has recently been moved from Servia, having been offered up as a sacrifice to Austria. He spoke gloomily of the future of the small nationality. Austria is bound to swallow her up, and that not long hence. He, of course, regrets our not taking a stronger anti-Austrian line, and renewing the warning of 'Hands off'. He declares that the English Government is losing its influence among the Servians, and that Mr. Gladstone himself alone retains a real hold over them.

The Queen was pleased with the letter which, at my reminding him of the date, he wrote to H.M. on the occasion of the anniversary of Her accession. He referred to the fact that H.M. had been now on the English throne within a few months as long as Queen Elizabeth, and expressed a hope that her present Majesty's reign would not only be longer than that of the Queen of the 16th century, but be associated with it in regard to the glory and happiness of the Empire and its people. In thanking him, H.M. dwelt on the length of time during which She had worn the Crown—a Crown (as She puts it) with many thorns, and concluded with an assurance that the objects of her life were the happiness of Her people and the glory of Her country.[4]

The Land Bill has not got on in Committee during this last week as well as it ought to have done. The acceptance of one or two amendments calculated to appease somewhat the jealousy of the landlords has roused the indignation of the extreme Irishmen, and a few more surrenders would be nearly fatal to the Bill. However, these may all be counteracted by the introduction of provisions dealing with arrears and leases and one or two of the other

---

[1] Alexander III.   [2] Alexander I.
[3] Louis Eugene Gould had been vice-consul and chargé d'affaires at Belgrade since 1879.
[4] For the exchange of letters see Guedalla, ii. 163.

points for which the most sensible Irishmen—the Ulster people—contend. I expect the distinction between present and future tenancies will be given up. If it were not that the change involved a considerable change of front, I should favour it. It would simplify the Bill, and please many of the Irishmen, while I do not believe the Tories would much object, because the surrender of the distinction might give better hope that the present settlement is a final one. On this point, I am to sound Pembroke, as Mr. G. would prefer the amendment to come from the other side.

Carrington has accepted Huntly's place. Lord Granville sounded St. Albans, but though pleased at the offer of office being renewed he would not accept, as I thought he possibly might.[1]

Sunday, 3 July.[2] (Wymondham) Down with the Wodehouses; he as strong a radical as ever. I trust he may manage to squeeze into political life.

Grant Duff has accepted India—I mean the Madras Governorship, which is a good thing. Rosebery is supposed to be willing to come in as Under Secretaryship [*sic*] at the Home Office; naturally Mr. G. is anxious to secure him in that place. This, however, of course entails Courtney being moved to the Colonial Office, and though in many respects he would probably be the best man, his transfer would probably be severely criticised, considering how committed he is on the Transvaal question, to say nothing of the objections which probably Her Majesty would raise. There might of course be a more general shuffle; for instance, it is understood that Brassey is useless at the Admiralty; but it is premature for shuffles, and even then the only Under Secretaryship available and at the same time carrying promotion with it to Courtney is the Colonial one. I shall be very glad to see Rosebery in the Government. He deserves it thoroughly, and I am sure it is the right thing for a politician to serve his apprenticeship in the ranks and not be lumped into the Cabinet.

The Duke of Bedford has intimated his inability to support the Irish Land Bill, and has therefore practically submitted the resignation of the Duchess from the Mistress-ship of the Robes. His letter had a very regretful tone about it. Mr. G. was much concerned and has begged that at any rate the Duke will reserve his decision for the present and has hinted that his line of action need not involve the surrender by the Duchess of her appointment. If so good a Liberal as the Duke can't stomach the Bill, its fortunes in the Upper House don't look promising.

The Bill has made only slow progress on the whole during the week. Once or twice things went well and fairly slided, but then a bad sitting comes like that of Friday evening; obstruction reappears, and all one's calculations are thrown out and sanguine hopes extinguished. The Great Man, however, does not cower under the difficulties. He retains his pluck, and what is worth still

---

[1] See 30 Dec. 1880 and 17 June 1881.　　　　[2] EWH wrote '*Sunday, July 2d*,'

more he retains his strength. He has been marvellously well the last few weeks. One only trusts it may last. He has taken to enjoy his Sundays out of town.

Heneage, one of the Whig 'Cave', told me the other day that, now that the Government had met him and his friends so satisfactorily on the questions of the Fair Rent and the access of the landlord to the Court, no further trouble would come from his quarter, provided only that the Government would provide a very strong and large Court. He complained bitterly of Harcourt's rudeness and abuse, and also of the scant courtesy he received from the Attorney General for Ireland.[1]

Tuesday, 5 July. Yesterday was the 18th day in Committee on the Land Bill, and the progress was anything but satisfactory. In short, no progress would be made at all were it not for the excellent forbearing behaviour on the part of the bulk of the supporters of the Bill. Mr. G. says that, in his long experience, he has never known such unsatisfactory transaction of business as to delay, confusion, and individual licence recklessly used in defiance of the general feeling of the House of Commons. There is a small number of Home Rulers and a small number of Tories (the last named apparently being beyond the control of Sir S. Northcote who seems, according to Mr. G., to be more or less compelled to regard their inclinations and play into their hands) who so assiduously waste time that the termination of the session is wholly a matter of speculation. The fact is these infernal sections in the House are bent upon breaking down Mr. G., and they will succeed, I fear, more especially if this exceptionally hot weather continues. He always feels heat greatly, and though he has been so extraordinarily well lately, I am apprehensive of the heat bringing on one of those diarrhoea attacks.

Thursday, 7 July. My birthday—the 34th—completing probably the most privileged and the happiest [year] of my life, at least up to the present time.

The Land Bill has been making rather better way the last 2 days. Clause 7— the kernel of the Bill[2]—was got through at Tuesday's morning sitting, being carried by a most satisfactory majority of 130, and its triumphant passage has apparently made its impression in the House by shewing the obstructive minority that the Bill and the whole Bill is to pass and can't be set aside by them.

In the afternoon Mr. G. had a little conclave to consider the question of manufacturing peers. The counsellors were Lord Granville, Lord Hartington, Lord Cork, Lord Wolverton, and R. Grosvenor. It was decided, and wisely as I think, to postpone submitting anybody till *the* Bill has become law. The immediate submission would look as if it were an endeavour, though a very ineffectual one, merely to give the Government additional strength in the

[1] Hugh Law.
[2] It was the clause of the bill defining Fair Rent. See Hammond, pp. 238-9.

House of Lords. The candidates who are the favourites are Lords Reay, Tweeddale, and Howth; D. Marjoribanks, Harcourt Johnston, and Sir H. Tufton. No great exceptions can be taken to these names, though if I had been Prime Minister I should have considered that Marjoribanks had, by his repeated personal applications, put himself out of court.

The annual 'massacre of the innocents' has taken place and unusually ruthlessly. Practically all other bills are thrown overboard. The fact is, the French phrase admits well of being paraphrased—'The Government proposes, the House of Commons disposes'. The rejected bills include the Parliamentary Oaths Bill. Bradlaugh has behaved so well that I am sorry he has had to go to the wall, but it is inevitable. There is no doubt a strong feeling out of doors against him, and only a limited feeling in his favour. He threatens to question the legality of the proceedings of the House of Commons in his case by resort to physical force, but little can come out of this. The worst of it is, however, the troubles which his case causes to the Government will be renewed again next session. The sore will be kept open, and the Opposition will continue to have a good and nasty 'stick' wherewith 'to beat' that 'dog' of a Government.

The great heat at the commencement of the week—92° were registered in the shade on Tuesday—has subsided.

The Eton and Harrow match. Eton are getting a horrible thrashing, and I never witnessed a match between the two great public schools which possessed so little interest. The match is on Thursday and Friday this year, instead of the orthodox Friday and Saturday, owing to the great volunteer review on Saturday at Windsor.

Friday, 8 July. The President of the U.S.—Garfield—who was so cruelly shot by a spiteful wretch of a disappointed placeman a week ago—seems to be in a fair way to recover.

The Land Bill is making somewhat better progress. The 'purchase clauses' are now being fought out. The Irishmen are going in hot and strong for a ruthless raid on the Exchequer. They want the whole of the purchase money, instead of three fourths, advanced to the tenant, and to extend the repayment over 52 years. Mr. G., as might be expected, is offering a strenuous resistance to this raid and is supported by the orthodox Opposition. It will be an extension of these purchase clauses which the House of Lords will probably go in for, only in another direction, i.e. enabling all landlords who want to get rid of their properties under these altered conditions of tenure to sell to the Land Commission whether the tenants are ready to buy or not.

Pembroke was authorised by those with whom he acts to endeavour to negotiate for making the Court of Appeal in Dublin the Court charged with dealing with all matters between the landlord and tenant, but Mr. G. and Forster don't believe that the Court of Appeal would command the confidence of the tenants, and so they are little likely to act on this suggestion.

Protection and bimetallism seem to be fads which are securing a deal of advocates, and I can't help fearing that protection will be a formidable cry to the front before long. A man bet me the other day 2 to 1 we should have a general return to protection within 5 years. There is no doubt that, what with bad trade, bad harvests, hostile tariffs, and a still more hostile tariff threatened by France on the termination of the present Commercial Treaty, greater exception is being taken now to free trade than at any time since its introduction into this country. Sooner than have a bad treaty with France we had much better have none. Mr. G. says he looks upon the Commercial Treaty of 1860 as exceptional. He has himself little faith in tariff treaties and much sense of the false position into which negotiators of such treaties are thrown. He considers the English nation strong enough in its commercial position to let the 'world wag', as the saying is, and take its own course, relying upon this, that every country which adopts protection thereby so far disables itself from effectually competing with us in the markets of the rest of the world.

Lord Salisbury, in bringing forward the sugar question last night in the House of Lords, disclaimed categorically that he had the smallest intention of advocating a return to protection, or resort to reciprocity and retaliation, but his speech amounted to a bit of special pleading, and not very ingenious, on behalf of doing 'something' for industries attacked by foreign tariffs; and that something can only be some contravention of free trade principles.

Thursday, 14 July. Three very bad days this week in Committee. On Monday the Irishmen led off with a very violent attack on Forster. Biggar out-Biggared himself by calling on Mr. G. to send Forster to Madras or better still to 'some hotter place'. Poor 'Buckshot',[1] however, came in for a large [measure] of sympathy as much from the Opposition as from his own side. Walter Long next tried to justify his charge against Parnell about rent-raising, but completely broke down with his proofs. He had got hold of the wrong end of the story and had jumbled up the brothers Parnell. Mr. G. said it would have been much better had Long frankly apologised to Parnell, instead of which, in endeavouring to establish his case, he gave Parnell an opportunity of a 'good crow'. The remainder of the sitting was taken up with the reclamation clauses.

These clauses likewise occupied the morning sitting of Tuesday. They were finally carried, and Mr. G. expressed himself much satisfied that the proposal to make the Land Commission redeem at the sole risk of the State was negatived without a division.

The emigration clauses formed the next bone of contention. The extreme Parnellites are deadly opposed to them. The evening sitting of Tuesday was wasted by discussion upon them as irregular as it was humiliating (so said

[1] A nickname for Forster. See Wemyss Reid, ii. 301.

Mr. G.). These clauses are valued highly by the Tories whose pet cure for all Irish evils is emigration; they are esteemed moderately by Ministers, i.e. the absence of any such provision in the Bill would (they regard) be a distinct shortcoming, but they doubt much whether it will have much practical working.

Wednesday's sitting too was devoted to the same wrangle and given up to obstruction by the Parnellites, sometimes covertly and at other times avowedly. Mr. G. is evidently low in his mind, and he reverts to the great urgency of large and searching reform in the procedure of the House of Commons and to the absolute necessity of such a step for the character and efficiency of Parliament. Of course prospects of terminating the session are now again in the clouds. Mr. G. still bears up well and bravely.

The reform of Parliamentary procedure must no doubt be soon taken in hand. Much I am sure might be done in the way of economising time without any very radical innovations, and for more drastic measures resort will have to be had to some form of the cloture, to a transfer of some of the work in Committee to Grand Committees (such work as supply) and to relieving Parliament of some of its purely local duties.

In Bulgaria the Prince[1] has triumphed and won his way. According to Austria it was a choice between the dictatorship of the Prince and the dictatorship of the Liberal chieftains (Zancow & Co.), and on the whole Sir H. Elliot thinks the former is the lesser of two evils.

Three men have been 'bagged' to serve on the Land Commission— O'Hagan, an Irish Q.C.; Vernon, Pembroke's agent; and Litton M.P., Q.C. Lord Monck and Shaw, likewise Law, have declined offers; the first named may perhaps reconsider his decision. Vernon's appointment will be immensely popular among the landlords, and ought not to be the reverse of commanding the confidence of the tenantry.

The question of the Under Secretaryship at the Colonial Office is to stand over till after the Transvaal debate. But as nobody has been able to find anything culpable in Courtney's former speeches, it is most probable that he will be the man, and that Rosebery will be his successor.[2]

Saturday, 16 July. We are having extraordinary heat. On Friday afternoon the thermometer outside my official room on a thick north wall, in the draught of the window and the door, registered just upon 90°. The official reading was as much as 96° and 97°—almost unparalleled.

The Irishmen carried on their game on Thursday night of sheer obstruction on the emigration clause. At midnight Mr. G. burst forth in his best and most impassioned style—he called it himself a 'violent speech'—in defence of the

---

[1] Alexander I.

[2] Courtney did succeed Grant Duff at the Colonial Office and Rosebery succeeded Courtney as Under-Secretary at the Home Office. See 11 Aug. 1881.

dignity of the House. He was cheered to the nth on both sides of the House, and by 4 o'clock in the morning the clause was added to the Bill.

Yesterday (Friday) the air was cleared and the Committee went on swimmingly.

Mr. G. still fresh and well. Gone down to Windsor. He stays at the Castle tonight, and tomorrow night at the Deanery.[1]

The Queen continues to have down Her ex-ministers, which seems rather extraordinary. No ex-Liberal minister, as far as I recollect, ever went down during the Beaconsfield administration.

Sunday, 24 July. The two principal events of the last week have been the death of Dean Stanley[2] and the passing of the Irish Land Bill through Committee.

There is probably no one in the Church whose loss would have been more sensibly and widely felt. He and Mr. G. were, of course, at the opposite poles of thinking, but Mr. G. had a great respect for him. In writing to the Queen to express his sympathy with her on the Dean's death, he said no one, however minded, could fail to admire the genial and attaching disposition, the boundless generosity, or the brilliant gifts and varied accomplishments of the man. He referred to a not uninteresting incident which was that both he and the Dean were educated at the same small school near Liverpool. He added that, whatever might be the difference of opinion respecting the Dean, such a man will long be remembered as one 'who was capable of the deepest and widest love, and who received it in return, and who unsparingly devoted his entire life and all his faculties according to the best of his knowledge towards promoting the honor of his Maker and the welfare of mankind'.

The Queen has evidently felt the death of Stanley keenly. To lose 'two such friends' in one year as the Dean and Lord Beaconsfield was almost too much to bear. Would that the latter had been as good a real friend to her as the former!

The appointment of a successor to Dean Stanley is exercising the Great Man's mind considerably. He will no doubt be most guided by the advice of the Dean of Windsor as he always is in these matters. At present he has under consideration more particularly two cases of what he calls 'transplantation', i.e. the Bishop of Manchester (Fraser) and the Dean of Christ Church (Liddell). The Bishop has long been known to contemplate resignation and to be minded, now that he has worked at Manchester 12 years, to 'give up bishoping' as he calls it. Mr. G. thinks that the Bishop would carry on all that is best of the traditions of Dean Stanley and make a most efficient head of so important a chapter. He has hardly perhaps the polished manners and the social position requisite for this great metropolitan piece of preferment, but

---

[1] i.e. with his friend Gerald Wellesley, Dean of Windsor.
[2] Dean of Westminster.

he is a fine preacher and his appointment would probably be popular. The Dean of Christ Church would possess the qualities for the post in which the Bishop is most deficient, and moreover it could afford Christ Church an opportunity of having some one more fitted to be the head of a college, but his transfer would involve a loss of income.

The Committee on the Land Bill was concluded on Friday night, the 32nd day, the longest recorded time for Committee since the great Reform Bill. The last week's discussion was conducted in a far more legitimate fashion. There was still plenty of garrulity but no covert or overt obstruction. That speech which Mr. G. made the week before, denouncing the obstructives in violent terms, cleared the air and apparently cowed the Home Rulers. Mr. G. also came out on Thursday with a slashing little speech in which he regularly 'slated' Northcote, and not undeservedly, for sneering at the successive 'messages of peace' to Ireland and their inutility.

On the last night of the Committee one of the most important of all the amendments was moved, which provided that the Land Commission should be compelled to buy if the landlord objecting to the statutory conditions wished to sell. It is impossible to overrate the gravity of the financial liabilities which such a proposal involves; and of course Mr. G. opposed it firmly. It had the support of the Tories and a section of the Irishmen. Northcote, being a purist in finance, evidently shied at the proposal, but when it came to voting he did not desert his own friends.

The marvellousness of the man who conducted such a measure through such a Committee is now the subject of universal comment. He has achieved many legislative feats, but none so immense and so difficult as this Land Bill. It is impossible to overrate the mastery of detail which he has shewn, the tact, judgment, and good temper which he has displayed, the outbursts of eloquence which he has occasionally made, and last (and not least) the extraordinary physical power he has exhibited. As the *Daily Telegraph* said the other day, whatever may be our political opinions we all 'must be proud' of such a man.[1]

Another week will see the Bill in the House of Lords. As the time for its advent to that House draws nearer, there does not seem to be any greater likelihood of a want of reason on the part of the peers. The general idea seems to be that the Bill will be very little touched by them. My own belief is that, after watching its career in the Lower House and the unwavering support it has received from the unbroken majority, the Lords are willing to give it a trial, however much they may object to much of its principle. As Donoughmore said to me the other day—and there has been no stronger opponent of the measure—'If the Bill when passed does for Ireland what its authors expect from it, I shall be the first to take off my hat to Mr. Gladstone and to be grateful to him for evermore'. It is, of course, absurd to suppose that on the

[1] *Daily Telegraph*, 22 July 1881, p. 5, col. 1.

passing of the Bill the country will all of a sudden be transformed into a fairy land, where landlord and tenant will 'lie down' together and where nothing but peace, prosperity, and plenty will prevail; but I shall be greatly disappointed if the Bill is not successful to the extent of giving to Ireland a short lease of comparative quiet and freedom from agitation. We shall see. There is no such thing, of course, as finality in parliamentary measures.

The names of the Commission,[1] though they were not enthusiastically received at their announcement, are now generally accepted as good sensible appointments.

Hicks Beach has been anxious to back out of his vote of censure on the Transvaal question, but the Government would not let him. They have only been prevented from taking up the challenge sooner on account of circumstances wholly beyond their own control, and they are anxious to have their case tried in Parliament, now that the passage of the Land Bill through Committee affords an opportunity.

The Transvaal Commission have nearly completed their labours and a very tolerable settlement of a most difficult and complicated question seems in prospect.

When that and the Irish question are out of the way—at any rate temporarily—we ought to have comparatively quiet and less anxious times. The political horizon is clearing all round, and the party continues to behave magnificently.

Bradlaugh is to have one more shot at his seat this session, but the steps he is about to take, which amount to a direct threat to the House of Commons by physical force, are damaging his own case seriously; so much so that probably the Government will not be very keen to make any further effort on his behalf. He will in short have forfeited their good graces.

The *Quarterly Review* for this month has broken out with a violent tirade against free trade, in other words 'unfair trade' as it is now called.[2] This is a sign of the times, but, in spite of the growth of economical heresies among classes and those chiefly the wealthier classes, I do not believe the masses will ever tolerate a return to protection or reciprocity to any serious extent. *Nous verrons*.

Wednesday, 27 July. The Transvaal debate on Monday fell rather flat. Several spoke well and ably, notably Beach, Rathbone, and Chamberlain; but there prevailed on both sides a sort of hollowness, the fact being that it was difficult for the annexers of the Transvaal to condemn, and it was not wholly easy for the Government to defend, though as a choice of evils they were

---

[1] See 14 July 1881. The names were announced and discussed in *The Times* on 20 July 1881, p. 12, col. 5.

[2] The article 'English Trade and Foreign Competition' (assigned by *The Wellesley Index* to Louis J. Jennings) is in vol. 152, pp. 141–59.

indubitably in the right. Mr. G. was not up to the mark. He was overstrained, feeling as he said like a sucked-out orange; (and after 32 days of Land Bill Committee no wonder). This, moreover, made him somewhat irritable at the unmannerly interruptions which emanated from the rowdy Tories. However, he wound up with a magnificent peroration worthy of himself and thoroughly worth hearing.

The whole of yesterday was devoted to the stage of report on the Land Bill. Everything went swimmingly and most propitiously with one exception, and that was E. Fitzmaurice's amendment to limit the operation of the Bill to holdings under £100, which carried off some 25 Whigs and reduced the ministerial majority to under 40. Mr. G. contended in most unequivocal terms that the amendment was most injurious and altogether inadmissable; and I don't wonder. Such an amendment was most unfortunate and ill-judged. I can well understand anybody objecting to the principle of the Bill, but when you have swallowed the Bill and admitted it at any rate as a dis-agreeable necessity, it seems to me most shortsighted to go and pare it down by lopping a piece off here and a piece off there. It will only be leaving open sores which will fester and give ground for future agitation.

Mr. G. is 'vexed and indignant' about Goschen. He voted with E. Fitz-maurice last night and abstained from voting on the Transvaal question. I fear he means mischief. Who knows? Perhaps he thinks he sees his chance of playing into the hands of the Tories and leading them!

Wednesday, 3 August. Last week Mr. G. offered the Deanery of Westminster to the Bishop of Manchester.[1] He declined on the ground that he did not feel fitted, more especially in a social sense, for the appointment; in short, he felt he had no 'call' for the place. After a day or two of doubt Mr. G. turned his thoughts to Canon Barry, whose place might be filled by Mr. Holland of Quebec Chapel. He submitted those names to the Queen for want of better. The Queen, however, did not much like them and said she would prefer the Dean of Christ Church.[2] She put her objections in so earnest and undicta-torial a manner that Mr. G. could not well decline to take them into con-sideration, and he has done so by sounding Dean Liddell through Dr. Acland. I doubt Liddell (now 70) liking to uproot himself at his age. In many ways he would be a most suitable man for the place, and in any case his appointment would be somewhat less eminently 'dull' than that of Barry. I can't think who the right man is.

One of the difficulties attending the acceptance of the Deanery of West-minster by Dean Liddell will be the filling up of Christ Church. The man clearly marked out for the place is Edward Talbot, and his appointment by Mr. Gladstone might be attended with some awkwardness.[3] If Dean Liddell

---

[1] James Fraser. See 24 July 1881.   [2] Henry G. Liddell. See 24 July 1881.
[3] Presumably because Talbot had married Lavinia Lyttelton, Mrs. G.'s niece.

declines, I should not be surprised if Mr. G. were to turn his attention to Mr. Hannah of Brighton instead of to Canon Barry.

Friday, 5 August. The 3rd Reading of the Bill having been completed on Friday last after a parting kick from Randolph Churchill consisting of a violent denunciation of the whole measure and all the Government, it at length reached the Lords. They devoted Monday and Tuesday to the Second Reading. There was considerable oratorical display, and the case against the Bill was put as forcibly as it well could be, more especially by the Duke of Argyll and Lansdowne, but there was necessarily a hollowness about the whole debate consequent upon the determination of the Opposition Lords not to reject it, in spite of their denouncements against the measure. They reached Committee yesterday and will probably finish it tonight. (That is the way to do parliamentary business). On the whole they have exercised more forbearance and good sense than could have been expected of them, notably in the case of the 'Fitzmaurice amendment', in which instance they showed a good example to the Opposition 'in the other place' and the renegade Whigs.

But however forbearing the Lords may be I cannot but think they have put themselves in a wrong position by amending in so much detail the Bill in Committee. There were two courses open to them; one to throw out the Bill, which would have been the most consistent alternative, though perhaps the most impolitic. The other was to throw the whole of the responsibility of the measure on the Government and to accept it under protest *sub silentio* practically *en bloc*. Instead of this, the Lords have taken the third course—they have swallowed the Bill and then criticised and amended it in great details, and accordingly they will now have a share in the responsibility of the measure.

Sunday, 7 August. (Glynde) The Lords completed their handiwork on the Bill in Committee on Friday, and it will come back to the Commons on Tuesday. Meanwhile the Government has to make up its mind what to accept and what not. There was a Cabinet yesterday, but I came away before I could know what had been decided. Several amendments of the Lords are, as Mr. G. says, extremely grave in their character, and most particularly one of Lord Salisbury's. It is quite impossible for the Government to accept any of the amendments but one or two of the least vital ones, and I understand the Peers are determined to be obstinate. Pembroke told me yesterday Lord Salisbury meant to be stiff, and I understand he has had a whip of an urgent description sent out begging their noble lordships on no account to absent themselves from their places when the Bill is returned to them in order that they may 'insist' on their amendments. These proceedings mean, I fear, blows between the two Houses. One knows very well which must have their way in the long run, but in the immediate future the crisis may be very grave. The Speaker[1] is very apprehensive. He leans towards giving the Lords a '*locus penitentiae*'; that is, adjourning the House for a couple of months and sending the Bill up to the Lords again in the autumn. He believes there is a precedent for this. The Government might also accept the amendments, giving an undertaking that a bill should be introduced next session amending the Act of '81 on the points on which the Lords had laid their hands most severely. Mr. G. might also threaten dissolution or the creation of Peers. But let us hope the Lords even now at the 11th hour may show wisdom.

Supply has made tolerable progress the last few days, but at the beginning of last week covert obstruction reappeared in all its virulence. It led Mr. G. to observe that such proceedings shew with what efficacy such obstruction can be practised, and how vain it is to suppose the House can be restored to proper efficiency for discharge of business by penal measures alone; and that nothing short of extensive readjustment of its machinery will suffice for that end.

Thursday, 11 August. I forgot to note the completion of the arrangements consequent on Grant Duff's appointment to Madras. Courtney is now installed at the Colonial Office, and Rosebery at the Home Office.[2] The Queen 'kicked' at Courtney,[3] but of course had to give way, more especially as the Under Secretaryships are not Crown appointments—they are strictly speaking selections of Secretaries of State—and it is merely a matter of courtesy taking Her Majesty's pleasure thereon.

I also omitted to jot down the Bradlaugh incident of last week. He attempted to assert his right to take his seat by force; and the attempt was met by force. Bright made a very injudicious speech on the occasion. The Government have undertaken to endeavour to adjust the unpleasant matter at the commencement of next session. The order excluding Bradlaugh being only a sessional one, the contemplated adjustment is to take this form, which is based on a suggestion (I believe) of the Speaker's: Assuming Bradlaugh to be alive (he is reported but probably with some exaggeration to be seriously ill), he will come to the table again next session. The leader of the Opposition would move that B[radlaugh] cannot take the oath, and the House will be invited to support the moving of the 'previous question'. The Government ought to be able to carry this indirect resolution for seating Bradlaugh, who certainly has been the best card an Opposition ever had to play.

The Deanery of Westminster is still an open question. Dean Liddell has definitely declined it. Butler is the obvious man and is thought to be by 'far the best' by the Queen, but he is a member of the 'Church Reform

---

[1] Henry Brand, EWH's host at Glynde.   [2] See 14 July 1881.
[3] See Ponsonby's letter to G., 3 Aug. 1881, and ensuing communications, Guedalla, ii. 165–6.

Association',[1] and this in Mr. G.'s estimation places him 'out of court'. In fact, we ought to hang out a notice on the doors of Downing St. to the effect that clerical personages belonging to that Association who want preferment 'need not apply'. This is a 'fad' of Mr. G., but one taken up in all seriousness and conscientiousness. Next to Butler, the Queen would prefer Bradley because he was a great friend of the Dean[2] and 'broad', and according to H.M. would best assume Stanley's mantle. Mr. G. does not at all like this dictation from the Crown, or rather these strong hints. He regards such action as tending to invert the Crown and the Minister. Moreover, Bradley, according to Mr. G., is too much of the schoolmaster type. (It is worth noting that apropos of the appointment, the Queen has admitted herself to be a *broad* Church-woman). The two favourites now are Hornby (Eton) and E. Palmer (Christ Church), the latter strongly for choice; and I cannot help thinking Palmer would be an excellent man to nominate.

Friday, 12 August. The Lords' amendments were finally disposed of last night in the House of Commons (the 49th day of Land Bill wrangles!). The spirit maintained throughout their discussion has been very determined. The Government majorities have been excellently maintained, notwithstanding the double fire to which the Government has been exposed, from the Opposition whenever an amendment of the Lords was rejected, and from the Irishmen whenever an amendment was accepted. The result has been that the most weighty of the Peers' alterations have been struck out. The Government could not possibly have done otherwise. The Bill as amended by the Upper House would have been treated in Ireland as so much waste paper. In short, the more important amendments destroyed all hope of breaking down the Land League and pacifying Ireland, the 2 main objects of the bill, without (as Mr. G. says) taking away the aspect of innovation which the measure in some respects presents.

We are brought now face to face with the Upper House, and I fear Lord Salisbury means fighting.

Monday, 15 August. (Wilton) As was to be feared, the Lords on Friday night stuck to their guns and threw out almost all the amended amendments of the House of Commons. So we have come to a deadlock. All the London press, and with few exceptions all the provincial press, are against the action of the Peers. All hope, however, of an arrangement is not yet at an end. I gather from Pembroke that the Lords will be squeezable, and that Lord Salisbury

---

[1] EWH refers here to the National Church Reform Union which was founded in 1873 to encourage the formation of parochial councils and to advocate, among other things, giving a larger role to laymen in Church affairs and the disuse of the Athanasian Creed. H. M. Butler was listed as a member of its Council in 1881 but in 1882 he wrote Archbishop Tait that after attending its first meeting '7 years ago or so' he had had no connection with it. See Lambeth MS. 1463, ff. 1–2; Tait MS. (Lambeth), vol. 92, ff. 127–30; and Butler's letter to Tait, Add. MS. (B.M.) 44308, ff. 197–9.   [2] i.e. of Dean Stanley.

has not taken this line with any view to force the Government to dissolve. It seems as if the Peers would not be unwilling to accept a compromise, and that the only point on which they will really fight to the death is the famous 'Clause 7' and the instructions to the Court about defining Fair Rent. Their contention seems to be this: that the present words of the Commons Bill, directing the Court without qualification to take into account the tenant's interest, must mean that the amount which he may have paid on coming in is to be taken into consideration as well as the value of his improvements, and that by this means the rent will gradually be eaten up. They would sooner be 'ruined outright', which the rejection of the Bill might involve, than be 'ruined by inches', which would result from the Commons directions to the Court. The omission, however, of all instructions might possibly be acceptable to the Peers. I fully expect a compromise, but the Lords will have to give a deal more than the Commons.

Sunday, 28 August. The week before last I was too idle, while at Wilton for the cricket week, to write down anything, and this last week I have been too busy.

The unparalleled session terminated yesterday—'the one or single *Bill* session' as it is facetiously, and may be truly, called. The great Lords crisis terminated in an extraordinary manner. It was one of the few arrangements ever made which not only gave satisfaction to both parties, but over which both parties claimed a triumph. In reality it was a very one-sided triumph, and that for the Government. Owing to the extraordinary tact and ingenuity of Mr. G., the Peers were enabled to beat a retreat with so little ignominy to themselves that they brought themselves to believe that they had wrung important concessions out of the Government. Even Pembroke—the most sensible of the lot—was quite contented. 'Mr. G. behaved like an angel', he said. Such concessions to the Peers, however, as there were, were purely nominal, not real. The *Pall Mall Gazette* & Co. were far nearer the mark when they called the issue of the crisis 'the surrender of the Lords'.[1]

Yesterday was likewise noted for the announcement of the new Dean of Westminster. Bradley's is a flat, dull appointment, and he would never have been appointed had Mr. G. had his own way. Mr. G. was, in fact, not his own master, and, strongly as is to be deprecated the interference of the Crown in any appointments, it is not unfair that H.M. should have a voice in the matter, considering the place itself and the surroundings, or rather its associations.

Wednesday, 31 August. The Westminster appointment has been received on the whole favourably—not enthusiastically, but that was not to be expected.

[1] Such was the tenor of the article 'The House of Lords—After the Crisis' in the issue of 24 Aug. 1881, p. 1.

In looking back at the session, of course the one prominent figure connected with it, standing head and shoulders and likewise body, above everybody else, will always be the Great Man. The other ministers had little chance of asserting themselves. Lord Hartington has done whatever he had to do wonderfully well and has commanded more than ever respect from both sides of the House. His best performance was undoubtedly his speech in the Kandahar debate; but his exposition of the Indian Budget shows that he has an excellent aptitude for business, including figures. Chamberlain has no doubt gone up in the political market by his 'free trade' speech recently made and other minor efforts. Harcourt's chief success has been treading on people's toes with a rudeness and severity even unwonted for him. Forster has regained much of the position he had lost before the meeting of Parliament. He has uniformly defended himself against attack with great ability and has won the sympathy of friends and foes alike in his disagreeable office. Outside the Cabinet the two men in the Government who undoubtedly have made most way and most mark have been Dilke and Law. Dilke has succeeded in making a considerable position for himself, and my firm belief is, health permitting, he is the real coming man in the party. Law, in spite of his bad voice and worse delivery, has 'come out' wonderfully and has exhibited a surpassing knowledge of the difficult subject of the Land Bill in which he took so prominent a part. Of the Opposition, Gibson has no doubt shewed up best. He has had, of course, great advantages from having such an intimate knowledge of *the* subject of the session, and he will unquestionably in future form almost the most powerful prop of his party. Healy has shewn great talent and considerable debating and criticising power.

I understand the Queen was very grumpy at Holyrood, where She held the Prorogation Council while staying there for the Volunteer review en route for Balmoral. She never even said a civil word to Lord Spencer after he had undertaken that long journey, nor did She even ask him to dine. Moreover, though H.M. invited all the Tory notabilities, male and female, to break bread with her, She never asked Lady Rosebery to accompany her husband to dinner.

The six new peers of the U.K.—viz. Tweeddale, Howth, Reay, H. Johnstone, Tufton, and Marjoribanks—have been fairly received. I am only sorry that the last-named should have got his honour after all his begging and praying.

Mr. G. still at Deal,[1] and work is slackening off a little, but with only two men (Horace S[eymour] and myself) the work is even now very heavy.

Thursday, 1 September. The dreadfully unseasonable and disastrous weather continues. After 3 weeks of almost unintermittent rain, we have got a cold

---

[1] G. was Lord Sydney's guest at Deal Castle from 25 Aug. to 3 Sept. 1881.

north wind, and we are shivering over a fire. The harvest prospects are most saddening. One can't help feeling quite depressed at the agricultural outlook. To have almost within grasp a better harvest than there has been for some years past, and then to have it all ruined, is really enough to crush every farmer in the kingdom, and I fear it will crush an immense number. Not only will half the farmers be bankrupt, but the bad times will give a momentum to the protectionist cries, and we shall have a flood of quack remedies proclaimed up and down the country. The great thing to do is to keep a cool head in the storm, and with certain adjustments of taxation and land reforms the agricultural interest will be set on its legs again.

We are in the midst of a series of election excitements. North Durham, North Lincolnshire, Cambridgeshire, Co. Tyrone, Co. Monaghan, and Berwick; and we must be prepared, I expect, to meet an electoral 'facer'. Sir George Elliot has swallowed all kinds of pledges to secure the Irish vote; Jim Lowther has promised all kinds of boons to the farmers, and so on; but too much importance must not be attached to these by-elections. Parnell is fighting to the death for his satellite in Co. Tyrone, and will probably so far succeed as to land the Tory candidate. One can't help hoping that this is a death struggle of a man who feels his power crumbling away and is making a desperate plunge. In the face of such unscrupulous, unprincipled ruffians as the Parnellites, how is it possible that their professed ends can be accomplished. Their professed aims are the release of the suspects under the Coercion Act and the repeal of the Union or self-government, to say nothing of the absolute spoliation of the landlords' property. But how can the prison doors be opened in the face of such threatening language? And how can the country be handed over to the even partial rule of such a set of miscreants?

The Duke of Bedford insists on the resignation of the Duchess from the office of Mistress of the Robes, in spite of its having been pointed out to him by Mr. G. that such a step is absurd *now*. His scruples about her retaining office are foolish. As Mr. G. tried to show him the other day, the time is *past* for taking such a step on account of His Grace's inability to support the Land Bill. There can *during the recess* be no measure fashioned on which a disagreement can take place, and as for the *future* there is no fear of an Irish Land Bill for England, and it is premature to part company over hypothetical measures in the future. I suppose Mr. G. will have to give way to the Duke, but he feels it is a great misfortune that there should be any dissociation of such a family as that of the Russells from what is 'obviously the national tone'.

Friday, 2 September. We have commenced in good earnest the 'facer' I expected. Jim Lowther has got in for North Lincolnshire by nearly 500.[1]

---

[1] Lowther was the Conservative candidate. He defeated Colonel Tomline, the Liberal, 4,200 to 3,729. In the general election the Liberal, Laycock, had won with 4,159 votes.

If any importance is to be attached to by-elections, it is an indicator not to be disregarded. At the same time, it is very strange that in an agricultural district, where there are no Irish and cannot be a great many publicans, there should be such a change of feeling in less than a year and a half. It has its cause no doubt, like everything else. Lowther is a first-class man for fighting a contest, and Tomline must be a bad one. Moreover, at a time of great agricultural distress and in view of very bad agricultural prospects, it is no wonder that the farmer should support the candidate who promises to increase the price of his corn. The election shows how dangerous this 'neo-protectionist' cry may prove, and as I am convinced that the adoption of such a policy would be most damaging to our commercial prosperity, the outlook is formidable.

Sunday, 4 September.[1] The result yesterday of the North Durham election was even worse than that of the North Lincolnshire election, the seat being lost by a majority of nearly 700 votes. The Liberal candidate in short polled something like 1500 votes fewer than he did less than a year and a half ago.[2] Elliot was no doubt a very strong candidate, and moreover, having promised to vote for the release of the Irish suspects, he carried the Irish voters with him. But this will not account for so great a change. It marks a distinct change in public opinion, however temporary such a change may be, and chiefly I believe due to the unfurling again of the old Protection cry, for fair trade as expounded at the recent election campaigns is really and openly Protection and nothing else.

Sir S. Northcote made a political speech on Friday and though he evidently wished to shirk the Protection cry as much as possible he could not avoid reference to it altogether. He did this somewhat ingeniously. He declared that he always had been and still was a 'Free Trader', but (a very ominous word) Free Trade, he said, should be 'universal and fair'. It will be curious to see whether he will swallow his convictions or part company with his party. He must do one of these two things, and I back that he will elect the former alternative. (He is both weak and needy). I shall be sorry, because I have always regarded him as eminently sound on all financial, fiscal, and commercial questions, and have thought that under his leadership, whatever other mistakes they might make, the Tories would do no harm in these respects. This will now all be altered if he follows the lead of the tail of his party. The best cure to this reciprocity craze, like for many other crazes, would be to give it a trial for a limited period, were not such a trial likely to be attended with such expensive and ruinous results. A short experience of a return to protection would probably cure its most ardent advocates of their hobby.

[1] EWH wrote '*Sunday. 5 Sept.*'
[2] Sir George Elliot, the Conservative who had lost the seat at the general election, recovered it by a majority of 632 over the Liberal, Laing.

Mr. Childers has been offered the political pension, and he will probably accept it.[1] He clearly has the best claim on Mr. Gladstone, who will now get over the difficulty in connection with the claims of Northcote and Cross. Mr. G. evidently felt that there would be great awkwardness in conferring the pension on a member of the Opposition, and in this old Lord Halifax, who was consulted about Childers, entirely agreed.

Not unfrequently of late has Mr. G. referred to his wish to retire finally from politics, and he said the other day positively that he would not meet Parliament again with two offices.[2] However, he can't be spared yet and will have to be dissuaded from contemplating such a step. These election 'facers' won't make him regard office with greater relish.

There are not unfavourable signs of good results pending from the Land Act—notably Dillon's remarkable speech about parting company with Parnell & Co. for giving countenance, however small, to the measure, and Parnell's frantic denunciations in Co. Tyrone, the violence of which Mr. G. thinks may be taken to be the measure of apprehension lest the Act should take the bread out of the mouth of traders on public confusion, like Parnell and his following, by tranquillising the mind of the public. I don't think we ought to expect any appreciable effect in Ireland till after the Act is in fairly good working order.

In writing yesterday to Knowles (*19th Century*) about an article of Harrison's on the deadlock in the House of Commons,[3]—a very spirited piece of writing and a valuable contribution to the important subject—Mr. G. made a somewhat curious admission, which was that, though the Land Bill had been a most *difficult* measure, he could not regard it as a *great* one. He evidently thinks that the line which the reform of parliamentary machinery should take must combine both restrictive measures and measures for giving the House more free action. To the latter he attaches most importance. In the same letter he expressed a fear that it would not be possible to keep any such measure of reform out of the vortex of party with such a 'weak leader' of the Opposition as Sir S. Northcote.

Foreign affairs are singularly tranquil. There has not been such a lull in European politics ever since 1874. The most likely cause of trouble, which moreover would specially affect us, is the action of France in North Africa. It will be very awkward if she goes to Tripoli.

In this, as in the Commercial Treaty, she has behaved very badly and very shortsightedly. It is inconceivable that she can really wish to get on bad terms with us, but she is trying us very hard.

[1] See 28 Apr. and 8 May 1881.

[2] i.e. holding, as he did, both the posts of First Lord of the Treasury and Chancellor of the Exchequer. He finally gave up the second office in Dec. 1882. See 26, 27 Nov., 1, 4, and 7 Dec. 1882.

[3] Frederic Harrison, 'The Deadlock in the House of Commons', *The Nineteeth Century*, x (Sept. 1881), pp. 317–40.

As for the Commercial Treaty, I rather hope negotiations which are now suspended will finally break down. There have been some remarkable letters of Lord Grey in the *Times*, in which I cordially agree.[1] He urges strongly the necessity for our reverting to our early free trade policy which was to have no bargains with any nation, and denies emphatically that we have derived substantial advantages from our French Treaty. (This Mr. G. will not have at any price.)

Friday, 9 September. Mr. G. came up from Walmer[2] on Wednesday. He seems to have enjoyed his stay by the East Sea coast, more especially at Deal. Lady Sydney appears to be a model hostess. He has been in great force; Mrs. G. better but not her real self again yet. I bagged him for dinner on Wednesday— the night on which I had promised to dine with Knowles (*19th Century*) at the Reform. It was a charmingly agreeable evening. Mr. G. full of talk. The three principal topics of conversation were (1) the historical associations of Littleberries (the place at Hendon which the Aberdeens have lately had); (2) earliest recollections of childhood, in connection with which he referred to the story my father was so fond of telling—the only untruth, according to Mr. G., my father ever told—about his remembering the cupping of his grandfather when he (my father) was only 6 weeks old. Mr. G. has a vivid recollection of an incident when he was one year and a half only; he remembers being called to crawl upstairs to his nurse on a certain occasion, and the dress in which she was attired; (3) the strides in science, and the marvellous discoveries of recent years. Mr. G.'s contention, however, is that they all sink into insignificance by the side of the marvel of nature—*man*. Broad and expansive as is his mind, he shuns anything which seems to give an additional lustre to scientific discoveries that may run counter to the Bible and its teaching.

Mr. G. went off early after dinner, and Knowles and myself sat on talking for a long time. He is a very agreeable talker, full of information and animation, a strong Liberal, and 'devoted admirer'. He is much disturbed in his mind at the effect on the party of the future of (a) the Bradlaugh business, and (b) the protection cry. I don't think he is much afraid of what will happen in Mr. G.'s time;—but afterwards? Protection will undoubtedly be preached by many and swallowed by many. No cry could be better calculated to catch votes, but I think it is bound to recoil on the heads of the party who take it up. I am certain that all the *thinking men* among the Tories will fall away from them, and therefore if the cry does infuse life into the Opposition, it will break their party up for them, I expect.

The Tyrone election yesterday[3] was a great victory and did much to wipe

[1] See *The Times*, 27 Aug., p. 8, col. 3 and 2 Sept. 1881, p. 6, col. 1.
[2] See 31 Aug. 1881. After leaving Deal Castle G. visited Lord Granville at Walmer Castle.
[3] The Liberal candidate received 3,168 votes, the Conservative 3,084, and the Home Rule candidate (endorsed by Parnell) 907.

out the defeats in North Lincolnshire and North Durham, if it did not wholly counterbalance them. It would have been satisfactory to beat either the Tories in such a stronghold, *or* the Land Leaguers put forward in their whole strength, singly; but to inflict a double defeat upon Tories *and* Parnellites is a really great satisfaction. Mr. G. delighted.

Sunday, 11 September. The most important and difficult question immediately in hand is that of the release of the Irish suspects. Mr. G. is evidently anxious to make some move in that direction, especially since the Tyrone election, which may be taken as a distinct manifestation in favor of accepting the Bill as a settlement of the land question and as the occasion for a return to law and order. He has been communicating with Lord Cowper and Mr. Forster on the subject, and the latter is hurrying home from abroad in consequence. If the policy of 'messages of peace' is to be tried (and who can really gainsay its trial?), the programme had best be complete, and the Land Act be followed up by at any rate a partial liberation of the suspects. Matters, however, in Ireland are still very threatening. The latest accounts of agrarian crime are bad. There is apparently no fall off, but rather an increase in the amount. Mr. G. went down to Hawarden yesterday.

Monday, 12 September. Mr. G. last week said more than once that, speaking for himself and from an English landlord point of view, he should not object to the introduction of tenant-right into England. It would solve the difficult question of compensation for improvements.

Mr. Childers actually wrote the other day suggesting that a public form of prayer should be used in this country for the recovery of President Garfield! Mr. Gladstone, I am glad to think, considered it a childish proposal. Fancy such a proposal coming from a responsible minister of the Crown! I am afraid the little incident will not improve my opinion of Childers.

The Deanery of Carlisle is vacant, and Mr. G. is busy consulting thereon with the bishop of the diocese, Dean of St. Paul's, and Dean of Windsor.[1] I think his mind hankers most after Oakley of Hoxton.

The titles of the new peers are at length decided and are ready to be submitted to H.M. Of course Tufton was not allowed to take the title of Thanet.[2]

Wednesday, 14 September. That obstinate old Duke of Bedford persists on the acceptance of the Duchess's resignation of her appointment which scarcely can be called political, and after the question on which he disagreed with the

---

[1] i.e. with Bishop Harvey Goodwin, R. W. Church, and Gerald Wellesley.

[2] Sir Henry Tufton took the title Lord Hothfield. In 1849 his father, Sir Richard Tufton, had succeeded by will to the estate of the Earl of Thanet whose illegitimate son he was. See *G.E.C.* xii (Part I), 698.

Government has been settled and done for.[1] I fear it looks as if he were intending to break with his party.

Forster has returned from abroad, having hurried home consequent on the receipt of Mr. G.'s letter about the release of the suspects. He is not despairing, and at the same time not sanguine about the outlook in Ireland. There seems to be a general disposition on the part of the tenants to accept the Act and be pleased with it. But it remains to be seen whether they will have the courage, or dare, to admit their satisfaction. On this depends wholly the working of the Act and the peace and quiet of the country. An Irish landlord told me the other night that he was convinced that not only were the tenants silent and under the thumb of the Land League, but that the enlightened, law-abiding, and educated class were on the eve of joining the national movement. In one way this would be an improvement on the present state of affairs, of which one of the worst features is that those who have and are acquiring all this hold over the people and who seek to have some form of home rule, are a set of ruffians absolutely unfit to have a share in the government of any country.

Friday, 16 September. The most important event for the moment is the Land League Convention which is being held in Dublin. Parnell's speech yesterday was ingenious and was that of an utter irreconcilable; perhaps not more violent than could be expected, and possibly the greater violence shown, the more his friends feel that their power is being shaken. A national form of government, a parliament in College Green, and all its concomitants, such as protection of Irish-made articles, or the 'boycotting' of foreign, especially English goods, preceded by a general all round reduction of rent by about 80%, and by a demand for the immediate release of all the suspects, is Parnell's programme. It certainly looks bad, but it is early days at present to prophecy nothing but evil. Come what may, even the best, Ireland is pretty certain to be the bane and curse and difficulty of the country for many a year to come.

There is one thing, yet untried, which might do good, and that is that some of the ministry should be told off this autumn to go about in Ireland, make conciliatory speeches, and so counteract the evil influence of Land League. I pressed this strongly on Mr. G. yesterday. In Great Britain the great statesmen of the day on both sides are always stumping about, making speeches, and thereby educating the people. In Ireland nobody ever goes and opens his mouth except the Land League lot. How can it be expected, then, that the Irish shall imbibe any other teaching than that of Parnell & Co?

Mr. G. has made up his mind to submit to the Queen Wood of Leeds, and as his 'second horse' Oakley of Hoxton, for the Carlisle Deanery.

We have narrowly escaped an ugly Egyptian business. The army broke out and made all kinds of demands. Much talk about sending Turkish troops or

[1] See 1 Sept. 1881.

of a joint occupation by France and England, but fortunately a settlement has been effected, which has dispensed with resort to either of these dangerous expedients. This will probably only last for a while, and there will be a recurrence of troubles, which we shall owe to the policy inaugurated by the late Government when they first bought the Suez Canal shares and then interfered in the affairs of Egypt's creditors in conjunction with France, thereby entangling ourselves and giving France a distinct 'leg up' in the country which she has always regarded with such jealous eyes.

A constitution for Cyprus is being developed and about time too. It is a wonder to me that there has not been more fuss made about the retention of that ill-starred island, which is to cost the country here a large round sum every year.

Monday, 19 September. Lord Carew's death has vacated an Irish Lord Lieutenancy (Wexford) and a St. Patrick riband. Lord Powerscourt is first favourite for the former; and the latter, as it has been declined by the Duke of Leinster, is to be offered to Lord Bessborough.

Mr. G. has manifested great interest in, if not excitement over, the secession of Canon 'Campbello's' (of St. Peter's, Rome) having seceded from the R.C. Church; and what he says he cannot understand is how an R.C. priest can bring himself to be connected with any sort of communion except with an historic church or unbelief. (This worthy divine seems to have fallen 'flop down' into Methodism).[1]

Poor President Garfield struggles on with continuous relapses. It is hardly possible to conceive his surviving. Mr. G. is much touched by the pluck the President has shewn in the prolonged fight.

Mr. G. is very anxious that Dr. Döllinger should be induced, in the cause of religion, to come over to this country to attend some theological conclave which is to take place soon at Cambridge, and at which several foreign divines are to put in an appearance.

Matters are still tided over in Egypt, but it is a great rock ahead, which will be rendered all the more dangerous by the determination of Italy to have 'a finger in the pie'.

In writing to Lord Halifax today Mr. G. referred with great satisfaction (and no wonder) to the bloodless 'emancipation of Thessaly'. The importance of this great transfer of territory, effected mainly by the instrumentality of the present Government, has not been nearly enough appreciated.

Mr. G. is incensed at the account to which the Tories are turning this wretched hollow Fair Trade cry. However, Northcote must show his hand soon, as he is advertised to speak within the next few weeks at several places. Mr. G. thinks it fortunate that the demands on Northcote's 'backbone' are not as great as those on his speaking. I hope Mr. G. will go in for denouncing

[1] See 25 Nov. 1881.

the Fair Trade cry as strongly as he can put it at Leeds, where he is due early next month for the purpose of paying, or at least of acknowledging, the debt which the great constituency owe him. Mr. Kitson, the Liberal organiser at Leeds, has kindly invited me down for the occasion. I shall hope to take advantage of his invitation. I expect it will be one of the greatest demonstrations ever given to a public man.

That wretched 'Green imprisonment' business drags on. There was some hope that Green was becoming physically, if not mentally, affected by the continued imprisonment, but as Harcourt said, 'What are you to do for a man who will so unfeelingly put on 10 pounds weight during his incarceration'?[1]

Have been, and am, much worried about C. & W. M.[2]

Thursday, 22 September. Poor President Garfield succumbed (as I anticipated) on Monday evening. After such a prolonged and plucky struggle, quite a halo of heroism surrounds him, and the sympathy manifested in this country over the event is most marked. The order which is issued today for Court mourning will be greatly appreciated—as much appreciated as it is becoming. Few circumstances attending the death of the President strike one more than the fact that, though the reigning spirit of one of the greatest nations in the world, he should die worth only $25,000—say £5,000! What a reflection!

Here is an instance of the versatility of the Great Man. The other day when he was writing to Forster on Ireland, to Lord Granville on public affairs generally, to Blennerhassett on Dr. Döllinger and religion, he was also writing to some American professor on the cosmology of Homer and expressing a hope that the time would soon come when he would be able to test thoroughly the theories propounded by the Yankee.[3]

There seems hope that the Fair Trade bubble is pricked. The arguments used by the Trades Union delegates at their recent Congress form a striking answer to the appeal of the Fair Traders to the working man for support.

The outlook in Ireland is dreary beyond description. Whatever may be the ultimate results of the land legislation, in which I still have confidence, there seems to be no doubt that we have a very ugly winter ahead. People talk vaguely about stronger measures being taken by the Executive, forgetting

[1] The Revd. Sidney F. Green had been sent to prison as a result of court action taken against him for ritual offences under the provisions of the Public Worship Regulation Act of 1874. See 6 and 23 Nov. 1881 and Gardiner, i. 384–6.

[2] Probably a reference to some family problem relating either to his sister Constance or his brother Clement.

[3] On 27 Aug. 1881 Professor William Fairfield Warren, President of Boston University, sent G. a copy of his article which had just appeared in the *Independent* entitled the 'True Key to Ancient Cosmology and Mythical Geography'. Add. MS. 44471, ff. 127–8. The question that G. raised in his reply to Warren of 20 Sept. 1881 was whether Homer had conceived of the Earth as a plane or as a spherical or convex surface. Add. MS. 44545, f. 25.

wholly the difficulties there are in reaching the evil. It is not like as if the country were in open rebellion, where you could order troops out and after proper warning open fire upon the insurrectionists. It is the system of silent proscription—of 'boycotting'—which is striking terror in the country, and with which it is almost impossible to cope. Mr. G. has, I see, nearly reached boiling point with Parnell and is inclined to denounce him at Leeds as 'an enemy of the Empire'.[1] Notwithstanding the state of affairs in Ireland, there seems to be, judging from the best accounts, a suppressed feeling of satisfaction at the Land Act; and even those landlords who denounced the measure most are beginning to admit that under the new regime they will not be as bad off as they expected.

Sunday, 25 September. The Queen has of herself re-opened the question of filling up the vacant Garter. The two men she suggests are the Duke of Grafton, who she thinks would be sure to decline the honour, and the Duke of St. Albans. She does not, of course, mention Lord Derby, and though Mr. G. would like most to confer the riband on Lord Derby, he seems inclined to let the matter stand over for the next vacancy. I think this is wise, but it is a great question whether there are not weightier claims than those of St. Albans.

The Court of Common Council[2] propose to present Mr. G. with an address accompanied with a request that he will sit for a bust. There was a certain amount of opposition displayed to the proposal, and Mr. G. does not much like the idea of accepting anything which has been made the subject of contest. But as the opposition proceeded from men of no influence or weight among the Corporation, I don't see well how he can refuse.

The forthcoming retirement of Lord Justice Bramwell will create a vacancy in the Court of Appeal. Mr. G. is desirous to offer the place to Holker, for whom he appears to have a 'sneaking liking' and of whose abilities he evidently entertains the highest opinion. Coleridge does not think Holker would accept,[3] and is strongly in favour of the promotion of a Puisne Judge. His idea is that the judges of the first instance should be the really strong judicial bench.

Wednesday, 28 September. (Wilton) Lord Hartington appears to have written direct from Balmoral to Hawarden respecting army matters which appear to be assuming an acute form, including the Wolseley business and the Duke of C[ambridge]. In replying to Lord H[artington], Mr. G. opened out his mind pretty freely about his intentions for the future as well as on the situation generally. Apropos of the Wolseley business, which is further complicated

[1] G. was scheduled to make some speeches at Leeds on 7 Oct. 1881 and in one of his speeches he did denounce Parnell, who shortly afterwards was imprisoned under the Coercion Act. See 7, 11, and 16 Oct. 1881.
[2] Of the City of London.
[3] But he did. See 14 Jan. 1882.

now by the proposal to make him Adjutant General, Mr. G. thinks that where there are personal objections and recommendations only, much weight may be given to reason, or even unreason, of the Sovereign; but when there are reasons of public policy closely involved, then he holds that for the Prime Minister to give way is an abandonment of duty and a commencement of the process of sapping the constitution. As regards the Wolseley peerage, the normal course for him to take, now that he has been dragged into it by Childers, would be to force the appointment on threat of retirement. And, of course, one knows very well what would follow—H.M. would give way. But what Mr. G. now feels is that, as the surrender of his intention to retire ere long is out of the question, to take such a course now with the Queen would be acting towards her under false pretences; because if he forced her hand now, and retired a few months afterwards, She might fairly turn round and say, 'You forced my hand about Wolseley under more or less false pretences, as you threatened me with resignation which you had in view at the time'. Therefore his position is far more difficult than it would be were it under ordinary circumstances. In his letter to Hartington he dwelt again on the fact that when he took office last year he did not consider it was an abandonment of the scheme he shaped for himself in 1875.[1] He regarded his resumption of office as a temporary expedient, simply to deal with complications, and then to leave the conduct of affairs to those to whom he considers it rightly belongs viz. Lords Granville and Hartington.

Sunday, 2 October. Accounts from Ireland continue very bad. The Executive seems paralysed, and the Land League paramount. And yet one does not see what can be done further, unless it be to govern Ireland by martial law, and this would require Parliamentary powers which simply would not be given. There is no doubt, as Lord Derby puts it in a very striking article in the *XIXth Century*,[2] that except in Ulster there is no feeling, nor is there likely to be any feeling, of gratitude, wrung out of the hands of the Imperial Parliament by agitation and intimidation as the Land Act was. The fact is, the mis-government of Ireland can be summed up in two words—'Too late'. Every act of redress, every message of peace, has only come after it was too late to be of use.

Wood of Leeds has declined the Deanery of Carlisle. Oakley has been submitted to the Queen, but she may kick at it, as he is believed to be a 'disestablishist'.

Monday, 3 October. The Thistle which has become vacant by the sad and sudden death of Lord Airlie, one of the few staunch Liberal peers, is placed

---

[1] i.e. his plan to retire as leader of the party.
[2] 'Ireland and the Land Act', *Nineteenth Century*, x (Oct. 1881), pp. 473–93. See also 24 Oct. 1881.

at Rosebery's disposal. I should not wonder if he declined it. Failing Rosebery, Roxburghe ought to be the man.

As regards the Lord Lieutenancy of Ross-shire, I think Sir K. Mackenzie will get it, and A. Matheson, the other big county Liberal magnate, will be made happy by the promise of a baronetcy.

The Queen appears to have sent a ciphered message to Hawarden yesterday cautioning Mr. G. as to what he says at Leeds this week. Surely such interference is not becoming in a constitutional Sovereign? If her First Minister is not to be trusted in a matter of this kind, She had better dismiss him at once. Mr. G. as usual took it exceedingly well and returned the message by a most loyal and temperate explanation, which was to this effect: After commenting on the unfortunate fact of having to make a speech when public affairs are in such an uneasy state, he confided to H.M. that there were 3 things which specially weigh on his mind.

(1) State of incapacity for work to which House of Commons had been reduced.

(2) The proceedings of Parnell—'by no means an insignificant person' (as Mr. G. says)—aiming manifestly at separation and even hostility between the two countries.

(3) The strange revival of protection under guise of Fair Trade, to get rid of which it cost the country nearly a quarter of a century of legislative existence.

On these points he told H.M. he should speak strongly.[1]

Friday, 7 October. (Leeds) Arrived here yesterday about an hour before the special train which brought Mr. and Mrs. G. and Helen G. Mr. Kitson, with whom they stay, kindly offered to put me up. The reception on arrival was very enthusiastic; all the streets up to Kitson's house were lined with crowds who cheered enthusiastically. The demonstration however was, I believe, merely a foretaste of what the more formal demonstrations of today and tomorrow will be—yesterday's reception was called 'semi-private'. Mr. G. seemed remarkably well yesterday, though somewhat oppressed by the Transvaal news, which amounts pretty well to a rejection of the Convention by the Volksraad. This morning, however, he has unfortunately got a little touch of lumbago, which is truly unlucky.

Later. Returned from the first speech in the Town Hall. Tremendous enthusiasm all along the route as well as in the Hall, and organisation perfect. Mr. G. spoke for 1 hour and 35 minutes. He confined himself almost entirely to land and Fair Trade, and in his denunciations of Fair Trade absurdities and the shuffling conduct of Sir S. Northcote in regard to it, he was in his most powerful and happiest humours.

---

[1] For the exchange, see Guedalla, ii. 169–70.

Tuesday, 11 October. (Dalmeny) Came on here on Saturday night from Leeds.

The banquet on Friday was very striking. Mr. G. spoke in his gravest and most forcible manner, confining himself entirely to Ireland and denouncing Parnell in very strong terms. What was still more striking was the torchlight procession homewards. All the streets were packed, despite a drizzling rain, with dense throngs cheering vociferously, and were lined by torchbearers who, on our passing, fell in behind and formed a sort of rearguard of fire.

On the Saturday morning we drove again down to the Town Hall amid renewed cheers. Mr. G. gave the Chamber of Commerce an hour and a half on Free Trade v. Fair Trade in the unrivalled style in which he manipulates figures and dresses them up in a wholly new light. He is firmly convinced in his own mind that Fair Trade will never get beyond an electioneering delusion. After the speech came the banquet given by the Liberal Club, and after the banquet we reached the crowning point of the demonstration, namely the mass meeting in the specially built hall estimated to hold 25,000 people. The reception accorded to Mr. G. on his arrival was beyond description and quite overwhelming, what with the shouts, the clapping of hands in time (called the 'Kentish Fire'), the singing of 'He's a jolly good fellow'. It was arranged that several speakers were to precede Mr. G., but nobody, except Herbert G. who was tremendously cheered and acquitted himself extremely well, could get a hearing. Mr. G. spoke for about an hour and apparently commanded the whole audience. It was a declamatory speech on strictly party lines, but perhaps hardly equal to his other performances. After the mass meeting, a progress was made through the streets to the house of Mr. Barran, the other M.P. for Leeds,[1] and on dining there Mr. G. with Mrs. G. and Helen took his departure by special train for Mrs. Meynell Ingram's near Burton-on-Trent.

Those were indeed two memorable days. One will probably never see anything at all approaching to them again in one's life.

Found several people here—'Lady A.',[2] Col. and Mrs. Oliphant, Mrs. and pretty Mrs. Arthur Sassoon, Lady Reay, Lord Young. A nice place charmingly situated.

The accounts of the Lord Chancellor[3] are anything but good; in fact, quite bad enough to make one speculate about his successor upon whom it would certainly be difficult to light. Of course Jessel, the greatest judge on the bench, is out of the running.[4] There is Coleridge, who probably would be no great accession of strength to a Cabinet. Sir Henry James would have claims, but I am inclined to back Harcourt. He is probably as good a lawyer as Brougham was or had the reputation of being.

---

[1] Herbert Gladstone being an M.P. for Leeds also.
[2] i.e. Maria, Marchioness of Ailesbury, widow of the 1st Marquess.
[3] Lord Selborne.
[4] Presumably because Jessel was a Jew.

Sunday, 16 October. (Mayen) Came on here on Wednesday, and been seedy since my arrival.

The great news has been the decision of the Cabinet last week in regard to Ireland, which has resulted in the arrest of Parnell, and this step is being followed up and will be still further followed up by the arrest of other Land League notabilities. Perfect unanimity appears to have prevailed in the Cabinet. It remains to be seen what the effect will be of resorting to these further penal measures.

Mr. G. at Leeds the other day pointedly alluded on more than one occasion to the consignment of the leadership of the party to the hands of Lord Granville and Lord Hartington at no distant date. The allusion met with but scant approval, the names of both being received in silence. However, there is no doubt that the bent of Mr. G.'s mind is on resignation in the course of next year. A short time ago he opened out his mind on this question to Bright. In so doing he commenced by referring to the reasons which he had formed during his withdrawal from the leadership before the General Election of last year against returning to office. He thus summarised those reasons.

1. His age and probable failure of his faculties.

2. The probable exasperation of the tone of party strife to which his return would give rise.

3. His position relatively to Her Majesty.

4. The just claims of Lord Granville and Lord Hartington.

5. His natural disinclination to resume the reins, which under ordinary circumstances would have justified his refusal.

He told Bright he wished now to 'take stock' of these reasons.

As to No. 1, perhaps he need not say much. (Indeed he need not, for never were his faculties in more perfect and vigorous working order).

As to No. 2, he admitted that he could not see that party strife had been specially embittered by his return—a fact which was a relief and satisfaction to him.

No. 3—his relations with Her Majesty were greatly worse than he ever anticipated.

No. 4, he felt with increasing strength; and

As to No. 5, he only accepted the mission last year as special and temporary.

In most questions he considered that as much progress had been made as he had anticipated. Ireland, however, still looms very large. This question and that of the Transvaal still hang in the balance. From neither could he run away. He must remain chained to the oar until each had reached a settlement. Then it will be suitable and becoming for him to retire. He may have to take share in endeavouring to put into working order the organisation of the House of Commons, but this should be done within the next 6 months.

What then seems to be the bent for the moment of Mr. G.'s mind? He wishes to carry out his original determination to retire and make over the leadership to Lord Granville and Lord Hartington. This he would naturally do in the middle of next year, making the reform of parliamentary procedure his final political stroke. *But* is it possible to conceive Ireland quiescent within the next 6 or 9 months, and how can he surrender his trust until he has seen the country through the Irish difficulties? Therefore on Ireland would seem wholly to depend his future plans. Supposing he does make up his mind and give out his intention to retire next year. One of two things probably will happen: either the country will insist on his remaining at the helm provided he has strength and health to do so, *or* the party will come to grief, that is, it will for want of enthusiasm for its leaders 'run riot', or the Lords will pluck up courage in his absence to resist all Government measures and force the hands of the Government to dissolve before the franchise is extended to the counties. The outlook accordingly is gloomy. There is one point on which I have no notion of the bent of Mr. G.'s mind and that is what he will do when he does retire. He won't take a peerage. Can he wholly terminate his political connexion by withdrawing from Parliament? And can he remain in the House with another leading? All 3 alternatives seem impossible.

Wednesday, 19 October. (Mayen) The strong measures of the Government in Ireland have met with very general approval throughout Great Britain, and no remonstrance has come from even the extreme Radicals. The Tories never can see that to take such drastic steps as these the Government must have the country unanimously at its back (which, had the Government resorted to them earlier, would certainly not have been the case)—otherwise a very sensible part of the country would have sided with Parnell & Co. The exercise of patience has been most necessary in this instance. Of course the Opposition will now ridicule the Government for having at last to resort to force, which Bright declared was no remedy a year ago. Those words, however, of Bright are greatly distorted. What, of course, he meant was, that force could be no *permanent* remedy, nor more it can be—in short any more than a diet on blue pills could cure a patient with a bad liver. The occasional use of them does good and may be resorted to in chronic disorders, but their perpetual use must in the long run impair the constitution, which has been Ireland's fate.

Monday, 24 October. (Mayen) The arrests have been followed up by the proclamation of the Land League as illegal. The League by their last move, counselling the non-payment of any rent, played into the hands of the Government. The latest accounts of Ireland are, I hear, decidedly better.

Lord O'Hagan has resigned, for private reasons, the Lord Chancellorship of Ireland. He will be no loss, as he has been a palpably weak vessel, and has literally rendered no assistance whatever either in the House of Lords or outside it to poor Forster. I hear he is to be succeeded by Sullivan, Master of the Rolls, which will be a considerable accession of strength to the Irish Government. I know Mr. G. always entertained the highest possible opinion of Sullivan, who was Mr. G.'s right hand man throughout the handling of the Land Bill of 1870, when Sullivan was Attorney General.

I forgot to note that the Thistle vacant by Lord Airlie's death is to be conferred on Dalhousie. Rosebery again declined it. He is callous of ribands, and Dalhousie deserves it as an excellent supporter, more especially as he has lost his Home Office work in the House of Lords by the appointment of Rosebery to the Under Secretaryship and behaved extremely well about it. Such a contrast, as Mr. G. said at the time, to Courtney, who never even thanked Mr. G. for his promotion to the Colonial Office, whereas Dalhousie expressed satisfaction at the arrangement which deprived him of *his* office.

Mr. G. has had a cold, but is reported convalescent again. He goes to pay Lord Derby a visit this week—a notable event. Lord Derby's article in the *19th Century* on the Irish Land Act has excited much attention, and deservedly so.[1] He has a knack of giving such a sterling common-sense complexion to all he writes, and in the present instance has contrived to treat with real freshness a subject which has been so worn and thrashed out. It is not hostile or inoffensive [*sic*] towards the Government, but Mr. G. was afraid it might tend to damage public interests by emboldening agitation and weakening the law.

Friday, 28 October. (Mayen) Accounts from Ireland continue to be encouraging. The extensive arrests and the summary suppression of the Land League seem to have broken the neck of the agitation and system of terrorism, while the landlord class are taking heart and responding to the call which Mr. G. addressed to them. I am afraid Sullivan is not to be the new Lord Chancellor of Ireland. Law, I understand, has pressed his claim as Attorney General, which is undeniable.

Harcourt and Chamberlain have this week both made big speeches.[2] Chamberlain confined himself almost wholly to Ireland, and made a most powerful defence of the action of the Government as regards remedial and coercive measures, and as to the exact time to which resort was had to those measures. Harcourt slashed out against Salisbury and Northcote, and shewed in the way he reviewed the Government policy at home and abroad that he has the power of defending as well as of hitting in the most telling manner possible.

These speeches have done decided good, I think, and may have had something to do with the Berwickshire election, in which the Liberal candidate,

---

[1] See 2 Oct. 1881.
[2] On 25 Oct. 1881 Harcourt spoke at Glasgow and Chamberlain at Liverpool.

though a Roman Catholic and not supposed to be a good candidate, simply 'romped in'.[1]

Saturday, 29 October. Reports from Ireland still good. A story comes from Herbert G., who is now getting into official harness in Dublin as Forster's assistant, that a celebrated Land Agent went to Cork to collect rents last Saturday week and did not get a penny. He went again *last* Saturday and had the best rent paying day he ever had *in his life*! Tenants appear to be literally flocking into the Land Court.

I hear Herries has finally made up his mind to retire. Poor West! He will never get over it if Mr. G. does not appoint him Herries' successor. I trust this will be done, and I think Mr. G. *will* do it.[2] He would probably then offer a Commissionership to Arthur Godley. This would make a serious change in Downing St, as A.G. would, I think, be sure to accept.[3]

Monday, 31 October. Returned to town. Occupied part of the day in 'taking stock' of what has been going on, more especially in reading up the correspondence, i.e. the copies of Mr. G.'s letters written during my absence.

He seems quite to have recovered the effects of his cold, which he attributes to the exertions at Leeds—'the greatest physical effort he ever made', he says. No part of the Leeds proceedings evidently gratified him so much as the reception accorded to Herbert—''erbert' as the Leeds folk familiarly called him.

The Knowsley visit was clearly a great success. Mr. G. alludes to it more than once with great satisfaction. 'Nothing could have been more friendly and hearty than were both Lord and Lady Derby'. The visit ought to be the means of making the political tie strong and lasting. For years past I have always looked upon Lord Derby as a 'fish out of water', while allied to the Tories, but one little thought 3 years ago that the change would be so complete.

As to Lord Salisbury's recent speech in the North, Mr. G. alludes to it 'as the worst speech he had ever known delivered by the leader of a party'.[4]

The Wolseley imbroglio continues serious. The Queen appears to tackle each Cabinet Minister on the subject as She comes in contact with him. She and also Prince Leopold entered upon it at great length with Harcourt at Balmoral the other day. The appointment of Wolseley to the Adjutancy

[1] Hubert Jerningham, the Liberal, received 1,046 votes to his opponent's 529.
[2] He did. See 11 Nov. 1881 when EWH notes that Algernon West is to be Chairman of the Board of Inland Revenue.
[3] In fact, when an offer was made, Arthur Godley declined. See 7 and 13 Dec. 1881. But he eventually became a Commissioner of Inland Revenue in the summer of 1882. See 5 June, 17 July, and 12 Aug. 1882.
[4] Lord Salisbury and Northcote had used Newcastle as the scene of a series of speeches just after G.'s visit to Leeds. One of Salisbury's speeches was an especially bitter attack on G.'s policies.

General would make the Duke of Cambridge resign, which desirable as it might be on many grounds, might lead to serious difficulties. It would be putting the military 'fat into the fire with a vengeance'. The latest means of excape from the wretched business seems to be what I ventured to suggest a month ago, namely, that Sir J. Adye should be made Adjutant General, and that Wolseley should become Surveyor General, in which capacity he might receive his peerage. It is extraordinary that a man with a grain of self-respect and good feeling should not flatly decline to receive any honour or to take any post the bestowal of which is attended with so much embarrassment to the Government and is regarded with such ill favour by the Queen and the Duke.

There has been a row about Knox Little. He most injudiciously at the moment of his being appointed Canon of Worcester interviewed and took up the cudgel of the imprisoned Rev. S. F. Green.[1] By the judicious interposition of the Dean of St. Paul's,[2] K[nox] Little appears to have been brought to his senses and to have intimated his willingness to resign. Mr. G. seems satisfied with the intention, and the matter will probably now be allowed to drop. Oakley of Hoxton is to be Dean of Carlisle, and Rowsell seems first favourite for the stall at Westminster vacant by the death of poor old Leighton.

I see Mr. G. still harps upon the merits of *John Inglesant*, a romance of the 17th century.[3]

Cabinets are not to commence before the 9th. Mr. G. had serious thoughts of shirking the Lord Mayor's dinner, but Lord Granville is too gouty to take his place and so Mr. G. will go. I don't quite like the accounts of Lord G[ranville], who seems to be in anything but a satisfactory condition.

I hope that the sessional programme will mainly consist of reform of parliamentary procedure, the readjustment of imperial and local taxation, and the extension of Local Government Boards.

I expect '*Land*' will have to stand over, and certainly the extension of the franchise in counties, though Chamberlain is for giving precedence to the franchise question over Land reform.

I have made up my mind—though speculations are useless—that it will be the county franchise question which the House of Lords will select to throw out so as to force the hands of the Government to dissolve before they enlarge the electorate.

Wednesday, 2 November. Municipal elections have gone against us. It is probably as foolish to make much of the result as to take no heed of it. Of course the Irish vote is now 'solid' against the Government, and so it will be whenever another General Election comes, and this cannot fail to be an important consideration.

[1] For some information on S. F. Green, see 19 Sept. 1881.
[2] R. W. Church.
[3] This book, written by Joseph Henry Shorthouse, had been published in May, 1881.

There is an extraordinary mortality among Liberal M.P.'s, quite out of proportion to the majority in which they stand in the House of Commons. Tiverton and Stafford are now vacant by the deaths of Massey and Macdonald, the working man—a worthy but rather repulsive individual. Tiverton seems safe for Ebrington, who comes forward as a staunch Liberal (in contradistinction to his father's wishy-washy Tory-Liberalism) with a good certificate of conduct from Lord Spencer with whom he has been working as private secretary. Stafford will probably be lost. The Conservatives are ready with an excellent man in the person of Mr. Salt, who held office under the late Government, and the Radicals will require a very strong candidate to beat him. Probably the best man will be G. Howell, who would carry on the 'working man's' traditions of the constituency.[1]

An article in yesterday's *Standard* announcing pending changes in the Cabinet, which would comprise Mr. Gladstone's immediate resignation of the Chancellorship of the Exchequer to be followed by his early total withdrawal from the ministry, has set the world somewhat agog.[2] Of course it has no further foundation than Mr. Gladstone's own declaration at Leeds. In the case of the *Standard* as also in Mr. G.'s own case, I am inclined to believe that as regards the immediate future 'the wish is father to the thought'. No doubt he does not intend to go on with both or either offices indefinitely, but this he is repeatedly giving out; and therefore the announcement in the *Standard* was merely giving a startling complexion to a stale piece of news. His future plans must really mainly depend on Ireland.

Lord Granville, whose last attack of gout has, I fear, been more serious than usual, is better; as also is reported to be the Lord Chancellor,[3] but I have no confidence in his recovery.

The Queen wrote again today on the Wolseley business, specially exercised in her mind.[4] She hears that the result of the interview last Saturday between the Duke of Cambridge and Childers was to force down H.R.H.'s throat Wolseley for the Adjutant Generalship, which She maintains must lead to the resignation of the Duke. This version of the story does not at all tally with that which I learn from Nevy Lyttelton. The interview was supposed to have been very satisfactory; for, though no final decision was come to, the Duke of C[ambridge] was very friendly and by no means disinclined to withdraw his objections to the proposed appointment, and certainly never hinted at resignation. The natural conclusion to arrive at is that the Duke holds one language to H.M. and another to Childers. This makes him doubly difficult to deal with.

[1] On 14 Nov. 1881 the voters of Tiverton returned Lord Ebrington, the oldest son of Lord Fortescue, by a majority of 252. On 19 Nov. at Stafford Thomas Salt won out over the Liberal, G. Howell, by 297 votes. See 22 Nov. 1881.

[2] *Standard*, 1 Nov. 1881, p. 4, cols. 6–7.

[3] Lord Selborne.

[4] Guedalla, ii. 171.

R. Churchill continues to 'star' in the provinces, and there is no denying that he is making a position for himself. It is sickening to think that a man of such unscrupulousness and with such utter want of seriousness should be coming to the front in politics and would on the formation of a Tory Government be entrusted with governing this country. If politics were merely a question of men, not measures, I can conceive no serious-minded politician being anything but a Liberal. The Tories are bad enough as regards measures, but they are worse as regards men, commencing with Lord Salisbury and the weak-kneed Northcote down to such men as R. Churchill and J. Lowther, with whom politics is a burlesque.

Pembroke has sent me the speech he made the other day to the Warminster farmers on the agricultural distress and its remedies—thoughtful, sensible, and moderate as is all that he says. He is no Tory, and yet tremendously anti-radical. He ought to belong to the Commonsense party, in which (if there were one) he would almost persuade me to be a convert.

Thursday, 3 November. Mr. G. was told by Lady Derby the other day at Knowsley that it was all right about the Duke of Bedford; he intended remaining staunch notwithstanding the resignation of his Duchess, which he now declares is not on political grounds![1]

The main question for the Cabinet next week, Mr. G. says, will be: is precedence to be given next session to parliamentary procedure over all other business? Such a measure divides itself into two parts and two distinct parts:

  1. the restraint of individual members,

  2. the devolution of a portion of the duties of Parliament.

In writing to Lord G[ranville], Mr. G. comments on the present lull in what he calls 'over-sea affairs', resembling that which preceded the Franco-German war in 1870.[2]

Two fresh instances today of the varied objects of interest which engage the versatile mind of the Great Man. He is much excited about a religious census which has been taken in Liverpool,[3] and has been descanting on the girth of oaks.[4]

Madame Novikoff is over here again. Mr. G. has promised her a visit next week. In writing to thank her for putting him in possession of the opinion which two distinguished diplomatists hold regarding him and his policy,[5] he

---

[1] See 1 and 14 Sept. 1881. [2] Ramm, i. 308.

[3] Alfred Billson, Honorary Secretary of the Southwest Lancashire Liberal Association, had sent G. a copy of the *Statistics of Church Attendance in Liverpool* 'taken by the Liverpool *Daily Post*'. Add. MS. 44472, f. 203.

[4] On 2 Nov. 1881 G. wrote Lord Halifax about the dimensions of some large oaks in England. Add. MS. 44545, f. 46.

[5] The 'two distinguished diplomatists' were Count Be'ust, whom Mme Novikoff had seen recently in Paris, and the Dutch Minister, Count Byland, who had declared to her that G. was '"a genius, SIMPLY(!) a genius"', Novikof to G., 25 Oct. 1881, Add. MS. 44268, f. 243.

remarked that he and Lord G[ranville] had, besides having stopped up some special sources of ill-will, done nothing abroad with a merely selfish aim or in a spirit unfriendly to any person or country.

The negotiations with France have come to another standstill. Cotton and wool still form the staple difficulties. It is evidently no use proceeding with the matter till the new French government is formed and is at work. Gambetta with Leon Say ought to be willing to better the terms. Otherwise, of course, the treaty will not be concluded. Mr. G. says he should regret the failure of the negotiations mostly on political grounds, though we can afford the loss better than France can. He believes that apart from those grounds we are in a commercial sense so strong in the command of the general market of the world as to be independent of all huckstering—a matter, he says, much more suitable for those who have not yet extricated themselves from the 'arid labyrinth of protection'.

He alluded, in writing to Chamberlain, to the *Standard* article about himself and his future plans, and assured him that the matter has not gone a hair's breadth beyond this—that his return to official responsibility last year was for a special purpose, and that a great part of that purpose, though not the whole, seems to be accomplished.[1]

The danger for the moment in Ireland seems to be the overflooding of the Land Court.

The Queen has approved Rowsell for the Westminster stall.

Friday, 4 November. The result of the elections both in France and Germany have gone liberal. Gambetta has had a great triumph which will entail his assuming at last the responsibilities of taking the lead, and Bismarck has met with a not inconsiderable defeat.

The two first things for Gambetta to do are (1) to get out of the Tunisian mess as best he can, and (2) to come forward with terms which will enable a treaty to be made with this country.

The political importance of a treaty is greater for France than it is for us. She is practically isolated now in Europe, and that isolation has received a signal mark recently by the visit of the King of Italy to Austria.

There are rumours of a rising in Arabia, and of the setting up of a rival caliph. This may be the beginning of the realisation of Wilfrid Blunt's dreams and fond wishes, which have always been that the only solution of the Eastern question, so far as this country is concerned, is that the spiritual power of the Sultan should be divorced from his temporal power, thus reducing his significance in the eyes of the Mahometan world.

Sunday, 6 November. The Dean of Wells (Johnson) is dead, and Mr. G. has submitted the name of Dr. Plumptre to Her Majesty. Dr. P[lumptre] is a

[1] See 2 Nov. 1881.

distinguished man, and his appointment will greatly please the Archbishop of Canterbury.[1] As an instance of Mr. G.'s thoughtfulness—the moment he received from the son the intelligence of the Dean's death, he wrote off to the Bishop of Bath and Wells[2] to say that, if (as was probable) the widow was left ill off, a sum of £200 or £300 should be forthcoming.

The case of Green is hopeless. The Bishop of Manchester[3] has done his best to extricate the stubborn man out of his difficulty, but the imprisoned gentleman is not to be moved by his diocesan's tact, kindness, and liberal-mindedness; and so he will have to abide his time in jail. Mr. G. hopes that if any substitute for imprisonment in these cases is proposed, it will not be deprivation—the punishment of all others which seems to be most suitable.

Mr. G. has written at length to Dodson on the general subject of local taxation and local government. He evidently hankers after substituting for the present grants in aid the allocation of certain imperial taxes. He suggests the appointment of a small Departmental Committee to thrash out the subject.

Monday, 7 November. I am afraid, from what Lord F. Cavendish said to me this afternoon, Mr. G. has quite made up his mind against promoting Algy West to the Chairmanship of the Board of Inland Revenue.[4] It will be a truly bitter disappointment to West, and I believe his energy, diligence, and straightforwardness would amply make up for any want of absolute brilliancy and constitute him a very efficient chairman. I am very sorry about it, and a great difficulty will arise as to who can be put over him. Lord F. C. seemed to think it would be better and easier to secure a parliamentary man. If not, the only man I can think of for the moment is Sir J. Lambert.

Childers' interview with the Duke seems to have been satisfactory on Saturday. The Duke is said to have expressed his willingness to withdraw his objections to Wolseley for the Adjutant Generalship. Therefore, unless the Queen makes a difficulty, this matter will be tided over.

Tuesday, 8 November. Mr. and Mrs. G. arrived this afternoon—he in great force and she very much better.

The Duke of Bedford has withdrawn the Duchess's resignation after all.[5] Lady Derby seems to have had a hand in the reconciliation; for, notwithstanding what Lady Derby said the other day, it was evidently on political grounds, chiefly connected with land, on which the Duke wished to sever his indirect connection with the Ministry. However, his apprehensions have been removed. Mr. G. has written to him to express satisfaction, telling him that he could conceive nothing more unlikely than the application to England of the

[1] A. C. Tait. [2] Lord Arthur Hervey.
[3] James Fraser. For the Green case, see 19 Sept., 23 Nov. 1881, and 12 Aug. 1882.
[4] But he hadn't. See 11 Nov. 1881. [5] See 1, 14 Sept., and 3 Nov. 1881.

Irish Land Act. It is true that the Agricultural Holdings Act in principle introduced into the relations between landlord and tenant the action of a public authority, and this is probably inseparable from any legislative recognition of any rights of the tenant even for improvements, but this is totally different from a court which Mr. G. reaffirms that he adopted with the greatest reluctance for Ireland; and he reminded the Duke of the provisions as to future tenancies under which there is no right of application to the court for fixing rent.

The Bishop of Durham[1] has been staying at Hawarden. Mr. G. was greatly pleased with him. They had a talk over the new Newcastle see.

The great Brighton railway murder case has terminated today in a verdict of guilty, contrary (I think) to general expectation.[2]

Wednesday, 9 November. Just returned from the Lord Mayor's dinner, which was less of a scramble than that of last year. The wind had been rather taken out of Mr. G.'s sails by his recent speech in the City, and accordingly there was somewhat of a lack of interest in his speech on the present occasion. However, it was good and stately, and he was able to give a more rosy hue to it than he could last year. Lord Granville spoke at too great length, and I heard him too imperfectly to judge of the speech, but it bored the audience and he did not exhibit that lightness of hand for which he is noted in after-dinner speeches. My neighbours at dinner thought the speech had a touch of senility about it, for which I am extremely sorry.

Sir C. Herries came and resigned this morning, and I think West's chances of promotion to Herries' place are improving.[3]

The Speaker[4] next had an audience on parliamentary procedure which Mr. G. will certainly take up in real earnest.

He was followed by Forster, and then came a confab with Lord G[ranville] and Childers on the vexed question of the staff appointment at the War Office, which ended in my having to write to Ponsonby to say that if the suggestion he made in his last letter to me could be authoritatively put forward, the matter might arrange itself; the suggestion being that a few months' grace should be allowed during which Sir C. Ellice would be retained as Adjutant General, and that in the meanwhile the Duke of Cambridge should make up his mind to swallow Wolseley as Sir C. Ellice's successor.

Friday, 11 November. Yesterday's Cabinet was almost entirely taken up in the consideration of the question of parliamentary procedure, which they decided should be put in the front rank of next session's business. There are

---

[1] J. B. Lightfoot. See 12 Mar. 1882.
[2] On this day Percy Lefroy Mapleton was convicted of the murder on 27 June 1881 of a Mr. Gold on the Brighton Railway.
[3] See 4 Apr., 29 Oct., and 11 Nov. 1881.   [4] H. B. Brand.

to be no more Cabinets till after Christmas, and Parliament is not to meet till the ordinary time—about the 7th February.

Mr. G. is in tremendous force. I never saw him looking better or more cheery.

Poor West is out of his misery, and, in spite of all that has been said to the contrary, he has got the Chairmanship.[1] A. Young, Secretary of the Board, is to be put into the deputy chair, which will be a great strength to the Board— an arrangement which I think more than any other induced Mr. G. to get over his scruples as to West's appointment. I am sincerely glad for West. What a truly lucky fellow he has been! Everything has turned up trumps for him.

I never knew till yesterday that Goschen had been sounded for the Chancellorship of the Exchequer and that he declined. It must be pure huffiness, for I am assured he has no intention of 'ratting'. He has, I suppose, never got over his mortification at not being offered a seat in the Cabinet originally, or, at any rate, not receiving an intimation that but for his views on the franchise question he would have been numbered among the ministers.

Tuesday, 22 November. (Hawarden) Another horrible hiatus in the diary. Arrived here today with my mother from Great Budworth, where I have been staying since Saturday so as to be present at the christening of my first nephew.[2] Previous to that I was two days at Charlie Tudway's—an excellently 'well appointed' house, good shooting, good cooking, and good company— where we had the Normantons, Walronds, and several people of local connection.[3]

They are quite alone here with the exception of one of the Bowden Miss Gladstones.[4] I enjoy it, as it gives one the chance of having the Great Man a little to oneself. He descanted this evening after dinner on the excellencies of his present secretariat and its working, and specially on the merits of Arthur Godley, of whom he certainly has the highest opinion, and no wonder. He told me that he thought the best recipe for a shaky Liberal was May's *Constitutional History*, and this led up to the dissection of Sir T. E. May himself. I told Mr. G. he ought to make May a P.C., and he said he would willingly, were it not for the difficulty which might arise from his being placed in the same rank with the Speaker and Chairman of Committees. He evidently has the profoundest respect for May, and he said he had always regarded it a great slight on Lord Beaconsfield's part when he (Lord B.) passed over May for the Clerkship of the Parliaments.

[1] i.e. of the Board of Inland Revenue. See 29 Oct. and 7 Nov. 1881.

[2] EWH's sister Alice and her husband Robert Moberly lived at Great Budworth. The nephew is their son Walter Moberly.

[3] Charles Clement Tudway lived at Stoberry Park, near Wells, Somerset.

[4] i.e. one of the daughters of Captain John Gladstone of Bowden Park, Chippenham, G.'s elder brother.

The Stafford election on Saturday was a disagreeable facer.[1] However much is due to the local popularity of the Tory candidate, it won't account for the full extent of the change, and it must be numbered among the early signs of a waning popularity, which is inevitable; the Tories are becoming more courageous and proportionately rabid, the Whigs more timid and suspicious, and the Radicals more disappointed and impatient.

Accounts from Ireland are bad. Applications are pouring in to court, but outrages—and bad outrages—are more prevalent. In short, November is keeping up its Irish bad reputation. Meanwhile rents are being very generally and considerably reduced. Assuming the administration of the Act to be fair (and one has no right to question the justice and impartiality of the decisions) one may deduce from this that there was greater need for an Irish Land Act than was generally supposed. What the Opposition will assuredly 'run for' next session will be compensation for loss of rents. The plan would 'take' to a certain extent, but being wholly and entirely impracticable it ought not to assume very formidable proportions. Mr. G. certainly would not give a penny, nor would any other Prime Minister. It is one of those cries excellent for Opposition, but perfectly useless, because impracticable, to the Government of the day.

Wednesday, 23 November. (Hawarden) Mr. G. is in wonderful force. He was in one of his most agreeable talkative humours at breakfast. It is certainly one of his most remarkable attractions that he lays himself out just as much for 'nobodies' as he does for the greatest and the most intellectual in the land. He is much concerned at the news from Ireland; another murder reported this morning for payment of rent. In spite of all the strong measures which are being taken, there seems to be no check on crime, which is committed daily with the greatest impunity. The constabulary never seem to be in the right place. It is astonishing that no one who commits these outrages is ever arrested. It shows an alarming state of demoralisation throughout the Irish community, which excites Mr. G.'s gravest apprehensions. Unless a country is governed by martial law, it is impossible that the Executive should do everything.

Mr. G. this morning got upon the P[ublic] W[orship] Reg[ulation] Act and Mr. Green's case this morning.[2] He sees no solution for the latter. The deadlock all lies at the door of the 'iniquitous' Act. He does not believe that it ever would have become law had Bishop Wilberforce lived,[3] and he commented on the extraordinary behaviour of Disraeli in 1874 in taking up, and positively preferring to public business, this ecclesiastical bill, which no one

---

[1] See 2 Nov. 1881.   [2] See 19 Sept. and 6 Nov. 1881.
[3] Bishop Wilberforce died as a result of a fall from his horse in 1873. The bishops under the leadership of Archbishop Tait played an important role in initiating the Public Worship Regulation Bill in 1874.

of his colleagues hardly approved and some of them heartily disapproved. I have understood that Disraeli lived to regret his action in regard to this ill-starred measure, and that to no measure passed during his Government did he attribute a larger share of last year's defeat at the polling booths. Next to the assistance it received from the Prime Minister of the day, Mr. G. considers that the passing of the bill owed most to Harcourt, who struck out so hard for the defence of Protestantism.

From Disraeli's part in connection with this Act, we passed on to Dizzie's character generally. It is certainly very remarkable, after the sensational manner in which Disraeli's death was received in this country, how little has been said of him subsequently. As he lived, so he died—all display with an absence of reality and genuineness. Mr. G. commented on the paucity of biographical notices of Disraeli; so unlike the case of Sir Robert Peel, when articles and books without end appeared reviewing and dissecting the states-man's life and character. In the case of Disraeli this must be probably attributable to the difficulty of handling the subject. Mr. G. is afraid that there never will be anyone who will be able to portray the extraordinary character of his opponent. Had Bagehot been alive, he probably might have best succeeded in the difficult task; Goldwin Smith might be able to overcome the difficulties, but his animosity would probably warp his judgment. Mr. G. suggested to Lord Derby the other day that he (Lord D.) should take the work in hand, but apparently Lord Derby did not 'seem to see it'. One of the most striking characteristics of Disraeli was, according to Mr. Gladstone, the utter absence in him of a love of liberty. A conversation which Mr. G. had a year ago with Mrs. Stonor, daughter of Sir Robert Peel, evidently impressed him much. It appears that Disraeli one day came and sat down by the side of Mrs. Stonor, and after paying her some fulsome compliments, proceeded to laud her father up to the skies. On her contrasting such language with the part which he (Dizzie) played against her father when alive, Disraeli unblushingly admitted that he led the attack merely as a means—and the only apparent means open to him—of advancing his own position.

Mr. G.'s mind continues to work on the question of disentangling himself from office. My own belief is that he may plan his future as much as he likes but that the matter will arrange itself—that is, he will be forced to remain at the head of affairs, as it is quite impossible for him to desert the helm so long as Ireland remains in this critical state, and that it will be a far more considerable [time] before she settles down again than he, with too sanguine expectations, reckons. I am certain he inadequately appreciates his own position at the present moment. He thinks the country got on well enough without him in 1874 to 1876 before the Eastern question came to the front, and believes that it can do the same now. He also calls to mind the prevalent belief at the time of Lord Palmerston's death that there was no one to take Palmerston's place and the prevalent prophecies that Lord Palmerston's

removal would mean the destruction of the Liberal party, beliefs and prophecies which were falsified by events. But times have changed. Mr. G.'s
position at the present moment is wholly unlike that of anyone this century.
The Liberal party is in enormous ascendancy, but in a very disjointed
ascendancy; and he is the sole cohesive power. He inspires confidence in the
Whigs, and he is the moderating influence with the Radicals.

The disagreeable business about the War Office appointments seems to be
gradually arranging itself. The result of our negotiations will probably lead
to the acceptance of Wolseley by the Duke of Cambridge as Adjutant General
coupled with a disclaimer of any change in the relative positions of the Commander in Chief and the Adjutant General, and an assurance from Wolseley
that he will (as Ponsonby puts it) 'love, honour, and obey'. There will then
be a temporary end to the royal threats about retirement. Poor Childers,
though I doubt his having displayed too much tact or judgment, told me that
his position was getting gradually perfectly unbearable. He could get nothing
done, and he was thwarted in every turn—not that he appears to have received
a different treatment to his predecessors. They seem all to have fared much in
the same way at the hands of the Royal Duke, who was always wanting to
have his own way and threatening to resign—a threat which he actually
carried out when Lord Cranbrook was at the War Office as Gathorne Hardy.
Childers is not one of those who desires to get rid of the Duke. He attaches
much importance to the retention of the office of the Commander in Chief
by a Royal Duke as a buffer between the army and the War Office; and he
feels sure that if the Duke of Cambridge resigned the public would not stand
the transfer of the duties on a future occasion to any other member of the
royal family.

Lord Lyons has been made a viscount. The Queen wanted to make it an
earldom, but Mr. G. and Lord G[ranville] did not think that precedent would
admit of this, as it was not for any extraordinary services but merely for
valuable ordinary services.

Mr. G. wants to make Sir R. Phillimore a baronet; or rather perhaps it
would be more correct to say Sir R. P[hillimore] wants Mr. G. to make him
a baronet. Mr. G. is always rather too much inclined to do something for his
own personal friends and contemporaries—a charming and natural trait in
his character, but one which has its dangers in that in the eyes of the world
it savours (and not without reason) of jobbery. Sir R. P[hillimore] is, I fear,
not a favourite of mine, and still less so is his son.[1]

Mr. G. has been again lately concerned about apparent leaks, which are
impossible to trace. They must, however, have some common origin as they
all make their appearance in the same quarter and that a very unfriendly one

---

[1] Sir Robert Phillimore was made a baronet in Dec. 1881. His son was Walter Phillimore
(after 1918 Baron Phillimore).

to the Government—namely, the *Standard*. Suspicion rather points its finger at Forster's adopted son, Arnold Forster.[1]

I learned from Sellar the other day that the average number of seats which become annually vacant in Parliament is 25, i.e. one a fortnight. This is a higher average than I had any idea of.

Later. This afternoon I did the proper thing for Hawarden and partook in chopping trees in company with Mr. G. and Willie. It is wonderful to behold the vigour with which the Great Man of nearly 72 sets to work, and the accuracy with which he accomplishes it.

Nothing special transpired at dinner time. Mr. G. predicted, à propos of the publication of Bishop Thirlwall's letters, that *the* letters of this century when they come to be published will be those of Dr. Newman. Mary G. prophesied that Lord Acton would gain the second place. Mr. G. criticised at length the ecclesiastical preferments of Lord Beaconsfield, which were specially numerous among the Bishops; and he admitted that some of the appointments were very good, while others—notably to the see of Liverpool (Ryle)—were very bad. He fancies that Bishop Wordsworth must have been one of Lord Beaconsfield's principal advisers.

Thursday, 24 November. (Hawarden) The Lord Chancellor,[2] who seems to be getting stronger and to have a fair chance of recovering, is becoming very anxious and uneasy about the proceedings of the Land Commissioners in Ireland and has been writing to Mr. Forster. The Lord Chancellor evidently thinks that there is being established a case for compensation of the landlords which will be difficult to resist. Mr. Forster's reply, with which Mr. G. was much pleased, was to the effect that one must not jump too hastily to conclusions. Most of the judicial decisions have been in the North, where Griffith's valuation is known to be higher than in the South. Only a small percentage of estates have been dealt with and these are probably cases of exceptionally highly rented tenants. Mr. Forster has always expected a large reduction of rent, a greater number of estates being rackrented than is generally supposed. He quotes Lord Waveney in the case of 2 decisions to which especial exception has been taken but which are 'perfectly intelligible' on the spot, who adds that the Commissioners are 'proceeding with great care'. Mr. G. says all depends upon whether the Commissioners are proceeding judicially or whether they are acting under a bias which warps their judgment, and that to this point the Irish Law Officers must direct their special attention. Men like Montgomery[3] are, to judge from a letter which I received this morning from him and which I showed Mr. G., are getting frightened. They fear the

[1] Hugh Oakeley Arnold-Forster was his adopted father's private secretary. See 3 Dec. 1881 and 24 Apr. 1882.
[2] Lord Selborne.
[3] Most probably Hugh de Fellenburg Montgomery, an Irish landowner, occasionally in correspondence with G. and with EWH.

only alternatives will be ruin or compensation. He attributes the unexpectedly great reductions of rent not to any unfair bias on the part of the Commission but to the subsection which Healy got inserted in the Act in regard to improvements,[1] and the effect of which was not fully foreseen by the Government. This uneasiness on the part of moderate men like Montgomery, coupled with the continuance of outrages, cannot fail to make one feel very uncomfortable.

Friday, 25 November. (Woodcote) Left Hawarden this morning. Before I came away Mr. G. presented me with a copy of Sir F. Doyle's lectures delivered at Oxford when he was professor of poetry. He made me the present in return for a little book I gave him giving an account of Canon Campello's conversion to Protestantism, which I knew would interest him.[2] He based the appropriateness of the gift on the ground of the great intimacy between my father and Sir F. Doyle.

Mr. G.'s 'parting words' had reference to his contemplated retirement on which he is continually harping, and on which he harps too much. He said that in order to make only one 'disturbance' (as he called it) in the Government he should probably not lay down the Chancellorship of the Exchequer separately, and I gathered that as at present minded he would retain both offices till next autumn and then finally retire. I am sure it is important that he should be more discreet as to his intentions or wishes. If all his colleagues only knew his firm determination to withdraw from office, it would take all the heart out of their work.

I much enjoyed those two quiet days at Hawarden. It gave one an excellent opportunity of seeing Mr. G. as he lives at Hawarden within his family circle. His life is very regular. He rises a little before 8 o'clock and walks off to service at the parish church. On his return he opens his letter-bag and after giving it a glance reads the *Pall Mall Gazette*, the only paper he can be got now to look at. He then comes in to breakfast, at which he is always specially agreeable, and which he does not hurry over. After breakfast he returns to his own room—'the temple of Peace' as it is called—and gets to work. His letters with occasional dives into books occupy him till luncheon, when he again gives one the benefit of his conversation. He returns to his letters and books till about 3.30, when he goes out either for a walk or for a 'chop' in the woods, returning in time for 5 o'clock tea, which is a special fondness of his. Having devoted about half an hour in the drawing room to a cup of tea and a little chat, he once more goes back and alternates reading with his letters up till dressing time (which he makes a marvellously short

---

[1] Section 8 (9) of the Land Act protected tenants against being charged increased rents for improvements they had made.

[2] The books exchanged were Sir Francis Doyle's *Lectures on Poetry . . . Second Series* (London, 1877) and Count Campello's *An Autobiography Giving his Reasons for Leaving the Papal Church* (London, 1881). See 19 Sept. 1881.

business of). At dinner, though in a general way he perhaps hardly lays himself out so much for conversation as at breakfast, he is never silent and is always bright. The power of throwing off all his work and anxieties is among his chief wonders. If one fails to take into sufficient account this power, one might be tempted to think that the cares of government and responsibilities of office sit too light upon him, in almost an unbecoming manner. After dinner he soon resumes his book again, which will occupy him till bedtime (11.30). I doubt if any public man ever read one tenth part of the amount he does. It is simply marvellous the masses of books which he gets through, especially considering that he is not a rapid reader; on the contrary he reads everything, no matter what, with the greatest deliberation, as the pencil marks in the margin show; it is the amount of time he daily, hourly, and minutely devotes to books of every kind, from the 'tuppenny' tract to the stiff theological work, that enables him to get through the amount he does. His library at Hawarden is very large and very varied as may easily be imagined. It is beautifully arranged; and the arrangement, on which he prides himself, is all his own.

One of his little hobbies, on which he was touching yesterday, is his horror of waste in food. I don't think this 'fad' (as one may call it) proceeds from stinginess but simply from a genuine feeling that waste is wrong and unnecessary.

Monday, 28 November. (Woodcote) A very pleasant visit here. Excellent sport and excellent company—a male party including Rosebery who has been perfectly charming and delightfully agreeable. He fascinates me greatly.

Wednesday, 30 November. Back at work again. Ireland is most disheartening. In spite of the strong repressive powers and the vigorous use of them, contemporaneously with the Land Court, matters don't mend; on the contrary, outrages increase, and these for the most part are made in cases of rent payments and occasionally even in cases of application to the Land Court. The cry is for stronger measures and compensation to landlords. Abolition of trial by jury is advocated, but what is the use of having a new machinery for administering justice if there is no one arrested and no one to be tried? As to compensation, it is simply and absolutely impracticable unless the option of the purchase by the State is given; and moreover, why should a man who has rackrented and drawn much from his tenants get compensation while those who have been contented with moderate rents should get nothing?

Thursday, 1 December. Mr. G. came up from Windsor today whither he went for an audience yesterday, mainly to try and arrange the business about the War Office appointments. We seem within a measurable distance now of an arrangement; and it is probable that the Duke of Cambridge will raise no further difficulties about the appointment of Wolseley as Adjutant General next March, on the understanding to which Mr. G. and Childers agree that a paragraph should be inserted in the newspapers announcing the intended appointment with a disclaimer that any change is contemplated in the relations between and relative positions of the Commander in Chief and the Adjutant General.

H.M. appears to have been gracious, as she generally is on the occasion of audiences. I can't make out whether she likes or dislikes the engagement of Prince Leopold.[1] Mr. G. thinks she is pleased, but at the Council on Tuesday she would not make the smallest acknowledgment of the congratulations tendered by Lord Spencer. Parliament will, of course, have to be asked to provide a marriage portion. I am very curious to see what line Dilke will take in the matter.[2] If he is consistent, he will oppose the grant or at any rate absent himself and decline to support it. In either case he would entirely jeopardise his promotion; as the Queen might fairly object to having as Minister one who could not support a proposal to make the ordinary provision for one of her children on his marriage. If he is wise, however, he will forget his previous conduct and vote like any other member of the Government.

Mr. G. wrote a long letter the other day to Lord Ripon, who by the by seems rather at loggerheads with his financial minister, E. Baring. In that letter Mr. G. again alluded to Northcote and his present bearing—to the 'deplorable want of manhood which places him (Northcote) under the command of his tail'. As to India, Mr. G. remarked that he was one of those who think that to the 'actual as distinguished from the reputed strength of the Empire India adds nothing'; and he expressed a belief that by our Indian Army arrangements we at home have made India the means of fastening upon us large military expenditure which might well have been avoided. 'We have, however', he added, 'undertaken a most arduous and noble duty, and we are pledged to India and also mankind to its performance'. He also implied that, were he to consult his own wishes—vainly, I feel sure, conceived—he would be packing up and making way for Lord Granville and Hartington.

Friday, 2 December. The Duke of Argyll has opened fire again on the Irish Land question,[3] and this time his abuse of the measure is coupled with abuse of the Commissioners. This is rather a strong order of things; indeed, 'a very grave charge', as Mr. G. has told him. Such a charge amounts to a declaration that the Commissioners who are appointed to act as judges are not acting

---

[1] On 29 Nov. 1881 the Queen formally announced the engagement of Prince Leopold to Princess Helen of Waldeck.   [2] He abstained. See 26 Mar. 1882.

[3] See a part of his letter of 29 Nov. 1881 in his *Autobiography and Memoirs* (London, 1906), ii. 382.

judicially, while they pretend to do so. If this be true, (Mr. G. says) every man of them should be impeached and probably those who appointed them as well. The Duke characterises the Act again as barbarian. Mr. G. readily admits it is not a 'highly civilised' measure, but those like the Duke should remember that the most violent character of the Bill—the interference with rents—rested on the recommendation not only of two mixed Commissions,[1] but also of a mainly Tory Commission (Duke of Richmond's majority). Whether good or bad is to result from the Act in the long run, I shall always say that, whatever may be said to the contrary, the vague concluding paragraph of the report of the Duke of Richmond and his associates had most effect on Mr. Gladstone in the drafting of the measure.

Saturday, 3 December. Mr. G. went off early this morning—back to Hawarden. The Tory press are commenting on the 'indecency' of the absence of Cabinet meetings in the present state of things in Ireland. I confess I somewhat share the feeling. At the same time, Forster is able to communicate with his colleagues in other ways than by Cabinets in Downing St., and it is far better he should be on the spot at this crisis. Moreover, what would be the use of deliberation? Nobody can suggest any practical means of bringing about a better state of things.

Thring brought me today an interesting communication—a letter from Mudford, the editor of the *Standard*—addressed to the Queen's Printers referring to the startling leakage which took place last April in connection with the premature disclosure of the Irish Land Bill.[2] They were anxious to be acquitted of all suspicion; whereupon he has given them this assurance on his word as a gentleman that the document was not communicated by anybody connected with the firm, and (what is more) by anyone connected with the public service. This is extremely satisfactory. Thring has no doubt in his own mind, and I have little, that the culprit was the Chief Secretary's '*foster-son*'.[3] It is not unlikely that similar divulgences may be traceable to the same quarter.

We have at last brought to a close the extremely unpleasant business about the Duke of Cambridge and the new Adjutant General. H.R.H. has finally accepted Wolseley as Sir C. Ellice's successor next April, on the understanding that a paragraph is inserted in the newspapers stating that no changes in the relations of the Adjutant General with the Commander in Chief are contemplated. The wording of the paragraph is now agreed to; though I had some difficulty in persuading Mr. Childers to concur in the terms of the paragraph as altered after submission to H.M. But *pacis causa* prevailed; and it is to be hoped that things at the War Office will now go on more smoothly.

[1] i.e. the Bessborough Commission report and the minority report of the Richmond Commission which recommended the '3 F.s.'.

[2] See 6 Apr. 1881. The printers involved are the firm of Eyre and Spottiswoode.

[3] See 23 Nov. 1881.

8223242　　　　　　　　　H

Old Bass, who declines to have a baronetcy himself, is very anxious that one should be conferred on his eldest son with remainder to the younger and his issue. Mr. G. is rather averse to such an arrangement, which amounts (he says) to giving *two* baronetcies. However, I have found a precedent (Salomons in 1869) which may induce Mr. Gladstone to entertain the proposal.

Monday, 5 December. In writing yesterday to Lord G[ranville], Mr. G. referred to his visit last week to Windsor. As regards his relations with Her Majesty, he said they were perfectly defined and implied that they might be summed up thus: extreme civility, but 'keep your distance'.[1]

The other day at Lady Derby's he came across L. West's daughters, which has rather exercised his mind. They are the children of a woman with whom he lived abroad, and whether he was ever married to her or not the girls are illegitimate. Their existence was at one time thought to be a bar to his going as Minister to Washington. But the difficulty, as far as the Court here and the people in America are concerned, is got over, though Mr. G. still regards the whole circumstances as fishy and likely to lead to mischief.

The bothersome business about the appointment of Sendall to the Governorship of Natal has terminated. He has resigned; and as his resignation came on the top of the Natal resolution to vote the higher (£4000) salary, Lord K[imberley] has been able opportunely to accept it. It was a perfectly innocent appointment. Sendall was merely singled out because he was thought to be the best man for £2500 post, but the Natalians had got their backs up about him so much (dreading as they do federation with the Cape) that his position there would have been untenable. Lord K[imberley] can't make up his mind whom to send. He thinks of Buller—likewise of E. Wood. The latter would be the most popular with the colonists.

Wednesday, 7 December. Mr. G.'s friend, the author of *John Inglesant*, Shorthouse, sent his book on Wordsworth's Platonism.[2] Mr. G. agrees with Shorthouse in his estimate of the poet and his 'sacred teaching', or (as another person[3] once termed it) 'sabbatical writings'. He regards Wordsworth as a great teacher and a great blessing to mankind. This was not the only book for which Mr. G. thanked yesterday with his own hand. He acknowledged a book on 'Middlesbrough' in appropriate and humorous terms.[4] He also wrote to a Mr. Graham in high praise of his *Creed of Science*, with which Mr. G. seems to be much attracted, both as regards the lucidity of the style

[1] Ramm, i. 315.

[2] Joseph H. Shorthouse published *On the Platonism of Wordsworth* in 1882.

[3] Sir James Stephen had said to G. 'nearly 50 years ago' that '"Wordsworth is the most sabbatical book I know"'. G. to Shorthouse, 5 Dec. 1881, letterbook copy, Add. MS. 44545, f. 66.

[4] H. G. Reid had sent G. a copy of *Middlesbrough and Its Jubilee: a History of the Iron and Steel Industries with Biographies of Pioneers.*

and the mastery of the subject displayed. In his letter of thanks, he confessed himself to be a believer in the harmony between science and religion—a belief (he said) which he should carry to his grave, though he was sensible of the fact that some 'forms of thought, which religionists had invented and have taken for parts of religion, had been and will be roughly handled by the light of modern research'. This is an instance of Mr. G.'s power of devouring books on wholly different subjects—a poet, a philosopher, and local historian, all in one day.

A. Montgomery having resigned, Mr. G. has offered Godley the vacant Commissionership at the Inland Revenue. Godley hesitates about accepting, and I expect it will end in his declining the offer.[1]

Errington, who is endeavouring to invoke the good services of the Pope in Ireland, and whom suspicious people regard as a probable diplomatic agent at the Quirinal, seems (according to Lord G[ranville]) to be going rather too fast ahead. Lord G[ranville] has given him a snub.[2] The importance of this honorary mission is certainly greatly exaggerated. It is surely not out of the way to ask the Pope to place himself on the side of law and honor in Ireland.

Thursday, 8 December. The Derry election, which resulted in the return of the new Solicitor General for Ireland,[3] is one of the few crumbs of comfort which have come from that country of late, and is highly satisfactory, administering as it has a just rebuke to the Tories and a slashing defeat for the Land Leaguers.

Forster is cheered by it, and he is in slightly better heart at the latest state of things, which, however, are still bad enough. It is a cruel thing to say anything disparaging of the landlord class in the midst of their troubles, but there is no doubt, whatever is said to the contrary, that they do not show the bold front in this crisis which they ought to have. There is a want of cooperation, despite the unlimited assistance which the Government is prepared to afford them; and there is a deplorable absence of pluck and a horrible pervading spirit of demoralisation among other classes of the community, who can have, if for no other reason than that of self-interest, nothing in common with the revolutionary party. It is all very well to say the Government is responsible for law or order. So it is. But there are limits to that responsibility and decided limits to the means at the disposal of the Government. The Government requires assistance from the community as much as the community requires assistance from the Government. Whenever there have been serious disturbances in this country, has everything been left to the Government? Certainly not. The country has contributed its own share of police in the shape of special constables &c.

---

[1] He did. See 13 Dec. 1881 and also 29 Oct. 1881. But then see 5 June, 17 July, and 12 Aug. 1882 for his final acceptance of a commissionership.

[2] See Ramm, i. 317.   [3] Andrew M. Porter.

The Government is taken to task for not having Cabinets and for having intimated that they have no intention of summoning Parliament till February. I admit that there is some force in this not unnatural outcry. But what is wanted now is that the Chief Secretary and his Law Officers should be on the spot exercising firmness, instead of wranglings and clamour in Parliament with abortive results. It is not as if there were any specific ready at hand, which only required the sanction of Parliament. No two people are agreed as to what more can be done. The most common prescription is the suspension of trial by jury, but to that many, including one of the Tory Irish judges (Fitzgerald) takes exception, and the greatest opposition would be raised in the House of Commons. Moreover, even a greater difficulty than conviction is the production of evidence, and without evidence judges with summary jurisdiction would be unable to bring people to justice. At the same time, it is not improbable, considering how ordinary coercive measures have by constant application lost their deterring effect, that one conviction resulting in a good hard sentence would be more efficacious than a score of arrests under the Coercion Act; and for this reason I have always held that a suspension of the jury laws might with advantage have been substituted for the stereotyped suspension of the Habeas Corpus; but the difficulties would have been very great, if not insurmountable.

Lord Ripon has been quarrelling more or less with his financial adviser (Baring), who seems to have been wanting to make some great coup in his budget by abolishing some customs duties and reviving the income tax. However, according to the latest (telegraphed) news a compromise has been effected, the more radical portions of the financial scheme having been given up.

Sunday, 11 December. (Glynde) The Speaker[1] is evidently very keen about the contemplated reforms of parliamentary procedure. He, like Mr. Gladstone, wishes it to be the closing episode of his public life. He is confident that the necessity for the clôture exists, distasteful though it may be to English ideas.

Mrs. (or rather Lady) Brand, good Liberal as she is, is frantic about Ireland. It is not to be wondered at that the Government should come in for abuse, and the state of Ireland is undoubtedly having a very damaging effect upon the Government. At the same time, it is difficult to see what materially different steps they could have taken; and as to the idea that a Tory Government could have done better—(of course their contention is that under their rule the country would never have fallen into its present disturbed state)— I believe on the contrary that without having passed a remedial measure the Executive Government would be—and properly so—so thwarted by a large section of the British community that bad would even be worse and we should

[1] Sir Henry Brand, EWH's host at Glynde.

have something like open revolt countenanced more or less on this side of St. George's Channel.

The recent grant of a charter to a large Borneo Co. has an ugly look about it and smacks disagreeably of annexation or at any rate of contingent annexation. I know nothing of the real merits of the case, but I expect trouble is likely to come of it. One can't conceive what Lords Granville and Kimberley have been up to.

Lord Ampthill says that the French Ambassador at Berlin predicts a rapid downfall of the Gambetta administration.[1] Lord Lyons is evidently not quite easy in his mind as to Gambetta's policy.[2] Will Gambetta be able to resist the temptation of a spirited foreign policy? The coast is no doubt clear for him to take the opportunity of flattering the national vanity of France— neither Germany nor France apprehend an attack. Accordingly he is free to direct the attention of the country in other directions than towards Alsace and Lorraine. Will he do so? It is probably part of Bismarck's plan for securing German supremacy to push France into the Mediterranean, as well as to push Russia into Asia, and Austria towards Salonika. The danger to us, of course, is that if France does fall in with Bismarck's plan and become specially active in the Mediterranean, the Egyptian question will be cropping up awkwardly.

The Northcotes have been at Windsor again. How different is Her Majesty's treatment of the present Opposition Ministers to that of the late Opposition Ministers!

F. Millbank, M.P., wants a baronetage. No exception can probably be taken to this. Mr. G. is thinking of offering a like honour to Darwin, which would probably give great and general satisfaction in scientific circles. He is said to be a wealthy man.

Monday, 12 December. Mr. G. has been pouring out his heart about the U.S., while returning thanks, in terms of admiration, for a centennial address on the occasion of the anniversary of Yorktown sent him by the author.[3] He holds that it is impossible that anything should be happier than the relative position of America and this country, and comments on the stupendous destiny in store for the great Western Republic. He refers to the happy circumstances that in *that* country the strength of the nation is equal to the labour. *Here* we have undertaken a task beyond *our* strength. But even to *endeavour* to fulfil that task is an arduous and elevated vocation, provided we can manage to adopt a policy on the lines of justice. Mr. G. says that the paths of the two nations ought no more to clash 'than two parallel lines in space'.

[1] Knaplund, pp. 236–7.
[2] Lord Newton, *Lord Lyons* . . . (London, 1913), ii. 263–5.
[3] Robert Charles Winthrop.

Tuesday, 13 December. Forster seems a little more hopeful and has in contemplation one or two new measures which may be effective—a division of the country into districts with a sort of Chief Commissioner of Police to be answerable for the peace of each, an increase of constabulary, and a more extensive use of the military for protective purposes. Meanwhile the feeling, however unreasonable, that the Government should bestir itself more daily increases, but nobody has anything practical to suggest. They merely expect Cabinets, which means the withdrawal of Forster from Dublin, from his post where he is so much wanted, and would end in nothing; and they comment on the lengthened prorogation of Parliament, the summoning of which would likewise entail the absence of Forster from the Castle and endless wrangles in Parliament. Others, like Sir Harry Verney this morning, clamour vaguely for 'stronger measures', but when it comes to particulars none are forthcoming. Are we, as Mr. G. asks Sir Harry, to spend another 3 months in trying to obtain stronger coercive measures? As to the favourite recipe of suspending trial by jury, which Mr. G. says would be 'obvious folly', even the judges are against this resort; and juries, so far as the winter assizes have proceeded, are positively convicting.

Godley has finally declined the Commissionership of Inland Revenue.[1] I am very anxious Horace Seymour should get it, and I have been trying to work it through Mary G. However, this particular post may not be available for an immediate appointment, as old Jim Howard has resigned and Mr. G. appears to contemplate the possibility of extensive departmental changes by abolishing the Chairmanship of Customs and removing the incompetent DuCane to the Woods and by endeavouring to effect a union between the two Revenue Boards. I fear such a scheme is premature.

Wednesday, 14 December. Her Majesty has made it known (by a line from Ponsonby to me) that She will not open Parliament in person next February. She does not feel equal to the exertion. Mr. G. says he shrinks, after his many vain attempts, from urging upon her the personal of public duty, [*sic*] though he admits it is perhaps unmanly of him not to do so. I find H.M. opened Parliament once during Mr. G.'s first administration, and *three* times during the reign of the late Government. Will she do it at all during the present Parliament?

Mr. G. is concerned at the report about a contemplated Austrian conscription in Bosnia and Herzegovina, which he considers would be 'impolitic, cruel, and of most doubtful title'. He fears that Austria will be egged on southwards by Bismarck; and if she provokes a conflict with Russia in the Balkan peninsula she will probably come to grief. She can never commend herself to an Orthodox or even a Slav population as against Russia, and Russia has more to offer Turkey.

[1] See 29 Oct. and 7 Dec. 1881 and 5 June, 17 July, and 12 Aug. 1882.

The course which the Government should take in regard to the Lord Mayor's movement in support of the Irish Property Defence Association is not at all free from difficulty. If they come forward and subscribe, they will lay themselves open to the charge of taking up the side of a particular class, and will be said to admit their own effeteness in governing the country. If they hold aloof, they will be blamed for their want of charity and will be told that they are throwing cold water on a praiseworthy attempt on the part of landlords to exert and cooperate among themselves. Forster is most anxious that the movement should succeed, but he and Mr. G. on the whole incline to think that the Government should remain neutral, and that it is not becoming for them to take any active part in promoting it. Hartington is for distinctly countenancing it. Whatever the Government do, they are sure to be loudly abused, but on the whole I believe the neutral course is the wiser one. Judging from the tone of the meeting yesterday and the constituent parts of the Committee, which, contrary to the Lord Mayor's intention, can hardly fail to give a party colour to the movement, I doubt its success.

Mr. G. says the Duke of Argyll is in a 'white heat' over the Land Act, i.e. a heat the colour of his face, not of his hair. Despite the general clamour in Tory and landlord circles, the accounts on which most reliance can be placed tend to show that, though there have been some unwise declarations made by the Sub-Commissioners, yet their decisions are on the whole just, cautious, and defensible. No doubt the reductions on the cases which have been up to the present time settled are larger than anyone, including the Government, expected, but that by no means proves that they have been partial and unfair. Rackrenting very likely, as I have always believed, may have been far more universal than was generally supposed. I hear Lord Powerscourt, apprehensive of the decisions in the North, determined to revalue his estate himself so as to have some test against the decisions of the Commissioners when they came to deal with his estate, and the result of that private valuation has been, contrary to his expectations, to lower the rents by 25%!—a pretty good defence for the Land Act.

I hear the Tories are determined to fight the Bradlaugh business to the bitter end; they will not only oppose his taking the oath but also any measure which will provide the alternative of affirmation.

Powell, M.P., who got carried off on Saturday in a balloon by himself out to sea, has not been heard of since. He must, I fear, be lost. What an awful end to come to!

Friday, 16 December. Sir Montagu Smith having retired, there is a judicial life peerage, carrying with it £6000 p.a., at Mr. G.'s disposal. He has offered it to the Attorney General, but I doubt James's accepting it. James, it is believed, prefers political life and its uncertain prizes to the legal plums, but the attraction of the peerage may be too strong for him.

Chamberlain, in view of his having to speak next month, has written to get the cue and to ask whether his ideas on the situation in Ireland are in consonance with those of Mr. G.[1] He presumes compensation to landlords is out of the question, which he is certain would invoke great clamour in this country; and he maintains that the working of the Land Court affords unexpected evidence of the necessity of the Land Act. He can see no reason for further coercive measures, with the demand for which he is certain there is no real sympathy. Mr. G. has said *ditto* to him in reply and has told him that he cannot conceive that any further measures will be necessary or will be taken, unless it be to ask Parliament for power to *fine* the district in which outrages are committed. This is Herbert's[2] hobby.

Mr. G. has been exercising himself about what he calls the 'false genitive', that is, the use of the participle after a noun; thus: 'Mr. Gladstone going to Knowsley was a notable event'. It is clear that 'going' here is a noun and should be preceded by the genitive as it naturally would be in the case of a pronoun. No one would think of saying anything but 'his going'; and accordingly it is clearly wrong to say anything but 'Mr. Gladstone's going'. However, the other form is no doubt very common. Mr. G. says he has traced this vulgarism back to Charles the Second's time, but it is nowhere to be found in the Bible, or Shakespeare, or such men as Addison or Swift or Johnson or Macaulay; and he doubts if it can be found in poetry.

Sunday, 18 December. Gambetta is said to favour the promotion of good will between England and Russia with a view to making both countries useful friends to France, and a counterpoise to the German-Austro-Italian alliance. Lord Lyons is in favour of our responding cordially to such overtures if they are made.

An action of libel was brought the other day in France against the newspaper *Intransigeant* for imputing all kinds of stock-jobbing transactions to the Tunisian policy of the late Government. The jury acquitted the editor of the newspaper, and, as the verdict is tantamount to a denouncement of the recent Tunisian policy, the late Government are furious at the acquittal.

Mr. G. has written to Cardinal Newman on the subject of the conduct of the Irish priesthood. He disclaims any attention [*sic*] of inviting the Pope to interfere on behalf of Ireland, as was done in 1844.[3] But he holds that the Pope is responsible for the priests. Mr. G. maintains that if the Irish priests plainly denounced the decrees of 1870, the means would be found for pulling

[1] Garvin, i. 346.

[2] i.e. Herbert Gladstone's.

[3] For the correspondence, see Francis H. Herrick, 'Gladstone, Newman, and Ireland in 1881', *Catholic Historical Review*, xlvii (1961–2), pp. 347–50. In 1844 William Petre, a member of a prominent Roman Catholic English family and an attaché at Florence, went to Rome on the instructions of Lord Aberdeen, the Foreign Secretary, in order to urge the Papacy to act in a co-operative fashion over the issue of the Bequests Act.

them up; and accordingly he implies that like measures should be taken when they fail to confine their teaching within the four corners of law and order.

It is, however, not only the priests in Ireland who misconduct themselves; it is the community at large. Apart from the landlords, from whom (despite their untoward position) one might have expected a firmer front and more self-exertion, what has become of men like Shaw, Blennerhassett, M. Henry, the whole tribe of Liberal and Conservative M.P.'s? All through these troublous times they have never as much as opened their mouths; and in Dublin and Cork where among the educated classes one might have expected better things, freedoms of the City are bestowed upon the miscreant leaders of the Parnellites.

Tuesday, 20 December. The Tories seem to be a little over-confident and over-sanguine. Playfair the other day interviewed Raikes, his predecessor in the chair of Committees, and Raikes admitted that he was in Town to discuss the aspect of affairs with the leaders of his party who profess to be troubled at the prospect of office coming so soon to them. 'Before the middle of next session', Raikes said, 'we fully expect to put the Government in a minority and to force a dissolution sooner than we wish it to come; but we do not know how to avoid it'.

Rather an annoying thing happened today about the Solicitor General. I wrote last night to Mr. G., assuming the probability of his offering the vacant 'legal plum' to Herschell, to point out how, apart from the great loss which Herschell would be to the Government, his appointment might be attended with untoward circumstances, Herschell's own seat at Durham being very unsafe and that of Davey, who would probably be his successor as Solicitor General, being extremely uncertain. The loss of two seats would at this juncture have a singularly bad effect. Moreover, Herschell is young and has everything before him. This morning there arrived from Mr. G. a letter offering Herschell the life peerage with its seat on the Judicial Committee. Thinking possibly my letter might make Mr. G. change his mind, I kept back the note to Herschell till nearly noon on the chance of receiving a telegram. No telegram having arrived, I thought it was safe to let the note go forward, and I accordingly despatched it. Half an hour afterwards a telegram *did* come directing the suspension of the offer and implying that Mr. G. was inclined to consider favourably Lord Young's claims, which I told Mr. G. yesterday Rosebery was anxious should be weighed. Meanwhile the note, I found, had been delivered to Herschell, so it was too late to do anything, which was extremely annoying; all the more so, as I had not put forward the offer thoughtlessly. My hope still is that Herschell will decline. I know James will do all he can to dissuade him. If Herschell does accept, he will owe his splendid berth to me, or rather to an accident.

Harcourt is very anxious to press forward next session his scheme for reforming the government of London and has drawn up his ideas in a singularly able memorandum. Such a measure ought no doubt to be passed in connection with county government.

Zetland is said to have withdrawn his subscription from the local Liberal Association. Another defaulting peer; we shall soon have no House of Lords.

Wednesday, 21 December. The Solicitor General has, thank goodness, declined the judicial peerage. The Attorney General[1] told me this morning that what actuated both himself and the Solicitor General in refusing was 'loyalty and affection' for the Great Man. He said he could suggest no one for the berth; there was not a single Liberal on the bench or connected with the Bar worthy of the place. I hinted at looking outside the English Bar, and he said that the appointment of Lord Young, looking to the preponderance already of the Scotch element, would probably create great dissatisfaction at the Bar and with the public. He did not take the same exception to the Irish Master of the Rolls, Sullivan, whom I have suggested to Mr. G.

Lord Hartington made another excellent speech on Saturday. He taunted the Tories with thinking more of the Irish difficulties for party purposes than for (what they were a few years ago so fond of terming) patriotic motives. The Tories complained of the strong language and high words used by the Opposition when they were in power and confronted with difficulties. They now show that they can use the same weapons, and with far greater bitterness as far as personalities are concerned, e.g. hinting, as Lord Salisbury did, that Mr. G. is as much entitled to be in Kilmainham as the Parnell lot, and implying that the difference between Mr. G. and Parnell on ideas of rent was merely a difference between 'Tweedledum and Tweedledee'. Not only do the Tories curse and scream, but the Whigs (Brooks's)[2] grumble. So we live in troublous times, between many fires. However impossible it may have been for the Government to have acted otherwise than they have, the broad fact remains—Ireland is in a horrible condition; and however little or much the Government may be really to blame, it matters next to nothing—the fault is laid and naturally laid at their door.

Thursday, 22 December. I saw an interesting letter from the O'Donoghue today. He is a good-for-nothing fellow, a bankrupt, and has played a low game. But it is fair to say that he has broken off with Parnell & Co. since the 'No Rent' manifesto. He holds that there are two parties at present directly responsible for the troublous state of affairs in Ireland. There are the extreme Land Leaguers, who for political purposes are doing their might and main to prevent the use of the Land Act; and there are the landlords, who will do nothing to facilitate the execution of the Act and are holding out in the hope

[1] Sir Henry James.   [2] i.e. the Whiggish club.

that the prolonged confusion will lead to a change of Government, which might lead to changes in the Act and the admission of their claim to compensation. This claim, the O'Donoghue says, is perfectly monstrous; and he says that what is now going on is merely proving what his own belief has always been, that is to say, that high-renting has been the rule in Ireland, not excepting his own property.

Saturday, 24 December. Lord Spencer, who has been over in Ireland on the business of the Clifden Estate,[1] is not unhopeful. He has met with encouraging signs and is sanguine of a good result from some of the more recent measures which the Irish Government (tardily, however, I fear) have taken. He appears to be anxious that Law, the present Irish Lord Chancellor, should be created the Lord of Appeal, in order to be of use in the House of Lords on questions affecting the administration of the Land Act.

Shaw has finally separated himself from the Land League. His severance from that party, as well as the severance of many others, formerly extreme men, such as O'Connor Power, is one of the few causes for satisfaction and of which not sufficient account has been taken. Without the Land Act all these men to a man would have been against the Government and siding with Parnell & Co.

Old Thomson Hankey has written to 'draw' Mr. G. on bimetallism and has succeeded in eliciting an emphatic repudiation of any sympathy with the bimetallists. Mr. G. says he looks upon bimetallism 'as a departure from the very nature of a standard' and declares that, if he lived to the age of Methuselah, nothing would induce him to propose a measure which had any leanings in the bimetallic direction.

The Lord Mayor[2] has managed to make a thorough bungle of his fund in aid of the Property Defence Association. He managed to misrepresent Mr. G.'s views on the subject, has got a committee almost wholly composed of Tories or 'wishy-washy' Liberals, and has at present received but a very feeble response to his appeal for funds.

The recent severe sentences for bribery at Macclesfield and Sandwich have created a good deal of strong feeling; but Harcourt seems inclined to stand firm, which is as well, for it would be awkward for a Government who is pledged to introduce strong measures against corrupt practices to give way on the first occasion on which the judges have put their feet firmly down on very bad cases.[3]

Francis Knollys told Lady Spencer the other day that the question of the Prince of Wales' debts could not be postponed much longer. That will be an awkward matter for the Government to deal with. It is sure to raise a very

---

[1] The Irish estate inherited by Spencer's nephew, the 4th Viscount Clifden, who was at this time a minor.   [2] J. Whittaker Ellis.

[3] See H. J. Hanham, *Elections and Party Management* . . . (London, 1959), pp. 267–70.

strong feeling against the Queen, who (it will be thought and not unfairly thought) should have made some allowance to H.R.H. in consideration of the extra expenses which fall upon him by reason of her seclusion.

The despatch of Mr. Blaine, the late American Foreign Minister, which seeks to upset the Clayton–Bulwer Treaty of 1850, guaranteeing the neutrality of the Panama Isthmus, has excited Mr. G.'s wrath. The gravity of the aspect seems a good deal to depend on whether the despatch in question has been adopted by the new Presidential Government, of which Blaine is not a member.[1] Mr. G. considers that the terms of the despatch amount to an 'audacious repudiation', equal to and indeed in some respects worse than the line taken by Russia in 1870.[2]

The juries in Ireland against whom such onslaught has of late been made have acquitted themselves in a most praiseworthy manner. The system has, in short, been tried and not found wanting.

Christmas Day. For the first time in my life I have spent, I believe, a useful Xmas Day. There was an exceptionally heavy amount of work, and I gave eight hours, and eight hours uninterruptedly, to it. I made a good impression upon it.

I have eaten my Xmas Day at the Sturgis'—that hospitable house. I found myself next to Sir W. Harcourt. Whenever I meet him he always launches out against the Treasury in the most aggrieved and unpractical manner. I believe he thinks the Treasury is a mere Register House, i.e. an office established to register the decrees of the Home Secretary and other Ministers. He always seems to me to be as injudicious in Society as he is tactless in the House of Commons. He is perpetually cursing his 'infernal office'; and to those who don't know the man he must appear to be perfectly callous as to the fortunes of the Government—as a man whose only idea is to exchange public for private life.

Mr. G. is hesitating as to the time for Cabinets. They ought really to meet on the earliest possible day, if it were merely to disabuse the public mind of the strange illusion that not only are the Government indifferent to the state of Ireland, but that they are also half-hearted about their legislative programme. I have put my word in for an early day.

Monday, 26 December. I received a charming little note from Mr. G. this morning in acknowledgment of my Xmas wishes. If he is what he calls him-

---

[1] The new president was Chester Arthur, Garfield's vice-president. Blaine had been Garfield's Secretary of State. He went out of office in December and at that time published a note he had written to the American Minister in London, James Russell Lowell, on 19 Nov. 1881. See *Foreign Relations of the United States*, 1881, pp. 554–9.

[2] In Mar. 1871 Russia abrogated the clauses of the Treaty of Paris of 1856 relating to the Black Sea.

self, 'a ferocious master', he certainly is the kindest, the most thoughtful, and the most ready to give credit when credit is due.

The Sultan[1] seems to be coquetting with Germany—or (as Lord Dufferin terms it) 'wooing' Bismarck in the hopes of getting Tunis restored to the Porte. France is now Turkey's '*bête noir*', what with interference in Egypt as well as in Tunis.

Russia (according to Sir E. Thornton) is ready and content to bide quiet for the present.

Lord Lyons says that Gambetta has got very well through his first short (honeymoon) session, and has displayed great vigour and tact as a parliamentary leader. He (Gambetta) has been pleased by the reception he has got in the Senate. The Minister who seems to give most offence and excite most alarm among the conservative and moderate people is the Finance Minister (Tangé) [Allain-Targé]. Lord Lyons continues to be very keen, on political grounds, for the conclusion of a Commercial Treaty, and were it not that Tirard, the late Minister of Commerce, had greatly hampered the hands of the French Government, the negotiations would probably be brought to a successful issue. Gambetta and Tirard are both well disposed to us.

Mr. G. thinks well of Lord Granville's proposed reply to the U.S. on the Clayton–Bulwer Treaty business. It has only been seen by one or two Ministers at present, of whom the only one who has criticised as yet is Bright, and he, curiously enough, went so far as to hint that exception might be taken to it on the ground that the tone adopted was hardly in a lofty enough strain. His own idea is that a greater waterway like the projected Panama Canal and the Suez Canal should be guaranteed neutral by all the powers.

Tuesday, 27 December. There are rumours in the air that the Tories intend to move an amendment to the Address. I hope they will, as it will be the means of rallying the Liberal party.

Mr. G. has written a letter to Mr. L. Morris, who was one of the Liberal candidates in the field at Carmarthen, and who has retired in favor of another Liberal. Mr. G., in patting Mr. Morris on the back, has had a little fling at the Tories by twitting them on their promises to restore a Corn Law, as was the case in Lincolnshire, and on their engagements to vote for the liberation of the suspects, as was the case in Durham—all done in their eagerness to obtain seats. I know his fingers have been itching to make this little 'score'.

Lord Acton has been invited to come over from abroad to pay a little visit to Hawarden. There are few people to whose judgment Mr. G. so bows. Lord Acton is one of those who have been fighting Mr. G. on his resolve to retire; and Mr. G., in writing to him, expresses his hope and belief that he will persuade Lord Acton that, when the great specialties are disposed of, he (Mr. G.) is 'outwardly free and inwardly bound' to ask for his dismissal.

[1] Abdul Hamid II.

'The oracle has been worked', and a Cabinet is to take place next week.

Mr. G. has written to Childers to beg that the Army Estimate may be carefully pruned.

From what I hear, I don't think it is probable that Lord Cowper will stay on much longer in Ireland. If he does go, I agree with H[orace] S[eymour] that it would be desirable if possible to relieve Forster. Forster appears to lack decision in Ireland; he is shifty and changeable—so much so that he has gained for himself at the Castle the nickname of the 'pendulum'.

Wednesday, 28 December. Another judge dead—Lord Justice Lush. It is extraordinary how great has been the mortality among judges of late. It is curious that there should have been all these vacancies in the judicial bench, and not one on the episcopal bench.

The practice of publishing all letters in Mr. G.'s name, however trivial may be the subject, is becoming a perfect nuisance. One finds one's name in print almost daily; and what is worse, more often than not the stupid newspapers go and insert one's letters with gross blunders and make nonsense of one's little harmless effusions.

There has been a squabble between the Office of Works and the Master of the Horse on the subject of the Rangership of Hampton Court Park. There seems to have been a want of courtesy on both sides. The Works first go and issue an order respecting Park timber without apprising the Master of the Horse, and then the Master of the Horse goes and countermands the order without letting the First Commissioner know.

The Ladies' League in Ireland promises to be very troublesome.[1]

Thursday, 29 December. Lord Cowper has virtually resigned with a certain reservation as to time. He has not resigned in a huff, or because he desires to part company with the Government. On the contrary, Mr. G. says Lord Cowper's letter is very 'good-tempered, high-minded, and considerate'. But he dislikes and is bored by his position. The fact is, I fancy, he finds himself under Forster's regime too great a cipher. Forster is an essentially vain man and keeps everything in his own hands. I wish we could dispose of him elsewhere. He is wrecking the Government with Ireland as he did formerly with education.

I dined with the Roseberys tonight, who have just settled themselves at Lansdowne House. I expect it must have been a bitter pill to Lansdowne to let it. He said plaintively the other day he only 'hoped Mr. Gladstone would not introduce fixity of tenure within the next three years'. It is certainly one of the most charming houses—if not *the* most charming house—in London. It

---

[1] A Ladies' Land League had been founded by Parnell's sister. Its violent militancy was too much for Parnell and Dillon who were instrumental in its abolition in 1882. See 29 Aug. 1882.

has all the appearance of a country house deposited in the best part of Town. It just suits the Roseberys. They dislike and have outgrown their house in Piccadilly; and while they occupy Lansdowne House, Rosebery will have time to build on his new site at Knightsbridge.[1]

Friday, 30 December. (Salisbury) There is a rumour from Constantinople that there exists some arrangement between Russia and Austria for the partition of the Balkan peninsula. Mr. G. thinks that we ought to place on record some protest against any move by any Power to interfere with the growth and development of the Balkan nationalities.

Dilke has written again (rather nastily) about the Borneo charter business. He says it involves duties in regard to slavery and opium which are impossible to undertake, and that he is ready to make room for someone else to defend it. He maintains that to have granted the charter without any reference to the House of Commons amounts to the straining of the prerogative. He takes no notice of the record we have that he expressed an opinion once which was not adverse to its grant.

There is another rumour, which is probably absolutely groundless, that the Porte is willing to hand over to Germany Crete and Rhodes for Bosnia.

Yesterday was Mr. G.'s 72nd birthday. May the new year on which he has just entered see the termination of the Irish troubles and his labours on behalf of that thankless country rewarded as they should be. It is certainly on the fulfilment of that wish that alone his escape from office will be possible, unless the downfall of the Government comes. It is hardly conceivable that the Government will be placed in a minority this next session in the House of Commons; and the Lords are hardly likely to have a measure presented to them on which the Government would stake its existence and on which they would be justified in exercising their power of forcing the hands of the Government. So one's apprehensions as to the fate of the Government ought not to be realised; but there is no saying. It would be a most frightful responsibility to incur to throw Ireland, already confused enough, into worse confusion by the turmoil of a General Election.

Work has been very heavy lately; so a little reprieve is not unwelcome. At the same time I don't like being out of the swim even for a short space.

Forster's plan of dividing the disturbed counties into districts under special Commissioners on whom the duties of the Executive will be devolved seems to be well received. But why was this not done sooner?

Saturday, 31 December. The year just closing will always be a black one in the Liberal calendar. Nothing has gone right for the Government in internal

---

[1] The Roseberys had lived at 107 Piccadilly. They had acquired some land west of Albert Gate in Knightsbridge but, instead of building there, they moved to Lansdowne House and lived there until 1888. See Lord Crewe, *Lord Rosebery* (London, 1931), p. 118.

affairs; it has been a perpetual series of troubles—a perfect sea of them. As far as internal politics are concerned, they are summed up in one word—Ireland. Ireland was the great trouble on the 1st January; it is as great a trouble on the 31st December, in spite of all the strong distasteful measures taken and the scarcely less strong distasteful remedies which have been applied, and at present applied with little avail. What is to be the end of it? In reviewing the course taken by the Government it is difficult to see how they could have acted very differently if they had the year to spend over again. The coercive [measures] were bound to be taken, and the Land Act, founded as it was on the recommendations of all those best entitled to advise, supported as it was by the whole bulk of Irish representatives Tory as well as Liberal, and framed and developed as it was by the Great Mastermind of the age, was equally inevitable. The expectations formed of its effect have certainly not as yet been realised; and all one can say is that matters might be worse. The Land Act has had two good results: (1) it has kept Ulster loyal; (2) it has enabled the Executive Government to resort to strong measures with the support (probably for the first time in history) of the unanimous voice of Great Britain.

In 'over-sea' affairs (to use Mr. G.'s phrase) better fortune has attended the Government. The horizon is tolerably clear abroad. There is a complete lull in Europe; we are on excellent terms with all our neighbours; we have escaped fairly well from our Indian difficulties, thanks to the firmness and courage of Lord Hartington; we have patched up the unfortunate South African business; we have drawn closer together the ties between this country and the United States.

1882

Sunday, 1 January. (Salisbury) May this year be a more prosperous one for the Government and for the country at large, more especially the other side of St. George's Channel.

Had a long 'go in' with Pembroke and her Ladyship on politics. She is by far the fiercer partisan of the two. He is wild on the subject of the working of the Land Act. His main contention is that they have been deceived by the Government. In this way—they were led to suppose at the time of its passing that the landlords' interests would be in the hands of the 3 Commissioners named in the Act, and that it was only from having confidence in those Commissioners that the Lords allowed the Bill to pass. Instead of this, the rents are adjudicated upon by sub-commissioners, in whom they have no confidence, whom on the contrary they wholly distrust and to whose appointments they take the greatest exceptions. Moreover, the right of appeal will in practice avail little. To begin with, it is impossible that those 3 Commissioners can review the decisions of all the sub-commissioners; and further than this, any general upsetting of the rulings of the sub-commissioners would produce a revolution.

A more serious matter on which Pembroke touched in confidence was that Vernon[1] was appalled at the decisions of the sub-commissioners, and that some of the appointments had been made against his will. If Forster has not selected trustworthy men, he will be most justly to blame and deserves to be arraigned. I can't believe this.

Tuesday, 3 January. (Salisbury) I hear H.M. has written a very complaining letter about Ireland, saying that officials made the best of things, that order was not restored, and that if more troops were wanted they should be sent— 'in fact', says H[orace] S[eymour], 'quite in her worst style'.[2]

A most interesting letter came to hand this morning from Wilfrid Blunt, who is devoting his annual visit to the East this year to Egypt and intercourse with Arabi, Colonel of the Egyptian army and head of the National party. He says the views of that party have been greatly misrepresented. They are not in league with, and are not the tools of, the Sultan. They are honest and

[1] John Edward Vernon, one of the Land Commissioners, was also agent for the Pembroke estates in Ireland. See 14 July 1881.
[2] Guedalla, ii. 174.

sincere patriots. He speaks highly of [the] intelligence, earnestness, and disinterestness of Arabi, who disclaims any other intention than that of temporarily guarding the national rights of Egypt till the Parliament can do this. He reminds Mr. G. of what he once said—that on the spontaneous resumption of national will the regeneration of Egypt would depend, and W. B[lunt] says this has now occurred. He now solicits Mr. G.'s sympathy on the side of the struggling nationality. He represents the situation to be this:

(1) The National party under Arabi is purely political. They accept the existing relations with the Porte as the basis of their movement, but are determined to defend their national rights and trust to the Protecting Powers to guarantee their administrative independence.

(2) They profess allegiance to the reigning Khedive and will support him as long as he rules in conformity with his recent promises.

(3) They recognise and are grateful for the services of England and France, and regard the European control as a necessity until their debts are redeemed. They, however, wish to protest against the abuses and extravagance of the controlling system and take exception to the exemption of Europeans from taxation.

(4) They consider the army as the only available instrument whereby the national liberties can be protected; and to ensure this, something more than a passive attitude is required. Accordingly the efficiency of the army must be maintained. When the people have established their rights, the army will abandon their present attitude.

(5) Their general aim is the intellectual and moral regeneration of the country.

W. Blunt's articles on Islamism, concluded in the January number of the *Fortnightly*, have attracted much attention.[1]

Tuesday, 10 January. (Salisbury) Been to Wilton and Iwerne Minster (the Wolvertons) since my last entry—the two opposite extremes in politics. Pembroke reiterated at length his troubles at the political outlook. He is alarmed at the growth of democracy and apprehensive about the safety of property. If he could, he would sell every bit of land of which he is possessed. The landlords' property is to be conveyed to the tenant without the title deeds (to use Auberon Herbert's expression). Wilton is to be despoiled, cut up and subdivided among the masses. A reign of communism is to be set up. Class is to be set against class, and such like eventualities.

At Iwerne, everything must be right as well as safe and sound in Mr. G.'s hands. Lord W[olverton] has given very tangible proof of his feelings by embarking in a huge property and building a huge house, which except for the site and its surroundings is a great success and very striking. Nothing

---

[1] Wilfrid S. Blunt, 'The Future of Islam', *Fortnightly Review*, xxx (1881), pp. 204–23, 315–32, 441–58, 585–602; xxxi (1882), pp. 32–48.

could be kinder than were Lord and Lady Wolverton, and one could not have better hosts.

The short session of Cabinets is over. Parliamentary procedure has been thoroughly well discussed, the Speaker[1] and May having been called into counsel.

The speeches of Bright and Chamberlain last week at Birmingham were moderate; and they were neither of them indiscreet.

Thursday, 12 January. (Salisbury) I understand that Mr. G. holds very strongly that the cloture on the 2/3 principle will make it useless and that to be serviceable it must be on the principle of a simple majority. I doubt if the latter proposal would ever be accepted by the House.

The *D[aily] News* and *Standard* have both apparently been receiving inspiration of late. When can the inspiration come? It is a rare puzzle.

Saturday, 14 January. (Salisbury) There seems to be little or no news stirring in Downing St. Work appears to be in a tolerably quiescent state, so much so that I am going to prolong my holiday for a few more days. By that time I shall have taken in a stock of down air which ought to last me through all the session until the autumn. J. A. G[odley] says Mr. G. is hammering away at the idea of making Collier the judicial peer; I hope this will be exploded. Collier gave quite enough trouble in Mr. G.'s first administration.[2]

The Government can never do anything right in the eyes of the Tories. The joint Anglo-French Egyptian circular was first considered dangerous before its contents were properly known; now that it is published they call it a 'cave in'. Holker's appointment to the Lord Justiceship is regarded as a step to get rid of a formidable opponent.

Guy Dawnay is running for the North Riding as the Tory candidate. All one's friends run Tories.

Wednesday, 18 January. (Montacute) This is a most beautiful old Elizabethan house—quite perfect in its kind. The Phelips' very kind and hospitable.

I don't like the outlook of affairs at home or abroad. Northcote in his usual note of summons to his supporters to be in their places at the opening of Parliament refers to the 'critical' state of affairs, which no doubt it is. Egypt is a nasty difficulty. This country ought never to have been placed in the predicament of having to interfere so far in the internal affairs of Egypt as to warrant the issue of the collective note.

Ireland apparently gets no better, and the country (judging from public opinion reflected by the London and provincial press) does not take kindly

---

[1] Sir Henry Brand.
[2] The complex case of Sir Robert Collier is explained in Morley, ii. 383–6.

to the idea of the cloture. If, however, the Irishmen carry out their intentions of moving a resolution about every one of the suspects, the necessity for taking strong measures may be better recognised.

The fight in Yorkshire promises to be a hot one. If it is won by the tenant farmer, it will be at the expense of a considerable defection of Whigs. Lord Grey has finally broken away.[1]

The troubles and anxieties connected with Downing St. certainly go far to counterbalance the delights and interest of one's present berth.

Russia is coming out with horrible 'atrocities' in their dealings with the Jews, which greatly delights the Tory Russophobists.

Austria is threatened with troubles in the Balkan peninsula.

Friday, 20 January. Returned to Town yesterday. Somewhat cheered by view taken in Downing St. of political outlook.

Forster appears to be more hopeful about Ireland.

As to Egypt, the situation is certainly in a very delicate, if not critical, state. I rather fancy Malet has lost his head a little and has somewhat misled the Government. The great aim of the Government appears to have been, and to be, to maintain the *status quo*, for which the late Government is responsible. The *combined* interests of Egypt and England are what the Government are striving to serve, as well as to keep on friendly relations with France. Mr. G. is surprised at the development of the national sentiment and would evidently like to give scope to 'Egypt for the Egyptians', were this feasible and attainable without risk. Difficulties, however, seem to attach to every alternative. The single occupation of the country by England or France, or a joint occupation, would be alike very objectionable—in fact so strongly does Malet feel against intervention that he would consider it would be better to leave Egypt to itself. A Turkish intervention might possibly be the least evil, but this would be strongly opposed by the French and resented by the Egyptians. Another alternative, far less objectionable *prima facie*, is to establish a Committee of Control composed of representatives of all the European Powers; but Lord Lyons sees great difficulty in this from the jealousies of France.[2] What we ought to have done a year or more ago was to have endeavoured with the aid of the Powers, when they were acting in concert together, to obtain a declaration of neutrality so far as the Canal is concerned, which is the real important matter to us. We then could have extricated ourselves from the control difficulty and have obtained the guardianship of this waterway which is our principal (and indeed only real) interest in Egypt.

Gambetta is somewhat in a hole by forcing on the '*Scrutin de Liste*' some-

---

[1] A tenant farmer, Mr. S. Rowlandson, opposed the Tory candidate, Dawnay, for the vacant seat for the North Riding. Grey's letter explaining his departure from the Liberal ranks is printed in the *Annual Register*, 1882, p. 6. Dawnay won. See 26 Jan. 1882.

[2] Lord Newton, *Lord Lyons . . .* (London, 1913), ii. 270–1.

what prematurely, but Lord Lyons expects and favours the continuance in power of Gambetta.

Progress has been made with parliamentary procedure reform; and I do not expect any very drastic measures will be proposed. Mr. G. says nobody has approached the introduction of the closure principle with greater reluctance than he has, and that it is only the bare necessity of the case which has forced him to countenance it. As long as the cloture proposals are drawn very mild, there is fair hope of carrying them.

Poor Lord Kenmare seems to be in great straits. He says that the only thing that can keep him on his legs is a huge Government loan of £300,000. It seems, however, to be impossible to entertain such a proposal.

I find that Mr. G., being under the impression that Bishop Moberly is about to resign, has offered the see tentatively to the Dean of St. Paul's (Church).[1] I believe Mr. G. 'is counting on his chickens before they are hatched', and I have told him so.

Lord Lytton has been firing off a most reckless speech. Heaven defend the country against falling into the hands of such an utterly unscrupulous man.

Sunday, 22 January. The atrocious treatment of the Jews by Russia, equal to that of the Bulgarians by Turkey, is exciting much attention. People are either 'at' Mr. G. to move in the matter, or else taunting him with his silence and contrasting his behaviour towards his friend Russia with the line he took towards the 'unspeakable Turk' in the matter of the Bulgarian atrocities. He feels very strongly on the subject; and, were he a free agent, he would probably be (what is called) raising an agitation or a crusade against Russia. As it is, his hands are tied, more especially as he could only direct in his present position his denouncements against the Russian Government, and he holds strongly that in a case of this kind it is not by inter-governmental remonstrations, but by raising public opinion, that any real impression can be produced on the Power with whom the blame rests.

Edward Marjoribanks and Firth have been asked to move and second the Address. They are good selections and I am very glad Marjoribanks is to be paid the compliment, but I object to these persistent 'askings' by the Marjoribanks *père* and *mère*. They go on the principle (and find it pay) with a vengeance that 'nothing ask, nothing have', or 'ask and ye shall have'.

A characteristic *mot* of Lowe's. Apropos of the reading in the revised version of the sentence 'Deliver us from the evil one' in lieu of 'Deliver us from evil', he is reported to have said at Lambeth one day: 'I always said the Devil would never be contented till he was introduced by name in the Lord's Prayer'.

Encouraging accounts from the North Riding. To win a seat now would

[1] Bishop Moberly of Salisbury remained in that see until his death in 1885 when Lord Salisbury had the responsibility of nominating his successor.

have an excellent effect. James and Harcourt spoke in very good heart and forcibly yesterday at Burton-on-Trent.

Despite the rumours about a break-up of the Liberal party, there are excellent accounts of the condition of it.

Thursday, 26 January. Mr. G. arrived with Mrs. G. and Helen on Tuesday in great force. Though the fight in the North Riding was a very close one, we failed to carry the Tory stronghold, and Guy Dawnay was returned.[1] My feelings are mixed. A win would have been a great coup and a splendid fillip, but I am truly glad so excellent a fellow as Guy is in the House and thereby saved from returning to that fatal Africa. After the sanguine accounts we had of the contest, Mr. G. could not fail to be disappointed; but he takes the result with equanimity and his accustomed pluck. It was not a *loss*, which is something. At the same time, it is ominous of the beginning of the end of the high tide of Liberal prosperity and will put the Tories in such excellent heart.

The most amusing feature of the week has been the obscene misprint in the *Times* report of Harcourt's speech last Saturday at Burton. The sentence was inserted by a malicious compositor.[2] Copies of the edition containing the absurd insertion have been selling at all sorts of fancy prices. Lord Wolverton says they were fetching 20s at Brighton yesterday. Harcourt will never hear the end of it. I understand the *Times* has never sent him a line of apology.[3]

There was a Cabinet yesterday. The course of business in the House of Commons formed the first topic. An amendment to the Address is expected from the Parnellites. Another from the Tory Opposition is possible. They also discussed South African affairs. Natal is to be given a responsible government. But the main subject under consideration was Egypt. It seems to be impossible with the responsibilities we have incurred to yield in any appreciable degree to the demands of the national party. Rivers Wilson says that W. Blunt has been misled and is misleading Malet as to the nature of the so-called national movement. In spite of the objections which Lord Lyons has stated with much force against the invocation of the aid of the European Powers jointly, such as the appearance it would have of a denouncement of the good understanding between this country and France, the delay which it would involve, and the cumbrousness of the machinery, I expect a proposal will be made for the issue of an European Commission, on which France and

[1] See 18 Jan. 1882.

[2] *The Times*'s account of Harcourt's speech read at this point: "'I saw in a Tory journal the other day a note of alarm, in which they said, 'Why, if a tenant-farmer is elected for the North Riding of Yorkshire the farmers will be a political power who will have to be reckoned with.' The speaker then said he felt inclined for a bit of fucking. I think that is very likely. (Laughter).'" *The Times*, 23 Jan. 1882, p. 7, col. 4; but most copies now in libraries have the corrected version with 'the sentence' omitted. The 'obscene misprint' is quoted in Peter Fryer, *Mrs. Grundy. Studies in English Prudery* (London, 1963), p 73.

[3] But see 28 Jan. 1882.

ourselves would be more specially represented. The great difficulty is the mode of active intervention in Egypt, should unfortunately the necessity for it arise. I trust that at any rate the idea of a Turkish intervention will be abandoned.

There is no doubt just now that our relations with Foreign Powers are not as cordial as they might be, excepting of course France. Italy is jealous of our interference in Egypt. Bismarck views the *entente cordiale* between us and France with suspicion. Austria, though her hands are full with impending difficulties in the Balkan peninsula, is huffy. Turkey is mortally offended. Russia is exercised at the strong feeling to which this country is giving expression anent the atrocious treatment of the Jews in Russia. Holland is wounded about Borneo.

Friday, 27 January. A notable evening. West and myself carried out a little project I had for some time formed, which was to get Mr. G. to dine at Brooks' now that the club has been thrown open to 'strangers' when Parliament is not sitting. The dinner went off exceedingly well. The invited who could not come (Erskine May, the Speaker, Lord Arthur Russell, Sir H. James, Herschell, Sir F. Doyle) all expressed an everlasting regret at being obliged to decline. Our little party consisted of 9, who were thus placed at table:

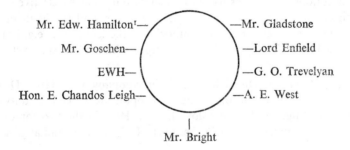

Mr. Edw. Hamilton[1]—	—Mr. Gladstone
Mr. Goschen—	—Lord Enfield
EWH—	—G. O. Trevelyan
Hon. E. Chandos Leigh—	—A. E. West

Mr. Bright

The company fitted in extremely well, and the dinner was excellent. It was a difficult *bill* of fare to draw, as I had two conditions to fulfil; (1) plainness, in order to suit Mr. G.'s tastes, and (2) goodness, in order to be worthy of the entertainment. Mr. G. was in great force and extremely agreeable, and towards the end of dinner Bright warmed up and was very interesting. Bright was immensely engrossed over the old club betting book and read out pages of it. Fox figures in nearly 9 out of 10 cases in the first 15 years of Brooks's existence. Besides the extreme pleasantness of the company, the occasion of the first entry into the club of Mr. G. and Mr. Bright cannot fail to be of lasting interest in one's life.

[1] i.e. EWH's uncle Edward.

Saturday, 28 January. The *Times* yesterday did tender an apology to Harcourt after all, and the paragraph of course has drawn more attention than ever to the compositor's obscene line.[1]

Gambetta has fallen with a terrible crash, having come a fearful cropper over the '*Scrutin de Liste*'. It is a tremendous upset. One thought last autumn that France had at last got hold of a Government, now that he had assumed command, which would have real stability about it; but his reign has been shorter even than that of his predecessors. Freycinet is to form an administration. The fall of Gambetta has come most inopportunely as regards this country, when we are so near the expiration of the old French Commercial Treaty and when we are working the Egyptian business in close company with France.

The North Riding election came to be a contest of a corn duty versus land reform. It is probable that the sanguine view which the Liberals took of the result was due to their reckoning that some 1000 voters who had promised to support Guy [Dawnay] would under the ballot support the tenant-farmer.

The Cabinet yesterday confined their main attention to the consideration of the Local Government Board Bill. Some progress was made. The County Councils, as the plan now stands, are to be elected by the ratepaying constituency voting directly, secretly, and singly; but each owner having a vote in his capacity as owner as well as that of occupier. The intention is to fortify local institutions in counties like in municipal boroughs by elective corporations, to commit to the Councils important duties, and to aid them within limits by monies raised under the authority of the legislature, e.g. house tax and assessed taxes. They are also to be charged with the licensing system.

Monday, 30 January. Dined last night in company with Guy [Dawnay]. Argued at length with him on his quack proposal to place a 5s duty on all foreign, as distinguished from colonial, corn. He said the two topics which seemed to excite most interest in the North Riding were Bradlaugh and the law of distress.

Another Cabinet today. Business wholly confined to parliamentary procedure. The Speaker[2] and May were summoned. They said there was complete accord among Ministers. The new rules are assuming more definite shape. They include *a* cloture, but a very mild one.

In connection with an article in *Contemporary Review*, Mr. G. sent the writer a line today to say, in answer to some words attributed to him, that he had never laid it down and never believed that the religion of authority was incompatible with freedom of thought.[3] He referred to the fact that Lord

---

[1] *The Times*, 27 Jan. 1882, p. 9, col. 6. See 26 Jan. 1882.   [2] Sir Henry Brand.
[3] G. wrote W. S. Lilly, the author of 'Free Thought—French and English' in the *Contemporary Review*, xli (Jan.–June, 1882), pp. 221–47. The reference to G. is on pp. 223–4. See Add. MS. 44545, f. 96 for a copy of G.'s letter to Lilly.

Macaulay, 45 years ago, had severely criticised Mr. Gladstone for maintaining the contrary, which he said he had always held and endeavoured to set forth.

Wednesday, 1 February. A very long Cabinet—from 2 to 7 P.M.—followed by a Cabinet dinner in the evening. The Speaker and May were again in attendance. The Speaker by the by addressed his constituents yesterday and addressed himself to the delicate task with great tact and judiciousness. What he said plainly in favor of some form of cloture should be helpful to the Government. Of course the Tories will now set to work and, as far as decency will permit, abuse him. At the Cabinet procedure again occupied chief attention. The proposed clôture stands as settled on Monday. It is more stringent than I expected as regards the putting of the question. There are two alternative limits, in effect to provide (a) for a full House and (b) for a small one; that is, when there is a full House 200 members must be found voting for the closing of the debate, and when the House is small there must not be more than 40 against. Apart from these limits, the voting will be by a bare majority. Today the discussion turned mainly on Grand Committees, the principle of which is accepted, and Mr. G. seemed pleased with the progress made.

Telegrams received this afternoon from Egypt also entailed much consideration. A crisis which will necessitate some outside intervention is expected, and I am afraid as a choice of evils the Porte will be moved to send troops. It seems very objectionable to invite the interference of the Sultan and thereby give the Turkish Government a distinct 'leg up' in a country, which in spite of the suzerainty of the Porte the object has been to emancipate from Turkish rule; but joint or single intervention by France and England or by France or England would probably be worse.

The Bradlaugh business still greatly worries Mr. G. His position in regard to it is so misunderstood. He is of course accused of patronising Bradlaugh, but in reality his only desire is (as he said the other day) that the case should be submitted to the Courts of Law, which refused Bradlaugh the power to affirm and which would now, if permitted, give him no more or less than the law gives. Mr. G.'s contention is that if the matter does not go to the Courts of Law, there will be a sense that injustice is done under the name of religion, which would promote or rather encourage unbelief.

Thursday, 2 February. The 'speech' is pretty well drafted. It is wonderful with what rapidity Mr. G. 'throws it off'. Paragraph after paragraph has made its appearance without apparently any effort. There is, as might be expected, no surprise in it. The programme is very unexciting.

Forster came in to my room today in quite an excited manner to warn us to be careful (as he said) about opening letters, which meant this—that Burke had had a letter brought to him with a suspicious-looking substance which had oozed through the envelope. He sent it down to the police who had it examined by a chemist, and the 'suspicious-looking substance' turned out to be a very explosive matter, which had been damped in order not to go off in its transit, but which when dry would be liable to explode with sufficient violence seriously to damage, if not to kill, the opener of the letter. We are not, however, alarmed by this specimen of diabolicism.

Friday, 3 February. The Cabinet today was to settle the Queen's speech, and Mr. G.'s draft was accepted with but few alterations. They also further discussed parliamentary procedure, more specially the plan of delegating bills of a certain character to Grand Committees to be entrusted with the duties of Committees of the Whole House. The Government have determined to propose the constitution of such Committees as a tentative and experimental measure. The resolutions of what may be called a restrictive nature underwent little further alteration. The Queen had offered to negotiate with the leaders of the Opposition on the subject of these resolutions. Considering, however, how unfavourably the Opposition leaders have criticised the supposed proposals of the Government, the Cabinet thought that negotiations which might (and probably will) end in failure should not be conducted by the Sovereign, and that an 'inferior instrument' (as Mr. G. called it) should first, in any case, be made use of. The 'inferior instrument' was to send Sir S. Northcote a copy of the draft resolutions, with the hope that, as the question of parliamentary procedure was of great common interest to both sides, a concurrence of opinion might possibly be obtained, or that at any rate the points of difference might be reduced to a minimum. An offer has been made that Northcote, with one or other of his colleagues, should personally confer with Mr. G. and Lord Hartington. It will be curious to see what Northcote says. I expect he will be frightened at the action of his 'tail'.

A new idea for meeting the Bradlaugh difficulty has been started by Bright (I believe), which appears to have a good deal to commend in it. It is something of this kind: that on Northcote's motion to prevent Bradlaugh from taking the oath, a counter resolution should be moved by the Government which would instruct the Speaker to ask if Bradlaugh admitted that he felt morally bound by the oath, and that if Bradlaugh replied in the affirmative, the question of his taking the oath would settle itself.

A question has been raised as to the necessity of appointing Lords Justices during the intended absence of Her Majesty abroad. The general opinion of the Cabinet seems to be that such a course would be unnecessary (looking to precedents) and would merely tend to annoy the Queen.[1]

[1] See 18 Feb. 1882.

Saturday, 4 February. Northcote's reply was not unsatisfactory. He is not unwilling to see what can be done towards narrowing beforehand the discussion on the procedure rules, though he hinted that it might be thought preferable to thrash the subject out on the floor of the House. He was to meet his colleagues tonight at the Smith banquet and sound them. I expect his party won't like the idea of resorting to any means which will shorten the fight. Their object is to stifle legislation, and the longer the rules of the House are debated, the shorter will be the time for consideration of measures.

The crisis in Egypt does not become less acute. The national party have ousted Sherif. The Government are certainly in rather an awkward position. The joint note, if it meant anything, meant that as a *dernier resort* there should be some kind of joint occupation; but not only is this Government against taking such steps, but so also is the new French Government. Waiting on events, which is always an unsatisfactory course to take, seems to be the *môt*. The great difficulty appears to be to know how far the so-called national movement is in the nature of a genuine feeling in favor of 'Egypt for the Egyptians'. W. Blunt, who has written again to the *Times*, insists strongly on the national character of the movement.[1] So also does Sir W. Gregory. Rivers Wilson, on the other hand, denies *in toto* that there is any real national feeling in the uprising.

Tuesday, 7 February. The parliamentary dinner last night went off very well. There was not [a] hitch, and everybody seemed in good heart. The party in the evening was also successful and well attended.

The session opened badly this afternoon, which does not augur well for the prospects of the Government. The Bradlaugh business came on early, sooner than was expected, before even Mr. G. had arrived. As was agreed at the Cabinet this morning, Northcote's resolution was met by the 'previous question', which Harcourt moved in Mr. G.'s absence. Bradlaugh himself spoke at the Bar very coarsely, in bad taste, and far less effectively than on former occasions. Mr. G., to make up for his non-appearance at the commencement of the debate, spoke subsequently and argued the case with extreme ingenuity from the Government point of view, which was simply this—that the question whether a man like Bradlaugh, who attached no force to the words in the oath referring to a Deity, had a right to take the oath was a legal question and as such should be relegated to the decision of the Law Courts in the same way as on a former occasion was the question of his having the right to affirm in lieu of swearing; that such a question could not be determined by Parliament and moreover, even if Parliament had the power, it had no capacity, as being a heated party assembly it had no qualifi-

---

[1] Blunt wrote *The Times* about this on 9 Jan. 1882, p. 9, col. 6. Again on 3 Feb. 1882 *The Times* published one of his letters (p. 3, cols. 2–3) and commented on it in a leading article (p. 9, cols. 2–3).

cations for acting as a tribunal. Northcote and his followers had a larger majority than was expected—58—and they crowed proportionately. I think the Government have messed the business. They had much better have washed their hands of it altogether; or given an undertaking that, so soon as the new rules in the House had been disposed of, they would do their best to legislate by introducing a one clause bill to enable people to affirm or swear *ad lib*. Such a bill, especially when accompanied by an undertaking from Bradlaugh (which he was willing to give) that if it were passed he would vacate his seat, might have had a very fair chance; and the consumption of a few Government nights over such a bill would have been, from a political point of view, amply made up for by making a genuine and honest attempt to get rid of the beastly business, which is doing incalculable harm to the party in the country. As it is, we have got no nearer the end of it than we were in April '80. It is the one thing of all others which is genuinely disagreeable and distasteful to Mr. Gladstone. Of course now he will in Tory circles be held up to be Bradlaugh's champion and the propagator of atheistic and disgusting doctrines. There certainly never was such a card for an Opposition to play.

A stall at Canterbury vacant. Mr. G. thinks of Westcott, or Holland, or Boyd-Carpenter. He ought to find a Low Church man, but the difficulty is to find a good one.

Wednesday, 8 February. After the Bradlaugh debate, the Irishmen opened the campaign by endeavouring to raise a question of privilege about the arrest of Parnell and his brethren. They did not make much of it, and a division being taken, there was time to move the Address. Marjoribanks and Firth (specially the latter) seem to have acquitted themselves well, but I left the House after the Bradlaugh division. (In the Upper House I hear Bingey Lawley spoke capitally in seconding the Address). In writing to the Queen Mr. G. summed up the question at issue on the Bradlaugh business in this way—that on the Government side, it was a contention of the maintenance of legality, and on the other side a contention of profanation.

Today the debate on the Address was resumed by Northcote, and I shall eternally regret not being present to hear Mr. G.'s reply, which according to all accounts seems to have been one of his very finest efforts. He even owned himself that he was good, which is very unusual for him. He said to Herbert,[1] after his speech, with much emotion: 'You will never hear anything better from me'. He was pleased at the line taken by the non-Parnellite Irishmen— P. J. Smyth, O'Connor Power, and Colthurst.

Thursday, 9 February. All agree who heard the speech that it was magnificent.

The cloture rule is received very unfavourably by the London press, but that does not count for much. Many have misunderstood its working, which

[1] i.e. his son.

comforts me, as I was taken in by it myself. I ventured to hint when it was under consideration that the wording of it was not clear and open to mis-contruction, but in spite of the admission of the Speaker[1] that the criticism was not unfair, no amendment was made. It would have been very easy to alter the terms of the resolution. The saving clause might have run thus, that 'the Question when put should not be considered to be decided in the affirmative if, when there were not 200 in the majority, there were as many as 40 in the minority' or something of that kind. The Tories intend to oppose the resolution 'tooth and nail', and some of the Liberals will no doubt wince under it. It is a pity that the resolutions were given baldly to the public without being explained by Mr. G. in submitting them to the House. The Government may accept certain qualifications, but they must stand or fall by the principle of a bare majority. Any attempt to introduce a proportion such as two-thirds would, according to the Speaker and May, render the resolution nugatory. The objections to it are mainly sentimental. It is hardly conceivable that it can be abused, if the Question cannot be put unless the Speaker or the Chairman of Committees consider that the *evident sense of the House* is in favour of the closing of the debate.

The anti-Gladstonian feeling becomes more and more bitter in Society, and no language is strong enough for their use. The Tories may pride themselves on being the aristocratic party, but they certainly do not possess what one may consider to be the primary attribute of the aristocracy—the behaviour of gentlemen.

Rosebery came to me today much exercised in his mind as to further proof of Mr. G.'s walking in the streets at night. It is a terribly unfortunate craze of his, and the only wonder is that his enemies have not made more capital of it. It is quite an unpardonable indiscretion for a man in his position. Rosebery is prepared to say a word about it, and as he is almost the only man who has ever dared to broach the subject of Mrs. T. with Mr. G.,[2] probably he would be the best spokesman in this instance. I recommended him, however, first to talk to Lord Granville. My own fear is that whoever talks on this subject to Mr. G. might as well talk to a door.[3]

Princess Louise came this afternoon to hear M. and C. play.[4] They acquitted themselves admirably.

Friday, 10 February. Heard a remarkable maiden speech this evening from Porter, the new Irish Solicitor-General. He made a capital defence for himself in the matter of the Derry election and for the Government on their Irish policy generally.

[1] Sir Henry Brand.
[2] Mrs. T. was Laura Thistlethwayte, *née* Bell (d. 1894). For further identification see M. R. D. Foot's forthcoming edition of G.'s diary.
[3] See 10 Feb. and 9 May 1882.
[4] i.e. EWH's sisters Maud and Constance.

Rosebery spoke to Lord G[ranville] yesterday on the walks after dark and their accompaniments. Lord G. was horrified to hear of their recent recurrence and quite agreed something ought to be said. He and Rosebery tossed up as to which of them should undertake the disagreeable and delicate task. Rosebery, having lost, came this morning and, having made an excuse for an interview, courageously broached the subject. Mr. G. took it in good grace and was apparently impressed with Rosebery's words, which will (I am in hopes) have a good effect.[1]

Saturday, 11 February. Mr. G. thought very highly of the speech of the new Solicitor-General for Ireland[2] last night, as I expected he would. As to R. Churchill, who preceded the Solicitor-General, and whom I also heard, Mr. G.'s comments upon his speech were that it was 'hotter in tone and weaker in argument than usual, without any statesmanlike features in it, acceptable to the Opposition and also to the Land Leaguers in certain passages'. Gibson, who spoke early in the evening, made a 'warm assault', according to Mr. G., but at the same time spoke very impartially as to the improved state of Ireland. The Land League party were more or less moderate on the whole.

Mr. G.'s short speech the night before last about Local Government for Ireland, in which he in reality merely repeated what he had said before on the subject on more than one occasion, has been laid hold of by the Opposition and been looked upon as a surrender to the Home Rulers. Though there was but little in the speech to which real exception could be taken, his words were certainly somewhat injudicious and ill-timed, and are words of which we shall hear a deal for some time to come. Whatever he says is sure to be distorted by the Tory party.

The Cabinet met today and were mainly occupied about the procedure rules, and came to the conclusion that the Government must use all its authority in Parliament to maintain the main (i.e. the clôture) proposal of the Government.

Notwithstanding the contentions of the *Times* and other London papers, that the cloture will not be passed, R. Grosv[enor] spoke confidently this morning of the amount of support which will be accorded to the proposals. Moreover, it seems to be the general opinion that a little pressure, savouring of a hint that the result will be regarded as a vote of confidence, will keep would-be 'Adullamites' straight.

Sunday, 12 February. The letter which I expected would come from the Queen arrived this evening.[3] It has no disagreeable tone about it. She assumes that Mr. G., in his remarks the other night on P. J. Smyth's amendment, had no intention to encourage the hopes of the Repealers; but She deplores the words he used as likely to give fresh impetus to agitation, more especially at this

[1] See 9 May 1882.   [2] Andrew M. Porter.   [3] Guedalla, ii. 176.

time when (this is an unexpected statement) the new Land Act in Ireland should be allowed 'to take its course' quietly and calmly. She would have preferred that Mr. G. had avowedly discountenanced any proposal which had the smallest savour of Home Rule.

Lonsdale's sudden death has naturally been the subject of much talk the last few days. On the whole one cannot regard the termination of his life as anything short of a mercy, as it appears he had taken again quite recently to his drinking habits, which was affecting his head. The circumstances are sad and almost tragic—his wife away in the South of France, and the man himself seized with his fatal illness in the house which he had provided for his 'Gaiety' friends.

Paid many calls this afternoon, among them to Sybella Lyttelton and Lady Reay—a striking contrast; Lady Lyttelton frantic with Mr. G. and charging him with having broken faith over the Land Act because (for this is what it amounts to) the opinion he hazarded as to the effect it would have upon rents has not been fulfilled; Lady Reay full of genuine admiration for the Great Man, as might be expected. Lord Arthur Russell was calling at Lady Reay's at the same time. Mr. G. has few men among the Whigs more devotedly attached to him than is Lord Arthur. He and men like Sir T. Acland (with whom I had a long talk at the House the other night) are among the sensible men who appreciate the genuine 'safeness' of the Great Man. Some day or other even the Tories will find out how instinctively conservative is Mr. G. in reality. Lady Reay spoke to me about a certain person (she would not give names) who had the ear of the Queen, and who maintained that H.M. has all along been most anxious to make friends with Mr. G., but She found this was not possible. The unknown person also said H.M. had complained that a letter of importance which she had addressed last summer to Mr. G. had been left unanswered for 3 weeks. I place no belief in either of these tales. Mr. G. never leaves unacknowledged for 3 weeks a letter from the most insignificant individual, much less from the highest personage in the realm, to whom he is, if anything, overscrupulous about writing and replying immediately. And as to the relations between him and the Sovereign, any strain or reserve that there may be is certainly not due to any want of courtesy or attention on his part. He never stoops to flatter or toady, it is true; but he is always most civil, considerate, and respectful.

Monday, 13 February. In view of the occurrence of a vacancy on the episcopal bench,[1] Mr. G. has made inquiries as to the truth of rumours that Wilkinson, of St. Peter's [Eaton Square], would not exchange his parochial work for a bishopric, in order that he may know whether or not he is to consider Wilkinson 'in the running'.

[1] Through the creation of the diocese of Newcastle out of a part of the diocese of Durham.

Though the *Times* and all the London Tory press continue their frantic screams against the cloture proposal, the prospects of the Government are supposed to be brightening. Grosvenor is sanguine. The reported defections seem to be exaggerated. There is an immense amount of sentimental talk on the subject. One would suppose that the idea had never been broached before; whereas as long ago as in 1848 the Speaker of the day—Shaw Lefevre—recommended a sweeping cloture.[1] Mr. G. is in good heart.

Tuesday, 14 February. Went down to the House to hear Mr. G. wind up the debate on the Address and found to my surprise the House had been counted.[2] This is a reflection on the 'Whips' and will greatly annoy Mr. G. There certainly ought to be in the new rules a provision against a 'count out' during dinner hour.

There seems to be no real apprehension as to the issue of a division on the famous No. 1 Procedure Rule, and the *Times* and *Standard*, who have been maintaining that the passing of it was a simple impossibility, will have quietly to eat their words. It seems to be one of those questions which, (as so often happens) when they are received very badly at the outset, improve and are found to 'wash' easily after the first criticism has subsided. The contrary is not less frequent.

I did not like Mr. G.'s reply yesterday to H.M. about his Home Rule references.[3] Though civil, it yielded not an inch and made no allowance for her (in this instance) not unnatural misgivings. His line of argument was that to say '*non possumus*' on a question of this kind was merely to array some 70 Irishmen against the British Government of the day; that he went no further than he had on many previous occcasions; and that as regards the form of local government he intended no more than what Scotland might have for the asking of it. I don't complain of the gist of his contention, but what appears to me to be injudicious is the occasion. The Government have by the Land Act succeeded in breaking up the Irish political party. To hold out a hope about local government, however right that may be, and however difficult it may be to formulate and impracticable to work, may have the very effect of uniting the Irishmen again, which Mr. G. wishes to guard against. I think he might have contented himself by assuring H.M. that he had said and meant no more than he had said and meant before, and that any new interpretation placed upon his words was, like with many other things he said, a distortion of facts.

The choice for the Canterbury stall fell upon Holland of Quebec Chapel, who accepted very gratefully and whose appointment will give great satisfaction to many and can give offence to no one.

It is today, I believe, on which Mr. G. has completed a term of premiership

[1] See Josef Redlich, *The Procedure of the House of Commons* . . . (London, 1908), i. 82–4.
[2] See 17 Feb. 1882. [3] Guedalla, ii. 176–8.

equivalent to that of Lord Beaconsfield. It is satisfactory to think that he has not been outdone by Lord B. even in this (secondary) respect.[1]

Friday, 17 February. Went down on Wednesday to Oxfordshire to see Frank Parker through at his marriage with Miss Gaskell, a nice, pretty, cheery little girl.

The collapse of the debate on the Address, which exhausted itself and was not due to a count out as I at first imagined, has been followed by an unexpectedly lengthy wrangle on the Report of the Address.[2] Jim Lowther opened fire, for the first time since his re-election, last night. He made some good points, but his speaking is more suited to the hustings than the House. He has any amount of 'brass' and works up his case well, but he is not over-fluent and has no statesmanlike or oratorical qualities. It was a 'memorable' speech (as Mr. G. termed it) in one sense, as it elicited from an ex-Chief Secretary for Ireland[3] a declaration of *Tory* Irish policy. He had 2 panaceas for Ireland: (1) the suspension of the jury laws, (2) emigration or (what he preferred to call) migration to English colonies. Lowther was followed by a short and very telling speech from O'Connor Power, which made a great impression upon me. Mr. G. then rose. He was not at his best, though he wound himself up well. He had some slight chill upon him and had remained in bed all day till after dinner when he came down to the House. He 'slated' Jim Lowther with some effect, but the most important part of his speech was his explanation of the words he used the other day in regard to Home Rule, to which (not unreasonably) so much exception has been taken. His explanation consisted in a reference to previous analogous statements of his on the subject. It is not difficult for him to clear himself from the charge of inconsistency; he has so often insisted on the necessity of decentralisation and the justifiableness of according to Ireland the same measure of local government as he would accord to Scotland, England, or Wales; but there is no doubt that his recent utterances were singularly inopportune. What he said with impunity out of office, cannot be said now in his present position of responsibility without awaking false hopes, and without laying himself open to an extra amount of distortion. They will always be memorable words and will for a long time be incessantly laid hold of for different motives by the Tories and the Irish party.

Mr. G. seems all right again. Work has been very active. We have received during the last 6 days about 550 letters, which is in excess of the average.

[1] According to a memorandum in Horace Seymour's hand, G. surpassed Beaconsfield in length of office on 2 Feb. 1882. Beaconsfield's first administration, according to that paper, lasted 285 days, his second 6 years and 67 days. G.'s first administration lasted 5 years and 73 days, his second by 2 Feb. 1882 1 year and 280 days. This was a continuing concern of G. and his secretaries. For Seymour's paper see Add. MS. 44775, f. 255.

[2] See 14 Feb. 1882.

[3] i.e. Lowther himself, who was Chief Secretary, 1878–80.

The Channel Tunnel question is to the fore and is exciting the mind of the public. So much has been said lately against the project that the Government have determined to inquire into all the bearings of the case, though the matter was practically settled and assented to by their predecessors.

The Taunton election yesterday went very badly. The Tory candidate not only won but gained votes, while the Liberal candidate lost votes. These bye-elections are disagreeably significant.[1]

Errington's unofficial communications with the Vatican, for the purpose of endeavouring to bring some pressure by the Pope on the Irish Catholic clergy, have excited not a little comment due to the absurd suspicions still lurking about with regard to Popery.

Saturday, 18 February. The debate on the Address terminated last night after nine days of it.

The Lords played the fool last night. On the motion of Donoughmore they carried against the Government a resolution entailing the appointment of a committee to inquire into the working and administration of the Land Act. It is hardly possible to conceive a greater piece of 'tom-foolery'. Even in their own interests, it must be a mistake. They must know that any amendment of the Act is outside the range of practical politics, and, if evidence be taken fairly, the result may and very probably will be to show that the decisions of the sub-Commissioners are perfectly sustainable, and that high renting is far more general than was anticipated. Moreover they will inevitably be running another nail into their own coffin. On broader grounds, the decision of the Lords is deplorable. It will weaken confidence in the Act and *pro tanto* weaken the main power of the Government to re-establish law and order in the country. It also involves the objection that judicial decisions will be subjected to discussion and review by a political body and a strong class interest.

So dangerous do the Government regard this move of the Peers that it was decided at the Cabinet today to move a resolution in the House of Commons to the effect that any inquiry into the Act just now would be most inopportune and detrimental to all interests. I am not sure that this is a wise step. (It is probably initiated by Forster, who is sure to be advising the wrong thing.) It will provoke more or less a conflict between the two Houses, which is to be deplored. It will involve an interminable discussion and waste of many valuable Government nights. The Government will run the risk of being defeated by Tories and Parnellites combined. The motion being agreed to, it surely would be wiser for the Government to wash their hands of it, allow it to take its course, and let the Lords stew in their own mess. The Tory Peers are, I understand, not all very easy about it. Some think they have got hold of a 'white elephant'.

[1] The Conservative, C. Allsopp, had 1,144 votes to Lord Kilcoursie's 917.

The Cabinet decided to advise H.M. that no steps should be taken in regard to the appointment of Lords Justices during her absence abroad.[1]

They have made up their mind to introduce some modification in the proposed closure rule, which is that, in the case of there not being 200 in the majority, the 40 minority should be held to veto the 'putting of the question', provided there be not 100 in the majority. This will probably disarm some of the opponents to the proposal; at the same time it has a disagreeable smack of surrender to the Tories.

Lord Ripon's proposal to send a Mahommedan envoy to the Ameer[2] was agreed to.

Mr. G. seems all right again. The Tory press are trying to make out that he was shamming on Thursday and stayed in bed to avoid an interview with the Queen.

Tuesday, 21 February. Last night Mr. G. brought on his procedure rules. The notice about the motion aimed at the action of the Lords fell like a thunder-clap on the House and gave rise to an angry, disagreeable wrangle. Mr. G. was, I think, pretty well at his best. The structure of his eloquent and persuasive speech was very fine. There was a wonderful dignity about it; even solemnity. Northcote, for whom I could not stay, followed Mr. G. and seems to have been rather weak, at the same time moderate and temperate. Marriott, the ex-cleric-legal-turncoat M.P. for Brighton,[3] who had the first hostile amendment on the paper, spoke later in the evening with great warmth, vehemence, and declamation. Goschen gave the resolutions staunch and useful support.

Wednesday, 22 February. Last night witnessed a fresh development of the Bradlaugh case. Labouchere moved that as Bradlaugh was not allowed to take the oath, a new writ should be issued for Northampton. It was made clear to the House that the seat could not be regarded as vacant, and the motion was accordingly rejected. Immediately after the rejection there followed an extraordinary scene. Bradlaugh stole a march upon the House, walked quickly in a bare-faced manner up to the Table, produced a bible out of his pocket, and subscribed to the oath with due formalities on his own hook; whereupon he announced that he had complied with the law. The Speaker ordered him to withdraw below the Bar, which he did; but he subsequently took his seat inside the House. It was, as Mr. G. said, 'an

---

[1] See 3 Feb. 1882.

[2] Abdur Rahman of Afghanistan.

[3] Marriott, having been a deacon in the Established Church, renounced his orders in 1861, became a student in Lincoln's Inn and a successful barrister. His career as a turn-coat had only begun. By 1882 hostile to G.'s policies, he finally in 1884 deserted the Liberal Party and sought re-election for Brighton successfully as a Conservative. See 1 and 13 Mar. 1884.

extraordinary scene of the utmost scandal'. Randolph Churchill, perceiving more quickly than anyone else the temper of the House, moved that Bradlaugh had by his own action vacated his seat. The Government pleaded for time to consider the new situation and adjourned the debate.

This augmented insult to the House, which had aroused among all side of the House [sic], afforded the Government an opportunity for taking a fresh departure in the case. We did what we could to make Mr. G. see the situation in a new light, but after conferring with the Cabinet this morning, Mr. G. stuck to his guns and threw the responsibility of solving the question on the Opposition majority. I never was more convinced that a political mistake was made. Any strong action of the Government would have been supported enthusiastically by the bulk of the Liberal party. Northcote thereupon moved that Mr. Bradlaugh be expelled from the precincts of the House. A little later Bradlaugh again took his seat, and this enabled Northcote to move a resolution expelling the man from the House, which was followed by another motion issuing a new writ. Both resolutions being carried, there is an end of Bradlaugh for the time being; and one can only hope that he will not be returned again, even though it will involve the loss of a seat. But the matter terminated most unfortunately for the Government. They all acted at 'six and sevens'; some voted in the majority, some in the minority, while others walked out of the House, among whom was Mr. G. himself. Moreover, Mr. G. maintained his conscientious consistency at a very heavy loss. The bulk of the party are thoroughly sick of Bradlaugh. He has tried them hard enough already, but the latest phase of the matter put an end to almost all sympathy with the man. He may now, of course, be sued by any common informer, which is evidently what Bradlaugh himself wished. The decision will be interesting.

Friday, 24 February. One certainly lives in a continued atmosphere of difficulty and excitement combined. Now that Bradlaugh is disposed of, we have on hand the resolution of the Lords for an inquiry into the Irish Land Act. The counter-move made by Mr. Gladstone is, of course, regarded as a revolutionary step. 'Now that he is gagging the House of Commons, he is about to collar the House of Lords'. 'He won't die happy without abolishing the Upper House'. Nothing of the kind is in reality farther from his thoughts or intentions. He would give anything if the Lords would come to a compromise, either by postponing their inquiry or altering the terms of the reference of inquiry. The Government are quite prepared to stand specific charges; and are not the least apprehensive as to the result. But what they cannot brook without a protest is a vague investigation conducted by Tory landlords, which is certain to shake the confidence of the Irish in the Land Act, and accordingly weaken the only material weapon there is for fighting the Land League. Lord Salisbury has taken the bit in his teeth and won't budge an inch. He will no doubt some day have reason to regret this ill-advised step of his brother peers. As a counter-resolution in the House of Commons can't stop the inquiry, I feel sure this move is a mistake, as it will create unnecessary alarms and stop the course of business. All that was necessary in my judgment was an emphatic statement by Mr. G. that, no matter what the Lords did or reported, the Government intended to stand by the Land Act. However, there it is, and nothing could be more unfortunate for the Commons as well as for the Lords.

Sunday, 26 February. Things have changed for the better from a party point of view. The idea of a conference of Mr. G.'s supporters agreed to yesterday is looked upon very favourably, and the prospect of it tomorrow has placed the party in good humour. Moreover, the Peers' action, since they declined to take advantage of the bridges which the Government built for them on Friday last, is regarded as so uncompromising and ill-advised, that the feeling of the Whigs has become as strong against the Lords as that of the Radicals. Even Lord Shaftesbury wrote to say he was horrified at Lord Salisbury's wilfulness. Accordingly, from a party point of view, the counter-action of the Government in the Commons will to all appearances act as a good rallying cry, and in this respect compensate for the disadvantage and discredit which the interruption to public business may entail. At the same time, so unwilling are the Government to bring on a collision between the high authorities of the State, and so anxious are they to avert an exhibition of weakness in the legislature at this moment in Ireland, that they have informed the Opposition that they will even now drop the hostile Commons resolution, if the House of Lords will consent to amend the terms of reference to the committee to the extent of excluding from their inquiry the judicial administration of the Land Act. Mr. G. is in good heart and talked most cheerfully this morning of the prospects of the party. Marvellous and extraordinary man! there he was quietly in his room perusing in turns Noel's *Philosophy of Immortality*, an annotated edition of the *Book of Wisdom*, and a non-conformist collection of hymns, with tomorrow in prospect.

Monday, 27 February. At last a 'red letter' day in the Liberal Calends. The meeting of Liberal M.P.'s this afternoon was a tremendous success and answered its end splendidly. It was very well attended and most enthusiastic as well as perfectly unanimous. Mr. G. (who had been down to Windsor at the Council in order to see H.M. to explain the situation) jumped upon a chair like a boy and spoke briefly and very forcibly. He told the meeting how anxious he had been, and still was, to avoid a conflict in the legislature at this time, but that so serious did the Government consider the action of the Lords, that if no compromise were forthcoming, they would feel bound to persist with their resolution. Dillwyn, Richard, Givan, Hussey Vivian, Whitbread,

Goschen and others spoke; all to the point, all in most loyal terms, and some extremely well. H. Vivian told Kensington that he had never witnessed a meeting of the kind which was so enthusiastic and unanimous. It certainly rallied the party most effectually, and I never was more glad about having pressed a point.

Went down immediately after to the House. Northcote did not attempt to defend his resistance to the postponement of the Orders of the Day, which was purely obstructive. A division was taken after about an hour's debate, which resulted much to the surprise of everybody in a majority for the Government of no less than 133. Northcote had failed to carry his party with him. Mr. G. then moved his resolution, Northcote having declined to show any sign of being willing to compromise. The speech in which the resolution was moved was simply superb and magnificent from beginning to end, moderate and yet most vigorous, dignified and emphatic but not menacing, and a perfect wealth of eloquence throughout. One is always inclined after hearing a speech from him to say it is the finest one ever heard from him, but I really think that this is the speech of all others that have impressed me most. I could have cried like a child. It was enthusiastically received. The effect of the preliminary meeting was most apparent in the House. The fact which has to be realised is this: we are face to face with the most formidable conspiracy that has ever confronted the Executive Government. No force can compel the payment of rents; and without the Land Act, what answer would there be to the better disposed tenants in Ireland, who might say, 'We don't object to paying just rents; what we do decline to do is to pay more than we consider fair'? With the Land Act, the Government can point out that the decision of what is justly due rests with a tribunal, and once shake the confidence of the people in that Act and the game is up; it would be 'surrender to the Land League'. This is what the landlords would do well to realise.

Tuesday, 28 February. It is generally—I may say universally—admitted that the Government 'scored' heavily yesterday. The rally of the party has come with special opportuneness.

The Lords' committee have selected Lord Cairns as chairman, and he has, in the name of the committee, been appointed to preside. He has written to request Forster to attend, and in writing has stated that the committee consider that the judicial administration of the Land Act *is* excluded from the committee's inquiry. The Cabinet, however, have thought the statement insufficient and unsatisfactory and have not considered it proper or dignified to treat it as they would have treated an amended reference by the House of Lords to the committee. Accordingly the debate in the Commons will have to proceed. A nice point arises as to whether Forster should obey the summons. As at present minded, the Cabinet are, I think, against his appearing before the committee. Possibly they may leave it to the discretion of the

House of Commons, whose leave has to be obtained before one of its own members can appear before a committee of the other House. I can hardly think it dignified for him to accept the invitation. If he is attacked on matters connected with the Land Act, the proper place for him to defend himself in is the House of Commons.

Friday, 3 March. Yesterday afternoon about 6 o'clock, a telegram came from Ponsonby to say that a shot was fired at H.M. on her leaving Windsor station, but that fortunately it had no result.[1] The Queen was not alarmed and behaved with perfect composure. Mr. G. at once sent a message of congratulations on her escape. It appears from later accounts that the shot came from a revolver loaded with bullet [*sic*], which was fired by one MacLean. He is not an Irishman; and as he was discharged from a lunatic asylum last year, it is more than probable that he was labouring under some aberration of mind. The attempt has created very naturally immense stir and elicited much sympathy from all classes and everywhere.

The question was raised this morning whether an Address expressive of abhorrence of the deed and of thankfulness for the escape should be moved in Parliament. As on no similar occasion since 1842 have such steps been taken, Mr. G. and Lord Granville came to the conclusion that perhaps it was better not to propose an Address. Ponsonby, however, was communicated with, and, by a telegram received this evening, it is evident that the Queen herself would rather like to be condoled with and congratulated by Parliament. Under these circumstances I very much hope Mr. G. will take the necessary steps, but he is such a 'stickler' for precedents that I expect he will not easily allow himself to be put in motion.[2]

Bradlaugh was, unfortunately for most reasons, again returned for Northampton yesterday. His majority had slightly declined, but he polled more votes than he did at the previous election. We shall accordingly be confronted once more with this infernal business. The proper course to pursue seems to me without doubt to be, to introduce a bill giving the option of swearing or affirming; and my remedy to meet the difficulty would be to bring forward such a bill and to hold Saturday sittings for its discussion till it was passed. If no decided step be taken this time, we shall get into fresh trouble, and shall be risking a renewal of disorganisation in the party.

Forster is over in Ireland and has gone himself to Clare where the state of the country is specially disturbed. If the difficulties there can be tided over, he is not the reverse of sanguine as to the outlook in the country. The Cabinet have advised him to decline to comply with the request made by Lord Cairns that he will attend the Lords Committee of inquiry into the Land Act, and he has acted on this advice. It was thought this possibly might lead to the

[1] Guedalla, ii. 179.   [2] But see 5 Mar. 1882.

abandonment of the Committee, but at present there are no indications in this direction.

Last week Mr. G. received an invitation to a Sunday 'at home' from Mrs. Langtry. He did not avail himself of it, but he went and called at her house. He did not even see her, but all kinds of rumours are already abroad about his intimacy with the 'professional beauty'. These rumours would have had much greater currency and better foundation, had he gone to the evening party, out of which I think we managed to frighten him and the card for which I first thought of hiding and saying nothing about. Certainly Rosebery spoke not a day too early about the night walks,[1] which are now openly talked of in Society.

Saturday, 4 March. I never noted the return the other day of Davitt for Meath, which is an ill-omened sign of the times. Of course he can't sit as a convict and the election is void. His place is to be taken by Egan, hardly a whit better than Davitt. The Irishmen tried on Tuesday last to make out a case for inquiry by select committee before the new writ was issued, but of course failed. The debate was remarkable for the warm testimony to Davitt's ability and honesty given by Shaw. To Davitt no doubt is due the credit of the original organisation of the Land League, and that without him it never would have been developed to the pitch it since has attained. Those who let him out of prison on 'ticket-of-leave' must take a considerable share of the responsibility of the proceedings resulting therefrom on their shoulders—that is, more particularly Cross.

As regards the Lords' Committee, which is getting quite stale, the Government have been taken to task a good deal by the Tory and half-hearted (e.g. *Times*) papers for not making Cairns' letter to Forster the basis for a compromise and for a withdrawal of the vote of censure. But a mere assurance from the Committee, on their own responsibility only, that they would not question the grounds of the decisions already given, could not possibly be held to correspond with the condition which the Government declared was essential to their not proceeding with their resolution in the House of Commons. On Thursday when the debate was continued, the Tories loudly denounced the Act as unjust to the landlords, while the Parnellites maintained with equal emphasis that it was cruel to the tenants. This double shot is really a high compliment to the Act, and good testimony to its fairness and justice. The new Solicitor General for Ireland[2] spoke again that night, and Mr. G. was much pleased with the speech. He (Porter) is evidently a very considerable acquisition and will soon very possibly be a match for Gibson. Mr. G. thought that Plunket, who followed Porter, most ingeniously shewed in his speech all signs of a foregone conclusion against the Act and clearly demonstrated the true tendency and aim of the Committee. The moving of the 'previous

[1] See 9 and 10 Feb. 1882.   [2] Andrew M. Porter.

question' by the Opposition, though a somewhat mild form of negativing the resolution, is probably the wisest course the Tories could take, as it prevents the putting of the Parnellite amendments, and displays better tactics than those which landed the Opposition on the preliminary motion in the same lobby as the Land Leaguers and under the whip of the Land Leaguers. By the way, Mr. G. was very pleased with Harry Brand's speech the first evening of the debate. I wish a place could be found for him in the Government.

I have omitted to note the meeting at St. James' Palace convened by the Prince of Wales for the purpose of starting a Royal College of Music—a Conservatoire—last Tuesday. It was a great success; the addresses of H.R.H. and the Duke of Edinburgh (especially that of the former) were extremely good; the speeches were admirable, particularly those of the Archbishop[1] and Rosebery; Mr. G. was in his usual eloquent form and Sir S. Northcote was amusing. Started under such favourable auspices, the project will probably succeed. Subscriptions are coming in very well.

Sunday, 5 March. The Queen is much pleased that the Government are going to move a joint address in Parliament congratulating her and expressing thankfulness on her escape at Windsor on Thursday.[2] Mr. G. hesitated at first about taking this step, because there was no precedent for it since 1842 and because such attempts on the Queen proceed from men of weak and morbid minds, to which the highest reward and inducement to do the deed is notoriety, and a parliamentary Address specially partakes of this. However, I am very glad it is going to be done. The Tories would have made capital out of the omission; (they have already been hinting at Windsor that *they* would like to move an Address) and as far as notoriety is concerned, any steps which Parliament may take can't add much to that.

The post of late has been very heavy, letters averaging about 90 a day, mainly consisting of addresses of confidence and approval of the Government.

Forster writes very hopefully from Ireland. He says there is an undoubted break in lawless agitation, that rents are being paid even in the worst districts, and that the very bad characters are bolting. He admits, however, that there are in the West a few very hard cases of evictions, for which it seems to be next to impossible to provide a remedy. Though he wishes to be let off returning in time for the debate on the vote of censure upon the Lords, he authorises a statement to be made that he will welcome any attack made in a constitutional fashion as regards the Sub-Commissioners.

The Queen has just erected a tablet in Hughenden Church to the sacred memory of Lord Beaconsfield with a garbled quotation from Proverbs, which

[1] A. C. Tait of Canterbury.
[2] See 3 Mar. 1882 and Guedalla, ii. 181.

has an almost snobbish ring about it.[1] I wonder whether, when the fatal day arrives, (if She lives to see it), she will erect a tablet to Mr. G. ?[2]

As regards the French Commercial Treaty, the lengthy and intricate negotiations came to nought in the end. The French Government would not come to reasonable terms. The result, however, is somewhat more favourable than might be expected; and if it were not for political reasons, we are undoubtedly well rid of a tariff treaty. Though there is to be no direct treaty, the French Government have by voluntary act consented to admit our trade and our subjects to the privileges of a most favoured nation so long as our tariff is not changed injuriously to France, and of this there is little likelihood.

Thursday, 9 March. The parliamentary week opened with a renewed Bradlaugh debate. Northcote insisted on bringing it on, despite the Address to the Queen which would be interrupted and Bradlaugh's own non-appearance. This move savoured much of obstruction to business on a Government night. The Government, instead of moving the 'previous question', supported an amendment of Edward Marjoribanks', which he brought to me in the morning as one of his own creation and with which Mr. G. was rather pleased and decided to adopt. It was to give expression to an opinion that it was expedient to amend the Parliamentary Oaths Act so as to give members the option of affirming or swearing. The debate occupied some hours and was attended (as Mr. G. said) with the indecent excitement which has so characterised all previous discussions on the subject and which is always belying the judicial character belonging to the occasion. This change of tactics lessened considerably the majority against the Government, but the result in the end was the same, which was to prevent Bradlaugh taking the oath, and so we are in the wretched position of 'as you were'. There is only one real way out of the difficulty and that is by legislation. This is regarded as impracticable and so it probably would be if it partook directly and solely of the nature of a 'Bradlaugh Relief Bill', but I believe as far as the House of Commons is concerned it would have been feasible to pass a measure to amend the Oaths Act, had advantage been taken at the commencement of the session of Bradlaugh's not unhandsome offer to vacate voluntarily his seat if such a bill were introduced and seriously taken up. Mr. G., however, will not swerve from the strictly legal line he has pursued from the commencement, and he has the Speaker and May on his side, who hold that, though it was impossible to prevent Northcote's interfering with the taking of the oath by Bradlaugh, such interference is *de facto* unconstitutional and illegal.

[1] The inscription on the Queen's tablet is: 'To the dear and honoured memory of Benjamin Earl of Beaconsfield this memorial is placed by his grateful sovereign and friend Victoria R. I. Kings love him that speaketh right. Proverbs xvi, 13. February 27, 1882.' The King James version of Proverbs xvi, 13, is: 'Righteous lips are the delight of kings; and they love him that speaketh right.'
[2] She did not.

Friday, 10 March. Last night witnessed the conclusion of the debate on Mr. G.'s resolution to counteract the determination of the Lords to inquire into the working of the Land Act. Mr. G. thought that Chaplin's and Lewis's speeches were the most effective on the attacking side yesterday. He noted, however, that both speeches were couched in terms of unequivocal condemnation of the Act. Accordingly, in their minds, inquiry into the Act meant a foregone conclusion. Mr. G. left Hartington to wind up the debate for the Government. Hartington, though forcible and at times humourous, was not to my mind quite at his best. He was followed by Northcote who was moderate and who excited no stir among the Tories. It struck Mr. G. that Northcote was sensibly labouring under the difficulties of a false position. The divisions which ensued were decisive, but not larger than was expected. On the first division (the previous question) the Parnellites abstained from voting, but they joined in against the Government on the main question and accordingly *pro tanto* decreased the majority of the Government. Mr. G. thought the most noteworthy circumstance in the debate was the further accentuation which it brought out of the differences among Irish members.

Mr. G., when down at Windsor on Wednesday evening, was touched by Her Majesty's sensibly increased apprehensions regarding the safety of Her own person consequent upon the recent attack upon her or rather futile attempt to do her harm.[1] The disposition of the Queen induced Mr. G. to go down personally himself again today to assist in presenting the Address of congratulations on Her Majesty's escape. So much for the charges that he neglects to pay her the respect due to her.

Mr. G. consulted with Harcourt and the Law Officers yesterday on the trial of MacLean, the would-be assassin. He reported the result to the Queen. They hold that the important end to secure is the power of imprisonment without limit of time. The indictment against MacLean is to be intent to murder. This charge, if proved, amounts to treason, which means capital punishment and thus imprisonment for life. The defence will probably be insanity, and this the Law Officers will not resist *à l'outrance*, because insanity secures imprisonment *ad libitum*; whereas, if the other plea of intent to alarm were set up, as assuredly it would be if that of insanity failed, and were such plea proved, the term of imprisonment would be limited.

Sunday, 12 March. Wilfrid Blunt, who has for some months past been living in company with Arabi Bey and the nationalist party in Egypt, has returned somewhat unexpectedly in order to see what he can do to plead the cause of the nationalists. He maintains with great assurance that the movement *is* a national one; that Arabi & Co. intend to respect all international engagements and have the power and capacity to do so; that the only point on which

[1] See 3 Mar. 1882.

they will insist is the reduction of the number of European employes and a more economical administration; and that all will go quietly and well in Egypt provided that the Egyptians are left to themselves and a word of encouragement is said on behalf of national and parliamentary institutions. Mr. G. has been unable to see him himself, but he has had interviews of Lord G[ranville] and Dilke, and he (W. B.) is certain that both are under influences directly hostile to the nationalists; and that, if nothing is done to correct this, intervention, which would result in national disaster and which *can* now be avoided, will become a disagreeable and hateful necessity.

The parliamentary outlook is very bad. Five weeks of the session have been consumed, and no work has been done. One night only has been devoted to procedure, and the necessities of supply entail a further postponement of its consideration. What is still more disheartening is that, if all the new rules of procedure had become law, one does not see how the sessional work would have been better advanced. There has been no occasion on which the power which the Government propose of closing a debate could have been exercised. My belief is that far more radical changes are required to put the machinery of Parliament into decent working order:

(1) There should be a power of closure, such as Lord Eversley advocated years ago, enabling anyone with due notice to move without debate at the commencement of the sitting that the question under discussion should be put at the termination of the evening's sitting. Such a power would have met the difficulties with which the Government are confronted when nine nights are consumed in the Address to the Throne and four nights are consumed in bringing to an issue a resolution such as Mr. G. has been moving and has carried to counteract the effect of the Lords' Committee of inquiry into the Land Act.

(2) The days allotted to private members should be curtailed. There is a deal of false sentiment about the right of private members which is well exemplified by the fact that the subjects brought forward by them are not of sufficient public interest to enable them to keep a House on two of the nights this session appropriated to their use.

Resort to such proposals may be thought dangerous and liable to abuse, but they would be dangers and abuses to meet still greater dangers and abuses—unlimited loquaciousness and inability to legislate.

It is to be hoped that the introduction of Grand Committees will ease the work of the House, which is an absolute necessity now that every year the demands on the Executive and for legislation increase at a frightful ratio.

Mr. G. is very anxious to exercise his right of appointing a bishop and is impatient that the arrangements for giving final effect to the endowments of the new See at Newcastle should be concluded.[1] He has been in consultation

[1] See 8 Nov. 1881 and 13 Feb. 1882.

with the Bishop of Durham[1] on the subject. The Bishop is divided in his mind between Canon Barry and Mr. Wilkinson (of St. Peter's). Mr. G. decidedly favours the latter and will no doubt make the offer to Mr. Wilkinson.

Mr. G. has been in wonderful force. As an instance of his extraordinary energy, he went down yesterday morning, after a late night in the House, at 8.30 to Dover with a party to view the Channel Tunnel works (Watkin's) which interested him greatly. The night before, in the midst of his parliamentary calls, he attended the Opera on the pressing invitation of Carl Rosa and Randegger.

One of the nights on which the House has been counted out was last Tuesday, and this was on the occasion of what Mr. G. called the 'puerile proposal' to raise a 'fair trade' discussion. This shews how sensibly has the 'fair trade' cry diminished in importance.

The Queen was much pleased by the Address of both Houses, and also at Mr. G.'s going down to present it himself.

Forster's speech the other day in Ireland is considered to have done good. The Irishmen liked the pluck he displayed, and the homely and manly way in which [he] spoke to them, though they were 'home truths' which he spoke. Why did he not do this months and months ago? I entreated him last autumn to speak himself and get others to speak as well, to counteract the nefarious teaching of the Land Leaguers. The poor old man was blackguarded more than usual by 'Humpy Joe' (Biggar) last week, who accused him of going to Ireland now, as he did in famine times of 1846–7, in order to witness suffering. The Speaker stigmatised the accusation as atrocious and demanded that the charge should be withdrawn. He should have coupled the demand with requiring Biggar to apologise to the House for such language on pain of being 'named' instantly.[2]

Evans, the correspondent of the Manchester *Guardian*, son-in-law of Freeman, and of Montenegrin notoriety, has been arrested by the Austrian Government on a supposed charge of treason.

An interesting despatch came under my notice today giving an account of an interview with the Czar.[3] The interviewer described the Czar as a prisoner of state; and, though resolute and calm, as anxious to abdicate were it not for the danger which would attach to the throne by the long minority of his son.[4] He was further represented to be inexperienced and perfectly conscious of his inexperience and unfitness for his Imperial position. He seems to have made up his mind upon two points, namely that economy must be enforced and peace maintained at all costs. No one has any influence over him. The *status quo* cannot last much longer; radical organic changes are indispensable and must come.

---

[1] J. B. Lightfoot.
[2] Biggar's attack occurred on 10 Mar. 1882. *Parl. Deb.* cclxvii. 620–1.
[3] Alexander III.   [4] Nicholas (later Nicholas II), who was born in 1868.

Monday, 13 March. Despite all his engagements, all his work, and all his anxieties, Mr. G. never passes a day without getting through a very considerable amount of extraneous and varied reading. In short, he reads every moment he is not actively engaged. It is his method of taking the strain off his mind. One of the last books on which he has been engaged is *Atlantis* by Donnelly, to whom he has addressed a long letter of thanks personally.[1] He (Mr. G.) says he is himself disposed to believe in an 'Atlantis'.

Today is almost the first day on which he has given signs of the approaching Budget. His mind is turning on the 'Death Duties' again, and he seems to be becoming a convert to our uniform duty—i.e., one duty instead of Probate *and* Legacy, and payable at the same rate by all alike.

Lord Ripon has written at considerable length to explain his action in connection with the recent North Riding election, which has been somewhat commented upon.[2] The long and short of the matter is that, though perhaps any peer's subscribing is strictly speaking an infringement of the Commons' rights, yet Lord Ripon in giving £1000 did no more than hundreds of other peers do on other similar occasions. The only mistake was that the fact should have got out.

In answering him, Mr. G. referred to Lord Ripon's administration in India as 'a standing source of comfort and justification' to him. He told Lord Ripon that the one great difficulty at home now was the deadlock in the House of Commons which many Tories labour to aggravate and most appear to contemplate with satisfaction.

Friday, 17 March. Very little way has been made with real work this week, the necessities of supply having interfered with other business. Monday night was given up to Army Estimates, but preliminary motions occupied the sitting up till midnight. 'Part of these', Mr. G. said (in effect) in writing to the Queen, 'were put forward for the purpose of obstruction, which has now reached such a height that the House must take its choice between putting down the mischief by wise expedients and a practical abrogation of most of its duties'. It was past midnight before Childers got up to make his army statement, which is very evident proof of itself of the condition of 'impotence to which the House is now reduced by the gratuitous action of its individual members'. Childers made a clever and clear speech. He is certainly very handy with anything connected with figures. After he sat down, a desultory conversation ensued, interspersed with obstructive divisions and accompanied by extremely ill-mannered attacks on Mr. G. for insisting that the vote for men should be taken. He sat through it all till after 4 o'clock in the morning, and

[1] Ignatius Donnelly, an American, was the author of this book; he also was a leading advocate of the Baconian authorship of Shakespeare's plays.

[2] Joseph Cowen accused Ripon of a breach of privilege in contributing £1,000 to aid the Liberal candidate in the by-election for the North Riding of Yorkshire. *Parl. Deb.* cclxvi. 787–9.

triumphed in the long run—so much so that all those who had used strong language, notably Percy, Sclater-Booth, and Lord E. Cecil, all apologised in turn. It is a most unusual thing to do to question the arrangements about supply, which the Government of the day, in the judgment of the Treasury, regard as necessary. What the Tories wanted to prove was that the Government were pushing on Supply merely to bring on the 'hateful procedure business' on the following Monday. They bungled over their dates and took no account of the extra time required by reason of the absence of the Queen abroad.

Tuesday ended in another 'count out'—a further proof of the absurd talk about the sacredness of Private Members' rights and of the expediency of allocating more parliamentary time to the Government. Previous to the 'count out', Broadhurst had brought forward a motion on a matter connected with Government employes. He spoke to it, as Mr. G. said, according to his custom with 'utmost modesty and propriety which might well teach a lesson to many, and with no small ability and clearness'. Mr. G. considers that Broadhurst and the other working man's candidate—Burt—do real honour to their class. It is certainly curious that the moderation and sobriety in Parliament should proceed from such men and all the heated talk, personal recriminations, and abuse should be found in the speeches of the scions of noble houses.

Thursday was devoted to Navy Estimates; and G. Trevelyan made a very remarkable statement. Hardly anyone among the 'coming men' has improved his position so conspicuously as has Trevelyan and is making a greater mark for himself.

Sunday, 19 March. Friday's sitting was wholly occupied with the discussion of the expediency of the grant of a Royal Charter to the North Borneo Co. Mr. G. defended it, but the debate was marked by the taking of strong exception to the grant by many of the radicals as well as some Tories. The Government, however, had a two to one majority, contrary to expectation, for Wolff declared confidently that they would be placed in a minority. Northcote did not vote, and in Mr. G.'s judgment 'beat himself in shabbiness' by his conduct.

Nothing of any special interest transpired at the Cabinet yesterday.

We are having the most extraordinarily lovely spring weather for the time of year. Mr. G. told me that he understood on the highest authority that there had not been such weather for 57 years.

Irish outrages are very bad. The Coercion Act seems to have failed so far as the commission of outrages is concerned, and yet, what can be done? The continued imprisonment of these hundreds of suspects is producing increasing irritation without any compensating effect. Juries are again failing to convict. My belief is that the establishment of some different tribunal to that of judge and jury will become a necessity for agrarian crime.

There seems to be a growing consensus of opinion that some steps will have to be taken for making the purchase clauses in the Land Act more effectual. Some such system as that advocated by W. H. Smith and O'Hara for issuing land debentures which will cover the *whole* of the purchase money seems to be required; but the *sine quâ non* of such a proposal must be, as Mr. G. says, the establishment of an Irish fund either by means of a special tax or some Baronial guarantee. I hope this may be taken in hand.

The Dean of Windsor[1] rather inclines to Boyd Carpenter for the new See of Newcastle, but Mr. G. sticks to Wilkinson.[2]

Courtney, in spite of all the persuasive power of Mr. G., declined point blank to be put in nomination for the vacancy in the East Cornwall representation. Assent would no doubt have been a great self-sacrifice on the part of Courtney; but had he less bluntness and more patriotism he probably would have answered to Mr. G.'s call. 'Stumpy' Acland has consented to run.

There are rumours about the intention of Austria to annex Bosnia and Herzegovina, but there has been no confirmation of them in official quarters. At the same time Mr. G. feels not a little uneasy lest where there is smoke, there should be some fire.

Mr. G. opened his mind the other day in replying to a letter received from Sir A. Gordon, for whom he has the highest regard and with whom he is on most intimate terms. He expressed pleasure that Sir A. G. approved of the 'modifying and undoing work' which it was the special mission of the Government to accomplish and which since their accession to office has been their special aim. He admitted that Ireland was mending far less rapidly than the Government had expected. As to the state of the House of Commons, the necessary reforms had grown to incredible dimensions, which he considered is due not only to the hostility of the Irish faction but to the passage of the Tories into opposition, for 'the unscrupulousness generated and made habitual under the regime of Lord Beaconsfield has affected many of them and terribly aggravated the indirect and latent means of opposition'. He maintained that he still clings to the idea of 'stopping with 50 years', but whether he alluded to his parliamentary or his official half century is not clear, which makes a difference, as, though he completes his 50 years in Parliament this year, his official career did not commence till 1834.[3]

Lord Salisbury has been 'letting out' most frantically in short epistolary ejaculations, attributing directly to Mr. G. all kinds of sinister motives, which certainly were absent from Mr. G.'s charges, however strong they were, during the Eastern question times.

---

[1] Gerald Wellesley.
[2] See 12 Mar. 1882.
[3] Paul Knaplund, ed., 'Gladstone–Gordon Correspondence, 1851–1896', *Transactions of the American Philosophical Society* . . . (Philadelphia, 1961), p. 85.

Thursday, 23 March. Lord Salisbury this week surpassed himself in his denunciatory notes. He even went as far as to comment on Mr. G.'s 'uncontrollable temper' and 'overweening vanity', and to bracket Mr. G. with Bradlaugh. Lord Granville took the opportunity this afternoon, on the motion for the 2nd Reading of Lord Redesdale's Swearing Bill, of giving 'Old Sarum' a dig about these letters. Lord Salisbury evidently winced a little, and after the debate he crossed the floor of the House and told Lord G[ranville] that the particular letter to which reference had been made was not *his* composition but that of his secretary Henry Manners, 'an inexperienced youth', though the Peerage shows that he has seen 30 summers, and that he (Lord S.) could not throw over his secretary. This line was no doubt creditable; but, however rash and tactless Henry Manners may be, it is inconceivable that he should have used such language had Lord S. not been continually applying strong epithets to Mr. Gladstone in his hearing; and what is more, some of Lord Salisbury's other letters signed by himself are little less ill-mannered. The only comfort is that by resort to such low devices Lord S. can do little harm to anyone but himself.

Sunday, 26 March. Last Monday Raikes renewed the cloture debate in a strong party spirit. The House might have expected to be enlightened by a man of such experience in procedure as Raikes; but he preferred to make personal attacks on Mr. G., who (he said) was the last person in the world that ought to have proposed a closing power when no one had occupied the time of the House by his verbosity so much. Raikes accused Mr. G. of having spoken at such length on the Divorce Bill that his speech or speeches cover 15 columns of the *Times*—a totally unfounded allegation, which on being brought to book he had to withdraw and apologise for, but which shews the sort of reckless things even men in responsible positions will say to damage Mr. G.[1]

Hartington followed in an excellent rattling speech—thoroughly *con amore.*

Tuesday was occupied by the County Franchise question brought on by A. Arnold, who has assumed to himself in this respect Trevelyan's mantle. Mr. G. thought the speeches of Arnold and Elliot (the seconder) both marked by much ability. The House declined to allow a division to be taken on the main question, so the Government had to show their strength in voting against the adjournment.

The resolutions relating to the marriage grant to Prince Leopold were moved by Mr. G. on Thursday. Labouchere led the opposition, founding himself on references to proceedings in the reign of George III, which were not in point, as the basis and amount of the Civil List is quite different now to what it was last century. Broadhurst followed him on the same side, but his speech was, in Mr. G.'s opinion, neither in spirit nor in language open to any

[1] Raikes referred to the debates on the Divorce Bill of 1857.

just exception. Mr. G. thought Healy and Storey extremely offensive. He considered the division perfectly satisfactory and thought nothing could have been better than the general spirit of the House. Dilke and Fawcett were the only men in the Government who abstained from voting, and considering what an active part Dilke had played on former occasions, perhaps abstention was the most that could have been expected of him.[1]

After the resolutions, the cloture was again discussed. Beresford Hope led off against it and spoke (as Mr. G. said) in his usual quaint manner and not ineffectively. Hicks Beach was the spokesman for the Opposition, and Mr. G. thought the speech the best that had been yet made from the front Opposition bench. He said it was marked by 'moderation, non-party spirit, candour, and closeness of reasoning'. Harcourt followed Hicks speech.

Friday was taken up by a Fair Trade debate raised on a motion of Ritchie. Protection was disclaimed, but Mr. G. said notwithstanding it was an effort to promote reciprocity or retaliation, and as such the real meaning of the discussion was that protective duties should be imposed, though the object of it was disavowed. Northcote and his followers actually all supported Ritchie! which will certainly mean that they have lost caste at the Treasury. Mr. G. rapped Northcote very smartly over the fingers.

The prospects about the cloture division are certainly not good, but the Government seem to be assured of *a* majority on Marriott's amendment which is held to be aimed at *any* closing power. The majority for the Government mainly depends on the action of the moderate Home Rulers, over whom the greatest tyranny is being exercised by the Parnellites. They want to establish that closure of any kind means coercion, i.e. no closure, no renewal of Coercive Act.

It is too soon to discuss the propriety of renewing the Protection of Life [and] Property Act, but Mr. G. is beginning to believe that in present circumstances a pure renewal of that Act is not possible, and that whatever is required must be met by supplementing the ordinary law in other forms.

My own belief is that the present means of coercion have wholly failed except as regards shutting up prominent political agitators. For these the Act was not really intended; while for those who commit outrages such 'kid-glove' confinement is rather a pleasant change. In spite of the difficulty of getting evidence which might even be enhanced when there was less likelihood of acquittal, I should be inclined to try the effect of substituting a Judicial Commission for trial by jury in agrarian cases.

Tuesday, 28 March. Litton, the Land Commissioner, has been summoned to appear before the Lords Committee and is actually coming over. Mr. G. is evidently not a little annoyed, after all that has been said on subject.

I had an interesting dinner at the Breadalbanes on Saturday at their new

[1] See 1 Dec. 1881.

house—Harcourt House in Cavendish Square—which they have done up in beautiful style. Besides ordinary social folk, we had Chamberlain, O'Connor Power, John Morley, and Sir W. Gull. I was very glad to make the acquaintance of O'Connor Power. In spite of a very unprepossessing appearance—(his features are all smallpoxed)—he is an attractive-mannered man. He spoke in uncertain tones about Ireland. He had not words enough to express his sense of the greatness and beneficence of the Land Act; he remains utterly opposed to coercion and is dead against any closing power. Chamberlain (who by the way is by far the best hated man in public life now) told me what had struck him most in his official life was the great ability and loyalty of the permanent Civil Service. Gull was saying he detected in Chamberlain a strong likeness to W. Pitt, according to the pictures.

The Baronet list was submitted yesterday—9 in all. It appears, somewhat curiously, that the roll of baronets has decreased since 1840, despite the increase of wealth and population. I am afraid more will be disappointed than pleased. That is the worst of all honours. For every one you please, you offend 9 others.

Wednesday, 29 March. Mr. G. was astir quite early this morning and wanted me before I was downstairs. He was considerably exercised in his mind about the impression which Forster's speech yesterday had produced that the Government had in contemplation further, i.e. more stringent, coercive measures.[1] This is impossible, as the Government have not yet considered the matter, nor could they consider it, having regard to the changes in the state of Ireland from week to week. It could only (as Mr. G. said) be a premature conclusion, and accordingly in all probability an erroneous one. That something will have to be done as the time for the expiration of the Coercion Act draws near is pretty certain, but I do hope the measures which may have to be taken will partake more of the nature of strengthening the ordinary law and even suspending trial by jury temporarily than that of arresting on suspicion, which has lost its terrorism in Ireland and is worse than useless (because it is irritating) for dealing with the outrage-mongers.

A very lengthy letter arrived from the Queen today.[2] It was mainly about royal marriage grants. She was pleased with Mr. G.'s speech on the Prince Leopold grant and naturally horrified at Healy's and Storey's speeches. She referred also to the necessity of taking into early consideration the question of provisions for the Prince of Wales' children, and also expressed a strong desire that an undertaking should be given that Princess Beatrice, whom she evidently intends keeping permanently by her side, should in the event of her surviving Her Royal Mother be treated like her other sisters. She commented on the abstention of Dilke and Fawcett in the division list on the

[1] See *Parl. Deb.* cclxviii. 199–203.
[2] See her letter from Mentone, 26 Mar. 1882, Guedalla, ii. 182–3.

Leopold grant, characteristically observing that it was unfortunate that 'such people' should be in the Government and that their conduct on this occasion must be an effectual bar against their becoming Cabinet Ministers. Mr. G. admitted that Dilke and Fawcett ought certainly to have communicated with him about their abstention, which however he believed was solely due to their desire to avoid embarrassment from the previous votes they had recorded.[1] The other matters will be considered by him in concert with Lord G[ranville] and Hartington.

Saturday, 1 April. Thursday evening was an exciting one and exciting till a late hour. The adjourned closure debate was resumed by Bright who was very fine and impressive. It takes a great deal now to 'wind him up', but when he is wound up he has, despite of a somewhat weakened voice, lost little of his charm of manner and language—his simple sentences and clear diction. He was conciliatory and unprovocative, rubbed up no one and [is] said even to have turned two votes (the Fitzwilliams). I came back to the House after dinner. Mitchell Henry was speaking well and made some excellent points by quoting Butt's language a few years ago. He was followed by Sexton, who was very eloquent, very vituperative, and very dangerous, as well as displaying great bad taste in his references to Bright. Northcote wound up for the Opposition. He was less humdrum than usual, made some good points, and altogether quite lively for him. He was followed by Mr. G., whose speech was closely reasoned, fiery, and combined in high degree the two great qualities of debating and oratory. After a few bitter words from Healy, the division was taken with a better result than was expected, the majority for the Government being 39. There were some dozen Liberal abstentions; but only two Liberals in addition to the Tellers (Marriott and Joseph Cowen) found their way in the Tory lobby—John Walter and P. Taylor. I hope the 'Times' liked his company.[2]

The Cabinet met yesterday. They have determined for the present to stick to their guns; at any rate not to *declare* any intention of qualifying the form of the First Resolution. They detest the 'two-thirds' majority proposal, which would no doubt make the closing power more acceptable to many; but, as the Government are likely to be pressed very hard by Lubbock's amendment for a proportional majority, I expect some concession will have to be made. I still think the best course would be to propose two closing powers. One—to meet the plethora of talk—consisting of the present Government proposal with the bare majority principle, but with notice beforehand. The other—to meet *bonâ fide* obstruction—consisting of a simple two-thirds majority without qualifications. The Government would then be adhering to their bare majority; would secure a more effectual weapon; and would be making the

[1] See G.'s reply, Guedalla, ii. 183.
[2] John Walter was the proprietor of *The Times*.

closure more palatable to many Liberals and less distasteful to many Conservatives.

The prospects of finance are by no means brilliant. There is a small surplus of revenue on the account for the year just ended, but on the present basis of taxation, there is only just an equilibrium of income and expenditure for the new year. Indeed, it looks as if some additional taxes will have to be imposed. Mr. G. seems to contemplate the possibility of finding this addition out of assessed taxes; query carriages.

Duleep Singh has been *at* Mr. G. again about his private affairs which seem rather desperate.[1]

I have been concerned again about the Langtry affair. Mr. G. presented her with a copy of his pet book, *Sister Dora*.[2] She is evidently trying to make social capital out of the acquaintance which she has scraped with him. Most disagreeable things with all kinds of exaggerations are being said. I took the occasion of putting in a word and cautioning him against the wiles of the woman, whose reputation is in such bad odour that, despite all the endeavours of H.R.H.,[3] nobody will receive her in their houses.

Sunday, 2 April. (Salisbury) Had a long walk and talk with Fawcett this afternoon. He regrets very much that the closure has been made so much of by the Government; that in short they went so far as to stake their existence on such a question. He believes no vote was ever given more unwillingly by a party, and hopes very much that the Government will now treat them with a light hand; in other words grant the two-thirds, making such a closing power a sessional order. He is quite conscious that the Ministers are deeply committed against a proportional majority, but nevertheless thinks under the circumstances it would be far preferable to say that, though they still hold that the bare majority proposed with its safeguards is in their opinion the best form on which to base the closure, they are willing to defer to the strong feeling in the House and to give the two-thirds closing power the trial of a session. It would then be good policy for all sides to join in making such a closing power work well. If the Government on the other hand stick to their present proposal and force it down the throats of the House, it will be the object of the House to show that it is liable to abuse and to put obstacles in the way of its working.

Fawcett thinks there is no doubt that the great impetus which has been given of late to thrift and the extended facilities which have been afforded to

---

[1] This deposed (but pensioned) Maharajah of Lahore was in persistent financial difficulties and complained of them loudly, publicly and privately. See 7 Aug. 1883 and 10 Dec. 1884.

[2] *Sister Dora: a Biography* by Margaret Lonsdale, first published in 1879, was an account of a nurse, Dora Pattison.

[3] The Prince of Wales.

saving by the instrumentality of the P[ost] O[ffice] have had a very sensible effect on the revenue derived from excise and customs. I think Mr. G. must bring this out in his budget.

In regard to Ireland he touched on rather a striking point. It is remarkable that in the disturbed state of the country and in the midst of the raids made against property, there is no instance of the destruction of any *Government* property, such as mail bags and telegraph wires. This would look as if the agitation were aimed wholly against landlords and not against the English Government.

He would evidently like to go in for extended P[ost] O[ffice] and telegraph facilities, and (not without reason) thinks it questionable how far the postal and telegraphic services should be made a means of taxation.

He takes a dismal view of party prospects. He thinks any appeal to the country in the immediate future would result in greater disaster for the Government than in 1874; and he is certain that if the Government risk their existence, the Tories would immediately dissolve and make out that the action of the Government was a confession that their Irish policy had failed and an admission that they were unable to deal with the Irish problem.

He commented on the absence of any strong popular feeling for legislation or reforms. The country will never take up more than one question at a time, and that question now which wholly absorbed public attention was Ireland.

Wednesday, 5 April. Another terrible murder in Ireland this week—this time a woman of the upper class is the victim, which makes the deed the more atrocious. This makes the second agrarian murder within a week. The two unfortunate victims are Mr. Herbert and Mrs. Smythe. The country seems to be in a worse state than ever. It is going through by far the most terrible social revolution (the tithe revolt in 1832 which most resembles the present one not even excepted) that has ever disturbed that wretched island. Public opinion is demanding fresh measures and not unnaturally. The difficulty is to know what to do. Some call out for the replacement of Forster by someone else; others for martial law. One thing is clear; coercion has practically failed, though without it things might have been worse. There are all kinds of objections to suspending trial by jury, not the least of them being the difficulty of obtaining evidence; but I think the attempt ought to be made whereby agrarian crime should be tried before a Commission of 3 judges. Like at cricket, a change of bowling is required; and as in that game it is not always the best, fastest, or deadliest bowling that gets wickets, so possibly the institution of such a Commission might do more good than that horrible system of arbitrary arrest.

Forster thinks, and Mr. G. strongly agrees with him, that the Executive *must* be strengthened. Cowper's intended resignation must be close at hand

and will offer an opportunity of sending a really strong Lord Lieutenant. Old 'Buckshot' actually suggested the idea that he should be made Lord Lieutenant or rather 'Lord Deputy' with a seat in the Cabinet and the Viceroyalty in commission! This of course Mr. G. cannot hear of. He turns his attention to Lord Spencer, who I expect, poor man, will feel it his duty to go and will have to go. Many people are calling out for Forster's resignation; and if it be really desirable, there can be no doubt that the Government have no business to be mealy-mouthed or too tender-hearted, and that however disagreeable and distressing it may be, they ought to sacrifice the poor old man for the good of the country. But against this, there is the strong objection which always attaches to 'swopping horses when crossing a stream'; while his removal would be looked upon by a large section of the community as a mean resort of the Government to shift the responsibility on the shoulders of one individual and to make a scapegoat of him; and moreover there is no one specially marked out as his successor.

Thursday, 6 April. The Queen continues to be very wrath with Dilke and Fawcett for not voting for the Leopold grant. They certainly I think ought to have communicated previously with Mr. G. and to have asked his leave to abstain; but to have changed their front suddenly would have necessitated explanations and would have probably led to very disagreeable remarks. Dilke sticks to it and has even told the Prince of Wales that he could not have acted differently and had no intention under the circumstances of making anything like a public recantation. Lord Granville and Mr. G. have endeavoured to allay the susceptibilities of H.M. by referring to Dilke's assurances on taking office, which though expressive more or less of regret as to the past were confined to an undertaking that he would desist in future from opposing such grants.

Harcourt made a fool of himself the other day in the lobby with Anderson about Anderson's declining to support the closure, and seems to have used most injudicious and even threatening language. What a pity it is Harcourt has not got a little more suaveness and tact!

The Queen takes exception to the number of baronets submitted. She thinks nine is too large a batch. However, precedents are all against her, and so I suppose She will give way.[1]

Affairs in Egypt have the appearance of trouble ahead. Freycinet objects to Lord G[ranville]'s proposal to send out experts from here and France to look into the cost of administration of government. He is also strongly against including the Porte in the European Powers for the purpose of joint action in Egyptian affairs. He considers that the present difficulty is mainly due to the effeteness of the Khedive and suggests another man, Hakim.

[1] See 28 Mar. and, for the Queen's acquiescence, 20 Apr. 1882.

H. Murray's appointment to the Secretaryship of Customs has given rise to much criticism outside and inside the House, and to considerable disappointment among revenue officers. There never was an individual appointment which was made so entirely on public grounds, which were simply these—Walpole, though a clever man and recommended by his Board for the post, was not considered the right man, and the Department was greatly in need of being strengthened particularly at a time when great changes were going on for amalgamating the two Bonding systems of the Inland Revenue and Customs. So that the present occasion was a singularly unfortunate and inopportune one for raising the question of the shewing of too great preference to Treasury clerks and to ex- and present private secretaries. Mr. G. never was on stronger ground as regards the making of an appointment, and a 'job' was never further from being perpetrated, notwithstanding the lines in *Vanity Fair* and their irreverent allusions to Horace [Seymour] and myself.[1]

Saturday, 8 April. Mr. G. wrote again yesterday to the Queen on the Dilke affair.[2] The ground he took up was that Dilke's not voting in the Leopold grant division should be regarded as an abstention by way of transition from the stage of opposition to support, and that his action under the circumstances was preferable to explanation. Mr. G., however, admitted that abstention from voting on such a question by a member of the Government had not in principle been condoned and the Government certainly could not bind themselves to acquiesce in it in future. Mr. G. will take an opportunity of having a little talk with Dilke.

A reference to the memorandum drawn up by Mr. G. in 1862 and adopted by Lord Palmerston's Cabinet on the subject of provisions for the Royal Family, which has been uniformly acted upon by successive Governments, appears to Mr. G. to govern and amply provide for the case of Princess

---

[1] In *Vanity Fair*, 8 Apr. 1882, p. 190, there appeared the following verse:

'The Job at the Customs'
Said honest Sir Charles, 'It is only fair play
That Walpole should have it, and so I shall say.'
'Stop! Stop!' said the Colonel, 'don't be in a hurry:
P'rhaps Horace might gain if they gave it to Murray.'
So Reggie and Cobbie and Algy—and all
Of the 'ring', who arrange when the Great Man shall rob
From others for them, gave to Herbie the call—
And Young Hopeful suggested Old Hopeless's job.

Sir Charles DuCane was the Chairman of the Board of Customs; Colonel Frederick Romilly was the deputy Chairman and Horace Seymour's father-in-law. Horace Seymour eventually became a Commissioner of Customs. See 7 Nov. and 24 Dec. 1884. 'Reggie' is Reginald Brett, Hartington's private secretary; 'Cobbie' is EWH, and 'Algy' Algernon West. *Vanity Fair* was fond of calling Herbert G. 'Young Hopeful' and G. 'Old Hopeless'. See for 1882, pp. 136 and 255.

[2] See G.'s letter to Ponsonby, 6 Apr. 1882, Guedalla, ii. 184–5.

Beatrice, about which the Queen expressed herself so much concerned; and that accordingly no further action and no further undertaking are necessary.[1]

The Prince of Wales has again recurred to the subject of a baronetcy for Freake.[2] Mr. G. thinks that a knighthood would be sufficient and preferable, especially having regard to the reported wild habits of Freake *fils*, and the political proclivities of Freake *père*.

Mr. G. kicks rather against the continuance of police surveillance at Hawarden; and as it is a matter on which the Home Office cannot interfere with the local authorities, he has dropped a hint to the chairman of the Flintshire Quarter Sessions that the caretaking should be dispensed with, believing as he does that there is not a 'shadow of a shade of danger' and willing as he would be to walk from one end of Ireland to the other.

It is most remarkable how strongly the present Irish agitation against rent resembles that of 1833–4 against tithe. The Parnellites have adopted with extraordinary accuracy the tactics of the anti-tithe men; and notwithstanding the application of coercion and the adoption of remedial measures, the outrages on the whole have kept up and even increased in number.

Lord Spencer has returned from Mentone. He has expressed his willingness to bow to Mr. G.'s strongly expressed wishes as regards his going to Ireland, and so to prefer duty for the public good to his own natural inclinations; but it does not appear so clear that Cowper would be willing after all to turn out now, as his resignation at a time when there is no real lull in Irish affairs might be considered to imply a grave reflection on his competency.

Wednesday, 12 April. Forster's report on the situation in Ireland comes to this:[3]

(1) The November rent recently due has been generally paid with some bad exceptions, notably where the arrears question is most severely felt.

(2) There is no open resistance to the law, and the Land League may be considered in a great measure defeated.

(3) There is less boycotting.

(4) Outrages are, however, very bad, especially as regards serious crime, which may be attributed to
    a. the fierce passions evoked by the struggle,
    b. impunity from punishment.

(5) Witnesses won't come forward, and juries won't convict; but it is possible that more evidence would be obtained if there were a greater certainty of conviction to make it worth the while of the witnesses to risk the consequences.

[1] The Cabinet Minute of 24 June 1862 set out the financial arrangements which should be made for the Queen's children. According to the Minute princesses should receive an allowance on the occasion of their marriage or upon the demise of the Crown, whichever is first. A copy of the Minute is in the Palmerston Papers, Broadlands.

[2] See 11 Apr. 1881 and 20 Apr. 1882.   [3] See Wemyss Reid, ii. 415–19.

His proposals are:

(1) That to secure convictions, agrarian offences must be tried by special commissions.

(2) That an appeal should be made to localities for material aid, such as the enrolment of special constables.

(3) That fines be imposed for connivance at outrages.

(4) That districts be made to pay for any special police charges rendered necessary by the prevalence of disturbance.

(5) That compensation should be paid to the victims of outrages or their relatives.

(6) That men out at night should be liable to be arrested under suspicion.

Even with these additional powers, he at present does not see his way to being able to dispense with a renewal of the Coercion Act. If the power of arrest does not deter criminals, it at any rate enables the Government to put murderers out of the way by locking them up.

He likes Mr. G.'s suggestion which is to have a law applicable to the U.K. to enable the proclamation in a district of a combination intended to conduce to illegal acts.

Mr. G. foresees immense difficulty in obtaining a renewal of the Coercion Act.

As regards suspending trial by jury, he thinks it may be worth considering whether the law of unanimity might not be dispensed with in England and Ireland, in the same way as it at present is in Scotland.

Under his Anti-Contract Association scheme, he would try all members of it by judges; and so this would probably meet the case of agrarian offences in Ireland which proceed from the Land League.

Whatever coercive measures may be decided upon, these with others to extend the purchase clauses of the Land Act and to deal with arrears (both of which questions must be taken in hand) will absorb all the remaining legislative time of the session; and all the Government measures will have to be thrown overboard.

Mr. G.'s forecast of the programme of the session is:

(a) Necessary finance and procedure till Whitsuntide (he is sanguine who thinks procedure with the necessary interruptions will be disposed of by that time).

(b) Refer to Grand Committees any non-party measures.

(c) Serious Irish legislation until the bitter end.

As regards the Irish Executive, Mr. G.'s idea is that if Lord Spencer takes Cowper's place it should be regarded as a temporary appointment, and he should be allowed to retain his seat in the Cabinet, Lord Carlingford being told off to do his departmental work.

Lord Spencer evidently less likes the prospect the more he thinks of it. He is afraid that with Forster his position might be so difficult as to be untenable. A quarrel of course would make bad worse and lead to fresh complications, but though Forster may have the bit very strongly between his teeth and be liable to bolt accordingly, it must be remembered he has never had anyone yet to assert himself against him (Forster). Cowper has evidently been a pure cipher and afraid to stand up against Forster. A letter of his to Spencer gives one a fair idea of how little he seems to rise to the occasion. He has literally nothing to suggest, except it is the suppression of the Ladies Land League, which he says Forster is afraid to do owing to the effect such a step might have upon the Radicals. If, however, Cowper is convinced of the necessity for it and is thwarted, he should appeal to Mr. G. He is evidently not equal to the post, and Mr. G. says he read Cowper's letter with melancholy. It gave one the idea that he (C.) was 'hopeless'.

Everybody was startled the day before yesterday by the news of Parnell's release, but it turned out that he had been merely liberated on parole to enable him to attend the funeral of his nephew.

Old Gortchakoff has at last finally retired. Giers takes his place. Thornton says that the change may be regarded as a blow to Ignatieff and his Slav party.

Thursday, 13 April. Lord Salisbury and Northcote delivered their philippics last night at Liverpool. Personal abuse was conspicuous by its absence, and the charges were not very overpowering. Lord Salisbury rested his main arguments on false grounds. He contended that there never had been an agitation against property until the iniquitous policy, dating since the Land Act of 1870, had been inaugurated of transferring the property of one class to another. He conveniently forgot the great tithe agitation 50 years ago, which resembles so strongly the present attacks against property. He also argued as if to the Liberal policy of the last 15 years was due the creation of [a] new kind of proprietorship in land—a joint proprietorship, likewise conveniently forgetting that it had existed in Ireland for years and years and in those parts of Ireland where there had been greatest prosperity and least disturbance, namely in Ulster. Northcote's tone towards Mr. Gladstone was sneering and in singularly bad taste. He and Lord Salisbury both announced their advocacy of an extension of the purchase clauses of the Land Act, and announced it as if it were 'their own child', instead of being a foundling at which they had for years persistently turned up their noses. I think I am right in saying that in 1879 Lord Monck strongly pressed the late Government to go in for the creation of a peasant proprietorship and to utilise some of the Irish Church surplus funds in accomplishing this end; but they declined point blank to have anything to say to the idea.

The main charge brought against the Government by their political opponents about Ireland is that they did not in 1880 renew the Peace

Preservation Act, which expired a few days after the Liberal administration was formed. To this the Opposition attribute all the subsequent evils. This is, of course, pure supposition, and it is fair to meet it with counter-suppositions. Supposing then the Act had been renewed in 1880; what might and probably would have been the consequences?

(1) A disruption probably in the Government and certainly in the Liberal party, when it was essential that both the Government and its followers should be united.

(2) An immediate issue of the no-rent manifesto. (Blennerhassett told me lately he knew it was ready for issue at that time.)

(3) The creation of a strong sympathy in Great Britain with the so-called Irish party.

(4) The addition of Ulster to the No Rent party.

(5) The absence of the only powerful engine with which to meet the no-rent cry—a Land Act. (To meet the cry against non-payment of fair rents is difficult enough; to meet the cry against non-payment of unjust or supposed unjust rents would have been impossible.)

(6) A certainty of less rent.

(7) A feeble Coercion Act; and with its existence, far greater, if not insuperable, difficulty in obtaining subsequently stronger powers to meet the subsequent necessities.

(8) A united Parnellite party, instead of a diminished and broken up one; and the sympathy of all the Irish Liberals inside as well as outside Ulster.

The main things which are now occupying Mr. G.'s attention are (1) how to deal with the pressing question of arrears; (2) how to extend the purchase clauses of the Land Act. He is inclined to think the latter can't be worked without a simultaneous extension of local government—the creation of some local bodies with whom the Government could deal; but this is touching upon dangerous and most delicate ground.

Sunday, 16 April. Mr. G. has been more than once harping on the question of creating new local machinery through which to work the purchase clauses when extended. He considers that the turning point is in the arrangement rather than in the pecuniary responsibility. The Irish tenant cannot be accepted as the debtor to the Imperial Treasury. The political objections are insurmountable apart from the financial ones. To make his responsibility real there must be bodies of real weight on whom to throw the working of the clauses. The Irish are too strong to be governed by an agency which has a purely English character like 'the Castle' and Whitehall. In the circumstances the safest course is probably a bold one, namely to call into existence 4 provincial bodies 'according to Lord Russell's idea'. (I don't know when that was projected). The great objection to attempting to go in for such a bold course seems to be the want of time in which to mature a plan.

It seems pretty certain that Spencer *is* to go to Ireland. Mr. G. considers him a better man for the place than Lord Carlingford, who is the only other Minister who would do and who could probably be pressed into going; and it seems necessary to secure a *Minister* with whom to replace Cowper in order to soften down the blow. Poor Lord Spencer goes most unwillingly and I don't wonder at it. Forster seems ready to make with him a division of duties, which would probably leave Spencer in charge of the Executive.

Old Forster has within the last few days become more alarmed and is afraid that strong and immediate legislation will be unavoidable. He never seems to know his own mind from day to day. One day he thinks it best to carry on as he is; three days later he says he must have this and that at a moment's notice.

Her Majesty was not unnaturally annoyed that the Irish Government never apprised her of the circumstances connected with Parnell's release on parole, and telegraphed here in a great state of mind on the presumption that it could not be true. It was just one of those stupid omissions to give her information which she has a distinct right to have.[1]

Parnell seems to be scrupulously anxious not to contravene in the smallest way the conditions of his parole. Among the few of his friends he saw while passing through was O'Shea. This man has been writing to Mr. G. to remind him of the overtures he made last summer with a view to securing the support of the Parnellite party to the Land Act, and has been asking Mr. G. whether he does not now regret having refused the offer. He (O'Shea) has taken the opportunity of offering to negotiate again; but he admits that he has not now the same authority to do so as he had last year. He makes himself out to be Parnell's special confidant, and as having been offered the leadership of the Irish party 2 years ago. His principal terms are (1) a settlement of arrears by a *grant* and (2) an extension of the purchase clauses. In return for this, the Parnellites to exercise all their moral power to stop outrages (as if they were not bound to do so now in any case) and to cease all parliamentary opposition. It may be as well to know what the views of the Irish party are; but it seems impossible to have any direct dealings with them. They are probably not the least to be trusted. I expect O'Shea himself is, though a gentleman by birth and a brother-in-law of Sir E. Wood, not of the 'straightest'.

I had a long letter yesterday from Willie Compton who has just returned from visiting Clifford Lloyd, the special magistrate for Co. Clare. He says he can only characterise the landlords as a parcel of funks, and the magistracy he describes as hopelessly rotten and equally cowardly and cowed. The magistrates decline to convict even in the face of evidence, and the constables naturally become disheartened. One magistrate out of sheer fright went and signed a petition for the release of a suspect whom he knew to be a leader of the intimidation party of his own district—the local 'Capt. Moonlight'.

[1] Guedalla, ii. 185-6.

Compton says he never could have believed without seeing how great is the effect of threatening letters. To them he greatly attributes the state of collapse and the success of the agitation.

Thursday, 20 April. Mr. G. returned from Hawarden on Monday. He is well with the exception of a slight cough which is hanging about him.

The Queen has at last approved the immediate creation of the baronets submitted to her, with the addition too of Freake, whom the Prince of Wales has so persistently and somewhat questionably (if not 'fishily') pressed on Mr. G. She has only given her assent grudgingly and after the precedents of batches of similar dimensions had been more than once brought home to her. Why she should be so apprehensive of the effect of the simultaneous announcement of 9 or 10 gentlemen for the commonplace honour of Barts. is not easy to understand.[1]

She is much disconcerted about the verdict of MacLean, who fired the shot at her on leaving Windsor Station a few weeks ago. The moment she had received the result of the trial yesterday evening, she fired off to Mr. G. a long cipher telegram, which reached me after I had gone to bed. If half-cracked men of such dangerous propensities are to be acquitted on the ground of insanity, there will never be an end to them till they have wounded or killed her. One can't help sympathising with these very natural fears of a Sovereign and woman combined, but detention in custody during Her Majesty's pleasure, which was comprised in the verdict and which means indefinite confinement in the Criminal Lunatic Asylum, is a sentence not far removed in severity from a charge of high treason and its consequences, which would have meant penal servitude. The Attorney General[2] told me this morning that in face of the medical evidence no other verdict was possible; he was perfectly satisfied with it and so also are all the Press.

Mr. G. has at last been devoting a little attention to the Budget, out of which nothing can be made. Expenditure is very heavy, and the revenue if not retrogressive is sluggish. It is against expenditure which the Tories might fairly level their attack. The cry of economy is a thing of the past. The want of it is the worst characteristic in the modern Liberal or Radical, and makes him in this respect compare badly with the old Whigs, with whom economy and retrenchment was part of their creed. Mr. G. sighed over this the other day. In writing to Rosebery about the salaries of the Scotch judges, he said that in matters of economy nowadays he considered himself an 'old mouldy

---

[1] See 11 Apr. 1881 and 6 Apr. 1882. On 21 Apr. 1881, G. wrote letters offering baronetcies to Henry Hussey Vivian, Charles J. Freake, Charles E. Adam, Michael Arthur Bass, Joseph Pease, J. G. Richardson, Alexander Matheson, Thomas Ashton, Frederick Milbank, and John Bennet Lawes. Add. MS. 44545, ff. 124–5. In all of these letters, except that to Freake, G. remarked on the reason for the offer and the pleasure its acceptance would bring. Only to Freake did he write a bare note making the offer in the briefest manner. See 30 Apr. 1882 for refusals.   [2] Sir Henry James.

landmark on a deserted shore'. To return to the Budget, the revenue on its present basis would exactly meet the expenditure for the new year with a moderate margin, were it not that the Government are pledged to give something towards the relief of the maintenance of highways, which will have to be found, though local taxation cannot be dealt with this session. In order to provide the requisite money for this purpose, Mr. G. proposes to raise the carriage duty, and he would like to hand over part of the tax thus increased to the local authorities instead of making the relief an additional grant-in-aid, but there seem to be insurmountable difficulties as to doing this.

Yesterday was the anniversary of Lord Beaconsfield's death, which according to the *St. James' Gazette* Mr. G. singled out for entertaining some of his advanced parliamentary supporters.[1] The memory of the world, especially perhaps of the political world, is short—'out of sight is out of mind'—but I should say that this has been remarkably the case with Lord Beaconsfield. One seldom now hears his name or his doings quoted.

The death of Canon Pearson, who was a remarkable man in his way, has placed a stall at Windsor at Mr. G.'s disposal. He did think of offering it to Dr. Butler, whom I think he now regrets not having placed at Westminster as Stanley's successor;[2] but as the Dean of Windsor[3] says that the Queen has a special predilection for Boyd Carpenter and as the Windsor canonries have always been regarded as the special perquisite of the Sovereign, Mr. G. has submitted Mr. Boyd Carpenter's name. Carpenter is, I believe, a Broad *Low* Churchman, and it is about time some preferment were given by Mr. G. to one of the Low Church School.

Goschen wrote the other day deprecating the present practice of M.P.'s memorialising the Government on questions of the day, which is quite an innovation. Mr. G. agrees with him that the practice is a decidedly objectionable one, but thinks it is probably due to the fact that in the present state of public business, when the best support which the followers of the Government can give is silence, memorialising is the simpler, if not the only, way in which they can give expression to their views.

No one has yet been found for the Governorship of the Isle of Man. Harcourt, in whose gift the appointment really rests, offered it to Sir E. Wood as a small mark of appreciation by the Government of his services in the Transvaal. Sir E. Wood, however, has declined the post. He prefers his military career. The only persons Mr. G. has been able to suggest to Harcourt are Colonel Romilly (he is too old) and Spencer Walpole Jun., the author.

Forster has put before the Cabinet in a clear memorandum his views of the situation in Ireland. They are much the same as those he expounded to

---

[1] The *St. James's Gazette*, 20 Apr. 1882, p. 4, noted that G. 'celebrated the occasion' by having 18 gentlemen to dinner, 'selected . . . from the more advanced section of Mr. Gladstone's followers'.   [2] See 11 Aug. 1881.

[3] Gerald Wellesley. See also 25 Oct. 1882 for the question of Windsor canonries.

Mr. G. and which I have already noted (April 12th). They briefly amount to this as regards his proposals:

(1) That the clauses of the Westmeath Act of 1870 should be re-enacted, i.e. those relating to fines and the quasi-curfew.

(2) That for all agrarian offences excepting serious ones against the person, the resident magistrates' summary powers should be enlarged.

(3) That murders and other serious outrages against the person should be tried by a Legal Commission.

He is still not sure that these additional powers will suffice without a re-newal of the Coercion Act, but he seems to be willing to allow the question of its renewal to depend upon the state of the country later on and upon the effect of the new powers which he seeks to obtain. Meanwhile he is prepared to let out the suspects by degrees.

Chamberlain has written strongly in favour of making an attempt to effect something of a conciliation between the Government and the Irish party by adopting in the main the Land Act Amendment Bill of which Healy & Co. have given notice. Mr. G. regards the bill itself as an indication of moderation on the part of the Parnellites, who by their bill practically endorse the Land legislation of the Government. The bill is not an extravagant one. It provides for a better definition of the tenants' improvement clauses, for dealing with arrears, and for extending the purchase clauses. In short it does not materially differ from what the Tories have themselves promised to go in for.

The question of replacing Lord Cowper is still in abeyance. I am not sure whether it would not be wiser on the whole to leave things as they are. The Tories will say of him in a small way what they would say of Forster were he to be removed, that the Government having failed in their Irish policy are offering up as a sacrifice the poor unfortunate Viceroy; and the Irish will swear that it is an avowal that coercion has failed and that his removal and replacement by a man of avowedly greater parts is merely bolstering up still more the 'Castle' which is so hateful to them.

Mr. G. begged Lord G[ranville] the other day to instruct Lord Dufferin to give the Sultan a strong nudge about the Armenian question which he (the Sultan) is evidently now trying to shuffle out of, and which he will probably succeed in shelving as long as he can play off one Power against another; and that is his game now, which is made easy for him to play by the action of Germany.[1]

The outlook in Egypt is not brilliant. There seems to be a fear that Arabi Bey is not strong enough to hold his military party, who are likely to break away from him if they do not put an end to him. Wilfrid Blunt shewed me the other day some very striking letters he had had from Arabi. If one is to judge from those letters, nothing can be more charming or better disposed than the

---

[1] See G.'s letter of 13 Apr., Ramm, i. 359.

man is himself. He writes in a most enlightened manner, full of professions to respect Egyptian obligations, to reform the administrative evils and to create a national Egypt.

Mr. G. hinted to Lord Granville today that if anything were to be gained by the change he would willingly and gladly surrender the Chancellorship of the Exchequer. He is evidently somewhat overcome by the pressure of work, and not unnaturally disappointed at the materials at his disposal out of which to form his Budget; but I don't see how his immediate surrender of the office would facilitate any changes in connection with Irish administration.[1]

Went on Tuesday to see Mrs. Langtry in *She Stoops to Conquer*. She is certainly lovely on the stage in appearance and very passable as an actress. I went with Lady Rosebery, whom I like and who is very kind to me.[2]

I am afraid the intimacy on paper with Mrs. Langtry is increasing. She has evidently been told to resort to the double-envelope system which secures respect from our rude hands;[3] and she is now making pretty constant use of this privilege. I regret this much, and I must try and find out how far she is making capital out of this privilege and boasting in proportion.

W. B. Richmond's picture of Mr. G. for the hall of Christ Church is reported by Watts in the most generous terms to be a great success.

Saturday, 22 April. Rosebery told me yesterday that the Prince of Wales had been mooting to him the question of the vacant Garter. H.R.H. mentioned Lord Sydney as a very proper and worthy recipient of it; he said Lord Sefton had made known to him his (Sefton's) strong desire for it; he (H.R.H.) also hinted at St. Albans, in the same way as the Queen did last year. As regards these candidates, Lord Sydney and the Duke of St. Albans have already been politically rewarded by Lord Lieutenancies. Of the three I should be inclined to take Sefton for choice, were it not that the next Garter must go to Lord Derby and that would mean two Garters following presented to Lancashire notabilities; moreover solicitations through H.R.H. are rather against Sefton.

Mr. and Mrs. Gladstone have been invited to Windsor for two nights this week—an unparalleled civility—on the occasion of the Leopold marriage.[4] They are pleased and gratified by the attention.

The Government have determined to take morning sittings on Tuesday— high time too. Tuesday evenings have up to the present time been practically

[1] Ramm, i. 362.

[2] Here there is a sentence so heavily inked and pencilled over as to be almost illegible— indeed the last word is illegible. The sentence reads: 'It is a thousand pities that in her great position she should have "no . . .".'

[3] G. allowed certain people to correspond with him in absolute privacy by enclosing a note and envelope in another envelope. Only the outer envelope would the private secretaries open. See also 5 May 1882.

[4] i.e. the wedding of Prince Leopold, the Queen's youngest son, to Princess Helen of Waldeck, which was to take place on 27 Apr. 1882. See 30 Apr. 1882.

wasted by successive counts-out. The rights of private members under such circumstances are all moonshine. Wednesdays and one night (say Friday) would be ample time to give up for the airing of the crotchets by private members.

Monday, 24 April. Mr. G. delivered himself of his Budget this afternoon. Considering that, with the exception of a small addition to taxation—an increase in the carriage duty—practically no changes were proposed, and that the materials were so slight, my belief is that his last (as I fear it will be)[1] Budget statement will as a financial exposition compare favourably with any of its predecessors. The construction was masterliness itself; and the touches of interest and life which he gave to an unvarnished tale and to dry figures were extraordinary. What must have been the essence of dullness in the hands of anyone else succeeded in engaging the wrapt attention of the House for fully 2 hours.

Irish matters don't progress, though they occupied almost the entire time of the Cabinet on Saturday. They seem to have determined to deal with arrears at any rate; and as regards stronger measures, they are inclined to try what further strengthening of the law will do, and to let the renewal of the Coercion Act depend upon the effect of such new measures. Lord Cowper has written about his position. It appears that Forster, wholly unauthorised and entirely off his own bat, broached with Lord Cowper the subject of placing temporarily a Cabinet Minister as Lord Lieutenant. Lord Cowper says he can't submit to such terms, but in the most angelic, gentlemanlike, and good-tempered manner offers to resign if he is wanted to do so.

There was a disagreeable-looking 'leak' in the *Daily News* this morning. I am inclined to credit Arnold Forster with it.[2]

Sunday, 30 April. (Charters) Came down here on Friday having been rather out of sorts. It has not been an uneventful week.

Mr. G. was, I think, not dissatisfied with his Budget speech, as indeed he well might be, and was up at his usual hour on Tuesday, bright and in good spirits, and apparently none the worse for his efforts over-night with the exception of being a little husky.

---

[1] Because of G.'s intention to resign his second post as Chancellor of the Exchequer which he did in December. See 1 Dec. 1882.

[2] The leader in the *Daily News*, 24 Apr. 1882, pp. 4–5, cols. 8, 1–2, stated that the subject of the Cabinet meeting on 22 Apr. had probably been the government of Ireland. It remarked on the unsatisfactory nature of the division of authority between Cowper, characterized as a cipher, and Forster and urged a new and more powerful viceroy, namely Spencer. On 29 Apr. G. wrote Forster about these leakages and concluded: 'I think you will have observed that this leakage happens specially in Irish matters.' See letterbook copy, Add. MS. 44545, f. 127. See 23 Nov. 1881 for EWH's suspicion of Forster's adopted son and private secretary, H. O. Arnold-Forster.

Tuesday was devoted to the Corrupt Practices Bill. It is not received with avidity, the general impression being that though excellent in intention it may by being too severe overshoot the mark and fail in its object.

Wednesday was quite an important day, as it was taken up by the discussion of the bill brought in by the Parnellite party with the name of Parnell himself on the bill, who is the reputed author of it, to amend the Land Act. It is the first step which that party have taken to recognise the Land Act, and its introduction is taken to mean that they will now accept the measure with certain modifications and withdraw their No-Rent Manifesto. Mr. G. declined to have anything to say to the clauses which affected the tenure sections of the Land Act, and as he postponed shewing his hand about the purchase clauses he confined his remarks to conciliatory generalities and a practical undertaking to take up and deal with the arrears question. On the whole his speech produced a fairly good effect, and the Irish party were more civil than they had been for many months past. The speech was taken to imply (as it was intended to do) a somewhat different departure now that the Parnellites had determined not to thwart the operation of the Land Act.

Since Wednesday the proposals about the Irish Executive have been matured, and it has been finally determined to replace Lord Cowper by Lord Spencer, whose work during his absence in Ireland (which will, for the present at any rate, be regarded as temporary) will be done by Lord Carlingford, Lord Privy Seal. The announcement of the change was, of course, blurted out prematurely by Forster, and the consequence was that there was no opportunity of explaining privately to the Press supporters the reasons for the change, which was unfortunate. It would have been hardly possible for Mr. G. to have announced the decision to Lord Cowper in nicer and more considerate terms than he did. There has been certainly the highest display of good feeling and gentlemanly behaviour on all sides. The decision does not mean the dismissal of Lord Cowper, or the supersession of Forster, or the admission of failure of policy in the past, or of itself any change of front or new departure. It amounts to no more than this—that in these critical times it is very desirable to have on the spot in executive authority a man of Cabinet *Ministerial* responsibility and position; that the Chief Secretary can't be running backwards and forwards every week, and must during the remainder of the session be in attendance at the House; that such a change which might have been most difficult if not impossible to effect has been rendered practicable by the wish and willingness of the present Viceroy to be relieved of his duties; and that by this means the further advantage is obtained of securing a man of tried and successful experience in Ireland, with whom Forster will be willing to share the duties of government, and who will be able to hold his own against Forster, in the place of a man like Lord Cowper, who, though able and talented and in many respects well-suited for the place—(especially as regards the possession of a charming and beautiful wife)—was young in administrative duties, unduly diffident about his own powers, and inclined to let the Chief Secretary have his own way entirely.

It seems to be almost certain that the political suspects will be let out after tomorrow's (Monday's) Cabinet. The moderate Home Rulers approve the idea; so also does a man like Lord Monck. I am certain that on the whole it is the right thing to do.

The wedding of Prince Leopold with Princess Helen of Waldeck went off brilliantly on Thursday. I was very sorry to have been prevented going down to see the sight, which to all accounts was brilliant and most impressive. The only other political people staying at the Castle for the two nights besides Mr. and Mrs. G. and Lord and Lady Granville were Lord and Lady Salisbury, Sir S. and Lady Northcote, and *Rowton*! (H.M. seems to be under the impression that Dizzie's spirit is now embodied in Monty Corry.)[1] All the other Ministers were, of course, invited to the ceremony and the banquet, as likewise were one or two others of the late Government—e.g., Sir R. Cross. Four years ago the Queen declared there was no precedent for inviting any members of the Opposition but the Leaders in both Houses, and accordingly it was impossible to include Mr. G. in the invitations! But things have changed since then and precedents have presumably been unearthed. I hear the Queen was in an extremely good humour on Thursday night, and after the banquet conversed most affably with all the Ministers including Bright and Chamberlain.

The Lords' Committee have given birth to their first child in the shape of a report confined almost wholly to recommending a sweeping extension of the purchase clauses as one expected.[2] It is worthy of remark that this Select Committee of the House of Lords, according to newspaper report, formally took the late Cabinet into consultation in drawing up their recommendations, which seems a strange proceeding!

I had a talk with Vernon on Wednesday. Though he has always been an advocate of peasant proprietors, he does not believe in the sudden and wholesale and compulsory transfer of proprietary rights from one class to another. It must be gradual and a voluntary change; and pending the accomplishment of that change the operation of the Land Court is a necessity. I asked him point blank his opinion of the Sub-Commissioners. He unhesitatingly said that he believed their work on the whole had been extremely creditable and done with impartiality. Out of about 250 appeals to the Chief Commissioner, under 50 had alone been reversed; in the case of 10 of these the rent had been actually further reduced, and in the other cases, where the rent had been raised, the increase had been not material.

A rather curious small question cropped up the other day. A Canadian R[oman] C[atholic] archbishop wished to be presented at Court, and the

---

[1] Montagu Corry, Lord Rowton, had been Disraeli's private secretary from 1866 until his death.   [2] *Parl. Papers*, 1882, xi.

Secretary of State naturally expressed himself ready to do so. It turned out, however, that there was no precedent for the presentation at Court of any R.C. Church dignitary, and the Queen referred the matter to Mr. G. He very naturally said he could see no grounds on which the archbishop's request could be refused; but it is curious that in these days there should still in practice be any distinction between the dignitaries of one church and those of another. It is probable that the absence of any precedent is due to the fact that Cardinals being foreign princes cannot be presented and that therefore as far as England and Ireland is concerned it would be awkward for lesser R.C. luminaries to appear where their superiors could not.

The baronets have had a good effect, and the announcements have been well received. Two to whom baronetcies were offered declined the honor—Richardson (Irish Quaker) and Ashton (English Quaker, supported by Bright). The other Quaker, by the by, Joseph Pease, accepted with avidity.[1]

The *Times* has been quite recently more and more anti-Government.

Thursday, 4 May. The last few days have been very stirring, interesting, and anxious times; in short, a ministerial crisis. Events have passed so rapidly that even behind the scenes it has been difficult to follow them step by step with exactness.

Simultaneously and wholly unconnected with the change of Viceroy, a very grave and difficult question presented itself to the Government, namely, how far the Government, without the smallest idea of bargaining, were justified in assuming a different attitude towards the Parnellites owing to the concurrence of two circumstances. These circumstances have been:

(1) The introduction last week of the Land Act Amendment Bill by the Parnellite party, which is practically an open admission that they are prepared now to cooperate in the working of the Land Act with certain stipulated modifications, especially as to arrears of rent.

(2) Certain private overtures made by O'Shea (who addressed himself direct to Mr. Gladstone) and by other members of Parnell's party who have endeavoured to approach the Government through Chamberlain.

It was next to impossible for the Government to disregard this change of front on the part of the Parnellite party, and yet it was most difficult for the Government to meet that party even halfway without laying themselves open to the charge of surrender to the Land Leaguers.

The difficulty became enhanced by the fact that they (the Government) were obliged to make up their minds in so short a time in view of the challenge, of which Sir J. Hay had given notice, against the policy of arresting without trial.

O'Shea went over last week on his own responsibility to see Parnell so as to get from him if possible his 'terms', which he succeeded in eliciting and

[1] See 20 Apr. 1882.

which O'Shea communicated to Forster. Parnell declared in effect that, if the Government would practically accept the Land Act Amendment Bill, he would do all in his power to stop the outrages, and implied that the no-rent manifesto would be withdrawn and that he would give his support again to the Liberal party. This no doubt was an indirect admission that Parnell had connived at, even if he had not instigated, outrages; but, considering the quarter from which such a proposal emanated, Mr. G. put a good construction on it. He is always inclined to take the most sanguine view of things, and wholly to disregard the taunts of the Opposition. Moreover, considered *per se*, there is much to be said in favour of releasing now the political suspects. All the Irish Liberals were in favour of the course, besides many moderate men like Lord Monck, English Whigs like Harry Brand, and even Tories as Sir J. Hay.

On Monday the Cabinet took the situation into consideration, and though they did not come to any absolute decision in the matter, the position of affairs at the end of the sitting seems practically to have stood thus:

All members of the Cabinet, Forster only excepted, agreed to (1) liberate political suspects, (2) not to renew present Coercion Act or the Act at any rate in its present form, unless they are forced to do so by the increased activity of secret societies, but to take immediate steps to strengthen the operation of the ordinary law and the administration of justice.

Mr. G. evidently was in hopes that a few hours' grace would bring Forster round to the views of himself and colleagues. He, however, remained obdurate and declined to avail himself of any of the bridges which Mr. G. had made for him to enable his retreat to be effected.

His contention was that he could not take upon himself the responsibility of releasing the suspects without a distinct assurance that the no-rent manifesto would be withdrawn, and that to require such an assurance would be tantamount to bargaining with the Parnellites.

Accordingly on the reassembling of the Cabinet on Tuesday at 12, Mr. Forster finally resigned; whereupon Lord Granville went down at once to Windsor to explain the situation to Her Majesty.

Nobody can fail to regret his withdrawal from the Ministry, which must thereby be weakened. He has many shortcomings as a Minister, more especially his want of decision, his tendency to blunder and blurt out the wrong thing in the wrong way, his bluff manners amounting to positive rudeness; but there can be no question of the honesty and straightforwardness of his intentions, his kindly nature *au fond*, and his courage.

It is a great blow to Mr. G. to part with him. As far as he (Mr. Forster) himself is concerned, he could not have chosen a better way of laying down his office. Instead of being considered a failure, he retires now in a halo of conservative glory and carries with him a very general feeling of sympathy. It is perhaps unkind to say so, but his vanity, which I think is undoubted, may have had something to do with his availing himself of this favourable opportunity of relinquishing a thankless post. We shall probably gain one thing by his retirement from the ministerial scene, namely, the avoidance of further 'leakages' which have been as discreditable as they have been frequent and have suspiciously always related to Irish matters.[1] The news of his resignation was received with the greatest hostility by the Opposition, which was only natural.

The Queen gave a very reluctant assent to the proposals of the Government, and expressed considerable apprehension as to the upshot of them, but in her letter there was nothing disagreeable or uncivil; she only hoped she might be wrong in her forecast.[2]

Mr. G. himself won't admit that there has been any new departure. 'Of a new departure', he wrote to R. Grosvenor (who has been away seedy), 'we know nothing; but of new hopes we know much. If wrong in our behalf, we are very wrong and must soon go to the right about'.

As possible successors to Forster, Mr. G. made out on his list Goschen, Whitbread, Lefevre, Trevelyan, Shaw, Chamberlain, Dilke, F. Cavendish, and Porter. The public made up its mind that Chamberlain was to be the man. Why, Heaven only knows, unless as seems probable Chamberlain gave out himself that he would be ready to accept the offer, were it made to him. Mr. G., I believe, hardly for a moment ever contemplated the idea. He summoned Lord Granville, Lord Spencer, and Lord Hartington for consultative purposes. He evidently would have liked to find an Irishman, but Shaw, it was known, would be essentially disagreeable to all the Irishmen, save a few Irish Liberals. The only other fitting Irishman was Porter; and to Porter the offer was first made, but he declined, chiefly on personal grounds. The choice next fell upon F. Cavendish, who after some hesitation accepted. Of the other men whom Mr. G. had jotted down, Goschen and Whitbread were practically not obtainable; Lefevre, though most hardworking and well versed in Irish affairs, commands no following and is singularly unsympathetic; Shaw and Porter were out of the running for the reasons just stated; Chamberlain would probably have struck terror among the would-be law-abiding Irish people—they would have thought the game was over and would have thrown up the sponge; Dilke was too much the counterpart of Chamberlain, and the submission of his appointment would, after his recent conduct on the Leopold grant, been useless.[3] This narrowed the selection down to Cavendish and Trevelyan; and F. Cavendish was, by his more lengthened official experience, considered to have prior claims.

Friday, 5 May. The House was all in a fever yesterday afternoon when it met; and the excitement was not lessened by the announcement first of Cavendish's appointment, which was received with no little derision, and secondly of the

[1] See 24 Apr. 1882.   [2] Guedalla, ii. 188.   [3] See 29 Mar. 1882.

intended release of Davitt, which was loudly cheered by all the Irishmen and was of course regarded as a further surrender. Forster then made his statement. It was somewhat unnecessarily lengthy, but drew forth very loud cheers from the Opposition benches. His contention was that he could only have assented to the liberation of the political suspects on one or other of 3 conditions, none of which were fulfilled. (1) A distinct disavowal by Parnell & Co. of the no-rent cry; (2) an improved condition of things in Ireland; (3) fresh coercive powers. Parnell spoke subsequently. His speech might have been better and might have been worse. Mr. G., though not pleased with it, thought it would 'pass muster'. Parnell certainly admitted that as soon as the question of arrears had been satisfactorily settled there would be an opportunity for himself and his party to endeavour to put down the outrages, and he expressed a belief that matters would mend. The debate continued the whole evening. The Opposition were white with rage and taunted the Government with complete surrender. Hartington replied later in the evening in a sensible, forcible, sober-minded speech. It is to be noted, as Mr. G. said to Her Majesty, that last night the Opposition kept on violently abusing the Parnellite party, which they had up till now studiously refrained from doing so long as they found the extreme party in their own (Tory) lobby. Mr. W. H. Smith announced at the commencement of yesterday's sitting that he would not proceed with his much talked of resolution for extending the purchase clauses. He gave no specific reasons, but it is probable that when the Tories came to formulate a specific plan for giving effect to the resolution they found themselves unable to agree. This would tally with what Lord Eustace Cecil told me last Tuesday (when I was dining at his house) that the report of the Lords' Committee had excited no little apprehension in many Tory circles.

F. Cavendish's appointment has been unfortunately received generally with marked disfavour. Everybody seems surprised and disappointed that the place which is just now of such transcendent importance should be filled by a man who was so little known to the public and who had given no public promise of success in so difficult a position. It has certainly not reassured the Whigs and the Tories; and the Liberals and Irishmen fail to comprehend what is meant by such an appointment. It is most unfortunate, but I should not be surprised if F. C[avendish] gradually but surely succeed[ed] in justifying his own appointment. I own, however, that as regards this and the whole turn of events, I feel decidedly uneasy. It may be all right, but it seems to me we are on very perilous ground, and, little as we depend upon the Parnell party, we shall find our hopes in regard to their future action completely frustrated.

The removal of F. C[avendish] from the Treasury, where he has been such a tremendous support to Mr. G., has induced Mr. G. to make up his mind to lay down the Chancellorship of the Exchequer. He evidently does not turn his mind to Goschen, and he has not committed himself any further to Childers. He makes the offer to Hartington, who will no doubt be admirably suited to the place, and who will in holding that place be all ready for the future leadership of the party. Hartington will no doubt accept. The India Office will then probably be offered to Lord Derby or possibly Rosebery. The Treasury will be offered to Trevelyan. Next to Trevelyan, Campbell-Bannerman comes next for promotion. The vacancy which will be created among the minor ministerial appointments will I hope be filled by Harry Brand who, with E. Fitzmaurice next to him, is considered 'first choice out' or 'twelfth-man'.

The Queen was much exercised in her mind about the release of Davitt.[1]

Mrs. Langtry's letters are becoming more and more frequent.[2]

Monday, 8 May. How little did I think when I made my last entry which specially related to the new Chief Secretary for Ireland that within 24 hours he would be no longer. The horrible assassination of poor Freddy Cavendish and Burke has been like a hideous nightmare. It has been the most horrible occurrence of recent, or almost of any, times. I was at home on Saturday evening, and about ¼ to 11 outside my door I heard my name called by a voice I did not recognise, and to my surprise appeared Sir W. Harcourt. He said, 'I have the most appalling news. Read these telegrams. I received them at dinner at the Austrian Embassy and could not make known their contents to Mr. and Mrs. G. (who were also dining there). You must break the news to them on their return. I must go in search of Hartington'. I had about half an hour to wait. Mrs. G. had gone from the Austrian Embassy to the Admiralty party, and Mr. G. was walking home. Mrs. G. was the first to arrive. She had been told at the Admiralty to go home in consequence of bad news, and had come back post haste very agitated, escorted by Baring. She suspected something had happened to poor F. C. in Ireland, and said she must know the worst. I briefly told her the news, and no sooner had I done this than in came Mr. G. There was no chance of breaking it to him by degrees. The worst was obliged to transpire almost at once. They were naturally completely stunned and wholly overcome. They first threw themselves on their knees in the inner hall, and[3] as soon as they had partially recovered themselves, they at once set out for poor Lady Frederick's. They found that the appalling news had already been told her by Lady Louisa Egerton. Kensington and several others came down to Downing Street to inquire the truth of the horrible rumours which were already abroad; and I shall not easily forget that night.

The facts were briefly these: Poor F. C., after getting through his installation and his first official work at Dublin Castle, set out on foot for the Viceregal Lodge. He was caught up by T. Burke in the Phoenix Park who was in a car, and both were walking along the broad open roadway through the Park

---

[1] Guedalla, ii. 189.

[2] This sentence is crossed over in pencil. See 20 Apr. 1882.

[3] The sentence up to this point was interpolated in pencil.

in sight of the Viceregal Lodge when they were suddenly attacked by 4 men with daggers and after a desperate struggle stabbed to death. The assassins, after their bloody deed, escaped on a car, and no trace of them has yet been found.

The general belief is that it is the deed of Fenians at the instigation of Ribbon (Secret) Societies and executed by Irish-Americans—O'Donovan Rossa's satellites.

All yesterday was a very trying and exciting day—people calling all day, Ministers in and out, telegrams backwards and forwards. Mr. G., though deadly pale, was perfectly calm and collected. He has never for a moment lost his head. I fear the after effects upon him.

Lady Frederick is behaving as the personification of courage and goodness combined. She is more than marvellous.

The Opposition have behaved very well. Northcote wrote a particularly nice letter yesterday morning, expressing the strongest sympathy and saying that the services of himself and his colleagues were at the disposal of the Government.

Old Forster, with the kindest intentions, offered to go back to Ireland during the interregnum temporarily, but Lord Spencer declined the offer, thinking that it might be open to misconstruction.

The Opposition have withdrawn, at any rate for the present, the motion of censure of which Beach gave notice on Friday, insisting that the *whole* Irish policy of the Government should be considered at once. This motion was to have been taken today and tomorrow. Mr. G. thought it not a little remarkable that after all the furious denouncements of the Tories they should have made no allusion to the release of the suspects in formulating their resolution and indeed have embodied in it no terms of censure.

In view of this resolution and the evident necessity for proceeding as soon as possible with Irish measures, the Cabinet had determined to offer to make a concession on procedure by accepting Gibson's amendment which introduced the two-thirds in addition to the safeguards attached to the Government proposal. Under the altered circumstances, procedure has to go overboard, and the Government proceed at once with their pacification measures for Ireland, to be immediately followed by a bill dealing with arrears.

Tuesday, 9 May. The Chief Secretaryship was offered to Dilke yesterday, and he declined it on the ground that the offer did not comprise a seat in the Cabinet. Mr. G. was surprised and not a little annoyed; and no wonder. It is not a little discreditable that at such a juncture as this a man should decline to undertake a duty of great trust and responsibility because (for to this it amounts) he considers that his dignity is not fully consulted. He certainly will lose caste by this step, and will be thrown back in his political course. Even had it been desirable to offer the price of a seat in the Cabinet in order to

secure Dilke's services, it would have been perfectly useless to submit such
a proposal to the Queen. She would not for one moment assent just now to
the promotion of Dilke to the rank of a Cabinet Minister. After he was so
recently unable to support the marriage grant for Prince Leopold, it is certainly not unnatural that she should object. Whether it was not Dilke's best,
if not in the circumstances his only, course, matters little; the fact that he was
absent in the division list remains unaltered. It is true he has spoken to Mr. G.,
or rather Mr. G. has spoken to him, and after explaining his difficulties (which
seem to be mainly founded on the fact that these marriage portions were not
like the civil list, the arrangement of Parliament, but were only privately
agreed to by Lord Palmerston's Cabinet in 1861–2 as embodied in a Cabinet
Minute drawn up by Mr. G. himself)[1] he gave Mr. G. to understand that he
would take an early opportunity of restating publicly his opinions on the
subject so as to enable him to support such grants in future. Apart, however,
from the temporary difficulty about Dilke in the eyes of Her Majesty, it is
certain she would decline point blank to admit him in the Cabinet on the
ground that in her belief the Cabinet is far too radical as it is. She seems to
imagine either that there are 13 Chamberlains in the Cabinet, or to labour
under the delusion that instead of being nearly lag both in choices and in
influence Chamberlain is the right-hand man, or sole adviser, of Mr. Gladstone. It shows how prejudiced she is, and how determined she is to see all
that relates to him in false colours. She must know that it is on men like Lord
Granville, Hartington, Spencer, Northbrook[2] on whom Mr. G. relies and to
whom he defers.

On Dilke's declining the Chief Secretaryship, the offer was made to Trevelyan who accepted it at once, and accepted it in the nicest possible manner.
So far from grasping at a Cabinet seat, he told me he was only too delighted
the post was outside the Cabinet. He had no wish to force himself prematurely into the Cabinet; he would prefer for the present to remain outside as
the spokesman of the Ministry.

Mr. Gladstone's ideas this afternoon for meeting the changes consequent
upon Trevelyan's transfer were:

Campbell Bannerman to the Admiralty vice Trevelyan

Courtney to the Treasury vice poor F. C.

Evelyn Ashley to the Colonial Office vice Courtney

Holmes to the Board of Trade vice Ashley

H[erbert] J. G[ladstone] to go up a step on the Treasury Board, i.e. become
a paid Lord vice Holmes.

Harry Brand to the War Office vice Bannerman.

I feel that the arrangements as regards Herbert G. are open to the greatest
exception, and I took upon myself to write and tell Lord Granville so. All

[1] See 8 Apr. 1882.
[2] EWH had written 'and Childers' but it has been heavily inked out.

kinds of disagreeable remarks would be made thereon. It would be slipping him in on the sly into a paid place by a backdoor (as it were); and far more objectionable than plumping him straight into another paid office.

But little progress has as yet been made towards detecting those vile assassins, but Lord Spencer evidently does not despair.

Nothing could be better or more sensible than Lord Spencer's letters. In spite of the position of unparalleled difficulty in which he has been placed, he seems never to have lost his head for a moment. He takes by no means a despairing view of affairs. He has already proceeded to strengthen his Executive. He has replaced Hillier by Colonel Brackenbury as Head of the Constabulary. (I have always believed that Hillier was a weak vessel); and has secured an Indian officer, Colonel Bradford, to assist in the secret police work and so to supply a want which has, I know, been felt for long, but to which Forster always turned a deaf ear. My namesake at the Admiralty— R. G. C. H[amilton]—of whom I have the highest opinion, has been secured, at any rate on trial, to succeed poor Burke.

By the by, Lord Northbrook got Mr. G.'s permission to endeavour to persuade G. Lefevre (who is very disappointed at not having been offered the Irish Secretaryship) to return to the Admiralty, but he has not been successful nor was it to be expected he would be.

The feeling everywhere is intensely strong, and letters and telegrams of sympathy (of which nearly 200 arrived yesterday) flock in from all parts of the world. Opinion in the country seems to be less excited than might have been expected, and the press is on the whole sober and sensible, if we except one or two London papers, especially the *Times*, which had a most blackguard article in it yesterday reported on the highest authority to have been inspired by Forster![1] Even Mr. G.'s bitterest enemies show, I think, that they are sensible of the terrible loss he has incurred, though some may regard it more in the light of a deserved punishment. I did not go down to the House yesterday afternoon, but from all accounts the short preliminary speeches before the adjournment of the House were very impressive and the whole scene very tragic. Mr. G. screwed up courage enough to move the adjournment himself. It was an awful effort to him, but I think he would have felt very disappointed afterwards had he failed to do so.

It is impossible at present to judge of the effect of the awful catastrophe and its consequences upon the Government. I am inclined to think it is most likely to be the deathknell of it. Of course if Ireland rapidly mends and quiets soberly down, things may go much better for the Government, but if the state of the country does not improve and improve rapidly, I expect that in the autumn there will be a general outcry for a dissolution which would be certain to mean the total and complete rout of the Liberal party. The 'new

[1] EWH probably refers to *The Times*'s leader of 8 May 1882, p. 11, cols. 1–2, which praises Forster.

departure' has no doubt given a rude shake to the confidence in the Government of many. Lord Fitzwilliam finally last week renounced his allegiance to the party, and even Rosebery told me that, had he been in a more responsible position, he could not have remained in the Government (but then he probably does not know all the *pros* and *cons*). I confess that, notwithstanding the acquaintance with all the facts which one has, it requires a very resolute exercise of faith in Mr. G. and his colleagues not to have qualms, which I confess I cannot wholly banish. I have no apprehensions as to the actual policy taken, but I have the greatest apprehension of anything which implies a belief in the integrity and straightforwardness of any one of the Parnellites including O'Shea, though he does seem like a gentleman.

The arrangements for the new see of Newcastle are at last complete, and Mr. G. has an opportunity of gratifying his desire of making a bishop.[1] He was previously prepared, after consultation last December, with his man, namely Mr. Wilkinson of St. Peter's. It appears, from what the Dean of Windsor[2] says, that Her Majesty will not have Wilkinson at any price. She has the greatest possible distrust of him. She believes him to be an extreme sentimentalist, and to be possessed of an excessive greed of power. Mr. G. was evidently greatly annoyed at the difficulties which were raised. He was glad that the refusal to accept his nominee had only come indirectly, and is taking time to consider what he shall do. Meanwhile, he is by inquiry informing himself on these two points respecting Mr. Wilkinson's character.

This and other indications of the Queen's unfriendly disposition towards him have evidently weighed heavily upon him. He rarely *says* anything, but (according to Mrs. G.) he did yesterday when on this subject remark despairingly, 'She will never be happy till She has hounded me out of office'.

Very greatly to my distress and annoyance, the most disagreeable question of the night walks has come to the front again.[3] One had hoped that after the mention of the subject by Rosebery they had been dropped. Alas, however, this has not been the case. On Saturday night last, he was seen to be accosted by and to be talking to a woman near the Duke of York's column. The scene was witnessed by Tottenham, M.P., who, I imagine, tracked Mr. G. and acted as a spy upon him, and of course the incident was at once noised over London. A lady[4]—a perfect stranger, evidently a great admirer—wrote to me with the nicest possible intentions to ask whether I could not flatly contradict what she believed to be a foul calumny against Mr. G. After consulting with Rosebery, I determined to show Mr. G. the letter. He was perfectly frank about the affair, as I knew he would be, and promptly related everything he remembered of the incident, which was merely that this woman had followed

---

[1] He had not been able to make an appointment to the episcopal bench since coming to office in 1880. He was impatient to do so. See 12 Mar. 1882.

[2] Gerald Wellesley.   [3] See 9 and 10 Feb. 1882.

[4] Mrs. Philip Henry Pepys wrote EWH about it on 7 May 1882. Add. MS. 48607. See 11 May 1882.

him and begged to be allowed to talk to him on the plea that she had a communication to make, and that on finding that her tale was an idle one, he
passed on. Of course the story had been dressed up; 'they were walking arm-
in-arm, etc'. I took courage and put in an imploring word that, as it was open
to the gravest misconstruction for a man in his position to talk to anyone in
the street, he would discontinue this practice of parleying with people in the
streets. He gave me three opportunities of putting in my word; all three of
which I availed myself of. He quite admitted the force of my warning word,
and implied that he would really give up these night encounters. I do trust
that some good may have come of this.[1] The whole matter worries me more
than I can say; though I know for certain that it is only from high, unselfish,
and kind motives and from no others that he addresses himself to women in
the street, in the hope (which he says has often been realised) of reclaiming
the poor creatures from their fallen position.

Thursday, 11 May. Poor F. Cavendish's funeral at Chatsworth today. The
meeting of the House was postponed till 9 o'clock in order to enable members
to pay their last token of respect. Large numbers availed themselves of the
chance. I am sorry to have been prevented going down, but what with the
extra pressure of work and being unwell, as well as the superior claim of
Horace S[eymour] to go, it was well nigh impossible. Mr. and Mrs. G. started
off by the special train this morning. They were to stay the night in order
slightly to lessen the fatigue. It was a frightful effort for them.

Letters and telegrams are pouring in at the rate of over 200 a day. It will
be impossible to answer all.

I answered the kindly disposed but inquisitive lady admirer yesterday.[2] As
Lord G[ranville] knew of the matter and had been spoken to by Rosebery
about it, I thought it might be prudent to submit my reply to him. He weighed
the matter well and brought all his tact and 'knowledge of the world' to bear
upon it. He made one or two slight suggestions, and I despatched it. From
a line I got today, the reply seems to have answered its purpose. The difficulty
was not to admit too much, and yet to avail oneself of his (Mr. G.'s) simple
frankness.

Lord G[ranville] fully agreed with me as to the unadvisability of the idea
which crossed Mr. G.'s mind to take the opportunity of putting Herbert G.
up a step in the Treasury. I quite hope now that Mr. G. has abandoned the
idea. The only other change in the programme, since I noted it on Tuesday,
has been that at Childers' request the Financial Secretaryship at the War
Office has been given to Arthur Hayter. He and Lady Hayter both seem much
pleased at the change and promotion. He is a very good fellow, and, having
always taken an interest in army matters from having been a soldier himself,

[1] See 13 June 1882.   [2] See 9 May 1882, note 4.

he is well fitted to the post. Lady Hayter's charm in manner and looks deserves to have her husband promoted.

I had an opportunity yesterday of letting fly a word to Ponsonby which I could not help seizing. Nobody could be more sensible and better disposed than he is, but I fear his influence is but small. I don't know whether he showed my letter, but he thanked me for it in a way which looked as if he had made *some* use of it.

Mr. G. has sounded the Bishop of Durham and the Bishop of London[1] as to Mr. Wilkinson's supposed sentimentalism and love of power, and, having received satisfactory answers to his inquiries, he will I expect proceed to press the appointment,[2] unless he is deterred from so doing by the account of Wilkinson's health, which seems to be none of the strongest.

Matters in Egypt look serious. The so-called National party have fallen foul of the Khedive over the sentences passed by the courts martial on the Circassian officers whom Arabi and his friends seem bent upon putting out of the way. Arabi & Co. seem determined to take the reins entirely into their own hands, depose the Khedive, and make themselves governors of Egypt pure and simple. Intervention of some kind seems on the verge of being absolutely necessary, but Heaven knows what that is to be or what it can be.

Friday, 12 May. According to all accounts, the funeral at Chatsworth yesterday must have been a most impressive scene. There are said to have been some 50,000 persons present. All the poor mourners from Lady Frederick and the Duke[3] downwards seem to have on the whole borne themselves wonderfully. Mr. and Mrs. G. stayed the night at Chatsworth. He saw the Duke and found in him nothing morbid or unnatural, but it must have been a very rude shake to the poor old man, who was specially devoted to Lord Frederick and who leant greatly upon him.

Mr. G. returned about 3 and went off to Buckingham Palace to have an audience. H.M. seems to have been kind and gracious and insisted on his sitting down. She apparently is always nicer and more considerate in conversation than in writing.

Rather a remarkable letter was circulated today from Howard Vincent. He gave an account of an interview he had had with Davitt. He said Davitt seemed in great earnest to do all he could to put down outrages in Ireland, was ready to go and work hard, and emphatically disowned all his former Fenian tendencies and connection. He (H. Vincent) believes that there never was such an opportunity of giving a death blow to Feniasm through the instrumentality of Davitt, and he is confident of the future.

The London world is of course rabid; they talk of nothing but 'the surrender', 'the treaty of Kilmainham', 'the compact with traitors'. It certainly

[1] i.e. Bishops Lightfoot and Jackson.   [2] To the see of Newcastle. See 9 May 1882.
[3] Duke of Devonshire, Lord Frederick Cavendish's father.

was most unfortunate and could not be otherwise than risky in its appearances that anything should have passed between the Parnell party and the Government. I think the Government should under the circumstances have declined to lend an ear to their advances, though they could not fail to take heed of information tendered to them uninvitedly. The Government no doubt, it seems to me, were right to release Parnell, as soon as he gave an undertaking that he would no longer thwart the operation of the laws of the land and was anxious to aid in putting down outrages; but the Government should have stopped there and have declined to give Parnell any idea of their intentions. Some of the Irish Liberals—P. J. Smyth and Shaw—entirely disapprove the proceedings so far as those proceedings went further than the act of release; but then they do not of course understand the real situation or know all the facts.

The new measure for strengthening the administration of the law and for the better prevention of crime was introduced into the House last night by Harcourt. He was very theatrical and highflown in his language, as might have been expected. The provisions are very stiff no doubt; and it seems a question whether they do not err on the point of severity; but I am convinced that some such measure will have a much better chance of producing good than the measure of last year. The present measure seems to be on the right lines. Its passage, accompanied with a reorganisation of the police force, ought to restore peace and order.

Wednesday, 17 May. The last two days (Monday and Tuesday) have in Parliament been almost wholly devoted to the discussion of the so-called 'negotiations', 'compact', or 'treaty' with the Parnellites. The Tories have all been up in arms; they have raved and ranted; and their ravings and rantings culminated yesterday in a speech from Arthur Balfour, who went so far as to denounce the Government as a 'Government of infamy'; and this denouncement was made by Arthur Balfour of all people in the world—a man who for many years has been on the most intimate terms of friendship with the Gladstone family and who has received from them and conferred upon them probably more kindnesses than any other Conservative. To such a pitch has party rage reached! I can't help thinking that the Tories 'over-reached' themselves yesterday, and that a reaction may ensue. Unquestionably, however, the upshot of the denouncement of the transactions connected with the release of the Parliamentary suspects has been very damaging to the Government, in the country at any rate if not within the circles of the party. There is no doubt a disagreeable appearance on the face of these transactions, such as to warrant searching criticism by the Opposition; but the real nature of the proceedings has been grossly exaggerated. There has really been nothing underhand in them, and nothing to be ashamed of. The Government did not take the initiative. The views or supposed views of Mr. Parnell were tendered uninvited to the Government by Mr. O'Shea in the first instance. He gave them to understand that Parnell was no longer bent on thwarting the operation of the law; and this was openly corroborated by the recent introduction of the Land Law Amendment Bill, which had the countenance of Parnell. This, then, amounted to an assurance that Parnell and his friends intended no longer to range themselves on the side of illegality and disorder; and how could these facts be disregarded by the Government? How could they fail to influence the policy of the Government? Parnell and the other imprisoned M.P.'s were not undergoing a sentence of law. They were merely put out of the way under the extraordinary powers invested in the Government by the Act of last year, because their being at large was supposed to be dangerous to law and order in the country; and as soon as that danger ceased to exist or was supposed to cease to exist, what title or right had the Government to keep them in prison any longer?

Hopes of detecting the Dublin assassins seem very slender, and practically to have vanished. It is a horrible reflection on the country. Trevelyan is getting into his new harness. He came over today, and he does not take an unhopeful view of the country, nor does Lord Spencer. Meanwhile every kind of illnatured thing has been said of Mr. G. in connection with the horrible murders. 'Fancy! Mr. G. went to church the day after (Sunday) the murders and actually stayed for the sacrament!' 'Would to God the assassins' knives had been plunged into Mr. G'. 'He does not feel the blow the least, &c, &c'. One's pen revolts from recording the unkind sayings.

The last few days, overtures have been made to Lord Derby to join the Government. Lord G[ranville] has been sounding Lord D[erby] himself. Mr. G. has been trying to negotiate through Lady Derby. Lord Derby is very friendly. He has admitted that no political difficulty exists, as he has absolutely renounced for good and all the Tory party; and though Mr. G. after his interview with Lady Derby was not very hopeful, yet he thought yesterday the door was not finally shut. Last night at Lansdowne House, where I was dining, Lord G[ranville] again tackled Lord Derby; but Lord Derby told Lord G. that, willing as he was to support the Government, he could not bring himself to join the Cabinet. He hinted at 'private and family reasons' as a bar to his assent. What these were Lord G. himself was at a loss to understand, unless it were that the Duke of Bedford had been using his powers of dissuasion. Lord G. again pressed Lord Derby this morning, but it appears to have been without any good result. This afternoon Mr. G. wrote to Lady Derby (a most charming letter it was too) to say what a 'horrible blow' Lord Derby's decision was to him (Mr. G.). He knew it was not a political severance, which was a comfort to him; and he admitted that, considering that the ship was labouring in waves (though he has not lost his faith in the future), an overture in such circumstances was more of a request than an offer. What he deplored, however, was the loss to the public. So long as Lord

Derby remained outside the precincts of the Cabinet, all his power, ability, and influence must be neutralised. What Mr. G. felt himself most was that, as his political hourglass was nearly run out, his last hope of serving in the Cabinet with Lord Derby was by Lord Derby's decision now gone. A further (and as he admitted a more personal and selfish) reason which made him regret that Lord Derby could not bring himself to join the Government was that he (Mr. G.) must now give up the hope of laying down his second office— the Chancellorship of the Exchequer; such a change now, he thinks, would only dislocate without conferring any compensating advantage. Accordingly, the upshot has, as matters at present stand, been that the Government has no one with whom to recruit the Cabinet (Mr. G. will not unfortunately, it seems, turn his attention to Goschen) and the arrangements for handing over the Chancellorship of the Exchequer will have to be abandoned. This is much to be regretted. Evidently Mr. G. would be greatly relieved if he could rid himself of one of his offices; and just at this moment the Government require to be strengthened, which probably the accession of Lord Derby would encompass.

The outlook certainly looks dreary; but the drearier it appears, the more marvellous does Mr. G.'s own pluck and courage stand out. He never seems to lose heart or faith. What concerns me most and haunts me continually is that in the close of his official career that great man should be so beset with difficulties and be made the subject of such unmitigated abuse and unfounded charges, and that his policy should be so little crowned with success, when it is directed from the highest and purest motives and with intent to mete out justice to all classes.

The Arrears Bill was introduced on Monday by Mr. G. It can't possibly be defended on principle, and yet it seems inevitable, demanded as it is from all sides by Irishmen, Liberals, and landlords. The Tories seem inclined to oppose it virulently, which can hardly best please the landlord section of them.

Forster, by the way, has during the last few days done his best to injure the Government—in all probability not intentionally, I believe, but certainly he has succeeded in doing it with great effect. It is partly, I think, due to that utter want of tact and judgment which characterises him, and partly due to his determination to do his best to damage Parnell.

Holmes is to go to the Board of Trade. His removal together with that of Hayter's creates 2 vacancies in the Treasury Board. There seems to be a strong feeling that the new man intended for whipping work should be one who will more or less represent the radical section of the party. Arnold Morley has been submitted to the Queen, and if the other vacant Lordship is filled up, Duff seems to run a good chance of getting it. It is unfortunate that the two vacancies should be offices which entail vacating of seats, as this excludes the possibility of securing a place for Harry Brand, on whom Mr. G. looks very favourably and whom he would like to bring into the Government.

On the strong advice of the Dean of Windsor, Mr. G. has determined to abandon the idea of fighting the Queen about Wilkinson for the Newcastle see, though he regards the objections taken to the nomination as very 'obstructive'. He has now 3 men in view—the suffragan Bishop of Bedford, Ernest Wilberforce, and Canon Clarke of Battersea (the last named for choice).

Last week the letters and telegrams which we received amounted to nearly 1200—an average of 200 a day!

Sunday, 21 May. Of the 3 men Mr. G. thought might do for the see of Newcastle, he has selected Ernest Wilberforce, of whom he has had personal experience at Seaforth and of whom the Bishops of Chester and Winchester and the Dean of Windsor[1] think highly. His youth and name will probably 'tell' in the North.

The fatality among judges continues. Holker has broken down and has resigned his Lord Justiceship. I expect Bowen will probably succeed.[2] Lord Selborne supports him, and though young for so big an appointment, he will probably do well. Moreover he is a Liberal.

Nothing more settled about the Treasury Lordship, or more properly speaking the Treasury Lordships. A. Morley declined. Grosvenor now thinks of Richardson, M.P. for Armagh, who will probably accept, if his seat is considered safe.

The Crime Prevention Bill was read a 2nd time on Friday afternoon. There was no sign of obstruction, and Mr. G. considered the tone of debate satisfactory. Parnell's speech was moderate. Mr. G. is under the belief that Parnell from his manner and behaviour contemplates the abandonment of land agitation. Sexton spoke with great eloquence and made an allusion to Lady F. Cavendish's letter to Lord Spencer, which pleased Mr. G. greatly. Mr. G. said it was done with genuine feeling and 'with the grace and felicity of diction of which Sexton is a perfect master'. Certainly the innate power of oratory among these Irishmen is extraordinary. This man Sexton has become one of the most finished and eloquent speakers in the House. He has only been in Parliament 2 years, previously to which he was, I believe, a humble clerk in a mercantile office.

In the evening sitting on Friday, there was a debate on Museum opening on Sundays. The motion, however, met with very small—unexpectedly small —support. The fact is, the promoters of this innovation are far in advance of public opinion; it is one of those subjects which it must be left entirely to public opinion to deal with; and as public opinion moves very slowly, it will probably be a long time before we see any radical changes in the observance of Sundays publicly recognised.

Mr. G. has gone down with Mrs. G. and Mary and Spencer L[yttelton] to

[1] i.e. Bishops Jacobson and Harold Browne and Dean Gerald Wellesley.
[2] He did.

a small farm to the north of London which the Aberdeens have.[1] She looks in more need of care and change than he even does.

The Egyptian crisis is tided over. The Khedive,[2] by standing firm, has brought the Arabi ministry to terms, and now that the French and English ships have arrived at Alexandria, he will probably be able to take a still more decided line of his own and to get rid of the present ministry and the army. I am afraid Wilfrid Blunt and all his enthusiasm for the 'National' party in Egypt has been shewn up. He sent some extraordinary telegrams to some of his Egyptian friends to the effect that, if they did not stick together, support Arabi, and behave themselves quietly, they would find their country annexed by Europe. He came to me in glee with the replies to these telegrams, from which it certainly might have been inferred that the Egyptians were all united in their support of Arabi & Co. Unfortunately, however, it transpired that, so far at any rate as one of the replies was concerned, it was sent at the dictation of the military ministry and in direct variance with the sentiments of the sender. This is rather a death blow to Wilfrid's ideas and his positive assertions that the *national* feeling was in favor of the present ministry.

Nothing special from Ireland, but Mr. G. is every day more and more impressed by and has more and more confidence in Lord Spencer.

Tuesday, 23 May. The pressure of the political atmosphere was abnormally heavy last week, and there has, since then, been a slight rise in the Government barometer. The breeze, however,—or rather storm—over the O'Shea transaction has not wholly blown over. Mr. G. said yesterday that if he was troubled much more with impertinent questions and imputations, he should tell Northcote that if he liked to move for a committee of inquiry, he (Mr. G.) would second the motion and come before it as first witness. There was an attempt in the House of Lords to get up a row about the same business, Waterford having been put up (presumably by Lord Salisbury) to ask a question worded with extreme disagreeableness about the (so-called) 'Treaty of Kilmainham'. It was withdrawn because there was not a sufficiently large house—a good enough 'gallery'—to witness the fun.

This is one of the many instances in which one can't help being struck that parliamentary warfare has been of late and is rapidly being degraded. The object of the Opposition does not seem to be to criticise or to attack boldly. It is not so much launched against the policy of the Government as against individual ministers. Its aim is to turn into ridicule grave statements of Mr. Gladstone and others; to scoff and laugh; to 'draw' the Prime Minister; to lay a trap for the Government; to have in short a bit of 'sport'; to get up a row; to provoke a scene; to do anything that will provide a transitory piece of amusement, a moment's excitement. And all this in view of the gravest possible state of things in one portion of the United Kingdom! And what is

---

[1] Dollis Hill.   [2] Mohamed Tewfik.

still more to be observed and deplored, this action proceeds from the party which comprises the men of gentler birth and superior education, and from whom one might have expected and rightly expected at any rate a decent show of good manners. When the political tables are reversed, of course, there will (and not unnaturally so) be retaliation, probably of a lower and more bitter description. How can men of the Storey, Joe Cowen, and Biggar type be expected to behave, when they have such examples set them by men like Lord Salisbury, Chaplin, Wolff, A. Balfour, Jim Lowther, George Hamilton and many others?

Last night obstruction broke out in the Conservative Opposition. The Arrears Bill (second reading) was moved last night. The principles it involves are no doubt exceptional and important, but if it is to be of any use at all its speedy passage is essential, which is already rendered difficult by the Prevention of Crime Bill which necessarily has to be pushed on. After about 8 hours' debate, the adjournment was moved. The Government said they would test the opinion of the House. The verdict was a majority against adjourning of more than 2 to 1 in a large House; and yet the Conservative Opposition insisted. It was a case in which the closing-power would have been advantageous, but without the two-thirds limit it would have been useless.

Davitt gave vent to his sentiments at Manchester on Saturday. It was a somewhat violent speech, but there was no taint of Fenianism in it, no allusion to repeal. It was aimed solely against landlordism; that is, it strongly advocated the expropriation of the landlords, prophecied failure for the Land Act, and denounced outrages.

I got a letter last night from Vernon, written with a view to elicit the wishes of the Cabinet regarding the intention of the Lords' Committee to summon over some 8 or 10 of the Sub-Commissioners in the midst of enormous pressure; and those singled out being the men to whose appointment special exception had been taken and whose decisions had been most widely found fault with by the landlord class. The Cabinet took the matter into consideration today. Mr. G. himself replied to Vernon. The Cabinet evidently wish to leave the decision on such a point in the hands of the Land Court, but he intimated very plainly that in the opinion of the Cabinet acceptance of the invitation was to be deprecated, and that a refusal if sent and subsequently questioned would be emphatically supported by the Government. I hope Lord Cairns will lay himself open to a good snub. There are enough complaints now about the decisions of the Sub-Commissioners made by the tenant class. Once let the Lords' Committee pick holes in the proceedings of the Land Court and the confidence in the Land Act will be fatally weakened. At present the inquiry has been harmless, or nearly so. Their duty has been, as Pembroke humourously describes it, to photograph Ireland, which won't sit still to allow of its picture being taken. Their photographing business is innocent amusement, but the dissection of individual Sub-Commissioners by Lords

Cairns and Salisbury might be a very serious affair, to say nothing of the grave interruption to an already overworked Court.

Wednesday, 24 May.[1] The morning sitting yesterday opened with a series of divisions on the question of giving precedence over the orders of the day to the Crime Prevention Bill, which the Irishmen sought to extend to the Arrears Bill. These divisions ended in disclosing serious differences of opinion between Parnell and some of his followers; and Mr. G. is fearful whether Parnell will be able to maintain his position and guide his party. His fall now would, in Mr. G.'s opinion, be anything but a public advantage. It would, no doubt, be a punishment for declaring himself on behalf of order; and some worse man would, though with weakened forces, succeed to his leadership. Parnell's position is a most difficult one. It is only fair to believe him to be in earnest; but it is probable that nearly all his power to do good has been taken from him owing to the action of the Tories who, by magnifying the importance of recent events and by implying that a compact has been made by the Government with him and that he has surrendered to them, have materially, if not fatally, weakened his influence in Ireland and his hold over his parliamentary followers. I should not be surprised if Parnell by slow degrees is supplanted and effaced.

The Government got the Arrears Bill read a 2nd time at the same sitting. The adjourned debate did not occupy as much time as was wasted the night before in fierce wrangles as to whether the debate should or should not then proceed. The bill though read a 2nd time by large majorities—there were 2 divisions—is not liked certainly, but that is not to be wondered at. Arguments are unfortunately mostly one way.

At the evening sitting the discussion raised by Cowen's amendment on going into committee on the Crime Prevention Bill was resumed, and it seems more than likely that a very lengthened criticism will ensue.

The Queen has telegraphed from Balmoral this evening taking exception to the decision of the Cabinet about the Sub-Commissioners and their being summoned to give evidence before the Lords' Committee. I should have thought that there could only be one opinion on this matter, but She seems to think differently. By raising frivolous objections of this kind to Cabinet decisions She only weakens her position and lowers herself in the estimation of her ministers.

Egypt is again in the acute state. Arabi & Co. decline to give way, and it seems probable that something more material in the shape of force than Anglo-French ironclads will be requisite to bring the National-Military party to their senses. There seems to be no doubt that the country from the Chamber of Notables downwards is against them and would be glad to be free of their military despotism. It is in the diagnosis of the real feeling of the

[1] Derby Day, but there was no parliamentary recess.

country that Wilfrid Blunt seems to have been so misled, unconsciously as I fully believe.

Mr. G. went and saw Lady Derby again today. The door does not now even seem to be finally closed as against Lord Derby. I am afraid he is one of those unfortunate men who can't make up their mind.

Wednesday, 31 May. Have been away for a few days, which I have spent pleasantly at Wilton and Salisbury. Harry Brand went down with me to Wilton. Nobody else there but the Sids[1] and Lord Mark Kerr. Heavenly weather and agreeable company, Lady P[embroke] specially so. Mooned about, sat about, fished about, and played lawn tennis—that was the order of the day. Monday being Whitmonday and thrown open to the public, we went over to see Melchet—Lady Ashburton's place. It is an extremely fine modern house full of beautiful things. She was as eccentric and as enormous as ever. Miss Baring is nice in looks and manner besides accomplished and well read, but seems delicate.

The latest excitement—that of the last few days—which has thrown Ireland even into the shade, has been Egypt. Arabi resigned on Saturday, but on Monday the Khedive was forced to reinstate him, at the risk (as was represented to His Highness and recounted to us here) of a massacre of the Ulemas. The Khedive's life as well as his deposition is threatened; the Europeans are greatly alarmed and are flying the country; Arabi is master of the situation; and the figure we have managed to cut jointly with the French is, I fear, rather a sorry one. We shook our fists in Arabi's face last week, and now that he has disregarded the menace we don't follow up the slight, and consequently the result has been something like a slap in the face. The fact is, there never was a question which was beset with greater difficulties, thanks to the unfortunate dual system of control established by the late Government. The course, however, which is generally thought to be the least objectionable, in the event of the requirement of material force, has all along been the intervention of the Sultan,[2] the rightful and acknowledged suzerain of Egypt; and quite recently the French, with whom it is right and expedient that we should if possible cordially pull together, gave their assent reluctantly to the adoption of this course. But, when the necessity is considered actually to have arisen, the French endeavour to back out of the idea of Turkish intervention; and they go in for reversing recent agreements by proposing an Anglo-French occupation and by harking back on the proposal to set up a new Khedive. The French have played a very shifty game and have put us considerably in a hole, the result of which will probably be that sooner or later we shall have to break with them—perhaps not an unmixed evil. Meanwhile the Government has been and is being abused pretty freely all round. The last idea seems

[1] i.e. the Sidney Herberts.
[2] Abdul Hamid II.

to be a conference at Constantinople of the ambassadors who represent the powers there, with a view of settling the limitations and conditions under which the despatch (if necessary) of Turkish troops should be safeguarded.

Wilfrid Blunt is not the least shaken in his own belief. He maintains that Arabi is occupying in Egypt the exact position which Garibaldi occupied in Italy when Italy was bestirring herself with a view of becoming a nation. In short, that the movement in Egypt is national, notwithstanding all that is said to the contrary which he implies and even asserts are falsehoods. It comes nearly to this, that one must (or rather he wishes one to) put his opinion against the opinions of all others, many of whom would be too glad if they could to call the movement national. He was bent on going out to Egypt himself to counsel Arabi, but I have talked him over this afternoon by a judicious admixture of flattery and remonstrance, and dissuaded him from undertaking that journey.

Thursday, 1 June. Whitsun recess over. Mr. G. returned from the Durdans and went straight to the House. Interpellations about Egypt passed off more quietly than could be expected. The intention to summon an European conference was announced.

Lord Derby is finally 'off'. He has decided absolutely against joining the Government, not from any want of confidence but apparently from want of resolution and pluck more than anything else. The consequence of this is, the idea about Hartington's taking the Chancellorship of the Exchequer is given up, because he does not care about leaving the India Office and only assented with readiness with a view of vacating a suitable office for Lord Derby. Mr. G. is none the less determined to relinquish his second office, and the successor to it will be the inevitable Childers. I am afraid his advent at the Treasury will not be greatly welcomed. Mr. G. won't hear of Goschen for the place. He seems to be prejudiced against Goschen for this place, believing, as he says, that no man connected with the City can make a good Chancellor of the Exchequer. He has, however, placed the War Office at Goschen's disposal. I don't believe for one moment Goschen will accept. He will be disappointed by the offer, if he wants and feels at liberty to take office, and will not be I think smoothed down by the way in which the offer is made—this being bluntly put to him with an intimation that he must swallow county franchise. The only chance of 'bagging' him, as I imagine, would have been by wheedling and coaxing him, regretting his exclusion hitherto, hoping that he now thought differently on the one subject about which there was a real difference &c, &c. However, we shall see. I hope devoutly I am wrong. His accession to the Government would be an unquestionable accession of strength.

Pembroke's letter on the Irish policy of the Government, which he was concocting when I was at Wilton, appeared in yesterday's *Times* (in large type).[1] It is an extremely able statement of the case from his particular point of view, which is a sort of mixture of the philosopher and doctrinaire with the common-sense man. It is the most powerful thing I have yet seen from his pen. In theory his arguments are excellent and incontrovertible; in practice, however, they would utterly have failed;—such is my belief. How would migration and emigration, reclamation of waste lands, and gradual increase of peasant proprietorship have prevented the realisation of the dangers which, bad as times have been, I verily believe, we have escaped? Viz:

(1) The union of Ulster on the side of disorder with the rest of the country.

(2) A general strike against rents, which it would have been impossible to resist.

(3) An unbroken Irish (Parnellite) party.

(4) A strong sympathy in Great Britain with Ireland.

We have avoided these dangers so far.

To go back a week—I forgot to note Dillon's speech delivered on Wednesday, which Mr. G. c haracterised as so heartbreaking. It was directly countenancing outrages. The next day Parnell gets up and disavows, before Dillon himself, the doctrines that have been preached the day before. Mr. G. thought Parnell's speech was 'skilful and important'. He spoke decisively against outrages. He admitted that payment for the land must precede possession. It is clear from this that any efforts that were on foot to dislodge Parnell from the leadership have disappeared. This is probably a matter of congratulation.

George Russell followed Parnell that afternoon in a very smart speech which pleased Mr. Gladstone, and for which he got general credit. He has been thought of for the vacant Whip's office, but somehow or other he is not very popular. *I* always like him.

Friday, 2 June. Goschen declines, as I imagined he would. He says it is quite a delusion to suppose that he has changed his mind on the county franchise question. This being the case, gratified as he professes to be by the offer, his accepting office is out of the question. To whom Mr. G. can now turn for the Cabinet I can't imagine. There is no one. He had much better hold on as he is. He is still sanguine enough (so he told the Duke of Argyll) the other day to think that tomorrow's official birthday dinner will be his last; that is, that he will be able to shake off office altogether by that time. If that be the case, it is hardly worthwhile his making two bites of the cherry, which he would be doing were he to lay down one office now and the other a few months only hence.

The appointment of Ernest Wilberforce to the see of Newcastle gives Mr. G. a good canonry at Windsor. He is thinking of Furse (of Cuddesdon); failing him, of Overton or Butler (Liverpool College). The Dean of Windsor

---

[1] *The Times*, 31 May 1882, p. 10, col. 3.

evidently does not much like either of these men. He suggests Teignmouth Shore, which probably would be a very popular appointment. The man appointed ought to be a Low Churchman. Mr. G. has shewn the High and the Broad Church too much favour. It is extraordinary the trouble he takes with making these clerical appointments. I doubt if a Prime Minister ever was so conscientious on this matter before or took so much pains or had so much personal knowledge of individual clerics.

In the House last night but very small progress was made with the Crime Prevention Bill. They stuck over an amendment moved by Horace Davey for striking out of crimes 'triable' by the special Commission, *treason* and treason felony. I expect it was a mistake to attempt to apply these extraordinary powers to any other crimes but agrarian, but when treason and treason felony had once and deliberately found its way into the Bill it was felt to be impossible to give way on the point. If Mr. G. had had his own way, such crimes would never have been included I am sure. The Government accordingly find themselves on the horns of the usual dilemma; viz., if they give way, it is regarded as an act of weakness, of fear, of surrender &c. If they don't give way, they are called dictatorial, bad managers, injudicious &c.

I fear the Arrears Bill is gaining in unpopularity. The fear is that it will demoralise those who have hitherto not been dishonest or disloyal by discouraging them from continuing their good ways. At the same time, no one says arrears ought not to be dealt with. The question has been called by landlord and tenant, Radical and Tory, the one thing which blocked the operation of the Land Act. It was bound to be more or less a charge on the taxpayer, whether the Government proceeded by loan or gift, and it should be remembered that it is hoped the measure will do something towards quieting down Ireland and thus relieving the taxpayer of a part of the heavy charge which is incurred by the large extra sums required for military police. However, I don't like it.

Mr. G. seems much revived by his little Whitsun holiday. He is looking better and brighter. There is nothing more marvellous than the temperament of the man. Instead of being weighed down by anxiety, worried and soured by events, and even swearing at the bad luck that certainly dogs the steps of this Government, he is always calm, hopeful, sanguine indeed to a fault, perfectly good-tempered, free from *arrière pensée*, confident in his own judgment, never at a loss, encouraging and soothing to others.

Sunday, 4 June. Yesterday being the day on which H.M.'s birthday was appointed to be kept, we had the usual dissipations of early parade, those horrible guns, and the evening entertainments. Our dinner in No. 10 went off very well. H.R.H. was in good humour and (according to St. Albans) was pleased and enjoyed himself. I got Jacko (Durham) and Bingey Lawley (Wenlock) to sit beside me and had a very pleasant evening. The former did evidently not enjoy the companionship of Ilchester out in India. In fact, one man could hardly use more disparaging and disdainful words of another.

Mr. G. is now turning his attention to seeing if he can entice Whitbread into the Cabinet. It is believed that his health has much improved since the Government was formed, when he declined office;[1] and it is proposed that the offer should be accompanied with an undertaking that he should not be required to sit up late at night. His joining the administration will be an undoubted accession of strength to the Government; no man carries more weight and is more generally respected in the House, though this of course is greatly due to the independence of the position which he has always occupied; but I rather doubt his accepting.[2]

Ireland is for the moment slightly quieter. I had a long and interesting talk yesterday with Mr. Leahy, Lord Cork's agent, who impressed me much as a man thoroughly conversant with the wants of the country and the ways of the people. He takes a hopeful view of things, provided the working of the Land Courts can be expedited, as he holds that the settlement of the rental of Ireland is the key to the whole position. He is strongly in favor of including within the operation of the Act *all* leaseholders. As to the Arrears Bill, he would have preferred a loan to a gift; but admits the necessity of dealing with the question and says that the successful working of it wholly depends upon the way the Act comes to be administered.

Her Majesty telegraphed yesterday advocating the application of 'urgency' to the Crime Prevention Bill,[3] but there is no bonâ fide obstruction and some of the questions raised are very important ones, to say nothing of the time which it would take to secure 'urgency'. Such a proposal in fact would be as inexpedient as it would be unwarranted.

I read today a good portion of the latest papers about the Central Asian question. For some time it has been mooted and discussed with Russia and Persia. There have been two courses advocated. One, by Lord Hartington, which has been to endeavour to arrange with Russia that a strip of territory bounding Afghanistan on the north and nominally belonging to Persia should become regular Persian territory, such as Persia could with the assistance of England and Russia assert full authority over. This is what Lord Ripon calls the 'Persian buffer scheme'. The other course, advocated by Lord Ripon, is not to trouble about marking out frontiers, but to obtain from Russia a treaty in which she would agree to respect absolutely the independence of Afghanistan subject to the predominating influence of this country, and in which the territory of northern Afghanistan should be in a similar position with regard to Russia. Both courses, however, are likely to break down, as Russia cannot bring herself to adopting the 'Persian buffer scheme', nor does she hold out much hope of being able to agree at a treaty. The treaty seems far preferable

---

[1] See 29 Apr. 1880.   [2] He did not accept. See 8 June 1882.
[3] Guedalla, ii. 198.

to the 'buffer scheme', and one is almost surprised to find Lord Hartington being outdone in common sense by the Indian Government. Russia evidently looks ahead and thinks she must take into account the fact that some day, not so long hence, she may have the Russophobist and anti-Russian party in power again in this country. She would gladly fall in with the wishes of the present English Government, were it a permanent one; but she must hold her hands free against the future and the possible recurrence of an unfriendly British Government. This being the case, our strength in India must be made dependent on our present frontier, which *faute de mieux* is stronger than one that stretches into a wild and hostile country such as Afghanistan.

Monday, 5 June. Not only have we the likelihood of great changes in Downing Street by reason of the separation of Mr. G.'s two offices but I am afraid we have also less indubitably in prospect changes in our happy secretariat. Alfred Montgomery's 6 months' grace is nearly up, and the vacancy which his retirement will make in the Board of Inland Revenue will no doubt be again offered to Godley, who this time will I expect elect to take a permanent appointment.[1] His great powers will be somewhat wasted on an old Revenue Board, but the fact is his physical strength is hardly equal to the wear and tear of this place. He is nervous about himself, and his own people are nervous about him. His loss here will not only be irreparable to Mr. G., but also to his colleagues and especially myself. One's own responsibilities will be trebled, and one certainly will never be able to replace Godley. I hope, however, that, if this change comes off, it will be arranged that Horace Seymour should remain on, though it will be unusual that the Prime Minister should have both his first Private Secretaries from the Treasury.

Thursday, 8 June. Mr. G. saw Whitbread on Monday afternoon, and after taking a night to sleep over the offer, Whitbread declined but evidently gratified.[2] His health seems to weigh with him, and moreover he, I expect, much values his independent position from which he feels he can render as much service to the Government as if he were in the Cabinet. This is certainly not the case. He would be an immeasurable strength to the Government. Curiously enough Fawcett last night was saying to me what an immense gain the addition of Whitbread would be to the Cabinet and was lamenting his having refused office when the Government was formed, which is now pretty well known.

Upon Whitbread's declining, Childers made a suggestion with a view to the attainment of the object of his wishes—the Exchequer—which would have been, if acted upon, as disastrous as it was foolish,—namely that Harcourt should move to the War Office, and Henry James made Home Secretary. The

[1] See 13 Dec. 1881 and 17 July 1882.
[2] See 4 June 1882.

latter appointment would probably do very well, but Harcourt's transfer would mean almost a general mutiny in the Army. The proposal would be enough to make the Queen's hair stand on end and would finally have disposed of the Duke of Cambridge—perhaps not an irreparable loss.[1] It is needless to say the suggestion met with no countenance from Mr. G. or Lord Granville. The upshot is that no changes will take place, and Mr. G. will have to hang on to the Exchequer for the present at any rate. It is evidently a disappointment to him. He said to me this morning he regretted the inability to give up his second place more in the public interests than on private grounds. He feels that Exchequer interests are being to a certain extent sacrificed. There are no doubt many matters which perhaps require more careful attention from a Chancellor of the Exchequer than what he can possibly give, but the little he does do is so far better than could be done by anyone else that it is almost more to the public advantage that he should do a little than that someone else should do much. It was only last night that Fawcett was saying that, greatly impressed as he had been again and again by Mr. G., he had never been more impressed by the marvellous powers of the man, both mental and physical, than he was last Saturday when he (Fawcett) had an interview about his bill to extend the P[ost] O[ffice] annuity business. It was the morning after a very late night at the House. Fawcett said Mr. G. exhibited all the vigour and freshness of youth and showed that his knowledge of detail on this technical point was perfectly surprising, exceeding as it did that of his own (Fawcett's) and Rivers Wilson put together.

Next to no progress has been made this week with the Committee on the Crime Prevention Bill. On Monday Mr. G. said that, though there was a great amount of unnecessary loquacity, yet there was no palpable obstruction. Since then the Irishmen have carried their opposition to the verge of open obstruction; and they now threaten to resume their pranks of last year, if no concessions are made especially on the clauses defining 'intimidation'. It is impossible for the Government to give way. They must make the provisions against 'boycotting' thoroughly effectual. 'Urgency' is being advocated by many; but it is hardly conceivable that better progress would be made were urgency resorted to—so long and stubborn would be the fight on the motion for getting 'urgency'.

Friday, 9 June. It having been impossible to find a Radical ready to accept, and presentable enough to take, Hayter's Whip, the choice has finally fallen upon Duff. The radical section will be disappointed, but it will please Scotland, which has indeed claims on the Government. Mr. G. declines at present to fill up the other Lordship of the Treasury, vacant by Holms' transfer, though he has no intention of giving Herbert [Gladstone] the paid place.

---

[1] This last phrase is crossed out in pencil.

I think it is a mistake his not filling up the appointment. To say nothing of the loss of a chance of giving office to one of the many hungry and worthy candidates for Government place, the arrangement will be open to the not unnatural construction that the place is not filled up because it is intended to benefit Herbert ultimately if not immediately. This is very objectionable, considering how quick the unkind world is to lay hold of anything done by Mr. G. which has the smallest appearance of a job.

There is indeed no language strong enough for the Tories to employ in abuse of the Great Man, e.g. Lord Wharncliffe said the other day that 'Mr. G. was the greatest curse the country ever had; that he had done more to ruin the character of the country and degrade political principles than any other man living or dead'. No such unmeasured abuse was ever employed before in political warfare, at least in modern times; and this is the language held by men of high station, good breeding, and education.

According to Labouchere, who unfortunately is made by Parnell to be his spokesman, Parnell is in great difficulty. There is a great breach in his party. He has fallen out with the extreme men and openly quarrelled with Egan. Unless he manages to get the credit apparently of extorting some concession on the Crime Prevention Bill from the Government, he will, he says, lose his hold over the dangerous section of his party; and having lost his hold, he will have to withdraw. This would be a very serious matter, and consequently the outlook is bad.

Another horrible double murder in Ireland—a landlord, Bourke by name, and his bodyguard, a soldier, both shot yesterday in broad daylight. There have also been other outrages reported today of a very serious character, which have made the Agrarian Crime Calendar look blacker than it has since the dreadful Phoenix Park assassinations.

Brackenbury, who has been appointed as sort of head detective in Ireland, has drawn up a report about the secret societies, which are clearly in a terribly rampant state. He says the only chance of breaking them up is by means of money. He wants about £20,000. With this amount of 'secret service', he is sanguine of being able to do real good, and the money will have to be got somehow.

Saturday, 10 June. The Cabinet met today, but only for a short time. They discussed the parliamentary difficulties connected with the Crime Prevention Bill. There seems to be some chance that the Government will be able to accept an amendment concocted by Healy, which will not really weaken the provisions aimed at intimidation and which will materially assist the progress of the Bill. If the same loquacious, if not obstructive, tactics continue, a continuous sitting will be taken on Thursday next in lieu of attempting to resort to voting 'urgency', which would probably not in the long run save time. Should stronger steps notwithstanding prove necessary, I should be for getting through the closure according to Gibson's amendment, which would secure a permanent advantage.

Egypt was shortly discussed also at the Cabinet. There is nothing particular which can be done for the moment. The Turkish Commissioner,[1] who has arrived at Cairo, seems to be likely to be able to restore the *status quo ante* recent events. The danger seems to be that the Turk will increase his hold too much upon Egypt, and the necessity for the conference is apparently all the more pressing in order that the action of the Porte may be safeguarded by the control of the European powers. We are a long way off, I fear, a settlement, and even if that is attained without bloodshed, there is the danger that we shall split with France; but perhaps this would not be an unmixed evil.

Lord Lyons says that the Freycinet ministry is very shaky. What, however, can take its place is not very evident.

It has been deemed wise, for fear of aggravating the threatened troubles in Zululand, to postpone Cetywayo's visit to this country. The poor old dethroned barbaric monarch seems to be in a very dejected state of mind accordingly.

I went on Tuesday to hear for the first time *Meistersinger* as given by the German company under the direction of Richter. It is certainly a noble work. No operatic work (*Lohengrin* only excepted) ever made such an impression upon me at first hearing. The principal subjects are Wagner at his best, which is saying a great deal. It is decidedly amusing as well as impressive. The performance was magnificent—the orchestra (especially the brass) splendid; the acting of a uniformly high standard; the singing of the chorus the best I ever heard; the mise en scene excellent; and the greatest care bestowed on details. I went with Lady Brand and Miss Maudie [Brand] and enjoyed myself greatly.

Dined on Wednesday with Fawcett. He lives in a nice little house the other side of the water down the Lambeth Road, west of Vauxhall Station. She is a very nice attractive ladylike little person and bears no trace of the 'strong-minded female' about her. There is something singularly straightforward, manly, highminded, and sensible about him, to say nothing of the pluck with which he has overcome his physical difficulties. He made himself very agreeable. It is unfortunate that he has got such a very harsh coarse voice and that he should make such very loud use of it. The absence of sight seems to have deprived him of all ideas of perspective (so to speak). He expatiated at considerable length on the marvels of Mr. G. One of the points on which he dilated with much force was the growing practice to which ex-ministers now resorted of mixing themselves up in City companies and business concerns as soon as they are relieved of office. He took strong exception to this and very rightly. As an illustration, which happened to be singularly apposite for the moment, he took the case of Childers, who, when out of office, was chairman

[1] Dervish Pasha.

of the Royal Mail Steam-packet Company. 'Supposing', he said, 'Childers were appointed Chancellor of the Exchequer. How could he be in a proper position to settle the subsidy when the contract expires, which is next year?' Mr. G., to whom I mooted this point the next day, admitted readily the objections to the practice, but said that, provided a man kept clear of any second-rate concerns, it was most difficult to avoid resort to it and that a chairman of a company of that kind was not in a very different position from a man who had a large share in stocks.

Sunday, 11 June. There is reported tonight a riot at Alexandria in which several Europeans have been killed and others, including the British Consul,[1] wounded. This portends very ominously. There is certainly no end to the troubles and crises which befall this ill-starred Government.

This morning another letter arrived from the Queen expressing great apprehension as to the tardy progress of the Crime Prevention Bill in committee and urging that steps be taken to expedite matters.[2] As She sent word it was to be delivered to Mr. G. wherever he was, I sent it down to Dollis Hill, the Aberdeen suburban retreat at Willesden, where he is spending the Sunday. Mr. G. has written again at length to her, fully admitting the serious loss of time and the importance of expedition, but expressing renewed doubts, in which the Chairman of Committees[3] fully shares, whether 'urgency', were it possible to get it voted, would save much time, if any. He took the opportunity of thanking H.M. for the anxiety she had shewed, in the message she sent by Lord Carlingford, with respect to Mr. G.'s personal safety. He said he could not treat as visionary the more or less widely prevalent impression that political assassinations may be attempted in this country, the most likely signal for them being the passage of the Coercion Bill. He is not, however, 'troubled by any fears, great or small' for himself, though he thinks it is his duty to exercise as much prudence as he can when he is out and about.

Tuesday, 13 June. Last night the 'intimidation clause' of the Crime Prevention Bill was at last got through, not without, however, further prolonged wrangling and a final and very significant kick from Redmond about the effect of the passing of the clause, viz. that it would make assassinations one of the institutions of the country. Redmond is one of the worst and the cleverest of Parnell's followers. His father was in Parliament and to oblige his father the Speaker kindly gave him a clerkship in the House of Commons which he suddenly threw up to enable him to join the Irish parliamentary party. He is a gentleman and good speaker, very quick and most audacious.

At the request of Harcourt and Howard Vincent, I have broached the subject of police surveillance with Mr. G. At present the watching of him is very difficult and haphazard. It should be on a more regular and more recognised

---

[1] Charles A. Cookson.   [2] Guedalla, ii. 198–9.   [3] Lyon Playfair.

footing. Stress is laid upon 2 points; one, that he should confine his walks to the principal thoroughfares; the other, that he should have someone in plain clothes always following him. He was extremely good-natured and submissive and has consented to the proposals without demurring. I learnt from Vincent that since the 6th ult. there have been no further reports of any incidents connected with night walks.[1] There seems to be no real cause for alarm, but precautions seem to be absolutely necessary.

Egypt is a great puzzle. It is next to impossible to know what to believe. I am regularly sandwiched between Wilfrid Blunt with his nationalists and the Foreign Office with their clientele headed by Malet. I suppose between the extremes there must be a *juste milieu*, but as to where it is I am at sea. There must be a great amount of truth in W. Blunt's story, exaggerated though it may be; and yet it is in direct contradiction to almost all the information which one hears and reads of elsewhere. He declares that owing to a telegram he sent off secretly yesterday, Arabi has made it up with the Khedive; that the Turkish Commissioner[2] will now go home; and that all will settle down quietly provided Arabi is not interfered with. The landing of Turkish troops, however, would be a signal for real fighting in Egypt and for a religious war which would extend over half the Mussulman races. What complicates matters so much is the impossibility of knowing what is the real game of the Sultan. The other day he had a fit of admiration for this country, declaring that he wanted the Egyptian business to be settled in a friendly way towards England, entirely irrespectively of France; that England was after all his best ally &c, &c.

Tuesday, 20 June. A gap of a whole week, chiefly attributable to a resumption of evening entertainments and late hours.

Nothing satisfactory, of course, has transpired during the last week. Nothing ever does here. The Crime Prevention Bill has 'draggled' on. *Some* progress has been made, but not near enough; and yet the difficulty is to know how to expedite its progress. There is, of course, a certain legitimate amount of discussion; and to meet the illegitimate part of it by resort to continuous sittings or to urgency would, it is feared, merely illustrate the old proverb— 'the more haste, the less speed'. The Queen has been constantly telegraphing and writing to urge greater expedition, as if the Government really wanted to spin out the passage of the Bill through committee to an interminable length! From time to time there have been offers made directly or indirectly by the Parnellites, but they have either been wholly unacceptable or have led to no good result. Labby, who at times has taken upon himself to act as a sort of ambassador between the Parnellites and the Government, has (it is said) been really the means of organising obstruction more than the Irish care about. O'Shea has tried his hand again and with prudence and moderation, though

[1] See 9 May 1882.   [2] Dervish Pasha.

not with equal success. Mrs. O'Shea has also been making some attempt, and has actually inveigled Mr. G. into seeing her. She seems to be on very intimate terms with Parnell; some say his mistress. It would have been far better for Mr. G. to decline point blank to see her or communicate with her; but he does not take the view of the 'man of the world' in such matters. He never attributes false motives to other people, and so never makes allowance for the effect which the attributing of false motives to himself has. Were the fact of his having seen this woman known, it would give encouragement to the supposition that the Government pay too much attention and heed to the Parnellite party.

Lord Spencer is fearful of some terrible outrages on a large scale immediately. They can get hold of no definite information, but tidings from certain sources give rise to these apprehensions. He regards the position as extremely critical.

I had a long interview the other day with Brackenbury, who has the charge of the new detective department in Dublin. With £50,000 at his disposal, which he declares is indispensable and which accordingly must be forthcoming by way of Secret Service, he is hopeful if not sanguine of being able to undermine the secret societies in the course of the next 2 years. I have far more faith in this mode of going to work to break up the secret organisations than in such measures as the Crime Prevention Bill. He spoke strongly of the dreadful 'administrative chaos' and over-centralisation which existed in Dublin Castle —the work chiefly of poor Burke.

A large discovery of arms was made in Clerkenwell last Saturday. The man who was storing them was arrested, and their destination was undoubtedly Ireland.

Last week on one day (Thursday) the questions asked in the House of Commons before the Orders of the Day reached one hundred! To such a pitch has this system of cross-questioning (necessarily often followed by crooked-answering) been abused! Mr. G. thinks that this is partly due to remissness on the part of the Speaker;[1] that is, so far as questions growing out of questions, and questions without notice, are allowed to be put.

The inefficiency of Playfair as Chairman of Committees is a good deal commented on. Of his ability there can be no question, but he seems unsuited for the place. He is rather deaf and rather blind and fussy and faltering. How to remove him is a very different pair of shoes.

Sunday, 25 June. (Charters) Down here for Sunday. Uncle Edward unwell. Nothing really serious I hope. A severe cholic attack only, from which he is rallying.

Mr. G. went down yesterday to Eton for the Sunday—to stay with Edward Lyttelton who is installed as a master there. Though most Eton boys are

[1] Sir Henry Brand.

Tories, I expect they will give him a worthy reception—feeling for an old Etonian predominates among them over politics. I hope he will take the opportunity of getting an audience of Her Majesty; he has not seen her since her return from Scotland. I have hinted at this to Ponsonby. Mr. G. himself certainly won't ask for one. He treats Her with scrupulous conscientiousness, but will not go out of his way to have the appearance of servility or flattery. Audiences are good things, as Her graciousness and friendliness come out much more when face to face with Her Ministers than when She has the pen in her hand; the feelings of the *Lady* necessarily predominate in oral communication. When seeing Lord Granville last week, H.M. seems to have again taken exception to the wording of some of Mr. G.'s reports of Cabinet proceedings; that is, She thinks they often contain what amount to 'decisions' or 'conclusions' instead of 'advice' or 'opinions'. Mr. G. says he has been scrupulously on his guard against the use of words which have the appearance of arrogation on the part of himself and his colleagues on matters where She has constitutionally Her say. He has begged Ponsonby to keep an eye on this and pull him up if he offends unconsciously in this respect. The fact is, when decisions really rest with Ministers and only nominally require the approval of the Sovereign, it is not very easy to steer clear, in the use of words, of passing by the Sovereign as well as of flattering Her in an unconstitutional and meaningless way. (This was probably Dizzie's mode of approaching Her.)

The book which has afforded Mr. G. the latest excitement has been Mozley's history of the 'Oxford Movement'.[1] It is really marvellous the amount of reading which he will get through. It seems *the* thing which rests his mind, and consequently when tired, instead of throwing himself down on a sofa or bed as most people would do and doing nothing, he takes up a book, and frequently a book which would tax most people's powers to master.

The irreverent and impertinent designation for Mr. G. which was devised by Labouchere—that of 'the Grand Old Man'—has been freely adopted by the Tory party and even quoted publicly by Northcote; but in so doing they have given rise to the rather happy, though disrespectful, appellation by way of retort for Northcote—'the Grand Old Woman'. Mr. G. is much alive to the excellence of Northcote's conduct of late over the Egyptian business as compared with that of most of his followers, who have become too unruly for him to hold and whose unruliness is directly countenanced by Lord Salisbury (to judge from his speeches in the House of Lords). Every afternoon the free lances of the Opposition—Chaplin, Wolff, J. Lowther, Gorst, Ashmead Bartlett, De Worms and such like—open a fire of questions at Dilke, most of which are exceedingly indiscreet and are put without notice. Dilke is first class at dealing with these hot-headed Jingoes and rarely satisfies their curiosity. He is always perfectly calm—never gets flustered or blurts out

[1] Thomas Mozley's *Reminiscences of Oriel College and the Oxford Movement* was published in 1882.

anything he ought not to, and generally keeps his temper in spite of the daily persistent bullying to which he is subjected. He is always brief and though certainly not unctious is never discourteous. Mr. G., being unable to acknowledge publicly his obligations to Northcote, has written Algy West a line with a view of its being shewn privately to Walter Northcote.[1]

A small berth in the Government is about to become vacant. W. Carington accepts the appointment of equerry to the Queen and so has to give up Parliament and the parliamentary groomship in waiting which he holds. Several names occur to one as good and fitting successors, provided their seats admit of being vacated for re-election—notably, Fred Tracy, Robert Cunliffe, R. Bruce, Bobby Spencer, Albert Grey, Monty Guest, F. Lambton, and others.

There is also a likelihood of another and rather more important vacancy occurring, i.e. office of Judge Advocate General, as Osborne Morgan has applied for the vacant Charity Commissionership, and if it is to be filled up his claims could hardly be passed over. He would not, I think, be any great loss to the Government. He is not popular in the House. He has rather a conceited manner, is apt to give foolish answers in the House, and magnifies unnecessarily the importance of his office and its duties. There would be no difficulty in getting a good lawyer to succeed him.

I had a small dinner at the Bristol this last week—where one really gets an excellent dinner, the best certainly one ever has at a restaurant in London. Lady Brand and Miss Maudie, Lady Hayter, Guy Dawnay, Almarus Digby, Albert Grey, and Grannie Farquhar. The Brand family always attracts me and so does Lady Hayter.[2] She is a great godsend to the Liberal party and is one of the few who exercise a good political influence. It is more than ever pleasant to come across a charming woman who thinks alike with one in politics at such a time when 'all the world and (especially) his wife' indulge in such perpetual abuse of Mr. G. and the Government. It makes one almost dislike to go into some houses; and from what others tell one, I fancy I don't hear half the worst. Ireland has been up till now the chief cause of their violent language; now it is Egypt as well. 'The British flag is being trailed still further in the dust'. 'Our prestige in the East as well as on the Continent is vanished'. 'We are the laughing stock of Europe'. (They forget France is exactly in the same boat as we are). 'Every Englishman is ashamed'. 'We have been kicked out of Egypt'.

I don't wonder that the policy of the Government is somewhat severely handled; for we are certainly in rather a plight in Egypt. The lives of our countrymen have been endangered; some indeed have been killed. There has been a general exodus of Europeans. The control is practically at a standstill.

[1] West and Walter Northcote were both at the Board of Inland Revenue.

[2] EWH originally wrote and then altered by heavily crossing out the italicized words: '*Most charming company. There is no family, barring the Herbert family, like* the Brand family, *and no more* attractive *woman than* Lady Hayter.' He then added the additional words that now appear in the text.

Arabi, whose banishment we demanded as a *sine qua non*, not only remains in Egypt but is master of the situation and the *de facto* Government. The Egyptian army has gathered strength and taken courage and is more than ever likely to show real fight in the case of intervention. The Porte has practically patched it up with Arabi and is prepared to recognise and accept the new ministry, in which Arabi is the moving spirit. The business of the country is at a standstill. The chances of the payment of the next coupon become daily and disagreeably less. This is the present situation. And what is to mend matters?

The conference, it is true, has met and is being attended by representatives of all the Great Powers, Turkey herself alone refusing to take part in it. But there seems little likelihood of any practical good resulting from the conference. Our aim is:

(1) The retention of the Khedive on the Egyptian throne.

(2) The reestablishment of the *status quo ante*.

(3) The maintenance of the control and respect of international obligations.

(4) The non-interference with the Suez Canal.

(5) The prudent development of local institutions.

To secure these ends, our recommendation to the conference will be that the Porte should be urged to send troops to Egypt; and that if she declines, the conference should be asked to provide for or sanction some other intervention, that is, English or Anglo-French, while we must be prepared to defend our own interests on the Canal.

Intervention of any kind whether Turkish or non-Turkish will mean serious resistance on the part of the Egyptians and all the horrible consequences of a country laid low with war. And all for what? (And this seems to me to be the difficult question to ask). For compare our aims with the programme of the new Egyptian ministry, accepted by Arabi and prompted by the Khedive, and they will be found to be practically identical. But by the policy we have pursued, we have landed ourselves in this dilemma—namely, that to recognise the new ministry would be eating our own words when we demanded a few weeks ago the expulsion from the country of Arabi, and that to decline to recognise the new ministry means an Egyptian war while the points of difference in the terms we demand and the Egyptians profess are to all intents and purposes *nil*. Moreover, on the two horns of the dilemma we find ourselves confronted with the risk of losing our prestige among the Mussulmen on the one side, and on the other with the risk of incurring the enmity of the Arabian race. We have no doubt been face to face with one of the most difficult questions with which a Government ever was faced—the difficulty being greatly enhanced by the great discrepancy in the accounts of the real attributes and intentions of Arabi's party; and our hands have been greatly

tied by the dual system and by our very natural and proper dislike to terminate
it and thereby break up our intimate relations with France, our nearest neigh-
bour and most appropriate ally. But notwithstanding all this, I can't help
thinking great mistakes have been made by the Government, and that all
things considered the line they should have taken should have been this:—
they should have from the first recognised Arabi and his party, and should
have held toward them this language: That it made no difference to this
country of whom the Egyptian ministry was comprised, and who was the
moving spirit in the ministry, *provided* the Khedive's throne was supported,
international obligations were respected, the control were maintained; and
that with these provisions respected we were ready to assist in developing
within prudent limits local institutions. We should then have put ourselves
in a position which without committing ourselves would have enabled us to
interfere, or require interference, the very moment when any one of these
conditions failed to be regarded.

There are rumours, which apparently have some foundation, that, if intervention takes place, the Egyptians mean mischief on the Suez Canal, and this
is a point on which the country will insist upon a firm line being taken, and
of which the Government are quite alive to the importance. We must defend
it at all hazards, notwithstanding that in these days when steamships are
being so much improved in speed the advantage of it to us as the quickest
means of communication is not so transparent as it used to be.

There were rumours last week that the contemplation of active intervention in Egypt involved the loss to the Government of Bright and Chamberlain. The rumours were probably put abroad for stock-jobbing purposes
and in fact had no foundation whatever. The south-east corner of the Mediterranean is the one point of all others where our interests have always been
admitted and rightly admitted to be really material even by the most fanatical
of anti-Jingoes.

Hints have been thrown out this week that the Government cannot postpone the procedure rules to another year. Therefore, they must be got through
now, before the end of the present session, or an autumn session will have to
be held. This is still an open point and is dependent on the progress (if it can
be called progress at all) of public business during the next few weeks. It is
also an open point whether the Government will stick to their original
closure proposal or will accept the Gibson amendment, which is tacking the
two-thirds on to the safeguards which already exist. Of course whichever line
they adopt they will be open to attack; they will either be called obstinate and
insensible to the real feeling of the House, or they will be termed squeezable,
weak-minded, and more alive to the opinion of their opponents and less good
supporters than to that of their most trusty followers. On the whole I believe
the wisest course to be under the circumstances a compromise, that is to say,
to accept the two-thirds limit on trial, and to insist upon this and the other

rules (at any rate all those other than involving delegation of work by Grand Committees) being passed this session. This will probably take less time than having a special session in the autumn with all the lengthened discussions which now attend the Queen's speech &c. Chamberlain is the only man who has spoken out against this course at present. But he is too timorous as to what his Associations will say and how the Liberal press will take it, and attaches too much importance to the effect of 'agitation' in the country. The great drawback to the advanced men of the present day seems to me excess of sensitiveness to public opinion, which thwarts their judgment and unduly influences their actions. His idea about procedure is that if the Government compromise about the closure and so draw the teeth of the Tories, the opposition to the passage of the rules will then be directed to the Grand Committee proposals or devolution rules; so that the Government would gain little in time, while they would lose caste in the eyes of their most trusty supporters. Moreover, between now and the autumn session, there would be plenty of time to make the opinion of the country properly felt by 'agitation'. Therefore, he is for sticking to the proposals in their entirety and passing them in the autumn.

Monday, 26 June. Mr. G. seems to have enjoyed his Sunday at Eton. No audience came off. When Mr. G.'s whereabouts were made known to the Queen She threw out no hint that She would like to see him; She merely told Ponsonby that if he saw Mr. G. he might make inquiry about Cetywayo! However, Hartington was there for the day; so perhaps she thought the sight of one minister was enough at a time.

The outlook of affairs in Zululand is bad. There seem to be four alternatives, each one of which is apparently fraught with danger and difficulty.

(1) Leave things as they are.
(2) Withdraw our Resident.
(3) Restore Cetywayo.
(4) Support the loyal chiefs which practically means annexation.

According to Guy Dawnay, if either of the first 3 courses is taken, a civil war in Zululand is certain to ensue either immediately or in a very short time; and a civil war will inevitably lead to grave troubles from the natives in Natal.

Objections to No. 4 which would entail the extension of our rule in South Africa are strong and evident enough, but G. D[awnay] believes that in the long run it would be the least dangerous and the least expensive. This, however, is a course to which the present Government will, I am sure, never lend themselves. *Primâ facie*, the restoration of Cetywayo looks the most reasonable of the alternatives.

Wednesday, 28 June. Egypt still continues to be the object of greatest public interest for the moment. It has temporarily even eclipsed Ireland. Last Sunday the Sultan made a startling proposal to Lord Dufferin. His *bête noir* just now is France; and in order to shut her out or pay her off, and also with a view probably of meeting some of the financial exigencies of the Porte, he proposed that a convention should be concluded with this country on the basis of the Anglo-Turkish convention about Cyprus, whereby Egypt should practically be handed over to England. It is needless to say that Lord Dufferin, while expressing himself sensible of the friendly spirit of the Porte, threw at once cold water upon the idea; and of course his refusal to entertain such a project has been warmly endorsed at home by the Government. Mr. G. thinks very highly of Lord Dufferin's diplomatic qualities at these difficult times.

As to the question of the hour—the immediate situation of events in Egypt —it is next to impossible to get at the truth. One moment it is reported from Constantinople that Dervish Pasha is temporising with Arabi, and only waiting his opportunity not only to send for Turkish troops but to kick Arabi clean out of the country. Another moment news comes from Alexandria to the effect that Dervish is patching up matters with Arabi, and that his instructions are to come to terms with Arabi—a story to which the fact of the decorating of Arabi by the Porte gives credence and seems to me to be by far the most likely version. Meanwhile, as far as the country of Egypt is itself concerned, the official telegrams which we get say that confidence among the Europeans daily decreases—that the country is being ruined financially and commercially—that the panic among the Europeans increases—and that distress is imminent among the lower classes. Probably a Jingo policy would temporarily be popular; but what right have we to interfere at all? Our plea must be to rid the country, in which we have a great interest and with which we are by firmans specially connected, from a military dictatorship and all its disastrous consequences.

Friday, 30 June. Hideous news again from Ireland. Lord Clanricarde's agent and agent's servant both shot dead yesterday, and two other single murders elsewhere have been reported within the last few days. It really is too terrible; and what is to mend matters? The Crime Prevention Bill would not have averted the dastardly boldness of assassins in broad daylight, or have made the people in the locality surrender these hellish villains. So the outlook is indeed black. However, the bill, as its name implies, is directly aimed at these terrible occurrences, and yet in spite of them it gains no motive-power. For each clause done, several new pages of amendments appear. I think the committee began their labours with 13 pages of amendments. Those labours have now continued for 20 days, and at the end of that time there are 16 pages of amendments still to be got through. There is to be a long sitting tonight; and, if decent progress is not made, an attempt to obtain urgency on Monday will be instituted. Erskine May thinks that this is the only chance of expediting matters. He has no confidence in the efficacy of continuous sittings, which he says will only provoke overt obstruction instead of covert obstruction. My own belief is that the greatest need of all is a new chairman of committees, who would be a real despot in the chair.

Mr. G. went down to the Council yesterday, as Her Majesty expressed a wish to see him. She certainly never exhibits any thoughtfulness. If she had only accorded him an interview on Sunday, she might have saved him the trouble and racket of going down to Windsor specially. But consideration for others is not one of Her best qualities. The audience seems to have been satisfactory—so much so that in writing last night Ponsonby commented on the misfortune it was that interviews were not accorded more constantly. 'They seem', as he said, 'to understand each other so much better at the end of them'.

There has been a good deal of discussion as to who is to do the entertaining of the Party this year. As for Mrs. G., whatever she does, she is sure to be abused. If she gave parties, she would be said to be unfeeling; and if she gives no more, she will be called stingy and lacking in duty. So it really did not make much difference, but it was thought on the whole that all things taken into consideration she might properly be let off. Lady Emma Baring and Lady Aberdeen have both offered their services; and so also has Lady Breadalbane, which will do admirably. She professes to be alarmed; but really with such a house and such a charming presence herself her alarm is rather groundless. I hinted that Rosebery should do more, but he declined and declined on grounds which at any rate do honour to his taste. He told me he could not bear the thought of being considered to be pushing and going out of his way—of assuming as an Under Secretary the position of a Minister. He further said that in view of promotion in the future the one thing of all others he wished to avoid was a charge similar to that brought against Lord Carlingford when he was married to Lady Waldegrave—that he had 'dined himself into the Cabinet'. Rosebery also said he wanted to economise a little. He had determined to pay the last General Election expenses to which he had been put out of income, and these amounted to £50,000!

Sunday, 2 July. Yesterday was another black-lettered day in parliamentary annals. It had been determined on Friday to push on the bill by an unusually prolonged sitting, and the Whips were ready with relays to meet any emergencies. The discussion on the 17th clause was prolonged for 15 hours, and there seemed no prospect of any speedier progress with the remaining clauses. About 10 o'clock, however, yesterday morning, Playfair startled the Government as well as the House with a *coup de main*. Presumably with the concurrence of the Speaker,[1] but without previous communication with or even

[1] Sir Henry Brand.

notice to the Government, he suddenly named some 16 of the Irish members for obstruction. On their being named, there was nothing to be done but for Childers, who was left in charge of the House, to move the suspension of the whole lot; but as the batch included one or two (notably Dillon and Marum) who had taken little part in the proceedings of the long sitting it was rather a drastic step to take and one to which ample exception will probably be taken by the Irish members. But it must be remembered that it was not for merely obstructing at that particular sitting that they were suspended but for persistent obstruction (carefully veiled no doubt) during 20 days. Playfair's move lashed the Parnellites into a frenzy. O'Donnell deliberately called his being himself named 'an infamy'. Parnell privately gave Playfair the lie. Callan called Edward Marjoribanks 'a white-livered devil', &c, &c. The remaining Parnellites, on the resumption of the committee on the bill, proceeded at once to move the adjournment and to report progress. After this game had been carried on a little time, and the Government had announced that they would take all the rest of the clauses which stood in the bill as originally introduced and would move 'urgency' on Monday for the post-poned clauses and subsequent stages of the bill, 10 others brought themselves under the suspension rule and were 'run in'. Their removal being effected, the remaining clauses were got through and the House adjourned about 8 in the evening after 28 hours' sitting.

Mr. G. was a little annoyed at first about Playfair's sudden move, which he had kept so dark that even R. Grosvenor himself had no inkling of its being about to take place. But Mr. G. soon came round to the conclusion that under the circumstances Playfair had been justified by the step he had taken on the joint responsibility of himself and the Speaker.

The Conference makes no way. France continues crazed against Turkey. It seems as if she would almost prefer English intervention in Egypt to Turkish or Anglo-Turkish intervention. Lord Lyons says Freycinet takes his cue entirely from Bismarck, who is sure to do his best to keep him (Freycinet) in power for fear of Gambetta's succession.[1]

Friday, 7 July. Aetate 35! We have been living at the mouth of volcanoes again this week. Crises on Egypt. Crises on Ireland.

First as to Egypt. Events follow so quickly one another that it is not easy to describe the situation. The Conference is making little way; Arabi shows no signs of giving in; the Porte still plays a totally dark game; and France cannot properly be relied upon. Mr. G. summarised the other day the points on which there could be no doubt the Cabinet were agreed, viz:

(1) Reparation must be insisted upon.

[1] See Lyons to Granville, 20 June 1882, Lord Newton, *Lord Lyons* . . . (London, 1913), ii. 286.

(2) A definitive course of action must be deferred till the Conference is over.

(3) There can be no negotiations with Arabi apart from the Khedive, as hinted at by France in what Mr. G. termed a very 'strange' manner.

(4) The instructions to Lord Dufferin must be adhered to.

Further, the Cabinet agreed to instruct Beauchamp Seymour to destroy the earthworks at Alexandria if they were recommenced or pushed on. But this step was not sufficient in the view of some members of the Cabinet, notably the representatives of the War Office and Admiralty and of India.[1] They appear to have been in favour of sending off troops at once to the Canal for its protection. To this proposal Mr. G. declined point blank to be a party on the ground that

(1) no danger to the Canal had actually arisen,

(2) the interference with the Canal is interference with a highway of the world, and as such requires the sanction of all the Powers,

(3) we are bound to await the deliberations of the Conference,

(4) it is impossible under present parliamentary difficulties to ask for a vote of credit.

Besides the above-named Ministers, Chamberlain, being the *alter ego* of Dilke, is said to be Jingo-ish. Indeed Mr. G. intimated that the only Minister who cordially supported him was Harcourt. Bright also must have sided with him.

Harmony, however, was re-established on Wednesday by the usual resort to a compromise. Two further regiments were to be despatched to the Mediterranean to take the place of two regiments now at Malta, which were to be passed on to Cyprus! It is a little unfortunate that the present Government should be having to make use of that possession.[2] So much for the Egyptian crisis.

As regards Egypt—apart from the question of the Suez Canal—I am rapidly coming to the conclusion that, if force is necessary for the re-establishment of the *status quo* &c, English or even Anglo-French intervention is preferable to Turkish intervention. The Turk when once admitted into Egypt will be difficult to turn out, and we may find ourselves in the long run driven to fight the Egyptians *plus* the Turks.

Saturday, 8 July. Now for the Irish crisis. Yesterday afternoon the report of the committee on the Crime Prevention Bill was to be taken. In the course of the sitting the proviso limiting the right of search by night to cases where there was reasonable suspicion of the meeting of Secret Societies (which Mr. G. had in deference to the strongly-expressed wishes of the Parnellites

---

[1] i.e. Childers, Northbrook, and Hartington.

[2] Before EWH pencilled emendations of this sentence it read: 'It is unfortunate that the present Government should be making use of that worthless possession.'

promised to propose) came on for consideration. This proviso, designed to exclude from the clause what might be deemed unnecessary invasions of liberty and homes, was founded on the advice of Lord Spencer. Notwithstanding the strong feeling manifested against the minimising effect of the proviso on the search clause, Mr. G. announced that he could be no party to the clause without it, and that if the proviso were rejected he should hold himself personally free to consider his position. Those wretched Parnellites, after accepting the pledge, absented themselves, and by dint of their absence and the default of over 20 Whigs, the proviso was rejected by 13 votes and the Government accordingly defeated. On the result being made known, Mr. G. said that under ordinary circumstances he should ask for an adjournment of the House; but owing to the pressing nature of the bill, he would proceed with it and reserve his action. The point which the Cabinet will have to decide today will be what course should be taken in respect to a division carried against the Government where (to use Mr. G.'s own words) the 'House of Commons, which is the special guardian of liberty, has, in the interest of real or supposed order, forced provision restrictive of liberty on the Executive Government, who are the specially responsible guardians of order'. There seems to be a general feeling that on such a point of detail, so long as Mr. G. redeemed his pledge or did his best to redeem it, there was no necessity for him to fight on the proviso with so high a hand. It is impossible for him to provoke seriously a ministerial crisis just now, and therefore his action was open to the objection of threatening when it is impossible to carry out the threats. What will probably happen is that Mr. G. will announce his readiness to carry on, so long as that power which the Executive did not ask for be not exercised.

Sunday, 9 July. The Cabinet assembled yesterday and as was to be expected the crisis was tided over. It was agreed that Mr. G. should make a short statement on Monday and, without going into particulars, remind the House that the power of search as it now stands in the bill was, like all other powers in it, a discretionary power; that the Government hoped there would be no necessity for exercising this particular power; but that if the necessity arose they would act with respect to it as to any other powers in the bill. Mr. G. has always been perfectly calm ever since the division; in the most placid of humours as if nothing had happened. He is convinced that he was right in the course he took. Good will come out of evil. The tactics of the Parnellites show how useless it is to attempt to have any dealings with them. The Whigs have blown off steam—had their little fling—and will probably take a lesson. It is rather absurd for them to complain of party despotism and haughtiness of the Prime Minister in the way that F. Lambton declaimed in a maiden and uncouth speech on Friday, and then to prove their liberty of action by going and voting just as they please.

It was decided at the Cabinet yesterday that the House should sit again in the autumn for the exclusive purpose of considering procedure. Parliament will not be prorogued; it will be merely adjourned as soon as the necessary business has been disposed of in addition to the two Irish bills and the Corrupt Practices Bill with which it is intended to proceed.

From what I can gather, I am inclined to think that if one had to bet one should bet that the Lords throw out the Arrears Bill. Their action, though not yet finally determined upon, depends as far as I can make out on two things— the support which the bill receives in the Lower House, and judging from the division on going into committee on the bill last Thursday that support will be such as to somewhat encourage the rashness of the Peers. The other consideration will be the wishes of the Irish landlords themselves; and my belief is they are becoming indifferent to the fate of the bill. They will very likely prefer to run the risk of its rejection to countenancing what they consider to be the demoralising effect of the measure in Ireland.

Monday, 10 July. Beauchamp Seymour, having detected the Egyptians at work again on the Alexandrian fortifications yesterday, had no other alternative but to send his ultimatum. So unless Arabi placidly submits, the bombardment will commence tomorrow; and we shall wake up to find ourselves at war with Egypt. The hope is, and the chances are, that the explosion of one or two shells will send all the earthworks to glory, and there will be an end for the moment of the matter. But it is impossible to predict. According to W. Blunt, the Egyptians are a formidable enemy. On the result of the bombardment hangs the fate of Bright. If the fire spreads into conflagration he will resign; and his resignation will be a blow to the Government. He represents the Peace party which is a large and increasing party, and which is numbered among the most trusty supporters of the Government. His loss just now and under these circumstances will be a greater blow than the loss of Chamberlain would be. His influence with the Dissenters is very strong. If, however, the bombardment is over immediately and it practically brightens the chances of peace, then he will probably be persuaded to stay on. He certainly will not leave Mr. G. in an hour of difficulty if he can help it. Mr. G. wrote to him today and begged him at any rate to do nothing in a hurry.

Tuesday, 11 July. Mr. G. made his promised announcement yesterday, which finally set at rest any apprehensions about a ministerial crisis. Arthur Balfour had previously during question time jumped up and asked Mr. G. if he had by that time 'reconsidered his position'. These special acts of rudeness from Arthur Balfour are singularly unfortunate and regarded (as they rightly should be) to be in the worst possible taste. I can't conceive what possesses him to go out of his way to insult Mr. G. as he does, considering what the intimate relations between the two once were and the mutual acts of kindness have been. Arthur Balfour is, I fear, as detestable politically as he is attractive socially in inverse ratio. With his antecedents his public behaviour and public associates should certainly be different.

According to Dilke (so Rosebery tells me) the gossip in the House last Friday when Mr. G. threatened resignation were[1] that, if he gave effect to his threat, Hartington would naturally be sent for, but that the conditions imposed upon him by the radical section of his party would be too onerous (that is, presumably, they would insist upon being represented too strongly and upon too extreme a programme) and that without the cooperation of the whole party he would decline to form a Government, or at any rate would fail to carry it on for any appreciable time. What the alternative was did not transpire. It could hardly be imagined that 'Jo'[2] would be sent for? He is the best-hated man in the country now; and (I can't help thinking) has much lost his power and influence during the last two years. Two years ago I should say that the radical wing of the party was in ascendancy; now I think the Whigs have the greater influence of the two sections. This country gets easily frightened; and it will be some time before we see the radical party reigning alone and supreme. A material shuffling of parties will probably take place first; and the signal for the commencement of the shuffle will be probably the retirement of Mr. G.

Harcourt yesterday gave vent to his feelings on the present state of Ireland. It is no wonder he regards it with such grave apprehension and outspoken disappointment. By one of those sudden changes of front, for which he seems to be rather conspicuous, he has come to the conclusion that all the remedial measures at which the Government has tried its hand have proved to be dead failures, and that an iron rule is now the only alternative. He seems to forget entirely how instrumental he was himself in 'screwing up' the Land Bill (as he called it at the time) and in egging on Mr. G. I quite think there is to be little change for the better for a long time to come; O'Connor Power is very likely right when he said to me on Saturday, 'Things will get even worse before they are better'; there is nothing to shew that the new Coercion Bill will put an end to the worst agrarian or political outrages. But it is absurd to condemn the Land Act as a failure yet. As a matter of fact, it has won the confidence of the majority of the Irish tenantry, and it is well known that the Land Courts have been the most powerful instruments in the hands of the Government with which to combat and practically overcome the Land League since last August. Without it, indeed, matters might be even worse, and even if the ministerial measures do in the end prove unsuccessful, it would have been quite impossible for a Liberal Government not to give them a trial. It must be right and just to endeavour first to correct abuses and amend unfair laws. If the endeavour fails, then show no mercy. No doubt the introduction of these remedial measures have been in great part due to agitation

---

[1] EWH had originally written a plural noun where 'gossip' now is.   [2] i.e. Chamberlain.

and its horrible accompaniments. But what great reforms have ever been accomplished in this country without agitation? Mr. G. may perhaps be liable to the charge of excessive sensibility to such outside action, but to attribute wholly the state of Ireland to his 'squeezable' nature is absurd. There might be some truth in it, had Ireland been prosperous and content under a different regime; but history tells continuously a wholly different tale.

Mr. G. has circulated Harcourt's letter. He evidently did not much like the tone and drift of it, but it will not be without its good effect if it tends to open Mr. G.'s eyes to the real state of Ireland and prevent his drawing sanguine conclusions from returns of daily, weekly, and monthly outrages.

The Arrears Bill is now well in committee. The majorities of the Government are not what they should be; and unless they improve, the Lords will probably take heart and reject the bill. If the termination of this Government is to be the forcing of their hands by the Lords, one can hardly conceive a more favourable opportunity for the Peers to do so. The bill is one disliked by the Government themselves, loathed by the Tories, regarded apparently with indifference by the Irish party and with something more than indifference by the Irish landlords, and there could hardly be a measure with which the Government could go to the country with greater unpopularity.

The bombardment of the Alexandrian forts commenced early this morning; and as the ironclads seem to have done their work well and the reply of those forts not immediately silenced to be very feeble and ineffective, the business of bombarding ought to be all over today. If it is brought to so speedy a conclusion, without any damage to our ships and without much loss of life on shore, it will be a creditable business, and one which will redound to the honour of the Government. Except among the extreme Peace party, the action of the Government seems to be generally approved, and, taken in combination with the preparations of a military character which have been silently and earnestly made, it will have a good effect in Egypt and in the East and will raise us in the estimation of our European neighbours. It will show that a Liberal Government can and will act, if necessity arises, as firmly as a Government under Lord Beaconsfield, only with less bounce and less fluster.

The Roseberys somewhat to their surprise were invited to Windsor last week. They have never quite got over the slight which they think they received last autumn when the Queen was at Holyrood and seemed studiously to avoid showing them attention. Lord Sydney, however, assured me the other day that it was the want of room in Holyrood Palace, and the necessity of entertaining those connected with the Volunteers (on whose account Her Majesty stayed in Edinburgh) which was the cause of any seeming discourtesy. At the same time, if it be true, as Rosebery says, that Lord Sydney himself was called upon to make an 'explanation' after he had entertained Mr. G. last autumn at Deal,[1] it is not unnatural that Rosebery himself, specially bound up as he

[1] See 31 Aug. 1881.

is with Mr. G., should conclude that absence of attention or courtesy was intentional.

I am always omitting social events. Dined last night with the Wolvertons. He is just as enthusiastic about Mr. G. as ever. He hoped to get Mr. G. to go yachting with him this autumn, which is a capital idea if it can be managed. Nobody gives one a much better dinner. There have been plenty of dinners going on lately. I had [a] particularly pleasant one last week at the Cowpers in their beautiful house in St. James' Square to which they acceded just before they went to Ireland. They seem to be both thoroughly glad to be back again in this country, freed from the cares of viceregal life. We had there among others the Baths, Pembrokes, Droghedas, Lady Bradford (to whom I sat next and who displayed no political animosity,[1] Sydneys, Lady M. Alford, A. Balfour, &c. The night before that I dined with the Brabournes—at the house in Queen Anne's Gate which he bought in order to entertain in it as Home Secretary![2] Never did a man certainly show in so pronounced a way his disappointment. I can understand anyone changing his opinions, but I cannot understand a man first accepting the high honour of a peerage from the Minister whom he subsequently denounces and renounces.

Lady Aberdeen and Lady Breadalbane both commenced their political parties last week, and both did them in the very best of styles. There was a somewhat insufficient response to the invitations in both houses.

Wednesday, 12 July.[3] Both sittings of the House yesterday were again devoted to the committee on the Arrears Bill. Progress was extremely slow; practically no faster (as Mr. G. said) than that made with the Crime Bill. Mr. G. attributes the resistance to the Arrears Bill in great measure to the sore and exasperated feeling which the atrocity of the crimes in Ireland has raised in this country and which has slackened the interest and zeal in support of legislation favourable to the people of Ireland. The majorities for the Government, with the assistance of the Parnellite votes, kept at the moderate level of about 70. The stubborn resistance which the Tories are offering to the bill in the Commons looks as if they were preparing the way for its rejection in the House of Lords; otherwise their opposition to it would be for the most part a mere *brutum fulmen*. The more one thinks of it and the more one hears, the more probable does it appear that the Lords will throw out the bill. If they do resort to this extreme measure, I cannot conceive that the Government will not resign. If the Opposition accepts the responsibility of forming a Government, they must appeal to the country and run the risk of throwing it into the turmoil of a dissolution. Harcourt told me last night he hoped the

[1] She had been a close friend and intimate correspondent of Disraeli.
[2] See 9 May 1880.
[3] EWH dated this entry '*Tuesday, 11 July*'. It was on the 11th that the Commons *again* sat in committee on the Arrears Bill.

end was near. He is sick or pretends to be very sick of office. If the bill is allowed to be thrown out, the Tories certainly ought to be ready to accept office; and in spite of all their professed unwillingness to return to power just now, I expect with all the many hungry souls for places that they will exhibit readiness to do so. It seems certain that a dissolution will mean the return of some 70 or 80 followers of Parnell—probably of even more determined disposition than the present men. These would probably hold the balance. With an extensive scheme, however, of expropriation of landlords dangled before their eyes by the Tories, it is quite possible they might be more tolerant of a Conservative Government for the moment than of a Liberal Administration. Accordingly, the Tories might carry on for a time. Moreover, they would be in possession of strong powers, without incurring the odium of having created those powers. Possibly, therefore, when once the dangers of a General Election were over, the Tories might be in a more favourable position to govern Ireland with effect than the Liberals. It will be a grim satisfaction at any rate to see them try their hand at the Irish and Egyptian difficulties. I would indeed submit with a good grace to the change were it not for the acute feeling of disappointment that Mr. G.'s final rule should not have been attended with less troubles and better results.

The Alexandrian bombardment seems to have been a complete success and worthy of the British navy; our loss was trivial: the practice of the huge guns wonderfully accurate, the frightful smoke which they make one of the greatest drawbacks to them. Charlie Beresford and Tom Brand seem to have both distinguished themselves with their respective gun-boats.[1]

I have omitted to note the fate of the bill introduced the other day by the Duke of Argyll to give the alternative of swearing or affirming. It was rejected by the Lords with the most sovereign contempt. This shows how little use it would have been for the Government to have attempted to meet the case of Bradlaugh by legislation.

Thursday, 13 July. 'The apprehended letter from dear old John' (Bright)—as Mr. G. put it in writing to Lord G[ranville]—arrived yesterday, in which he says his resignation must be tendered to Her Majesty.[2] All his affection and loyalty for Mr. G. cannot get over his scruples about the action of the fleet off Alexandria. Such action is wholly inconsistent with the tenor of his political life, and he cannot be a party to it. He moreover views with the greatest apprehension the possible consequences of the bombardment. Mr. G. has used all his persuasive powers I fear in vain, and there seems no prospect of Bright's reconsidering his position. Mr. G. has tried to make him look

---

[1] In the sections about guns and smoke there were verbs including the words 'seems to'. At the end of the paragraph EWH wrote '(Four "seems" in 8 lines!)'. But he eliminated two 'seems' and the final remark by pencilling over them.
[2] Ramm, i. 392 and G. M. Trevelyan, *The Life of John Bright* (London, 1925), p. 433.

upon this military step as one really conducive to peace and order. Bright's loss will be very great. It will be severely felt by Mr. G. himself, who will probably feel parting with Bright more acutely than any one of his other colleagues save Lord Granville. It will be a great blow to the Government. He is sure to carry with him all the Peace party and a large number of the Dissenters; and his resignation will be interpreted even outside that circle as foreboding still more decided intervention to come.

Curiously enough, when we are practically at war with a subject state of the Porte, Mr. G. dined last night with Musurus. Mr. G. was pleased with the tenor of the language held by Musurus, who expressed himself pretty confident that the Sultan would send troops after all to Egypt and send them for the purposes we want. Mr. G. evidently 'slipped it into' Musurus, to whom he pointed out that our action had cleared the way for the Sultan's troops; that the Sultan had now a great opportunity; and that for the Sultan the present was a supreme moment for the Ottoman Empire, indeed probably the last. Mr. G. seems to have met at Musurus's dinner table with nothing but sympathy and indeed satisfaction from the other foreign ministers present.

Meanwhile the news from Alexandria is bad. Arabi has apparently withdrawn under the flag of truce himself and his army, and left the city to the prey of fanatic Bedouins and released convicts, who have looted and nearly destroyed the city and have also massacred the Europeans who were still left behind. This is a serious business. It makes the action of the Government far more open to criticism. It makes the military situation more difficult; as now, if we have to follow up the naval action by the landing of troops, we shall have probably to march up to Cairo; and that at this time of year would be a very serious matter.

Dined last night at the Aberdeens—a pleasant dinner; among the company we had the Enfields, Belpers, Hayters, Harcourts, Lady Ridley, Lord Balfour, Chandos Leighs. Went afterwards to the Army (Childers') and Navy (Northbrook's). Lord Kenmare does not think the Lords will resort to rejection of the bill; but I still hold to my prophecy, all things considered. The departure of Bright and its effect on the Liberal party would be an additional inducement for the Tories to have their fling at a General Election.

Friday, 14 July. Bright still lingers on; but, though he has not taken the final plunge yet, I can't believe he can possibly remain, especially after what he said to Rosebery at the Marlborough House garden party yesterday. He spoke in the most open-mouthed manner. He denounced the Egyptian business as worse than anything ever perpetrated by Dizzie. 'It is simply damnable'. But he is still *of* the Cabinet. Mr. G. had a lengthened interview with him this morning, and this afternoon repeated the gist of his conversation in writing.[1] The arguments Mr. G. used came in effect to this: 'You

---

[1] Morley, iii. 84–5.

can't be one who believes that all use whatever of force is unlawful. You are one who detests wars, and believes wars to have been generally unnecessary. In this I agree myself. As to any particular use of force you would look first to a justifying cause, and then endeavour to appreciate the actual effect. What has been the case with the present resort to force? Egypt had reached such a state of disorder that all legitimate authority had been put down, and the situation of force could only be met by force. What did we do? What we tried to bring about was that, if force were to be employed, it should be employed by the Sovereign (the Sultan) and under the highest possible authority—the authority of the Great Powers of Europe. While this was proceeding and maturing, a bye-question arises. The British fleet, lawfully present in Alexandrian waters, is menaced. It naturally requires the surrender of the menacing forts, and on being refused proceeded to destroy them. By this act we are responsible for the loss of a certain amount of life in the batteries; but the real destruction—the pillaging and conflagration of Alexandria which followed the bombardment was not attributable to our shells, but to the seemingly wanton wickedness of Arabi. What has been the reception or effect of this act of bombardment of ours? No one disapproves it. It has struck a heavy blow at the violence of Arabi; it has shewn the fanaticism of the East that Europeans can't be massacred with impunity; it has advanced the European[1] question towards a peaceable solution'. Mr. G. wound up by referring to the value of Bright's cooperation in the Cabinet in the cause of peace, and to the great blow to peace which the withdrawal of that cooperation would entail.

The badgering in the House yesterday at question time knew no bounds. Question after question was fired off. Neither Northcote nor Cross took any prominent part in this. The cross-questioning was left to their subordinates—Gibson, Beach, and Smith seem to have divided the honours.

The House made very poor progress last night in committee on the Arrears Bill. It was, Mr. G. said, deplorably slow—even worse than that of the Crime Bill. Its progress in committee of this bill certainly illustrates most strikingly the breakdown of parliamentary procedure. Here is a bill, important no doubt and one to which free exception may justly be taken, but comparatively short and simple, and not obstructed by the Irishmen; and yet it has taken already 5 days in committee to discuss the first clause, and the end has not yet come!

I hear on all sides that the way in which Harcourt conducted the Crime Prevention Bill through the House has added much to his parliamentary position and will always redound much to his credit. He shewed far more consideration and good humour than ever could have been expected.

Mr. G. has been summoned to Windsor next Sunday. He is only, however, asked for one night. She seems to have asked the Dean[2] to give Mr. G. a bed

---

[1] So EWH writes, but G. of course wrote 'Egyptian'.
[2] Gerald Wellesley of Windsor.

for the other (Saturday) night, because she is to take the sacrament next Sunday and likes to be quiet over-night.[1]

Monday, 17 July. Bright finally resigned on Saturday morning; and, while professing the greatest reluctance at having to part political company with Mr. G., he stated that his views on the subject of foreign intervention were more at variance with those of Mr. G. than he anticipated or had any idea of. Thus in all probability terminates the active political career of John Bright! His departure will be a great blow personally to Mr. G. and cannot fail to damage the Government. He represents a large and growing section of the political followers of the Government, and his name is more widely known in the country, next to that of Mr. G., than anyone else's. It is a household word among numbers of electors, who hardly know Lords Granville and Hartington, and in whom these statesmen at any rate fail to elicit any enthusiasm. Mr. G. has given no sign as yet of what his intentions are about filling up Bright's place. There is no one specially marked out for a seat in the Cabinet. Dilke, if he could be taken from the Foreign Office just now, is out of the question. The Queen would certainly not 'look at' him. Trevelyan is probably the best entitled to promotion in the Cabinet. If it is not considered necessary to make another Cabinet Minister, the Chancellorship of the Duchy of Lancaster might at the end of the session be offered to Playfair? It might offer a means of replacing him by a more competent man in the chair of committees.

The situation in Egypt is changed little for the better. The destruction of Alexandria is nearly completed. Little is known of Arabi's whereabout or intentions; though, according to Wilfrid Blunt, he (Arabi) is bent on repeating the process of destruction throughout Egypt, if he is not allowed to have his own way. As might be expected, no assistance comes from the Porte. In the midst of such a state of things, the only suggestion made by the Sultan to Lord Dufferin is the substitution of Halim for Tewfik as Khedive!—as if a change of Khedives could re-establish law and order in the country, and as if we could possibly assent to the overthrow of a viceroy who had behaved loyally towards us and to whom we were wholly pledged.

Mr. G. (I hear) told Sir W. James last week that he looked forward confidently to slipping out of office this year. I have always thought that to attain this object has been one of the primary reasons for his arranging an autumn session. He is committed to procedure; and indeed can't go before. When this is settled, he will consider himself free. Whether it is possible, and whether it can be right, for him to contemplate such a step with so little prospect of a settlement by that time of either the Irish or the Egyptian difficulties is another and very serious matter.

[1] EWH has written but then heavily crossed out: 'What a [trying?] woman she is!'

Pembroke thinks the Lords after all will *not* throw out but merely alter the bill.

I am sorry to say the loss of Godley is really in prospect and indeed imminent.[1] His loss to us will only be second to his loss to Mr. G., which will be untold. To the state of his health, to his nervousness about himself, to his unambitious nature or excessive modesty, and to his desire for permanent employment, his acceptance of a Commissionership of Inland Revenue is due. But one can't help feeling that in taking this step he is throwing himself rather away and that his brilliant talents might be turned to better account. It is impossible to overrate his charm as a colleague; always ready, never put out, never excited; while his modesty, simplicity, genuineness, unselfishness, and brilliancy are irresistably attractive.

Tuesday, 18 July. Old Bright yesterday made a short statement in the House in deference to its decidedly expressed wishes. He did it in the best possible taste, and succeeded in doing a disagreeable task without damaging himself or his colleagues—very unlike Forster 2 months ago. Mr. G. made a brief response, greatly to the point and in equally good taste.

There was a Cabinet this morning. They agreed to admit in the Arrears Bill an amendment to promote by means of loans through the Unions the emigration of those willing to leave. I was afraid Mr. G. would hold out against it; but in view of certain defeat had the Government declined to take up this question, he allowed himself to be overruled by his colleagues. This will probably ease the passage of the Arrears Bill, the prospects of which in the House of Lords looks more promising. The Cabinet agreed to the despatch of another regiment to Alexandria for police purposes. They also discussed the question of the very hostile tariff of Spain; but they naturally declined to assent to the only remedy suggested, which was retaliation by a rearrangement of the Wine Duties.

The Porte still dallies. No answer can be got out of the Sultan, and the hope now is that he will decline to send troops or else continue to dally so as to make it possible for the Powers to act independently and appoint other mandatories to settle the Egyptian question.

In the midst of all the present press of business on Mr. G. he has found time to indite a line of sympathy to Mr. R. J. Herbert, R.A., on the loss of his son.

Thursday, 20 July. Dined last night with the Cavendish Bentincks. We were 28, and I think (barring 2 foreigners who don't count) I was the solitary Liberal. I am sure if I had been a Tory all my life the bitterness and narrowmindedness of my friends would have converted me to Radicalism. It is all indiscriminate abuse. Everything that Mr. G. does must be wrong and

[1] See 5 June and 6 Aug. 1882.

wicked, and everything wrong and wicked that happens must be attributable to Mr. G. He has created all the difficulties in Egypt and Ireland. His one object is to ruin landlords, plunder bondholders, and to destroy, in short, the country. Went afterwards to the Aberdeens and Hayters.

There are limits to forbearance and patience, and the forbearance and patience of the Government with the Porte are at last exhausted. They yesterday sent the Sultan an ultimatum. If he declined to reply to the request of the Conference to intervene in Egypt within 12 hours, some independent action would have to be taken. This morning a characteristic response came from the Porte, avoiding the point at issue and merely intimating a readiness to join the Conference. The Government have determined to send out troops to Malta and Cyprus so as to bring up our available force to 15,000 men, ready for active intervention in Egypt either alone or in concert with France. It is much better we should now take our own independent line, but the difficulty is that having summoned a conference we can't disregard the European Concert and also our relations with France established by the late Government. A vote of credit is to be moved on Monday so that we may be all ready the moment we can cut in or are driven to cut in. This probably means an extra 1$^{\rm d}$ on the income tax.

Brackenbury has had the bad taste to prefer his own interest to those of the public, and actually applied to Lord Spencer for leave to go on active service to Egypt.[1] Lord Spencer wisely took his proposal as a resignation. Mr. G. is shocked at Brackenbury's behaviour.

Friday, 21 July. Foster, formerly of the Treasury and now manager of the Ottoman Bank at Constantinople, came here yesterday. He is well behind scenes at the Sultan's Palace, and he told me he is convinced that Arabi has all along been the tool of the Sultan, who has instigated the so-called national movement in order to get rid of the European control in Egypt for fear of its leading to practical annexation.

The Lords had their meeting today. It is believed they are not going to move the rejection of the 2nd reading of the Arrears Bill but are to amend it pretty freely in committee. That is, they will probably endeavour to emasculate it so as to make it useless.

The question of the hostility of the Spanish tariff came before the Cabinet the other day. 'Joe' actually made a proposition to *retaliate* by means of our wine duties so as to compel Spain to behave herself better towards us! These very unorthodox views, however, met with no support from anyone else. To propose retaliation is of course absurd. A readjustment, however, so as to coax Spain to treat us better might be possible to entertain, were it not for the difficulty of taking any step which would involve a loss to revenue.

Lord Spencer has been pressed by some people to obtain a renewal of the

[1] See 9 and 20 June 1882.

PPP Act[1] of last session; but at present he sees no necessity for this and, though he leaves himself quite free to apply for it in the autumn session, he hopes to be able to get on with the Crime Prevention Act alone. It would be dreadful, if not useless, to go to Parliament again for further powers, particularly after the very partial success only which the act of last year had.

No progress made at Constantinople; and the news from Egypt is more and more disquieting—more Englishmen are said to have been massacred, Arabi to be bent on and actually working mischief, and his forces to be rallying and increasing.

Tuesday, 25 July. We are in for it; and are practically embarked in an Egyptian war. Moreover the brunt of it will fall upon us alone. France declines to do more than assist us in the protection of the Suez Canal. The Porte—though at the last moment she characteristically gives some indication of an intention to send troops at the eleventh hour—will probably render little, if any, assistance. There is a chance of the co-operation of Italy. At least she is to be invited, in spite of the Anglophobia which she has recently been displaying; (Her Majesty does not at all like the idea of the invitation); but the odds are, I think, rather against her 'cutting in' now. This being the case, we are to send out some 15 or 17,000 men from here, and about 10,000 Indian troops are to come from India to join ours.

Active intervention having been decided upon, Mr. G. had yesterday to move the vote of credit, of which he had given notice on Friday. On making the motion he delivered a statement in review and in defence of the Government policy in Egypt. He was well up to the mark. The construction of the speech was masterly. He left nothing almost unsaid and met all the points most liable to attack energetically and skilfully. He referred just enough to the responsibility of the late Government in bringing about the present state of things; but judiciously made no strong party attack. He was followed by Northcote, who was unusually weak and who begged for an adjournment of the debate till today.

Mr. Gladstone's statement had been preceded by a most unseemly scene of arrant obstruction and abusive language to which his moving that precedence should be given now on every day to Government business gave rise. Healy and O'Donnell were the principal offenders. Anything more monstrous or audacious than their conduct it is almost impossible to conceive.

In the House of Lords last night there was also an Egyptian debate. Lord Granville does not seem to have been 'in form'. According to Pembroke he quite lost control of his brain and tongue several times—quite painful to witness.

For the moment the action of the Government in regard to Egypt is fairly popular, but it is not until lives are lost and pockets are pinched that John Bull hollows out; and no doubt he will hollow loud enough over the war later

[1] i.e. the Irish Protection of Person and Property Act.

on. From a national point of view, active intervention seems to have been inevitable; from a political point of view, I think it means another and very large nail in the ministerial coffin. It appears to me that the fatal mistake we have made all along has been not to have declared from the first that the internal affairs of Egypt, notwithstanding our controlling powers, were of insufficient moment to entail active intervention, so long as the Suez Canal was not endangered, and that for the safeguarding of the Canal we were ready to make any sacrifices, but for this only.

Garnet Wolseley is to have chief command. Sir J. Adye also goes out. Likewise all three of Childers' private secretaries, including Nevy Lyttelton. In short the whole military staff of the War Office is going out, which seems to be rather an extraordinary arrangement.

It will be another 3 weeks at least before business commences; and the fear seems to me to be that some terrible catastrophe will happen in the meanwhile—wholesale massacres and destructions of property.

It has been determined not to appoint for the moment a new Chancellor of the Duchy of Lancaster. There was an idea first that Childers should hold the seals provisionally—he having once before held them; but he is too greatly occupied just now to undertake additional duties, and a nice point might have been raised about his seat had he taken a new office. Accordingly Lord Kimberley is to be an interim Chancellor. When the place comes to be filled up permanently, it will be an extremely difficult matter to know what to do with it. If an addition is to be made to the Cabinet, I am not sure whether on the whole, despite his physical infirmities, Fawcett is not the man who would command greatest confidence. He is a force in the country. He would alarm no one—not even the timid Tories; and would please immense numbers. His honesty, straightforwardness, and good sense are universally admired.

Thursday, 27 July. Everything is now Egypt. The Prince of Wales has volunteered to go out. This is the latest news. Ponsonby telegraphed this morning to Mr. G. to know what his views were.[1] Mr. G. naturally and properly threw cold water upon the proposal, to which H.M. is averse. He said it was contrary to precedent, and that H.R.H. would run some risk especially from fever, and that, while the Prince's patriotic feeling would be much appreciated by the country, the objections far outweighed the advantages. It appears that H.M., regarding the matter as 'non-political', has also taken the advice of Lord Cranbrook and Northcote about it; and it is said, which I can hardly credit, that they favour the project. It surely is a most extraordinary proceeding that on a public question of this kind the Queen should consult with the leaders of the Opposition, and even before her First Minister! Mr. G. has not noticed this openly, but it certainly sounds unconstitutional.[2]

[1] Guedalla, ii. 202.   [2] See 31 July 1882.

The Egyptian debate still proceeds. It was resumed on Tuesday by Stanley, who Mr. G. said spoke 'temperately'. Lawson followed, launching out strongly against interference generally. Dilke replied later on in a speech which Mr. G. thought extremely able, and which was regarded with evident favour by the House generally. No one certainly next to Mr. G. has such a power of stating a case luminously. He marshals his facts so well and states his arguments so clearly. He is always calm and collected. Gorst afterwards treated the House to what Mr. G. called 'a minute and ingenious criticism, but in the spirit more of an advocate than of a legislator'. Cross contended that the Government ought to have taken the Egyptian question under its sole care many months ago and settled it by military force without reference to the wishes or the title of other Powers. Chamberlain followed and wound up. He went so far as to say—and Mr. G. could not make out what his object was in saying so—that, had there even been no control, we should be under the circumstances still obliged to do what we are doing.

In the debate yesterday, Bruce—Conservative M.P. for Portsmouth—is supposed to have spoken well and with some weight. The only other speech of importance was that of Goschen, who evidently spoke with great success and of course with great authority.

There was a rumour reported the day before yesterday that Arabi or rather some of his friends and allies were getting a little tired and alarmed at the prospect. But there is probably little chance of their really coming to terms.

Sunday, 30 July. The vote of credit debate terminated on Thursday and was carried by an overwhelming majority. The small minority was made up of about 10 Lawsonites, 1 Tory (P. Wyndham), and a few of the irreconcilables, *told* by Biggar and O'Donnell. The debate was a good illustration of the plethora of talk which now curses every discussion in the House of Commons. It was a simple question—important, no doubt, and one on which many had a right to speak, but not seriously opposed—and yet it absorbed 4 whole days! Mr. G. wound up the debate. While admitting the difficulties of Lord Salisbury and the benefits resulting from the control of Egypt, he pressed it home on the Opposition that the arrangements made by Lord S[alisbury] directly favoured the action of the disturbing parties and helped to render necessary the recent steps taken in Egypt. The only point which Mr. G. thought the Opposition made with some effect against the Government was that by yielding to the French we aggravated the Egyptian difficulties. Otherwise their attack was not formidable. The Tories are so very inconsistent. They first abuse the Government for having isolated England, and then strongly advocate isolated action. They denounce resort to Turkish intervention, and then attribute all difficulties in the East to a want of cordiality with the Sultan.

The Prince of Wales is very anxious to go to Egypt. He even hinted in the event of refusal of resigning his commission and going out as a civilian. One appreciates his pluck and patriotism, but the proposal is open to the gravest objection, as the Government think, on military and political grounds as well as on many other grounds. The Queen is naturally very much opposed to it, and She will therefore be glad to have the Cabinet's concurrence in her views. Wolseley has actually allowed the Duke of Teck to be attached to his staff. It really savours of turning a very serious business into a joke.

I am afraid the Lords mean business, and a very mischievous business, with their amendments in the House of Lords. Pembroke tells me Lord Salisbury fully intends to stand by his two amendments, viz. (1) the joint application of landlord and tenant, and (2) the tenant-right an asset. He is reckless as to the result and indeed is pledged to fight, as it was only in consideration of fighting in committee that the Lords consented to read the Bill a second time. They seem to me to have taken up a most untenable position. There would be something to be said for their rejecting the Bill. They would have quashed a measure which in principle is admitted by all to be open to great objection; they would have prevented the establishment of a bad precedent; they would have avoided any demoralising effect which it may have. Instead of this, however, they retain the principle of the Bill, which is its worst feature, and then propose to emasculate it so that it will be useless in its operation. In short, the upshot would be a maximum of mischief and a minimum of good. It is impossible that the Government can accept the 'joint application' amendment and so make the Bill optional. Gift *and* compulsion were the essence of the Bill. If the Lords and Government come to loggerheads and the Bill is lost, Mr. G. has hinted that he would prorogue Parliament for a week and re-introduce the Bill.

Ireland is for the moment tolerably quiet. Outrages are falling off; but there are not the best harvest prospects; and any failure of crops producing special distress would probably fan the smouldering fire into flame again this autumn and winter. Just now they are cowed by the new Crime Act; and the Land Act seems to continue to command increased confidence and produce gradual and growing good. R. G. C. Hamilton—the acting Under Secretary, the most sensible and able of men—says, 'Whenever the land question is settled and a satisfactory arrangement come to between landlord and tenant, the district quiets down'.

Next to no news from Egypt. The rumours about Arabi's capitulating seem to be at any rate premature, and nothing more has come of it. Lesseps appears to be 'playing old Harry' out there. He has been coquetting with Arabi and taking upon himself to promise that, so long as the Canal is not interfered with, no intervention by either France or Italy need be feared.

Monday, 31 July. The usual French crisis. Such is the uncertainty of French politics! Freycinet beaten on the vote of credit by an overwhelming majority!

I must make two corrections in my yesterday's entry.[1] The Queen did not consult the leaders of the Opposition about H.R.H. until the ministers had been first communicated with. Lord Cranbrook never [?] replied. Northcote was much averse to H.R.H.'s going. Ponsonby in explaining this refers to the precedent of 1804, when the Prince of Wales at that time desired to take part in the Peninsular War. The Government of the day was against compliance with his wish, and the Prince's case was taken up by the Opposition (Sheridan) and consequently the matter was made a party question.

Tuesday, 1 August. The Queen is greatly exercised in her mind—and no wonder—at the behaviour of the Sultan.[2] She characterises his demand for the withdrawal of our troops from Egypt as most 'insolent'. It is quite impossible we should agree to Turkish intervention except on the most stringent conditions, under which the Turk would assist us merely in the work which he ought to do himself and ought to have done long ago. The Government are very firm about this, and Her Majesty much approves their firmness. But what if the Turk insists on going in [for] the exercise of his suzerain rights? This always seemed to me to be the rub and was a probable contingency, whether or not the Porte's cooperation in Egypt had been invited.

Sunday, 6 August. (Yacht Palatine. Off Swanage.) Came down with Lord Wolverton to his yacht at Cowes on Wednesday evening. She is a magnificent 3-masted yacht—steamer and sailing vessel—450 tons—formerly Lord Wilton's. The Brouns (Alice Leighton of old Oxford days)[3]—pronounced Broons—and Col. Williamson, R.H.A. are the only others on board. Lord W[olverton] was pilled last week for 'the Club'—R.Y.S.—a really monstrous shame. He has taken the pilling very good naturedly. We came on here last night from Bournemouth where we had spent the day to enable Lord W. to run over to Iwerne for a few hours. Lady W. unfortunately cannot stand yachting.

We are having most lovely weather and I am enjoying the change immensely. This little holiday just fitted in with Godley, who does not take his final departure till next Saturday.[4] Spencer L[yttelton] is to be our new assistant, which is very nice. Certainly as far as I am concerned it is the most agreeable arrangement of any which could be made.

The amendments which the Lords inserted in the Arrears Bill on Monday last are to be taken into consideration next Tuesday. The Government will be

---

[1] EWH had repeated in his entry for 30 July the statement about the Queen consulting Cranbrook and Northcote but because it was a repetition of what he had written on 27 July he had crossed it out.

[2] Guedalla, ii. 203.

[3] Mrs. Montague Broun was the daughter of Francis Knyvett Leighton, Warden of All Souls, 1858–81.

[4] See 5 June and 17 July 1882.

prepared to give way on one or two minor points, but they will certainly remain firm about the 'joint application'; that is, they cannot possibly accept the amendment requiring the application of both landlord and tenant, which makes the Bill optional instead of compulsory, and in short completely transforms it and strikes at its very root. Lord Salisbury has evidently taken the bit between his teeth and is going to bolt down a reckless course heedless of all consequences. What the upshot of this eventually may be Heaven only knows. It may for the moment displace the Government, but in the long run it must most seriously affect the position of the House of Lords. It is now perfectly impossible for a Radical or even Liberal Government to pass any measure, or pass any measure without its being serious[ly] crippled, so long as the House of Lords takes up this very hostile attitude. Some reformation in the constitution of that august body must be in store before long, and such reform will probably take place during Lord Salisbury's reign.

As all hope of a compromise seems at an end, the Bill will presumably drop; and as soon as supply is got through, Parliament will be prorogued. A new session will be held in the course of a week or so for the sole purpose of re-introducing the Arrears Bill and giving the Lords another chance of passing it. We shall, of course, hear a great deal about Mr. G.'s imperiousness and such like. The common belief is that he is a perfect autocrat and acts off his own bat always, instead of consulting, as he always does, with the moderate men in his Cabinet, Lords G[ranville], Hartington, and Northbrook.

Later. Just heard from Downing St. Godley says the parliamentary situation looks better. The Cabinet have hit on what they think a good amendment to Lord Salisbury's first amendment (the joint application one), and as to the second they intend to accept it, only limiting the period within which the sale of the tenancy must take place if the landlord is to have a slice out of it in respect of arrears. Good divisions in the Commons are, I hear, reckoned upon. There is also further good news:—It is thought we shall be able to stave off intervention in Egypt altogether, even if the Sultan issues the necessary proclamation against Arabi, which is doubtful.

If after the assumption by the Government of this conciliatory attitude towards the Lords, and Lord Salisbury still remains obstinate with a view to force on a dissolution, the programme which such obstinacy would invite should be, I think, as follows: Prorogue Parliament, re-introduce the Arrears Bill again; on its being rejected, adjourn the House till November; pass the Corrupt Practices Bill and introduce a simple measure equalising the county and the borough franchise, which, of course, the Lords would contemptuously dismiss; then dissolve. The cry would then be naturally and properly the reform of the House of Lords as well as of the House of Commons.

The Government are naturally charged with inconsistency for their proposal to employ Indian troops in Egypt at the cost of India. No doubt the circumstances connected with Afghanistan and Egypt are by no means identical, and there is much to be said for charging India with a part of the cost of an expedition which is undoubtedly taken to a considerable extent in the interests of India. But I confess I should, were I in the House, give a very reluctant support to the Government proposal, if I gave it at all.

Friday, 11 August. (Off Cowes.) Last Sunday, when at Swanage, we drove over to see Corfe Castle—the finest ruin I ever saw. The stonework is marvellous. It was destroyed in the Civil War, and the masonry is of such magnificent solidity that huge masses have fallen perfectly intact.

On Monday we came round the south of the Isle of Wight, back round to Southampton. Lord Wolverton had to go up to Town on Tuesday, when I went over via Newport to Freshwater where Mother, Ethie, and Concie are. C[oncie] seemed rather better, poor little girl. On Wednesday we came back to Cowes. Yesterday we amused ourselves in the new steam-launch. Today we are off to Weymouth. I have put off returning till Sunday.

The Arrears Bill fighting is all over. Mr. G. was in his most conciliatory mood. The Government made sundry concessions, but practically rejected the most important amendment of the Lords which converted the Bill into an optional measure. The Government had first-rate majorities, and 'Old Sarum'[1] has had to cave in. It is said that he was for continuing the fight, but was not allowed to do so by his party. He accordingly had to confine himself to making a fighting speech and complained that he had no majority! So we have tided over the crisis, which is a great comfort.

The Mansion House dinner took place on Wednesday. Mr. G. seems to have spoken well, but H[orace] S[eymour] says the other speeches were not good at all. Childers lengthy and overdone; Northbrook halting and feeble; Dodson inaudible; and the Lord Chancellor[2] prosy. So one did not miss much by being absent.

What I am rather sorry to have missed was the reception by Mr. G. of Cetywayo. John Arthur [Godley] says the conversation was interesting; Cetywayo's utterances were quaint and eloquent after a fashion; his gesticulations like those of an excited Frenchman. Everybody, Godley says, was pleased with Cetywayo and his manners. When Mr. G. gave him his photograph, he roared with laughter, but this was his way of expressing pleasure.

Playfair has intimated his intention to resign.[3] His resignation is, I am sure, a necessary part of making the rules of the House more effectual; but it won't be easy to find a successor and especially a really competent successor. Probably in most respects Courtney would be the best man; but would he take it? The place should certainly be better paid. It is one of the most burdensome of all offices.

[1] i.e. Lord Salisbury.   [2] Lord Selborne.
[3] As Chairman of Committees and Deputy Speaker of the House of Commons.

The life of yachting is so demoralising and lazy-like that it is next to impossible to get through anything in the shape of reading beyond the newspapers; but I have been trying to read Mozley's reminiscences of Oxford and the Oxford 'Movement' which so excited Mr. G.[1] It is interesting but not overpoweringly so. I have also been reading a short novel which has been talked about a great deal—an American political tale entitled *Democracy*.[2] It is written with much power and vivacity; but I have been slightly disappointed.

Sunday, 13 August. (London) Returned to Town this afternoon. We had a most enjoyable steam-sail on Friday to Weymouth. I think it must be something like 28 years ago since I was last there. For fear of a roll we went over yesterday to Portland Harbour. In the afternoon we paid a visit to the prison. I had got the Home Office to telegraph down special permission for us. We paid a second visit there this morning by attending service at the convict church. Looking down from a gallery pew upon 1400 convicts was a very strange and sad sight. The service was very impressive. There was every appearance of devotion and attention. No one looked round on us, and only a few of those sitting at right angles as much as glanced up at us. The singing was most hearty. The man who played the harmonium had murdered his wife. It was a strange company to be in. Discipline very smart and striking. Cleanliness wonderful. Saw Sunday dinner served out. The Sunday meal consists only of bread and cheese. The order being given, each cell door was unlocked. At the word of command, 'One step to the front', each man advanced and took up the plate containing his meal which had been deposited on the floor opposite his cell-door. At the further command, 'One step to the rear', each convict stepped back into his cell and simultaneously closed his iron door which shuts with a spring. It was like a roar of cannon. Some of the men exhibit great ingenuity. Some beautifully designed and executed tablets on slate were the work of one man with the aid only of the roughest tools made by himself. Another produced some fine carving in stone; a third some carved work in wood. We saw the various implements with which attacks had been made from time to time on the Governor and warders, attended in some cases with fatal results. Not the least interesting part of what we witnessed were the fossils excavated in the quarries—animals of prehistoric age and trees found in the stone, bark and all, 27 feet deep, the date of which is absolutely inconceivable. The Governor was apt to 'draw the long-bow' somewhat and to flash in our faces the many royalties from whom he had received attention; but he was very courteous and interesting. (Clifton is his name.) He gave us two instances of persons whom he had himself conducted over the prison as visitors and who at no great interval of time had found their

---

[1] See 25 June 1882.   [2] By Henry Adams.

way into the prison as convicts—one remarkable case, a clergyman convicted of forgery.

Here one is back again after a most pleasant 10 days' trip. Nobody could have been kinder than Lord Wolverton. It was too bad his being blackballed for 'the Club'. I am sorry to find that he thinks he has been passed over. He evidently considers himself much aggrieved—that he ought to have at least had such an office as the Chancellorship of the Duchy of Lancaster, with even a seat in the Cabinet! It is certainly strange how badly some people gauge their own *métier*.

Saturday, 19 August. The House is at last adjourned. It has certainly been a most vexatious and most disappointing session; but, thanks in great measure to Old Sarum and his brother peers, who played completely into the hands of the Government, the Government come out of it stronger than they went in, and Mr. G.'s own personal position is greater than ever it was. Mr. G. was in excellent spirits this week and would have gone away yesterday in high glee had it not been for the unfortunate affair of Mr. Gray, M.P., who was committed to prison and fined for contempt of court by Judge Lawson. Gray's offence consisted in his having, as proprietor and editor of the *Freeman's Journal*, questioned the sobriety of the jury who had convicted a 'moonlighter' for murder. It was a very grave offence no doubt, but the committal will, it is feared, have a most irritating effect in Ireland. Lawson was no doubt right to visit the offence severely, but the general opinion seems to be that the punishment is out of proportion to the offence; and, though he did the right thing, he did it in the wrong way (as Herschell said to me) as he certainly ought to have allowed Gray to appear with counsel. Almost all the House having left town, and it being the eve of the adjournment, it was impossible to take any parliamentary step in the matter such as appointing a committee of privilege, for which there were precedents. Moreover, it seems to be a great question whether Parliament or the Crown has power to interfere with a sentence of this kind. Mr. G. is much concerned by the occurrence, as is also Lord Spencer. He thought it one of the worst pieces of luck which have befallen the Government.

Outrages are again terribly to the front in Ireland as far as atrocity is concerned. Yesterday there was a quadruple murder—a man, his wife, his daughter, and his mother. One of the man's sons has since died of his wounds, and another is supposed to be fatally injured. This is surpassing in horror all previous outrages.

Mr. G. went down to Osborne yesterday. He went on board Lord Wolverton's yacht today and is to spend Sunday at Portland. Mrs. G., Mary, and Herbert accompanying him. Ponsonby says the Queen was pleased with his visit. They always seem to get on well together whenever they meet.

Sunday, 20 August. The general impression seems to be that the position of the Government is at this moment very good. It is very strange that it should be so. They are at war; they have been baffled in legislation; they have lost 2 very influential members of the Cabinet; they have had to raise the most unpopular taxes. It is almost entirely due to the marvellous power of one man, which unites his friends and baffles his foes. The more hated he is by society, the more loved he is by the masses.

It was announced this last week that Cetywayo is to be sent back to Zululand under certain conditions. Lord Salisbury & Co. of course are furious. 'It is another reversal of policy'. 'It is again undoing the work of their predecessors'. 'How can there be continuity of Government'? The fact is if the work of the Conservatives is not to be undone, they must take care to do it better. The arrangements made by the late Government had completely broken down. There were only two alternatives to which, according to the most sober-minded and unprejudiced persons, resort could be had. These were restoration of Cetywayo or annexation. Annexation is of course out of the question. So the restoration or partial restoration of the old Zulu monarch was really 'Hobson's choice' amidst immense difficulties. He seems to have exhibited a good many signs of intelligence; notably when on drinking the Queen's champagne at Osborne he pronounced it excellent and complained of the champagne given him by the Colonial Office as a *caution*, or the Zulu equivalent, which turns out to have been procured at 36/ a dozen. He also seems to have the inherent qualities of a courtier. When at Marlborough House, after he had been made known to the young princes and princesses he asked where was the Princess of Wales. He declined to believe that the lovely young woman he saw before him was the mother of such tall children. On Mr. Gladstone's showing him a picture of Bright and describing it as the portrait of 'our Great Orator', Cetywayo at once demurred and said he always had understood that the 'Great Orator' was before him.

The rules of procedure are to be submitted as they stand when October comes. The wisdom of this decision, but taken only after careful communication with the Speaker, Grosvenor, and Lord Hartington, may be questioned; but it is absurd, as some say, that in reverting to the original cloture proposal, Mr. G. is breaking faith with the House. When on the 6th May—the afternoon of that noted evening—he proposed to accept Gibson's two-thirds proviso tacked on to the Government proposal, he distinctly said it was to enable the Government to carry the rules *at once* and reserved full liberty of action if anything unforeseen should occur, which unfortunately did occur, to prevent this.

The Prince of Wales brought his sons here on Wednesday last to show Mr. G. According to all accounts they are remarkably nice boys and greatly improved by their 2 years' cruise in the *Bacchante*. Prince 'Eddie', the eldest, is the tallest and most taking; Prince George the cleverer of the two.

The Lord Chancellor[1] before going away wrote to propose to Mr. G. that there should be appointed a Royal Commission to inquire into the marriage laws and possibly to include in their inquiries the laws relating to divorce. Both questions are said to be in an extremely unsatisfactory position as far as the law is concerned. Mr. G. has thrown rather cold water on the idea. He has got over his scruples about the Deceased Wife's Sister, but he does not seem to have yet shaken off his strong opinions about divorce—at any rate that he is the last person by whom the question should be re-opened.

Mr. G. has offered Whitbread a Privy Councillorship, and also Otway, according to promise. It is unkind to say so perhaps, but have not the occasional notes professing confidence and attachment which have proceeded from Otway had something to do with this coveted honour?

Nothing has yet transpired as to Mr. G.'s intentions about reconstructing the Cabinet. Rosebery, I know, has pressed upon him the desirability of doing this and doing it soon, but I fancy Mr. G. himself, clinging as he does to the hope of escaping from office at the end of the year, would prefer to leave things as they are so that the Government may not be weakened by two reconstructions. At the same time, a letter which Dilke has written to Mr. G. [sic] looks as if something in the shape of changes was in the air.[2] The letter was evidently written to order with the view of eliciting a statement from Dilke as to his position with regard to grants to royalties. Without something approaching to a recantation it would be useless to press Dilke on the Queen for the Cabinet, and I much doubt if what he has said will be deemed sufficient, though it is difficult to say what more decisive expression of opinion could be extracted from him. He says he has consulted with Chamberlain—his 'alter ego'. He can't volunteer a recantation. It would look as if he were buying himself into the Cabinet. Moreover, his opinion as to the wisdom of an inquiry into the Civil List and royal allowances remains unchanged. He feels, however, the collective responsibility of the Cabinet, and even without such inquiry he would go with his colleagues were he a minister. If he remained a subordinate member of the Government or were a private member he should, pending such inquiry, be silent and not vote, except in what he considers a perfectly clear case, namely, the case of providing for the Prince of Wales' eldest son.

Considering what took place when Dilke declined the Chief Secretaryship for Ireland, is his claim to Cabinet office now paramount? Is it not superseded by Trevelyan's claim? It would, moreover, be extremely inconvenient and indeed difficult to take Dilke away from the Foreign Office at such a time as this.

No news of any moment from Egypt. Wolseley's plan of campaign is not known; but he is making his way round to Ismailia or Suez with the bulk of his forces; and it is therefore probable that the attack on Arabi will be made

[1] Lord Selborne.   [2] See 23 Aug. 1882.

from the rear. The Sultan declines to accept the military convention as revised and agreed to by his ministers. Dufferin continues to hold very stiff language. Unless, therefore, the Sultan runs the risk of sending troops contrary to the conditions which we impose—and this is hardly likely—we shall probably be left to do the work entirely by ourselves.

Went yesterday to see Lady de Vesci and Mrs. Reggie Talbot, both of whose husbands are gone out. They naturally are keen for any scrap of news. Both were in fairly good heart. They intend going out to Malta the end of the month, unless the whole thing is over within the next few days, which is possible but I fear unlikely.

Monday, 21 August. The Canal has been occupied with little opposition. At Port Said the few rebel troops there were there laid down their arms. Near Ismailia there has been a little *brush* which has terminated brilliantly according to the accounts to hand—between one and two hundred of the enemy killed and no casualties to speak of on our side.

The Porte not only continues to make difficulties about the proclamation and convention but forbids the exportation of mules and other animals. It is evidently the Sultan who is *nasty*, not his ministers. The latter wish to be friendly, and the fear is they will be dismissed. Lord Dufferin, however, is replete with threats—'all friendly assurances will be withdrawn'. 'When the final settlement comes, the annoyance to which H.M. Government have been exposed will not be forgotten'—and so forth. The three ministers remaining in Town—Lord Hartington, Lord Northbrook, and Childers—have gone so far as to suggest as the only means of bringing the Sultan to his senses that we should discontinue holding communication with him and his representatives at the Porte and no longer communicate with Musurus. There are, I believe, precedents for resorting to such steps without meaning actual bellicose intentions. But it is straining the relations between the two powers rather severely.

The new Russian Ambassador at Constantinople[1] seems to be behaving in a somewhat unfriendly manner. It is difficult to imagine what it means, unless his country wishes to stir up strife between Turkey and this country in order to further her own ends by having the Turk busily occupied and the coast cleared for her own games.

The Green business is again to the front—the time after which he becomes deprived of his living having expired or being just about to expire.[2] All seem agreed that no royal power can grant a pardon. His liberation, therefore, from prison can only take place on the application of his prosecutors, who having succeeded in depriving him of his living ought to be satisfied with the punishment they have inflicted.

---

[1] Nelidoff.
[2] See 19 Sept., 6 and 21 Nov. 1881.

Tuesday, 22 August. The action of Nelidoff, the new Russian Ambassador at Constantinople, seems due to the Emperor,[1] but His Majesty is reported to be in better humour again now.

Mr. G. is wind-bound in Portland Harbour and accordingly goes with the rest of the party today to Iwerne. He was greatly impressed by his visit to the prison, especially by the service in the convict chapel which he attended. He was struck by the extent of the Governor's duties and responsibilities, the perfect organisation and apparent efficiency.[2] He has asked Harcourt if he shall not recommend the Governor for the C.B. He is probably a good and conscientious man, but I rather expect him to be a little wee bit of a humbug and toady.

As regards the Gray case,[3] which still continues to be the main topic of the moment, it appears that Sullivan (Master of the Rolls) has interviewed Judge Lawson and there is a probability that Judge Lawson will release Gray as soon as the Commission now sitting in Dublin is terminated, that is, as soon as the special jury have got through their cases. The release would, of course, be conditional on Gray's entering into recognisances for good behaviour.

Another horrible murder reported yesterday. This time it is an agent near Kenmare. This fresh outbreak of outrages is probably intended to *answer* the Crime Prevention Act. The Labour League seems likely to give trouble in Ireland this winter. It is evidently intended to serve as a peg on which to hang fresh agitation now that the Land League is practically broken up.

Went this afternoon to hear Hubert's new symphony rehearsed for the Birmingham festival next week.[4] It is very advanced and high-pitched and therefore difficult really to judge on a first hearing, but I heard sufficient to indicate that the work is one of very high order—extremely broad in its conception, some of the motives most original and grand. It is worked up in different places in truly magnificent style worthy of Brahms. One of the orchestra called it 'sublime'.

Wednesday, 23 August. What passed the other day between Mr. G. and Dilke as to the latter's position with regard to royal grants evidently had reference to Dilke's future generally, not to any particular offer of the Cabinet in view.[5] In order to put himself right, Mr. G. thinks Dilke might confine himself to making allusion to the past when an opportunity occurs. Dilke's objection to the Royal grants—and Mr. G. admits that it is not an unsound one—has been the omission to appoint a committee for considering them. Now that all the sons, and all the daughters but one, of the Queen have been disposed of, Mr. G. thinks Dilke might in referring to the past course he has taken

[1] Alexander III.
[2] See 13 Aug. 1882 for further reference to Clifton, the governor of the prison.
[3] See 19 Aug. 1882.   [4] i.e. Hubert Parry's 1st Symphony in G.
[5] See 20 Aug. 1882.

treat it as a closed chapter. When a *new* set of cases comes up the question of a committee will naturally arise, which Mr. G. hopes will be entertained. It is quite clear that the Prince of Wales, whose means are already strained to the utmost, cannot possibly make provision for his sons when they come of age (which is close at hand) and for his daughters when they come to be married (which is not far distant). Some arrangement to meet their cases will have to be made. It will be a delicate matter and will not admit of any very lengthened postponement.

From a letter received today from Henry Primrose it is evident that the Indian Government are greatly exercised in their mind at the prospect of having Indian revenues charged with the expense of the Indian contingent sent to Egypt. I confess I still sympathise much with the contention of the Indian Government.

There seems every reason to suppose that the Irish Government have bagged and have evidence against the fiends who perpetrated the horrible atrocity of murdering the Joyce family.

The Sultan seems to be coming to his senses. The prohibition against the exportation of mules for our expedition in Egypt has been removed.

Friday, 25 August. Mr. G. has returned to London somewhat unexpectedly, and I expect he will make his escape hence to Hawarden. He would evidently prefer being there to resuming his cruising operations, unless he were perfectly sure of his weather. He came up from Iwerne, which evidently pleased him much and likewise astonished him considering what a new-made place it is. He seems very well. He has begun to kick out strongly against being any longer body-guarded. He wishes to be able to move again 'without his shadow' (as he calls it).

Lord Lyons reports France to be anxious to keep up the *entente cordiale* which he thinks should be done but only in a general way and without committing ourselves.

Italy abounds in friendly assurances, but she seems to be playing rather a humbuggy part and given to brag. She promises to be a 'good child' now and give us no more trouble.

News has come in this evening of the first real encountre with Arabi's forces. Wolseley moved westwards from Ismailia in order to take possession of a dam constructed by the enemy across the freshwater canal. He took with him the Household Cavalry and 1000 of the line with a few guns and some mounted infantry. He seized and held the post against overpowering odds. It seems to have been quite a brilliant little affair. The Household Cavalry made a gallant charge, and all the troops under Wolseley behaved, he says, excellently well. Casualties few.

It is a very exciting though anxious time. I feel quite Jingoish for the moment. It is, of course, the craze of the Tories now that Mr. G. (or the

'Grand Old Man' as he is universally called now) has adopted their politics and taken leaves out of their books, which he cut up to pieces so when in opposition. His policy has in reality as much resemblance to Jingoism as cheese has to chalk. Expression is well given to this craze by a caricature which is exhibited in St. James' St., representing Mr. G. as disguising himself as Dizzie. It is a clever drawing.

The Government have got and are continuing to get great *kudos* for the admirable manner in which the Egyptian expedition has been fitted out. There has been no hitch, no bustle, no flurry, and great expedition.

Saturday, 26 August. Mr. G. still in Town—highly pleased at the march of events in Egypt of which, however, no further news whatever has been received today. He seems bent on making his escape to Hawarden on Monday unless unforeseen events crop up to detain him. Poor Lord Wolverton will be greatly mortified, I fear.

The Great Man is much taken up at the announced illness of the Archbishop of Canterbury.[1] There have been rumours before this illness of his intended resignation, and it is thought that this attack will probably make him fulfil his intention. The question of his successor has already begun to occupy Mr. G.'s thoughts. He has written to his clerical adviser—the Dean of Windsor[2]—on the subject. I went through the Bench of Bishops with him this afternoon. The field of possible selection is very limited. The Bishop of Winchester[3] stands first, but he is over 3 score years and ten. Next to him comes the Bishop of Durham.[4] What with age and other objections the remaining candidates would probably be Ely, Truro, and Exeter[5]—the latter is hardly eligible.

The cases of *Green* and *Gray* between them have made Mr. G. come to the conclusion that the law of contempt of court is a scandal and requires drastic reform.[6]

Rosebery turned up this afternoon, having come all the way down from Dalmeny to attend the funeral of his groom who was thrown from his horse the other day while accompanying D.[7] and killed on the spot. He went back to Scotland tonight.

Went tonight to the theatre with Mrs. Cavendish Bentinck who must be in Town if anybody is. Her energy is certainly marvellous, only equalled by her good nature. Miss Venetia is an excellent girl.[8]

London is, as usual this time of year in my opinion, very pleasant. There are more people than usual owing to the presence of poor 'grass widows'. There are always plenty of men to dine with at the clubs.

---

[1] A. C. Tait.   [2] Gerald Wellesley.   [3] Harold Browne.
[4] J. B. Lightfoot.   [5] J. R. Woodford, E. W. Benson, and Frederick Temple.
[6] See 21 and 22 Aug. 1882.   [7] i.e. Rosebery himself.
[8] These last two sentences are crossed out in pencil.

Sunday, 27 August. No news all day from Wolseley—in fact none since Friday evening. Anxious wives and relatives are greatly disappointed. Poor Lady Pembroke is in a great state of mind about her brother Reggie [Talbot]. Mrs. Reggie, however, had a telegram today to say 'all right'.

Dined on Friday night with Wilfrid Blunt at St. James' Club and had a long Egyptian talk with him. He considers that he has been grossly mal-treated by the Foreign Office at home and by Malet and Colvin, who he contends have thrown him over and repudiate entirely having made use of him last winter. He still sticks to his friend Arabi or rather maintains that the Egyptians are really in arms for national purposes and no others. As long, however, as they get freedom eventually—that is, so long as they cut adrift from the tyranny of the Porte and secure a substantial development of local government—he professes indifference as to what happens. Unfortunately for him there is damning evidence against Arabi. Some of Arabi's letters have fallen into Lord Dufferin's hands. So far from Arabi's working to throw off the tyranny of the Porte, it transpires from these letters that he has been directly coquetting with the Sultan, to whom he professes abject obedience and attachment. The papers further show a bitter spirit of antagonism to the Khedive, a strong denouncement of the European control in any form what-ever, a profound jealousy of this country, a determination indeed to oppose the Khedive and to get rid of all foreigners, and an assurance of increased tribute to the Porte! This is strangely at variance with the innocent pro-gramme to which Wilfrid has contended the national party were attached.

Saw Sid[1] today. He has had a narrow escape of losing an eye, having been plugged in the face by Newport while grouse driving at Wharncliffe's.

To return to Wilfrid for a moment—he is convinced in his own mind that annexation or something very much akin to annexation will have to take place—and for this reason, that the material for forming a Government by Egyptians will be entirely destroyed. There will be chaos in the country, and the governing powers will consist solely of the Khedive and the few around him, who without external support will be unable to carry on. There is probably a good deal in this; but time alone can show. There is only one thing of which one may be pretty sure, and that is that there will be no annexation. This is the last Government to annex, and it is certain that Europe would not permit annexation, were England ever so eager for it.

Tuesday, 29 August. At last at the eleventh hour, according to Turkish custom, the Porte has expressed its readiness to sign the convention on our terms; and the question which Mr. G. had yesterday to decide in consultation with Lord G[ranville], Lord Northbrook, and Childers—the only other ministers in Town—was whether we should now accept the convention. We don't want now the Porte's assistance. The issue of the proclamation

[1] Sidney Herbert.

denouncing Arabi a rebel, which was the important preliminary to the admission of Turkish cooperation and which might have had a powerful effect on many of Arabi's followers, comes too late. There is the inconvenience which must attach to any joint intervention without any compensating advantages. On the other hand, it is not good policy, and the Government have no wish, that we should estrange ourselves with the Porte more than can be helped.

(All that has taken place at Constantinople clearly shows how impossible it is to deal with such a knave—and a clever knave too—as the Sultan. He never knows his own mind two days or even two hours together—much less can anyone else, be he the minister of the Porte or a foreign ambassador, understand or answer for the vagaries of that Eastern Potentate. If anybody could manage him, it would be Lord Dufferin who has exhibited throughout these difficult times extraordinary diplomatic acumen and great firmness.)

What was determined yesterday with respect to the convention, at Mr. G.'s instance, was that the convention should be accepted but only on the following conditions, viz:

(1) Immediate release of animals, supplies, and persons for the British army, and a promise to aid in forwarding them to Egypt.

(2) Assurance that no impediment will be hereafter offered.

(3) Immediate issue of the proclamation.

(4) British officers to be sent to concert modes of operation with the Turkish officers at Crete or Constantinople.

An attack on the British position at Kassassin Lock is reported this afternoon. It was repulsed with heavy losses. Wolseley calls it brilliant success. No particulars yet known. But it looks as if the enemy were not so entirely routed as was supposed.

Mr. G. had finally to give up the idea of rejoining Lord Wolverton's yacht owing to the continuance of most unsettled weather; and he took himself off this afternoon to Hawarden. He was very sorry to have to throw over poor Lord W. but he is always happiest at Hawarden. He went away in great force and high spirits, in holiday costume—light grey suit—looking more like 60 than 73. Marvellous man!

He gave Mrs. O'Shea another interview this morning at her earnest solicitation. It appears that what she wanted most to press on the Prime Minister was the consideration of her husband's claims to be appointed Under Secretary for Ireland in case my namesake[1] does not retain the place permanently! (This or some other place is very likely what has been at the bottom of O'Shea's overtures and negotiations and friendly professions all along.) Mr. G. thinks the Government is under *some* obligation to O'Shea. I can't admit this at all. There never befell a greater misfortune than to have to take heed

[1] R. G. C. Hamilton was *acting* under-secretary for Ireland at the beginning of his tenure of that post in May 1882. He became the under-secretary and held the post until 1886.

of that man's information. Mrs. O'Shea told Mr. G. that Parnell had broken up the Ladies Land League, had stopped their supplies, had laid hold of the Land League funds—that is, invested them, amounting to £60,000—and was determined to confine himself within bounds of legality.[1] (We shall see how far he sticks to his word in the matter of the Labour League which seems to be making headway and promises to give trouble.) She also said that Davitt and Dillon were both 'in great dudgeon' (as Mr. G. termed it) with Parnell by reason of his restricted action on land and national questions. She regards Davitt as the incarnation of vanity and Dillon as a *tête montée*. She, of course, reflects Parnell's views, and in so doing admitted the improvement of the state of Ireland.

Mr. G. was not a little exercised in his mind at Courtney's having taken himself off to Russia for 5 weeks without saying a word to his chief. Rather cool!—particularly at such a time when what with Egypt and Ireland there are so many urgent questions.

The Queen had another shot gently fired at her yesterday about Dilke. Mr. G., after referring to what had passed before on the subject, told her he was able to give Her an assurance that, if at any time Dilke should be submitted for the Cabinet, he (Dilke) would always go with his colleagues in the matter of royal grants. Mr. G. expressly told Her that his communication had no reference to any specific or immediate proposal affecting Dilke. Indeed he has no intention of 'replenishing' the Cabinet till the autumn, which probably means that he will make no changes until he sees the way clearly to his own position.

The Dean of Windsor is evidently inclined to prefer the Bishop of Durham to the Bishop of Winchester for the See of Canterbury, should it unfortunately fall vacant.[2] The Bishop of W. is rather too pronounced a ritualist, in the Dean's opinion, and lacks firmness. The Dean thinks that Winchester might be too easily led by the advanced party. Moreover, he (the Dean) questions whether Harold Browne would be acceptable to the Queen who has never much appreciated him as Her Diocesan at Osborne. Lightfoot, he (the Dean) regards, is though broad free from latitudinarian tendencies and though less experienced is younger and more vigorous. Mr. G. sees every good but nothing *great* in Bishop of Durham.

Thursday, 31 August. The Porte has swallowed the conditions on which H.M. Government expressed their willingness to accept the convention. The Sultan's ministers, however, put in a final plea that the Turkish troops should be allowed to land on their way to Aboukir at Alexandria. Lord Dufferin is half inclined to advise that we should concede this to them in order not to rub up the Sultan more than we can help. Mr. G. is disposed to agree; but Lord Northbrook and Childers, with whom I communicated, are strongly opposed,

[1] See 28 Dec. 1881.   [2] See 26 Aug. 1882.

especially having regard to the decidedly expressed wishes of the Khedive on this point; and as regards political advantages they think that much more is to be attached to compelling the Turk to land at a place like Aboukir, which would bring him into direct conflict with the rebels, than to respecting the susceptibilities of the Sultan.

The Queen is 'alarmed' at the acceptance of the Turkish convention. She is convinced the Sultan, whom She has always been calling 'our faithful ally', will play us false.[1]

Russia in the person of her ambassador at Constantinople[2] seems inclined to be nasty. On my commenting on this the other day Mr. G. said, 'It is only natural. We did all we could to thwart her when she was waging a just war on behalf of the Slavs; it is her turn now to thwart us when we are waging a just war in Egypt'.

Whitbread has again declined to receive any recognition of his parliamentary services. He won't take the Privy Councillorship offered him by Mr. G. He thinks it is not becoming an independent private member. As to the other candidate for the Privy Council—Otway—Mr. G. hesitates, as he is informed by Lord Wolverton that Otway is a great 'stag' in the City.[3]

Prince Leopold has been ill again. He has been suffering from gravel producing hemorrhage; but is reported better again.

The Queen is much pleased by the candle reflector with which Mr. G. presented Her the other day.

Mr. G. wrote a long letter today in Italian to some old padre to ask him to criticise the translation which he (Mr. G.) recently made in Italian of an English hymn.[4]

The Irish constabulary and Dublin police are likely to give trouble. The matter is most delicate. A real strike would be serious in the extreme, and the Irish Government are naturally anxious to avoid it at all costs; and yet there is the difficulty of appearing to make concessions to agitation and mutinous conduct. Mr. G. is inclined to be very stiff; but one must defer to the Executive on such a matter, especially when the Executive consists of such men as Lord Spencer, Trevelyan, and R. G. C. Hamilton, which is probably the strongest and most competent trio that 'the Castle' has ever had.

Fancy a party on the 30th August! Mrs. Childers was 'at home' last night. There was but a limited concourse to meet the Duke of Cambridge who had been dining there—principally diplomats and officials. She is supposed to stand much on her dignity as the wife of the War Minister.

Last night Mrs. Cavendish Bentinck and Miss Venetia dined with me at the

[1] Guedalla, ii. 207.
[2] Nelidoff.
[3] i.e. that he is a speculator seeking quick profits through dealing in shares of stock.
[4] G. wrote Luigi Tosti about the translation G. had made of Cowper's 'Hark, my soul! it is the Lord'. The translation, beginning 'Senti, senti, anima mia', eventually appeared in the *Nineteenth Century* (Sept. 1883), xiv. 357–60.

Bristol, where one certainly gets by far the best restaurant dinner in London. It really is very good. We went afterwards to the Promenade concert.

No further news from Wolseley today.

Friday, 1 September. The principal item of news today has been a further long telegram from Dufferin giving a detailed account of the latest shifts and changes of that shifty and changeable old Sultan.[1] He (the Sultan) has cried '*peccavi*' unreservedly and says that if only we will allow his troops to land at Alexandria to be passed on direct to Aboukir he will be forever our firmest friend and ally, and as an earnest of his good intentions he professes to be willing to reduce considerably the number of the troops he will send, to place Baker Pasha second in command, and to put the contingent under the direct control of the English generals. Meanwhile a telegram arrived from Wolseley in which he says that Aboukir is an impossible place for the Turk to land; that a landing there would mean heavy naval losses and the release of a strong garrison which Arabi could bring into the field against us; that he thinks it best, and indeed would rather like, that the Turkish troops should be sent round to him in the Canal where he could usefully employ them (which as Lord Northbrook said in my room this evening looks as if Wolseley were in need of further forces), and that failing the Canal the position of Mehs is the best destination for the Turkish troops. Mr. G. is still inclined to give way to the Sultan, in accordance with the strong recommendation of Lord Dufferin, about Alexandria; but he is willing to defer to the judgment of Northbrook and Childers. Accordingly Lord Dufferin has been told to suggest to the Sultan that Wolseley's proposal should be adopted.

Mr. G. has told the Queen that what swayed him in favour of following Lord Dufferin's advice was:

(1) the desire to support and assist an ambassador who, in circumstances of the greatest difficulty, had shewn himself a 'master of his profession' as a diplomatist,

(2) the belief that the landing at Alexandria could be effected in batches and so would be comparatively harmless,

(3) the fear of souring and exasperating the Turks by forcing them to land at a place like Aboukir, which is frowned upon by a strong fortress and which is at best an only partially sheltered shore, within easy reach too of a safe landing place; and accordingly of putting them in a bad temper before the slightest good had been derived from their assistance.

There is much to be said for this; but the Canal has carried the day for a landing place.

Saturday, 2 September. Lord Spencer has had to resort to a bold measure in the matter of the Dublin police, which Mr. G. entirely approves and from

[1] *Parl. Papers*, 1882, lxxxiii. 439.

which he anticipates great advantage. In spite of being promised an inquiry into their grievances and in spite of being warned that their attendance at further meetings would involve grave consequences, over 200 of the Dublin force assembled the night before last and alluded in menacing language to their superior officers as well as increased their demands. It was determined yesterday to dismiss summarily those insubordinate men; and the act of their dismissal was followed by the resignation of the force *en masse*. Accordingly Dublin is police-less. Every precaution for maintaining law and order by swearing in special constables and by the employment of the military has been taken, and the peace has not been broken. The question of engaging the services of some of the London police force has been raised, but the Home Secretary has no power to tell off on duty metropolitan police outside their district, and it is thought that practically none would volunteer to exchange London for Dublin, especially as there are but very few Irishmen in the force to whom a transfer to Dublin from local and personal connection might be an attraction.

In the midst of Irish and Egyptian affairs Mr. G. found time yesterday to write a long letter to Dr. Döllinger, to whom he is much devoted. The main object of his writing was to call Dr. Döllinger's attention to the reprint of a book of an old Archbishop Hamilton in the 16th century—Primate of Scotland—entitled a *Catechism*.[1] Mr. G. attaches great weight to the work and seems specially impressed with the omission in it of all allusion to the Pope when it was setting forth the substance of the Christian religion, and also with its avoiding the use of the term 'transubstantiation' and speaking of the 'God's Board'. He also dilated to Dr. Döllinger on the importance of a new edition of Palmer's *Church* which at his (Mr. G.'s) instance MacColl has in hand.[2]

Mr. G. is greatly pleased that the Lord Chancellor[3] is taking in hand so promptly the revision of the present law of contempt of court at which Mr. G. is greatly exercised in his mind *a propos* especially of the cases of Green and Gray.

Nothing from Egypt, except a few more details of last Monday's engagement and a good report of the healthiness of the climate and the cheerfulness of the troops.

Hubert's symphony seems to have been a great success at Birmingham, excellently performed and well received.[4]

Sunday, 3 September. In the absence of Lord Lyons, Plunkett reports secretly from Paris that Duclerc, the new French Prime Minister, was closeted the

[1] A new edition of the 1552 catechism of John Hamilton, Archbishop of St. Andrew's (1511?–71), was published in 1882 in Edinburgh. Another edition was published in 1884 by the Clarendon Press with a preface by G. See 16 Oct. 1884.
[2] See 14 Dec. 1884.   [3] Lord Selborne. See 26 Aug. 1882.
[4] See 2 Aug. 1882.

other day with Gambetta and that, as far as foreign affairs were concerned, they determined to act together on the basis of the closest friendship with this country.

I have got Mr. G. to sound the Queen through Ponsonby as to whether, considering that there is no fitting person for the Parliamentary Groomship who is willing to risk his seat, She will not take Fred Tracy, although She has the brother—Sudeley—already in Her household. He is anxious for the place, has a safe seat, and would probably do very well for the post.

Wolseley says he can't make a further advance until the railway is in good working condition, without which he could not make sure of his supplies.

Mr. G. wrote the other day a capital letter to Mr. Richard putting the war in Egypt in a light which would be likely to convince the strongest 'peace-at-any-price' person. But as it was sure to be published, and it made references to secret (Salisburian) despatches and to the intercepted despatches of Arabi to the Porte, I doubted whether it should go forward. Lord Granville agrees with me.[1]

Called this afternoon on Lady Donoughmore (Dowager) who is always most cordial and agreeable. She has both her sons-in-law in Egypt.

The Primate[2] seems to be sinking slowly. I don't see why the Bishop of Peterborough[3] should not be thought of as another possible candidate; he is probably the best preacher on the Bench and is certainly second to hardly anyone as an orator in the House of Lords. There is also the Bishop of Truro[4] who will have to be considered.

Tuesday, 5 September. Yesterday and today there has been a slight rally at Addington;[5] though it is possible that it means recovery. Mr. G. thinks the Bishop of Peterborough quite out of the running great as his oratorical and exegetical powers may be. According to Mr. G. the Bishop lacks what he calls ἦθος and weight. The Dean of St. Paul's[6]—the other clerical adviser, who has been called in—favours the Bishop of Winchester most as the best qualified all round. The Dean thinks that the highest interests of the Church would hardly be safe in the hands of the Bishop of Durham in the event of the occurrence of some difficult question of creed or formulary to decide. Sooner than the Bishop of Durham the Dean would have the Bishop of Truro. But above both of these bishops the Dean is inclined to place the Bishop of Ely, though he admits that this appointment might perhaps be too venturesome.[7]

---

[1] G.'s letter to Henry Richard of 31 Aug. 1882 was sent only after the last paragraph, referring to 'covenants, some of them not known to the world' and to the Government having 'the best means of knowing' that Arabi had been trying 'to *sell* to the Sultan . . . the acquired liberties' of Egypt, was excised. Add. MS. 44545, f. 187. See also 5 Sept. 1882.

[2] Archbishop Tait.   [3] William C. Magee.   [4] E. W. Benson.

[5] The Archbishop of Canterbury's country house near Croydon.

[6] R. W. Church.   [7] See 26 Aug. 1882.

A propos of the letter I referred to above to Mr. Richard, which Mr. G. has altered, having cut out all allusion to secret treaties and intercepted despatches, he (Mr. G.) has not been able to let slip the opportunity of expressing himself very freely to Lord G[ranville] about 'Old Sarum' and his secret treaties which he (Mr. G.) regards as the most outrageous of all Lord Salisbury's outrages including his fibs.[1] Mr. G. believes that Lord Salisbury is the only author of secret treaties this century and would evidently like to denounce him publicly on the subject again, though he admits that how, when, and where to do so is not easy to determine. Mr. G. thinks that in justice to Parliament and the country steps should be taken sooner or later 'to make such things as secret treaties impossible'. In addition to the well-known Schouvaloff agreement and Turkish convention, Mr. G. alludes to others, of which it is believed there are records. These are:

(1) An agreement with Austria before going into Congress at Berlin that in return for her cutting down the limitations of Bulgaria, he (Lord S[alisbury]) would support the transfer to her of Bosnia.

(2) An agreement with the Khedive that if he would support the arrangements connected with the joint control in Egypt, he (Lord S.) would prevent the introduction into Egypt of the predominating influence of any other power than France and England.

(3) A hint, not a formal agreement, that France might go to Tunis if she did not interfere too much with us in Egypt.

The Sultan has, it is believed, signed the convention, having accepted the Canal as the place of disembarkation for his troops. The hope now must be that with her accustomed dilatoriness and with the difficulty he will meet in getting together men and money, our decisive blow will have been struck at Arabi before the Turkish troops reach Egypt, when we could say we have no longer call for their services. Her Majesty says she was 'terrified' at the idea of allowing the Sultan to land his men at Alexandria and quite sufficiently 'alarmed' at their landing anywhere. How *can* the Sultan be now believed to be sincere? She thinks that the epithet she once heard Mr. G. use about the Sultan fully justified—that is, 'scoundrel'. She apprehends danger to our troops from the presence of a Turkish contingent.[2] (It is almost amusing to think of Her having become so anti-Turk).

Another despatch of Arabi to the Porte has been intercepted in which he is represented to 'blow' very loudly. He says he has 100,000 men under arms who will fight *à l'outrance* and has already on several occasions defeated the English.

I came across today an interesting letter which Lord G[ranville] sent over from Macdonell, our representative at Munich. It appears that the Princess Royal has had a long and interesting conversation with him about Bismarck and disposition towards this country. She said that our prompt action in

[1] See Ramm, i. 413-14 and 3 Sept. 1882.   [2] Guedalla, ii. 207-8.

Egypt has given Bismarck intense satisfaction, and that he is thoroughly pleased at the business-like way we have gone to work. He believes that our greatest misfortune would be the acceptance of the co-operation of the Turk and if we were to shut our eyes to the intrigues of Russia. He is very anxious to come to a more friendly understanding with this country. She confessed she had recently quite changed her opinion about the man and was beginning to believe and admire him. She was convinced that England is the only country for which Bismarck *au fond* entertains a sincere sympathy and admiration. He hates Russia, can never understand France, despises Austria, and ignores Italy. She expressed herself as being sorry that the prejudice against Bismarck was so deeprooted in this country 'in some quarters'.

Thornton at St. Petersburg reports as to Russia that, if we were to attempt any aggrandisement in Egypt, she would no doubt endeavour to gain something; but that, as we are pledged against this ourselves, she will probably confine herself to attempting to get the Treaty of Berlin revised on the first opportunity. It is with regard to that treaty and the part we took at Berlin during its conclusion that she is sore, very sore. She will not allow herself to be outwitted by Germany at Constantinople, but is evidently sincerely desirous, if possible, to avoid complications.

Wednesday, 6 September. The police difficulties in Dublin are practically at an end. By his firm conduct Lord Spencer has brought the malcontent force on their knees. They have apologized unreservedly and, excepting the ringleaders, will probably be readmitted. Mr. G. thinks that Lord Spencer's conduct has been quite admirable.

In recurring to the subject of the despatch of Turkish troops to Egypt Mr. G. has admitted to the Queen that the 'perfidy' of the Sultan (he can call it by no other name—'insincerity' is too weak a term) leaves him not a 'shred of claim' to take any part; but yet Mr. G. thinks something is due to the feelings of the Sultan's men and the danger of irritating them, and that we ought to be loathe to have a row with Turkey for fear of reopening the whole Eastern question and giving an opening to the 'land-hunger' of some, if not all, the Powers.

Malet says the Khedive is alarmed at the prospect of the arrival of Turkish troops. Arabi will very likely surrender to them in order to put himself right in the eyes of the Islamic world, and the consequence would be the Khedive would never be secure on his viceregal throne. The Khedive's fears are to be calmed down by pointing out that probably Wolseley will have struck his decisive blow before the Turks can possibly arrive; and Wolseley has been told that in the event of a victory and surrender the arrangements for landing the Turkish troops anywhere in Egypt are to be suspended.

Harvest prospects are somewhat gloomy. It will continue to rain, and the fear is that in many parts fine crops will be seriously damaged.

Had quite an assemblage at tea this afternoon of ladies with husbands and relatives in Egypt—Lady de Vesci, Mrs. Reggie Talbot, Lady Pembroke, Lady Donoughmore, and Lady Margaret Hamilton.

Thursday, 7 September. The convention is not yet signed after all, and the latest little game of the Sultan has been to alter the wording of the proclamation in some not immaterial points! Dufferin seems to be in doubt whether this seemingly extraordinary conduct on the part of the Porte is attributable to perfidy or to stupidity. Considering that there is a report from Malet that the Sultan is at his old games of intrigue in Egypt—this time asking one Cadre Bey if Arabi could 'give guarantees'—the former alternative is the most probable. However, further trickeries of the Sultan mean further delays as to the signature of the convention; and delays with regard to the convention mean the postponement of the despatch of the Turkish contingent, which is all in our favour. If the Turks are ever to be despatched and are ever to land, Mr. G. made a good point, when, in writing again to the Queen yesterday, he said that the danger of their landing would probably be less on the Canal than any other place such as Aboukir because if landed at Port Said or Ismailia they would be under Wolseley's eye and be really at a greater distance from the front and from the enemy than anywhere in the Mediterranean.

Dined tonight with D.[1] at the St. James'. He made himself most agreeable. There is certainly something extraordinarily attractive in him to me. We went together afterwards to Drury Lane to see a very high-class melodrama called *Pluck*. I can't help thinking, from what he has said to me on more than one occasion, that he contemplates leaving the Government whenever Mr. G. leaves it. I hope not. He should remember that his service is due to the country, not only to Mr. G. personally.

Sunday, 10 September. There was a reconnaissance in force by the enemy yesterday which resulted in some sharp fighting. The enemy were driven back with loss and 4 guns were captured. Our casualties not heavy. This took place westward of Kassassin. But the great fight has still to come, for which we shall probably have to wait some days yet, though the railway is now in fair working order.

The Queen continues greatly exercised in Her mind at the prospect of the Turkish intervention. She telegraphs and writes her fears daily. She is convinced that the reason why the Sultan has agreed to sign the convention is his intention to come to a secret understanding with Arabi, who might be made to surrender to *him* (the Sultan). To allow the Turks to land now would be, moreover, going expressly against the Khedive's wishes. She can't understand Dufferin's 'altered language' and professes a total inability to trust the Turks

[1] i.e. Rosebery.

'a yard'. Mr. G. has been endeavouring to calm her fears. He is quite willing to admit that the question of finally concluding the Turkish convention is as nice as it is grave. But it must be remembered that up to a certain point we are committed and can't take a new departure without real ground for change; that the Khedive naturally only regards the matter from an Egyptian point of view; and that we on the other hand have to weigh the consequences of an open breach with the Sultan from an European and international point of view. Mr. G. does not believe much in the prophecies of alarmists as to the attitude of the Mussulmen in India; but he is very apprehensive of what may be the consequences of such a breach on the peace of the Levant at a time when the Great Powers are almost all likely to want to prosecute their own interested views.

Having regard particularly to the 'fidgetty' state of Her Majesty, and to the views of Lord Northbrook and Mr. Childers, with regard to the Turkish convention and what is to follow from it, which are not quite identical with the views of Lord Granville and himself, Mr. G. has determined to summon a Cabinet for next Wednesday. The Queen can't see *two* sides to a question sufficiently. She sees one side and sees it very clearly. All along, however, she has been in perfectly good humour. She does not make sufficient allowance for the *pros* of this question. There is Austria (in addition to the other reasons) who is most anxious for the conclusion of the Turkish convention. In her opinion for us to break off with the Turks at the eleventh hour would be to increase the danger of our operations in Egypt by giving a complexion to the war of a Xian campaign *versus* the Islamic world, and probably also to play into the hands of Russia. Russia might very likely be willing to sell Egyptian interests against some boon to herself, totally regardless of Egyptian liberties.

As regards the future in Egypt, Mr. G. thinks it reasonable to conjecture that if the military matter is got well over, our position there will naturally be something like that which Russia occupies now in Bulgaria—the result not of stipulation but of effort and sacrifice crowned by success. Mr. G. says this with special reference to France. Having backed out of taking active part in the settlement of the country, she (France) has no right to expect that her influence will be as paramount as ours will probably be.

There have been reports of 'keel-hauling' and the practice of other tortures in Alexandria. At the demand of Lord Granville, searching inquiry has been made with the result that in only one case it is believed such atrocities have been published, and stringent injunctions have been issued at our instance by the Khedive to prevent the recurrence of any such barbaric practices.

Ireland, according to all accounts, is slowly but surely settling down and recovering from the effects of the recent horrible social upheaval. Rents are generally being paid, and outrages are steadily on the decrease. The Dublin police difficulty is fairly at an end, thanks to Lord Spencer's firmness and good judgment. Mr. G. was very pleased that resort had been had to special constables—one of the matters which, he says, he repeatedly pressed on Forster without the smallest effect.

Mr. G., I am glad to say, has written Lord Ripon a long letter in which he argues forcibly the case of saddling India with a portion of the cost of the campaign. His argument is in effect this: he admits that we are discharging in Egypt single-handed an European duty, and moreover that India has not been consulted on the political issue, and her material interests only are in question. He comments with some emphasis on the enormous Indian estimate of the cost as compared with the English one. If the vast excess in the Indian cost be unavoidable, he grants that this fact may be taken into account as regards the share of the expense which shall ultimately fall upon India's shoulders, though to determine this share we must await the total charge. He maintains that unquestionably the connection with Egypt affects Indian as well as British interests. The material interest for both countries is the interest in the Canal. It is very specially the interest of India. No trades gain in the same degree as Indian trades. The Canal is an unmixed and enormous benefit to India. To England the canal is a great but mixed benefit; it has indeed taken away from this country branches of our former *entrepôt* trade. Apart from the quantity of our several interests, the quality is the same, both military and commercial. Apart from the Canal we have no interest in Egypt which would warrant (in Mr. G.'s opinion) intervention. But the safety of the Canal can't consist with illegality and military violence in Egypt. The exclusion of India from a proportion of the charge of the war can only be affirmed on the ground that the entire business of maintaining communications with India through the Canal is British and India has no such interest.

Such is the gist of Mr. G.'s argument. Were I an Indian the exception I should take to it would be something as follows: granted that the communication through the Canal is in reality a greater boon and of greater advantage to India than to England. Accordingly it is our (Indian) duty to defend, or at any rate to assist in defending, that route. But the question is this—Is the route, or has the route ever been, in danger? What matters it to us in India whether Arabi or the Khedive is ruler, provided the Canal itself is not meddled with? If the Canal is threatened, we (Indians) will readily share in warding off those dangers. All we maintain is that a case of danger has not been sufficiently made out.

Monday, 11 September. The Queen won't have Tracy for Her Parliamentary Groom. She will adhere to Her rule as to not having two brothers in Her Household; and if a member of Parliament is not forthcoming, She will fill the vacancy by a non-political man.[1]

Now that the Cabinet has been summoned out of special deference to the

[1] See 3 Sept. 1882.

Queen, she has begun to be alarmed at the possible effect of a meeting of ministers. Mr. G., however, has told her that according to his belief the impression of a Cabinet will on the whole be favourable. He remembers that in the Crimean War a lengthened intermission of Cabinets was, though with good reason, bitterly attacked.

Bismarck's son, Count Herbert, has returned to this country and has been charged by his father to say that he (Prince Bismarck) cordially approves the line we have taken, and that the German interest in Egypt is so small that it matters little to her (Germany) what the settlement is provided we maintain our friendly relations with her. He is even not opposed to our annexing Egypt; nor would even France be. But it should be avoided if possible, retaining only real preponderance, and having regard to French susceptibilities. He (Bismarck) strongly countenances the conclusion of the convention, with a view especially of avoiding a rupture with the Porte, which would in these circumstances be a great misfortune.

By the way, in writing to Lord Ripon Mr. G. took an opportunity of 'harking back' on the old subject of retiring the end of this year. He is probably sanguine enough to believe that by that time procedure will be satisfactorily dealt with. Ireland will have practically quieted down, and the Egyptian business will in the main have been settled. The wish, I fear for him, is in this instance father to the thought, and there is very small likelihood of its being fulfilled.

Tuesday, 12 September. Plunkett reports from Paris that the French Government consider that England should recognise the state of things in Tunis, in return for French acquiescence in the progress of English influence in Egypt. Otherwise, to restore her prestige, France must resort either to a spirited colonial policy or come to terms with Germany.

The disposition of the Powers at the present moment towards this country seems to be, when summed up, something as follows: Germany and Austria cordial and respectful; France anxious to retain a close *entente cordiale* with us but desirous of obtaining a *quid pro quo* in return for her inevitable declension of power in Egypt; Italy jealous of our resuming close relationship with France; Russia hungry and on the look out for a plausible excuse of getting the Berlin arrangement reviewed in a sense more favourable to herself.

Wednesday, 13 September. Today has been an anxious, an exciting, and a great day. The newspapers got hold of the capture of Tel-el-Kebir about eleven this morning; but no personal details. Accordingly waiting for the official confirmation was very anxious work. What must it have been for the poor wives and close relatives? The confirmation arrived this afternoon. It was evidently a very brilliant and very decisive affair, and the losses as compared with the result have not been heavy so far as they are known at present.

The plan of assault seems to have been as gallantly carried out as it was brilliantly conceived, and the rout of the enemy complete. Arabi escaped on horseback, but the cavalry were in hot pursuit when the report of the battle was sent off. Wolseley was within two days of the calculation he gave to Childers, which was that he should strike his blow at this very place— Tel-el-Kebir—on the 15th of this month. I sent off many telegrams and notes to allay the apprehensions of anxious wives and relatives. The result of today may, one may hope, be the practical collapse of the rebellion. Moreover, the brilliancy and gallantry of the action ought to close the mouths of the old military croakers who are always crabbing Wolseley and declaring the British soldier can no longer fight.

Mr. G. arrived in the middle of the day for the Cabinet in great force and high spirits over the news which greeted him on his arrival. The Cabinet decided that the convention with the Porte *was* to be signed, provided the conditions regarding the issue and wording of the proclamation and the landing of the troops be agreed to.

Friday, 15 September. The war is over. The capture of Tel-el-Kebir has been followed by the occupation of Cairo and the surrender of Arabi and what remained of his followers as well as of the Kafre-dowar contingent. There never was a more brilliant little campaign, achieved with as great a success and as small a loss. Mr. G. is naturally in the highest possible spirits, pleased with our generals, our admirals, our officers, our men, and our military arrangements. We are at last reaping the fruit of the reform of our little army initiated some 12 years ago, on account of which the Liberals have incurred so much odium all this time. Mr. G. with his usual thoughtfulness wrote poor old Cardwell a line tonight to congratulate him, to whom so much of the original credit is due. I hope he will be of sufficiently sound mind to appreciate the attention.

Peerages, to which Her Majesty readily assented, have today been offered by telegraph to Wolseley and Beauchamp Seymour, to whom Mr. G. has also written congratulatory letters.

Wolseley speaks in the highest terms of all the men under him from generals down to the rank and file. In a letter to Lady Wolseley the other day which I saw quoted, he said: 'As to the Life Guards, there are no finer body of men in the world'. Some grumbling may be expected from the Guards owing to their not having been given a more prominent place in Wednesday's battle, the reason for which will no doubt be put down to the arrangement to which so much exception was taken whereby the Duke of Connaught was given the command of their brigade.

Dined last night at the Garrick with Welby in company with Mr. G. and Lord Granville, after which we went to see *Patience* at the Savoy. They thoroughly enjoyed it and laughed heartily. Mr. G. was well cheered on his arrival at and departure from the theatre. He is probably the only man to whom such a mark of recognition has ever been given. It is curious too that any popular signs should be manifested in his favour in a London theatre of all places, where the audience is certainly not much given to Gladstonianism.

The war being over, Mr. G. has already sketched out his ideas roughly for the settlement of Egypt—something as follows:

I. *Military settlement.* (For consideration of England)

(1) Disband rebel forces.
(2) Try the criminals.
(3) Withdraw as soon as possible our occupying force.
(4) Organise small military force; also police force.
(5) Egypt not to bear any cost of war; but possibly to be debited with the expense which the retention of any of our forces in Egypt for a time may entail.
(6) Dismantle the fortifications.

II. *Political settlement.* (For the consideration in the main part of the Powers)

(1) The sovereignty of the Porte, which has failed in its purpose *de jure* and *de facto*, to be modified.
  a. Tribute might be continued.
  b. Homage to the Sultan might be required of the Sultan [*sic*].
  c. The Sultan's title to command the service of Egyptian troops should be terminated.
  d. Likewise his title to nominate the ruler of Egypt.
  e. The suzerainty might be more on the basis of the Balkan and Rouman suzerainties.

(2) As to the political settlement of the country internally.
  a. Firman privileges should be made irrevocable between Egypt and the Porte.
  b. The territory might be neutralised.
  c. A firm stand must be made by us for the development of self-governing institutions.
  d. Europeans must no longer be exempted from taxation.

(3) The use of foreign officers might be retained; but their tenure should be no longer dependent on the consent of their respective Governments.

(4) As to the Canal.
  a. The conduct of the Company must be reviewed.
  b. The question of its neutralisation might be referred to a Committee.

Saturday, 16 September. Mr. G. returned to Hawarden this afternoon. I never remember to have seen him in higher spirits. All the time one was with him he was animated in conversation and constantly telling anecdotes. He was quite disappointed at leaving before the guns in honour of the Egyptian victories had been fired, which was his own suggestion, and about which he was quite childishly keen.

The first thing this morning he wrote off to the Archbishop of Canterbury's secretary[1] and the Archbishop of York[2] about issuing directions for thanksgivings in church tomorrow. (The Archbishop by the by is making a wonderful fight of it with his marvellous constitution, and seems in a fair way to rally.)

Reverting again today to the Egyptian settlement, Mr. G. is inclined to think it might be well to send out at once some civilian to work at that part of it which belongs essentially to this country. He suggests Goschen, and possibly Lord Derby? (The latter would hardly do. He has not got sufficient purpose or active-mindedness.) Somebody of considerable position must clearly go. Excellent as Wolseley is as a general, he has not shewn himself either in South Africa or Cyprus a good civil administrator.

Fawcett wrote today about his position on the Egyptian question so far as it affects India. He has to address his constituents soon, and he wanted to know whether he might say without embarrassing the Government that so far as he was concerned he could not support any proposal which involved saddling India with the *whole* cost of the Indian troops employed in Egypt. Mr. G. has told him such a suggestion would be impossible, as it would be totally inconsistent with his (Fawcett's) position in the Government. But he also pointed out that nothing was yet definitely settled, and that it was unnecessary now for Fawcett to commit either himself or the Government. While writing this letter he gave vent to his ideas about Fawcett. He is evidently not a great believer in Fawcett and does not think Fawcett will or can ever rise to the front rank of statesmen. He considers that Fawcett is totally unable to work in concert with others—essentially 'idiosyncratic' in temperament, to which possibly his physical infirmities have partly conduced. I can't say (and I told Mr. G. so) that I agree in Mr. G.'s estimate of Fawcett, whom I believe to be far-seeing, right-judging, fearless, and independent; and I am convinced Mr. G. underrates Fawcett's position in the country. It is a small matter and does not indicate much, but I remember Rosebery telling me that at Chatsworth on the occasion of poor Freddy Cavendish's funeral the person who attracted most attention among the assembled multitude, next to Mr. G., was unquestionably Fawcett.

Monday, 18 September. Two great dignitaries of the Church—very different in every respect—have died within the last 2 days: Dr. Pusey and the Dean of Windsor (Wellesley). The death of the latter will be a great loss to the Queen, the country, and those who enjoyed his friendship—to no one more than Mr. G. By his death Mr. G. has lost not only an old and valued friend but also a wise counsellor—as has certainly likewise the Queen. The Dean was

[1] Randall Davidson.   [2] W. Thomson.

almost the only man left who exercised a real influence, not confined only to Church matters, with the Queen. His successor will indeed be difficult to find. It is a Church appointment in which of course the Queen has a special voice. It is almost impossible to think of anyone. Might Butler of Harrow by chance do? How about Lord Alwyne Compton?

The Egyptian business has given a great 'fillip' to the Government. It was about time this hitherto ill-starred Government had a turn of luck. One of the Egyptian forts (Damietta—held by the determined black regiment) declines to surrender. An early difficulty will be how to deal with the rebels— from Arabi downwards. They will probably be tried on suspicion of being implicated in the Cairo *emeute* last summer and in the destruction of Alexandria. A further charge independently of this will have to be preferred against them for their conduct as traitors to the Khedive. There will probably be a strong sentimental feeling in this country against their being put to death; and yet anything short of most summary punishment may be fatal to the authority of the Khedive.

One of the most satisfactory outcomes of the war has been the sudden and complete collapse of the so-called National party, which proves how radically wrong Wilfrid Blunt, plausible as he often led me to think him, was in his estimate of the movement. According to Rivers Wilson, who has certainly proved right in his judgment throughout this complicated business, the fundamental error underlying Wilfrid's contention has been that he formed his opinion of Arabi and his party from observation of the Bedouins. This information he applied to the Egyptians who are said to be totally distinct in every respect from the Arabs. He has confused the Fellah for the Arab, who in reality despises the Egyptian. Mr. G. thinks that it has been 'too bad' of Wilfrid to have combined 'so much fanaticism with so little information'.

Wednesday, 20 September. Mr. G. has felt the Dean of Windsor's death terribly, as I knew he would. He regards it as a 'sore and grievous blow' to the Queen, the Church, and himself. It is impossible for Her Majesty to fill his place. The Dean, Mr. G. believes, was cognisant of every Church appointment for upwards of a quarter of a century. It is difficult, says Mr. G., to overestimate the influence exercised by the Dean's 'large heart and deep insight for the best interests of Crown and Church'. He was as 'pure as gold and true as steel'. His was the 'most precious life in the Church of England'. Sir H. Ponsonby told me yesterday that Her Majesty hopes Mr. G. will not take the initiative in submitting a name. She seems to look (and not unnaturally) upon the appointment as her particular perquisite—a contention which I am not sure that Mr. G. will admit.

Sir R. Cross has again applied for a political pension, one being vacant by the death of Sir George Grey the other day. Mr. G. in talking about it the other day did not seem to be inclined to look favourably upon the application, were it to be renewed. He doubts if there is a precedent (which he is always in search of for everything) for awarding a political pension to a political opponent. But I know of no likely candidate on the Government side of the House who is eligible.

Harcourt is at Balmoral. He is rather at sea as to the line to be taken with the Queen about Egypt. Her Majesty seems minded to insist that we should keep a strong hand in Egypt, 'not exactly annexation, but something very like it'. Everything was 'couleur de rose' at Balmoral until the sad news of the Dean's death arrived, which threw a gloom over everything.

The Duke of Cambridge has written his congratulations to Mr. G., and Mr. G. in thanking H.R.H. for them had an opportunity of bearing testimony to the conduct of all the military arrangements at the War Office, to which great credit from Childers downwards is due. Lord Northbrook too and his department have done admirably.

The Guards, according to all accounts, are frantic with Wolseley for having kept them rather in the background, whether intentionally or not. If intentionally, this has no doubt been due to the necessity which he very naturally felt for exercising extra precaution with regard to the brigade which the Duke of Connaught commanded. It was a great mistake, involving some injustice, to have sent the Duke in any command and still more to have given him the command of the Guards brigade.

The Egyptian business has evidently given this country a great lift in the estimation of Europe, and it is comforting to think that British prestige has been heightened without any bluster or swagger on our part.

Friday, 22 September. Mr. G. left Hawarden at cock-crow yesterday morning to attend the funeral of Dr. Pusey at Oxford. Wondrous energy! It was certainly not very prudent of him, and I doubt its being judicious. I should not wonder if half the nonconformist world is up in arms at his attending the grave of the Great High Priest. I suppose it may be considered for the High Church party a set-off against his visit some months ago to Spurgeon's tabernacle, at which they in their narrow-mindedness were all agog.

According to Harcourt who is still enjoying the delights of Balmoral and basking in the sunshine of royalty, much to his liking, the prejudices against Dilke in the highest quarters are greatly removed, and it is probable that the same obstacles as to Dilke's promotion when broached again will not be made.

Poor Tenterden died suddenly last night. He had been ailing for some time, but his end was not expected. He will be a great loss to the Foreign Office. He had great experience; he was thoroughly loyal; he possessed much common sense besides great ability; he had great command of his pen. Pauncefote will be his most likely successor. The other possible candidates are presumably Philip Currie and Sanderson.

Tomorrow is the poor Dean of Windsor's funeral. Mr. G. is staying at Sir Robert Phillimore's near Henley and intends going thence to Strathfieldsaye. It is almost impossible to think of anyone for the Deanery. Mr. G. says he knows of no clergyman who possesses Her Majesty's confidence unless it be the Archbishop of Canterbury; and he is still almost *in extremis*, and it is hardly possible to conceive his becoming Dean of Windsor.

There is an idea on foot that some of the Indian troops should be brought over here from Egypt to receive medals—an idea to which Mr. G. is not averse.

Work has of late been certainly heavy, but Mr. G. found time the other day nevertheless to write a longish letter to Mr. Rutherford commenting upon a book as to the estimate in which Homer was held by the classic Greeks.[1]

Went tonight to see Mrs. Langtry act in Tom Taylor's *Unequal Match*. She really plays the part of Hester with much grace and cleverness. She is certainly above the average of actresses.

Saturday, 23 September. The Queen is keen for the hanging of Arabi. Mr. G. thinks that, apart from rebellion, his (Arabi's) complicity with either the massacre at Alexandria last June, or the incendiarism of Alexandria in July, or the base use of the flag of truce after the bombardment, or the depriving of the town of its water supply, if proven, would constitute a case of 'off with his head'. Perhaps even Arabi's betrayal of the liberties of Egypt to the Sultan and his holding the Khedive in prolonged fear should also, if proved, be charges involving sentence of death. Indeed, Mr. G. would be glad if Arabi could be hung without *real* inclemency.

The Queen is not unnaturally averse to the early withdrawal of troops from Egypt, but if Wolseley is ready, as he says he is, to send home about half his forces, there can be no reason for our retaining them out there; and Mr. G. hopes early steps will be taken in this direction. I understand that the Queen is anxious that the Guards should not be among the first to come home.

The appointment of Dr. Pusey's successor to the Regius Professorship of Hebrew is occupying much of Mr. G.'s thoughts. No Prime Minister I am sure ever took so much pains, or was so conscientious, about ecclesiastical appointments. In this case the field of choice is naturally very limited—the names at present before him are Cheyne, Sayle, Nutt, and Driver. He is in consultation with the Deans of Christ Church and St. Paul's.[2]

Mrs. O'Shea will continue to volunteer writing under the inspiration of Parnell. It is a great piece of impertinence; and yet difficult for Mr. G. to forbid it.

[1] EWH refers here to William G. Rutherford's *The New Phrynichus*, published in 1881.
[2] i.e. Deans Liddell and Church.

Friday, 29 September. (Kiplin) Left Downing St. on Monday for this place which is very nice. It is a comfortable old house of medium size; Walter Carpenter is a charming host, and we have had an agreeable little party consisting of Miss Mundy (his sister-in-law who plays the part of hostess for him), Lady Marian Alford, Charlie Compton, J. Pollen and his wife, and Guy Sebright (Coldstreams) and his bride, a pretty, very fair girl.

No news of any interest has reached me from Downing St., and there has been nothing stirring in the way of public events. Mr. G. has gone to Penmaenmawr, where Lady F. Cavendish is staying. He is no doubt ruminating over the Windsor Deanery, though I think he is quite prepared to let Her Majesty make the first move. He is not disinclined for Lord Alwyne Compton. He has not forgotten either Dean Liddell; but he (Liddell) would probably not care to move from Christ Church to Windsor, anymore than he cared to move to Westminster.[1] After Dean Wellesley's funeral last Saturday Mr. G. divulged to the Duchess of Wellington that about 12 years ago when the Archbishop of Canterbury was supposed to be failing that he had the Queen's permission to offer the see of Canterbury to Dean Wellesley. The Archbishop has, wonderful to relate, made a great rally; but it is hardly conceivable that he will rally sufficiently to enable him to continue to discharge his archiepiscopal duties.

Wednesday, 4 October. (Escrick) Came on here on Monday after lionising York for several hours. The minster is splendid and grandly impressive. The coloured glass is magnificent. Here there are staying Ham Cuffe and Lady Margaret, Mr. and Mrs. Pointer (he the R.A.), and Charlie Mills. The house is very comfortable and roomy. One or two of the rooms have recently been done up by Lady Wenlock in truly aesthetic style with much success.

The Queen, who has taken the Windsor Deanery entirely into her own hands, seems to be most inclined for Canon Connor, Her Isle of Wight man. She is reported to be greatly disconcerted at the prospect of an early withdrawal of all the troops from Egypt (except those required for temporary occupation); but it is clear that this step must be taken. In spite of the masterly manner in which the military operations were conducted, I am afraid there is serious ground for complaint as regards the Commissariat and the Army Medical Department. Mr. G. has been staying at Penmaenmawr with Lady F. Cavendish for a few days, and in spite of having had a bit of a cold is said to be quite flourishing.

It seems unfortunate for the Government to have approved the employment in Egypt of a man like Baker Pasha, who was cashiered.

The harvest, which has been pretty well gathered in in most parts of the country by this time, may be put down as very fair on the whole, especially in comparison with the last few bad years. It is remarkable that the corn

[1] See 3 and 11 Aug. 1881.

should be so good as it is, considering how little sun and very little heat we have had this summer.

Saturday, 7 October. (Carolside) Left Escrick early this morning after a very pleasant little visit there. Bingey Lawley makes the most delightful of hosts, and Lady Wenlock is certainly most fascinating. Ham Cuffe and Miss Lawley acted a little play last night excellently well. We had good sport. Bingey is, I think, the best and most sportsmanlike shot I have ever seen. I fancy he is very little behind DeGrey, whom I unfortunately just missed at Escrick, for which I was very sorry as I have always been so anxious to see him shoot.

Reay is away in Holland. Lady Reay, always agreeable, is alone here with her mother.

Sir S. Northcote is 'starring' in Scotland. He fired off a long but dull speech at Glasgow, that Liberal stronghold. There was nothing in it to which an opponent could take exception. He is certainly always very fair in his criticisms; but I imagine he is pleasanter to have as a political opponent than one's political leader. He lacks so lamentably hard-hitting, and must fail wholly to inspire enthusiasm, both as regards the matter he speaks and the manner in which he speaks it. The Egyptian successes have evidently been a thorough damper to the Tories, who have to fall back upon the miserable expedient of charging the Liberals with eating their words and bagging their clothing; and this ought to be equivalent to eliciting Tory approval, which of course the Tories are slow to admit. As yet there has been but little 'out of Parliament' speechifying. It is remarkable that one hears no more of 'fair trade' this year. That bubble has effectually bursted. It has never recovered [from] the blow which Mr. G. administered to it at Leeds just a year ago.[1]

Saturday, 14 October. (Haddo) Arrived here on Tuesday. We have had a pleasant party and a cheery one—somewhat too cheery I think for the host and hostess.[2] Among those who have been here are Lord and Lady Kintore, the Dalhousies, Keith Falconers (he the ex-manager of the Conservative machinery), Sant the painter, Sandhurst, Hugo Charteris, some Duffs, an ex-moderator and his wife. Aberdeen has made the house very comfortable and by reason of the range of ground which it occupies it makes a fine pile. There is a magnificent new room—a library, and the internal arrangements generally of the house are excellent. It is *bien montée* in every respect. There is a chapel, in which there are daily prayers after presbyterian fashion night and morning; it contains a fine organ, for which there is a tame organist. Aberdeen, though always fussy and a little too particular, is the kindest of hosts. We have had rather bad weather but had two days' very fair shooting. Lady Dalhousie was looking lovely but rather shocked the Aberdeens. Lady

---

[1] See 7 Oct. 1881.   [2] Lord and Lady Aberdeen.

Kintore is a very taking person. Aberdeen is said to have spent £100,000 on the house in alterations, additions, and decorations.

I am quite newsless here. A letter from Mary G. today says that the Prime Minister is well and in great force at Hawarden.

The Tories are having a campaign in Scotland. Northcote and Gibson have been endeavouring to rouse the apathetic Scotch Conservatives, but they have selected a bad season and some uncongenial soil on which to 'waste their sweetness'.

Country house life is certainly attractive, and no one enjoys it more than the official.

The Aberdeens are splendidly enthusiastic about Mr. G.

Wednesday, 18 October. (Taymouth) Came on here Monday with Sandhurst. This is a truly glorious place. There is a mixture in it of grandeur and beauty which can hardly be surpassed, and it would be difficult to see it under more favourable circumstances than with the autumn tints and shades. Lady Breadalbane is a charming hostess—as charming as she is beautiful. Breadalbane is a very good fellow. He is a good Liberal and a staunch admirer of Mr. G. We have here Lord Kenmare and his nice young son, Castlerosse; Lord Suffield, a regular devotee of Lady B[readalbane]; Newport; the Edward Guinesses, he of porter repute and she of London ballroom fame; Cochrane Baillie, Lord Lamington's son; M. Lister; and one Sartoris; besides Sandhurst and myself; also Miss Paget, the Maid of Honor. There were to have been other ladies, but they failed at the last moment. One of the most striking features in the house is a splendid lantern which runs up to the top of the house. There is a very nice room called the Banner Hall in which most of the sitting is done and which contains a fine organ and good piano. We are treated every night to bagpipe music at dinner, and the pipers wind up their programme with a march round the table three times. We have been on the hills every day, grouse driving; but the bags have not been very large, chiefly owing to a want of straightness of powder.

Before I left Haddo Lady Aberdeen confided to me she was most anxious that Aberdeen should get some place which would give him a little official work and a foothold on the political ladder.

Northcote's speech at Inverness fell very flat, even among his own supporters, e.g. the *Standard* which came down upon him for his dullness and his want of rallying powers. No news from Downing Street.

Sunday, 22 October. Arrived in town early this morning. I feel like a boy returned to school. I quite lost my heart to Lady Breadalbane. There is something truly ennobling about her besides fascinating. I never came across anyone in her position who seemed so anxious to fulfil all her duties in the highest manner. As for him, he is the most model landlord to all appearances that can be conceived. He concentrates all his attention and time on his vast property. Would that there were more such landlords! The landed interest would then have little to fear. I took a charming trip with him up the loch on Friday in the new steamer which he has put on and is running himself on his own beautiful lake.

I found Mr. G. this morning very well and flourishing. He said he was, however, much bored at the prospect of the renewal of active parliamentary work and harked back on his favourite theme of the necessity of early retirement from official duties. I very much fear that he will really carry into effect his intentions, which will surely mean the destruction of the Liberal party for a long time to come. He has thrown his thoughts into a letter addressed privately to Lord Spencer, to whom he lately conversed much on the subject of the future. After reviewing in that letter the position of independence and irresponsibility which he occupied in 1875-80, he reasserts that he assumed office two years and a half ago solely for the purpose of meeting a state of facts on which the General Election turned, and that as such state of facts has been practically met it is time that the lead of the party should revert to what he terms the legitimate possessors of it. He maintains that the time for his relinquishing the lead really arrived a year ago; but other special circumstances, three in number—namely, Ireland, the entanglement of Egypt, and the state of the House of Commons—had temporarily intervened. He considers that the advance which has been made in the settlement of the first two questions has been sufficient to determine the detaining force and that as regards the third he is about to try his hand to accomplish something. He argues then that the right moment is near at hand when he ought to give effect to his intentions of retiring and when it may be allowed to him, a man of 73 years old and of 50 years' public service, to relieve himself from the life of contention which he now leads and to devote his time to employments more appropriate and less imperious than those in which he is now engaged. Moreover, he feels that he has a growing disinclination for work, which he knows is the sign of diminishing power. He compares himself to a half-exhausted singer whose notes are flat, which everyone perceives except himself. He does not contemplate parliamentary extinction for the moment, but I can hardly believe that Lord Hartington would lead with Mr. G. behind him as a free lance in Parliament. He can't be allowed to go to the House of Lords, and accordingly there are, to my mind, only two alternatives—one, that he should remain on as Prime Minister and leader of the House of Commons; the other, that he should retire from public, official, and parliamentary life finally and wholly.

Monday, 23 October. There has been what Mr. G. terms an 'open Cabinet' today for consideration of procedure. By this he means a more or less informal Cabinet which ministers may attend according as they like and as the business to be discussed concerns them individually, and of which he does not send a report to the Queen. The Speaker,[1] May, and Whitbread were called in council. The business was mainly confined to the discussion of details of the procedure rules and the maturing of the Grand Committee scheme, the main question of closure having been previously settled, and settled after much consideration in the direction of sticking to the original proposals. Curiously enough Lord Hartington, notwithstanding the very strong line he took up on this matter early in the session, has been in favour of a compromise, though still clinging to the belief that the 'bare majority' is the only right system in principle. He has admitted that his mind is influenced by a desire to soften party differences and to avoid the evil effects of extreme bitterness, of which he professes to be very conscious. Mr. G., though he originally thought the proposal to take power to close debate hardly worth squabbling about, and its importance exaggerated, is dead against the Gibson—'two-thirds'— amendment, which the Speaker holds is practically unworkable. Such an amendment Mr. G. regards as an open recession, and the principle of it utterly bad. He thinks it amounts to handing over to the Opposition the power to say whether the closing power should be used. Mr. G. is not himself averse to asking that the closures should be merely a *sessional* order. But the Cabinet, after hearing the arguments *pro* and *con*, have determined to persevere with the resolutions as originally proposed. The members of the Cabinet who advocated adhesion most strongly were Harcourt, Childers, and Chamberlain.

Mr. G. wanted Childers to take the G.C.B. in consideration of his 'signally successful' (?) War Office services; but he declined—wisely I think. Acceptance would have been ape-ing too much the late ministers, Cross & Co. He wanted the K.C.B. for Morley, who is believed to have acquitted himself excellently well, but Mr. G. thought that the reward for Morley's services should partake of promotion and not of ribands. It is to be feared that poor Childers has knocked himself very much.

Wednesday, 25 October. The opening day of the autumn session yesterday was favourable. Randolph Churchill fired off what he thought was going to be a big constitutional gun. He moved the adjournment of the House on the ground that there was no precedent for the sitting of the House after the Appropriation Bill had been passed. But Mr. G. 'smashed and pulverised' (as he called it) R. Churchill's contention. To begin with there was a very direct precedent for an autumn sitting subsequently to the Appropriation Act, viz. in 1820; and after all, no principle could have been involved—at most a practice was departed from; and surely if there ever was a reason for a departure from practice by the House of Commons it would be when the House was to take into consideration its own rules and regulations.

---

[1] Sir Henry Brand.

Contrary to expectation, the head (the front Opposition bench) followed the tail (R. Churchill & Co.) into the lobby! They (the minority) were supported by the Parnellites, but *minus* their speeches. After this digression, a committee was appointed to inquire into the case of Mr. Gray's arrest,[1] and Mr. G. secured precedence for the discussion of procedure *de die in diem*. So the House will now plunge *in medias res*.

The Tories will evidently fight to the death any closure power. Mr. G. told H.M. that he would like to have been able to make a concession so as to secure the support of the Opposition, but he was obliged to admit that the reception accorded by the Tories to his proposal last May (viz. the acceptance *pro tem.* of Gibson's amendment) indicated no willingness on the part of the Opposition to meet the Government half way. The resolutions were not discussed and decided on without the counsel of Whitbread, whom Mr. G. regards as *the* greatest independent authority on procedure matters.

Mr. G. was speculating to Richard Grosvenor this morning about the future, on which Mr. G. seems to have made up his mind, when he said that on his own departure from official life, Lord Derby would be sure to join the Cabinet, and the choice of another peer would have to lie between Rosebery and Morley.

George Leveson, according to all accounts, acquitted himself first-rate last week on the platform down at Bodmin, much to his father's delight. He ought to do well in the political world. He will have had an admirable start and an excellent apprenticeship to assist him.

In appointing a successor to poor Dean Wellesley the other day, Mr. G. made a sort of arrangement with the Queen, of course not binding upon but for the guidance of his successors, that, if the choice of the Dean at Windsor is to be left to H.M., the canonries should be filled up in the ordinary way, to which at one time she laid a sort of special claim.

Friday, 27 October. The votes of thanks in both Houses were moved yesterday to the forces employed in Egypt. Mr. G. in moving the vote in the House of Commons spoke for a whole hour. The speech was arranged in his usual masterly manner, and at times he grew most eloquent and most impassioned. It was, however, perhaps a little overwrought and too elaborate for the occasion. Sir W. Lawson by way of entering his protest against the war moved the previous question, and in so doing he amused the House greatly, however inappropriate and unnecessary such action on his part might have been.

Scarcely any progress has been yet made with procedure, though all Wednesday and yesterday's sitting after the vote of thanks had been moved was devoted to it. The Tory party has, now that R. Churchill has returned, got quite out of hand, and Northcote has like the rest of them to follow the new Tory leader. There seems, however, to be a general sort of belief that the fight

[1] See 19 Aug. 1882.

of the Tories will collapse, and that the new rules will be got through sooner than is ordinarily supposed. My own belief is that the sitting will drag its weary way along until the second week in December.[1] A great deal of nonsense and misconception about the closing power prevails. The real exception to take to the Government proposal is that it has been whittled away by reason of the many safeguards with which it has been fenced round. Those safeguards must prevent the abuse of closure; but even if they prove not to be as effectual as is supposed, it would surely be better that the closing power should be abused now and again than that the House should continue to be perpetually subject to the tyranny of the minority.

Today Mr. G. sent Lord Granville and Lord Hartington a copy of his secret manifesto addressed to Lord Spencer reviewing his position. This subject (viz. that of Mr. G.'s intended retirement) perpetually haunts one. As far as Mr. G. is personally concerned there is little doubt that, unless unforeseen circumstances arise, no more favourable opportunity for his making his bow could be found than the close of the present year. He will have quieted down the great social upheaval in Ireland; he will have conducted the most difficult question of Egypt towards a fair way of settlement; he will have placed the House of Commons in a condition again to resume legislative work. He would hand over his party to Lords Granville and Hartington *unbroken* after steering them through some of the most dangerous shoals that ever confronted the political bark. Moreover, there would be a certain appropriateness in his retiring from public and official life at the conclusion of his half-century of public service. His departure now could not be put down to his wishing to run away at a time of difficulty to his party. He would retire amidst a halo of glory and in the zenith of his power. He would quit the public stage before there were any apparent signs of failure of either mental or physical powers.

When regarded, however, from a party and also a public point of view, his intended retirement presents a different aspect. He is not only the sole man who can hold together the many sections of the Liberal party; he is the cohesive and modifying power. He impels the sluggard Whig and holds in check the impulsive Radical. It is difficult to say what might be the effect of his removal from the public stage upon the forces at work both politically and socially. Moreover, his own future would be a great difficulty. Why should he be banished from the political world when his powers are so unimpaired? Why should he be made to relinquish prematurely the trust which the Midlothian electors reposed in him for the present Parliament? And yet, it is difficult to conceive that Lord Hartington would undertake the leadership of the House while Mr. G. remained in it an untrammelled critic and with an undiminished influence of a kind such as no public man in this century has possessed. He (Mr. G.) would doubtless have the most loyal

---

[1] He was wrong, but not by much. See 3 Dec. 1882.

intentions towards Lord Hartington; but what would happen if points of difference arose? And with his impulsive and susceptible character, how could the formation of cliques and cabals around him by some of the most unruly members of the party be prevented or avoided? It is not yet known what Lord Granville and Lord Hartington will say to Mr. G.'s proposal; but it is not unlikely that when brought face to face with the awful responsibilities of governing the country and of leading the party they will decline to undertake them and will put any amount of pressure upon Mr. G. to induce him to reconsider his determination. From what Lord Wolverton told me the other day after a conversation with Lord Granville, it seems that sooner than lose Mr. G. Lord Granville would be willing to relinquish the lead he has so long held in the House of Lords and make way for Mr. G. But how could Mr. G. bring himself to oust Lord Granville from the position he has so long and so conspicuously held in the House of Peers? And last, but not least, what could be more inappropriate than for Mr. G. to be relegated to the Upper House? He *must* go down to posterity—untarnished by coronets and undecorated by ribands—as plain 'William Ewart Gladstone'.

Sunday, 29 October.[1] There seems to [be] reason to fear that we are not out of our difficulties in Egypt. News has arrived, which is calculated to raise grave apprehensions, that the so-called 'false prophet'[2] in the Soudan is, with large forces at his back, about to march upon Egypt; and Egypt being army-less, who are to act as the defenders of Egypt but our forces? This may mean a most serious business. It may retard indefinitely the withdrawal of our troops from Egypt; it may indefinitely destroy the hopes of a speedy settlement of Egypt; it may mean difficult and disastrous work for our garrison in Egypt.

Difficulties too with France seem to be ahead. She does not like the proposals we have as yet made in regard to Egypt.

Within the last few days there have shewn themselves some dangerous revolutionary symptoms in France.

R. Churchill and his followers have been in nearly open revolt with poor Sir Stafford. R. Churchill, in moving a foolish amendment on Thursday to the closure resolution, confided to R. Grosvenor that he had merely divided the House to see how many fools there were in it. Hitherto the Irishmen have been assisting the Opposition in the procedure discussions; and perhaps this is as well.

I see Mr. and Mrs. G. just returning from church across the Parade, surrounded by an admiring and respectful throng.

Sir G. Wolseley arrived yesterday. Mr. and Mrs. G. went to meet him at Charing Cross Station.

---

[1] EWH wrote '*Sunday. 30 Oct.*'
[2] i.e. the Mahdi.

Monday, 30 October.[1] A letter came from H.M. today expressing herself greatly pleased with Mr. G.'s speech in moving the Egyptian vote of thanks, and most particularly his references to the services of the Duke of Connaught.[2] She also expressed herself horrified at the Wilfrid Lawson faction—that 'Radical or in other words revolutionary party'. She called special attention to the alleged breakdown of the Medical Department in Egypt. It seems no doubt to have been at fault and to have shewn itself very deficient in organisation. But according to sensible men like Nevy Lyttelton, its shortcomings have been greatly exaggerated and the charges brought against it have mostly proceeded from Tories and anti-Wolseley-ites, whence H.M. generally draws her information. Childers is about to institute searching inquiries into the system; but he is dead against reverting to the old regimental system, which was strongly condemned by a Committee appointed by the late Government.[3]

An excellent move has been made, which is to get Lord Dufferin to go to Egypt temporarily to assist Malet in the present very difficult times. We here have never formed a very high opinion of Malet's capabilities or judgments; but few men have been placed in more difficult positions; and he now shows himself to have the good sense to welcome the cooperation of Lord Dufferin.

Duclerc, the present French Premier, seems to be a man of some determination and courage. He is not alarmed much at the revolutionary signs which have recently shewn themselves in France and is confident that he can cope with them without difficulty. The French will probably grumble at whatever we propose with regard to Egypt, but they are likely to content themselves with endeavouring to strike a bargain by obtaining a *quid pro quo* in the matters immediately affecting her and which are outstanding for settlement—namely, the Newfoundland fisheries question, Madagascar, and Tunis.

Lord Ampthill reports a conversation he has had with the Crown Prince of Germany in which the latter expressed himself strongly in favour of our annexing Egypt![4]

The rains have been appalling of late, and floods are already higher at Eton and Oxford and elsewhere than they have known to have been for years.

London seems fairly full; and if one were to judge the time of year by Mrs. Cavendish Bentinck's Sunday luncheon party yesterday, one might imagine oneself back again in the Season. Charlie Beresford was there. He seemed to take a very sensible view of the situation in Egypt. He told me the Khedive had offered him the Governorship of the Soudan, which he (C. B.) did not seem disinclined to accept temporarily.

[1] EWH wrote '*Monday, 31 Oct.*'
[2] Guedalla, ii. 217–18.
[3] Presumably EWH refers to the 'Report of a Committee of General and Other Officers of the Army on Army Re-organization', *Parl. Papers*, 1881, xxi, pp. 185 ff. The committee was appointed in 1879 and reported in Mar. 1880.
[4] Knaplund, pp. 277–8.

Tuesday, 31 October. The Queen has been quite in a state of mind about the famous Dante illustrated by Botticelli, which belongs to the Duke of Hamilton's library.[1] She was properly anxious that the British Museum should purchase it; and it appears they were anxious to acquire it, if possible; but quite on the sly, and unbeknown even to the auctioneer, the Duke of Hamilton disposed of the great collection of MSS *en bloc* to the German Government for the (reputed) sum of £50,000, thus never giving the English Government the refusal of any of the lots.

A letter came from Lord Granville today in reference to the copy of Mr. G.'s letter to Lord Spencer explaining his (Mr. G.'s) intentions as to the future.[2] Mr. G. handed it to me to read. I had only time to take brief stock of its contents. From a cursory glance over it, which was written in Lord G[ranville]'s best and most persuasive style, I gathered that Lord G. pooh-poohed the idea of Mr. G.'s retirement; referred to Mr. G.'s unimpaired powers; and said that nothing would induce him to aid or abet Mr. G.'s sinister intentions of retiring.

I was reminded this evening of a story told by Henry Calcraft to Lord Beaconsfield a few years ago, by which Lord B. was much taken. It was that at a certain supper at which certain 'ladies' had assembled, Nelly Bromley was asked what she would like to do best in the world; whereupon she replied, 'To be Mr. Gladstone's mistress'. 'And why'? 'Because I could then desert him'.

Thursday, 2 November. The House of Commons reached Gibson's amendment on Tuesday. Mr. G. followed the mover and made a great speech—considered to be one of his best. Though he 'smashed and pulverised' the amendment and declared that a closing power dependent upon an artificial majority was worse than no closing power, he gave out that, as the question at issue was one essentially for the House itself to determine, he should not treat an adverse vote like a vote of want of confidence. He was much struck in the debate by the zeal and determination of the Government followers. Sir J. Lubbock was the only Liberal who spoke against the Government proposal. Whitbread argued in favour of it with great force. Mr. G. considered the tone of the debate very temperate, though there was no disposition of a compromise indicated by the Opposition. Yesterday the debate was resumed, chiefly remarkable for a clever and characteristic speech by Randolph Churchill, who again threw off all party allegiance and declared himself unwilling to support Gibson, though ready to resist to the death all closing power. A good division is expected tonight, and a majority, counting the Irishmen, of some 70 is anticipated.

The Queen seems disposed to grant the remainder of Wolseley's peerage to

---

[1] Guedalla, ii. 214–15.
[2] Ramm, i. 450.

the female line, as he has only a daughter; but it is doubtful if there is any modern precedent for this.

In deference to the Prince of Wales, Oscar Clayton has been submitted for knighthood. It is to be hoped that no disagreeable stories will come out about him.

An interesting but hugely long letter arrived from Lord Ripon yesterday. The exception he takes to the proposal about charging the expenses of the Indian contingent in Egypt to Indian revenues is twofold: he denies that the interest of India in Egypt is sufficient to warrant so heavy a charge; he says that the resources of India must be husbanded. He gave a detailed account of the many questions he has in hand—primary education, local self-government, freedom of the press, development of local industries &c. He admits that he is regarded as a tremendous Radical by the Indian Council—'the most conservative body in Europe'. He alluded to the excessive Toryism of Sir J. Ferguson. Lord Ripon wound up by expressing great dismay at the hint Mr. G. gave him of his intention to resign the end of the year.

Went last night with the Cavendish Bentincks to hear Gounod's new oratorio, *The Redemption*, which was given at the Albert Hall. I was disappointed with the work; it never really rose to anything like sublimity and is very devoid of real melody.

Dined tonight with the Algy Wests—Mr. and Mrs. G., the Normantons, and Mr. F. Leveson were present.

Sunday, 5 November. (Charters) The division on Gibson's amendment on Thursday was better than was expected—a majority for the Government of 84. This included a considerable number of Parnellites, whose accession to the Government ranks was of course attributed by the Tories to some unholy alliance—some further compact. There were about 16 weak-kneed Liberals who found their way into the lobby of the minority, including J. Walter (of course), Albert Grey, J. Dundas, three Fitzwilliams, Sir E. Colebrooke &c. It is deplorable that Albert Grey should so constantly be a defaulter. He has, I fear, got all the Grey 'crankiness' in him. Mr. G. was regretting that a young fellow like Albert Grey should be throwing away his political career in the way he does. It is difficult to have patience with a fellow who does not ride off on small issues and trifling hobbies but is always electing crucial questions for the occasion on which to desert his party. One would have thought that if ever there were a question on which he could trust his leaders it would be on a subject so essentially one for experience of parliamentary life and knowledge of parliamentary ways as that of procedure. The debate on Thursday did not close without some interesting speeches. Mr. G. was struck by Arthur Balfour's ingenious reply to the leader of his (Fourth) party, R. Churchill. He thought Bobby Spencer's maiden speech highly effective, and the wind up of the debate by Lord Hartington an admirable exposition (though also apparently rather dull) of the true nature of freedom of debate. Labouchere sought to put forward in a light and airy manner the view which the Democratic party took of parliamentary debate—that view being that the duration of Parliaments should be shortened and that the legislature should pass without any discussion (to speak of) such measures as had been demanded by the constituencies at the General Election—in fact, that Parliament should become a registration office, which should register the decrees of the people. J. Walter naturally defended in the House the line he had taken in his paper[1]— and it is to be hoped that he will soon give up calling himself a Liberal—he is now neither fish, flesh, nor fowl; 'a Liberal', as Mr. G. described him in his parliamentary letter, 'who never votes with the Liberals'. Parnell spoke to explain the vote which he intended to give and had persuaded most of his followers to give—namely, against the 'two-thirds' proposal. Mr. G. thought the speech a masterpiece of ingenuity.

On Friday the dreary debate on the closure continued. Some purely obstructive amendments were moved in favor of more complicated arithmetical proportions than the two-thirds; and these when disposed of were followed by an amendment of W. H. Smith which sought to provide for those who might think the closing power was unfairly put into force a means of formally recording the next day their protest on the Journals of the House.

The division on Northcote's resolution to negative the closing power altogether is not expected to be reached till next Thursday!—though every argument has been worn threadbare which has any relation to every form of closure. The Tories are determined to have a good final fling, and to be considerate enough to prove beyond demonstration the absolute necessity of making an attempt to curb this accursed plethora of talk when the bounds of legitimate discussion have been well passed. As regards the closure, however, when it is obtained and is in working order, it is likely that the hopes of its friends will be disappointed and the apprehensions of its enemies unfulfilled. Mr. G. himself has never thought that it will be anything like as effective in saving the time of Parliament as the adoption of a system of devolution by Grand Committees. He believes it will very rarely be put into force; and then when put into force it will only be so after great and evident waste of time.

There was a Cabinet on Friday. The chief business was the consideration of draft instructions to Lord Dufferin in Egypt, where affairs certainly don't march—at present they only crawl. The question of the Skye crofters was also discussed. Lord Macdonald, owing it is believed to bad management and want of tact, has got into trouble with these small tenants of his and wants to serve processes of eviction upon them. The service of these processes is to be resisted, and the magistrates have asked the Government for the use of military and naval forces. To this the Cabinet decided not to accede, and the

[1] i.e. *The Times.*

magistrates have been told that, if *force majeur* is necessary, they must increase the *civil* force.

The first number of the *Fortnightly* under its new editorship, which has been transferred from J. Morley to Escott (the *Standard* man), has made its appearance this month. It is an extremely good number. Among several good articles in it, there is a clever and incisive one from the pen of Healy; it is war to the knife against the English Government until the demand for Home Rule has been met or partially met, when the millennium is assured.[1]

That bothersome woman Mrs. O'Shea will go on writing for an appointment for her husband, and Mr. G. most unfortunately admits that the man has some claim on the Government for his services. There never was a man who played a difficult part more awkwardly, and who unconsciously so discredited those he intended (as I believe) to assist, but to assist with motives of self-advancement. Mr. G. will not get much sympathy on this account from his colleagues.

In trying to mend the ways of procedure, would to goodness that the Government would try and find some means for checking the multiplicity of questions asked, which is a really wicked waste of time. The number on the notice paper last Thursday amounted to 60!—and these were augmented by subsidiary questions (questions out of questions) and others put without notice.

I can't help feeling very anxious about Uncle Edward. He is greatly altered, having shrunk to nothing comparatively, and has grave disorders internally, I fear. He is, however, fairly bright and happy, and quite resigned.

Thursday, 9 November. Went to the Lord Mayor's dinner this evening, which was much the usual scramble. Mr. G. having to leave early in order to return to the House, the speeches were cut shorter. Lord Northbrook replied appropriately, briefly, and forcibly for the Navy; and poor Childers—who is looking wretchedly ill, is thoroughly knocked up, and whose only chance is complete rest—returned thanks for the Army in a speech which was evidently a great effort and was literally read out. Mr. G. spoke for about 20 minutes. He was extremely impressive, in great voice, and eloquent beyond himself throughout. He was well received. It is any odds, I suppose, that it was his last appearance at this festivity.

After the dinner I went on to Mrs. Speaker's,[2] where there was a pleasant little assemblage.

Last night one was most dissipated. Dinner at Lord Suffield's with music afterwards; Mrs. Gladstone's party which was quite a success; and a dancing party at Mrs. Cavendish Bentinck. The Downing St. dinner and party was in honour of Wolseley.

[1] T. M. Healy, 'The Irish Parliamentary Party', *The Fortnightly Review* (Nov. 1882), xxxii. 625–33. [2] i.e. Lady Brand's.

Childers wants a baronetcy for Sir J. Adye. But there seems to be insufficient means. One would have thought a G.C.B. would have sufficed and been most appropriate. Mr. G. suggested a Privy Councillorship.

The Queen thinks Lord Northbrook and Childers should both have the G.C.B. Both, however, have been previously sounded, and both were against it.

The wretched closure debate drags on. The first resolution has now occupied 16 or 17 days, which ought to be of itself pretty conclusive proof of the necessity of a closing power. The House is now in the thick of the debate on Northcote's motion to reject the resolution *in toto*. The Tories have really placed themselves in a most inconsistent position. They first supported *a* form of closure—that by 'two-thirds'—and then they propose to negative all closure. Every available Tory has been pressed into speaking. Among these has been Sidney Herbert, who appears to have acquitted himself very tolerably. Mr. G. mentioned him to the Queen as one of those who had maintained the debate with ability. All this spun-out talking is next door to obstruction and is at the best perfectly needless and most dilatory.

Sunday, 12 November. (Bushey Park) Down here for Sunday, which is very pleasant. Mostly the Paget family, with the addition of Grannie Farquhar and Miss Capel.

Friday saw the end of the closure debate. The last night's talking was chiefly remarkable for Cowen's eloquent and virulent attack, which naturally drew down storms of applause from the Opposition. He is the representative of the Tory Democrat school and an eccentric politician, but his 'faculty of speech', as Mr. G. admits, is wonderful. Cowen's main idea is hatred of Mr. G. It is said that this hatred and defection from the Liberal party are due to an incident in the House of Commons about 5 years ago. He had been ill, and on his return to the House after his illness he was in the lobby being congratulated on his recovery and was passed by Mr. G. unnoticed. Shortly after, Dizzie came by and on seeing Cowen grasped him by the hand and inquired tenderly after his health. From that moment he transferred his allegiance from Mr. G. to Dizzie.

The only other speech of any note was by Sexton, whose command of phrase Mr. G. regards as marvellous and of whom one may be sure one will hear much in the future. His oratory and power, however, are not considered by Mr. G. to be equal to the oratory or power of either O'Connell or Sheil.

The majority (44) was excellent and larger by several votes than was expected on the most sanguine estimate. Only 3 men defaulted—Marriott, Courtauld, and P. A. Taylor. Mr. G. was much pleased with the result. It is, of course, said that if the party had dared to vote as they really pleased they would not have carried any closing power, but the Tories are the last people who ought to throw stones at party fidelity. Their house of allegiance is all glass—none of them ever vote wrong.

The Opposition seem inclined to take up Bourke's vote of censure about the surrender of Arabi to the Egyptian authorities.

Lord Spencer has in an excellent and sensible letter stated his views about Mr. G.'s threatened intention to retire at the end of the year. If Mr. G. is determined to carry out his intention, he had better not try and argue his case, because he is driven to defend himself by harking on his inability to *construct* legislation, of which others are better judges. Lord Spencer's views coincide with ours in Downing Street. He is sure Mr. G. underrates greatly the effect of his retirement on his party, who never recognised his withdrawal from the leadership in 1875. Moreover, those who called him into office in 1880 did not call him back merely for the purpose of putting straight the crooked doings of Lord Beaconsfield. They called him back because they wanted certain measures of first importance, e.g. Local Government and County Franchise, passed, which he alone could pass; and there would be profound disappointment were he to take himself off without tackling one of these measures. There is no saying when divisions of opinion may not creep into the party again, and Mr. G. is the only man who can possibly heal those divisions. If he cannot face the task of construction, he must devolve it upon others and confine his labours to criticism and supervision. If he and Lord Hartington were to differ, *he* would be sure to carry with him the bulk of the party. Fancy, therefore, Lord Hartington's difficulties! However much Mr. G. may struggle to retire, my belief is he will find it impossible to do so *yet*.

Monday, 13 November. This morning's post brought a letter from Lord Hartington written at Sandringham containing the first expression of his views of Mr. G.'s pronounced intentions.[1] He maintains that the leadership of the House of Commons in its present temper is an impossibility for anyone but Mr. G. himself. The advanced section of the party would require stronger measures from Mr. G.'s successor than from Mr. G. himself—measures which he (Lord H.) would not be prepared to initiate. Were he (Lord H.) to make room for someone else who would not feel the same difficulties in this respect—a step which he (Lord H.) would consider no sacrifice—the moderate section of the party would be sure to break away. In short, there is no arrangement conceivable which would afford any prospect of success or permanence. Mr. G.'s retirement would certainly lead to the speedy, if not the immediate, dissolution of the Government and the party.

This is pretty plain speaking. It is in effect saying to Mr. G. that he (Lord H.) will be blowed first if he will undertake the leadership. Every fresh expression of opinion, then, enhances Mr. G.'s difficulties in giving effect to his

[1] Bernard Holland, *The Life of . . . Devonshire* (London, 1911), i. 377–8.

very natural wishes. There is a further consideration which bears in one way upon the inopportuneness of Mr. G.'s retirement now, and that is, he is on too high a pinnacle of glory. His departure now would look as if he had chosen to end his political career in a halo of success.

We had an interesting ceremony this morning. Mr. G. received the officers of the Indian contingent who have come over to receive the medal from the Queen's own hands. They were presented to him one by one by Sir H. Daly, who gave a short account of each man's antecedents. Mr. G. touched the sword of each, according to oriental custom, and shook hands. At the conclusion of the presentation he said a few appropriate words to them. He was immensely struck by their appearance, as he could hardly fail to be. They ought to be gratified by the reception they are receiving in this country wherever they go. The other night, when they appeared in the gallery of the House of Commons, the unprecedented step was taken of a spontaneous cheer in the House.

Mr. G. went on Saturday evening to see Tennyson's new play.[1] It seems to have been a most dreary failure; and going with Tennyson's son,[2] as he did, he evidently felt in a most awkward position.

Mr. G. has recently had in contemplation the grant of special art honours. His original idea was to offer baronetcies to Millais and Watts, knighthoods to G. Richmond and Herbert, and knighthoods to Woolner and Boehm. Such a project could not fail to give considerable offence—to say nothing of the difficulty of leaving out Leighton. If it is to be done at all, the honour ought to be given to the profession; and though he may not be so big a master, Leighton, as President of the R[oyal] A[cademy], ought to be the representative man to receive a mark of recognition. To confer honours on individuals means selection which is very invidious and open to strong differences of opinion. Indeed, the whole question is so beset with difficulties that I expect Mr. G. will have to give up his project.

Wednesday, 15 November. There was a Cabinet yesterday. The most important topic of conversation seems to have been how to deal with the question which the Porte is pressing of sending a commission to Egypt. That it should be counteracted seems to be a matter of necessity; and the Cabinet decided that the best mode of counteracting the plan of the Ottoman Government would be to threaten the Sultan with a suspension of diplomatic intercourse.

Mr. G. yesterday penned a line to Mrs. H. Tennyson[3] to serve as a sort of *solatium* for the bad reception which the Poet Laureate's new play had on

---

[1] *The Promise of May.*
[2] Lionel Tennyson. See 15 Nov. 1882.
[3] So EWH wrote, but the letter was actually to Mrs. Lionel Tennyson. See Add. MS. 44546, f. 35. Hallam Tennyson was unmarried at this time.

Saturday evening. He did not attempt to admire or criticise the work. He confined himself with much ingenuity to certain generalities. He pointed out to her that the Theatre requires a playwright as well as a poet; and that, if the two characters are to be combined in one, the poet instead of 'walking erect' has to 'stoop a good deal'. He referred to the fact that the London Gallery requires to be fed with 'milk rather than strong meat' and adverted to the craft of orators who are obliged to take the audience for their standard.

All yesterday's sitting was confined to the discussion of the second resolution, which deals with irregular adjournments of the House. Many purely dilatory amendments were moved; and the waste of time would have been, Mr. G. said, little creditable to a 'parish vestry' or a 'meeting of working men'. Almost all the amendments hitherto which have been moved, and which have had the support of the front Opposition bench, have emanated from the 'fourth party'.

The Arabi business is getting acute, and there seems to be a very prevalent impression that we had no business to be handing Arabi over to the Egyptian authorities. It would be an excellent thing were it possible [to] quash the judicial proceedings, which promise to be interminable, and to get him banished straight off.

Sunday, 19 November. The review by Her Majesty on the Horse Guards Parade yesterday was a really beautiful spectacle and went off most successfully. There never could have been an occasion when the proverbial fortune of the Queen as to weather was demonstrated with such extraordinary exactness. The morning opened with a dense white fog. It lifted about eleven; but there was still a veil of mist which precluded a sight across the Parade till the arrival of the Queen, when instantly the curtain as it were rose and the spectacle was lit up by the appearance of the sun. My windows commanded the prettiest view of all, I believe; and they accommodated among others Lady Suffield and Miss Harbord, Lady Alfred Paget and one of her girls, Lady Bety Herbert, Lady Katie Lambton, the Walter Hutchinsons, Miss Maudie Brand, and Mrs. Stanley Clarke. Mr. G. was quite delighted with the sight which he witnessed from the small stand which we had had erected in the garden. What struck him most was the magnificent appearance of the line regiments—an unanswerable proof against the charges of short service. In the evening Mrs. Childers gave a huge rout at the War Office, which was attended by all the Royalties and all the Egyptian heroes.

Colonel Stanley and Sir R. Cross have made overtures respectively to Sir W. Harcourt and the Speaker for the postponement of the resolutions relating to the constitution of Grand Committees. If the Government will only assent to their postponement, the rest of the resolutions shall be through next week; if not, the Opposition will fight as long as they possibly can. Mr. G., as is also the Speaker, is strongly against making the concession. To postpone the consideration of what Mr. G. terms 'devolution' would be to waste another session in remedying the evils from which the parliamentary machinery is suffering by reason of its being overclogged. Moreover, Mr. G. has committed himself over and over again to statements that it was devolution to which he looked as the real reform of parliamentary procedure and not the penal code. The Government must persevere. Any unnecessary opposition and obstruction to the Standing Committees must redound to the discredit of the Tories, and be a proportionate gain to the Liberal party.

Lord Hartington has circulated a long letter from Fawcett about the charge to which Indian revenues are to be subjected in respect of the expenses of the employment of Indian troops in Egypt. Fawcett declares that the decision of the Cabinet on this matter must affect his own position in the Government. Besides supporting all the arguments used by the Indian Government, he takes strong exception to the mode of procedure in giving effect to the section in the Act empowering the use of Indian troops outside India. He contends that as the resolution in the House of Commons is ordinarily worded, the Home Government obtain an 'unlimited credit'. The manner of defraying the cost should be definitely stated, and the troops to be employed on an expedition beyond the Indian frontier should be strictly limited. The question really at stake is whether the Egyptian expedition was for Imperial or Indian purposes; and he points out with much force that, if troops drawn from India be employed on an expedition which is even partly Imperial only and the expense of them be wholly maintained out of Indian revenues, the constitutional check on the employment of troops by the Crown is swept away. He lays great stress on the fact that India was not consulted before active interference in Egypt was finally determined upon. The members of the Cabinet who have seen the correspondence are pretty unanimous in their opinion that, though the circumstances of the Egyptian expedition are such as to justify the imposition of *some* charge on Indian revenues, yet a compromise with the Indian Government is desirable, and indeed difficult to resist, when regard is paid, as it must be, to the strong line taken by the members of the present Government, when in opposition, on the Afghan question. The reasonable and proper arrangement seems to be that the ordinary charge of the Indian troops employed in Egypt should be borne by India, but that all extraordinary expenditure connected with the expedition should be defrayed out of Imperial revenues. With this the Indian Government and Fawcett ought to and probably would be content; but it seems to be expedient to go even beyond this, for the sake of avoiding the possibility of Fawcett's resignation and bad impressions in India.

The Cabinet seem more and more inclined to compound for the exile of Arabi; and in this they have the support of Lord Dufferin.

A slow but sure progress has been made during last week with the procedure resolutions.

The Government have had to give way about a committee of inquiry into the Kilmainham business. It is unfortunate and is a bad precedent; but Mr. G., 'drawn' by the insinuations made regarding the transactions which took place, unguardedly committed himself.

Tuesday, 21 November. W. Grenfell lost Salisbury yesterday, having had to stand re-election on accepting the Parliamentary Groomship. This is most annoying, but only what, I confess, I expected. The Tory candidate, who is reputed to be not of the most refined, has been carefully nursing the borough these 3 years; and the borough has always been susceptible to *attentions*. The Tories, of course, claim the seat as a great victory—a protest against 'Gladstone's Gag'; a nail in the Government's coffin. But little, however, is to be inferred from a bye election, especially in a small borough, swayed by local influences and always evenly balanced.

The death of Lord Harrowby has placed another Garter at Mr. Gladstone's disposal, and Mr. G. is now sifting claims for the two Blue Ribands. He, of course, as was to be expected, puts Lord Derby first. The others who first occurred to him were Lansdowne and Lord Bath. Lord Granville has also suggested for consideration the Dukes of Leinster and Grafton. His latest leanings are towards Lord Derby and the Duke of Leinster. It is probable that exception may be taken to Lord Derby. It is certainly rather hard that he, a recent convert, should be preferred to others who have served long and faithfully in the Liberal ranks. Two men will certainly be disappointed—Lord Ailesbury and Lord Sefton; the latter, I know, asked H.R.H. to further his claims. Mr. G. thinks Lord Derby cannot possibly be objected to; independently of his great political position, he enjoys one of *the* oldest earldoms and is possessed of enormous property and wealth, both of which always count much in the disposition of the Garter. The Duke of Leinster has, as Mr. G. said today, been incomparably faithful. But will not Lord Northbrook and Lord Kimberley be reasonably disappointed?

Mr. G. has been rather *low* lately, owing to his seeing greater difficulties about escaping from office.

Thursday, 23 November. Sir S. Northcote is unwell and has to take himself off for a complete rest. W. H. Smith places his splendid yacht at his disposal. It is, I fear, a revival of a somewhat serious weakness of his—heart. Mr. G. wrote him a very nice note this morning of good wishes.

Lord Spencer has sent over some extremely interesting papers about secret societies. They have managed to get hold of a certain number of informers by dint of bribes and under pledge of secrecy. There appear to be two separate Assassination Committees in Dublin to which 900 members belong! A truly horrible disclosure. They condemn certain men to death, and then draw lots for the execution of the deed. Failure to carry out the sentence means certain death to the individual. Among those supposed to be included on their devillish list are Lord Spencer, Mr. G., Sir W. Harcourt, and some sort of blow is expected to be struck ere long. From information collected, it seems to be clearly established that it was Burke alone whom these devils intended to make away with, and that poor F. Cavendish fell a victim accidentally. It is something to have got together the information they have; but how to get more with a view of breaking up these horrible societies is a difficult matter. It is thought by some that the power of arresting on suspicion ought to be renewed; but the experiences of the last suspension of the Habeas Corpus are not encouraging, and any appeal to Parliament for further powers, which would have to be made ostensibly for the purpose of breaking up these societies, would probably put an entire stop to the flow of any information, to say nothing of the parliamentary difficulties which such an appeal would involve. On the whole it seems best to work out in secrecy with the present powers. With such a disclosure of facts, one can't help feeling uneasy that Mr. G. declines to be body-guarded.

There have been several more convictions in Dublin—All the perpetrators of the horrible Joyce murders have been sentenced. This ought to have a good deterrent effect, and it is satisfactory that these sentences have been obtained by juries.

Lord Hartington gave a great reception last night at the Foreign Office in honour of the Indian officers. It was a great success, and there was no lack of people, though it was the autumn.

The Government have determined to proceed with the proposal for Standing Committees, but Lord Hartington, to Mr. G.'s surprise, was rather in favour of dropping them.

Tonight a small party at the Speaker's—one is quite gay again.

Went last night before the Foreign Office *rout* to the Albert Hall with the Cavendish Bentincks. The *Elijah*.

Saturday, 25 November. There seems to be a good probability that the House will be up by the end of next week; and in view of this, Mr. G. has got the Queen's speech in draft. Its composition added to the exceptional parliamentary calls upon him—(5 days a week of Government business of which he has sole conduct)—has rather exhausted him; and he dreads more than ever the possibility (which is really a probability) of having to remain on in office. As a *dernier resort* to strengthen his case, he has asked Andrew Clark to call upon him in the hope that Clark may give him a 'Doctor's certificate'; rather a frail hope, I fear, for Mr. G. to lean upon. He opened out his mind for some time this morning to Richard Grosvenor, from whom almost alone he gets sympathy—a sympathy not untinged, I think, with selfishness, as R. G. evidently wants to get out of harness also, partly from a feeling of wearisomeness and partly from bad health.

The Archbishop of Canterbury[1] has had a relapse. It is to be feared that there can now be little hope of his recovery.

Mr. R. Lawley, a great bore, called here yesterday to press the claims of Lord Ailesbury for one of the vacant Garters. He has a story that Lord Beaconsfield offered Lord A. the Garter twice over, once orally and the other time in writing, on condition of his supporting the Tory party. This in common decency of course Lord A. declined! And now he wishes to get the reward due to his consistency and his refusal of so tempting a bribe!

Sunday, 26 November. After dining with Lady Freddy Cavendish last night, Mr. G. went and had a long talk with Lord Granville. The draft of the Queen's speech was doubtless considered; but the main topic of the conversation must have been Mr. G.'s personal position and the reconstruction of the Cabinet which in any case is unavoidable. He had jotted down on paper the offices which would have to be refilled. In this list he had included the *First Lordship of Treasury, Chancellorship of Exchequer, Presidency of Council* (Lord Spencer having, it is believed, foregone, with his usual unselfishness, his claims to return to the active duties of a Cabinet minister), *Chancellorship of Duchy of Lancaster, Surveyor Generalship of Ordnance* (to be vacated by transfer of Sir J. Adye to Governorship of Gibraltar), *Chairmanship of Ways and Means*, and (with queries) the *Postmaster Generalship*, in view of the possibility of Fawcett's parting company with the Government over the Indian-Egyptian business, and the *Speakership*, about which Sir H. Brand has as yet given no signs.

If Mr. G. still persists in his intentions and persuades himself that he will be able to effect his retirement, surely the reconstruction of the Cabinet must be the work of his successor? Here there is a slight inconsistency.

Assuming, however, that he has himself to reconstruct, Mr. G. evidently has in contemplation the offer of the Chancellorship of the Exchequer to Childers, provided his health will stand it and there is a fair prospect of his being fit to resume office work at an *early* date. To this offer he is no doubt much [?] pledged; but it is to be hoped that he will still revive the idea of last summer that Lord Hartington should assume the Chancellorship, for which I heard from a private source the other day Lord Hartington himself now wishes. Mr. G.'s further ideas are (1) Dilke for the War Office; (2) Morley, who has acquitted himself admirably at the War Office all this time and consequently 'gone up many places', for the Chancellorship of the Duchy of Lancaster; (3) Harry Brand for Under-ship at War Office; and (4) Edmond Fitzmaurice for Under-secretaryship at Foreign Office.

Lord Salisbury has been 'starring' this last week in Edinburgh; but it is hardly likely that he has made any very sensible impression upon the hard-headed stout Scotch Liberals.

[1] A. C. Tait.

Her Majesty objects to giving the baronetcy which Childers wants for Sir J. Adye, an objection for which she will get sympathy from here. All the Egyptian honours have been greatly overdone; and as regards Sir J. Adye, his services have already been pretty substantially rewarded by a G.C.B. and the appointment of Governor-Generalship at Gibraltar. Childers, as Lord G[ranville] yesterday remarked, is rather too fond of lavishing honours on everybody but himself.

One of the new Rules has been put twice to the test during this last week, viz. the Rule intended to provide against abuses of the privilege of adjourning the House to raise discussion on extraneous subjects. The two occasions have been (1) Parnell's debate on Irish matters, (2) Yorke's debate on the Kilmainham business and his motion for an inquiry into the circumstances of that business. The new Rule, watered down as it has been in deference to the wishes of the House, has been tried and I fear been found rather wanting.

Mr. G. and Lord G[ranville] are more hopeful as to the outlook in France and of her relations towards us in this difficult Egyptian business.

Lord Dufferin seems to be pulling excellently well with Malet at Cairo, which speaks volumes for the tact of both.

As regards the position of the Government generally towards the close of the session, there is no doubt that it is appreciably stronger than it was a year ago. This increased strength may be mainly ascribed to the improved state of Ireland and the rapid success of the Egyptian campaign. But one must not overrate the accession of strength and popularity. These 'fillips' are very ephemeral, and it is probable that so far as the Egyptian war has contributed to the successes of the Government, the new popularity is mainly confined to Pall Mall and the upper classes, and also the politically neutral class, on none of which can the Government rely to any great extent. Apart, however, from these fleeting causes of popularity, the increased prestige of the Government may be attributed partly to the belief (and this is far firmer ground), which has been slowly and surely maturing in the public mind, that in administrative matters the capacity of the Government as a whole is exceptionally good. Lord Spencer has done wonders in Ireland. Mr. Childers and Lord Northbrook have shewn marked efficiency in organising the fighting services. Lord Granville and Sir C. Dilke have displayed the greatest dexterity in steering the country through difficult foreign shoals. Chamberlain and Harcourt have done both well in their respective departments. Fawcett has acquired the fame of an administrator of the highest order and earned much popularity by his enterprising and judicious reforms.

Against, however, these administrative successes has to be set the failure of the Government as regards legislative work; and if, with increased facilities for accomplishing such work, this failure continues, this circumstance will tell greatly against the Government, and this force will have to be reckoned with.

Monday, 27 November. Clark called yesterday, and as was to be expected 'passed' Mr. G. perfectly sound. So he cannot very well plead broken health as an excuse for retirement.

He has, since my last entry, fired off two letters to Lord Granville in further relation to the future.[1] He has gone so far as to say that he is willing, if Lord G[ranville] and Lord Hartington like, to stay on till *Easter*, as he does not anticipate any serious legislative work till after Easter next year, that inconvenient moveable feast falling as it does so early in 1883.[2] He has proposed that Lord G[ranville] should again sound Lord Derby as to joining the administration. He has also laid it down that it is a mistake to suppose that the Chancellor of Exchequer's work is light. It is by rights, and Mr. G. himself found it so, one of the hardest places in the Government. In this I do not agree, except in the case of a man of enormous inventive power like Mr. G. himself. He made this remark apropos of the idea that it is the place to which Lord Hartington, with the reversion of the leadership of the House of Commons, should be appointed. Mr. G. is evidently willing that Lord Hartington should have the place if he wishes for it and should certainly be given it, should the vacating of the India Office make the best arrangements whereby Lord Derby would join. But apart from these considerations, Mr. G. would naturally look to Childers to succeed himself as Finance Minister. It is the office of Chancellor of the Exchequer which no doubt most immediately presses for consideration, and as regards Childers a certain amount must depend on his real state of health.

I attended the Cabinet today for a short while for the first time with special reference to the prorogation and reassembling of Parliament. It was interesting to get a glimpse into the way in which Cabinet business is conducted.

The two men now who ride the Opposition most in Parliament are Harcourt ('Jumbo') and Courtney. It is a great pity that Courtney is so bear-like in his ways. His ability is most marked.

Friday, 1 December. These are extra-interesting times. The work of reconstructing the Cabinet has commenced; and the construction is not to take place *minus* its head-piece, as has lately seemed to be most probable. Owing to the urgent representations of Lords Granville and Hartington, Mr. G. has, though very reluctantly, abandoned the idea of retiring for the present. He has promised Mrs. G. not to fret any more about it at any rate until Easter. The best and most important news is that the negotiations renewed in St. James's Square have been successfully concluded.[3] The conclusion is in no small part due to the tact of Lord Granville by whom the negotiations have been conducted. In short, Lord Derby has consented to join the Government. It may somewhat reflect upon his character that he declined to enter the

[1] Ramm, i. 458–9.   [2] Easter fell on 25 Mar. in 1883.
[3] Lord Derby lived at 23 St. James's Square.

Cabinet, when the Government was *down*, as it certainly was last summer,
and has consented to come in when the Government is *up*; but it is said on
good authority that his refusal last summer was due in the main to the action
of Lady D[erby], who is reputed to be very ambitious and to have thought
that last summer was an inopportune moment and that for *him* to have joined
then would have prejudiced his political career. He is to take the India Office.
The subsequent and necessary changes are still in embryo. Lord Hartington
has suggested 3 alternative courses.

1. Lord Derby to be Secretary of State for India. Himself (Lord H.) to
   become Chancellor of Exchequer.
2. Lord Derby to be Secretary of State for India. Mr. Childers to move to
   the Exchequer. Himself (Lord H.) to go to the War Office.
3. Lord Derby to be Secretary of State for India. Lord Hartington to
   become Chancellor of the Exchequer. Mr. Childers to take the Chancellorship of the Duchy of Lancaster. Lord Northbrook to be transferred
   to the War Office. Dilke to assume the First Lordship of the Admiralty.

Mr. G. expressed a decided preference for the *second* alternative. I confess
to leaning towards No. 3. Lord H[artington] seems no doubt to wish to come
to the Exchequer, and were it not that Mr. G. has so often promised Childers
the Chancellorship of the Exchequer, Lord Hartington's claim to become
Finance Minister would be paramount. Mr. G., however, feeling in duty
bound to make the offer of the Chancellorship to Childers and believing that
Childers has the greatest aptitude for the place, has written to say that the
Exchequer is at Childers's disposal. He qualifies the offer in two respects.
He implies that he must have a medical certificate from high authority to say
that Childers is fit to resume work again. Mr. G. has moreover told Childers
that Lord Hartington would *like* the choice of the Chancellorship open to
him.

Sunday, 3 December. Parliament was prorogued yesterday after (I think) 161
days in session, which makes it the longest session but two in the last 50 years.
The Opposition to the Grand Committee proposals unexpectedly collapsed
on Friday evening; and so all the new Rules with certain modifications, some
of which it is to be feared have not been improvements, are passed. The completion of the work is a great triumph for Mr. G. and will rank as one of his
greatest feats. He is convinced that without a session specially appropriated
to the consideration of procedure its reform would have been practically
impossible. He attaches great importance to the devolution of work to Grand
Committees and is sanguine of their eventful success. Nothing but experiment
of them can test their real value. The Tories look upon the establishment of
these Committees with great suspicion. Gibson went so far as to call the proposal 'revolutionary'; but why should so much alarm be manifested about
a proposal which has been advocated by the best authorities for a length of

time and by authorities of much moderation, such as ex-Speakers, the present Speaker, Erskine May, and which is admitted to be purely experimental? Time and experience will probably allay these apprehensions as it has allayed many other apprehensions regarding far more drastic reforms.

Mr. G. is in a great state of delight that the session has come to an end and that his (herculean) procedure labours are concluded. This consideration added to the prospect of Lord Derby's advent as a colleague has done much to make up for the disappointment he has experienced at having to postpone his retirement.

He has been twice down to Windsor this last week but has not broached with H.M. the subject of the coming administrative changes or the bestowal of the vacant Garters. It is to be wished that he would take Her more into confidence when he has audiences.

The Archbishop of Canterbury,[1] after the most protracted and lingering illness, passed away this morning. It appears that, taking all things into consideration, including the Archbishop's own dying wishes conveyed to Mr. G. by the Dean of Durham,[2] the choice of a successor to the see of Canterbury is most likely to rest between the Bishop of Winchester and the Bishop of Truro.[3] I expect the offer will be made in the first instance to the Bishop of Winchester, but it may be thought that he is too advanced in years.[4] Both, I fear, are far removed from being Liberals.

Poor Fawcett is lying dangerously ill with an attack of diphtheria and typhoid fever combined. His loss would be a very heavy one to the public and to the Government.

It has been decided that the Imperial Government should propose to contribute £500,000 towards the expenses incurred by the Indian Government in connection with the Egyptian expedition; this would leave some £600,000 odd to be provided by the Indian Government. I could wish that the Imperial Government had taken upon itself the whole expenses of the war; it would be a bit of generosity which would be highly appreciated in India and (I believe) popular in this country. But Mr. G. considers that to exempt India from all share of the expense (he does not mind so much what the exact amount is) in defending the highway to the East, in which India has far greater interests than this country, would be indefensible in principle and a monstrous injustice to the British taxpayer. It is to be hoped that the Indian Government will now accept the compromise in good grace.

H.M. wants a small representative force taken from the Indian Army to be permanently kept in this country to serve on state occasions. Mr. G. does not much like the idea but has not wholly rejected it. He merely remarked that it was characteristic of H.M.'s restlessness of mind. The decision had better be left to the new Secretary of State (Lord Derby).

[1] A. C. Tait.
[2] W. C. Lake.
[3] i.e. between Harold Browne and E. W. Benson.
[4] He was 71.

Monday, 4 December. Today the new Law Courts were opened. I drove down with Mr. and Mrs. G. He was very well received all along the route, and in certain places very loudly cheered. The ceremony in the central hall was very imposing, and Mr. G. presented a magnificent appearance in his Chancellor of the Exchequer's robes. Owing to his legal rank as Chancellor of the Exchequer, it was able to be arranged (mainly, I believe, by the Attorney General,[1] the most loyal and enthusiastic of men) that Mr. G. should have a place in the procession to which his position entitled him. He walked immediately in front of H.M. The Queen read her speech excellently, and her beautiful voice told wonderfully. The proceedings passed off without hitch, though Harcourt, who as Home Secretary was the minister immediately in attendance upon Her, did not know his lesson *pat* (as we used to say at Eton).

In connection with this marked day in legal annals, the Lord Chancellor[2] has, as head of the legal profession, been made an Earl. I suggested the propriety of the honour to Mr. G. on Saturday, and after consultation with Lord Granville, Mr. G. decided to make the submission. According to Lord Granville, Lord Selborne is not a favourite with H.M., but she made no difficulty about approving the proposal, though she approved professedly as a compliment to the Bar.

The Arabi trial is, thank goodness, over. As arranged by Lord Dufferin, all charges against Arabi were dropped but that of rebellion, and to this he pleaded guilty. The sentence was commuted to banishment, and it seems probable that Ceylon will be the place selected.

At a Cabinet this afternoon it was decided that the measures to be proposed *early* next session should be Bankruptcy, Patent Laws, Criminal Code, and Corrupt Practices; the first three of which, pursuant to the undertaking given in the House, are to be referred to the new Standing Committees. Accordingly, all contentious measures, which may find a place in next year's legislative programme, such as Local Government and Land Reform, will stand over till after Easter, between which and now the Cabinet will have ample time to develop their schemes.

Childers has accepted with avidity the Chancellorship of the Exchequer, which is to be regretted on more grounds than one. Having been told that Lord Hartington would like the place left open to him, Childers ought surely to have waived his claims? He has promised to submit himself to a further medical examination, and until that has been made his appointment to the Exchequer will of course remain uncertain.

Thursday, 7 December. (Wilton) Mr. and Mrs. G. went off to Harcourt's on Tuesday in the New Forest for two or three days, and I have run down here for two days' shooting. The party consists of the Brownlows, de Vescis, Reggie Talbots, Keith Fraser, J. Pollen, and Guy Dawnay. It would be very

---

[1] Sir Henry James.   [2] Lord Selborne.

difficult to find a more beautiful quartet of ladies than those present—Lady Brownlow, Lady Pembroke, Lady de Vesci, and Mrs. Reggie Talbot.

Rosebery yesterday confided to me his difficulties with regard to his position as well as his disappointment. Mr. G. had on Tuesday told him of the administrative changes in contemplation, and likewise intimated to him that:

(1) No change was to be made with respect to his office, though when he was appointed Mr. G. told him the arrangements were only temporary.

(2) There was no chance of his immediate promotion; and

(3) That Morley's claims to advancement would have to be preferred to his (Rosebery's) by reason of longer service.

He is greatly disconcerted and disappointed. He considers that the just expectations of Scotland to have their interests represented more effectually ought to be met; and he believed they would have been met. He had hoped that he might have been selected as the person to represent those interests in an improved manner. If length of service is to be the consideration entitling promotion, he will be the last to be promoted as he only joined the Government 16 months ago. From certain hints dropped by Mr. G., and from the peculiar relations which Rosebery has held with Mr. G., he had been led to expect that a step was in store for him. He is sure that his being kept on in his present post under the present arrangements will be greatly misunderstood in Scotland. It will be thought that he has been tried and found wanting. He finds the present arrangement, making him responsible for all Scotch affairs without any direct access to the Cabinet, is unworkable. In short, he is grievously disappointed at not getting Cabinet office, and I must say, taking everything into consideration, his disappointment is not without reason. He asks to be relieved of his present place as Scotch minister; he will, so long as Mr. G. remains on, continue to serve the Government in a subordinate place; he will then give up politics. He is evidently under the impression that Lord Granville does not like him and has put a spoke in his political wheel. I hope I have not misrepresented him. If anybody else had taken the line he has, I should have said it showed a want of patience, that it was unreasonable, and that it was overrating himself too high. But considering the estimate which Mr. G. has formed and rightly formed of Rosebery's abilities, and how often Mr. G. has let Rosebery know what that estimate was, I am not surprised at all at Rosebery's state of mind. The difficulty is this—if Mr. G. were now to reconsider the point and give Rosebery (say) the Chancellorship of the Duchy of Lancaster with a seat in the Cabinet and a special commission to administer Scotch affairs, it would be almost impossible for Rosebery to accept any such offer with proper regard to his *amour propre*, now that he has made a representation to Mr. G. on the subject of his own feelings.

He (Childers) has at the instance of Mr. and Mrs. G. submitted himself to Gull, who says that all that Childers requires is 6 weeks' rest, and so it is to be presumed that his health will not stand in the way of his taking up his place at the Exchequer. It is to be devoutly hoped that he will not wish to reside in Downing St., as to be turned bodily out of our present Chancellerie into No. 10 would be terribly inconvenient.

It seems clear that as at present minded Mr. G. will only bring into the Cabinet Dilke besides Lord Derby. The best way of bringing this about would be to transfer Lord Kimberley to the Presidency of the Council and give Dilke the Colonial Secretaryship. The other alternative is probably to move Lord Northbrook to the Council Office and to place Dilke at the Admiralty; but this would mean moving from the Admiralty one of the best and most popular administrators that have ever held the First Lordship. I am afraid Lord Derby and Dilke will be a nasty pair for H.M. to accept.

Mr. G. was much pleased with a note he got the other day from Trevelyan who had written to thank Mr. G. for his kindly appreciation of his (T.'s) conduct of Irish affairs in the House of Commons. In thanking Trevelyan for his letter, Mr. G. adverted to the question of a Local Government Bill for Ireland. He is convinced of the necessity of establishing a political system which may make Ireland feel that it has a Government of its own and not merely an alien one. He harks back on Lord Russell's (alleged) basis of working such a system by the 4 Provinces. Mr. G. admits that any such measure might be regarded as a concession, but he attaches far more importance to providing the Government with a bulwark against attacks carried on by charging the Empire and the Exchequer with all local wants in Ireland for want of local powers.

Sunday, 10 December. Returned to Town yesterday, as did also Mr. and Mrs. G. Childers presented himself, and as Gull thinks 6 weeks' rest will render his return to work possible, he is to become definitely the new Chancellor of the Exchequer. Fortunately he does not contemplate residence in his official house.[1] So we shall not be uprooted wholly from our present Chancellerie, and I shall not be turned out of my rooms.

Dilke is to have the Chancellorship of the Duchy of Lancaster and is greatly pleased at his promotion. The arrangement will have its advantages as it will obviate the necessity of a more extensive shuffling of places. Dilke seemed inclined to think that Evelyn Ashley would make his best successor. The men who stand best for the vacant minor appointments are Harry Brand, Edmond Fitzmaurice, and Illingworth (to represent the 'extreme left'). Of the young men, Dilke thinks most of R. Brett.

Mr. G. yesterday wrote to the Queen recommending the Bishop of Truro for the see of Canterbury. From private inquiries made, it is thought that the Bishop of Winchester's age and somewhat failing strength make it unadvisable to make him the offer of the Archbishopric. Probably, therefore, the Bishop of Truro is the right man.[2]

[1] No. 11 Downing Street.　　　[2] See 10 Dec. 1882. But see also 12, 14, and 17 Dec. 1882.

The quashing of Arabi's trial has deprived the Egyptian ministry of Riaz's services; but according to Lord Dufferin, Riaz's loss will not be very great, and there seems to be a fair prospect that Nubar's services will now be available. As regards Arabi, his counsel admitted to Lord Dufferin that, though there was no likelihood of the production of direct proof of Arabi's complicity in the massacres and burning of Alexandria, yet the weak point in his case was that he had done nothing directly to arrest the burning of the city or to punish the perpetrators either of that deed or of the murders of Europeans.

The Liverpool election was a great surprise and was as gratifying as it was unexpected. To have won Liverpool is worth the loss of a dozen Salisburys.[1] Mr. G. is much elated. The election seems to have turned wholly on men, not measures; that is, it was a question of confidence in Mr. G. or the reverse.

Tuesday, 12 December. Mr. G. went down on Monday to Windsor for an audience to broach the question of Lord Derby and Dilke for the Cabinet, for which he had prepared H.M. by a letter the night before, and to discuss further the candidates for the Archbishopric.

H.M. takes exception to the Bishop of Truro on the ground of his age, which is certainly younger than that of previous archbishops when appointed, and she greatly prefers the Bishop of Winchester.[2] Mr. G. is quite willing to admit that the question of the age of the former is a nice point—the Episcopal Bench being all ripe in years might resent having so young a man (53) placed over their heads; and Mr. G. is prepared not to press his recommendation till after he has instituted further inquiries. He is making those inquiries of the Bishop of Chester[3] to whom he wrote yesterday to consult secretly not only as to the Bishop of Truro but also as to the Bishop of Winchester. Were it not for his age and infirmity the Bishop of Winchester would make no doubt an excellent archbishop; but he could only be practically a stop-gap, and Mr. G. is evidently anxious to appoint a man who has a good many years before him and who is likely to make a mark as archbishop and to reflect credit on his nominee. The discussion as to the appointment is quite friendly, and, so far as it has been carried on in writing, Lord G[ranville] thought that it redounded to the honour both of H.M. and Mr. G.

As to the proposals for recruiting the Cabinet, H.M. appears to be quite prepared to accept both Lord Derby and Dilke; but unfortunately she objects to the offices for which they are respectively designated. She does not like Lord Derby's going to the India Office; She is presumably afraid that he is not a Russophobist sufficiently. She dislikes the idea of the Duchy of

[1] At Liverpool S. Smith, the Liberal, won over Forwood, the Conservative, 18,198 to 17,889. For Salisbury, see 21 Nov. 1882.
[2] Guedalla, ii. 219–20.
[3] William Jacobson.

Lancaster for Dilke, inasmuch as that office would naturally bring Her into constant and close contact with the 'ex-republican'. Mr. G. is anxious to meet her wishes if possible. The difficulty is how to do so. Lord Derby might go to the Colonies while Lord Kimberley was moved to the India Office—an idea to which Lord K. has no objection. But then what is to become of Dilke? Of course if anything happened to poor Fawcett, the Postmaster Generalship with a seat in the Cabinet would be the thing for Dilke. Mr. G., by the by, has determined not to press any longer the Garter for Lord Derby now that he is to join the Government, though the Queen had acquiesced in the proposal.

Dined at the Speaker's[1] tonight and discussed with him possible candidates to succeed Playfair as Chairman of Ways and Means. The man whom the Speaker thinks most fitted for the place is Courtney; but he is unwilling to shift from the Treasury. Mr. G. has already sounded him. Failing him, the Speaker seemed to think that the next best men were Lubbock, St. Aubyn, Hussey Vivian, and O'Shaughnessy.

Wednesday, 13 December. Mr. Gladstone's jubilee—this being the 50th anniversary of his return to Parliament for Newark. Letters and telegrams of congratulations have arrived from many quarters. The Greeks and the Greek communities outside Greece have been most active. They are certainly a grateful race.

Cabinet arrangements have not further advanced today. The Queen appears to dislike the idea of Dilke's accession the more she thinks over it.[2] She now not only takes exception to the appointment (the Duchy) designated for him, but to his taking *any* Cabinet office. Dilke last night went down to Birmingham to see if he could induce Chamberlain to swop offices in order to facilitate matters—which was, Mr. G. thought, a commendable piece of boldness on his part. Submission of his name for some other office would probably conduce much to lessen the fight.

The Bishop of Chester whom Mr. G. consulted as to the acceptability of the two candidates most eligible for appointment to the see of Canterbury. The Bishop is of opinion that Winchester, were it not for his age and infirmity, would be most generally liked, but that Truro under the circumstances would be best, and he is sure no objection would be raised to him on the score of his being younger than the usual age at which archbishops are appointed. But if he is young, the Bishop of Winchester is, according to precedent, too old. There is no record of the appointment of a man to the see over 70 years of age.

Thursday, 14 December. Another very bustling busy day. I have had about eleven hours of it consecutively.

There seems to be a possibility, if not a probability, of a disagreeable fight

---

[1] Sir Henry Brand.　　　　[2] Guedalla, ii. 220.

about the new Archbishop. The Queen made known this afternoon, through Sir H. Ponsonby, Her latest views on the subject. She admits that the Bishop of Winchester's age and infirmities are a serious drawback, but She still thinks the offer of the archbishopric should be made to him with possibly a hint that he is expected to refuse. Next to him, She places very decidedly the Bishop of Durham.[1] She thinks from what she has been told that the Bishop of Truro's appointment would give offence to the Episcopal Bench—certainly four of them. She does not disclose the authority on which she bases her conclusions, but it is probable that she has talked the matter over with the Dean of Westminster,[2] who has been down to Windsor this week. Mr. G. was greatly minded to put his foot down at once. He was not unnaturally very annoyed that, after She had narrowed the choice to two—and this merely on the ground of age—She should set up so decidedly a different opinion to that which he had formed after the most anxious consideration of the matter for months. It was as if She were the person really responsible for the appointment instead of himself, who would certainly be held wholly accountable for the selection. Considering that he had given way to Her in the matter of the Deaneries of Windsor and Westminster,[3] it looked as if She wished to take an ell when given a yard. He was almost inclined to fire off at once a serious threat.[4] I dissuaded him from doing this and got him to postpone his reply till tomorrow; meanwhile he authorised me to write to Sir H. Ponsonby hinting at the serious consequences which might result from the line she was taking and giving Sir H. P. an idea of his feelings, which were those of a man much hurt at this apparent want of confidence shown in him.

Poor Fawcett is making a gallant struggle against his horrible illness, and the latest accounts are hopeful. There is no man probably who could have elicited so much universal sympathy and interest on the bed of sickness as he has, save Mr. G. himself.

Sunday, 17 December. After all, the apprehended rumpus about the archbishopric ended in smoke. My letter of Thursday evening brought up Sir H. Ponsonby the next morning in hot haste. It appeared that, written in a hurry, his letter had entirely misled us; that what he had said was not intended to represent the Queen's views but merely those of an adviser[5] and those founded on inquiries which she had made; that H.M. never dreamt of Bishop Lightfoot Herself; and that She was coming round to the conclusion that Bishop Benson was probably the best choice; but she reserved her final say till She saw Mr. G. At the audience yesterday the matter was clenched, and the offer of the see of Canterbury was made to Bishop Benson. Accordingly Mr. G.

---

[1] J. B. Lightfoot.   [2] G. G. Bradley.
[3] See 20 Sept., 4 and 25 Oct. 1882 for the Windsor deanery and 24 July, 3, 11, and 28 Aug. 1881 for Westminster.
[4] 'of resignation' is crossed out.
[5] The adviser was Randall Davidson. See *Letters*, 2nd ser., iii. 375–8.

has had his way, and most properly so too. As Prime Minister he alone would be held accountable for the appointment, and therefore his responsibility is supreme. What he so much feared was that the Queen would desire to take the matter too much into Her own hands. She has already manifested a desire of late to take too much upon Herself in the matter of ecclesiastical appointments—She objected to Wilkinson for a bishopric; She pressed Dean Bradley for Westminster; She preferred Boyd Carpenter to Butler for the canonry at Windsor; She monopolised the appointment of a new Dean of Windsor. In all these points Mr. G. gave way. It was now time for Mr. G. to assert his responsible authority.

At yesterday's Council Childers was sworn in as Chancellor of the Exchequer, Lord Hartington as Secretary of State for War, Lord Kimberley as Secretary of State for India, and Lord Derby as Secretary of State for the Colonies. H.M. kicked up to the last moment about Lord Derby. She was much incensed about his Manchester speech; She even regarded his accession to the Government as a worse evil than that of Dilke, who was at any rate 'right about foreign matters.'[1] After further representations, however, by Mr. G., She gave way on Friday evening.[2] Lord Derby might present himself at the Council as Colonial Secretary; his appointment to that office was an improvement upon the original proposal to place him at the India Office; it was, however, more painful than She could say for Her to receive him again as Her minister 'under such very different circumstances', and he must not expect a cordial reception. Mr. G. took this last remonstrance in very good humour, though it would be difficult to put any other interpretation upon such words as 'under such very different circumstances' than that Lord Derby last presented himself as a minister in Mr. Disraeli's Government (1874), and he now presented himself as a minister in Mr. Gladstone's Government (1882) —a truly terrible change!

H.M. is prepared to admit Dilke into the Cabinet. It is only now a question of which office it is to be. Chamberlain is ready to exchange the Board of Trade for the Duchy of Lancaster in order to facilitate Dilke's admission; and this will probably be the arrangement made, though other alternatives have been suggested, such as Dodson's transfer to the Duchy, Chamberlain to the Local Government Board, and Dilke to the Board of Trade.

Mr. G. after the Council yesterday took himself off to Hawarden for a little comparative rest. He has been greatly harassed and overtired during the last week—these ministerial changes, and the bothers they give, try him a deal more than the House of Commons work. This last week he wished himself back on the Treasury Bench to be worried by the Randolph Churchills and Gorsts. After the tremendous bustle of the last week, it is pleasant to get again into smooth water and to breath a little rest. Mr. G. was much too kind yesterday about my work for him, which is indeed paid for at a fancy price

[1] Guedalla, ii. 221.   [2] Ibid., pp. 221–2.

by the great privilege of being constantly with him, seeing him, hearing him, and knowing his thoughts.

I am still greatly concerned at the prospect of Rosebery's carrying out his threat of retirement. I have been doing my utmost directly and indirectly to prevent his taking such a step, which would be ruinous to him personally, damaging to the Government, vexatious to Mr. G., and moreover be fatal to Scotch interests, which Rosebery maintains is the principal question at issue. He should confine himself to demanding improved arrangements for the conduct of Scotch business. I fear, however, he is inclined to be pig-headed.

Friday, 22 December. (Salisbury) Got away from Downing St. for a little holiday on Wednesday. Spent two nights at Wilton on the way here. Had a very enjoyable day's shooting yesterday in Langford Wood. No house party. Good sport and lovely weather.

The difficulty about Dilke has not yet been got over. The idea of an exchange with Chamberlain did not do. H.M. objected as much to Chamberlain for the Duchy as She did to Dilke.[1] Harcourt and others were in favour of inducing Dodson to become Chancellor of the Duchy and of placing Dilke at the Local Government Board or else Chamberlain. But Mr. G. considers that such an offer to Dodson would be insulting, unless Dodson could be promised the reversion of the Speakership which would be awkward. Moreover, neither Chamberlain nor Dilke would have any previous training for the Local Government Board. Another idea which struck both Seymour and myself was that Mundella should be got to take the Duchy and Dilke be made Vice President of the Council. This still seems to me to be the best solution. The Duchy might be regarded as promotion by Mundella, and he would have less office work, which is said not to be his *forte*. Dilke has not behaved with great propriety in the matter. He goes as far as to suggest and even to be inclined to dictate his own terms of admission into the Cabinet. One of his suggested combinations was that Lefevre should become Chancellor of the Duchy with a seat in the Cabinet, and he (Dilke) should assume First Commissionership of Works. To place Lefevre in the Cabinet (especially merely to suit Dilke) would inevitably and rightly give offence to Trevelyan and Fawcett, who I am glad to say is becoming convalescent.

Sir H. Ponsonby tells me that as regards Lord Derby Her Majesty's objections to him were deep-rooted. She thinks he is ready to sacrifice his country at any moment, and this is (according to Sir H. P.) to what she referred when she alluded to the pain it was to Her to receive him now again as minister under 'such very different circumstances'. Mr. G. does not think Lord Derby is conscious himself of H.M.'s strong aversion to him. When She received him at the Council, Mr. G. says 'her lips were pinched till they were as sharp

[1] Ibid., pp. 222.

as a knife's edge'. Sir H. P. told me that, but for Mr. G.'s judicious handling of H.M. in this matter, the difficulties would have been far greater.

When I left Town, the Rosebery business had not mended. He continued very obstinate and Mr. G. was becoming provoked. Mr. G. regarded the correspondence[1] as astonishingly foolish—a tempest in a tea-kettle—and thought it marvellous how so clever a man as Rosebery could be so silly. He had, however, not lost his patience with Rosebery and continued to treat R. with kindness and much tact. Rosebery has indeed placed himself in an awkward dilemma:

(a) If he rests his case on public grounds, it may be said that it is for him to propound a plan whereby Scotch business can be transacted on an improved basis, and not to go and threaten resignation which would deprive Scotland of its most popular member of the Government and its most useful administration and which would inevitably damage Scotch interests.

(b) If he rests his case on private grounds, his contention must come from pique and disappointment—two utterly untenable reasons for resignation—and reasons reflecting most seriously on his conduct.

Mr. G. very properly of course pins him to the first alternative. Whatever, however, happens, R[osebery] will, I fear, have damaged himself permanently in Mr. G.'s estimation.

Sunday, 24 December. (Salisbury) The appointment to Canterbury of the Bishop of Truro,[2] of whose final acceptance, however, I have not yet heard, has been well, though not enthusiastically, received by all parties. It is believed by some that the offer of the archbishopric was made in the first instance to the Dean of St. Paul's,[3] which was not the case.

I hear that Dodson has been sounded as to exchanging the Local Government Board for the Duchy and has loyally placed himself at Mr. G.'s disposal. He has by this unselfish conduct gone up in one's estimation as many places as Dilke by the tone of his behaviour has gone down. It will be a great comfort and an immense relief to Mr. G. if by this arrangement the Dilke difficulty is solved. The great objection to it is that it removes a man from the Local Government Board who, whatever may be his weaknesses, is well fitted for the place and knows the works of the office, while it puts a man into the Local Government Board with no sort of previous training for the work and quite ignorant of all County business. The country gentlemen are sure to be up in arms and will view with double suspicion any reform of Local Government initiated by a radical Townsman, which is unfortunate.

I also hear that H.M. has been writing warning letters about Lord Derby.[4] She conjures up all sorts of calamities by the entrance of Lord D. into the Cabinet and imagines that with Lord Granville's somewhat failing health,

---

[1] See Lord Crewe, *Lord Rosebery* (N.Y., 1931), pp. 125-8.
[2] E. W. Benson.　　　　[3] R. W. Church.　　　　[4] Guedalla, ii. 223-4.

Lord D.'s policy in foreign affairs may have a paramount influence in the policy of the Government!

I understand that Mr. G. is seriously contemplating the necessity of postponing his visit to Midlothian next month, if Rosebery continues in his present tempestuous state of mind. Scotland would never forgive Rosebery if it is through him that they lose the visit of their beloved Mr. G. This would put Rosebery in a great hole; so I hope with all my heart he may at any rate consent to postpone pressing his case till after Mr. G. has gone northwards.

I am reading the third and concluding volume of Bishop Wilberforce's life by his son. It is very interesting but unpardonably indiscreet. The imprudent disclosures are naturally giving great offence and evoking loud protestations.

The Duke of Grafton has been offered one of the vacant Garters at the special instance of Lord G[ranville]. It seems rather unnecessary to bestow so high an honour on a man who has so lately succeeded to the ducal honours. (The late Duke declined the Garter more than once). The only excuse can be to clench the present Duke's support.

The Duke of Bedford recently again sent in one of his periodical letters as to the necessity of the Duchess's resigning the Mistress-ship of the Robes owing to his being so feeble a supporter of the Government; and this time it seems unlikely that he will allow himself to be put off and prevented from carrying his threat into effect. The stock of duchesses from whom to choose a successor to the Duchess of Bedford is very limited. Query, the Duchess of Roxburghe?

Mr. G. wrote last week the nicest possible letter to the Bishop of Winchester to explain to him that it was only weight of years which prevented his receiving an offer of the archbishopric.[1]

The Chairmanship of Committees is still going begging. Stansfeld declined the place straight off and rather huffily. Lord Hartington seems rather in favour of offering the post to Raikes! This surely would be a great insult to the Government side of the House? The only Liberal that Lord Hartington could think of was Bryce.

Had rather a good day yesterday with Pembroke's harriers. He mounted me very comfortably. Sent for me and sent me back. There never was anything like the kindness I receive from them.

Tuesday, 26 December. (Salisbury) Wonderfully mild Xmas weather. Edward Ottley staying here. He certainly is an attractive and promising man. He ought to get on in the clerical world and make his mark. It is a treat to come across a clergyman who is so devoted a Gladstonian and so thoroughly liberal.

Rode over to Wilton today with Ethie.[2]

The Bishop of Truro has at last made up his mind to accept Canterbury.

---

[1] G. W. Kitchin, *Edward Harold Browne* (London, 1895), pp. 456-8.
[2] i.e. his sister Ethelinda.

Truro will now remain to be filled up. I expect Mr. G. will want to offer it to Mr. Wilkinson; but I hope just now he will not press Mr. W. on H.M.[1] She has had enough disagreeable pills to swallow lately in admitting Lord Derby and Dilke into the Cabinet. The arrangements as regards the latter are finally complete. Dodson most goodnaturedly makes room for him at the Local Government Board and is ready to accept the Duchy—my originally suggested way out of the difficulty, though it has its objections and very strong ones.

Mary G. holds out rather better hopes that a settlement of the Rosebery business will be effected. Lord G[ranville] is for dealing with him most tenderly and quite admits his preferential claims to the next vacancy for a peer in the Cabinet; he would give a sort of pledge to Rosebery. I am glad to say Rosebery now wholly disclaims any personal motives such as disappointment. I am truly sorry for him and have written him today a line of sympathy.

Wednesday, 27 December. (Salisbury) Hunted with Pembroke's harriers. Meet in the familiar country—Salterton Down. Ethie accompanied me. A good deal of running about, but bad scenting day and very muggy and damp.[2] It is delightful to see him with his hounds—so wonderfully keen. They are a really beautiful pack.

Spent a good bit of time in reading the 3rd volume of Bishop Wilberforce's life.[3] The amount of indiscretion displayed by the son, which has been so commented upon, is much less than I expected. It would have been easy for him to have eliminated it all at the expense of a certain amount of interest. The most indiscreet parts relate to the Bishop's animosity to Lord Beaconsfield, which rather surprises me. I was always under the impression they were rather friends. I remember he had no scruples in asking Dizzie to give me a nomination for the Treasury—this must have been early in 1868;[4] and though it never came to anything, as he quitted office not long after, he (if I recollect rightly) was disposed to look favourably upon the Bishop's application on my behalf, on the ground that he (Dizzie) was glad always to oblige the Bishop, at the same time rather demurring to benefit one who was the son of a spiritual peer who never supported him (Dizzie) and the nephew of a man who always strongly opposed him in the House of Commons. Bishop Wilberforce's political position was rather peculiar—not unlike that of my father's—a conservative by nature, but very averse to and distrustful of the leader of the party (Dizzie) with which he was naturally in

---

[1] See 9 May 1882.

[2] EWH then wrote, but it is heavily crossed out: 'Had much talk with Lady P[embroke] who actually has irresistible charms to me.'

[3] Reginald G. Wilberforce, *Life of . . . Samuel Wilberforce . . .*, vol. iii (London, 1882).

[4] EWH is correct. Samuel Wilberforce wrote Disraeli on his behalf on 8 Apr. 1868. Disraeli Papers, Hughenden, B/XXI/W/371.

sympathy and devoted to, and having the greatest possible confidence in, Mr. Gladstone.

Friday, 29 December. (Salisbury) Mr. G.'s birthday. The completion of his 73rd year, and yet he is as vigorous mentally and bodily as if the figures were reversed. Great indeed is my good fortune to have the privilege of serving such a man. There never was and never could be so delightful a master to serve. He has a great idea of discipline and is strict almost to being exacting, yet always making allowances for any shortcomings and always giving credit for even moderately executed work. If every post in the kingdom were open to me, I should elect the one I hold. It is probably the most interesting of all appointments. One is more behind scenes than any other Cabinet minister, except in respect of not being present at the Cabinet Councils; and yet even into those secret proceedings one gets an insight by means of the Prime Minister's report to the Queen.

The Duke of Grafton has not had the same scruples as his brother had and has accepted the Garter. I am rather sorry. He has not served long enough in the Liberal ranks, and his decoration will give offence to others who have served long and faithfully.

The endless Belt trial was brought to an end yesterday—the 43rd day!—and the plaintiff, Belt, obtained a verdict with damages (£5,000). There must have been some hard-swearing on one or the other side.

The Rosebery *fracas* is smoothed over, thank goodness, for the moment at any rate. He has withdrawn his threat of resignation pending the development of a scheme for the better administration of Scotch affairs. I believe that after a first touch of disappointment he has behaved disinterestedly. In evidence of this, Reay tells me Rosebery has expressed himself quite willing to accept the Under Secretaryship in a Scotch Department presided over by a man like Baxter. I am afraid, however, there is no denying he has acted somewhat foolishly; for he set himself to work in the wrong way.